CODE

CODE – THE LANGUAGE OF OUR TIME

CODE = LAW CODE = ART CODE = LIFE

Herausgegeben von
Gerfried Stocker
und Christine Schöpf

Ars Electronica 2003

Festival für Kunst, Technologie und Gesellschaft
Festival for Art, Technology and Society

Organization
AEC Ars Electronica Center Linz
Museumsgesellschaft mbH

Managing Directors
Gerfried Stocker / Romana Staufer

Hauptstraße 2, A-4040 Linz, Austria
Tel. +43 / 732 / 7272-0
Fax +43 / 732 / 7272-77
festival@aec.at
www.aec.at/code

ORF Oberösterreich

General Director
Helmut Obermayr

Prix Ars Electronica Coordination
Christine Schöpf

Prix Ars Electronica Organization
Gabriele Strutzenberger, Judith Raab
Europaplatz 3, A-4021 Linz, Austria
Tel. +43 / 732 / 6900-0
Fax +43 / 732 / 6900-24270
info@prixars.orf.at
http://prixars.orf.at

Directors Ars Electronica
Gerfried Stocker, Ars Electronica Center Linz
Christine Schöpf, ORF Oberösterreich

Producer
Katrin Emler

Assistant Producer
Manuela Pfaffenberger

Production Team
Wolfgang Almer, Ellen Fethke, Ingrid Fischer-Schreiber, Marcus Lust, Dieter Mackinger, Iris Mayr, Elisabeth Sachsenhofer, Klemens Maria Schuster

Curatorial Advisors
Ingrid Fischer-Schreiber, Iris Mayr, Christiane Paul, Casey Reas

Technical Director
Magnus Hofmüller

Public Relations
Ulrike Ritter

Press
Wolfgang Bednarzek

Ticketing & PR Assistent
Sonja Panholzer

Marketing, Sponsoring
Ursula Kürmayr, Doris Peinbauer

Consultant
Jutta Schmiederer

Ars Electronica Center System Administration & Technical Maintenance:
Christian Leisch, Christian Kneissl, Karl Schmidinger, Gerold Hofstadler

Architecture
Scott Ritter

Technical Expertise & Know-how
Ars Electronica Futurelab

Web Editor / Web Design
Ingrid Fischer-Schreiber / Joachim Schnaitter

Editors
Gerfried Stocker, Christine Schöpf

Editing
Ingrid Fischer-Schreiber

English Proofreading
Ian Bovill, Elizabeth Ernst-McNeil

Graphic Design
Gerhard Kirchschläger

Cover Subject
The CODE Logo is based on a design by Astrid Benzer and Elisabeth Schedlberger. A dictionary entry was used for the background text.

Printing
Gutenberg-Werbering

Published by
Hatje Cantz Verlag
Senefelderstraße 12
73760 Ostfildern-Ruit
Germany
Tel. +49/711/44050
Fax +49/711/4405220
Internet: www.hatjecantz.de

Distribution in the US
D.A.P., Distributed Art Publishers, Inc.
155 Avenue of the Americas
Second Floor
New York, NY 10013-1507
USA
Tel. +1 / 212 / 6271999
Fax +1 / 212 / 6279484

ISBN 3-7757-1356-5

Printed in Austria

25.00

ARS
ELECTRONICA 2003

Hatje Cantz

Das Ars Electronica Center Linz
ist eine Einrichtung der
Stadt Linz.
The Ars Electronica Linz Center is an institution of the municipality of Linz.

Ars Electronica Center Linz &
Festival Ars Electronica are supported by:

Stadt Linz
Land Oberösterreich
Bundeskanzleramt/Kunstsektion

Veranstalter / *Organization:*

ARS ELECTRONICA CENTER
MUSEUM OF THE FUTURE

Ars Electronica Center Linz

ORF

ORF Oberösterreich

Mitveranstalter / *Co-organizers:*

BRUCKNER HAUS

OK Centrum für Gegenwartskunst
Oberösterreich

Universität für künstlerische und industrielle Gestaltung Linz

---

Stadt Linz

Land Oberösterreich

Bundeskanzleramt/
Kunstsektion

SAP AG

Gericom AG

Telekom Austria

Bank Austria
Creditanstalt

ORF – Österreichischer Rundfunk

Quelle AG

Hewlett Packard Österreich

voestalpine

Österreichische
Brauunion

Sony DADC

FESTO

Mitsubishi Electric

Microsoft Österreich

Siemens Österreich

Prix Ars Electronica wird unterstützt von / *is supported by:*

Telekom Austria
voestalpine AG
BAWAG / P.S.K. Gruppe
Stadt Linz
Land Oberösterreich

Prix Ars Electronica Additional Support:

Österreichischer Kulturservice
Pöstlingberg Schlöss'l
Sony DADC

Additional support for Ars Electronica and Prix Ars Electronica by
Spring, 3Com, Lexmark, Austrian Airlines, KLM, Opel Günther, PANI Projection & Lighting, NRG Gstetner

Contents

Ars Electronica 2003

Principles of Indeterminism

CAMPUS

Ars Electronica Center Exhibition

CODE—the Language of Our Time

Gerfried Stocker

Is the language of the computers becoming the lingua
franca of the global Information Society?

Software is omnipresent; digital codes are the materia prima of our modern, global Information Society. And it is precisely its unlimited capacity to be programmed that turns the computing machine into the unique medium that has so successfully and so mightily pervaded all aspects of our life—one that can simultaneously function as an implement of war, economic tool and artistic instrument.

CODE = LAW

Software sets the standards and norms, and determines the rules by which we communicate in a networked world, do business, and gather and disseminate information. Upon closer examination, the global digital network consists not so much of computers and data transmission lines as of mutually compatible communication protocols.
Cyberspace as a social sphere and a new type of public domain derives its uniqueness not as a result of the data that are stored or exchanged within it abut rather from the specific possibilities and impossibilities of the program codes of TCP-IP, of the browsers and chat rooms, of the encryption programs. The Internet is no longer a lawless, chaotic, disorganized no-man's-land. It has long since become the target of substantial, systematic efforts aimed at rigorous regulation and control. Not so very long ago, it was above all the interests of the market economy that could function only under controlled conditions; since September 11, 2001, though, it is first and foremost the interests of homeland security that have set the tone. Copyright and privacy are leading slogans in the fight to achieve a knowledge-driven society.

How strong is the socially regulative and
normative power of the software monopoly actually?
If code assumes the status of law, which court offers us a forum
in which to challenge it? To whom do we go to demand our rights?
Who authors the Codex of Cyberspace?
What possibilities exist to evade it?

CODE = ART

For artistic work, software is a fantastic instrument. In digital simulation, there are no constraints placed upon the imagination and the creative urge. Nevertheless, it is not only the way in which artists work that has changed in the wake of computerization and the programmable model worlds to which it gives rise; far beyond these considerations, the result has been the emergence of a totally new form of art. Digital media art or cyberart—a hybrid term that has already taken root as a linguistic construction—has established itself as a distinct genre and diversified into a broad spectrum of highly varied artistic practices. Thus, digital technologies have finally instituted optimal preconditions for the implementation of the idea of art as an ongoing, dynamic process.Fostered by the public attention that has been focused on the so-called Digital Revolution, media art has assumed a fixed place in the art world. Parallel to this triumph, though, an essential discourse dealing with the processuality of media art and the accompanying valence shift from object to dynamic system has retreated into the background.

At present, the dominant concept of data is one that registers a clear analogy to the objects of real space. Data are indeed virtual: they fluctuate in telematic networks, and they can be copied and (re)modeled at will; nevertheless they ultimately remain entities that can be labeled and dealt with. On the other hand, a dynamic system as engendered by an interactive process reacts autonomously to the participants and their environment, whereby it is not merely made public but made publicly accessible. It is used and formed by all participants in their own individual temporal and experiential windows. Such an open dynamic structure can no longer be created in the sense of a work of art; instead, it can only be encoded as a framework.

The enormous speed with which media art has developed and spread over the last 10 years makes it a matter of utmost urgency to take up again and expand this fundamental discourse aimed at producing a media art theory that is in keeping with these times.

What, then, are the characteristics that define the essence of digital media art?

Is it digital data's formability that carries on an updated version of the criteria of traditional arts, or is it instead the dynamics and openness of interactive, cybernetic processes and generative algorithms that suggest an extensive break with conventional attitudes and expectations with respect to the production and reception of art?

How can we go about defining a contemporary digital media art that concentrates on these new practices but does not set aside its conceptual forerunners?

Is art programmable? Can software itself be art, and according to which aesthetic criteria are we to assess this issue?

CODE=LIFE

In the parlance of the Computer Age, code stands for control and programmability. Bioinformatics and digital biology are the names of the "hot new fields" that, in the wake of Artificial Intelligence and neurobionics, are the expected sources of the key technologies of the 21st century.With this vocabulary, mankind is going about the task of working out the genetic foundations of life and propagating a mode of understanding that would have us believe that life is controllable and programmable like the digital code of the computer.

Will we use this genetic alphabet to rewrite the Book of Life or to summon forth a biological Babylon?

A media art that is coherently and consistently conceived will never be limited to the artistic use of technical media. Beyond this, it is always aesthetic research, critical analysis and social critique of our scientifically, technically conditioned view of the world. Media art is inseparable from the technological developments of the age, and that makes it into a laboratory for the future. As a festival for art, technology and society, Ars Electronica sees its mission as providing a platform for an encounter with the art of our time.

CODE – the Language of Our Time

Gerfried Stocker

Wird die Sprache der Computer zur Lingua Franca der globalen Informationsgesellschaft?

Software ist allgegenwärtig, digitale Codes sind die Materia Prima unserer modernen, globalen Informationsgesellschaft. Erst durch die freie Programmierbarkeit wird die Maschine Computer zu jenem einzigartigen Medium, das mit großem Erfolg und großer Macht in alle Bereiche unseres Lebens vorgedrungen ist und gleichzeitig Kriegsgerät, ökonomisches Arbeitsmittel und künstlerisches Instrument sein kann.

CODE=LAW

Software setzt die Standards und Normen und bestimmt über die Spielregeln, nach denen wir in der vernetzten Welt kommunizieren, Geschäfte abwickeln, Informationen erhalten und weitergeben. Das globale digitale Netz basiert bei genauerer Betrachtung nicht so sehr auf Computern und Datenleitungen, sondern vor allem auf gemeinsamen offenen Übertragungsprotokollen. Der Cyberspace als sozialer Raum, als neue Öffentlichkeit gewinnt seine Eigenart nicht durch die Daten, die in ihm gespeichert sind oder ausgetauscht werden, sondern durch die spezifischen Möglichkeiten und Un-Möglichkeiten der Programmcodes des TCP-IP, der Browser und Chat-Rooms, der Verschlüsselungsprogramme. Das Internet ist kein gesetzloses, chaotisches, ungeordnetes Niemandsland mehr. Längst steht es im Zentrum von handfesten Versuchen, es einer lückenlosen Regulierung und Kontrolle zu unterwerfen. Waren es bis vor kurzem vor allem die Interessen der Marktwirtschaft, die nur unter kontrollierten Bedingungen funktionieren kann, so sind es seit dem 11. 9. 2001 vor allem die Interessen der Homeland-Security, die dabei den Ton angeben. Copyright und Privacy sind zentrale Schlagworte im Kampf um eine demokratische Wissensgesellschaft.

Wie stark ist also die gesellschaftsregulierende und -normierende Macht der Software-Monopole tatsächlich?
Wenn Code an die Stelle des Gesetzes tritt, vor welchem Gericht können wir ihn anfechten? Wo können wir unser Recht einfordern?
Wer schreibt den Kodex des Cyberspace?
Welche Möglichkeiten gibt es, diesen zu unterlaufen?

CODE=ART

Für die künstlerische Arbeit ist Software ein fantastisches Instrument. In der digitalen Simulation sind Fantasie und Schöpfungsdrang keine Grenzen gesetzt. Doch weit darüber hinaus hat sich im Sog des Computers und seiner programmierbaren Modellwelten nicht nur die künstlerische Arbeit verändert, sondern eine ganz neue Form der Kunst herausgebildet. Digitale Medienkunst oder „Cyberart“ – ein hybrider Begriff, der schon zu einer festen sprachlichen Wendung geworden ist – hat sich als eigenes Genre etabliert und in ein breites Spektrum sehr unterschiedlicher künstlerischer Praktiken diversifiziert. Die Idee von Kunst als einem fort-

laufenden, dynamischen Prozess hat mit den digitalen Technologien endlich die optimale Voraussetzung für ihre Umsetzung gefunden. Begünstigt durch die öffentliche Aufmerksamkeit, die der so genannten digitalen Revolution zuteil wurde, hat die Medienkunst inzwischen einen festen Platz in der Kunstwelt eingenommen. Parallel zu diesem Erfolg ist jedoch der zentrale Diskurs über die Prozesshaftigkeit der Medienkunst und die damit einhergehende Verlagerung der Wertigkeiten vom Objekt zum dynamischen System in den Hintergrund getreten.
Derzeit dominiert ein Datenbegriff, der eine klare Analogie zu den Objekten des realen Raums aufnimmt. Daten sind zwar virtuell und fluktuieren in telematischen Netzwerken, sie sind beliebig kopierbar und (um-)formbar, aber sie sind letztlich jederzeit etikettierbare und handelbare Entitäten. Ein dynamisches System hingegen, wie es von einem interaktiven Prozess gebildet wird, reagiert autonom auf die Teilnehmer und deren Umgebung und wird dadurch nicht bloß veröffentlicht, sondern öffentlich zugänglich. Es wird von jedem Teilnehmer in seinen eigenen individuellen Zeit- und Erlebnisfenstern genutzt und gestaltet. Eine solche offene, dynamische Struktur lässt sich nicht mehr im Sinne eines Werkes erschaffen, sondern kann nur als Framework gecodet werden. Die enorme Geschwindigkeit, mit der sich Medienkunst in den letzten zehn Jahren entwickelt und verbreitet hat, macht die Wiederaufnahme und Ausweitung dieser grundlegenden Diskurse über eine zeitgemäße Medien-Kunst-Theorie dringend notwendig.

Was also sind die wesensbestimmenden Merkmale einer digitalen Medienkunst?

Ist es die Formbarkeit der digitalen Daten, in der sich die Kriterien der traditionellen Künste fortschreiben lassen, oder sind es eher die Dynamik und Offenheit der interaktiven, kybernetischen Prozesse und der generativen Algorithmen, die eine weitgehende Zäsur mit gängigen Erwartungshaltungen über die Produktion wie Rezeption von Kunst nahe legen? Wie könnte sich eine zeitgenössische digitale Medienkunst definieren, die sich auf diese neuen Praktiken konzentriert, aber ihre konzeptiven Vorläufer nicht verdrängt?

Ist Kunst programmierbar? Kann Software selbst Kunst sein, und nach welchen ästhetischen Kriterien ist dies zu beurteilen?

CODE=LIFE

Code steht im Sprachgebrauch des Computerzeitalters für Kontrolle und Programmierbarkeit. Bioinformatik und Digital Biology nennen sich die „heißen Bereiche", die nach Artificial Intelligence und Neurobionik für die neuen Schlüsseltechnologien des 21. Jahrhunderts sorgen sollen.
Mit diesem Vokabular gehen wir an die Bearbeitung der genetischen Grundlagen des Lebens und reden ein Verständnis herbei, das uns glauben lässt, das Leben sei beherrsch- und programmierbar wie der digitale Code des Computers.

Werden wir mit dem genetischen Alphabet das Buch des Lebens neu schreiben oder ein biologisches Babylon heraufbeschwören?

Medienkunst, konsequent gedacht, wird nie auf die künstlerische Nutzung technischer Medien beschränkt sein. Sie ist immer auch ästhetische Recherche, kritische Analyse und gesellschaftliche Kritik an unserem wissenschaftlich-technisch indizierten Weltbild. Medienkunst ist nicht trennbar von den technologischen Entwicklungen unserer Zeit - und das macht sie zu einem Labor für die Zukunft. Als Festival für Kunst, Technologie und Gesellschaft versteht sich die Ars Electronica als Plattform für die Auseinandersetzung mit dieser Kunst unserer Zeit.

Main Entry: code
Pronunciation: 'kOd
Function: noun
Etymology: Middle English, from Middle French, from Latin caudex, codex trunk of a tree, document formed originally from wooden tablets
Date: 14th century
1 : a systematic statement of a body of law; especially : one given statutory force
2 : a system of principles or rules <moral code>
3 a : a system of signals or symbols for communication
b : a system of symbols (as letters or numbers) used to represent assigned and often secret meanings
4 : genetic code, Date: 1961, the biochemical basis of heredity consisting of codons in DNA and RNA that determine the specific amino acid sequence in proteins and appear to be uniform for all known forms of life
5 : a set of instructions for a computer
- code·less /-l&s/ adjective

Function: verb
Inflected Form(s): cod·ed; cod·ing,
Date: 1815,
transitive senses : to put in or into the form or symbols of a code
intransitive senses : to specify the genetic code <a gene that codes for a protein>
- cod·able /'kO-d&-b&l/ adjective,
- cod·er noun

Code oder wie sich etwas anders schreiben lässt

Friedrich Kittler

Codes sind nach Wort und Sache, was uns heutzutage bestimmt und was wir daher sagen müssen, schon um nicht unter ihnen zu verschwinden. Sie sind die Sprache unserer Zeit, gerade weil Wort und Sache Code viel älter sind, wie ich in einem kurzen Rückgang in die Geschichte zeigen möchte. Seien Sie nur unbesorgt: Ich komme bei der Gegenwart schon wieder an.

Imperium romanum

Codes entstehen in Prozessen der Codierung, als welche nach einer eleganten Definition Wolfgang Coys „mathematisch gesehen eine Abbildung einer endlichen Menge von Zeichen eines Alphabets in eine geeignete Signalfolge ist".[1] Diese Bestimmung macht bereits zwei Sachverhalte klar: Zum einen sind Codes, der umlaufenden Meinung zum Trotz, keine Eigenheit von Computertechnik oder gar Gentechnologie; als Folgen von Signalen in der Zeit gehören sie zu jeder Nachrichtentechnik, jedem Übertragungsmedium mithin. Zum anderen spricht vieles dafür, dass Codes erst denkbar und machbar geworden sind, seitdem es zur Codierung natürlicher Sprachen nicht nur Ideogramme oder Logogramme gibt, sondern wahrhafte Alphabete. Das sind, wie gesagt, Systeme von abzählbar vielen, identisch wiederkehrenden Zeichen, die mehr oder minder eineindeutig und tunlichst auch vollständig Sprachlaute auf Buchstaben abbilden. Ein Vokalalphabet vom Typ jener einmaligen griechischen Erfindung,[2] der mit Grund die „erste Totalanalyse einer Sprache" nachgerühmt worden ist,[3] scheint daher in der Tat eine notwendige Bedingung für das Aufkommen von Codes – und doch noch keine hinreichende. Denn was den Griechen abging – von sporadischen Anspielungen abgesehen, die sich bei Aischylos, Aeneas Tacticus und Plutarch auf den Einsatz von Geheimschriften finden[4] –, war jene zweite Bedingung aller Codierung: eine entfaltete Nachrichtentechnik. Es scheint mir daher nichts weniger als Zufall, dass unsere Nachrichten von geheimen Nachrichtensystem mit dem Aufkommen des römischen Kaisertums schlichtweg zusammenfallen. In seinen *Leben der Caesaren* berichtet Suetonius, der selber von Amts wegen einem großen Kaiser als Geheimschreiber diente, er habe beim göttlichen Caesar wie beim göttlichen Augustus unter ihren hinterlassenen Handakten verschlüsselte Briefe entdeckt. Caesar beschied sich damit, alle Buchstaben des lateinischen Alphabets um vier Stellen zu versetzen, also D statt A zu schreiben, E statt B und so weiter; sein Adoptivsohn Augustus dagegen soll nur einen Buchstaben übersprungen haben, wobei mangelnde mathematische Klarsicht das X als letzten Buchstaben allerdings durch ein doppeltes A ersetzte.[5] Der Zweck lag auf der Hand: Bei lautem Lesen Unberufener (und Römer waren nicht grad litterat) ergab sich nur noch Konsonantensalat. Als sei es aber mit solchen Innovationen der Verschlüsselung noch nicht genug, schreibt Suetonius Caesar unmittelbar davor die Erfindung zu, seine Kriegsberichte, wie sie aus dem Gallienfeldzug zum Senat nach Rom flossen, in mehreren Kolumnen, wo nicht gar Buchseiten abgefasst zu haben; Augustus fällt der noch höhere Ruhm zu, er habe über Reiter und Relaisstationen das erste strikt militärische Eilpostsystem Europas eingerichtet.[6] Mit anderen Worten: Es war das Imperium als solches, im Gegensatz mithin zur römischen Republik oder bloßen Kurzschriftstellern wie Cicero, auf dem der Zusammenfall von Befehl, Code, Nachrichtentechnik letzten Endes fußt. Imperium heißen zugleich der

Befehl und sein Effekt: das Weltreich. „Command, Control, Communications, Intelligence“ war daher im Pentagon noch unlängst imperiale Devise; erst seit neuestem, dem Zusammenfall nämlich von Nachrichtentechniken und Turingmaschinen, lautet der Schlachtruf C^4: Command, Control, Communication, Computers – vom Orontes bis vor Schottland, von Bagdad bis Kabul.

Nun hießen *imperia,* die Befehle der Kaiser, aber auch *codicilla,* kleine geschälte Blöcke aus Holz, in deren Wachsbeschichtung sich schreiben ließ. Das Stammwort *codex* wiederum, Altlateinisch *caudex,* mit unserem Hauen urverwandt, nahm in imperialer Frühzeit die Bedeutung von „Buch“ an, dessen Seiten sich, anders als bei Papyrosrollen, erstmals durchblättern ließen. So kam schließlich jenes Wort in Umlauf, das auf seinem Irrweg zum Französischen und Englischen uns hier in Linz bewegt: Code hieß, von Kaiser Theodosius bis zum Empereur Napoleon, schlicht das gebundene Gesetzbuch, Kodifikation also der juridisch-bürokratische Akt, ganze Ströme kaiserlicher Briefe oder Befehle, wie sie über Jahrhunderte die Eilpoststraßen des Reiches nur durchflogen hatten, zum Stillstand einer einzigen Gesetzsammlung zu verhalten. Aus Nachrichtenübertragung wurde Datenspeicherung,[7] aus puren Ereignissen serielle Ordnung. Insofern tragen *Codex Theodosius* und *Codex Iustinianus* noch heute, wo nicht gerade (wortwörtlich gemeint) das anglo-amerikanische *Common Law* tobt, einen Code alteuropäischer Rechte und Pflichten. Denn im *Corpus iuris* sind (um das Mindeste zu sagen) Copyrights und Trademarks, ob an einem Codex oder Code, schlicht Undinge.

Nationalstaaten

Bleibt nur die Frage, warum der technische Wortsinn von Code den juristischen derart verdunkeln hat können. Bekanntlich scheitern Rechtssysteme von heute regelmäßig daran, Codes überhaupt zu begreifen und folglich zu schützen: gleichgültig ob vor ihren Räubern und Aufkäufern oder ob umgekehrt vor ihren Entdeckern und Schreibern. Die Antwort scheint schlicht: Was immer wir seit den Geheimschriften römischer Kaiser bis zu den *Arcana imperii* der Neuzeit als Code verbuchen, hieß ab dem Spätmittelalter „Chiffre“. Unter Code verstand man lange Zeit sehr andere Kryptografieverfahren, wo die Aussprechbarkeit erhalten blieb, aber dunkle oder harmlose Wörter die geheimen schlicht ersetzten. Chiffre dagegen war ein anderer Name der Null, die damals aus Indien über Bagdad in Europa einzog und *sifr* (Arabisch: „das Leere“) zu mathematisch-technischer Macht verhalf. Seitdem gibt es (sehr anders als im Griechenland) für Sprachlaute und Zahlen völlig unterschiedene Zeichensätze: hier das Alphabet der Leute, da die Ziffer von Geheimnisträgern, die schon im Namen das arabische *sifr* ein zweites Mal nachbuchstabierte. Getrennte Zeichensätze sind aber fruchtbar: Miteinander hecken sie uns Wundertiere aus, die Griechen oder Römern gar nicht beigefallen wären. Ohne neuzeitliche Algebra keine Codierung, ohne Gutenbergs Buchdruck keine neuzeitliche Kryptologie. Battista Leone Alberti, dem Erfinder der Linearperspektive, gingen 1462 oder1463 zwei schlichte Sachverhalte auf: Erstens sind in jeder Sprache die Laute oder Lettern unterschiedlich häufig, was laut Alberti sich am Setzerkasten Gutenbergs beweist. Die Kryptoanalyse kann also schon aus den Frequenzen der versetzten Lettern, wie sie von Caesar und Augustus stammten, den Klartext von Geheimbotschaften erraten. Daher reicht es zweitens auch nicht mehr, beim Chiffrieren alle Buchstaben um einen selben Abstand zu versetzen – und noch bis in die Zeit des Zweiten Weltkriegs galt fortan Albertis Vorschlag, bei jedem weiteren Buchstaben im Klartext einen Schritt auch im geheimen Alphabet zu tun.[9] Ein Jahrhundert nach Alberti verschränkte François Viète, Begründer der modernen Algebra, aber auch Entzifferer im Dienst von Henri IV., Zahl und Letter noch viel enger. Erst seit Viète gibt es Gleichungen mit Unbekannten und allgemeinen Koeffizienten, bei deren bei der Anschrift Zahlen als Buchstaben codiert werden.[9] So hält es heutzutage noch jeder, der in einer höheren Programmiersprache schreibt, die zudem ja ebenfalls (mathematisch mehr oder weniger korrekt)

The Meaning of Code

Peter J. Bentley

The computer program has come a long way. Once the domain of obscure mathematicians, the code that drives computers is now as familiar to us as the cars we drive ourselves around in. It seems that everyone knows about the World Wide Web, whether they've surfed in its turbulent waves or not. Everyone knows about email, whether they're spammed to death every morning, or have not even had a single offer of millions from a dead Nigerian president's cousin. Everyone knows about windows-based operating systems, and can tell at least three horror stories of computer crashes that resulted in traumas to the poor victims. Everyone knows that the worst bugs are not the kind that are susceptible to insect sprays. Software runs our world. It keeps our money safe, makes our car engines run, allows us to talk to each other on the telephone, and helps entertain us through television broadcasting and films. Software is changing lives, and we even have movies about how software is changing lives. The words "you've got mail" will never mean the same thing again. Computers are everywhere, and so is the language of computers: code.

Somehow everything seems possible in code. There are no ambiguities, no hidden meanings. Problems are delicately pulled apart by master dissectors, and solutions are formed that magically instruct the computer to perform the necessary tasks. A good programmer is a virtuoso performer; his masterpieces are works of art as beautiful to comprehend as any concerto or poetry. But all his work is hidden within the mind of a computer; his audience is forever unaware of his skills. A bad programmer (and there are far more of these) is simply a "jack of all trades" with no more creativity or skill than someone "painting by numbers." The results are dire and never last long.

When you've been programming for long enough, when you've grown up programming computers, you think in a subtly different way. It's not a case of seeing ones and zeros in front of your eyes, as one memorable scene in "The Matrix" showed. It's a little more subtle than that. You become used to breaking down problems into smaller, easier parts. It becomes natural to think in this way, whether working out how to build a robot, or how to climb down from a tree. Good programmers are natural problem-solvers, for this is how we write code. But code can also dehumanise a person. There is no subtlety, no humour, no scope for emotion in code. While a programmer needs to be creative and artistic, he also needs to be very literal. If something is not working, it's not because the computer is annoyed, or has misinterpreted its instructions, or is bored. It is because the programmer is annoyed, or has misinterpreted his own code, or is bored. Code is so literal, so unambiguous, that it takes a while to train a mind to think in the same way. These limitations of code can produce side-effects in people that write it—a joke is lost, a philosophical point missed, an ambiguity the cause of excessive confusion. I used to be like this (and still am, sometimes), but learned to appreciate art, to love the ambiguities of language. In general, the effects of raw, undiluted code on people is not always a helpful thing. Try saying something deliberately ambiguous to a programmer and just watch how long it takes them to work out the meaning. Say the same thing to an artist and they won't even blink before responding.

Most of us are not up to our eyeballs in code every day, however. Instead, an increasing number of us are using the code. We are the users (a very derogatory term for a programmer) and we have to deal with all of the new opportunities that the software brings us. We are given so much freedom, so many options, that using software now threatens to turn our workplace into information-searching activities. We search through the hundreds of functions in the word processor (half of which helpfully make themselves invisible) in order to add a simple character such as " ï." (It took me 90 seconds to insert that through the menu system of my word processor, and I knew how to do it. With a pencil, I could have made the same symbol in less than one second.) We search through thousands of functions in an art package, just to draw a line with an arrow on the end of it. With the deterioration of email in recent years, we search through tens of unsolicited spam emails to find the real messages hidden amongst them. And although we have search engines for the Internet, we still search through the results of the search to find anything useful. Information overload is another side effect of code.

But code is not only bad for people, it's becoming bad for computers, too. Software is rarely written by virtuoso programmers any more. Code is now becoming "bloatware"—inefficient, slow, and containing vast quantities of old, out-of-date code (legacy code, as it is known). Rather than follow the computer processor industry's model and make the chips smaller, faster, more efficient and cheaper, software companies have opted for the stupid model and add more features to the product. It's like starting with a bad car, and keeping on adding new things to it until it can barely be driven, despite the ultra-fast new engine that is put under the hood. Some might argue that this sounds familiar—are our laws not created in a similar way? But this inefficient, cumulative build-up of unnecessary code is not what we see in art, or in biology. The best art is radical, new, and simple in concept. And although the genes of living creatures are written in a cumulative manner, efficiency is still paramount—they cannot survive if they are inefficient. So, from the viewpoint of a computer scientist who has grown up with code, the current froth of computer software is largely awful. The imagination has left the code. There is no efficiency, no elegance. Very few masterpieces are ever written these days. Contemporary, off-the-shelf software is not inspiring at all.

One reason for the downfall of code is what is sometimes termed the complexity ceiling. Software is now so complex that not even a huge team of well-trained people can get a handle on how it all works—or indeed if it all works. There are so many separate elements (subroutines, modules, files, variables) and they interact with each other in so many different ways, that it is simply beyond our abilities to cope with it. So current software is not delivered as a fully working product. It's delivered, and then continuously updated with "service packs" or "upgrades" to overcome the bugs in the original code. Today's code doesn't work. We've hit the complexity ceiling for software, and the only options are either to reduce the complexity, or find a different approach to writing code. (It is interesting to note that we're also reaching the complexity ceiling in other areas. For example, our wars have so many weapons and so many different armies, that the job of determining friend from foe in real time is becoming very difficult, especially when your enemy will sabotage any identification measures you may try to introduce. Friendly fire is becoming the biggest killer in modern warfare. We also see problems in major engineering feats: space satellites have suffered from the "too many separate elements" problems, with even basic problems such as a mix-up between imperial and decimal measurements. And the next problem will be the human genome project. Decoding the thousands of genes properly is simply beyond current technology—every gene affects so many others in millions of different ways. You can't work out what a single gene does in isolation, because it doesn't work in isolation.)

Traditional computer code may be doomed, but what else do we have? What could replace it? Here we must look to biology, for nature has its own code. This becomes very appealing when we study life, for natural systems are highly imaginative, creative, efficient and elegant. In addition, nature does not appear to be limited to any complexity ceiling (at least none that we can currently perceive).

Evolution is the master programmer in natural systems. Genes are nature's code. Evolution works by exploiting genetic novelty in populations of individuals. Those that are better suited to their environments because they have better genes are more likely to survive longer and reproduce. When they reproduce, they pass on shuffled copies of their genes to their offspring, producing new, good varieties. Human creativity is often thought of in terms of merging existing ideas in new ways, or coming up with new ideas that are a step up from previous ones, and this is exactly how evolution works. But the key thing about nature is that it is self-designing. There is no-one in control of evolution, it is an unthinking, uncaring process. What works is kept and stored in DNA, what doesn't work is discarded. It's a brutally efficient code-generating procedure.

And the next generation of computer code is based around these principles. Evolutionary algorithms are computer programs that evolve solutions to problems. Tell the computer a problem, and it will evolve you the solution, whether the problem is "optimise a jet engine turbine blade" or "compose a piece of music." These new types of computer code (which also include swarming algorithms and chaotic systems) are self-organising systems. They are the problem solvers, and they are tomorrow's computer programmers.

Or at least they will be, once we understand how to make them work properly. Once again, we are limited by a complexity ceiling: nature is simply too complex for us to understand. And it's hard to duplicate a natural process in a computer when we don't fully understand it. So while we are successfully evolving solutions to problems with our computers, we haven't broken through that ceiling yet. There's a limit to the level of complexity that our evolutionary algorithms can attain. To go beyond it, we either have to start guiding evolution ourselves, or we have to learn one last thing from nature.

That thing is this: Natural code is not quite the same as computer code. In our technology, we have a distinct separation between hardware and software. The hardware is predesigned, manufactured, and becomes a solid chunk of silicon—a chip. The software is more dynamic—it can be changed, rewritten, loaded and unloaded into the chip. There is no such distinction in nature.

This is important. Natural systems do not have hardware and software. Natural systems are both hardware and software combined. A living organism has its code predesigned by evolution. But that code is a physical molecule—a complex DNA molecule. The molecule enables the production of proteins, and as genes produce proteins, so proteins interact with genes and turn them on and off. The natural code is "executed" by the laws of physics, and it causes cells to divide, grow, move, change, extrude substances and die. Before long there is a fully formed multi-cellular organism. But there is no software in it, any more than there is hardware. The DNA will do nothing unless it is in exactly the right conditions—it must be integrated into the right cell, at the right temperature, with the right kinds of proteins surrounding it. DNA is not just information, it is physical. It relies on being physical to work. It relies on a billion other physical things, and physical laws, for it to mean anything. DNA is not really that much like our traditional computer code, which has meaning in (can be translated to work in) any computer. DNA is embodied within its environment—it forms an integral part of an organism, and it harnesses all the subtleties of every cell and protein it is among. In a different environment, the DNA loses its meaning. Move my genes into the cell of a mouse or a chimp, and they won't work. Maybe one or two might do something, but you can't grow a Peter Bentley on the back of a mouse (not unless the back of the mouse was effectively made into a human womb).

So the lesson from nature is that to really harness self-organising principles such as evolution, to create great code that knows no complexity ceiling, we need to lose this arbitrary distinction we have between hardware and software. We need to make code physical (or make hardware into software). If we blur the boundaries between code and computer, then the code becomes a million times more powerful. Imagine a device whose structure does the thinking and by changing its own structure it changes its thinking. It sounds extremely organic. Can art be defined by shape, and can it redefine itself by changing its shape? These are concepts that we struggle with, for we are so used to separating knowledge from things, just as software is separate from hardware. When knowledge and the object become one, what will we have created? A new type of computer? A new type of art? I don't know, but I'd love to find out.

Der Sinn des Code

Peter J. Bentley

Computerprogramme haben sich mittlerweile durchgesetzt. Einst das Revier verschrobener Mathematiker, ist der Code, der in jedem Computer steckt, mittlerweile so alltäglich wie das Auto, in dem wir umherfahren. Jeder scheint das World Wide Web zu kennen, gleichgültig, ob er auf dessen stürmischen Wellen gesurft ist oder nicht. Jeder weiß, was E-Mails sind, egal, ob er allmorgendlich mit Spams überhäuft wird oder nicht ein einziges Mal ein Millionenangebot von einem Cousin eines verstorbenen nigerianischen Präsidenten erhalten hat. Alle reden bei fensterorientierten Betriebssystemen mit und kennen zumindest drei Schauergeschichten, aus denen die Opfer eines Computerabsturzes traumatisiert hervorgingen. Jedes Kind weiß, dass die schlimmsten *Bugs* jene hartnäckige Spezies sind, denen man nicht mit Insektensprays zu Leibe rücken kann. Software steuert unsere Welt. Sie sorgt dafür, dass unser Geld sicher ist, der Motor in unserem Wagen läuft, wir miteinander telefonieren können und Fernsehsendungen und Filme uns reibungslos unterhalten. Software verändert unser Leben. Darüber gibt es sogar Filme. Der Satz „Sie haben Post" wird niemals wieder dasselbe bedeuten. Computer sind überall, und damit auch ihre Sprache: Code.

Irgendwie erscheint im Code alles möglich. Es gibt keine Zweideutigkeiten, keine versteckten Bedeutungen. Probleme werden meisterlich bis ins Kleinste seziert und Lösungen bereitgestellt, die den Computer wie von Zauberhand die notwendigen Schritte tun lassen. Ein guter Programmierer ist ein Virtuose. Seine Meisterstücke sind Kunstwerke – vergleichbar einem Konzert oder Gedicht. Doch sein ganzes Schaffen steckt unsichtbar im Inneren eines Computers, und dem Publikum bleibt sein Genie auf immer verborgen. Ein schlechter Programmierer (und davon gibt es wahrlich genügend) ist nur ein „Hansdampf in allen Gassen", kaum kreativer oder talentierter als jemand, der sich in „Malen nach Zahlen" übt. Die Ergebnisse sind schauerlich und nur von kurzem Bestand.

Hat man lange genug Computer programmiert, ist also quasi damit „aufgewachsen", dann eignet man sich eine differenzierte Denkweise an. Es erscheinen einem jedoch keine Einsen und Nullen vor den Augen, wie in jener unvergesslichen Szene im Film *The Matrix.* Es ist etwas subtiler. Man gewöhnt sich an, Probleme in kleinere, leichter lösbare Einheiten zu zerlegen. Das wird zur natürlichen Denkart. Und dabei ist es egal, ob man einen Roboter konstruieren oder von einem Baum herunterklettern will. Gute Programmierer sind Problemlösungstalente, denn so schreibt man Code. Code kann einen aber auch entmenschlichen. Code lässt keinen Platz für Feinsinniges, Humor oder Emotionen. Der Programmierer muss zwar kreativ und künstlerisch sein, er muss aber auch sehr buchstabengetreu arbeiten. Funktioniert etwas nicht, dann liegt es nicht daran, dass der Computer ärgerlich ist, die Anweisungen missverstanden hat oder sich langweilt, sondern dass der Programmierer verärgert war, seinen eigenen Code falsch verstanden oder sich gelangweilt hat. Code ist so wörtlich, so unzweideutig, dass man seinen Verstand erst darauf trainieren muss, ebenso zu denken. Diese Einschränkungen des Codes zeigen mitunter Nebenwirkungen bei den Menschen, die ihn schreiben – ein Witz kommt nicht an, ein philosophischer Gedanke wird verpasst, oder eine Zweideutigkeit verursacht unbeschreibliche Verwirrung. Auch mir ging es einmal so (und geht es gelegentlich noch immer). Ich habe aber gelernt, die Kunst zu schätzen und die Mehrdeutigkeit der Sprache zu lieben. Die Auswirkungen, die reiner, nackter Code auf die Menschen hat, sind nicht immer günstig. Sagen Sie einmal einem Programmierer absichtlich etwas Zweideutiges und beobachten Sie, wie lange er braucht, um die Bedeutung zu verstehen. Sagen Sie dasselbe einem Künstler, und er wird im Nu antworten.

Dennoch stecken die meisten von uns nicht tagtäglich bis über beide Ohren in Code; es steigt vielmehr die Anzahl derer, die den Code nutzen. Wir sind die *User* (eine sehr abwertende Bezeichnung für einen Programmierer) und müssen uns mit all den Möglichkeiten, die uns Software bietet, herumschlagen. Sie gibt uns so viel Spielraum, so viele Optionen, dass der Einsatz von Software unsere Arbeit zur bloßen Informationssuche verkommen lässt. Wir stöbern in Hunderten von Funktionen unseres Textverarbeitungsprogramms (von denen sich die Hälfte zum Glück selbst unsichtbar macht), um ein einfaches Zeichen wie ein „ï" einzufügen. (Über die Menüs meiner Textverarbeitung habe ich dafür 90 Sekunden gebraucht. Und dabei wusste ich, wie es geht. Mit einem Bleistift könnte ich dasselbe Zeichen in weniger als einer Sekunde schreiben.) Wir durchforsten Tausende Funktionen eines Grafikprogramms, nur um eine Linie mit einer Pfeilspitze zu erstellen. Im Zug der E-Mail-Inflation der letzten Jahre suchen wir in einem Wust unerwünschter Spam-Mails nach den wenigen wirklichen Nachrichten, die darunter verborgen sind. Und obwohl wir Internet-Suchmaschinen einsetzen, durchsuchen wir die Ergebnisse erst Recht wieder nach brauchbaren Dingen. Informationsüberschuss ist eine weitere Nebenwirkung von Code.

Code schadet aber nicht nur den Menschen, sondern in zunehmenden Maß auch den Computern. Software wird kaum noch von Programmiervirtuosen geschrieben. Code wird zur „Bloatware" – ineffizient, langsam, randvoll mit veraltetem Code (so genanntem Legacy Code). Statt dem Beispiel der Mikrochip-Industrie zu folgen, die immer kleinere, schnellere, effizientere und billigere Prozessoren erzeugte, wählten die Softwarefirmen ein unsinniges Modell und fügten immer neue Funktionen hinzu. Ähnlich wie bei einem schlecht konzipierten Wagen, der mit immer mehr Extras ausgestattet wird, bis er trotz seines extrem leistungsstarken Motors kaum noch zu fahren ist. Manchen kommt das bekannt vor? Werden nicht auch unsere Gesetze so geschrieben? Der Kunst oder der Biologie jedoch ist diese ineffiziente Anhäufung von unnötigem Code fremd. Die beste Kunst ist radikal, neu und beruht auf einem einfachen Konzept. Und obwohl die Gene aller Lebewesen auf kumulative Weise geschrieben werden, so ist Effizienz dennoch das oberste Gebot – sonst können sie nämlich nicht überleben. Aus der Sicht eines Computerfachmanns, der mit Code groß geworden ist, ist der Großteil der derzeit angebotenen Software schlicht scheußlich. Code ist fantasielos geworden, ohne Effizienz und Eleganz. Heute werden nur noch vereinzelt Meisterleistungen erbracht. Aktuelle Software von der Stange hat überhaupt keinen Pepp mehr.

Ein Grund für den Niedergang von Code liegt in der so genannten Komplexitätsgrenze. Software ist mittlerweile so komplex, dass selbst ein riesiges Expertenteam nicht in der Lage ist zu prüfen, wie alles funktioniert – oder *ob* überhaupt alles funktioniert. Es gibt so viele Elemente (Subroutinen, Module, Dateien, Variablen), die auf unterschiedlichste Weise miteinander interagieren, dass wir damit einfach überfordert sind. Daher wird Software heute nicht als voll funktionsfähiges Produkt ausgeliefert, sondern nach und nach mit „Service Packs" oder „Upgrades" aktualisiert, um die Fehler im Ausgangscode auszumerzen. Code funktioniert heute einfach nicht mehr. Wir haben die Komplexitätsgrenze für Software erreicht. Als Alternative bleibt uns entweder die Komplexität zurückzuschrauben oder neue Wege für das Programmieren zu finden.

Interessanterweise erreichen wir auch in anderen Bereichen bereits die Komplexitätsgrenze. So kämpfen z. B. so viele verschiedene Armeen mit dermaßen diversifizierten Waffen auf den Kriegsschauplätzen von heute, dass die Unterscheidung zwischen Freund und Feind im Gefecht fast unmöglich wird. Vor allem dann, wenn der Feind die Erkennungsmechanismen, die man zum Einsatz bringen möchte, sabotiert. In der modernen Kriegsführung fordert „freundliches Feuer" die meisten Opfer. Auch technische Meisterleistungen bleiben davon nicht verschont: Selbst Weltraumsatelliten sind vom Problem „zu vieler Einzelelemente" betroffen, die durchaus grundlegender Natur sein können, wie die Verwechslung von britischen und metrischen Maßeinheiten. Und als nächstes wird es das Human-Genom-Projekt treffen. Die exakte Dekodierung Tausender Gene übersteigt die heutigen Technologien, denn jedes einzelne Gen beeinflusst so viele andere Gene in millionenfacher Weise. Und es lässt sich nicht erkunden, was ein einzelnes Gen isoliert macht, denn isoliert funktioniert es nicht.

Das Schicksal des traditionellen Programmiercode mag besiegelt sein, doch was bleibt uns sonst? Womit sollen wir ihn ersetzen? Wir müssen uns an der Biologie orientieren, denn die Natur hat ihren eigenen Code. Das Leben zu studieren ist besonders attraktiv, denn die Systeme der Natur sind höchst fantasievoll, kreativ, effizient und elegant. Und darüber hinaus scheint die Natur nicht durch irgend welche Komplexitätsgrenzen eingeschränkt zu sein (zumindest keine, die wir mit unseren derzeitigen Mitteln wahrnehmen können).

Die Evolution ist ein Meister im Programmieren natürlicher Systeme. Gene sind der Code der Natur. Die Evolution nützt dabei genetische Neuerungen in Populationen von Individuen. Diejenigen, die aufgrund ihrer Gene ihrer Umwelt besser angepasst sind, überleben länger und vermehren sich. Bei der Reproduktion geben sie modifizierte Kopien ihrer Gene an ihre Nachkommen weiter und erzeugen so neue, bessere Varietäten. Die menschliche Kreativität stellt man sich oft so vor, dass bestehende Ideen neu zusammengefügt werden oder man eine neue Idee hat, die der alten einen Schritt voraus ist. Und genau so arbeitet die Evolution. Allerdings entwirft sich die Natur immer selbst. Niemand steuert die Evolution; sie ist ein sich selbst überlassener, zufälliger Prozess. Funktioniert etwas, wird es in Form von DNA gespeichert. Alles andere wird verworfen. Das ist eine geradezu brutal effiziente Prozedur zur Codegenerierung.

Auch die nächste Generation von Computercode wird auf diesen Prinzipien beruhen. Evolutionäre Algorithmen sind Computerprogramme, die Problemlösungen entwickeln. Gleichgültig, ob man dem Computer die Aufgabe „optimiere die Turbinenschaufel eines Düsentriebwerks" oder „komponiere ein Musikstück" stellt, er wird die Lösung dafür selbst finden. Diese neuartigen Computercodes (die u. a. Schwarmalgorithmen und Chaossysteme einsetzen) sind selbstorganisierende Systeme. Sie sind die Problemlöser und die Programmierer der Zukunft.

Beziehungsweise werden sie es sein, sobald wir herausgefunden haben, wie man sie wirklich zum Funktionieren bringt. Denn wieder stoßen wir an eine Komplexitätsgrenze: Die Natur ist für unseren Verstand einfach zu komplex. Und es ist schwierig, einen natürlichen Prozess im Computer nachzubilden, wenn man ihn nicht vollständig durchschaut. Während wir also erfolgreiche Problemlösungen mit unseren Computern entwickeln, haben wir diese Grenze noch nicht durchstoßen. Unsere evolutionären Algorithmen erreichen nämlich nur einen

bestimmten Komplexitätsgrad. Will man noch weiter, so muss man entweder die Evolution selbst steuern oder von der Natur noch eine letzte Sache lernen:
Natürlicher Code ist anders geartet als Computercode. Wir unterscheiden in unserer Technologie klar zwischen Hardware und Software. Die Hardware wird entworfen, dann produziert und manifestiert sich schließlich als ein Stück Silizium – ein Chip. Die Software ist da schon dynamischer: Man schreibt sie, ändert sie, lädt sie in den Chip oder löscht sie daraus. Die Natur kennt diese Unterscheidung nicht.
Das ist der springende Punkt. Natürliche Systeme bestehen nicht aus Hard- und Software, sondern vereinen beides. Der Code eines Lebewesens wurde von der Evolution entworfen. Aber dieser Code ist ein physisches Molekül, ein komplexes DNA-Molekül. Dieses Molekül ermöglicht die Produktion von Proteinen. Bei der Proteinproduktion durch die Gene interagieren die Eiweißbausteine mit den Genen und aktivieren bzw. deaktivieren sie. Der natürliche Code wird auf der Grundlage physikalischer Gesetze „ausgeführt" und veranlasst die Zellen sich zu teilen, zu wachsen, sich zu bewegen, zu verändern, Substanzen zu extrudieren und zu sterben. Ehe man sich versieht, ist ein vollständig ausgeformter, vielzelliger Organismus entstanden. Der enthält aber weder Software noch Hardware. Solange die Bedingungen nicht optimal sind, tut die DNA gar nichts – sie muss sich in der richtigen Zelle befinden, die Temperatur muss stimmen, und sie muss von passenden Proteinen umgeben sein. DNA ist nicht nur Information, sie ist *dinglich.* Sie funktioniert nur, weil sie physisch ist. Sie fußt auf zig anderen physikalischen Gegebenheiten und Gesetzen, um überhaupt eine Bedeutung zu haben. Daher ähnelt die DNA kaum unserem üblichen Computercode, der für jeden Computer Relevanz hat (in Arbeitsanweisungen übersetzt werden kann). DNA ist in ihre Umgebung eingebettet. Sie bildet einen integralen Bestandteil eines Organismus und nutzt die Feinheiten der sie umgebenden Zellen und Proteine. In einer anderen Umgebung verliert die DNA ihre Bedeutung. Verpflanzt man meine Gene in die Zelle einer Maus oder eines Schimpansen, so funktionieren sie nicht. Ein oder zwei werden vielleicht noch etwas bewirken, aber auf dem Rücken einer Maus wird kein Peter Bentley heranwachsen (sofern man den Mäuserücken nicht erfolgreich in eine menschliche Gebärmutter umgewandelt hat).
Die Natur lehrt uns also, diese willkürliche Unterscheidung zwischen Hard- und Software aufzugeben, wenn wir selbstorganisierende Prinzipien wie die Evolution nutzen wollen, um leistungsfähigen Code jenseits jeder Komplexitätsgrenze zu generieren. Code muss physisch werden (oder die Hardware in die Software integriert sein). Verwischt man die Grenze zwischen Code und Computer, so wird der Code millionenfach mächtiger. Stellen Sie sich ein Gerät vor, dessen Struktur denkt und das durch Veränderung seiner eigenen Struktur auch seine Denkweise verändert. Das klingt ausgesprochen organisch. Kann Kunst durch Form definiert werden und kann sie sich selbst neu definieren, indem sie die Form ändert? Mit diesen Konzepten haben wir so unsere Not, denn wir sind es einfach gewöhnt, das Wissen von den Dingen zu trennen so wie die Software von der Hardware. Wenn das Wissen und das Objekt eins werden, was haben wir dann geschaffen? Einen neuen Computertyp? Eine neue Kunstform? Ich weiß es nicht, aber ich würde es liebend gerne herausfinden.

Aus dem Englischen von Michael Kaufmann

The Battle over Control of Code is a Battle over Freedom

Howard Rheingold

The battle for the control of code is the decisive battle in a war that most people don't know about yet, a conflict that will shape the world we and our descendants will inhabit in coming decades—a war over the freedom to innovate. Most people in 2003 take for granted that we can all use personal computers and the Web today because people like Doug Engelbart and Tim Berners-Lee didn't have to ask for permission before they invented new media for thinking and communicating. Computers and telephones are not just power tools, but mind-power tools: the liberty to invent and deploy new communication media is significantly different from the license to invent other kinds of products and services. A television channel, a weblog, a java program, a World Wide Web is not a breakfast cereal, a railroad, a microchip—but an avenue for learning, a channel for communication, a means to persuade, and a vehicle to self-organize, all at the same time. The products of the media and communication industries are states of mind and social relations. When you can control or influence people's state of mind and social relations, you unlock the gateway to power over them.

The most important questions concerning the future of communication technology and the media they enable are, more than ever, questions of power and liberty:

- Who will be free to innovate? Entrepreneurs, or employees?
- Will people who purchase tools and experiences remain active users of technology, reshaping and evolving media to our own purposes, or will we be turned back into passive consumers, whose only choice is which brand to buy from a small number of vendors?
- Will mobile communication media and pervasive computing enable entire populations to organize collective action, or will such collective action be prevented, channeled, and metered by laws and code?

Legal, political, and regulatory moves to protect the owners of today's technology and yesterday's business-models are attempting to thwart the process of capitalistic "creative destruction" whereby cheaper, more powerful, more effective products and services replace older, less valuable ones:

- The move by incumbent license-holders to lock up radio spectrum, using laws formulated to regulate technology of the 1920s, rather than open large amounts of spectrum to WiFi, ultra-wideband, cognitive radio, mesh networking, and other potentially disruptive technologies is one front of the assault on the freedom to innovate. Spectrum is the real estate of the mobile-and-pervasive age.
- The battle to criminalize the sharing of computer resources over the Internet is about control of collective action of the kind that built the Web. Preventing p2p through legal and technical restriction could shut down distributed research into cancer cures, along with college students exchanging music.

- The already existing Digital Millennium Copyright Act in the USA and in its global versions, instantiated in near-future hardware through the "secure computing" schemes, along with the Broadcast Flag and other Digital Rights Management proposals, are battles over whether only certain existing companies or whether individuals and companies-to-be will be able to create and distribute cultural products—and whether lawmakers, under pressure from lobbyists, can force all future chip manufacturers to embed code police and police code in their hardware.
- The moves by broadband cable and telephone infrastructure operators that also own companies that sell broadband to compromise the Internet's end-to-end principle is an assault on the fundamental code architecture that enabled the Internet, and the Web to grow and flourish through the aggregated and coordinated invention of millions of people. The enclosure of the Internet commons is on its way to being encoded in the routers that move bits around—the hardware gateways that make the Internet possible.

Will tomorrow's artists, engineers, teachers, designers, political leaders, citizens, technology users, continue to be free to invent tools like the personal computer or the Internet, or will law and code restrict the freedom to innovate? Although the two most powerful instruments of code—the personal computer and the Internet—originated in the US military, and were built on infrastructure constructed by companies like IBM and ATT, ultimately the PC and the Internet became mass media because millions of computer and Internet users reinvented these media for their own purposes. From nineteen year-old Harvard dropout Bill Gates taking control of computers away from IBM, and equally young Steve Wozniak and Steve Jobs making PCs "for the rest of us"—computers that people who had never used computers started to use to do things computers had never been used to do—to Tim Berners-Lee creating the World Wide Web and giving it away, the PC and the Net have been shaped by its users. Unix, Linux, Usenet, Yahoo, Google—commercial and gift-economy—were created by individual inventors and tribes of collaborators.

The PC and the Net are not just technologies with their own significant powers, they are the means of production and distribution of new inventions, the instruments of "bootstrapping" Engelbart envisaged forty years ago. The explosion of invention that brought us from the Apple II to the Pocket PC, from the 300 baud modem to the multi-megabit/second broadband connection happened because affordable tools, willing tinkerers, and a legal and cultural atmosphere that encouraged individual innovation came together. We cannot assume that these conditions for grassroots innovation will continue to exist as we move into the most technically powerful media revolution: when billions of people walk around carrying or wearing multimedia devices thousands of times more powerful than today's desktop computers, linked to other people and devices through a wireless network thousands of times faster than today's broadband Web, will freelancers remain free to tinker—will people be free to self-organize our own ad-hoc networks of people and devices? Or will we have to work for one of a few global disinfotainment factories to be free to create and enable cultural production—but not to own them?

Especially in this age of mobile communications, the freedom to innovate—and the move to constrain that innovation—operates on the level of collective action as well as the level of individual initiative. The balance of self-interest and cooperation that made enterprises like markets, nations, constitutions and corporations possible also drove the growth of today's mediasphere. The companies that made the hardware, owned the connections, sold access, although they reaped profits, did not build today's mobile, self-evolving, self-organizing, datacloud. Hundreds of millions of people did that because others built tools that enabled people to communicate with each other in new ways through their PCs, to publish web pages, create new operating systems. At the core of the rapid evolution of the Net were tools created deliberately to afford collective action: Unix, TCP/IP, the Web, free/open source software all grew through the collective actions of those who built and used them. The end-to-end model conceded in the very architecture of the Internet that future users would think of things to do with the medium that its original architects never dreamed of, and wisely did not wall out.

Although the recording industry is interested only in its business model, and paints the post-Napster legislative and judicial attacks on peer-to-peer file-sharing as a battle solely over intellectual property, the liberty to interconnect our PCs and mobile devices into legitimate and powerful confederations like *http://folding.stanford.edu* is also at stake. Nobody today can imagine what kind of medical research, scientific exploration, technology development might be possible when the whole worldwide swarm of personal supercomputing communicators can pool their computation and communication power. But the kind of draconian control of peer-to-peer applications being pushed today by the recording and motion picture industries, if concretized into laws as bad as the DMCA, could severely hamper the freedom of computational association.

Increasingly, however, some of the software, communication, and entertainment interests that owe their power to these tools are combining architectural, legal, and regulatory machinery to prevent new enterprises and technologies from seizing that power. Western Union didn't succeed in stopping telephony. The motion picture industry didn't stop the production of VCRs, although it tried. No railroad barons or buggy-whip manufacturers were able to hold back the automobile. But today, immensely more powerful global enterprises, backed up by the politicians they help elect, are combining forces to create what sounds benign, like "Digital Rights Management," or "trusted computing," but what is aimed at restricting future technological innovation to this small number of large interests. The concentration of ownership of the news media essential to free societies is moving on to concentrate ownership of invention.

The freedom to invent and to use media to organize collective action is at stake. Whether we retain these freedoms is uncertain. And if a sufficient number of people are able to understand, organize, and act, winning that freedom is not a magic ticket to a benign future for technologically-amplified collective action. I called my 2003 book *Smart Mobs* because not every group who uses media to organize collective action has socially beneficial ends in mind. Super-empowered swarms of people can lend power to democratic collective action, or to fascist collective action. The printing press made science, medicine, and constitutions possible, but the enabling technology for population-wide literacy did not eliminate bad intentions, violence, or injustice. Indeed, technology makes the production of machine guns possible as well as the production of antibiotics. Ultimately, the question about control over the codes of collective action is about whether the powers of worldwide media would be used more wisely by a few, or by many.

Der Kampf um die Kontrolle von Code ist ein Freiheitskampf

Howard Rheingold

Der Kampf um die Kontrolle von Code ist die Entscheidungsschlacht in einem Krieg, von dem die Mehrheit noch gar nichts weiß. Dieser Konflikt wird die Welt formen, in der wir und unsere Nachkommen in den nächsten Jahrzehnten leben werden – ein Krieg um die Innovationsfreiheit. Der Gebrauch von Personalcomputern und dem World Wide Web ist im Jahr 2003 für viele eine Selbstverständlichkeit, weil ein Doug Engelbart oder ein Tim Berners-Lee nicht lange um Erlaubnis fragen mussten, ob sie neue Meinungsbildungs- und Kommunikationsmedien erfinden durften. Computer und Telefon sind nicht bloß Elektrogeräte, sondern elektrisierende Geräte: Die Freiheit, neue Kommunikationsmedien zu erfinden und einzusetzen, unterscheidet sich wesentlich von der Lizenz zur Erfindung anderer Produkte oder Dienstleistungen. Ein Fernsehkanal, ein Weblog, ein Java-Programm, ein World Wide Web sind keine Frühstücksflocken, keine Eisenbahn, kein Mikroprozessor, sondern gleichzeitig Zugang zu Wissen, Kommunikationskanal, Überzeugungsinstrument und Vehikel zur Selbstorganisation. Die Produkte der Medien- und Kommunikationsindustrie sind Geisteszustand und Sozialkontakt. Wer den Geisteszustand und die Sozialkontakte anderer kontrolliert oder beeinflusst, öffnet sich damit das Tor zur Macht über sie. Die brennendsten Fragen zur Zukunft der Kommunikationstechnologie und der Medien sind mehr denn je Fragen der Macht und der Freiheit:

- Wer hat die Freiheit zur Innovation? Unternehmer oder Arbeitnehmer?
- Bleiben die Käufer von Werkzeugen und Know-how aktive Anwender der Technik, die die Medien ganz ihren Bedürfnissen anpassen und entsprechend weiterentwickeln, oder werden wir zu passiven Konsumenten degradiert, die lediglich die jeweilige Marke aus dem Angebot einer kleinen Gruppe von Anbietern wählen dürfen?
- Werden die mobilen Kommunikationsmedien und der allgegenwärtige Computer ganzen Bevölkerungsgruppen kollektives Handeln ermöglichen, oder wird ein solches kollektives Handeln durch Gesetze und Code erstickt, kanalisiert und genau bemessen?

Zum rechtlichen, politischen und regulatorischen Schutz der Eigentümer heutiger Technologien und der Vertreter gestriger Geschäftsmodelle sucht man die kapitalistische „kreative Zerstörung" zu vereiteln, die die veralteten, weniger wertvollen Produkte und Dienstleistungen durch billigere, leistungsfähigere und effizientere ersetzen will:

- Unter Berufung auf Gesetze, die 1920 zur Regulierung der damaligen Technologien eingeführt wurden, frieren derzeitige Lizenzinhaber Funkfrequenzen lieber ein, anstatt ganze Frequenzbänder für Wi-Fi, Ultra-Breitband, Cognitive Radio, Mesh Networking und andere bahnbrechende Technologien freizugeben. Dieses Unterfangen ist nur ein Schauplatz der Unterdrückung der Innovationsfreiheit. Das Frequenzspektrum ist die Immobilie des mobilen Durchdringungszeitalters.
- Die Anstrengungen, die gemeinsame Nutzung von Computerressourcen über das Internet zu kriminalisieren, zielen schlicht auf die Kontrolle jenes kollektiven Handelns ab, das das Web überhaupt erst entstehen ließ. Unterbindet man Peer-to-Peer durch juristische und technische Restriktionen, so würde zusammen mit den Musiktauschbörsen der College-Studenten auch die verteilte Krebsforschung abgedreht werden.

- Auf einem weiteren Kampfschauplatz wird sich entscheiden, ob mit dem in den USA bereits verabschiedeten *Digital Millennium Copyright Act* (DMCA) und seinen globalen Varianten – in naher Zukunft noch durch digitale Sicherheitskonzepte in der Hardware unterstützt – sowie mit Broadcast Flag und weiteren Vorstößen zum Digital Rights Management nur mehr einige etablierte Unternehmen in der Lage sein werden, Kulturprodukte zu erschaffen und zu verbreiten, oder ob dies auch Einzelpersonen und noch zu gründenden Firmen möglich sein wird. Und ob der Gesetzgeber in Zukunft alle Chiphersteller dazu verdonnern kann, Code-Polizei und Polizeicode in die Hardware zu integrieren.
- Die Bestrebungen von Breitbandkabel- und Telefonie-Infrastrukturbetreibern, die gleichzeitig als Breitbandanbieter auftreten, das End-zu-End-Prinzip des Internets aufzuweichen, sind ein Angriff auf die grundlegende Codearchitektur, die das Internet ermöglicht und dazu beigetragen hat, dass das Web durch die gesammelten und koordinierten Erfindungen von Millionen von Menschen wuchs und gedieh. Schon werden Zäune um das frei zugängliche Internet errichtet, indem man die Router – jene Hardware-Gateways, die das Internet zum Funktionieren braucht, weil hier die Bits durchfließen – entsprechend codiert.

Werden die Künstler, Techniker, Lehrer, Planer, Politiker, Bürger und Technikkonsumenten von morgen weiterhin Werkzeuge wie den PC oder das Internet erfinden dürfen, oder werden Gesetz und Code diese Innovationsfreiheit beschränken? Auch wenn die beiden wichtigsten Instrumente des Code – PC und Internet – vom US-Militär stammen und deren Infrastruktur von Firmen wie IBM und ATT entwickelt wurde, so wurden sie schlussendlich zu Massenmedien, weil sie von Millionen von Computer- und Internetusern für deren Zwecke laufend neu erfunden wurden. Der PC und das Netz wurden von ihren Benutzern geformt; angefangen vom neunzehnjährigen Harvard-Abbrecher Bill Gates, der IBM die Kontrolle über die Computer wegschnappte, über Steve Wozniak und Steve Jobs, die ungefähr im gleichen Alter PCs für „den Rest von uns" machten – Computer, die von Leuten, die niemals zuvor einen PC bedient hatten, zu Aufgaben herangezogen wurden, für die noch nie zuvor ein Computer verwendet worden war – bis zu Tim Berners-Lee, der das World Wide Web kreierte und für die Allgemeinheit freigab. Unix, Linux, Usenet, Yahoo, Google – kommerzielle und Geschenkökonomie – wurden von einzelnen Erfindern und Heerscharen von Mithelfern geschaffen.
Der PC und das Netz sind nicht bloß bedeutsame Technologien, sondern die Produktionsmittel und Distributionskanäle für neue Erfindungen, die Bootstrapping-Werkzeuge, die sich Engelbart vor vierzig Jahren vorstellte. Die Entwicklungsexplosion, die uns vom Apple II zum Pocket-PC und vom 300-Baud-Modem zur Breitbandverbindung mit Übertragungsgeschwindigkeiten x-Megabit / Sekunde brachte, hat nur deswegen stattgefunden, weil leistbare Werkzeuge, gewiefte Bastler sowie eine juridische und kulturelle Atmosphäre, die innovative Ideen des Einzelnen begünstigte, zusammentrafen. Allerdings können wir nicht davon ausgehen, dass diese Bedingungen für grundlegende Innovationen ewig bestehen bleiben, wo uns doch die größte technische Medienrevolution bevorsteht: Wenn erst einmal Milliarden von Menschen tagtäglich Multimediageräte bei sich tragen, die tausendmal leistungsfähiger sind als heutige PCs, und untereinander und mit anderen Geräten über ein drahtloses Netzwerk verbunden sind, das tausendmal schneller ist als heutige Breitband-Internetverbindungen, werden dann die freien Mitarbeiter weiterhin nach Lust und Laune herumbasteln dürfen? Werden wir weiterhin die Freiheit haben, unsere Ad-hoc-Netzwerke zwischen Menschen und Geräten selbst zu organisieren? Oder werden wir für eine der wenigen globalen Disinfotainment-Fabriken arbeiten müssen, um ungehindert kreativ tätig sein zu können und Kulturproduktion überhaupt zu ermöglichen – die Werke jedoch nicht zu besitzen?
Vor allem im Zeitalter der mobilen Kommunikation passiert Innovationsfreiheit – und die Bestrebung, Innovation zu beschränken – sowohl auf der Ebene des kollektiven Handelns als auch auf jener der individuellen Initiative. Das Gleichgewicht zwischen Eigeninteresse und

Kooperation, das Märkte, Staaten, Regierungsformen und Firmen als Unternehmung erst ermöglicht hat, war auch die treibende Kraft der heutigen Medienwelt. Die Firmen, die die Hardware erzeugten, denen die Verbindungen gehörten, die die Zugangsberechtigungen verkauften und dabei satte Gewinne einfuhren, haben die mobile, sich selbst organisierende Datenwolke nicht geschaffen. Das haben die Abermillionen von Menschen gemacht, denen andere die Werkzeuge gebaut haben, die es ihnen ermöglichten, untereinander über den PC zu kommunizieren, Webseiten zu publizieren oder neue Betriebssysteme zu generieren. Im Zentrum der Evolution des Netzes standen die Werkzeuge, die bewusst für dieses kollektive Handeln entwickelt wurden: Unix, TCP / IP, das Web, Free- bzw. Open-Source-Software – und sie alle wuchsen durch das kollektive Handeln ihrer Entwickler und User weiter. Dieses End-zu-End-Modell führte zu genau jener Architektur des Internet, die es zukünftigen Nutzern erlaubt, das Medium für Dinge einzusetzen, von denen seine Architekten niemals geträumt, die sie in weiser Voraussicht aber auch nicht ausgegrenzt hatten.
Obwohl die Plattenindustrie nur an ihrem eigenen Geschäftsmodell interessiert ist und die gerichtlichen Schritte gegen den Peer-to-Peer-Dateiaustausch als Kampf um das geistige Eigentum darstellt, geht es dennoch um die Freiheit, unsere PCs und mobilen Endgeräte in legitimen und leistungsfähigen Netzwerken wie *http://folding.stanford.edu* zusammenzuschließen. Niemand kann heute erfassen, welche Errungenschaften in Medizin, Wissenschaft oder Technik möglich wären, wenn alle Personal Supercomputing Communicators der Welt ihre Rechen- und Kommunikationskapazität ein einem gemeinsamen Pool zur Verfügung stellten. Doch die von der Platten- und Filmindustrie geforderte drakonische Beschränkung von Peer-to-Peer-Applikationen könnte die Freiheit solcher Rechenverbände gravierend beeinträchtigen, wenn die Gesetze dazu so schlecht ausfallen wie der DMCA.
Gewisse Vertreter der Software-, Kommunikations- und Unterhaltungsbranche, die ihre Macht diesen Werkzeugen verdanken, setzen vermehrt auf strukturelle, juridische und regulatorische Mechanismen, um neue Unternehmen und Technologien an der Übernahme dieser Macht zu hindern. Western Union konnte das Telefon nicht aufhalten. Die Filmindustrie konnte die Produktion von Videorecordern nicht vereiteln, obwohl sie es versuchte. Kein Eisenbahnmagnat oder Pferdepeitschenfabrikant konnte den Siegeszug des Automobils stoppen. Unterstützt von Politikern, denen sie zur Wahl verhelfen, vereinen jedoch heute wesentlich mächtigere Unternehmen ihre Kräfte, um hilfreich klingende Errungenschaften wie „Digital Rights Management" oder „Trusted Computing" zu entwickeln, die letzten Endes darauf abzielen, zukünftige technische Innovationen auf diese kleine Gruppe mit ihren mächtigen Interessen zu beschränken. Wir bewegen uns von einer Konzentration der Nachrichtenmedien, die für freie Gesellschaften unabdingbar sind, zu einer Konzentration der Innovation.
Die Freiheit des Erfindens und des Einsatzes von Medien zur Organisation kollektiven Handelns steht auf dem Spiel. Es ist ungewiss, ob man uns diese Freiheiten weiterhin lässt. Und selbst wenn genug Menschen in der Lage sind zu verstehen, sich zu organisieren und zu handeln, so ist der Gewinn dieser Freiheit kein Freifahrtschein in eine rosige Zukunft des technisch unterstützten kollektiven Handelns. Ich habe mein 2003 erschienenes Buch *Smart Mobs* betitelt, weil nicht jede Gruppierung, die Medien zur Organisation kollektiven Handelns verwendet, sozial nutzbringende Ziele vor Augen hat. Überbefähigte Gruppen von Menschen können ihre Macht dem kollektiven Handeln demokratischer oder faschistischer Kräfte zur Verfügung stellen. Die Druckerpresse machte Wissenschaft, Medizin und Verfassungen erst möglich, doch die Technik, die potenziell Bildung für die gesamte Bevölkerung versprach, konnte böse Absichten, Gewalt und Ungerechtigkeit nicht eliminieren. In der Tat gestattet die Technik gleichermaßen die Produktion von Maschinengewehren und Antibiotika. Somit stellt sich letztendlich im Hinblick auf die Kontrolle über die Codes des kollektiven Handelns die Frage, ob einige wenige oder viele die Möglichkeiten weltweiter Medien klüger nützen würden.

Aus dem Amerikanischen von Michael Kaufmann

Meditations on Trusted Computing

Fred von Lohmann

In 1641, in his Meditations on First Philosophy, mathematician and philosopher Rene Descartes asked how it is that we can trust our senses. What if, he asked, everything we experience is actually part of a delusion created by an omnipotent demon bent on deceiving us?

It turns out that a similar question has been weighing on the minds of Microsoft, Intel, and a number of other computer companies. How do you know that your computer is actually what it seems? After all, hackers could have broken into your computer and replaced the software on it with software that imitates, in every particular, the software that was on your computer before. To you, things would appear unchanged. But now your computer is under the hacker's control, logging your every keystroke, copying your most sensitive information, and sending it out over your Internet connection.

This points to another nagging epistemic doubt—how can any software on your computer trust any other software running on your computer? For example, when you run an anti-virus program, how can it be sure that the operating system hasn't been subverted somehow? After all, software installed by the hackers could intercept any warnings before they were output to your display, replacing them with screens announcing "no problems detected."

In short, how can you be sure that everything you experience on your computer is not part of a delusion created by hackers bent on deceiving you?

These are not idle questions. Today, computer users are increasingly besieged by malicious, hard-to-detect software designed to subvert computers—viruses, Trojan horses, worms, and spyware, to name just a few. This specter haunts not only individuals, but also a wide variety of companies, including health care providers, movie studios, intelligence agencies, and others who routinely entrust valuable or sensitive information to computers.

Enter the Trusted Computing Group, comprised of Microsoft, Intel, AMD, and several other large computer technology companies. The TCG companies are working on technology that will let you trust that your computer is what it appears to be.

Trusted computing: What is it?

First, you'll have to buy a new computer (did you think for a moment that a plan hatched by the world's largest software, chip and computer companies could start any other way?) that will include a special chip containing cryptographic hardware and keys.

You can choose to ignore the new chip, and your computer will behave just like the one you have now. You are free to install any operating system you like, and any software. The chip remains dormant until you decide to take advantage of it.

If you elect to activate the "trusted computing" features made possible by the chip, and if your operating system has been updated to take advantage of it, then your computer is "virtually" split in two, divided into "untrusted" and "trusted" sides. Both "sides" share the same CPU, the same hard drive, the same keyboard, and the same display, but the trusted side has an additional, very special property—it cannot be subverted by other software running on your machine. In other words, on the trusted side of your computer, you can run software with a high level of confidence that the software is what you think it is.

How? Well, the story depends on a great deal of sophisticated cryptography. When the trusted side of your computer saves data to the hard drive or to memory on behalf of a particular trusted software application, it does so in a secure, encrypted format. This encrypted data can only be read by that software application, running on the trusted side of your computer.

Malignant software that may be running on your computer (whether on the trusted or untrusted side) will not be able to read the encrypted data that belongs to another trusted application. In addition, the trusted side has a secure, encrypted channel to your keyboard and display, so malignant software cannot intercept data or interpose itself between you and the trusted application.

All of this allows you to trust the integrity of the software that is running on the trusted side, and that data saved by this software will not be accessible to subverted software that may be running on the untrusted side. (You are still vulnerable if a hacker has access to your hardware, however, as the security can be breached by hardware-based attacks.) So far, so good.

Trusting computing: Troubling implications

Trusted computing, however, does more than allow you to trust your own computer; it also aims to enable *others* to trust your computer. The key to this capability is in a feature called "remote attestation." This allows another person to ask the software running on the trusted side of your computer to identify itself. Because the answer comes from the tamper-resistant hardware on the motherboard of your computer, the "attestation" is relatively reliable. This feature certainly has some desirable uses (for employees logging into corporate networks from offsite locations, for example).

But there is a dark side. If others are able to verify that particular software is running on the trusted side of your computer, then some may refuse to communicate with you at all *unless* you are running their software. In other words, companies may begin demanding that you install and run the software *of their choice* on the trusted side of your computer. This would effectively give them control over a portion of your computer. You would be free to refuse, but then you would not be able to do business with them.

In a competitive market, this might not be a problem, as vendors would avoid anything that might alienate customers. In a market where competition is compromised, however, trusted computing can dramatically increase the power of a monopolist or cartel to impose "take it or leave it" terms on the public, by giving them the capability to insist on a relatively unassailable beachhead inside your computer.

For example, imagine that Hollywood movie studios decide to release their movies in formats that can only be played by certain trusted media player software. "Remote attestation" would be used to verify that the media player software was, in fact, running on the trusted side of your computer and that it had not been tampered with. This would give the movie studios unprecedented control over how your computer interacts with their movies. Your continued ability to make copies, take excerpts, fast-forward and mute would all be entirely within Hollywood's control, and part of your computer would now answer to Hollywood, rather than to you.

The implications, however, reach far beyond "digital rights management" schemes pushed by entertainment companies. Other industries may also eagerly embrace the idea that they can demand a beachhead inside your computer as a condition of doing business

with you. For example, the dominant vendor for a particular software application (like Microsoft Word for word processing) could modify a future trusted version to prevent you from migrating your documents to a competing application.
As with many technologies, trusted computing has uses both for good and for ill, and thus should be viewed with a critical eye, lest the users end up, in Descartes words, "as the captive, who, perchance, was enjoying in his dreams an imaginary liberty, when he begins to suspect that it is but a vision, dreads awakening, and conspires with the agreeable illusions that the deception may be prolonged."

Meditationen über Trusted Computing

Fred von Lohmann

1641 stellte der Mathematiker und Philosoph René Descartes in seinen „Meditationen über die Grundlagen der Philosophie" die Frage, wie wir unseren Sinnen vertrauen können. Was, wenn alles, was wir erleben, in Wahrheit Teil einer Illusion ist, die von einem allmächtigen Dämon geschaffen wurde, um uns zu täuschen?
Tatsächlich beschäftigen sich Microsoft, Intel und eine Reihe anderer Computerfirmen seit einiger Zeit mit einem ähnlichen Problem. Woher wissen wir, dass unser Computer das ist, was er zu sein scheint? Es könnte ja sein, dass sich Hacker Zugang zu unserem Gerät verschafft und unsere Software gegen andere Programme ausgetauscht haben, die der Originalsoftware bis ins Detail ähneln. Wir würden keine Veränderung bemerken. Unser Computer wäre jedoch völlig in der Hand des Hackers, der jeden Tastenanschlag verfolgt, unsere intimsten Informationen kopiert und sie über unsere eigene Internetverbindung versendet.
Diese Überlegung lässt weitere erkenntnistheoretische Zweifel aufkommen – wie kann eine Software, die wir verwenden, den anderen Programmen auf unserem Computer vertrauen? Wie können wir zum Beispiel, wenn wir einen Anti-Virus-Check durchführen, sicher sein, dass das Betriebssystem nicht irgendwie unterlaufen wurde? Es könnte ja sein, dass die von den Hackern installierte Software sämtliche Virus-Warnungen abfängt, bevor sie auf dem Bildschirm erscheinen, und sie durch die Meldung „Keine Probleme festgestellt" ersetzt.
Wie können wir also sicher sein, dass nicht alles, was wir auf unserem Computer erleben, Teil einer Illusion ist, die von Hackern geschaffen wurde, um uns zu täuschen?
Das sind keine müßigen Fragen. Heutzutage sind Anwender in zunehmendem Maß heimtückischer, schwer zu entdeckender Software ausgesetzt, die dazu programmiert ist, Computer zu unterlaufen – Viren, Trojaner, Würmer und Spyware, um nur einige zu nennen. Dieses Schreckgespenst betrifft nicht nur Einzelanwender, sondern auch zahlreiche Unternehmen, zum Beispiel im Bereich der Gesundheitsfürsorge, Filmstudios, Nachrichtendienste und andere, die ihren Computern regelmäßig wertvolle oder geheime Informationen anvertrauen.
Genau hier tritt die *Trusted Computing Group* (TCG) auf den Plan, zu der Microsoft, Intel, AMD und einige andere große Computertechnologiefirmen gehören. Die Unternehmen der TCG arbeiten an Technologien, mit deren Hilfe wir uns sicher sein können, dass unser Computer genau das ist, was er zu sein scheint.

Was genau ist Trusted Computing?

Zuerst müssen wir uns einen neuen Computer kaufen (Sie haben doch nicht wirklich auch nur eine Sekunde gedacht, dass ein von den weltgrößten Software-, Chip- und Computerherstellern entwickelter Plan anders anfangen könnte?), der einen Spezialchip mit kryptografischer Hardware und Schlüsseln enthält. Wir können den neuen Chip nun bewusst ignorieren, und unser Computer wird genau wie der alte funktionieren. Wir können jedes Betriebssystem und jede beliebige Software installieren. Der Chip ruht, bis wir beschließen ihn zu nutzen.

Sobald wir die vom Chip gestützten Trusted-Computing-Features aktivieren und wenn unser Betriebssystem für den Einsatz des Chips aktualisiert wurde, wird unser Computer „virtuell" in zwei Teile gespalten, und zwar in einen „ungesicherten" und einen „gesicherten". Beide Seiten teilen sich CPU, Festplatte, Tastatur und Schirm, die gesicherte Seite hat jedoch eine ganz spezielle Zusatzeigenschaft – sie kann von keiner anderen Software auf unserem Computer unterlaufen werden. Mit anderen Worten können wir also auf der gesicherten Seite Software verwenden, die mit hoher Wahrscheinlichkeit genau das ist, was sie zu sein scheint.

Wie funktioniert das? Nun, das Ganze hat mit jeder Menge ausgeklügelter Kryptografie zu tun. Speichert die gesicherte Seite unseres Computers über eine bestimmte gesicherte Softwareapplikation Daten auf der Festplatte oder in den Speicher, so geschieht das in einem sicheren, verschlüsselten Format. Diese verschlüsselten Daten können nur von der Softwareapplikation auf der gesicherten Seite des Computer gelesen werden.

Eventuell auf dem Computer vorhandene bösartige Software (sei es auf der gesicherten oder der ungesicherten Seite) kann die verschlüsselten Daten einer gesicherten Applikation nicht lesen. Zusätzlich verfügt die gesicherte Seite über einen sicheren, verschlüsselten Zugang zu Tastatur und Schirm, sodass bösartige Software Daten nicht abfangen oder sich zwischen uns und die gesicherte Applikation stellen kann.

So können wir also der Integrität der Software auf der gesicherten Seite vertrauen und sicher sein, dass die über diese Software gesicherten Daten für möglicherweise manipulierte Software auf der ungesicherten Seite unzugänglich sind. (Der Computer ist jedoch weiterhin anfällig für Angriffe von Hardware-Seite, sofern der Hacker darauf Zugriff hat.)

So weit, so gut.

Trusted Computing: Beunruhigende Auswirkungen

Trusted Computing führt allerdings nicht nur dazu, dass wir unserem eigenen Computer vertrauen können. Die Technologie soll dies auch *anderen* ermöglichen. Der Schlüssel dazu liegt in einem Feature namens „indirekte Authentifizierung". Es ermöglicht einer anderen Person, die Software auf der gesicherten Seite unseres Computers um Identifizierung zu bitten. Die Antwort kommt von der gegen Manipulation geschützten Hardware auf der Hauptplatine unseres Computers, und die „Authentifizierung" ist daher relativ verlässlich. Dieses Feature hat gewiss nützliche Anwendungen (etwa für Mitarbeiter, die sich von außerhalb in Firmennetzwerke einloggen).

Es gibt jedoch auch eine Kehrseite der Medaille. Sobald Außenstehende feststellen können, dass auf der gesicherten Seite unseres Computers eine bestimmte Software zur Anwendung kommt, könnten sich einige überhaupt weigern, mit uns zu kommunizieren, wenn wir ihre Software *nicht* verwenden. Anders gesagt, könnten Firmen von uns verlangen, auf der gesicherten Seite unseres Computers die Software *ihrer Wahl* zu installieren, womit sie im Endeffekt die Kontrolle über einen Teil des Computers hätten. Natürlich könnten wir dies ablehnen, doch würden wir mit dem jeweiligen Unternehmen dann keine Geschäfte mehr machen.

Dieses Problem stellt sich möglicherweise auf einem wettbewerbsfähigen Markt nicht, da die Anbieter alles tun würden, um potenzielle Kunden nicht zu verlieren. Ist der Wettbewerb jedoch beeinträchtigt, so kann Trusted Computing es einem Monopolisten oder Kartell gefährlich leicht

machen, nach dem Motto „Alles oder nichts!" zu arbeiten, da sie mittels Trusted Computing auf der relativen Zugriffssicherheit unseres Computers bestehen können.
Stellen wir uns zum Beispiel vor, dass die Hollywood-Studios beschließen, ihre Filme in einem Format zu veröffentlichen, das nur über bestimmte gesicherte Media-Player-Softwareprogramme abspielbar ist. Über die „indirekte Authentifizierung" ließe sich feststellen, ob die Media-Player-Software tatsächlich auf der gesicherten Seite unseres Computers installiert ist und dass sich niemand daran zu schaffen gemacht hat. So hätten die Filmstudios eine beispiellose Kontrolle darüber, wie unser Computer mit ihren Filmen umgeht. Es wäre Hollywood überlassen, ob wir weiterhin Kopien machen und Ausschnitte herausnehmen, den Schnellvorlauf betätigen oder den Ton abschalten könnten. Folglich würde ein Teil unseres Computers nicht länger unseren Befehlen folgen, sondern denen Hollywoods.
Die Auswirkungen gehen jedoch weit über das „Digital Rights Management"-System hinaus, das die Unterhaltungsindustrie durchzusetzen versucht. Anderen Industriezweigen wäre es vielleicht ebenfalls nur allzu lieb, als Voraussetzung für mögliche Geschäftsbeziehungen einen geeigneten Brückenkopf in unseren Computer zu verlangen. So könnte zum Beispiel der marktführende Anbieter einer bestimmten Softwareapplikation (wie Microsoft Word für die Textverarbeitung) in Zukunft eine geschützte Version so modifizieren, dass wir unsere Dokumente nicht länger über die Applikation eines Konkurrenten bearbeiten können.
So wie viele Technologien hat auch das Trusted Computing positive und negative Implikationen und sollte daher kritisch betrachtet werden. Andernfalls endet der Anwender möglicherweise mit den Worten Descartes „[w]ie ein Gefangener, der zufällig im Traume einer eingebildeten Freiheit genoss, bei dem späteren Argwohn, dass er nur träume, sich fürchtet aufzuwachen und deshalb den schmeichlerischen Täuschungen sich lange hingibt."

Aus dem Amerikanischen von Elisabeth Wiellander

Towards a Society of Control?

Otto Leopold Tremetzberger / Radio FRO 105.0

New Digital Standards and their Impact on Freedom of Information

Current Consequences and Strategies for an Independent Public Sphere

This year's festival theme, "Code—The Language of Our Time," poses the question of the socially regulative implications of the digital codes that are omnipresent in modern Information Society. They define "the rules by which we communicate in a networked world, do business, and gather and disseminate information." [1]

Control Of Standards Means Control Of Content

Constraint of diversity is not the only hidden danger inherent in standardization. Not the least of its consequences are possibilities of comprehensive control such as those currently being discussed in conjunction with the process of adopting uniform copyright laws throughout the EU.[2] After all, whoever controls standards also controls content in many respects. The EU copyright law amendment follows the American lead in extending copyright protection to the new media and particularly the Internet and, above all, provides for stricter measures against evading protection technology.

For years—and even prior to its experiences with swap exchanges like Napster—the software and music industry has been demanding stronger copy protection provisions. The industry is now getting support from lawmakers who, in their copyright law amendments, are legally legitimating the interests of the software and music monopolists and protecting with legal sanctions the "technical protective measures" that prevent any form of copying—even, in certain cases, copying for one's own personal use.

The criticism of those who are skeptical about DRM, like Fred Lohmann of the Electronic Frontier Foundation, point out that DRM cannot prevent "Internet piracy"; instead, the barriers being erected hinder content and, in the final analysis, the very market that only seems to be protected by these steps.[3] Tendentious digital standards like DRM thus contribute substantially to the development of an elitist Information Society in which access to information is reserved for those who can afford it, and this to an even greater extent than is already the case. In this respect, systems like Digital Rights Management become a form of Digital Restriction Management[4] and the "question of information becomes a question of one's budget."[5]

Developing Open Spaces

The history of open spaces is also a story of control strategies and the exertion of influence. Notwithstanding the deluge of data and its much-discussed unmanageability, it is precisely the digital sphere that offers thorough and comprehensive possibilities for control and censorship. While surveillance systems like ECHELON comb through the digital universe in search of questionable keywords and, in the wake of proclaimed national security considerations, proceed to disappear from the public debate and thus for the most part from public consciousness as well, alternative communication platforms and

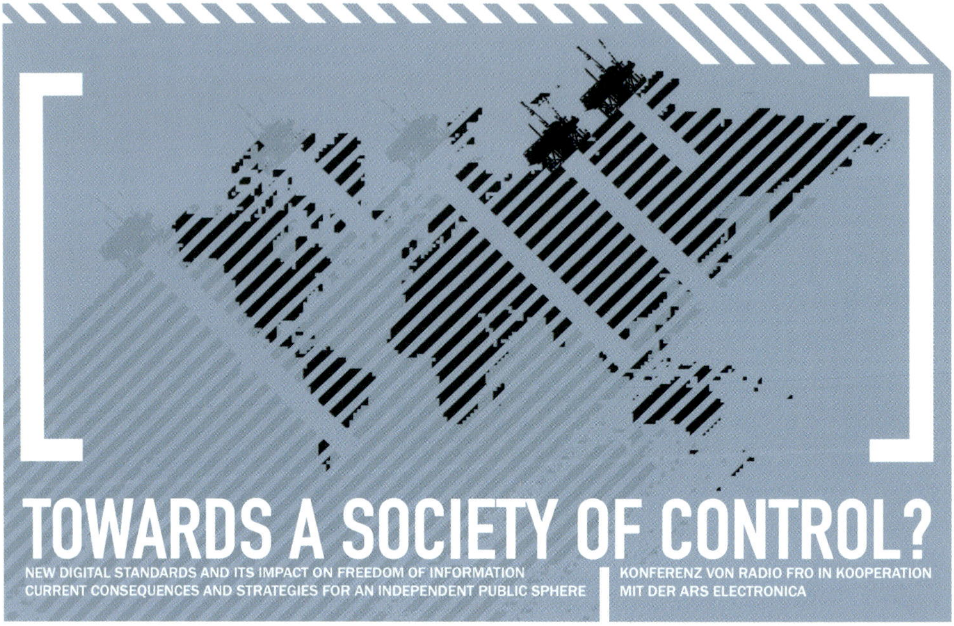

providers see themselves targeted by charges of illicit content. Parallel to the growing need for security, the preconditions for control—political and technological alike—are being put in place. "Digital human rights"—analogous to general human rights—freedom of information, privacy and the open access to information and the exchange thereof are the challenges now facing civil society.

"The great experiment of an unfettered communication space that the Internet as a public medium seemed to provide now seems more like a historical and temporary window of opportunity. If we still care about a common space of knowledge, ideas and information mediated world-wide by networked digital media, we can no longer accept that principle as a given; i.e. as 'naturally' embodied in the Internet."[6]

The emancipatory expectations that have been invested in the new media—first and foremost, the Internet—remain unfulfilled; their broad-based democratic, participative potential—said without any nostalgia—still has hardly been exploited and is stuck on the level of online voting. Experience shows that technological potential alone does not lead to democratization of information and knowledge; quite the contrary—completely in the interest of globalized markets, the "command/control" structure of technologies leads to increasing social homogenization.[7]

According to Eric Kluitenberg, the creation of independent "open zones" is now not only a matter of safe havens for data and a sort of "hygienic" (off) cyberspace but also of the formulation of strategies and tools for use in actual practice. After all: "the common space is defined and constructed through us. It is not given."[8]

Strategies and Purpose

A democratic society requires open access to information and knowledge as well as corresponding open forums and spaces in which this knowledge can be produced and published. Radio FRO poses the question of the interests, intentions and messages hidden behind digital codes. What consequences do digital and legal standards like DRM have on Information Society? What reactions to limitations and restrictions can be anticipated? If digital codes define the path that information and communication follow in global networks (and elsewhere as well), then what function do citizens' initiatives assume and what possibilities of reaction and subversion do they have? What is the impact of the rules of play in global communication and the multifarious regulative mechanisms on the existence and work of these initiatives? What strategies of evasion are currently available? What is the potential upshot of participation in light of developments in political policymaking and information technology that are increasingly oriented on regulation and surveillance? What possibilities are there to influence the course of events? If those who define the standards also control the content, then who controls these very groups? Instead of relieving the state of a burden, doesn't the privatization of responsibilities like security and privacy that have traditionally been within the purview of the state lead to the deprivation of the power of that state that legitimizes via legal guidelines the commercial interests of the giants of the software and music industry?

Festival Presentation

Experts in theory and practice discuss a wide range of issues including the implementation of EU guidelines (Digital Rights Management), changes in copyright law, the impact of digital standards on Information Society, current problems and issues, the interplay of technology, the economy and surveillance, as well as strategies of resistance. Radio FRO's panels at this year's ARS ELECTRONICA are an up-to-the-minute contribution to the debate on freedom of information and communication.

Panel A: Containing Information: New Digital Standards, Changes in Copyright and its Impact on Freedom of Information

The EU-wide legal legitimation of digital standards like DRM is in the interest of the software and music industry and leads to considerable restrictions on copyright. Tendentious digital standards are not only barriers to the free access to and exchange of information; they also put in place the technological infrastructure for future surveillance systems. Whoever controls the standards controls the contents too. Experts discuss the consequences of these developments for freedom of information and the interplay of technological, economic and political factors in the context of increasing restrictions in the world of the Infosphere.

Panel B: Digital Standards and the Public Domain: Consequences and Current Strategies For An Independent Public Sphere

Democratic societies need open access to information and knowledge, and open media domains in which this knowledge can be produced and published.
A confrontation with digital standards and their consequences for independent media and network initiatives. Current strategies, forms of resistance and restrictions, questions of privacy, copyright and censorship.

Translated from the German by Mel Greenwald

References cf. p. 56

Towards a Society of Control?

Otto Leopold Tremetzberger / Radio FRO 105,0

Information, die man sich leisten kann?
Digitale Standards und Informationsfreiheiten in der Infosphäre

Das Thema der Ars Electronica 2003 – „Code – The Language of Our Time" – stellt die Frage nach den gesellschaftsregulierenden Implikationen digitaler Codes: Digitale Codes sind in der modernen Informationsgesellschaft jederzeit präsent. Sie definieren „wie wir in den globalen Netzwerken miteinander kommunizieren, Geschäfte abwickeln, zu Information kommen und unser Wissen verteilen."[1]

Kontrolle der Standards ist Kontrolle des Content

Standardisierung birgt nicht nur die Gefahr der Einschränkung von Vielfalt. Sie bedeutet nicht zuletzt auch umfangreiche Kontrollmöglichkeiten, wie sie etwa gegenwärtig im Zuge der EU-weiten Anpassungen im Urheberrecht diskutiert werden.[2] Denn wer die Standards kontrolliert, kontrolliert vielfach auch die Inhalte. Die EU-Urheberrechtsnovelle dehnt nach US-amerikanischem Vorbild den Urheberrechtschutz auch auf die neuen Medien, insbesondere das Internet, aus und sieht vor allem auch verstärkte Maßnahmen gegen die Umgehung technischer Schutzeinrichtungen vor.
Vor den Erfahrungen mit Tauschbörsen wie Napster fordert die Software- und Musikindustrie bereits seit Jahren verstärkte Maßnahmen für den Kopierschutz. Unterstützung bekommt die Industrie nun von den Gesetzgebern, die in der Urheberrechtsnovelle die Interessen der Software- und Musikmonopolisten rechtlich legitimieren und „technische Schutzmaßnahmen", die jede Vervielfältigung u. U. auch für den eigenen Gebrauch verhindern, gegen Strafe schützen. Skeptiker des DRM wie etwa Fred von Lohmann (Electronic Frontier Foundation) kritisieren, dass DRM „Internet Piracy" nicht verhindern könne und stattdessen für den Content und letztlich auch für den nur scheinbar geschützten Markt selbst Barrieren aufgebaut werden (siehe Seite 48).[3] Einseitige digitale Standards wie das DRM tragen damit maßgeblich zur Entwicklung einer elitistischen Informationsgesellschaft bei, in der der Zugang zu Information jenen vorbehalten bleibt, die es sich leisten können, mehr noch und auf einer breiteren Basis als es bereits jetzt der Fall ist. An diesem Punkt werden Systeme wie das „Digital Rights Management" zu einem „Digital Restriction Management"[4] und die „Frage der Information wird eine Frage des Budgets".[5]

Offene Räume

Die Geschichte „offener Räume" ist auch eine Geschichte der Strategien von Kontrolle und Einflussnahme. Ungeachtet der Datenfluten und ihrer viel diskutierten Unüberschaubarkeit bietet gerade der digitale Raum gründliche und umfassende Möglichkeiten von Kontrolle und Zensur. Während Abhörsysteme wie ECHELON das digitale Universum nach fragwürdigen Schlüsselworten durchforsten und im Fahrwasser proklamierter nationaler Sicherheiten wieder aus der öffentlichen Debatte und damit weitgehend auch aus den Köpfen verschwunden sind, sehen sich alternative Kommunikationsplattformen und Provider dem Vorwurf illegalen

Contents ausgesetzt. Parallel zum wachsenden Bedürfnis nach Sicherheit werden auch die Voraussetzungen für Kontrolle – politisch wie technologisch – geschaffen. Analog zu den Allgemeinen Menschenrechten sind „Digital Human Rights“ – also Informationsfreiheit, Privacy und der offene Zugang zu Information und Informationsaustausch – die Herausforderungen der Zivilgesellschaft:

> The great experiment of an unfettered communication space that the Internet as a public medium seemed to provide, now seems more like a historical and temporary window of opportunity. If we still care about a common space of knowledge, ideas and information, mediated world-wide by networked digital media we can no longer accept that principle as a given; i.e. as "naturally" embodied in the Internet.[6]

Die emanzipatorischen Erwartungen an die neuen Medien, allen voran das Internet, haben sich nicht erfüllt, ihr demokratisches, partizipatives Potenzial auf breiter Basis bleibt – ohne Nostalgie – kaum ausgeschöpft und auf der Ebene von Online-Votings stecken. Die Erfahrung zeigt, dass allein das technologische Potenzial nicht zur Demokratisierung von Information und Wissen führt. Im Gegenteil: Ganz im Interesse der Globalisierten Märkte führt die „Command / Control“-Struktur der Technologien zu einer zunehmenden sozialen Homogenisierung.[7]

Mit Eric Kluitenberg geht es in der Frage der Schaffung unabhängiger „Open Zones“ nun nicht um sichere Datenhäfen und eine Art von „hygienischem“ (Off-)Cyberspace, sondern um die Formulierung von Strategien und Praxistools. Denn: "The common space is defined and constructed through us. It is not given."[8]

Strategien und Zielsetzungen

Eine demokratische Gesellschaft benötigt den offenen Zugang zu Information und Wissen und die entsprechenden offenen Foren und Räume, in denen dieses Wissen produziert und publiziert werden kann. Radio FRO stellt die Frage nach den Interessen, den Absichten und Botschaften, die sich hinter digitalen Codes verbergen. Welche Auswirkung haben digitale und rechtliche Standards wie DRM auf die Informationsgesellschaft? Wie sehen die Reaktionen auf Limitationen und Restriktionen aus? Wenn digitale Codes den Weg definieren, den Information und Kommunikation (nicht nur) in den globalen Netzwerken beschreiten: Welche Möglichkeiten der Reaktion und Subversion und welche gesellschaftspolitischen Funktionen haben Initiativen der Zivilgesellschaft? Wie wirken sich die Spielregeln der globalen Kommunikation, die vielfältigen Regulative auf die Existenz und Arbeit dieser Initiativen aus? Welche aktuellen Strategien des Unterlaufens gibt es? Was bedeutet Partizipation vor dem Hintergrund der zunehmend auf Regulation und Kontrolle ausgerichteten Entwicklungen in Politik und Informationstechnologie? Welche Möglichkeiten der Einflussnahme bestehen? Wenn diejenigen, die die Standards definieren, auch den Content kontrollieren, wer kontrolliert dann diese Gruppierungen selbst? Folgt mit der Privatisierung klassischer staatlicher Aufgaben wie Sicherheit und Privacy nicht die Entlastung, sondern die Entmachtung des Staates, der mit gesetzlichen Richtlinien die kommerziellen Interessen der Software- und Musikgiganten legitimiert?

Darstellung beim Festival Ars Electronica 2003

Expertinnen aus Theorie und Praxis diskutieren ausgehend von der Umsetzung der EU-Richtlinie (Digital Rights Management) zu Änderungen im Copyright über die Auswirkungen digitaler Standards auf die Informationsgesellschaft, aktuelle Problemstellungen, das Zusammenspiel von Technologie, Ökonomie und Überwachung sowie über Strategien von Widerstand. Der Beitrag von Radio FRO zur Ars Electronica 2003 liefert einen aktuellen Beitrag zur Debatte um Informations- und Kommunikationsfreiheit.

Panel A: Containing Information: New Digital Standards, Changes in Copyright and its Impact on Freedom of Information

Die EU-weite gesetzliche Legitimierung von digitalen Standards wie DRM führt im Interesse der Software- und Musikindustrie zu erheblichen Einschränkungen im Urheberrecht. Einseitige digitale Standards sind nicht nur Barrieren für den freien Zugang und Austausch von Information, sie stellen auch die technologische Infrastruktur für zukünftige Überwachungssysteme. Wer die Standards kontrolliert, kontrolliert auch die Inhalte. ExpertInnen diskutieren ihre Auswirkungen auf die Informationsfreiheit und das Zusammenspiel von Technologie, Wirtschaft und Politik vor dem Hintergrund zunehmender Restriktionen in der Welt der Infosphäre.

Panel B: Digital Standards and the Public Domain: Consequences and Current Strategies For An Independent Public Sphere

Demokratische Gesellschaften brauchen den offenen Zugang zu Information und Wissen und offene mediale Räume, in denen dieses Wissen produziert und publiziert werden kann.
Eine Auseinandersetzung mit den Digitalen Standards und ihre Auswirkungen auf unabhängige Medien und Netzinitiativen. Aktuelle Strategien, Widerstände und Beschränken, Fragen von Privacy, Copyright und Censorship.

---

1 *http://www.aec.at/code*
2 Siehe etwa den Artikel: „Mit Digital Rights Management direkt in den Zensurstaat":
http://www.heise.de/bin/nt.print/newsticker/data/anw-23.01.03-005/?id=62fd6699&todo=print
3 Fred v. Lohmann, "Digital Rights Management: The Skeptic's View:
http://www.eff.org/IP/DRM/20030401_drm_skeptics_view.php
4 Rene Pfeiffer, „Trusted Computing und Digital Rights Management": *http://www.ffs.or.at/artikel/tcpa_drm.pdf*
5 Andy Miller-Maguhn, Chaos Computer Club:
http://www.heise.de/bin/nt.print/newsticker/data/anw-23.01.03-005/?id=62fd6699&todo=print
6 Eric Kluitenberg, „Constructing the Digital Commons, A venture into hybridisation":
http://www.n5m4.org/journal.shtml?118+575+3411
7 Konrad Becker, „Tactical Reality Dictionary", Wien 2002
8 Eric Kluitenberg, „Constructing the Digital Commons, A venture into hybridisation":
http://www.n5m4.org/journal.shtml?118+575+3411

Protocol and Counter-Protocol

Alexander Galloway / Eugene Thacker

A proposition: code only "matters" when it is understood as being the substance of a network. For the last decade or more, network discourse has proliferated with a kind of epidemic intensity: P2P file sharing networks, WiFi community networks, terrorist networks, contagion networks of biowarfare agents, political swarming and distributed dissent, guerilla marketing, MMORPGs, PANs, cell phones, "generation txt" and on and on. Often, the discourse surrounding networks tends to pose itself both morally and architecturally against what it sees as retrograde structures like hierarchy and verticality, which have their concomitant techniques for keeping things under control: bureaucracy, the chain of command, and so on. But even beyond the field of technology, the concept of the network has infected broad swaths of contemporary life. Even the U.S. military, a bastion of vertical, pyramidal hierarchy, is redefining its internal structure around network architectures, as RAND researchers John Arquilla & David Ronfeldt have indicated in their work. They describe here the contemporary mode of conflict they call "netwar": "Netwar is about the Zapatistas more than the Fidelistas, Hamas more than the Palestine Liberation Organization (PLO), the American Christian Patriot movement more than the Ku Klux Klan, and the Asian Triads more than the Costa Nostra."[1]

These in/out lists are, of course, more fun to read than they are accurate political evaluations, but it is clear that the concept of connectivity is highly privileged in today's societies. In fact it is so highly privileged that it is becoming more and more difficult to locate places or objects which don't, in some way, fit into a networking rubric. The recent USA Patriot Act and other legislation allowing increased electronic surveillance further reinforces the deep penetration of networked technologies and networked thinking. As networks continue to propagate, it seems that there will not remain any sense of an "outside," a non-connected locale from which one may view this phenomenon and ponder it critically. Today's conventional wisdom cajoles us into thinking that everything can be subsumed under the warm security blanket of interconnectivity, but it hasn't yet told us quite what that means.

All of this fanfare around networks highlights for us the continued indissociability of politics and technology. There are several sides to the debate. The technophile perspective, such as that expressed by Howard Rheingold or Kevin Kelly, is an expression of both a technological determinism, and a view of technology as an enabling tool for the elevation of bourgeois humanism in a very general sense. The juridical/governance perspective, seen in the work of Lawrence Lessig, Yochai Benkler and others, posits a similar situation whereby networks will bring about a more just and freer social reality via legal safeguards. The network science perspective, expressed in popular books by authors such as Albert-László Barabási, portrays networks as a kind of apolitical natural law, operating universally across heterogeneous systems, be they terrorism, AIDS, or the Internet.

Yet this "network fever"[2] has a tendency to addle the brain, for we identify in the current literature a general willingness to ignore politics by masking it with the so-called black box of technology. Thus a goal of our current work is to provide ways of critically analyzing and engaging with this black box, with this ambivalence between politics and technology (in which, sadly, technology always seems to prevail).

The question we aim to explore here is: what is the principle of political organization or control that sews a network together? Writers like Michael Hardt & Antonio Negri have helped answer this question in the socio-political sphere. They describe the global principle of political organization as one of "empire." Like a network, empire is not reducible to any single state power, nor does it follow an architecture of pyramidal hierarchy. Empire is fluid, flexible, dynamic, and far-reaching. In that sense, the concept of empire helps us greatly to think about political organization in networks. But while we are inspired by Hardt & Negri's contribution to political philosophy, we are concerned that no one has yet adequately answered this question for the technological sphere of bits and atoms.

To this end, the principle of political control we suggest is most helpful for thinking about technological networks is *protocol,* a word derived from computer science but which resonates in the life sciences as well. Protocol abounds in techno-culture. It is a totalizing control apparatus that guides both the technical and political formation of computer networks, biological systems and other media. Put simply, protocols are all the conventional rules and standards that govern relationships within networks. Quite often these relationships come in the form of communication between two or more computers, but it can also refer to purely biological processes as in the systemic phenomenon of gene expression. Thus by "networks" we want to refer to any system of interrelationality, whether biological or informatic, organic or inorganic, technical or natural—with the ultimate goal of undoing the polar restrictiveness of these pairings.

In computer networks, science professionals have, over the years, drafted hundreds of protocols to govern email, web pages, and so on, plus many other standards for technologies rarely seen by human eyes. If networks are the structures that connect people, then protocols are the rules that make sure the connections actually work. Internet users commonly use protocols such as HTTP, FTP, and TCP/IP, even if they know little about how such technical standards function. In the world of biotechnology, protocols are employed at many levels, from the networks of protein-protein interactions in the cell, to the mixing of molecular protocols with the Internet (accessing a genome database), to the institutional and ethical protocols for the handling of biological materials in the lab. Protocol is both an apparatus that undergirds and facilitates networks and also a logic that governs how things are done within that apparatus. While, in our current network society, protocols are mostly understood within the context of information networks, we would add that a logic of protocological control exists in biological networks as well.

Today network science often conjures up the themes of anarchy, rhizomatics, distribution, and anti-authority to explain interconnected systems of all kinds. From these sometimes radical prognostications, and the larger technological discourse of thousands of white papers, memos, and manuals surrounding them, we can derive some of the basic qualities of the apparatus of organization which we here call protocol:

- protocol facilitates relationships between interconnected, but autonomous, entities;
- protocol's virtues include robustness, contingency, interoperability, flexibility, and heterogeneity;
- a goal of protocol is to accommodate everything, no matter what source or destination, no matter what origin, definition or identity;
- while protocol is universal, it is always achieved through negotiation (meaning that in the future protocol can and will be different);
- protocol is a system for maintaining organization and control in networks.

Each of these characteristics alone is enough to distinguish protocol from many previous modes of social and technical organization (such as hierarchy or bureaucracy). Together they compose a new, sophisticated system of distributed control. As a technology, protocol is implemented broadly, and is thus not reducible simply to the domain of institutional, governmental, or corporate power. In the broadest sense, protocol is a technology that regulates flow, directs netspace, codes relationships and connects life forms.

Networks always have several protocols operating in the same place at the same time. In this sense, networks are always slightly schizophrenic, doing one thing in one place and the opposite in another. Thus protocol has less to do with individually empowered human subjects who might be the engines of a teleological vision for protocol, than with manifold modes of individuation that arrange and re-dividuate both human and nonhuman elements. Protocol is a mode of control, and as such it contains within itself its own resistance. As we describe in more detail elsewhere, protocological control challenges us to rethink critical and political action around a newer framework, that of multi-agent, individuated nodes in a metastable (fluctuating within boundaries) network. Political action in the network, then, can be deliberately guided by human actors, or accidentally or "naturally" affected by nonhuman actors. Often, tactical misuse of a protocol, be it intended or unintended, can identify the political fissures in a network. Examples include computer viruses (protocol as biological) and emerging infectious disease (protocol as technological). We suggest that such moments, while sometimes politically ambiguous when taken out of context, can also serve as instances for a more critical, more politically-engaged "counter-protocol" practice. Protocological control brings into existence a certain contradiction, at once distributing agencies in a complex manner, while at the same time concentrating rigid forms of management and control. This means that protocol is less about power (confinement, discipline, normativity), and more about control (modulation, regulation, network identification). Whether counter-protocol practices can develop from this situation is, in part, dependent upon how we refigure the concepts of resistance, agency, and, in the end, "network affect."

---

1 John Arquilla & David Ronfeldt. *Networks and Netwars: The Future of Terror, Crime, and Militancy,* p 6. RAND, Santa Monica, 2001

2 See Mark Wigley's recent essay of the same name in *Grey Room* 4 (2001).

Protokoll und Gegenprotokoll

Alexander Galloway / Eugene Thacker

Eine These: Code hat nur „Bedeutung", wenn er als Substanz eines Netzwerks begriffen wird. In den letzten zehn Jahren oder mehr hat sich der Netzwerk-Diskurs mit nahezu epidemischer Intensität verbreitet: Es gibt P2P-Filesharing-Netzwerke, WiFi-Gemeinschaftsnetzwerke, terroristische Netzwerke, Netzwerke zur Verbreitung von Mitteln der biologischen Kriegsführung, politisches Swarming und verteilten Dissens, Guerilla-Marketing, MMORPGs, PANs, Mobiltelefone, „generation txt", usw. Oft stellt sich der ein Netzwerk umgebende Diskurs tendenziell sowohl moralisch als auch architektonisch gegen das, was er als rückwärtsgewandte Strukturen wie Hierarchie und Vertikalität erachtet, um die Dinge mit eigenen Techniken unter Kontrolle zu halten: die Bürokratie, die Befehlskette usw. Doch auch über den technologischen Bereich hinaus hat das Konzept des Netzwerks weite Teile unseres modernen Lebens bereits infiziert. Sogar das US-Militär, eine Bastion der vertikalen, pyramidalen Hierarchie, beginnt seine internen Strukturen mittels Netzwerkarchitekturen neu zu definieren, wie die RAND-Forscher John Arquilla und David Ronfeldt in ihrer Arbeit aufgezeigt haben. Darin beschreiben sie einen zeitgenössischen Konfliktmodus, den sie „Netzkrieg" nennen: „Beim Netzkrieg geht es eher um die Zapatisten als die Fidelisten, eher um die Hamas als die Palästinensische Befreiungsorganisation (PLO), eher um die American-Christian-Patriot-Bewegung als den Ku-Klux-Klan und eher um die Asiatischen Triaden als die Cosa Nostra."[1]

Solche In/Out-Listen sind natürlich eher amüsante Lektüre als präzise politische Bewertung, doch wird klar, dass das Konzept der Konnektivität in modernen Gesellschaften einen hohen Stellenwert hat. Dies geht tatsächlich so weit, dass es zunehmend schwieriger wird, Orte oder Objekte zu finden, die sich nicht auf irgendeine Weise in eine Netzwerk-Rubrik einordnen lassen. Der kürzlich in den Vereinigten Staaten beschlossene *Patriot Act* und andere Gesetze zur verstärkten elektronischen Überwachung lassen die Durchdringung mit vernetzten Technologien und vernetztem Denken noch tiefer gehen. So wie sich Netzwerke immer weiter verbreiten, scheint es fast, als bliebe kein Verständnis für das „Draußen", für einen nicht vernetzten Ort, von dem aus man dieses Phänomen betrachten und kritisch bewerten könnte. Das konventionelle Wissen der Gegenwart suggeriert uns, dass sich alles unter der warmen, schützenden Decke der Interkonnektivität subsumieren lässt, doch fehlt bisher die Erklärung, was wir uns darunter vorstellen sollen.

All das Getue um Netzwerke macht nur deutlich, dass Politik und Technik nach wie vor nicht voneinander zu trennen sind. Es gibt verschieden Aspekte dieser Debatte. Die technophile Perspektive, wie sie von Howard Rheingold oder Kevin Kelly vertreten wird, ist sowohl Ausdruck technologischen Determinismus als auch Interpretation von Technologie als Ermächtigungsinstrument für die Erhabenheit des bourgeoisen Humanismus in einem sehr allgemeinen Sinn. Die juridische und Governance-orientierte Perspektive, wie wir sie in den Arbeiten von Lawrence Lessig, Yochai Benkler und anderen finden, postuliert eine ähnliche Situation, in der Netzwerke mit Hilfe rechtlicher Schutzmechanismen eine gerechtere und freiere gesellschaftliche Realität schaffen. Die Perspektive der Netzwissenschaft – vertreten z. B. in den populärwissenschaftlichen Werken von Albert-László Barabási – bildet Netzwerke als eine Art apolitisches Naturgesetz ab, die universell über heterogene Systeme hinweg operieren – seien diese nun Terrorismus, AIDS oder das Internet.

Dennoch lässt dieses „Netzfieber"[2] das Gehirn tendenziell träge werden, da wir in der aktuellen Literatur eine allgemeine Bereitschaft feststellen, die Politik zu ignorieren, indem man ihr das Mäntelchen der so genannten technologischen Blackbox umhängt. So zielt unsere aktuelle Arbeit darauf ab, Möglichkeiten zu schaffen, wie man diese Blackbox kritisch analysieren bzw. sich kritisch mit dieser Ambivalenz zwischen Politik und Technik auseinandersetzen kann (in der die Technik leider immer die Oberhand zu behalten scheint).

Die Frage, der wir hier nachgehen wollen, lautet: Welches Prinzip der politischen Organisation oder Kontrolle hält dieses Netzwerk zusammen? Autoren wie Michael Hardt und Antonio Negri haben mitgeholfen, eine gesellschaftspolitische Antwort auf diese Frage zu finden. Sie beschreiben die globale politische Organisation als das Prinzip des „Empire“. Wie ein Netzwerk lässt sich das Empire nicht auf eine einzige Staatsmacht reduzieren; ebenso wenig folgt es einer Architektur pyramidaler Hierarchie. Das Empire ist fließend, flexibel, dynamisch und weit reichend. In diesem Sinn hilft uns das Konzept des Empire einen großen Schritt weiter, wenn es darum geht, sich politische Organisationen als Netzwerke vorzustellen. Doch während wir uns von Hardt und Negris Beitrag zur politischen Philosophie inspirieren lassen, befürchten wir gleichzeitig, dass noch niemand diese Frage im Hinblick auf die technische Sphäre der Bits und Atome ausreichend beantwortet hat.

Zu diesem Zweck schlagen wir ein Prinzip politischer Kontrolle vor, das in der Betrachtung technologischer Netzwerke höchst hilfreich sein wird, nämlich das *Protokoll* – ein Wort aus der Computerwissenschaft, das jedoch auch ins Biologische spielt. Protokoll kommt in der Techno-Kultur ausgesprochen häufig vor. Es handelt sich dabei um einen totalisierenden Kontrollapparat, der sowohl die technische als auch die politische Formation von Computernetzwerken, biologischen Systemen und anderen Medien lenkt. Einfach gesagt, stellen Protokolle sämtliche konventionelle Regeln und Normen dar, die die Beziehungen innerhalb von Netzwerken kontrollieren. Ziemlich häufig treten diese Beziehungen als Kommunikation zwischen zwei oder mehreren Computern auf, doch können sie sich auch auf rein biologische Prozesse (wie in dem systematischen Phänomen der Genexpression) beziehen. In diesem Sinn möchten wir den Begriff „Netzwerk“ auf jegliches System der Interrelationalität beziehen, sei dieses biologisch oder informatisch, organisch oder anorganisch, technisch oder natürlich – mit dem ultimativen Ziel, die polare Restriktivität dieser Paarungen aufzubrechen.

Im Lauf der Jahre haben Wissenschaftler in Computernetzwerken Hunderte Protokolle entworfen, um E-Mails, Web-Pages usw. zu verwalten, sowie zahlreiche andere Standards für Technologien, die das menschliche Auge nur selten erblickt. Wenn Netzwerke die Strukturen sind, die Menschen verbinden, dann sind Protokolle die Regeln, die sicherstellen, dass diese Verbindungen auch wirklich funktionieren. Internetuser verwenden normalerweise Protokolle wie HTTP, FTP und TCP/IP, auch wenn sie wenig darüber wissen, wie diese technischen Standards funktionieren. In der Welt der Biotechnologie kommen Protokolle auf vielen Ebenen zum Einsatz, von den Netzwerken der Protein-Protein-Interaktionen in der Zelle über die Vermischung von Molekularprotokollen mit dem Internet (Zugriff auf eine Genom-Datenbank) bis hin zu den institutionellen und ethischen Protokollen zur Handhabung biologischer Materialien im Labor. Das Protokoll ist sowohl ein Apparat, der die Grundlage für ein Netzwerk bildet, als auch die Logik, die die Abläufe innerhalb dieses Apparats bestimmt. Während in unserer aktuellen Netzwerkgesellschaft Protokolle zumeist im Zusammenhang mit Informationsnetzwerken verstanden werden, möchten wir noch hinzufügen, dass auch in biologischen Netzwerken eine Logik der protokollogischen Kontrolle existiert.

Heute beschwört die Netzwissenschaft oft Themen wie Anarchie, Rhizomatik, Verteilung und Antiautorität, um verbundene Systeme jeglicher Art zu beschreiben. Aus diesen manchmal radikalen Prognosen sowie dem breiter gefassten technischen Diskurs Tausender Weißbücher, Memos, und Handbücher in ihrem Umfeld können wir einige der Grundqualitäten des Organisationsapparats ableiten, den wir hier als Protokoll bezeichnen:

- Ein Protokoll erleichtert die Beziehungen zwischen verbundenen, jedoch autonomen Entitäten;
- zu den Eigenschaften des Protokolls zählen Robustheit, Kontingenz, Interoperabilität, Flexibilität und Heterogenität;
- ein Ziel des Protokolls besteht darin, alles unterzubringen, ganz egal, welche Quelle oder welcher Zweck, welche ursprüngliche Definition oder Identität;
- obwohl das Protokoll universell ist, kann es immer durch Verneinung erzielt werden (d.h. dass das Protokoll der Zukunft anders sein kann und wird);
- ein Protokoll ist ein System zur Aufrechterhaltung von Organisation und Kontrolle in Netzwerken.

Jede dieser Eigenschaften reicht für sich allein aus, um ein Protokoll von den vielen bisherigen Formen der gesellschaftlichen und technischen Organisation zu unterscheiden (wie Hierarchie oder Bürokratie). Gemeinsam bilden sie ein neues, raffiniertes System der verteilten Kontrolle. Als Technologie wird das Protokoll umfassend angewendet und lässt sich somit nicht auf die Macht von Institutionen, Regierungen oder Großkonzernen reduzieren. Im weitesten Sinn stellt das Protokoll eine Technologie dar, die Datenströme reguliert, Webspace verwaltet, Beziehungen kodiert und Lebensformen miteinander verbindet.
Bei Netzwerken sind immer mehrere Protokolle gleichzeitig am selben Ort aktiv. Daher sind Netzwerke immer leicht schizophren, da sie an einem Ort dies, an einem anderen Ort genau das Gegenteil davon ausführen. So hat Protokoll weniger mit autorisierten Einzelpersonen zu tun, die die Antriebskraft einer teleologischen Vision eines Protokolls darstellen könnten, sondern eher mit den zahlreichen Formen der Individuation, die sowohl menschliche als auch nicht menschliche Elemente anordnen und redividualisieren. Ein Protokoll ist eine Form der Kontrolle, und als solches enthält es in sich einen eigenen Widerstand. Wie wir dies anderweitig im Detail beschrieben haben, fordert uns die protokollogische Kontrolle dazu heraus, kritisches und politisches Handeln in einem aktuelleren Rahmen neu zu überdenken, nämlich im Hinblick auf individualisierte Multi-Agent-Knoten in einem metastabilen (d. h. innerhalb bestimmter Grenzen fluktuierenden) Netzwerk. Politisches Handeln im Netzwerk kann dann bewusst durch menschliche Akteure gelenkt oder zufällig bzw. „natürlich" von nicht menschlichen Akteuren ausgelöst werden. Oft kann der taktische Missbrauch eines Protokolls, sei er beabsichtigt oder nicht, die politischen Risse eines Netzwerks identifizieren. Man denke nur an Computerviren (biologisches Protokoll) und neu auftretende Infektionskrankheiten (technologisches Protokoll). Wir behaupten, dass solche Momente, wenn sie auch außerhalb des Kontexts politisch manchmal doppeldeutig sind, auch als Beispiele für eine kritischere, stärker politisch engagierte Praxis der „Gegenprotokolle" dienen können. Protokollogische Kontrolle ruft auch Widerspruch hervor, da sie einerseits auf komplexe Weise Agencies verteilt, während sie gleichzeitig strenge Management- und Kontrollformen einsetzt. Dies bedeutet, dass es bei Protokollen weniger um Macht (Beschränkung, Disziplin, Normativität) und mehr um Kontrolle (Modulation, Regulierung, Netzwerk-Identifizierung) geht. Ob sich unter solchen Voraussetzungen Gegenprotokoll-Praktiken entwickeln können ist zum Teil davon abhängig, wie wir die Konzepte Widerstand, Agency und letztendlich „Network Effect" refigurieren.

Aus dem Amerikanischen von Susanne Steinacher

---

1 Arquilla, John und Ronfeldt, David: *Networks and Netwars: The Future of Terror, Crime, and Militancy,* RAND, Santa Monica 2001, S. 6.
2 Siehe Mark Wigleys kürzlich unter demselben Titel erschienen Essay in *Grey Room* 4, 2001.

The Birth of MacroMind

Marc Canter

When we started MacroMind we had a vision of a world where PCs and other consumer electronic devices featured highly interactive computer graphic and music interfaces. This world was our version of the scene from *Blade Runner,* where the hero dives into the photo—navigating through the pixels at x1,000. We knew that the digital future would need tools and we were toolsmiths, experienced in producing development tools for videogames.

But when we started MacroMind, we didn't know anything about a GUI or mouse. We didn't know anything about the PC industry or selling software. All we knew was that the Macintosh had a whopping 128k of RAM and built-in audio and video cards—and that's all we needed to know.

We were videogame guys from Bally-Midway in Chicago. Our company was first called Chicago Software, until we decided three days later to name it after one of the characters in my co-founder Jay Fenton's game—GORF. We were working on its sequel Ms. GORF together when Jay and I, along with our other co-founder Mark Pierce, incorporated MacroMind in April 1984.

One thing we knew—that the world needed end-user "tools" that could be used by artists, musicians and designers—to create this "stuff"—this combination of graphics, text, music and interactivity that we knew was possible. Digital video was still a far away dream, but we knew what the potential of computer music and graphics was—as we all had been working with it—throughout the late 70's in Chicago.

But the only way to control computers to do musical or visual things back in 1983 was to program it with C, FORTH or some other programming tool.

So we set out to create videogame development tools that could be used by artists or musicians. We called ourselves a software rock & roll band and were represented by the Wm. Morris talent agency. We likened ourselves to modern day poets, rock stars or painters, crafting our tools like great gunsmiths or watchmakers before us.

This notion of an end-user tool that was the modern day violin/paintbrush is what was behind our original product SoundVision. But our publisher insisted that we separate the concept and create two products: MusicWorks for computer music (which became the MIDI and sampling software business) and VideoWorks for graphics and animation (which evolved into multimedia animation and authoring systems.)

MusicWorks was released in Oct. 1984 and featured the first music score, real-time timeline. It also had a piano keyboard timeline and an Overview window. As the music was playing, the end-user could plop down quarter notes or eight notes or draw on the piano scroll. This was radical stuff back in 1984 and drew the attention of Alan Kay, Steve Jobs and the Macintosh community. This was back before MIDI existed.

But within 12 months there were over 10 other Macintosh music products, and there were fewer than 100,000 Macs out there! Because such an inordinate number of programmers were also musicians, the Macintosh GUI was like a magnet for everyone who EVER dreamed of a real-time interactive music interface.

VideoWorks was released in June 1985—and that turned out to be our saving grace. By Xmas of '85 we had baked a tiny basic scripting language into the VideoWorks timeline and licensed it to Apple, to produce guided tour training discs which would ship with every Macintosh. VideoWorks' timeline synchronized multiple channels of moveable sprites with an audio channel. Any sprite could be moved at any frame, and as thousands of frames zipped by, designers found themselves with a dynamic world that could combine and move design elements and navigation controls along motion paths around the screen. A scripting system was interlaced with this synchronization mechanism enabling creative people to decide where a hot-spot was, what action would happen upon clicking on that hot spot and to completely redefine what menus were.

Each multimedia menu took on a character of its own, and thus was born "multimedia authoring." Hypercard was around at the same time, but because it was based on a non-time-based card system, it lacked the ability to author the dynamic nature of multimedia (but DID have database capabilities!) By re-defining what menus were and creating entirely new worlds of education, entertainment and visualization, multimedia designers had in their hands a tremendous powerful new kind of tool which could take them into any realm.

Empowering normal, non-technical people to author multimedia was what we stumbled onto, not by design or intent. We discovered multimedia authoring because that's what the market needed, what the world needed—at that point in time (mid-late 80's.) We just looked out around the landscape and saw what was possible, and sat down next to the people who were building these multimedia thingies—and we then gave them what they wanted and needed.

This was the secret to Director. We WERE multimedia developers. We kept our company going, doing gigs for Microsoft, Ashton-Tate, Lotus and Borland. We practically invented the concept of the floppy disc (later CD ROM) marketing and training disk. We did our first projects in 1985—and had to give up the practice in 1988 when the VCs entered into our lives and insisted that we not compete with our own customers.

So because we had a direct connection to the animators, designers and musicians who were using our tools, we knew exactly what features and capabilities they needed. We also put our programmers into our trade show booths and had them demo to potential customers. This made them understand how people were seeing and approaching their software. These were some of the reasons that Director evolved as it did.

But what was really going on was that we were participating in the first golden era of software development—which started with the release of Lotus 1-2-3. Pagemaker, Photoshop, Painter, Filemaker, Quicken, Sidekick, MORE, Quark Express, Word and Word Perfect. Productivity software took the power of microcomputers and put it into the hands of non-programmers. That was a big deal back in 1986!

Now in 2003 we look back and laugh. But we're not done yet.

The New Paradigm of Tools

We've barely moved forward since those days of word processors and spreadsheets. Since 1988, the only major new software categories that have been created are email, IM, browsers and blogging tools. For all the flack, noise and supposed development, we have barely innovated the initial concept of what a tool is.

And we've lost track of what some of the potential of digital media is.

Doug Engelbart talks about an augmented computer experience which improves the way human beings interact and work together. Don Norman talks about an invisible computer and activity based approach to user experiences. Nicholas Negroponte has talked about bits and the digital convergence. Only 3% of the world's fiber infrastructure is currently being utilized.

I have (over the past 11 years since I left Macromedia) done applied research in scalable content and developed various implementations of multimedia personalization. Whatever you call it, there is a new paradigm of tools coming which will jump forward as far from where we are today as did that jump from assembly language programming to productivity tools in the 1980s.

Tools today are still fundamentally based upon shrink wrapped product mentality. It goes on a truck to a warehouse, where it is distributed through a two-tier system to retail locations, where consumers come in cars and pay for the product—upfront. They then take it home, by themselves, read the manual, by themselves, and attempt to use the product. That product outputs traditional formats for traditional distribution systems—and you'll have to BUY any additional upgrades, improvements or retrofits to new technology.

That all seems pretty archaic to me.

In 1997 Dave Winer had a content management system called Frontier which had a web site framework and series of utilities surrounding it. Dave found that he needed various communications and data flow control, so he started to develop a sophisticated set of capabilities and functions that worked with a browser, on-line servers and a simple, outline based scripting language. He invented a protocol mechanism for sending and discovering any sort of XML data (XML-RPC.) He was in a zone.

As I sat next to Dave and watched this object database shuffle, filter and sort data, I wondered at how direct, simple and easy it was to manipulate (what I thought were) complex data structures and procedures. To my delight I saw a simplistic system of customization and templating that could be easily adapted to many of the things I wanted to do!

At that point I knew that these huge web creation engines (like Vignette, Broadvision, Interwoven, ATG had) were in fact just grown up versions of Dave's Frontier system. But these huge systems were relegated to building traditional web sites and ecommerce (partially because of their cost and complexity), and were not pushing the envelope as to what was possible.

But Dave (and a company named Pyra) stumbled onto something that WOULD push the envelope—blogging. By 1999 Dave had a hosted blog service called EditThisPage just about at the same time that Pyra released Blogger. These early blogging tools were the first of what I call this new paradigm of tools, where everything the end-user needs is right there in front of them—in the browser page.

As the blogosphere evolved, Dave released Radio Userland, which put the blogging tool on the client's machine and integrated a new aggregator with the tool. Thus was born the next step of this paradigm, kind of picking up where Napster (and the other P2P clients) leave off.

News aggregators were made possible because Dave and Netscape had developed a syndication standard called RSS and all of a sudden any blogger could have their blog's RSS channel subscribed to—off a list right next to the NY Times or the BBC's channels. Other standards like OPML and the MetaWeblogAPI came out and this all fueled what we know as the blogosphere today. These standards combined with XML-RPC led to the rise of news aggregators and a world of 100,000's of RSS feeds and blogs.

This blogosphere has enabled new kinds of communities and interaction, all based upon the simple premise of personal publishing. As Anil Dash declared it, this was the era of "micro-content," where smart, distributed chunks of content would usher in an era of customizable, sustainable ecosystems. New kinds of micro-content "browsers" would come into being, enabling whole new kinds of navigation and browsing. I had often dreamed of going beyond just linking that T B-L gave us. I've often wanted a 2-way link, or a video or audio link or a link that expressed what sort of link it was. I discovered (through the blogosphere BTW) that the dream of semantic web was coming into reality.

The blogosphere is based upon the principle of self expression as a new kind of amateur journalism, whether you are reporting on the Battle for Baghdad or in your backyard. What I began to see was how the technology, spirit, ethics and process of the blogosphere can be applied beyond to much larger areas of influence.
The syndication and alternative distribution systems that drive the blogosphere will give birth to much more than just amateur journalism.
Jonathan Peterson in his Corante.com blog "The Me in Media" writes about new trends in personal publishing and how individuals one day will generate the majority of on-line media. The belief in 'narrowcasting' is something that has inspired me for years, and we have put a NARROWCASTING button into our new tool WebOutliner—even though we don't really know what narrowcasting is and what it can do.
But we're confident that our end-users will tell us. Just like we learned from the early days of VideoWorks, we're planning on evolving with the market—just as soon as we figure out what it is! This process of iterative design was the secret behind Director and something that can't be formerly engineered, scheduled or Gant charted.

Open Standards

When I was a young entrepreneur I was introduced (by Dave Winer) to a book which became my marketing bible —Marketing Warfare—by Reiss & Trout. This book talked about erecting a new hill (which represented a new product category) and erecting barriers of entry on top of that hill, holding off your competition with machine guns and hand grenades. This is how we captured and held onto the nascent multimedia authoring tools business.
In fact that lock-in strategy of ours has done pretty well for Macromedia. 15 years later they have 97 percent of all the browsers running their Flash format.
But in 1994 a guy named Doc Searls said: *"It shouldn't be warfare, it should be a conversation,"* and thus a new trend was born, which was personified in a book called the ClueTrain manifesto. In this book Doc and his fellow Cluetrainers tried to explain that if you don't listen to and work with your customer, you'll be gone.
And in fact they're not your customers anymore. They're your partners, because without them, you're nothing. This new refreshing approach to how software is bought and sold has given birth to a new open world of standards and source code.
Open source and open standards have evolved over the past eight years, providing LAMP (Linux, Apache, MySql, Python/Perl/php) and an NEA kind of environment for all to use: No one controls it. Everyone can use it. And Anyone can improve it.
The Internet has blossomed into a rich garden of innovation and from that garden is springing a new paradigm for tools. It's a World of Ends—where the distributed power of people working together can conquer over the entrenched powers and infrastructure.
In fact it's a new kind of infrastructure that we're building.
Many people ask me how to make money in the open source world. I always point to the story of Jabber—which is both an .org and .com. We plan on offering our WebOutliner as "open source" and will ask only one thing from those who use the code: you have to link to us and give us credit.
We plan on making money selling our software based upon the principle of "pay for using." The WebOutliner will allow you to use it for free—as long as you save your files onto our servers. But if you want to save your files onto your OWN servers or local drives, then we'll ask for $ 40. You won't be ABLE to upload your media onto servers at all. You can dabble with the tool as much as you want, but the moment you start relying upon and caring about what you've created; then THAT's when we think we can ask for money.

Everything we need has been invented, now it's time to get it all to work together

OK—so all these trends are lining up, we've got open standards and lots of open source code (and more coming—thanks to Mitch and Andy!)

One of the most exciting evolutions I see coming is how the technical and social standards established within the blogosphere will spread around the world. This process will happen if for no other reason than because ISPs need to sell bandwidth and there's almost an unlimited amount of it. So they use software to differentiate their offerings.

The same goes with consumer electronics vendors and system operators. In fact there's almost an endless amount of entities that can benefit from these new kinds of tools and the functionality and content they enable.

But (of course) the best stuff will come from the digital artists and musicians (and others) who just wanna play with it. There's so much to do! Contributative and open galleries, collaboratories, Wikis, forumne entirely news, social networks and systems will be created to enable new forms of creativity.

If you can imagine a new kind of interactive TV show which originated on someone's PC, and which narrowcast itself out to a limited number of people—well that's just ONE thing that's gonna happen!

Virtual garage sales will enable folks to sell off their stuff—and go around eBay. New kinds of tools will enable the creation of new kinds of micro-content, while also providing a built-in on-line community of fellow micro-contenters.

One of the ways that this could happen is what Seb Paquet calls Structured blogging. This idea of micro-content can be applied to lots of other kinds of media and data types. A person's persistent digital identity profile can be thought of as micro-content. A media library or a collection of photos (albums) or music or video (playlists) are also micro-content types. These are the obvious new kinds of micro-content.

But there are also some rather revolutionary new kinds of micro-content. A conversation (whether it be from an IM or chat session, email interchange or message board or forum) can be micro-content. A review of a movie, record or restaurant can also be micro-content. And an entire on-line community can be encapsulated as micro-content.

Tim O'Reilly talks about new kinds of distribution systems. What we have to imagine is what happens when new kinds of tools create lots of new kinds of micro-content which enable new kinds of on-line communities.

This is what our company—Broadband Mechanics—is doing, and we hope that as many new tools and technology as possible will enter into this ripe arena. The idea is that all of us together can equal what Microsoft is working on, which they call Longhorn.

It's possible that an inter-connecting world of micro-content servers and RSS aware tools can create a distributed, open source, web services based People's Mesh.

Longhorn and Apple's iLife will be the litmus we will compare our People's Mesh to. The goal would be to equal their functionality, but have it free and open for us all to use.

Die Geburt von MacroMind

Marc Canter

Am Beginn von Macromind stand unsere Vision einer Welt, in der PCs und andere Geräte der Unterhaltungselektronik mit höchst interaktiven Grafik- und Musikinterfaces ausgestattet waren. Das war unsere Version jener Szene aus *Blade Runner,* in der der Held ins Foto eintaucht – und mit 1.000 Sachen durch die Pixel jagt. Wir wussten, die digitale Zukunft braucht Werkzeuge; und wir waren Werkzeugmacher mit Erfahrung in der Herstellung von Entwicklungswerkzeugen für Videospiele.

Allerdings hatten wir beim Start von Macromind keine Ahnung von GUIs oder Mäusen. Wir hatten keinerlei Kenntnisse von der PC-Industrie oder vom Softwareverkauf. Wir wussten nur, dass der Macintosh unglaubliche 128 kB RAM und eingebaute Audio- und Videokarten hatte – und mehr brauchten wir nicht zu wissen.

Wir kamen vom Videospielhersteller Bally-Midway in Chicago. Unsere Firma hieß zuerst Chicago Software, wir tauften sie aber drei Tage später nach einer Figur in einem Videospiel meines Kompagnons Jay Fenton – GORF. Wir arbeiteten gerade an der Fortsetzung *Ms. GORF,* als Jay, ich und Mark Pierce als drittes Gründungsmitglied Macromind im April 1984 gründeten. Eines war uns klar – die Welt brauchte benutzerfreundliche „Tools“, die es Künstlern, Musikern und Grafikern ermöglichten, jenes „Zeugs“ – diese Mischung aus Grafik, Text, Musik und Interaktivität – zu kreieren, das uns vorschwebte. Digitales Video war noch in weiter Ferne, aber wir wussten um das Potenzial, das in Computermusik und -grafik steckte – hatten wir doch in Chicago in den späten 1970er Jahren ständig damit zu tun.

1983 konnte man allerdings einen Computer nur mit C, FORTH oder einem ähnlichen Programmierwerkzeug dazu bringen, musikalische oder visuelle Leistungen zu vollbringen.

Deshalb machten wir uns daran, Entwicklungstools für Videospiele zu schaffen, die auch Künstler oder Musiker einsetzen konnten. Wir bezeichneten uns selbst als „Software-Rock-&-Roll-Band“ und wurden von der Agentur Wm. Morris vertreten. Wir sahen uns als moderne Poeten, Rockstars oder Maler, die wie ehedem die großen Büchsen- oder Uhrmacher ihre Werkzeuge selbst herstellten.

Wir hatten diese Idee eines Endanwender-Werkzeugs, eines modernen Violin-Pinsels, für unser erstes Produkt *SoundVision.* Doch unser Verleger bestand darauf, das Konzept zu teilen und zwei Produkte zu kreieren: *MusicWorks* für die Computermusik (wurde später zu MIDI und Sampling-Software) und *VideoWorks* für Grafik und Animation (entwickelte sich zu Multimedia-Animation und Autorensystemen).

Im Oktober 1984 erschien *MusicWorks,* das über die erste Echtzeit-Timeline für Musiknotation verfügte. Es gab auch eine Klaviatur-Timeline und ein Überblicksfenster. Während der Musikwiedergabe konnte der Benutzer Viertel- oder Achtelnoten direkt oder über die Klaviertastatur einfügen. 1984 war das eine Sensation und erweckte die Aufmerksamkeit von Alan Kay, Steve Jobs und der Macintosh-Gemeinde. Und das lange vor MIDI.

Doch innerhalb von zwölf Monaten gab es bereits zehn weitere Musikprodukte für den Macintosh, von dem noch nicht einmal 100.000 verkauft waren. Da ungeheuer viele Programmierer auch Musiker waren, wirkte das Macintosh-GUI wie ein Magnet auf jeden, der schon IMMER von einem interaktiven Echtzeit-Musikinterface geträumt hatte.

VideoWorks erschien im Juni 1985 – und wurde zu unserem Rettungsanker. Bereits Weihnachten 1985 hatten wir eine simple Scriptsprache in die Timeline von *VideoWorks* integriert

und an Apple lizenziert, die damit animierte Lernprogramme auf Disketten produzierten, die mit jedem Macintosh ausgeliefert wurden.
Die Timeline von *VideoWorks* synchronisierte mehrere Kanäle verschiebbarer Sprites mit einem Audiokanal. Jeder Sprite konnte zu jedem Frame verschoben werden und plötzlich fanden sich die Grafiker – mit Tausenden vorbeizischenden Frames – in einer dynamischen Welt, in der sie Grafik- und Navigationselemente beliebig zu einer Animation kombinieren konnten. In diesen Synchronisierungsmechanismus wurde ein Scriptsystem eingebunden. Damit konnten kreative Köpfe Hot-Spots gezielt setzen und festlegen, was passiert, wenn man sie anklickt, und eine völlige Neudefinition von Menüs vornehmen.
Jedem Multimedia-Menü wurde eine eigene Funktion zugewiesen und schon war das „Multimedia-Authoring" geboren. Zur selben Zeit gab es auch schon Hypercard, mit dem aber die dynamische Natur von Multimedia nicht machbar war (dafür lag seine Stärke in der Datenbank!), weil es auf einem nicht-zeitbasierten Kartensystem beruhte.
Dank der Neudefinition, was alles als Menü fungieren konnte, und der Schaffung völlig neuer Bildungs-, Unterhaltungs- und Visualisierungswelten hatten Multimedia-Designer ein extrem leistungsfähiges Werkzeug an der Hand, das sie in jede Sphäre vordringen ließ.
Eher zufällig ermöglichten wir es normalen Nicht-Technikern, Multimedia-Inhalte zu kreieren. Wir entdeckten das Multimedia-Authoring, weil der Markt und die Welt dies damals (Mitte bis Ende der 1980er Jahre) brauchten. Wir schauten uns um, erkannten die Möglichkeiten und setzten uns mit den Leuten an einen Tisch, die diesen Multimedia-Kram machten. Und gaben ihnen dann genau das, was sie wollten und brauchten.
Das ist das Geheimnis hinter *Director.* Wir *waren* Multimedia-Entwickler. Mit Aufträgen von Microsoft, Ashton-Tate und Borland lief unsere Firma prächtig. Wir sind quasi die Erfinder der Marketing- und Schulungsdiskette (bzw. später CD-ROM). 1985 absolvierten wir unsere ersten Projekte – und mussten sie 1988 einstellen, als die Videokonsolen auf der Bildfläche auftauchten und uns die Konkurrenz mit unseren eigenen Kunden untersagt wurde.
Weil wir einen direkten Draht zu den Animatoren, Grafikern und Musikern hatten, die unsere Werkzeuge einsetzten, wussten wir ganz genau, welche Funktionen und Fähigkeiten sie benötigten. Außerdem ließen wir auf den Fachmessen unsere Programmierer die Software den Interessenten vorführen. So lernten sie die Sicht- und Herangehensweise der User verstehen. Das sind einige der Gründe, warum sich *Director* letztlich so entwickelt hat.
Der glücklichste Umstand war jedoch die Tatsache, dass wir uns in der ersten goldenen Ära der Softwareentwicklung befanden, die mit der Veröffentlichung von Lotus 1-2-3, Pagemaker, Photoshop, Painter, Filemaker, Quicken, Sidekick, MORE, Quark Express, Word und Word Perfect begann. Mit der Produktivitätssoftware verlagerte sich die Macht der Mikrocomputer hin zu den Nicht-Programmierern. 1986 war das eine große Sache!
2003 blicken wir zurück und lachen. Wir sind aber noch nicht fertig.

Werkzeuge und ihr neues Paradigma

Allerdings sind wir seit diesen Zeiten der Textverarbeitungen und Tabellenkalkulationen kaum vom Fleck gekommen. Die einzig wirklich neuen Softwarekategorien seit 1988 sind E-Mail, IM (Instant Messages), Browser und Blogging-Werkzeuge. Trotz allen Tamtams und der vermeintlichen Entwicklung hat sich die ursprüngliche Idee, was ein Werkzeug ausmacht, kaum erneuert.
Und wir haben einige Möglichkeiten digitaler Medien aus den Augen verloren.
Doug Engelbart spricht von einer intensivierten Computererfahrung, die Interaktion und Kooperation der Menschen steigert. Don Norman sieht einen unsichtbaren Computer und setzt auf aktivitätsbasierte Usererfahrung. Nicholas Negroponte erörtert Bits und die digitale Vereinigung. Weltweit werden derzeit nur drei Prozent der Glasfaserinfrastruktur genützt.

Ich habe (seit meinem Weggang von Macromedia vor elf Jahren) angewandte Forschung im Bereich skalierbarer Inhalte betrieben und verschiedene Implementierungen einer Multimedia-Personalisierung entwickelt. Wie immer man es auch nennen mag, wir stehen an der Schwelle eines neuen Werkzeug-Paradigmas, das uns genau so weit nach vorne katapultieren wird wie damals in den 1980ern, als der Wechsel vom Programmieren in Assembler zu den Produktivitätswerkzeugen erfolgte.
Software-Tools werden auch heute noch vornehmlich fertig verpackt angeboten. Per Lkw kommen sie in ein Lager, von wo aus sie über ein zweistufiges Distributionssystem in die Läden kommen, zu denen die Kunden hinfahren und wo sie für das Produkt bezahlen müssen – im Voraus. Sie nehmen es mit nach Hause, lesen das Handbuch und versuchen die Software einzusetzen. Das Produkt liefert traditionelle Ausgabeformate für traditionelle Verteilernetze – der Kunde muss weitere Upgrades, Verbesserungen oder Implementierungen von neuen Techniken *kaufen.*
Das alles erscheint mir ziemlich altmodisch.
1997 hatte Dave Winer das Content-Management-System *Frontier* entwickelt, das aus einer Basis-Website und einer Reihe von Tools bestand. Dave wollte auch verschiedene Möglichkeiten der Kommunikations- und Datenflusskontrolle, weshalb er die Fähigkeiten und Funktionen für Browser und Online-Server weiter verfeinerte und eine einfache Scriptsprache integrierte. Er erfand ein Protokoll zum Senden und Aufspüren von allen möglichen XML-Daten (XML-RPC). Er war in einer Zone.
Während ich neben Dave saß und zusah, wie diese Objektdatenbank die Daten herumschob, filterte und sortierte, war ich von der Direktheit und Leichtigkeit, mit der die (wie ich dachte) komplizierten Datenstrukturen und Prozeduren manipuliert wurden, begeistert. Zu meiner Freude hatte ich ein einfachstes System für Maßlösungen und zur Erstellung von Vorlagen entdeckt, das sich leicht an alle meine Vorhaben anpassen ließ!
Plötzlich war mir klar, dass die riesigen Webapplikationssysteme (wie sie Vignette, Broadvision, Interwoven oder ATG anboten) de facto „erwachsene" Varianten von Daves System *Frontier* waren. Allerdings blieben diese Riesensysteme auf die Entwicklung von traditionellen Websites und E-Commerce-Lösungen beschränkt (zum Teil wohl auch wegen der Kosten und Komplexität) und hinkten weit hinter den Möglichkeiten her.
Doch Dave (und die Firma Pyra) stolperte über etwas, das ALLE Möglichkeiten ausschöpfte: Bloggen. 1999 hatte Dave ungefähr zur selben Zeit, als Pyra ihren *Blogger* veröffentlichte, seinen moderierten Blog-Service *EditThisPage* eingerichtet. Diese frühen Blogging-Tools waren das erste – wie ich es nenne – Paradigma von Werkzeugen, die alles, was der Endanwender benötigt, direkt vor seinen Augen auf der Webseite bereitstellen.
Im Lauf der Entwicklung der „Blogosphäre" veröffentlichte Dave *Radio Userland,* das das Blog-Werkzeug mit integriertem Aggregator auf dem Rechner des Anwenders installierte. Die nächste Stufe dieses Paradigmas war geboren und knüpfte dort an, wo Napster (und andere P2P-Clients) aufgehört hatte.
News-Aggregatoren wurden möglich, weil Dave und Netscape ein Standardaustauschformat mit der Bezeichnung RSS entwickelt hatten. Mit einem Mal konnten Blogs von jedem als RSS-Channel abonniert werden – aufgelistet neben den Channels der New York Times oder der BBC. Weitere Standards wie OPML oder das MetaWeblogAPI kamen dazu und förderten das, was man heute als Blogosphäre bezeichnet. Diese Standards führten zusammen mit XML-RPC zu News-Aggregatoren und Hunderttausenden von RSS-Feeds und Blogs.
Diese Blogosphäre hat neue Formen von Gemeinschaften und Interaktionen geschaffen, die alle auf der Prämisse privater Veröffentlichung fußen. Das war die Zeit des „Micro-Content", wie Anil Dash es bezeichnete, in der intelligente, verteilte Content-Brocken eine Ära maßgeschneiderter und widerstandsfähiger Ökosysteme einläuteten. Es sollten neue „Micro-Content-Browser" entstehen, die völlig neue Navigations- und Surfmöglichkeiten eröffneten.

Ich hatte oft davon geträumt, über die einfachen Links, die Tim Berner-Lee uns bescherte, hinauszugehen. Ich wollte Zweiweg-, Video-, Audio- oder selbsterklärende Links. Ich stellte (dank der Blogosphäre) fest, dass mein Traum vom semantischen Web Wirklichkeit geworden war.
Die Selbstdarstellung als eine neue Form von Amateurjournalismus, mit Berichten über den Kampf um Bagdad oder den eigenen Hinterhof, bilden das Grundprinzip der Blogosphäre. Mir wurde auch bewusst, wie man Technologie, Geist, Ethik und Prozesse der Blogosphäre auf größere Einflussbereiche anwenden konnte. Die Austausch- und alternativen Distributionssysteme hinter der Blogosphäre werden viel mehr als bloß Amateurjournalismus entstehen lassen. Jonathan Peterson schreibt in seinem Corante.com-Blog unter *The Me in Media* über die neuen Trends im Personal-Publishing und wie eines Tages Einzelpersonen den Großteil der Online-Medien stellen werden. Der Glaube ans „Narrowcasting"[1] bewegt mich seit Jahren, und ein Narrowcasting-Button ziert auch unser neuestes Tool *WebOutliner* – obwohl wir nicht genau wissen, was Narrowcasting eigentlich ist und was es leisten kann.
Wir sind aber zuversichtlich, dass uns die Endanwender ihre Wünsche mitteilen werden. Wie schon in den Anfängen von *VideoWorks* planen wir, uns mit dem Markt zu entwickeln – sobald wir herausgefunden haben, was es ist! Dieser Vorgang des iterativen Designs war das Geheimnis von *Director* und kann nicht im Voraus entwickelt, geplant oder in einem Gant-Diagramm dargestellt werden.

Offene Standards

Als junger Unternehmer empfahl mir Dave Winer ein Buch, das zu meiner Marketing-Bibel wurde: *Marketing Warfare* von Reiss und Trout. Man soll einen neuen Hügel errichten (was einem neuen Produkt entspricht), auf dessen Gipfel Sperren aufstellen und die Konkurrenz mit Maschinengewehren und Handgranaten in Schach halten. So nahmen wir den entstehenden Markt für Multimedia-Authoring-Werkzeuge ein und verteidigten unsere Stellung.
Nun, für Macromedia war diese Strategie des Sich-Verschanzens recht erfolgreich. 15 Jahre später läuft auf 97 Prozent aller Browser ihr Flash-Format.
1994 meinte ein gewisser Doc Searls: *„Ein Dialog wäre besser als Krieg",* womit sich ein neuer Trend entwickelte, der im Buch *The ClueTrain Manifesto* seinen Ausdruck fand. Doc und seine Co-Cluetrainer versuchten zu erläutern, dass man auf verlorenem Posten steht, wenn man nicht auf seine Klientel hört und mit ihr zusammenarbeitet. Sie sind auch nicht mehr bloß Kunden, sondern Partner. Denn ohne sie ist man nichts. Dieser erfrischend neue Ansatz, wie man Software kauft und verkauft, hat eine völlig offene Welt von Standards und Quellcode erschaffen.
In den letzten acht Jahren haben sich Open Source und offene Standards herausgebildet, die LAMP (Linux, Apache, MySql, Python/Perl/php) und eine NAJ-Umgebung zur allgemeinen Verwendung schufen: Niemand hat die Kontrolle. Alle können es nützen. Jeder kann es weiter entwickeln. Das Internet ist zu einem blühenden Garten der Innovation geworden, aus dem ein neues Paradigma für Werkzeuge entspringt. Es ist eine „Welt der Enden", in der die auf kooperierende Menschen verteilte Macht die sich verschanzenden Mächte und Infrastrukturen besiegen kann.
Tatsächlich bauen wir eine neue Infrastruktur auf.
Ich werde von vielen gefragt, wie man in der Open-Source-Welt Geld verdienen kann. Und ich verweise immer auf *Jabber,* das sowohl ein .org als auch ein .com ist. Wir wollen unseren *WebOutliner* als Open Source anbieten und die Nutzer des Codes nur zu einem verpflichten: einen Link zu unserer Site einzurichten und uns als Urheber anzugeben.
Wir wollen unsere Software nach dem Prinzip „Bezahlung bei Nutzung" anbieten. Man wird den WebOutliner gratis verwenden können – so lange man seine Dateien auf unseren Servern

speichert. Will man die Dateien jedoch auf eigenen Servern oder lokalen Laufwerken ablegen, werden 40 USD in Rechnung gestellt. Man wird gar nicht in der Lage sein, seine Medien auf Server hochzuladen. Man soll mit dem Tool nach Herzenslust spielen können; sobald man aber das Erschaffene gezielt einsetzen will, ist der Zeitpunkt gekommen, wo wir glauben, Geld verlangen zu dürfen.

Alles Notwendige wurde erfunden, nun ist gemeinsames Funktionieren gefragt

Gut – alle diese Trends fügen sich ineinander, es gibt offene Standards und eine Menge von Open-Source-Codes (und dank Mitch und Andy werden es noch mehr werden).

Als eine der spannendsten Entwicklungen sehe ich wohl die zukünftige weltweite Verbreitung der technischen und sozialen Normen an, die sich in der Blogosphäre herausgebildet haben – und wenn dies nur geschieht, damit die ISPs weiter Bandbreite verkaufen können, die fast unbegrenzt vorhanden ist. Denn sie werden Software einsetzen, um sich in ihren Angeboten zu unterscheiden. Dasselbe gilt übrigens auch für Anbieter von Unterhaltungselektronik und Systembetreiber. Eigentlich können unendlich viele Dinge von diesen neuen Werkzeugen und den Funktionen und Inhalten, die sie ermöglichen, profitieren.

Die besten Beiträge werden (natürlich) von den Digitalkünstlern und -musikern (und anderen) kommen, die einfach damit spielen wollen. Es bieten sich so viele Möglichkeiten! Gemeinschaftliche und offene Galerien, virtuelle Forschungszentren, Wikis, Foren, reine Nachrichten, soziale Netzwerke und Systeme werden entstehen, die neue Formen der Kreativität eröffnen. Stellen Sie sich eine neue Art interaktiver TV-Sendungen vor, die auf einem x-beliebigen PC entstand und per Narrowcasting nur einer begrenzten Anzahl von Zusehern zur Verfügung steht. Und das ist nur *ein* mögliches Szenario!

Auf virtuellen Flohmärkten wird man seine Sachen verkaufen können – und auf eBay herumspazieren. Neue Werkzeuge ermöglichen die Erstellung von neuem Micro-Content, die außerdem eine eingebaute Online-Gemeinschaft Gleichgesinnter bieten.

Ein Weg zur Realisierung könnte über das von Seb Paquet so genannte „strukturierte Blogging" führen. Dieses Micro-Content-Konzept kann auf viele andere Medien- und Datentypen angewendet werden. So kann man sich ein unveränderliches digitales Identitätsprofil einer Person als Micro-Content vorstellen. Eine Medienbibliothek oder eine Fotosammlung (Alben) sowie Musik oder Videos (Titellisten) sind ebenfalls Arten von Micro-Content. Dies alles sind offensichtliche Beispiele für diese neuen Formen.

Es gibt aber auch revolutionär neue Formen. So kann eine Unterhaltung (die von einer IM- oder Chat-Sitzung, von einem E-Mail-Verkehr, einem Message-Board oder einem Forum stammen kann) einen Micro-Content darstellen, ebenso eine Film-, Platten- oder Restaurantkritik. Sogar eine ganze Online-Gemeinschaft kann als Micro-Content abgelegt werden.

Tim O'Reilly spricht über neue Distributionssysteme. Dazu müssen wir uns vorstellen, was passiert, wenn neue Tools Unmengen neuer Formen von Micro-Content kreieren, die völlig anders geartete Online-Gemeinschaften entstehen lassen.

Genau das ist es, was unsere Firma Broadband Mechanics macht. Wir hoffen nur, dass so viele neue Tools und Technologien wie möglich die offene Arena betreten. Die Absicht dahinter ist, dass wir alle gemeinsam es Microsofts Projekt Longhorn gleichtun können.

Eine untereinander vernetzte Welt von Micro-Content-Servern und RSS-fähigen Werkzeugen kann ein verteiltes, auf Open Source und Webdiensten basierendes „Volksnetz" erschaffen. Longhorn und iLife von Apple sind die Latte, an der wir unser Volksnetz messen werden. Das erklärte Ziel dabei ist, die gleiche Funktionalität wie diese, aber kostenlos und für alle frei zugänglich, zu bieten.

Aus dem Amerikanischen von Michael Kaufmann

1 Anm. d. Ü.: Antonymische Wortbildung zu *broadcasting* (senden, übertragen).

Some Code to Die for
On the Birth of the Free Software Movement in 1887

Leo Findeisen

Morti por kodoj
Pri la naskiĝo de la movado por la libera fonto en la jaro 1887

Sterben für Codes
Zur Geburt der Free-Software-Bewegung im Jahr 1887

„It could be art's function to show that in the dimension of the possible, order is possible."[1]

Old Code and New Code

The following thoughts manifest in a code, letter by letter, syllable by syllable, and are then printed and thus materially stored as something which, for the sake of simplification, is categorized here as *Old Code*—the English. "Old Codes" go back approximately 7000 years[2] and are usually called "natural languages" or "human languages." These include all languages which support the coherency of social superstructures such as religions, ideologies or nations, and are found at all points in history. They are manifested each day in innumerable posters, school books and web pages, they resonate in larynxes and in the space between two faces: the *interface* of the Old Codes.[3] But in terms of a media history that is interested in codes related to language, we are in the year 2003, and amidst a new burst of development. The dynamics of this development are hard to reconstruct for a majority of us because they are quite untouched by most of what we used to under-

„La funkcio de la arto povus esti, montri, ke en la sfero de la eblas ordo."[1]

Malnovaj kaj novaj kodoj

La sekvaj pensoj estas – litero post litero, silabo post silabo – verkitaj, presitaj kaj tiel fizike konservitaj en kodo, kiu ĉi tie simplige estas klasifikita kiel „malnova kodo", la esperanta. Malnovaj kodoj pruvite ekzistas ekde ĉirkaŭ 7000 jaroj[2] kaj ankaŭ estas nomataj „naturaj lingvoj" aŭ „homaj lingvoj". Al ili apartenas ĉiuj lingvoj, per kiuj sociaj superaj unuoj kiel religioj, ideologioj kaj nacioj savis kaj savas sian koherecon en scioplena tempo. Ĉiun tagon ili manifestiĝas sur afiŝoj, en lernolibroj kaj sur retpaĝoj, resonas en laringoj kaj en la spaco inter la homaj vizaĝaj facoj, la „interfaco" de la malnovaj kodoj[3]. Laŭ komunikil-historia perspektivo, kiun interesas lingve parencaj kodoj, ni en la jaro 2003 tamen troviĝas jam meze en nova evoluondo de la signosistemoj. Ties dinamiko estas apenaŭ komprenebla por la plejmulto de la nuntempaj homoj, ĉar ĝi apenău tuŝas la leĝojn de kultur- ău natur-evoluo, kiujn ni taksis

„Die Funktion der Kunst könnte es sein, zu zeigen, dass im Bereich des Möglichen Ordnung möglich ist."[1]

Altcodes und Neucodes

Die folgenden Gedanken sind Buchstabe für Buchstabe, Silbe für Silbe in einem Code abgefasst, gedruckt und damit materiell gespeichert, der hier der Einfachheit halber als „Altcode" kategorisiert wird, dem Deutschen. Altcodes sind seit etwa 7000 Jahren nachgewiesen[2] und werden auch „natürliche Sprachen" oder „Humansprachen" genannt. Darunter fallen alle Sprachen, mit denen soziale Supereinheiten wie Religionen, Ideologien oder Nationen in polyhistorischer Zeit ihre Kohärenz bewahrt haben und bewahren. Jeden Tag manifestieren sie sich auf Plakaten, in Schulbüchern und auf Webseiten, resonieren in Kehlköpfen und im Raum zwischen Menschengesichtern, dem *Interface* der Altcodes.[3] In einer medienhistorischen Perspektive, die sich für sprachverwandte Codes interessiert, befinden wir uns im Jahr 2003 allerdings schon längst in einem neuen Entwicklungsschub der Zeichensysteme. Dessen Dynamik ist für eine Mehrheit der Zeitgenossen kaum nachzuvollziehen, da sie von den Gesetzen einer Kultur- bzw. Naturentwicklung, wie wir sie zu

stand as the laws of "culture" and "nature." These new developments are the programming languages which I shall call *New Codes.* These New Codes are, like all language codes, closed systems of semiotic elements. The texts which are formulated in these languages, or *programs,* are performative strings of signifiers that keep the alliance of mathematical theories and electromagnetic practices on course, they are the literature of information society. The New Codes are responsible for the inter-communication of *technical interfaces.* Remarkably, this term not only denotes that which is facing us (what is on the screen), but also devices such as the mouse or the joystick, as well as box-shaped hardware or even separate levels in a New Code.[4] And it is an open secret that in the technical underground of computers, not on the screen but de-facing us, one speaks Java and Javascript rather than Zulu, not Kanton but Tcl, neither American nor English English, but LISP and AutoLisp, not Hindi, but Pearl and C++, not Portugese, but Python.

New Codes —Qualities create *Communities*

The average life-spans of the New Codes are comparably short, because the specific functional demands of a New Code—its "environment"—is in a state of permanent flux and change. These changes in a code's environment are not only induced by well-known factors such as faster processors or stronger transmission bitrates, or by updates in operating systems. They may also take place, and this is a crucial

konataj. Temas pri la t.n. programlingvoj, kiuj ĉi tie estas nomataj novaj kodoj. Novaj kodoj estas, kiel ĉiuj lingvokodoj, fermitaj sistemoj de signoj. La tekstoj, verkitaj en tiaj lingvoj, la programoj, estas plenumaj signoĉenoj, kiuj kapablas stiri kunaĵon el matematika teorio kaj elektromagneta praktiko – kvazaŭ la teknika literaturo de la informsocio.

La novaj kodoj respondecas pri la komunikado inter la teknikaj interfacoj. Rimarkinde ke oni tiel ne nur nomas tion, kio aperas fronte al nia vizaĝo, sed same la muson kaj la stirstangon, skatolforman aparataron aŭ apartajn nivelojn en tia nova kodo mem.[4] Kai estas publika sekreto: En la teknika subgrundo de la komputiloj, nevideble al niaj okuloj, oni ne parolas la zuluan, sed Java kaj JavaScript, ne la kantonan, sed Tcl, ne usonan aŭ britan anglan, sed LISP kaj AutoLISP, ne la hindan, sed Perl kaj C++, ne la portugalan, sed Python.

La kvalitoj de novaj kodoj kreas „komunumojn"

Rilate al la vivodaŭro de la novaj kodoj, la specifaj funkciaj postuloj al ili, do kvazaŭ la „medio" de nova kodo, daŭre ŝanĝiĝas. Tiaj ŝanĝoj cetere ne nur estas kaŭzitaj de la konataj teknikaj faktoroj kiel pli rapidaj procesoroj, pli grandaj transig-rapidecoj aŭ ĝisdatigoj de la mastrumaj programoj. Povas ankaŭ okazi, kaj tion necesas emfazi en nia kunteksto, ke kodopoeto neatendite publikigas eĉ pli modernan novan kodon, eĉ pli

kennen glaubten, kaum tangiert wird. Gemeint sind die Programmiersprachen, die hier „Neucodes" genannt werden. Neucodes sind wie alle Sprachcodes geschlossene Systeme von Zeichen. Die in solchen Sprachen abgefassten Texte, die *Programme,* sind performative Zeichenketten, die einen Verbund aus mathematischer Theorie und elektromagnetischer Praxis steuern können, die technische Literatur der Informationsgesellschaft sozusagen. Und die Neucodes sind für die Verständigung von *technischen Interfaces* verantwortlich. Damit wird heute bemerkenswerterweise nicht nur das bezeichnet, was gegenüber unserem Gesicht erscheint, also am Bildschirm, sondern ebenso die Maus oder der Joystick, kastenförmige Hardwaregeräte oder gesonderte Ebenen in einem Neucode als solchem.[4] Und es ist ein offenes Geheimnis: Im technischen Untergrund der Rechner, unserm Gesicht abgewandt, spricht man nicht Zulu, sondern Java und JavaScript, nicht Kantonesisch, sondern Tcl, nicht amerikanisches oder englisches Englisch, sondern LISP und Auto-LISP, nicht Hindi, sondern Pearl und C++, nicht Portugiesisch, sondern Python.

Neucodes – Qualitäten erzeugen *Communities*

Was die Lebensdauer der Neucodes betrifft, befinden sich ihre spezifischen Funktionsanforderungen, quasi die „Umwelt" eines Neucodes, ständig im Fluss. Solche Veränderungen in Codeumwelten werden übrigens nicht nur von den bekannten technischen Faktoren ausgelöst wie etwa schnelleren Prozessoren, größeren Übertragungsraten oder Updates von Betriebssystemen. Es kann auch passieren, und dies gilt es in unserem Zusammenhang

point to my argument, because of the unexpected arrival of a poet of code who publishes a better New Code, a more sophisticated prototype of a cybernetic language.
The aesthetics of this code might be more inspiring to program in than the previous one, it may perform identical commands with fewer lines, or build alliances to mainstream net-applications more skillfully, more reliably and faster. Such a development saves precious time, is more fun and is likely to be used by the more skillfull and sympathetic programmers, and so contribute to the formation of a transnational *community* of highly specialized coders, the so-called *geeks.* Only then, as an active code-generated, code-generating collective are they capable of going the next step, which is to multiply the code's potentials and applications via the internet, and oversee its chances and dangers in this changeable environment. And even if the members of this collective may say „good night" to each other in Old Code or New Code, their Chats never seems to sleep. In a world-wide code-community there are always some developers on whom the sun is rising. All members are conscious of the fact, and this is obviously
a historical *novum,* that their global, self-reliant and horizontally organised code *Task Force* in which they know each other, meet each other and collaborate with one another, was constituted, at the beginning, by a code, and the hope for its successful elaboration and global dissemination. A recent example of such a New Code is the language *Python,* invented by the Dutch mathematician and computer scientist Guido van Rossum, which has been publicly developed over the last 10

maturan prototipon de kibernetika lingvo.
Ties logika estetiko povas ekzemple pli inspiri la programadon ol kutime ĝis nun, oni povas plenumi la samajn komandojn per malpli multaj kodolinioj, krei pli lerte la bezonatajn ligojn al vaste uzataj program-aplikaĵoj ktp. Tia evoluaĵo ŝparas valoran tempon, donas pli da plezuro kaj tial estas pli volonte uzata de la lertaj kaj simpatiaj kolegoj. Pro tio iĝas verŝajne, ke fulmrapide estiĝas unu de la supernaciaj komunumoj konsistantaj el alte specialiĝintaj fakuloj, en la angla la t.n. „geeks". Nur kiel de la kodo kreita, la kodon kreantan kolektivo eblas al ili la logike sekva paŝo, nome tra la Interreto multobligi la eblojn kaj aplikaĵojn de kodo en malmulta tempo, pretervidante nek ŝancojn nek riskojn en ĝia „medio" dum tio. Iliaj babilejoj, en kiuj oni deziras bonan nokton unu al la alia en malnovaj kaj novaj kodoj, ŝajnas mem neniam dormi – super kelkaj kreantoj ja ĉiam leviĝas la suno. Ĉiuj unuopuloj dume konscias pri tio, kaj tio historie ŝajne estas io nova, ke ilia tutmonda, memelektita kaj senhierarkie organizita kodo-taĉmento sin konas, renkontas kaj kunlaboras, ĉar je la komenco iam estis la kodo resp.
la espero pri ĝia sukcesa evoluigo kaj disvastigo en la tuta mondo. Aktuala ekzemplo de tia nova kodo estas la programlingvo Python de la nederlanda komputilmatematikisto Guido van Rossum, kiu ekde ĉirkaŭ 10 jaroj estas publike evoluigata. Lia lingvosistemo troveblas ĉe www.python.org, kiu mem jam estas la retejo de komunumo de lingve orientitaj evoluigantoj. Ĝi ne hazarde ciferece estas gasto ĉe la neder-

besonders festzuhalten, dass ein Code-Poet unerwartet einen noch aktuelleren Neucode publiziert, den noch ausgereifteren Prototypen einer kybernetischen Sprache. Dessen logische Ästhetik kann z. B. das Programmieren inspirierender gestalten als bisher gewohnt, er kann mit weniger Codezeilen dieselben Befehle ausführen, die notwendigen Allianzen zu verbreiteten Softwareanwendungen geschickter knüpfen, usf. So eine Entwicklung spart kostbare Zeit, bereitet mehr Lust und wird eher von den gewandten und sympathischen Kollegen benutzt. Deshalb ist es wahrscheinlich, dass sich blitzartig eine der transnationalen *Communities* aus hoch spezialisierten Fachleuten bildet, den sogenannten *Geeks.* Erst als vom Code generiertes, den Code generierendes Kollektiv ist ihnen dann der logisch folgende Schritt möglich, nämlich *via Internet* die Potenziale und Anwendungen eines Codes in kurzer Zeit zu vervielfachen und dabei weder Chancen noch Gefahren in seiner „Umwelt" zu übersehen. Ihre Chats, in denen man sich in Altcodes und Neucodes eine Gute Nacht wünscht, scheinen selber nie zu schlafen – über einigen Entwicklern geht eben immer die Sonne auf. Allen Einzelnen ist dabei bewusst, und das ist historisch offensichtlich ein Novum, dass ihre globale, selbst bestimmte und horizontal organisierte *Task Force* des Codes sich kennt, trifft und zusammenarbeitet, weil am Anfang einmal der Code bzw. die Hoffnung auf seine erfolgreiche Entwicklung und weltweite Verbreitung stand. Ein aktuelles Beispiel eines solchen Neucodes ist die Sprache *Python* des holländischen Computermathematikers Guido van Rossum, die seit etwa zehn Jahren öffentlich

years. The code can be found at *www.python.org,* itself web site of a language-oriented *community* of developers. It is no coincidence that this community is digitally hosted by the Dutch net-culture server *xs4all* („Access for all") and that the language is recommended by the team at Google. Building upon Python, other communities like *www.zope.org* or *www.plone.org* followed. In only a few years they have been able to collaborate in writing applications of a highly complex and technically superior nature. The rule which allows for this collaborative construction is as follows: Everything written in Python is generally seen as being under a Public License, and as such it becomes free computer literature. The "Source Code," the "digital DNS" of the programming language, is no secret and its author, though fully acknowledged as such, does not claim any copyright.

Two missing links at the end of the 19th Century

Yet as suggestive as this juxtaposition of the respective effects and functional environments of Old Code and New Code might seem, it is the main thesis of this paper to draw attention to two complexes of phenomena that serve as missing links between them. Meanwhile, it has become possible to discern these two complexes of phenomena that are unprecedented and as yet unrepeated in the history of media and communication. The following will thus thematize the *invention,* the socio-cultural *implementation* and the global *development* of planned languages as they emerged first in Western and then in Eastern Europe in the late 19th Century.
The fact that the main language-, semiotic- and media-theories of the

landa retkultur-servilo xs4all („access for all" – angle por „aliro por ĉiuj"). Sur la nova kodo Python, kiu estas rekomendata i. a. de la Google-teamo, povis baziĝi siavice aliaj komunumoj kiel ekzemple www.zope.org aŭ www.plone.org. En malmultaj jaroj ili kune skribis en Python alte kompleksajn, teknike superajn aplikaĵojn. Kaj la regulo, kiu permesas, reciproke bazi sian laboron sur tiu de alia, tekstas: Kio estas skribita en Python, estas ĝenerale libera, pluuzebla komputila literaturo, la lingvo estas senpaga, ĝia fonta teksto, la „cifereca DNA", ne estas sekreto, ĝia aŭtoro rezignas, simplige, pri sia aŭtora rajto.

Du mankantaj ĉeneroj je la fino de la 19a jarcento

La fokuso nun iru al la tezo, ke intertempe, t.e. en la historia rerigardo, montriĝas du mankantaj ĉeneroj inter malnovaj kaj novaj kodoj je la komunikil-historia horizonto. Ambaŭ estas en sia komunikadstrukturo unufojaj kaj ĝis nun neripetitaj eventkompleksoj de alta elstareco.
Temas pri la invento, la socikultura implementado kaj la tutmonda pluevoluigado de t. n. modernaj interkomunikaj lingvoj, kiuj je la fino de la 19a jarcento eliris unue de okcidenta kaj poste de orienta Eŭropo. Ke ambaŭ kompleksojn preskaŭ komplete ignoris la esencaj lingvo-, signo- kaj mediteorioj de la 20a jarcento, siaflanke provokas estontajn esplorojn.[5]

entwickelt wird. Sein Sprachsystem ist unter *www.python.org,* zu finden, selbst schon die Website einer sprachorientierten *Community* aus Entwicklern. Diese ist nicht zufällig digitial zu Gast beim holländischen Netzkultur-Server *xs4all* („Access for all"). Auf dem Neucode Python, der u. a. vom Google-Team empfohlen wird, konnten wiederum andere *Communities* wie etwa *www.zope.org* oder *www.plone.org* aufbauen. Im Verlauf weniger Jahre schrieben sie in Python hochkomplexe, technisch überlegene Anwendungen zusammen. Und die Regel, die es erlaubte, gegenseitig aufeinander aufzubauen, lautet: Was in Python geschrieben wird, ist grundsätzlich freie, anschlussfähige Computerliteratur, die Sprache ist kostenlos, ihr Quelltext, die „digitale DNS", ist kein Geheimnis, ihr Autor verzichtet, vereinfacht gesagt, auf sein Urheberrecht.

Zwei Missing Links am Ende des 19. Jahrhunderts

Ins Zentrum soll nun die These rücken, dass mittlerweile, d. h. im historischen Rückblick, zwei *Missing Links* zwischen Altcodes und Neucodes am mediengeschichtlichen Horizont Profil annehmen. Beide sind in ihrer Kommunikationsstruktur erstmalige und bisher unwiederholte Ereigniskomplexe von hoher Prägnanz. Die Rede ist von der *Erfindung,* der *soziokulturellen Implementierung* und der *globalen Weiterentwicklung* von sog. modernen Umgangssprachen, wie sie gegen Ende des 19. Jahrhunderts erst von Westeuropa und in Folge von Osteuropa ausgingen. Dass beide Komplexe fast durchwegs von den maßgeblichen Sprach-, Zeichen- und Medientheorien des letzten Jahr-

20th Century have almost entirely neglected them provides an interesting starting point for future research.[5]

Volapük–The first global manifestation of a *community* generated by a New Code

The first developer that experienced a world-wide dissemination of his New Code was a German Roman-Catholic priest, Johann Martin Schleyer from Konstanz in Baden. Not long after developing his "World Alphabet," merely a new compilation of letters, Mr. Schleyer had an apparition of his God in a dream telling him to go on with the good work and to let the alphabet evolve into a full world language. Schleyer, who was said to command 50 languages, was obedient to the word and soon had his *Volapük* ready.[6] The name of his new language pointed to his decision to follow the phonetics of English. Users should still recognize the term "World" in "vol" and the term "speak" in "pük," which together make *Worldspeak – Weltsprache – Volapük*. In 1879, 8 years after the end of the Franco-Prussian war, he published his textbook. From its cover it looked like a

„Volapük" – La unua tutmonda konkretiĝo de komunumo kreita de nova kodo

La unua kreanto, kiu povis sperti tutmondan disvastiĝon de sia nova kodo, estis Germano, la romkatolika prelato Johann Martin Schleyer el la badenlanda urbo Konstanz. Ne mallonge, post kiam li estis kreinta „mondalfabeton", do nur novkompilitan aron precipe da skribliteroj, iun nokton al sinjoro Schleyer aperis la Dio de lia religio en sonĝo kaj persone donis al li la taskon, pluevoluigi la bonan verkon al kompleta mondolingvo. La pastro, kiu laŭdire parolis 50 diversajn lingvojn, obeis kaj baldaŭ prezentis sian volapukon (Volapük).[6] *Jam la nomo malkaŝis, ke li decidis, bazi la inventon laŭsone sur la angla: La uzantoj en „vol" ankoraŭ rekonu la resonon de la angla „world" (mondo), en „pük" de la vorto „speak" (paroli), kune do „Worldspeak" – „mondparolilo" – „mondlingvo" – „Volapük".*

hunderts ignoriert wurden, ist seinerseits ein interessanter Ansatzpunkt für zukünftige Fragestellungen.[5]

Volapük – Die erste globale Manifestation einer vom Neucode erzeugten Community

Der erste Entwickler, der eine weltweite Verbreitung seines Neucodes erleben konnte, war ein Deutscher, der römisch-katholische Prälat Johann Martin Schleyer aus der badischen Stadt Konstanz. Nicht lange nachdem er ein „Weltalphabet", also lediglich eine neu kompilierte Menge v. a. an Schriftbuchstaben, erarbeitet hatte, erschien Herrn Schleyer eines Nachts der Gott seiner Religion im Traume und erteilte ihm höchstpersönlich den Auftrag, das gute Werk in eine vollständige Weltsprache weiter zu entwickeln. Der Pater, dem man nachsagte, er beherrsche 50 verschiedene Sprachen, gehorchte aufs Wort und legte alsbald sein *Volapük* vor.[6] Schon der Name verriet, dass er sich dafür entschieden hatte, die Erfindung am Klang des Englischen anzulehnen: Die User sollten in *vol* noch das englische *world* nachklingen hören, in *pük* das Wort

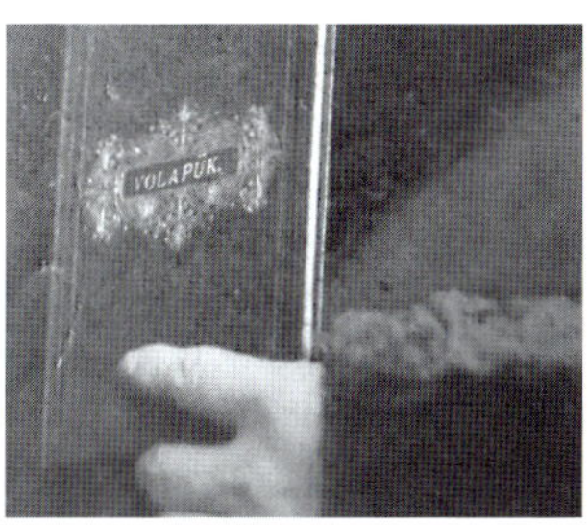

J. M. Schleyer is pointing at his *Schoolbook of Volapük*, 1879

J. M. Schleyer montras al sia lernolibro de volapuko, jaro 1879

J. M. Schleyer zeigt auf sein *Schoolbook of Volapük*, 1879

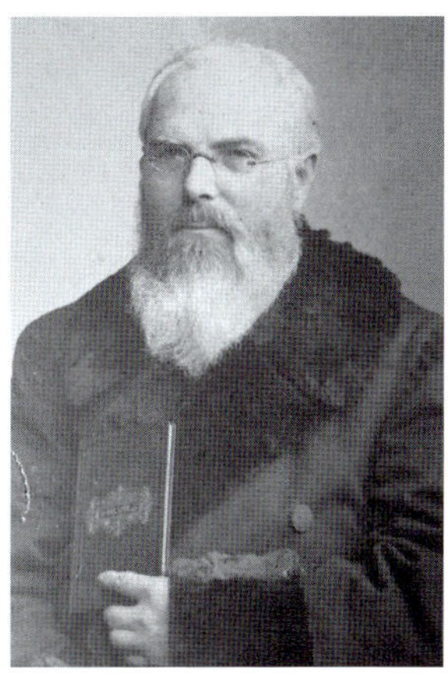

common school book for languages, but it invoked an unforeseen chain-reaction. Only 10 years later, this New Code had created a community of 283 *Volapük*-Clubs across Europe, America and Australia. They were connected by periodicals, organized *interface*-lessons, and their students graduated with diplomas. This geography of dissemination was an immediate result of Schleyer's opportunistic decision to rely on the global reach of the English language, and its limits–in Asia one was not really *understanding* this form of invitation. Nevertheless, the entire number of those involved in this first global *linguistic turn* is assumed to have been more than 100.000[7] – a success of *implementation*. But the further development of this *collective* directly failed because of the father himself. Bugs in the architecture of Schleyer's prototype gave the final blow to the future success of his New Code. For example, a certain Mr. Karl Lenze, the first diploma-holder and teacher of Volapük, was a man talented in theoretical mathematics. Elaborating on a bug-report protocol, he calculated that the code had „no less that 505 440 unprecise inflections of verbs, which are directly caused by the

En la jaro 1879, 8 jarojn post la fino de la german-franca milito, li publikigis la respektivan uzinstrukciaron, laŭ ekstera aspekto ordinara lingvolernolibro, kiu tamen kaŭzis mirigan ĉenreagon: Nur 10 jarojn poste ekzistis komunumo de entute 283 volapuko-kluboj en Eŭropo, Ameriko kaj Aŭstralio. Ili estis konektitaj per periodaĵoj, faris „interfacajn" kursojn kaj aljuĝis diplomojn. En la geografio de la lingvodisvastiĝo tuj respeguliĝis la oportuna inklino al la tutmonde realigita normo de la angla – en Azio oni malbone „komprenis" la inviton. Tamen la entuta nombro de personoj, kiuj kunfaris tiun unuan lingvikan turniĝon en loka memelprovo, verŝajne sumiĝis je ne malpli ol 100.000 volapukistoj[7] – tutŝajne sukcesa implementado. La pluevoluigado, la kolektiva kvalitkontrolo, tamen fiaskis pro la persono de la inĝeniero nomumita de Dio mem. Tial pliaj mankoj en la arkitekturo de la prototipo de Schleyer montriĝis komplete fatalaj al la sukceso de lia kodo. Ekzemple iu Karl Lenze, la unua diplomita instruisto pri volapuko entute kaj talenta en matematika teorio, verkis protokolan eraroraporton kaj elkalkulis „ne malpli ol 505

speak, zusammen also World-*speak – Weltsprache – Volapük.* Im Jahr 1879, acht Jahre nach Beendigung des deutsch-französischen Krieges, veröffentlichte er die entsprechende Betriebsanleitung, dem Anschein nach ein gewöhnliches Sprachlehrbuch, das allerdings verblüffende Kettenreaktionen auslösen sollte: Nur zehn Jahre später war eine *Community* von insgesamt 283 *Volapük*-Clubs in Europa, Amerika und Australien entstanden. Sie waren durch Periodika miteinander verbunden, hielten *Interface*-Kurse ab und verliehen Diplome. In der *Geografie* der Sprachverbreitung koppelte sich sofort die opportune Anlehnung an den weltweit etablierten Standard des Englischen zurück – in Asien *verstand* man die Einladung nicht so recht. Trotzdem dürfte die Gesamtzahl derer, die diesen ersten globalen *Linguistic Turn* im lokalen Selbstversuch mitvollzogen, nicht weniger als 100.000 Volapükisten betragen haben[7] – eine augenscheinlich gelungene *Implementierung*. Die *Weiterentwicklung* allerdings, die kollektive Qualitätskontrolle, scheiterte an dem von höchster Stelle berufenen Ingenieur persönlich. Weitere Mängel in der Architektur von Schleyers Prototyp wurden seinem Codeerfolg deshalb vollends zum Verhängnis. Ein gewis-

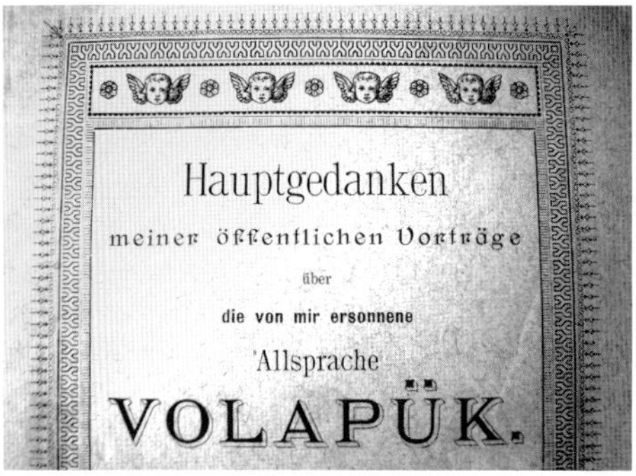

Frontispiece of the first Schoolbook of Volapük: "Main Thoughts of my public lectures on Volapük, the Universal Language conceived by me, Hans Martin Schleyer, Priest and Editor"

Frontispico de la unua lernolibro de volapuko: „Ĉefaj pensoj de miaj publikaj prelegoj pri la universala lingvo volapuko, elpensita de mi, de Johann Martin Schleyer, pastro kaj redaktoro"

Frontispiz des ersten Lehrbuchs des Volapük: „Hauptgedanken meiner öffentlichen Vorträge über die von mir ersonnenen Allsprache VOLAPÜK, von Johann Martin Schleyer, Pfarrer und Redaktör"

author".[8] Consequently, „numerous simplifications, restructurings, re-organisatons and heretical derivate versions"[9] were produced synchronically and transcontinentally, uncontrollable by the author and destroying the necessary consistency of the code. Schleyer, already known to be extremely vain and patriarchal in character, travelled widely attempting to confront all the derivative versions he could get hold of with his authoritative and original version. Soon, all the do-it-yourself co-authors stopped their cheeky improvements, and ceased enjoying their language-games in *Volapük*. After their long lasting enthusiasm the question had arisen, for the perfection of *whose* world exactly one had spent so much effort ...? And *voilà,* the first *community* exclusively generated by a New Code in Modern Times (or, to be even more precise, in the entire history of culture) had, in three decades, dissolved into a frustrated silence. "From Heaven, through the world, to Hell!" (J.W. von Goethe).
Some of this initial community had, however, accustomed themselves to the luxury of a potentially world-wide circle of friends, and after examining their options, changed systems: Possibly to the *Langue Universelle* of Menet (1886), or the *Bopal* of Max (1887), the *Spelin* of Bauer (1886), the *Dil* of Flieweger (1893), the *Balta* of Dormoy (1893) or the *Weltparl* of Arnim (1896).[10] These different codes not only gradually weakened the dissemination of *Volapük,* but also their own respective dissemination in relation to one another. The reason for this, to put it bluntly, in that in the long run there can only

440 malklarajn derivaĵojn de verboj, pri kiuj respondecas sole al la aŭtoro."[8] Kiel sekvo ekestis, – por la aŭtoro nekontroleblaj, ĉar samtempe verkitaj sur pluraj kontinentoj –, „multaj simpligoj, novstrukturadoj, reordigoj kaj herezaj idoj"[9] kaj detruis la necesan koherecon de la kodo. Schleyer, konata kiel ekstreme vanta kaj patriarka, siavice obstine postvojaĝis per vorta aŭtorstampo ĉiujn derivajn evoluaĵojn. Baldaŭ ĉiuj memnomumitaj kunaŭtoroj finis siajn impertinentajn plibonigajn projektojn, sed kun la sekvo, ke ili ankaŭ ĉiam pli tediĝis pri siaj lingvoludoj en volapuko. Post multjara entuziasmo ŝajne subite iĝis malklare al ili, al kiu apartenis la mondo, kiun ili celis plibonigi ... Kaj jen: La unua, sole per nova kodo kreita tutmonda komunumo de la moderna epoko, resp. pli precize de la kultur – kaj kodo – historio entute, malfondiĝis ĝis la komenco de la 20a jarcento en frustrita silentado. „De la ĉielo tra la mondo al la inferno" (J.W. von Goethe), en nur tri jardekoj.
Kiu en la komunumo alkutimiĝis al la lukso de amikara rondo, principe ampleksiĝanta la tutan mondon, trarigardis la oferton de la konkurenco kaj transiris al alia sistemo: Ekzemple al la „Langue Universelle" de Menet (1886), la „Bopal" de Max (1887), la „Spelin" de Bauer (1886), la „Dil" de Flieweger (1893), la „Balta" de Dormoy (1893) aŭ la „Weltparl" de Arnim (1896).[10] Ili tiutempe ne nur de jaro al jaro malfortigis la plian disvastigon de volapuko, sed ankaŭ la respektivan propran. Ĉar laŭ sistema vidpunkto validas por modernaj komunikadaj

ser Karl Lenze etwa, der erste diplomierte Lehrer des *Volapük* überhaupt und begabt in mathematischer Theorie, erstellte einen protokollarischen Fehlerbericht und errechnete „nicht weniger als 505 440 uneindeutige Ableitungen von Verben, die ausschließlich auf den Autor zurückzuführen seien".[8]
In Folge entstanden – für den Autor unkontrollierbar, weil gleichzeitig auf mehreren Kontinenten angefertigt – „allerlei Vereinfachungen, Umstrukturierungen, Neuordnungen und häretische Ableger"[9] und zerstörten die unverzichtbare Codekonsistenz. Der als äußerst eitel und patriarchal bekannte Schleyer selbst reiste verbissen allen Derivatentwicklungen mit einem verbalen Autorenstempel hinterher. Bald sollten alle selbst ernannten Co-Autoren ihre frechen Verbesserungsprojekte unterlassen, allerdings mit der Konsequenz, dass immer mehr auch ihrer Sprachspiele auf *Volapük* überdrüssig wurden. Nach jahrelangem Enthusiasmus schien ihnen schien plötzlich unklar geworden zu sein, für die Verbesserung von genau *wessen* Welt man sich da eingesetzt hatte ... Und *voilá:* die erste, ausschließlich durch einen Neucode erzeugte globale *Community* der Neuzeit, bzw. genau besehen der Kultur- und Codegeschichte überhaupt, löste sich bis zum Beginn des 20. Jahrhunderts – *Fin de Siècle* – in frustriertes Schweigen auf. „Vom Himmel durch die Welt zur Hölle" (J.W. von Goethe), in nur drei Jahrzehnten. Wer sich in der *Community* an den Luxus eines potenziell die ganze Welt umspannenden Freundeskreises gewöhnt hatte, sondierte nun das Angebot der Konkurrenz und stieg auf ein anderes System um: auf die *Langue Universelle* von Menet (1886), das

be one international language—as there is today with English, a fabulous Old Code which as such cannot be blamed for leaving a bitter aftertaste on a growing number of tongues these days.

Esperanto–A Code for all and none

During these years, however, another code-poet and his New Code appeared: Ludwig L. Zamenhof from Bialystok, today in the East of Poland, then in Lithuania under the administration of the Russian Empire. Very early, this talented boy had discovered his love for languages, such as the ancient languages, or the Russian language. But being constantly confronted by various animosities between speakers of the Old Codes, between Polish, Jewish, Russian, White Russian and German for example, he developed while still in his teens a "lingwe universala," a "universal language." At first, however, he decided to "hide his work from everyone," "foreseeing nothing but shame and ridicule."[11] Zamenhof elaborated on his invention for another 15 years, like a Swiss watch-maker, highly concerned with a pleasing sound, fine-tuning some of the strengths of its predecessor *Volapük*[12] and testing its expressive qualities by translating some of the most

lingvoj malgraŭ ĉiu afableco: Longtempe „povas ekzisti nur unu" – kiel hodiaŭ la angla, grandioza malnova kodo, al kiu mem oni ne povas riproĉi ke ĝi komencas postlasi amaran kromguston sur daŭre pli da palatoj.

„Esperanto" – kodo por ĉiu kaj neniu

Sed en tiuj jaroj plia aŭtoro publikigis sian novan kodon: Ludoviko Lazaro Zamenhof el Bjalistoko, urbo hodiaŭ situanta en orienta Pollando, tiutempe Litovio, administrita de la rusa cara regno. La altdotito jam frue malkovris sian amon por la rusa kaj la klasikaj lingvoj. Sed spertante la malamikecojn inter Poloj, Judoj, Rusoj, Bjelorusoj kaj Germanoj, forte kaŭzitajn de malnovaj kodoj, li jam kiel junulo konceptis iun „lingwe universala", „universalan lingvon". Unue tute por si mem, ĉar (kiel li mem skribis) „Antaŭvidante nur mokojn kaj persekutojn, mi decidis kaŝi antaŭ ĉiuj mian laboron."[11] *Zamenhof dum pliaj 15 jaroj fajlis sian inventon kvazaŭ svisa horloĝisto, zorgis pri la lingva belsono, poluris kelkajn fortajn flankojn de la antaŭinta kodo volapuko*[12] *kaj poste elprovis la esprimkapablon, tradukante diversajn aŭtorojn de la mondliteraturo al sia nova kodo. El la sorto de volapuko li lernis, ke eĉ la plej kohereca baza strukturo, la*

Bopal von Max (1887), das *Spelin* von Bauer (1886), das *Dil* von Flieweger (1893), das *Balta* von Dormoy (1893) oder das *Weltparl* von Arnim (1896).[9] Diese schwächten damals Jahr um Jahr nicht nur die weitere Verbreitung des *Volapük*, sondern auch ihre jeweils eigene. Denn systemisch gesehen gilt für moderne Umgangssprachen bei aller Höflichkeit: Auf Dauer *kann es nur eine geben* – wie heute das Englische, einem großartigen Altcode, dem als solchem nicht vorgeworfen werden kann, dass er auf immer mehr Gaumen einen bitteren Beigeschmack zu entwickeln beginnt.

Esperanto – Ein Code für alle und keinen

In diesen Jahren hatte jedoch noch ein weiterer Autor seinen Neucode am Start: Ludwig L. Zamenhof aus Bialystok, heute im Osten Polens, damals in Litauen, vom russischen Zarenreich verwaltet. Der Hochbegabte hatte schon früh seine Liebe für das Russische oder die klassischen Sprachen entdeckt. Doch angesichts der massiv durch Altcodes miterzeugten Feindseligkeiten zwischen Polen, Juden, Russen, Weißrussen und Deutschen entwickelte er schon als Teenager eine „lingwe universala", eine „Universalsprache". Zunächst nur für sich, denn „(...) nur Spott und Hohn voraussehend" beschloss er, seine „Arbeit vor jedermann zu verbergen".[11] Zamenhof feilte weitere 15 Jahre wie ein Schweizer Uhrmacher an seiner Erfindung, sorgte sich um den sprachlichen Wohlklang, unterzog einige Stärken des Vorgängercodes *Volapük* einem *Tuning*[12] und testete dann die Ausdruckskraft, indem er verschiedene Autoren der Weltliteratur in seinen Neucode transformierte.

established authors of world literature into his New Code. He had observed in the development and flaws of the *Volapük*-Movement that even a strong prototype had to be tested and optimized by the continual practise of many speakers in many countries in order to stay „alive". That means that in order to survive, his New Code had to exist in the *interface*-space of the Old Codes. One had thus to prepare for the emergence of a somehow collective but nevertheless moderated work on aspects like applicability or performance, in which individuals could guide themselves without any centralized organ of control, first of all without "the creator" or "the author." All had to, by free will, obey by themselves the Kantian Imperative of Coders: *Always alter elements of a New Code only in such a manner that the maxim of your alteration favours a structure of world-wide communication.* In other words: Language systems belong to the public sphere, so try not to modify at all, and if you modify, then rather a little than a lot, and only after asking for feedback. Never ever publish a derivative version!

In 1887, Zamenhof finally went public. His father, working as a censor at the time, played down his son's work as a „harmless couriosity"[13] to a Russian

prototipo, nur povas esti prijuĝata, plibonigata kaj viva, t.e. en la interfaca spaco de la malnovaj kodoj, tenata, per la lingvopraktiko de multaj parolantoj en diversaj landoj.

Tial gravis prepari kolektivan kaj gvidatan laboron cele al kompleteco kaj efikeco de la kodo, en kiu multaj unuopuloj per propra decido, t.e. sen centra kontrolorgano kiel „kreinto" aŭ „aŭtoro", respektos la kategorian imperativon de la kodistoj: Ŝanĝu elementojn de nova kodo nur tiel, ke la maksimo de viaj ŝanĝoj harmonias kun tutmonde komunikebla kodostrukturo.

Alivorte: Lingvosistemoj estas produkto kaj tial posedaĵo de la publiko, tendence do prefere tute ne ŝanĝu ion, prefere malmulton, prefere nur post redemando – kaj precipe ne lanĉu derivaĵon!

En la jaro 1887 Zamenhof fine eldonis sian verkon. Lia patro, kiu laboris en la rusa cenzuroficejo, malgravigis la verkon antaŭ sia kolego kiel „sendanĝeran sensencaĵon"[13] kaj ricevis presphermeson. Plie li enmetis je la komenco trilinian tekston, kiun oni povas legi ne nur kiel literaturseiencan dokumenton al la multe diskutata temo „morto de la aŭtoro", sed ankaŭ kiel la fondodaton de la strategio „publika fonto": „Internacia lingvo, simile al ĉiu nacia, estas propraĵo socia, kaj la aŭtoro por ĉiam forcedas ĉiujn personajn

Am Schicksal des *Volapük* hatte er ablesen können, dass ein noch so konsistentes Grundgerüst, der Prototyp, tatsächlich erst in der Sprachpraxis von vielen Sprecherinnen und Sprechern in verschiedenen Ländern beurteilt, verbessert und „am Leben", d. h. im *Interface*-Raum der Altcodes, gehalten werden würde. Es galt demnach, eine kollektive und moderierte Arbeit an der Vollständigkeit und Leistungsfähigkeit des Codes vorzubereiten, in dem viele Einzelne sich durch Selbstbindung, d. h. ohne zentrales Kontrollorgan namens „Schöpfer" oder „Autor", an den kantischen Imperativ der Coder halten würden: *Verändere Elemente eines Neucodes nur so, dass die Maxime deiner Veränderungen einer weltweit kommunikablen Codestruktur zuträglich bleibt.* Mit anderen Worten: Sprachsysteme sind Produkt und damit Eigentum einer Allgemeinheit, verändere tendenziell eher gar nicht, eher wenig, eher nur auf Rückfrage – und lanciere vor allem kein Derivat!

Im Jahr 1887 ging Zamenhof dann an die Öffentlichkeit. Sein Vater, der in der russischen Zensurbehörde arbeitete, spielte das Sprachlehrbuch bei seinem Kollegen als „harmloses Kuriosum"[13] herunter und die Druckerlaubnis wurde erteilt. Außerdem ließ er zu Beginn einen dreizeiligen Text anbringen, den man nicht nur als literaturwissenschaftliches Dokument zum viel diskutierten Thema „Tod des Autors", sondern auch als das Gründungs-

☞ Die internationale Sprache soll, gleich jeder nationalen, ein allgemeines Eigenthum sein, wesshalb der Verfasser für immer auf seine persönlichen Rechte darüber verzichtet.

Druck von Ch. Kelter, Nowolipie-Str. N. 11, Warschau.

The surrender of his author's right by Zamenhof, 1887

Die Erklärung auf Rechtsverzicht durch Zamenhof, 1887

La deklaro de la rezigno pri ĉiuj aŭtororajtoj de Zamenhof, jaro 1887

colleague and thus its printing was permitted. In addition, Zamenhof inserted a text of three lines at the very beginning of the manual, that can not only be interpreted as a literary document in the context of the widely discussed theme of the „death of the author“, but also as the foundational act of the Free Software-Movement: „An international language should be, as any national one is, be a common possession, which is why the author is here resigning for all time his personal rights over it.“[14] Thus, Zamenhof's code was not only published, it was also and at the same time actively liberated for further public elaboration and collaboration.

In the beginning, the New Code entailed only a minimal grammar, 927 roots and some exemplary texts, allowing it to evolve in the "community." From the last pages of the manual the readers could also cut out coupons for subscription, and distribute them to their circle of friends, who could sign them and send them back to Zamenhof's personal address . Thus, the readers and their friends could document their interest in the language and „promise“ to learn it when 10.000.000 others also expressed their interest in

rajtojn je ĝi."[14] *La kodo de Zamenhof do ne nur estis publikigita, sed ankaŭ ofertita libere por aktiva plua prilaboro.*

La kodo je la komenco konsistis nur el minimuma gramatiko, 927 vortradikoj kaj kelkaj ekzemplaj tekstoj, por ke la lingvo povu evolui ene de la komunumo. El la lernolibroj la legantoj plie povis eltranĉi etajn kuponojn, pludisdoni, subskribi kaj resendi ilin al la aŭtoro mem. Ili per tio skribe konfirmis sian intereson pri la lingvo kaj „promesis", lerni ĝin, se kaj kiam 10.000.000 aliaj far(int)os la saman.

La komunumo sekve unue estu antaŭfigurita kiel imagata adreskolekto en la fantazio de la unuopaj personoj,[15] *poste dokumentita reale en unu loko kaj fine realigita tutmonde – kiel t.n. „memkreiva evolufiguro", kiu renkonteblas ĉe alta nombro da diversaj kaj interdependaj eblaĵoj. La resendkuponojn oni povus rigardi kiel la unuan oferton de novaĵletero antaŭ la Interreto, tamen ankoraŭ sen la eblo de malabono.*[16] *Tiu strategio unuflanke vaste fiaskis, ĉar dum la sekvaj du jaroj alvenis nur ĉirkaŭ 1000 kuponoj al Zamenhof, aliflanke tio ne prezentis longdaŭran obstaklon kontraŭ la kododisvastigo. Unue en Rusio,*

datum einer „Free Software"-Strategie lesen kann: „Die internationale Sprache soll, gleich jeder nationalen, ein allgemeines Eigenthum sein, weshalb der Verfasser für immer auf seine persönlichen Rechte daran verzichtet".[14] Zamenhofs Code wurde also nicht nur publiziert, sondern aktiv zur Weiterbearbeitung freigestellt.

Am Anfang umfasste dieser lediglich eine Minimalgrammatik, 927 Wortstämme und einige Beispieltexte, damit sich die Sprache innerhalb der *Community* würde entwickeln können. Aus den Sprachlehrbüchern konnten die Leserinnen und Leser zudem kleine Coupons ausschneiden, weiterverteilen, unterschreiben und an den Autor persönlich zurückschicken. Sie bekundeten damit schriftlich ihr Interesse an der Erfindung und „versprachen", diese zu lernen, falls und wenn 10.000.000 andere dasselbe täten bzw. getan hätten. Die *Community* sollte demnach zuerst als imaginäre Adressenversammlung in der Phantasie der Einzelnen *präfiguriert,*[15] dann real *dokumentiert* und schließlich global *realisiert* werden – eine sog. autopoetische Entwicklungsfigur, die bei der Kommunikation einer hohen Zahl von verschiedenen und interdependenten Potenzialitäten auftritt. Die Rücksendecoupons könnte man auch als erstes *Newsletter*-Angebot vor dem Internet bezeichnen, aller-

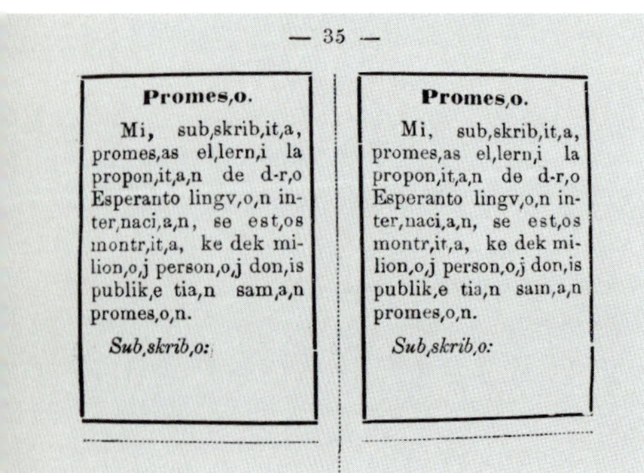

— 35 —

Promes,o.

Mi, sub,skrib,it,a, promes,as el,lern,i la propon,it,a,n de d-r,o Esperanto lingv,o,n inter,naci,a,n, se est,os montr,it,a, ke dek milion,o,j person,o,j don,is publik,e tia,n sam,a,n promes,o,n.

Sub,skrib,o:

Promes,o.

Mi, sub,skrib,it,a, promes,as el,lern,i la propon,it,a,n de d-r,o Esperanto lingv,o,n inter,naci,a,n, se est,os montr,it,a, ke dek milion,o,j person,o,j don,is publik,e tia,n sam,a,n promes,o,n.

Sub,skrib,o:

Adress Managment in the Code-*Community:* Start-up with 10.000.000 subscriptions

Adres-administrado en la kodo-„komunumo": starto kun 10.000.000 subskriboj

Adressenmanagement in der Code-*Community:* Start-up mit 10.000.000 Unterschriften

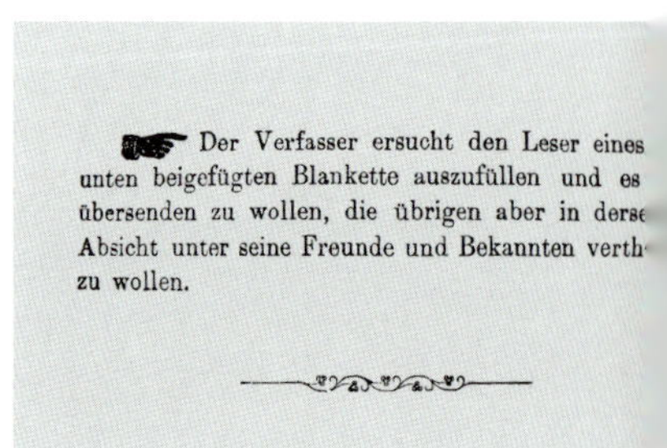

Der Verfasser ersucht den Leser eines unten beigefügten Blankette auszufüllen und es übersenden zu wollen, die übrigen aber in derse Absicht unter seine Freunde und Bekannten verth zu wollen.

the same way. The *community* was thus first *prefigured* as an imaginery assembly of adresses in the minds of the individuals,[15] and secondly, was *actualized* in documentation at Zamenhof's private home, and finally, as a third step to come, was to be *realized* on a global scale. This reflects an autopoietic figure of development, today a form that typically arises in communication when one is dealing with a high number of interdependent potentialities. The coupons were to function like our contemporary Newsletters offered on the Internet, except that the possibility to unsubscribe was not a technical option at the time.[16] Obviously, the strategy failed, as in the following two years only 1000 Coupons were returned—but that did not stop the New Code spreading. First in Russia, then in France and the rest of Western Europe „followers"of the New Code were making contact with each other. They managed the step from reading the code to using it in conversation and could thus initiate the first *interface*-tests. From these *community* members, Zamenhof was sent numerous ideas, contributions, and criticisms of his code. Yet he was serious about wanting to step back from his authors role: He

poste pli kaj pli en Francio kaj en la okcidento de Eŭropo troviĝis ĉiam kodo-„adeptoj", kiuj transiris de la legado al la parolado kaj tiel povis fari la unuajn interfacajn testojn. Baldaŭ multnombraj ideoj, proponoj kaj kodo-kritikoj atingis Zamenhof. Li serioze restis je la malakcepto de la aŭtora rolo: Li tuj insistis pri la starigo de komisiono, tamen devis atendi ne malpli ol 18 jarojn, ĝis oni forprenis de li la ŝarĝon de la kompleta respondeco.[17] *En Boulogne-sur-Mer, rekte ĉe la Maniko proksime al Calais, oni en aŭgusto 1905 okazigis la unuan Universalan Kongreson de Esperanto kaj 688 vizitantoj el 20 diversaj landoj dum unu semajno komunikis unu kun la alia kaj sin bonege komprenis, per la nova kodo kiel ununura komuna lingvo.*
La Franca matematikisto Louis Coutourat raportis: „(...) ne nur, ke ĉiuj sin komprenis, (...) ankaŭ la diferencoj en la prononcado estis tute sensignifaj kaj tute ne ĝenis. Plej ofte oni ne povis eĉ diveni la naciecon de la kunparolanto."[18] *Tiu kompleksa kaj sukcesa apliktesto de prototipo kunevoluita de la komunumo por la interfaco de la malnovaj kodoj estis io, kion Schleyer neniam spertis, sed ankaŭ neniu kodo-*

dings noch ohne die Möglichkeit zum *unsubscribe.*[16] Diese Strategie scheiterte einerseits zwar gründlich, da in den folgenden zwei Jahren nur ca. 1000 Coupons bei Zamenhof eintrafen, andrerseits tat das der Codeverbreitung auf Dauer keinen Abbruch. Zuerst in Russland, dann zunehmend in Frankreich und im Westen Europas fanden sich immer Code-„Anhänger", die vom Lesen ins Sprechen übergingen und somit die ersten *Interface*-Tests vornehmen konnten. Zamenhof erreichten bald zahlreiche Ideen, Eingaben und Code-Kritiken. Mit der Ablehnung der Autorenrolle blieb es ihm ernst: Er drängte sofort auf die Einrichtung einer Kommission, musste allerdings nicht weniger als 18 Jahre darauf warten, dass ihm die Bürde der Gesamtverantwortung abgenommen würde.[17] In Boulogne-sur-Mer, direkt am Ärmelkanal in der Nähe von Calais, wurde im August 1905 der erste *Esperanto*-Kongress veranstaltet und 688 Besucherinnen und Besucher aus 20 verschiedenen Ländern kommunizierten eine ganze Woche lang miteinander und verstanden sich blendend, mit dem Neucode als einziger gemeinsamer Sprache. Der französische Mathematiker Louis Coutourat berichtet: „ (...) nicht nur, dass sich alle verstanden, (...) auch die Unterschiede in der Aussprache waren völlig unbedeutend und störten überhaupt nicht. Meistens

Roll-on Roll-off-Verkehr /m/ MA10 en/ elŝipigo propaganda de veturiloj; RoRo
Rollprüfstand /m/ WT10 provbenko de fiksa deĵorejo
Rollprüfstand /m/ WT10 relmaŝino por ellaciĝprovoj
Rollschranke /f/ NT80 bariero rulebla
Rollsteig /m/ AT30 rultrotuaro
rollstuhlgerechter Reisezugwagen /m/ (Behinderte) MT52 pasaĝervagono rulseĝotaŭga
rollstuhlgerechter Wagen /m/ (Behinderte) MT52 pasaĝervagono rulseĝotaŭga

International Dictionary for Railroaders, German – Esperanto

Internacia Fervojista Leksikono, Germana – Esperanto

Internationales Eisenbahnerlexikon Deutsch – Esperanto

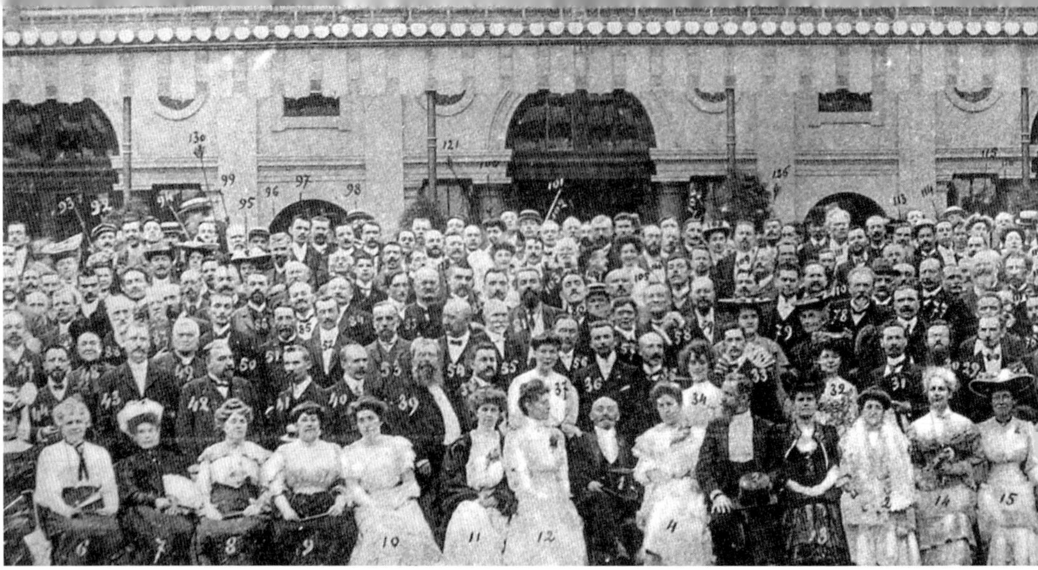

First international Esperanto Congess, Boulonge-sur-Mer, France, August 1905. The Autor in the middle, surrounded by women.

Unua internacia congreso de Esperanto, Boulonge-sur-Mer, Francia, Augusto 1905. Aŭtoro dekstre de la centro ĉirkaŭata de virinoj.

Erster Internationaler Esperantokongress, Boulonge-sur-Mer, France, August 1905. Der Autor rechts von der Mitte, umgeben von Frauen.

immediately asked others to set up a commission that should moderate the growth of the language, but he would have to wait for another 18 years to have this burden taken off his shoulders.[17] In Boulogne-sur-Mer, near the city of Calais in France, the first *Esperanto*-Congress was organized in August 1905 and 688 visitors from 20 Countries communicated for a week using only their New Code. The french mathematician Louis Coutourat reported in a letter: " ... not only have they all understood each other, (...) but as well the differences in articulation (dialect) were insignificant and did not at all disturb. Most of the time one could not even guess the nationality of ones partner in dialog."[18] A complex and successful test of a prototyp like this was something that Johann Martin Schleyer never experienced, and no code-poet since is likely to. At the same conference the community agreed on a "Fundamento" of the Code, in order to fire-wall it against derivates. This consisted of 16

poeto post Zamenhof. Je la sama kongreso la komunumo ankaŭ interkonsentis pri la „fundamento" de sia kodo por malebligi derivaĵ-evoluojn: 16 reguloj, 2644 vortradikoj kaj tekstkorpo kiel lingva modelo. Kaj vere: Nur 2 jarojn poste okazis la lanĉo de la t.n. „Ido", danĝera derivaĵo. Ties komunumo tamen poste pereis denove pro estiĝo de propraj derivaĵoj kaj daŭraj kvereloj – kiel jam antaŭe volapuko. Sed la nova kodo kun la nomo Esperanto ĝis hodiaŭ posedas elstaran pozicion inter la planlingvaj projektoj. Ĝi estas la nura, kiun ĝia komunumo finpoluris al komplete evoluigita kulturlingvo. Oni povas apliki ĝin en ĉiuj vivokampoj kaj en ĉiuj landoj de la mondo, la vortaroj intertempe enhavas pli ol 20.000 normitajn vortradikojn kaj la sekvaj Universalaj Kongresoj okazos en Pekino (2004) kaj Vilno (2005).

konnte man nicht einmal die Nationalität des Gesprächspartners erraten."[18] Dieser komplexe und erfolgreiche Anwendungstest eines von der *Community* mitentwickelten Prototyps für das Interface der Altcodes war etwas, das Schleyer nie erlebt hatte und kein Code-Poet nach Zamenhof so erleben sollte. Am selben Kongress einigte sich die Community auch auf das „Fundamento" ihres Codes, um Derivatbildungen zu verhindern: 16 Regeln, 2644 Wortstämme und einen Textkorpus als sprachlichem Modell. Nur zwei Jahre später wurde tatsächlich ein gefährliches Derivat, das sog. *Ido,* lanciert. Dessen *Community* ging in Folge allerdings wieder an eigenen Derivatbildungen und Dauerstreitigkeiten zugrunde – wie vorher schon das *Volapük*. Der Neucode namens *Esperanto* aber nimmt bis heute eine Sonderstellung unter den Plansprachprojekten ein. Als einziger ist er durch seine *Community* zu einer vollentwickelten Kultursprache abgerundet worden und kann in allen Lebensbereichen und in allen Ländern der Welt

rules of grammar, 2644 roots for words and a corpus of text as a language model. And indeed, only two years later a highly aggressive derivate called *Ido* was published, but its *community* stumbled over their own derivates and conflicts, similar to *Volapük.*
Looking back today, the New Code called *Esperanto* has achieved a special position in the family of constructed languages. It is the only one, whose *community* developed it into a full cultural language. It can now be applied to all walks of life, its dictionaries contain over 20.000 standardized roots, and the next World-Conferences will be staged in Peking (2004) and Vilnius, Lithuania (2005).

Some Code to Die for—What is the message of this medium?

The modern theory of linguistics gives us other categories than those used so far. In Noam Chomsky's generative transformational grammar for example, this New Code would be classified as a "possible natural language" as it is using the same generative mechanisms as other Old Codes, only in a stricter manner. *Esperanto* would thus be neither a New Code nor a programming language. Nevertheless, Ludwig Zamenhof deserves the *Golden Nica,* in the category for "Most successful Hack of Old Codes since the historical Pentecost." In this way he intervened,—as he was highly aware—, at the core of the power dispositives of the religious, pseudo-religious and post-religious phantasms of the Modern, the high-voltage area of cultural "production."
History proved in a cruel way then, that Zamenhof's father, who described the manual as a "harmless curiousity", could not have

Morti por kodoj–Kio estas la mesaĝo de tia komunikilo?

La teoriformado de la moderna lingviko intertempe enkondukis aliajn kategoriojn por lingvokodoj kaj tiel oni klasifikus Esperanton ekz. laŭ la transforma gramatiko de Noam Chomsky kiel „eblan naturan lingvon", ĉar ĝi estas generata laŭ la samaj bazaj reguloj kiel malnova kodo, nur pli strikte. Tial ĝi do ne estas nova kodo kaj tutcerte ne programlingvo. Tamen Zamenhof ekde 1905 meritas la premion „Ora Nica" en la kategorio „plej sukcesa rekodado de malnovaj kodoj ekde la historia Pentekosto". Li ŝajne tute konsciis pri tio, ke li per sia invento intervenis en la alttensia regiono de la kultura „produktado", en la potenclogika kerno de la religiaj, anstataŭreligiaj kaj postreligiaj fantasmoj de la moderna tempo. La plua historio ja ankaŭ poste en kruela maniero malpravigis la patron de Zamenhof, kiu nomis la unuan lernolibron „sendanĝera

Anwendung finden. Die Wörterbücher führen mittlerweile über 20.000 standardisierte Wortstämme und die nächsten Weltkongresse finden in Peking (2004) und Vilnius (2005) statt.

Sterben für Codes – Was ist die Botschaft eines solchen Mediums?

Die Theoriebildung der modernen Linguistik hat andere Kategorien für Sprachcodes eingeführt und so wäre *Esperanto* z. B. nach Noam Chomskys Generativer Transformationsgrammatik als „mögliche natürliche Sprache" einzustufen, da es nach denselben Grundregeln generiert wird wie ein Altcode, nur strikter. Es handelt sich also doch nicht um einen Neucode und erst recht keine Programmiersprache.
Trotzdem verdient Zamenhof seit 1905 die *Goldene Nica* in der Kategorie „Erfolgreichster Hack von Altcodes seit dem historischen Pfingsten". Mit seiner Erfindung konnte er demnach nicht umhin, und dessen war er sich wohl bewusst, in einem Hochspannungbereich kultureller „Produktion" zu intervenieren, im machtlogischen Kernbereich der religiösen, ersatzreligiösen und nachreligiösen Phantasmen der Moderne.
Die Geschichte sollte Zamenhofs Vater, der das erste Sprachlehrbuch

been more mistaken. The New Code of his son not only resulted in happy, travelling, reading and marrying users—but these users were also imprisoned, tortured and killed, especially under the dictatorships of Adolf Hitler and Joseph Stalin. Their new, neutralized communicative competence was obviously a strong threat to these powers, National Socialism and Sowjet Communism, who by this time had taken the respective Old Codes, German and Russian, hostage of their sense of mission.[19] Before the very eyes of our contemporary authors and writers of New Code for *technical interfaces,* (the term Hacker has become somewhat of an anachronistic touch), a second front has manifested in the last decades, and the conflict about the codes of tomorrow and the culture adequate to developing them is now emerging. An important contribution has been made by Vilém Flusser, in various aspects an invisible twin of Zamenhof, with his maxim: *from subject to project.*[20] It is of vital interest for our future societies that this second Clash of Code-Cultures is made more and more understood by the public in the years to come, the mainstream will appreciate it. In our more and more differenciated technical worlds and environments contact to those for whom one might have initiated a code-project is mediated to a very high degree. The manifold shiftings, partitions and juxtapositions of problems that the members of a contemporary code-community have to deal with (strong nerves are an advantage here), can be visited and studied in detail at *http://www.gnu.org/ people/ people.html.* There an author of a prototype for a free operation

sensencaĵo", ĉar la nova kodo de lia filo rezultis ne nur en feliĉaj, vojaĝantaj, legantaj kaj edziĝantaj uzantoj, ili ankaŭ milope estis enkarcerigitaj, batitaj kaj murditaj, precipe en la diktaturoj de Adolf Hitler kaj Joseph Stalin. Tiu nova, neŭtraligita lingvokompetenteco signifis sufiĉe rektan endanĝerigon de la potencaj sferoj, la n acisocialismo kaj la sovjetkomunismo, kiuj, kiel oni povas diveni, transformis siajn respektivajn malnovajn kodojn, la germanan kaj rusan, al komplicoj de siaj sendokonsciencoj.[19]
Antaŭ la okuloj de la konstruivaj aŭtoroj kaj verkantoj de la novaj kodoj, kiujn multaj miskomprene ankoraŭ nomas kodaĉantoj, estiĝas nuntempe dua fronto: La konflikto pri la kodoj de morgaŭ kaj la ĝusta kulturo por ilia evoluigado. Gravan kontribuon postlasis Villém Flusser, multrilate nevidebla samvojano de Zamenhof, per sia maksimo: De la subjekto al la projekto.[20] *Sed en la sin diferenciĝantaj teknikaj mondoj kaj medioj de la novaj kodoj, la kontakto al tiuj, por kiuj oni subjekte ekis siajn projektojn, estas altskale pli malrekta. Necesas pliklarigebli tiun duan kulturan batalon dum la sekvaj jaroj – la granda amaso dankos pro tio. Kiu posedas sufiĉajn nervojn, povas rigardi la multoblan dispartiĝon kaj ŝoviĝon de la problemoj en medio de teknikaj interfacoj laŭ plia komunumo kaj detale ĉe: http://www.gnu.org/ people/people.html. Tie ankaŭ klarigas aŭtoro de la prototipo de libera mastra programo, Richard Stallman, siajn motivoijn (http://www.gnu.org/ gnu/ thegnuproject.html).*
„La eĥo de la teknikoj provokas la homan inteligentecon, kvalifiki

als „harmloses Kuriosum" betitelte, dann auch in grausamer Form widerlegen, denn der Neucode seines Sohnes resultierte nicht nur in glücklichen, reisenden, lesenden und heiratenden Userinnen und Usern, diese wurden auch zu Tausenden eingesperrt, misshandelt und getötet, v. a. unter den Diktaturen von Adolf Hitler und Joseph Stalin. Die neue, neutralisierte Sprachkompetenz bedeutete eine ausreichend direkte Gefährdung von Machtbereichen, dem Nationalsozialismus und dem Sowjetkommunismus, die, man ahnt es, die jeweiligen Altcodes Deutsch und Russisch zu Komplizen ihres Sendungsbewusstseins gemacht hatten.[19] Vor den Augen unserer zeitgenössischen konstruktiven Autoren und Literaten der Neucodes und technischen *Interfaces,* von vielen noch missverständlich *Hacker* genannt, manifestiert sich derzeit eine zweite Front: Der Konflikt um die Codes von morgen und die richtige Kultur für deren Entwicklung. Einen wichtigen Beitrag hat Vilém Flusser, in vielem ein unsichtbarer Weggenosse Zamenhofs, mit seiner Maxime „Vom Subjekt zum Projekt"[20] hinterlassen. Doch in den sich ausdifferenzierenden technischen Welten und Umwelten der Neucodes ist der Kontakt zu denen, für die man subjektiv seine Projekte begann, um Potenzen vermittelter. Darum gilt es, diesen zweiten Kulturkampf um Codes in den nächsten Jahren besser verständlich zu machen, der *Mainstream* wird es danken. Wer die Nerven dazu aufbringt, kann sich en detail die vielfache Teilung und Verschiebung der Problemstellungen in der technischen Umwelt einer solchen Community unter *http:// www.gnu.org/people/people.html* ansehen. Dort erläutert auch ein Autor des Prototypen eines freien

system, Richard Stallman, explains his motivation (http://www.gnu.org/ gnu/thegnuproject.html.) „The feedback of technical dimensions provokes the human intelligence to qualify for the tasks of being an engineer on spaceship earth.“[21]
If one is, on the other side, confronted with the task of understanding why human beings would risk and lose their life for a „foreign“, or „neutral“ language, a new riddle in our *Second Modernity* (H. Klotz, U. Beck) manifests itself. *Some Code to die for*—a media theory which doesn't take its name for granted has an unexpected new theme to ponder. Its first horizon might be sketched here: For the first time, the Medium was actually congruent with its Message.

sin por la taskoj de inĝeniero surŝipe de la spacoŝipo tero“. [21] *Kiel oni aliflanke komprenu, ke homoj libervole riskis la morton por ja verdire „fremda“, ĉar „neŭtrala“ lingvo, ree prezentiĝas kiel enigmo en nia „dua moderna epoko“ (H. Klotz,U. Beck). „Morti por kodoj“ – „komunikil-teorio, kiu meritas sian nomon, jen ricevas plian neatenditan temon. Unua pensa horizonto eble povas esti konturigita: La unuan fojon komunikilo fakte estis kongrua kun sia komuniko.*

Betriebssystems, Richard Stallman, seine Motivation (http://www.gnu.org/gnu/thegnuproject.html). Das Feedback der Techniken provoziert die menschliche Intelligenz, sich für die Aufgaben des Ingenieurs an Bord des Raumschiffs Erde zu qualifizieren.“[21] Wie man sich allerdings auf der anderen Seite einen Reim darauf machen soll, dass Menschen für eine eigentlich „fremde“, weil „neutrale“ Sprache“ freiwillig den Tod riskieren, stellt sich als ein Rätsel in unserer *Zweiten Moderne* (H. Klotz, U. Beck) neu auf. *Sterben für Codes* – einer Medientheorie, die ihren Namen verdient, ist damit ein unerwartetes Thema aufgegeben. Ein erster Horizont konnte hier vielleicht angedeutet werden: Zum ersten Mal war ein Medium tatsächlich deckungsgleich mit seiner Botschaft.

For further information visit *www.paramediamind.org*
English translation by Leo Findeisen and Stephen Zepke. / Esperanto translation by Gunnar Fischer.
The author wants to express his gratitude to the staff at the Department of Planned Languages and International Esperanto Museum, Austrian National Library, Vienna, for their support. All imagery courtesy of the same.

1 N. Luhmann, *Weltkunst*, 38; in: *Unbeobachtbare Welt, Über Kunst und Architektur*, hrsg. von N. Luhmann, F.D. Bunsen und D. Baecker, Bielfeld 1990
2 D. Crystal, *Cambridge Encyclopedia of Language*, 17ff.
3 See P. Sloterdijk, "Zwischen Gesichtern, Zum Auftauchen der interfazialen Intimssphäre." in: *Sphären I – Blasen;* Frankfurt am Main 1998, 141f .; french: +Sphères I – Bulles+, Paris 2002, 152ff.; spanish: +Esferas I – Burbujas+, Madrid 2003, 85ff.
4 E.g. the so-called APIs, Application Programming Interfaces, that are providing programmers with a writable surface into a program
5 A late exception being U. Eco, *Die Suche nach der vollkomenen Sprache*, München 1997, v. a. 322ff.; english: *The search for the perfect language*
6 R. Centassi / H. Masson, *L'homme qui a défié Babel*, Paris 1995, 68
7 Centassi / Masson 68; Eco 324
8 Centassi / Masson 103, in der Übersetzung des Autors
9 a.a.O.
10 Eco 324
11 U. Lins, *Die Gefährliche Sprache*, Gerlingen 1988, 16
12 Lins 20
13 Lins 18f
14 a.a.O.
15 See one of the standard works for a media theory of Nationalism: B. Anderson, *Imagined Communities: Reflections on the origin and spread of nationalism*, Verso 1991
16 Lins 29ff.; Chrystal 354, Centassi 174ff.
17 a.a.O.
18 H. Mayer, *Das Kind des Esperanto: Briefe Louis Coutourats an Hugo Schuchardt (1901–1914)*, Wien 2001
19 Lins v.a. 90ff. und 215ff.
20 See V. Flusser, *Vom Subjekt zum Projekt. Menschwerdung*, hrsg. von St. Bollmann und E. Flusser, Bensheim und Düsseldorf 1994; see in english: *Writings*, University of Minnesota Press 2002; *The Freedom of the Migrant: Objections to Nationalism;* University of Illinois Press 2003
21 See P. Sloterdijk, *Sphären III – Schäume*, Kapitel 1 A, *Absolute Inseln*, Frankfurt am Main 2003; french: *Sphéres I – Ecumes*, Paris 2004

Towards a Language of Collective Intelligence

Pierre Lévy

The Ecology of Ideas

Language, with its different recognizable sounds, has opened up to humanity the possibility of asking questions, telling stories, and participating in dialogue. Language has allowed the emergence of unknown entities in animal societies: numbers, gods, laws, works of art, calendars, the technological adventure, and the entire cultural universe. I will designate here by the term "ideas" those complex forms that appear, reproduce themselves, and evolve only in the world of culture, in the space of signification opened up by language. Language has allowed human communities, as compared to hives, herds and packs, to make a leap of collective intelligence because language creates a stronger and more supple link of competitive cooperation than what insects or monkeys have in their respective communities. In putting the idea at the center of my model, I have chosen an approach to human collective intelligence that radically distinguishes it from the collective intelligence of other animal societies. From this perspective, language represents the limit or threshold beyond which ecosystems of ideas are constituted. These are like spiritual hypertexts living in symbiosis with the societies of talking primates we humans form. These ecosystems of ideas grow more complex, die out, diversify, or combine in such a way as to lead those societies that cultivate them down, the in part undetermined, road of cultural evolution. Teilhard de Chardin coined the term "Noosphere" to describe the world ecosystem of all the ideas which globalization and the development of the means of communication, whose culmination we see in cyberspace, have only begun to put at our fingertips.

Human communities can survive only by maintaining cultures, that is, semi-closed collective intelligences conducive to the breeding (reproduction and selection) of ideas. An ethical person, a corporation, an institution, a nation, a religion, a political party, a science, a virtual community or a tribe cultivates—*nolens volens*—ecosystems of ideas. In the course of its existence, a culture explores a viable evolutionary direction for its ideas.

Our mental representations give ideas their forms. In a way, representations are the face, or the mask, of ideas. Representations can be of all kinds; their variety is in theory unlimited : e.g. the images of our perceptions, such as those created by human works of art, music, symbols, and the structures of highly complex relations that have been constructed by means of language and many other sign systems.

Our intentions are the souls of ideas: the movement which animates the face. Intentions direct the mental representations toward particular destinations, or particular targets. They entrust ideas with a goal, which can be quite near, or even very far away, aiming at almost inaccessible horizons. We can think of intentions as the abstract structure of emotions, in other words, as vectors endowed with a force (intensity) and a direction (the "nature" of the emotion). Representations must be distinguished from emotions because the same representation, depending on the circumstances, can serve as a face for very different emotions.

Our skills and abilities are the reproductive, motor and nutritive organs that our minds offer the world of ideas. These are the human faculties by means of which our principal symbiotic partners—symbols—are conceived, reproduced and maintained. Thus culture "breeds" certain human qualities (in preference to others), or certain skills and abilities which are the particular organs of the ideas whose evolution the culture is exploring.

The symbiotic relation between populations and ecosystems of ideas (each feeding off the life of the other) has important consequences. Some populations allow for a more favorable reproduction of ideas, especially where writing, mass communications media, institutions and "values" are at work, since they facilitate collective intelligence and the flowering of the life of the mind. Such populations benefit in turn from those cultural means that support their demographic performance and health. Those ecologies of ideas that offer populations the best competitive advantages receive, by this very fact, the human resources and technologies that ensure their duration, abundance and diversity. On the other hand, populations that select ecosystems of ideas leading to their deterioration or self-destruction in one way or another, cannot for very long reproduce themselves, and consequently, will not be able to reproduce those very ecosystems of ideas. In a word, the process of cultural evolution essentially consists in a mutual selection of the two symbiotic (or symbolic) "halves:" ecologies of ideas and human populations, *without any fixed point or absolute causal endpoint.*

A new idea (a new circuit of complex cognitive acts) lasts or is reproduced only if its "repercussions" are favorable to the population of ideas that sustain it: those ideas without any positive cooperative repercussion are not "viable." Any idea which destroys the environment that nourished it by pillaging its resources without giving anything back is not "durable." The processes of mutation, reproduction and selection of ideas, just like the reciprocal influence which they exert on the populations that shelter them, are governed by multiple and complex rhythms and durations. *They also depend very much on historical and geographical contexts.* Thus the mission of the collective intelligence research community is not to pass "scientific" (much less "definitive") judgment on whether ideas are good or bad. From this perspective, the good and the bad are not stable, well-defined qualities of particular ideas. An idea is not good or bad "in itself." But in those circumstances where it arises, an idea helps or hinders the culture that shelters it according to the particular situation of a highly sensitive and complex ecological system. That's one reason why I've chosen the game as a model: a game-piece (an idea) is neither good nor bad; it is merely the vehicle of a certain power. On the other hand, in the course of a game, it is necessary to evaluate and hierarchize the value of possible moves which this game-piece (this idea) can make. In other words, an idea cannot be the object of an a priori moral evaluation. Only an act can be directly judged; an idea must have inspired many acts in the cultures and different situations before we can make an informed judgment about it. Ideas have value only in the long term effects of the acts they inspire, impacting the well-being of those who cultivate them.

The orientation that the evolution of ecosystems receive most often comes from the retroaction due to the effects (unfavorable after a period of time) produced on the human beings who cultivate these ecosystems. So, why do we want to create a science or deliberate cultivation of collective intelligence when "natural selection" happens automatically? Because another form of evolution is possible: *deliberately cultivating ecosystems of ideas so their evolution may result in an increase in collective intelligence,* and thus an increase in the health, economic prosperity, cultural capital, and spiritual refinement of the communities that care for them, raise them, and select them. This second option is in every respect more prudent, because it is less costly to human populations.

Having spent the better part of its existence living in the oral culture of nomad tribes, humanity took a giant step forward when it domesticated and deliberately selected animal and plant species. Humanity is today confronted by the challenge of organizing in a deliberate fashion the various disciplines of knowledge, intentions, and know-how that form the basis of the life and evolution of ideas. Today, as formerly, a decisive step will allow us to create a much more secure future for posterity. Beyond agriculture, the same evolutionary leap is responsible for creating the city, the state, and writing. In Mesopotamia, in Egypt, in the Indus valleys, in China, and in the great Pre-Columbian civilizations, the same steps seem to have been taken in succession: agriculture, city, temples, states, and in every case (most of the time independently of one another) the invention of an ideographic writing—the culmination of the process. In my opinion, we are once again experiencing the same type of innovation, but much faster and on a much greater scale. In combination with alphabetic writing, the invention of the printing press triggered a movement of global mutation in the ecosystem of ideas. The revolution of experimental science, coupled with the industrial revolution, destabilized the old Neolithic civilizations and led culture to a second massive mutation. The destruction of the family, mass urbanization, global economic integration, the multiplication of transportation and human contacts, and finally the birth of cyberspace as an interactive instrument of communication that goes beyond borders and reconfigures public space on a new scale and in a new form—all these events converge, in my opinion, on the birth of a meta-city. The continuation of all those movements now in process seem to point toward the appearance of new political, economic, and cultural forms for the generations who will come after us. The many conflicts tearing humanity apart express the extreme tension which this mutation is causing us to undergo, especially when we cannot see the "goal." In this time of uncertainty, a few major principles do seem clear, such as the desire to have ideas and knowledge henceforth constitute "the wealth of nations." It is this new phase of the human adventure that the science-art of collective intelligence wishes to support.

The first farmers of the Neolithic age furnished the name and the very model of culture, its relationship to time. Neolithic writing is itself an analogue for agriculture. Ideas are cultivated just like domestic plants. Signs are planted on clay, or on all kinds of earthen materials, whether heavy or fragile. Reading is like a harvest, the multiplication of the planted signs in the mind ... not to mention the multiplication of the ideas attached to these signs. Scientists in biotechnology today can decode genomes, reprogram them, and manipulate the workings of cells at the molecular level. Similarly, it is possible that the meta-writing (or super-language) of the future will be founded on the tridimensional manipulation in cyberspace of a kind of dynamic cultural code.

The shepherds and farmers who come after us will cultivate organisms and ideas in the same way, sowing and reaping to the rhythm of the seasons. We will manipulate ideas by means of the knowledge we have of their "code," and we will launch them in the market place or in the cultural environment, once we have run simulations of their ecological and economic effects. In response to this new "post-modern" condition, the science of collective intelligence (or the science of ecosystems of ideas) proposes to perform the simulations of the interactions among ideas. It is not unreasonable to imagine the essential characteristics of this new writing. It should express in a synthetic manner the ecological dynamics of a great many different ideas. It should allow the rapid verification of the viability of an ecosystem of ideas. Finally, it should contain in its very structure a decisive piece of information concerning the organization of the world of ideas. In a word, it could be a semantic encoding of the universe different from that of language, different as well from the writings inherited from the Neolithic age which over-coded orality on a fixed and durable base. The new encoding will certainly be visual, like classical writing, but it will also be tridimensional, animated and interactive, like a video game or the graphic simulation of a scientist in biology. The ideograms will play the part of elementary "characters" in a virtual world.

To repeat, in the metacultural framework I have here sketched, a prudent plan of action for collective intelligence consists in optimizing the "cultivation," for any given community, of the ecology of ideas with which it lives in symbiosis, and in judiciously orienting its evolution. The development of operative and testable models of collective intelligence is a means to this end, and the "language game" which I have here proposed is meant to exercise our minds in the dynamic modeling of the cultural ecosystem.

A Free Software: The Game of Collective Intelligence

To make collective intelligence a stable object of knowledge, it seems useful to make it *visible* by means of symbolic images. There indeed exists a much remarked link between the development of a science and the development of its instruments of observation, visualization, and representation. The telescope, the microscope, cartography, or the new images in medical science clearly illustrate this relationship. Furthermore, the great periods of cultural invention have often forged a strong relationship among drawing, "spatialization" and thought. To confirm this, we need only look to the ideographic writings that accompanied the birth of Egyptian and Chinese civilization, to the role geometry played in classical Greek culture, and the role that geometric perspective played in the Renaissance. Each of these great periods of cultural creation have likewise produced remarkable forms of urbanism, architecture, and monumentality.

In the twentieth-century, the digital image is inaugurating a new dialectic among space, vision, and reason. The number of scientific disciplines that use digital images to visualize their data is beyond reckoning. At the same time, in the industrial sector, the design and management of complex processes increasingly rely on computerized graphic simulations. Finally, the link between architecture, urbanism, and virtual worlds, already well under way, is destined to grow ever closer in the future. Traditional instruments of observation had opened the door to the infinitesimal, the far away, the immense, and the hidden. Today, computer technology lets us transform masses of digitized data into images, indeed, into universes yet to be explored, and thereby opening the door to the (indirect) vision of *the super complex and the abstract.* We may advance the following hypothesis: the universe of information, interests, knowledge, and expertise—i.e. semantic space—is destined to become formative with respect to other spaces. It naturally follows that we must envision the conception of software that calculates—from the flow of empirical data coming in from real communities—*visual representations of collective intelligence, its conditions of development and its environment.* These representations should be readable and explorable in virtual space in order to help people and groups orient themselves in abstract space (which is nonetheless influential), on which everything will increasingly depend. The project of the research network I direct is to construct such software and to test it using real data. The Game of Collective Intelligence (GCI) will include functions to help with the gathering and formatting of data, visual modeling, and interactive simulation. Using the information provided, the GCI will send the interested communities, as in a mirror, an explorable and reflective image of their collective intelligence. This image will give them some indication of the problems to be resolved (since the form of any collective intelligence has an intimate relation to its landscape of problems), and it will help the community to perfect their models of intellectual cooperation and to balance their cultural ecosystems. Of the many factors that figure in its composition, the model proposed here below, as will become apparent, assigns an important place to reflexivity, in other words, the information and ideas (organized in a coherent way) *which impact the cognitive functioning of the community in question.* The construction and the free Internet access to the GCI aims to contribute to a better "self-knowledge" of the communities that wish

to commit themselves to the adventure of cognitive self-transformation. Furthermore, the software—which as its name indicates is the platform for a "game of collective intelligence"—should encourage the apprenticeship of a strategic thinking adapted to a society of highly complex knowledge in the grips of globalization and rapid change.
The use of this software would follow these steps:

1 gathering the data concerning the economy of the knowledge of a community (plotting one's "position");
2 supplying the computer model with data so as to obtain a mapping of the structure and the position of the collective intelligence of this community (transfer its position onto the "map");
3 using this structure and singular position, the GCI will be able to simulate the different scenarios of the community's evolution of ideas toward an increase in collective intelligence (the "compass" points "north"). These simulations are meant to give pertinent indications as to the course to be followed in order to progress—in each different situation—toward an increase in collective intelligence.

In the GCI, ideas are represented by dynamic ideograms. These ideograms each have a characteristic visual image and are affected, according to their definitions, at specific zones of semantic space. They also have their own behavior allowing them to interact with one another, to combine, reproduce, and evolve in concert according to defined rules. Together the ideograms compose—on one hand—a language of animated images capable of *figuring* the infinitely varied facets of the universe of collective intelligence, and—on the other hand—they compose an instrument to simulate the ecology of ideas (or cognitive economies). Here, linguistic usage is an act, in other words, an event that has its origin in the intentions, knowledge and expertise of the agents intervening to particular ends, by manipulating symbols, in the given situation. The game will be able to suggest orientations for real agents, or simply indicate the easily foreseeable bad consequences of certain "moves." What is more, as a pedagogical exercise or just for fun, players will be able to go up against the computer and improve their proficiency in "the strategy of collective intelligence."

Translated from the French by Michael Taormina

http://www.collectiveintelligence.info/documents/0-REF-CI.doc
http://www.collectiveintelligence.info/documents/03-CIN.doc
http://www.collectiveintelligence.info/documents/Research-Outline-07-05-03.doc
http://www.collectiveintelligence.info/documents/02-FRENCH-JEU.doc
http://switch.sjsu.edu/~switch/nextswitch/switch_engine/front/front.php?artc=280
http://www.collectiveintelligence.info/documents/CI-THEORY-1.ppt
http://www.collectiveintelligence.info/documents/CI-THEORY-2.ppt
http://www.collectiveintelligence.info/documents/CI-THEORY-3.ppt
http://www.collectiveintelligence.info/documents/CI-THEORY-4.ppt
http://www.collectiveintelligence.info/documents/CI-THEORY-5.ppt
http://www.collectiveintelligence.info/documents/MOA-DATABASE.ppt
http://www.collectiveintelligence.info/documents/PLAYGROUND.ppt

Eine Sprache der kollektiven Intelligenz

Pierre Lévy

Die Ökologie der Ideen

Die artikulierte Sprache hat der Menschheit die Möglichkeit eröffnet, Fragen zu stellen, Geschichten zu erzählen und Dialoge zu führen. Sie hat das Aufkommen von Entitäten ermöglicht, wie sie in der Gesellschaft von Tieren unbekannt sind: Zahlen, Götter, Gesetze, Kunstwerke, Kalender, die Welt der Technik und der Kultur. Hier bezeichne ich mit dem Begriff „Ideen" jene komplexen Formen, die nur in der Welt der Kultur, im dem von der Sprache eröffneten Bedeutungsraum erscheinen und sich nur dort reproduzieren und weiterentwickeln können.
Verglichen mit Gemeinschaften von Tieren wie Bienenvölkern oder Herden hat die Sprache den menschlichen Gemeinschaften einen *Sprung in der kollektiven Intelligenz* ermöglicht, weil Sprache eine die wettbewerbsorientierte Kooperation unterstützende Bindung herstellt, die stärker und flexibler ist als jene, die z. B. die Gemeinschaften von Ameisen oder Pavianen zusammenhält. Ich stelle die Idee ins Zentrum meines Modells, weil ich mich für eine Annäherung an die menschliche kollektive Intelligenz entschieden habe, die sie sehr radikal von der anderer tierischer Gesellschaften unterscheidet. Aus meiner Sicht markiert die Sprache die Schwelle, und davon ausgehend bilden sich *Ökosysteme von Ideen* – eine Art spiritueller Hypertexte –, die in Symbiose mit Gesellschaften sprechender Primaten leben, wie wir Menschen sie bilden. Diese Ideen-Ökosysteme werden entweder komplexer oder sterben ab, sie diversifizieren oder mischen sich und führen dadurch die sie kultivierenden Gesellschaften auf einen Weg der kulturellen Evolution, der nur ansatzweise determiniert ist. Teilhard de Chardin hat das weltumspannende Ökosysteme aller Ideen „Noosphäre" genannt, die dank der Globalisierung und der Entwicklung von Kommunikationsmitteln, die im Cyberspace ihren vorläufigen Höhepunkt finden, nun für uns tatsächlich greifbar wird.
Die menschlichen Gemeinschaften können nur dann überleben, wenn sie über *Kulturen* verfügen, also über halb geschlossene kollektive Intelligenzen, die der Heranzüchtung von Ideen (d. h. ihrer Reproduktion und Selektion) förderlich sind. Eine moralische Person, ein Unternehmen, eine Institution, eine Nation, eine Religion, eine politische Partei, eine Wissenschaft, eine virtuelle Gemeinschaft oder ein Stamm kultivieren und pflegen – nolens volens – Ideen-Ökosysteme. Im Laufe ihrer Existenz sucht eine Kultur nach einer für die Entwicklung ihrer Ideen gangbaren Entwicklungsrichtung. *Unsere mentalen Repräsentationen* geben den Ideen ihre Gestalt. Diese Repräsentationen sind in gewisser Weise die Gestalt, das Gesicht, die Maske der Ideen. Sie können beliebige Formen annehmen, ihre Vielfalt ist im Grunde unbeschränkt: Es sind die Bilder unserer Wahrnehmung, also jene Bilder, die die Menschen in der Kunst, Musik oder in ihren Symbolen schaffen, aber auch die Strukturen ultrakomplexer Beziehungen, die durch die Sprache und multiple Zeichensysteme konstruiert werden.
Unsere Intentionen sind die Seele der Ideen: die Bewegung, die „die Gestalt" belebt. Die Intentionen dirigieren die mentalen Repräsentationen hin zu gewissen Zielen, und dieses *Ziel* kann sehr nahe, aber auch in sehr weiter Ferne liegen und auf einen fast unerreichbaren Horizont verweisen. Man kann die Intentionen als die abstrakte Struktur der Emotionen betrachten, d. h. als Vektoren, die eine Kraft (Intensität) und eine Richtung (die „Natur" der Emotion) aufweisen. Es ist wichtig, Repräsentationen und Emotionen zu unterscheiden, weil ein und

dieselbe Repräsentation je nach Umständen sehr unterschiedlichen Emotionen dienen kann. Unsere *Kompetenzen* sind die reproduzierenden, bewegenden und nährenden Organe, die unser Geist der Welt der Ideen schenkt. Sie sind jene menschlichen Fähigkeiten, dank der unsere wichtigsten Symbioten – die Symbole – erdacht, reproduziert und bewahrt werden. Die Kultur „erzieht" also gewisse menschliche Qualitäten oder Kompetenzen (und stellt sie damit über andere), die dann die speziellen Organe jener Ideen sind, deren Entwicklung diese Kultur verfolgt. Die symbiotische Beziehung zwischen Populationen und Ideen-Ökosystemen (wobei sich eines vom Leben des anderen nährt) hat weit reichende Konsequenzen. Gewisse Populationen machen es den Ideen leichter, sich fortzupflanzen, vor allem dann, wenn Schrift, Kommunikationsmedien, Institutionen oder „Werte" wirksam werden, die die kollektive Intelligenz und das Aufblühen geistigen Lebens begünstigen. Solche Populationen profitieren ihrerseits von kulturellen Mitteln, die ihre demografische Performanz und ihre Gesundheit stärken. Jene Ideen-Ökologien, die den Populationen die größten Wettbewerbsvorteile verschaffen, kommen allein schon auf Grund dieser Tatsache in den Genuss menschlicher und technischer Ressourcen, die ihnen Dauerhaftigkeit, Reichhaltigkeit und Vielfalt garantieren. Umgekehrt können Populationen, die sich für jene Ideen-Ökosysteme entscheiden, die zur Schwächung oder Selbstzerstörung dieser Populationen führen, sich selbst nicht lange halten – und daher können sie auch die betreffenden Ideen-Ökosysteme nicht lange reproduzieren. Alles in allem besteht der Prozess der kulturellen Evolution im Wesentlichen in einer wechselseitigen Selektion der beiden „symbiotischen" (oder symbolischen) Hälften: Ideen-Ökologie und menschliche Populationen, *ohne Fixpunkt oder absoluten kausalen Endpunkt.*

Eine neue Idee (eine neuer Kreislauf komplexer kognitiver Akte) ist nur von Dauer (und reproduziert sich nur dann), wenn sie günstige Auswirkungen auf die Ideenpopulationen hat, in der sie lebt. Ideen, die sich auf die Kooperation nicht positiv auswirken, sind nicht „lebensfähig". Eine Idee, die ihr Umfeld zerstört, indem sie alle Ressourcen plündert, ohne selbst etwas dafür zu geben, ist nicht „nachhaltig". Natürlich gehorchen die Prozesse der Mutation, Reproduktion und Selektion von Ideen sowie der Einfluss, den sie auf die sie beherbergenden Populationen ausüben, vielfältigen und komplexen Rhythmen und zeitlichen Verläufen. *Diese Prozesse sind außerdem in hohem Maße vom historischen und geografischen Kontext abhängig.* Die Gemeinschaft all jener, die sich mit kollektiver Intelligenz beschäftigt, fühlt sich also nicht im geringsten berufen, vorgeblich „wissenschaftliche" Urteile darüber abzugeben, was „gute" und was „schlechte" Ideen sind (und schon gar keine „definitiven" Urteile). Aus unserer Perspektive sind Gut und Schlecht keine fixen, definierten Qualitäten bestimmter Ideen: Eine Idee ist nicht an sich gut oder schlecht. Aber in dem Kontext, in dem sie auftritt, begünstigt oder schädigt sie die sie beherbergende Kultur, je nachdem in welchem Zustand sich das komplexe, ultrasensible Ökosystem befindet. Das ist einer der Gründe, warum ich das Modell des Spiels gewählt habe: eine Spielfigur (eine Idee) ist weder gut noch schlecht, sondern lediglich Träger einer latenten Kraft. Andererseits ist es im Laufe eines Spiels notwendig, mittels dieser Spielfigur (dieser Idee) den Wert möglicher Züge zu evaluieren und sie in Beziehung zueinander zu setzen. Mit anderen Worten: Eine Idee kann nicht a priori Gegenstand einer moralischen Evaluation sein. Nur eine Handlung kann direkt beurteilt werden; eine Idee muss zuerst also viele Handlungen in verschiedenen Kulturen und Situationen inspiriert haben, bevor man über sie ein qualifiziertes Urteil fällen kann. Ideen entfalten ihren Wert nur über die langfristigen Wirkungen, die die von ihnen ausgelösten Handlungen auf das Wohlergehen derer haben, die sie nähren.

Welche Richtung die Evolution von Ideen-Ökosystemen einnimmt, ist bis jetzt meist durch die Rückwirkungen jener (nach einer bestimmten Zeit negativen) Effekte bestimmt worden, die sie auf die Menschen haben, die eben diese Ökosysteme hervorbringen. Warum wollen wir also eine Wissenschaft oder eine eigene Kultur der kollektiven Intelligenz schaffen, wenn die „kulturelle Selektion" ohnehin automatisch stattfindet? Weil eine andere Form von Evolution möglich ist: *nämlich bewusst Ideen-Ökosysteme so zu kultivieren, dass sie sich in Richtung einer Steigerung der kollektive Intelligenz entwickeln* – was sich natürlich auch auf die Gesundheit, die wirtschaftliche Prosperität, den kulturellen Reichtum und die spirituelle Entwicklung jener Gemeinschaft positiv auswirkt, die sie „aufzieht" und selektioniert. Die zweite Option ist in jeder Hinsicht die weisere, da sie den menschlichen Populationen weniger teuer zu stehen kommt. Mit der bewussten Selektion tierischer und pflanzlicher Arten begann für die Menschheit, die den größten Teil ihrer Existenz in oralen Kulturen nomadischer Stämme verbracht hatte, eine neue Entwicklungsphase. Heute steht die Menschheit vor der Herausforderung, Wissen, Intentionen und Know-how, die die Basis des Lebens und der Evolution von Ideen bilden, bewusst verwalten zu müssen. Heute wie damals wird uns ein entscheidender Schritt erlauben, für unsere Nachkommen eine wesentlich sicherere Zukunft zu schaffen.

Ein und derselbe Entwicklungssprung hat nicht nur den Ackerbau, sondern auch die Stadt, den Staat und die Schrift hervorgebracht. In Mesopotamien, Ägypten, im Industal, in China und in den großen vorkolumbianischen Zivilisationen scheinen sich immer die gleichen Etappen wiederholt zu haben: Ackerbau, Stadt, Tempel, Staaten – und in jedem Fall (meist unabhängig voneinander) die Erfindung einer ideografischen Schrift als Krönung des Prozesses. Es scheint mir, als würden wir im Moment genau dieselbe Art von Fortschritt erleben, aber auf einem höheren Niveau und mit höherer Geschwindigkeit.

Kombiniert mit der alphabetischen Schrift hat die Erfindung des Buchdrucks einen globalen Wandel des Ideen-Ökosystems ausgelöst. Die Revolution in den experimentellen Wissenschaften hat im Verein mit der industriellen Revolution die alten neolithischen Kulturen destabilisiert und die Kultur an die Schwelle einer zweiten großen Mutation gebracht. Der Zerfall der Familie, die massive Verstädterung, die wirtschaftliche Integration auf globaler Ebene, die Vervielfachung der Kontakt- und Transportmöglichkeiten, die Entstehung des Cyberspace als grenzüberschreitendes interaktives Kommunikationsinstrument, das die Entstehung einer neuen Form des öffentlichen Raums markiert – all dies scheint mir in die Geburt einer *Metastadt* zu münden. Die Tatsache, dass sich diese im Moment stattfindenden Bewegungen fortsetzen, scheint auf das Auftreten neuer politischer, wirtschaftlicher und kultureller Formen für die uns nachfolgenden Generationen hinzudeuten. Die zahlreichen Konflikte, die die Menschheit auf die Probe stellen, sind Ausdruck der extremen Spannung, die diese Mutation in uns auslöst, vor allem dann, wenn wir kein „Ziel" erkennen können. Inmitten dieser Ungewissheit scheinen sich einige große Prinzipien abzuzeichnen, z. B. das Prinzip, dass nunmehr Ideen und Wissen den „Reichtum der Nationen" bilden. Und genau diese neue Phase im Abenteuer der Menschheit möchte die Kunst-Wissenschaft der kollektiven Intelligenz begleiten.

Die ersten Bauern des Neolithikums haben den Namen, das eigentliche Modell für die Kultur geliefert, ihre Beziehung zur Zeit. Die neolithische Schrift ist selbst ein Analogon zum Ackerbau: Man kultiviert Ideen so, wie man Nutzpflanzen kultiviert. Zeichen werden in Lehm oder einen anderen Boden gesät, sei er nun schwer oder krümelig. Lesen gleicht dem Einbringen der Ernte; es ist die geistige Multiplikation der Zeichen, die man ausgesät hat ... und damit der Ideen, mit denen diese Zeichen verknüpft sind. Heute entziffern die Genetiker die Genome, programmieren sie um und können die Funktion der Zellen auf molekularer Ebene manipulieren. Es ist möglich, dass sich die Meta-Schrift (oder die Meta-Sprache) der Zukunft ebenfalls auf die dreidimensionale Manipulation einer Art kultureller dynamischer Kodierung im Cyberspace gründet.

Die Schäfer und die Bauern, die ihnen nachgefolgt sind, haben die Organismen und die Ideen auf dieselbe Art und Weise kultiviert: Sie säten und ernteten im Rhythmus der Jahreszeiten. Wir werden Ideen dank des Wissens um ihren „Code" manipulieren und sie auf den Markt, in das kulturellen Environment bringen, nachdem wir ihre ökologischen und wirtschaftlichen Auswirkungen simuliert haben. Als Antwort auf diese neue „postmoderne" Situation schlägt die Wissenschaft von der Kollektiven Intelligenz (oder die Wissenschaft der Ideen-Ökosys-

teme) vor, die Interaktion zwischen Ideen zu simulieren. Es macht durchaus Sinn, sich die wesentlichen Züge dieser neuen Schrift vorzustellen: Sie sollte auf synthetische Weise die ökologischen Dynamismen großer Mengen verschiedener Ideen ausdrücken können. Sie sollte es erlauben, schnell die Tauglichkeit eines Ideen-Ökosystems überprüfen zu können. Letztendlich sollte sie auch in ihrer Struktur selbst eine entscheidende Information über die Organisation der Welt der Ideen beinhalten. Alles in allem könnte es sich um eine Kodierung des semantischen Universums handeln, die anders ist als die der Sprache – und auch anders als die aus dem Neolithikum ererbten Schriften, die die Oralität auf einem fixen, dauerhaften Träger überkodiert hatten. Die neue Codierung wird mit Sicherheit visuell sein, wie es auch die klassische Schrift war, aber sie wird darüber hinaus dreidimensional, animiert und interaktiv sein, so wie ein Videospiel oder die grafische Simulation eines Biologen. Die Ideogramme werden die Rolle elementarer „Personen" in einer virtuellen Welt übernehmen.
Ich wiederhole: In dem hier skizzierten metakulturellen Rahmen besteht das bewusste Vorgehen einer kollektiven Intelligenz darin, auf für eine Gemeinschaft optimale Art und Weise die Ökologie der Ideen, mit denen sie in Symbiose lebt, zu „kultivieren" und ihre Evolution mit Bedacht zu steuern. Die Entwicklung verifizierbarer, operativer Modelle einer kollektiven Intelligenz ist ein Mittel zu diesem Zweck, und das hier vorgeschlagene „Spiel der Sprache" möchte den Geist für diese dynamische Modellierung des kulturellen Ökosystems trainieren.

Ein Open-Source-Programm: das Spiel der kollektiven Intelligenz

Um aus der kollektiven Intelligenz ein gutes Wissensobjekt zu machen, scheint es angebracht, sie mittels symbolischer Bilder *sichtbar* zu machen. Wie oft betont wird, existiert eine Verbindung zwischen der Entwicklung einer Wissenschaft und der Entwicklung ihrer Beobachtungsinstrumente. Das Teleskop, das Mikroskop, die Kartografie oder die neuen Bilder der Medizin illustrieren diese Beziehung auf sehr eindringliche Weise. Außerdem haben die großen Epochen kultureller Erfindung oft eine starke Beziehung zwischen „Zeichnung", „Verortung" und Denken hergestellt. In diesem Zusammenhang sei nur an die ideografischen Schriften erinnert, die wesentlich an der Hochblüte der ägyptischen und chinesischen Kultur beteiligt waren, oder an die Rolle, die die Geometrie in der klassischen griechischen Kultur und die geometrische Perspektive in der Renaissance spielten. Alle diese Zeiten gesteigerter kultureller Kreativität haben bemerkenswerten Formen des Städtebaus, der Architektur und des Monumentalismus hervorgebracht.
Im 21. Jahrhundert scheint das mittels eines Computers berechnete Bild eine neue Dialektik zwischen Raum, visueller Wahrnehmung und Denken einzuläuten. Es gibt inzwischen unzählige wissenschaftliche Disziplinen, die digitale Bilder zur Visualisierung ihrer Daten benutzen. Parallel dazu erfolgen in der Industrie das Design und die Verwaltung komplexer Prozesse immer öfter über grafisch gestützte Computersimulationen. Letztendlich wird sich die bereits jetzt bestehende Verbindung zwischen Architektur, Urbanismus und virtuellen Welten in Zukunft noch wesentlich verstärken. Die traditionellen Beobachtungsinstrumente haben uns das Winzige, Ferne, Riesige und Verborgene eröffnet. Heute erlaubt uns die Computerwissenschaft, Massen digitaler Daten in Bilder zu verwandeln, ja, sogar in erforschbare Universen, und gewährt uns damit Zugang zur (indirekten) visuellen Wahrnehmung des Hochkomplexen und des Abstrakten. Man kann die Hypothese aufstellen, dass der semantische Raum – das Universum der Informationen, der Interessen, des Wissens und der Kompetenzen – in Zukunft *strukturierend* für andere Räume wirken wird. Wir müssen daher die Konzeption von Programmen erwägen, die anhand des Flusses empirischer Daten, die aus realen Gemeinschaften stammen, *visuelle Repräsentationen der kollektiven Intelligenz* errechnen. Diese Repräsentationen müssten im virtuellen Raum lesbar und erforschbar sein, um Personen und Grup-

pen zu helfen, sich im abstrakten (aber trotz allem sehr bestimmenden) Raum zu orientieren, von dem alles immer stärker abhängig sein wird.
Das von mir geleitete Forschungsnetzwerk plant, ein solches Programm zu entwickeln und es mit Echtdaten zu testen. Da „Spiel der Kollektiven Intelligenz“ wird Hilfefunktionen umfassen, die die Teilnehmer beim Sammeln und Formatieren von Daten, beim visuellen Modelling und bei interaktiver Simulation unterstützt. Auf der Basis der zur Verfügung gestellten Informationen wird das Spiel der Kollektiven Intelligenz den beteiligten Gemeinschaften wie in einem Spiegel ein erforschbares und reflexives Bild ihrer kollektiven Intelligenz liefern, und das wird ihnen Hinweise auf anstehende Probleme geben (da die Form einer kollektiven Intelligenz in engem Zusammenhang steht zu ihrer Problemlandschaft) und den Gemeinschaften helfen, ihre Modelle intellektueller Kooperation zu perfektionnieren und ihre kulturellen Ökosysteme auszubalancieren. Wie wir sehen werden, misst das unten vorgestellte Modell vor allem einem der vielen bei der Erstellung mitspielenden Faktoren einen besonderen Stellenwert bei: der Reflexivität, also jenen (auf kohärente Art und Weise organisierten) Informationen und Ideen, die sich auf das kognitive Funktionieren der betreffenden Gemeinschaft beziehen. Dadurch, dass das Spiel der Intelligenz gratis im Internet verfügbar sein wird, wollen wir zu einer besseren „Selbstkenntnis“ jener Gemeinschaften beitragen, die sich auf das Abenteuer einer kognitiven Selbsttransformation einlassen wollen. Außerdem sollte die Software – die, wie der Name schon andeutet, die Plattform für ein „Spiel der Kollektiven Intelligenz“ ist das Einüben eines strategischen Denkens fördern, das den Anforderungen einer ultrakomplexen, immer globaleren und sich immer schneller verändernden Wissensgesellschaft gerecht wird.
Die Implementierung dieser Software wird in folgenden Etappen geschehen:

1. Sammeln von Daten über die Wissensökonomie einer Gemeinschaft („Bilanz ziehen“);
2. Einspeisen der Daten ins Datenmodell, um Struktur und Position der kollektiven Intelligenz dieser Gemeinschaft zu kartografieren (um ihre Position auf der „Karte“ einzeichnen);
3. Anhand dieser singulären Struktur und Position kann das „Spiel der Intelligenz“ Szenarien für die Entwicklung der Ideen der Gemeinschaft simulieren, die auf eine Steigerung der kollektiven Intelligenz zielen („der Kompass zeigt nach Norden“). Diese Simulationen sollten relevante Hinweise auf den einzuschlagenden Kurs liefern, um – in den unterschiedlichsten Situation – eine Steigerung der kollektiven Intelligenz zu gewährleisten.

Im Spiel der Kollektiven Intelligenz werden die Ideen mittels dynamischer Ideogramme repräsentiert. Diese Ideogramme besitzen ein charakteristisches visuelles Bild und werden je nach ihrer Definition spezifischen Zonen im semantischen Raum zugewiesen. Außerdem weisen sie ein spezifisches Verhalten auf, das ihnen erlaubt, untereinander zu interagieren, sich zusammenzutun, sich zu reproduzieren, und zwar koordiniert und nach definierten Regeln. Als Ganzes bilden Ideogramme – einerseits – eine Sprache aus animierten Bildern, die die unendlich vielfältigen Fassetten des Universums der kollektiven Intelligenz *darstellen* können, andererseits bilden sie gemeinsam ein Instrument zur Simulation von Ideenökologien (oder kognitiven Ökonomien). Hier ist die Anwendung von Sprache ein Akt, also ein Ereigniss, das seinen Ursprung in den Intentionen, dem Wissen und den Kompetenzen seiner Akteure hat, die in bestimmten Situationen mit einem bestimmten Ziel intervenieren, indem sie Symbole manipulieren. Das Spiel kann den realen Akteuren eine Orientierung geben oder leicht vorhersehbare negative Konsequenzen gewisser Handlungen aufzeigen. Außerdem können sich die Spieler in einer spielerischen oder pädagogischen Übung an der Maschine messen und ihre Kompetenz in Sachen „Strategie der kollektiven Intelligenz“ steigern.

Aus dem Französischen von Ingrid Fischer-Schreiber

Referenzen: siehe Seite 92

Exe.cut[up]able statements: The Insistence of Code

Florian Cramer

The resurgence of code

Friedrich Nietzsche's aphorism that "our writing tools are also involved in our thoughts," put down after he first used a mechanical typewriter, has become an axiom of contemporary media theory. Applied to computer code and art, it could also be phrased as a question: How does code shape the aesthetics of digital art and technology?
"10 Programs written in BASIC ©1984", the title of a solo show of the Dutch/Belgian artists Jodi in Malmö/Sweden, June 2003, can be read beyond its specific description of the work exhibited as a programmatic statement that leads the digital arts back to the future. Consisting of vintage Sinclair ZX Spectrum computers running, quote, "ten programs in BASIC that the visitor can add and change things to", the exhibition shows Jodi's work at a radical peak of a development that began with net art and continuously evolved from web browser manipulations through HTML data, manipulations of computer games in sourcecode to increasingly abstract "variations" of simple BASIC program code. It dismantles the notion that, despite the boom of graphical user interfaces in the 1980s and 1990s, program code still is at the heart of computing and digital information technology and hasn't structurally changed since 1984, the year the Apple Macintosh computer was first sold. While artists had run software code in black boxes to drive work that didn't show the programming involved—interactive video installations, for example—, since the late 1990s, programming and program code have received increasing attention as artistic material in themselves.[1] Today, the Macintosh computer has likewise mutated into a flavor of the Unix operating system, exposing its code on a textual commandline interface and thus catching up with contemporary digital arts and its increasing use of computer code as material.
Perhaps the most radical example of computer code turned into artistic material is "Codeworks",[2] chiefly E-Mail-based Net.art written in private languages which hybridize English, program and network code and visual typography, like the following:

```
Exe.cut[up]able statements ---
::do knot a p.arse.r .make.
::reti.cu[t]la[ss]te. yr. text.je[llied]wells .awe. .r[b]ust.
```

In these lines, which were taken from the posting "Re: OPPO.S[able].I.T[humbs]ION! !" by the Australian net artist mez (a.k.a. Mary Anne Breeze) to the mailing list "arc.hive" on January 14th, 2003, the word „Exe.cut[up]able" becomes a self-describing executable sourcecode which expands, among other things, into "Exe" (the Microsoft DOS/Windows file extension for executable programs), "Executable" and, recalling the mechanized collage techniques of Brion Gysin and William S. Burroughs, "cutup". A poetic employment of computer code which adheres more literally to Unix, Perl or C syntax can be found in the E-Mail codeworks of Alan Sondheim, Jodi, Graham Harwood, Johan Meskens and Pascale Gustin.

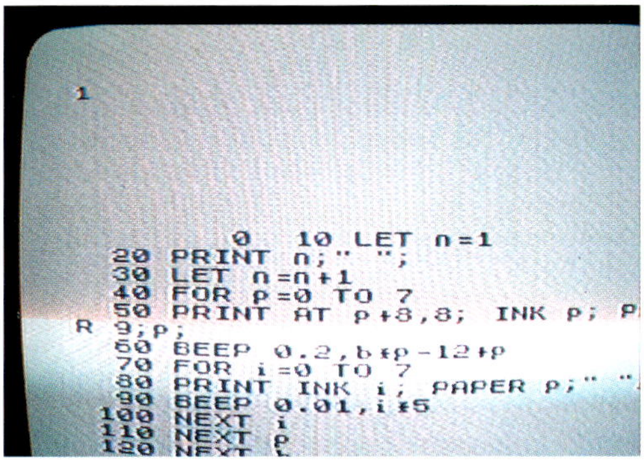

Jodi, installation screenshot of „10 Programs Written in BASIC (c) 1984), Malmö, 2003

Aside from the more narrow field of digital art and technology in which code appears as code, it can first be observed that the graphical interface paradigm in so-called end-user software scales only to a limited amount of complexity, thus creating the need for textual scripting extensions and programming interfaces in the software itself;[3] secondly, that artists (and also non-artists) who employ software for complex tasks and as part of their thinking and subjectivity tend to push its limits to the point where they start to extend, reprogram or re-implement its code. This tendency manifests itself today in two phenomena. One is Free (or Open Source) Software, as it has gained the attention of a larger public since circa 1998; the other one is software art, a topic in the digital arts since circa 2000. Both discourses intersect in such projects as *runme.org,* a software art website created after the model of Free Software download repositories, and sweetcode.org, a Free Software website referencing conceptually (and hence also artistically) interesting computer programs.

From utopia to user computing

Investigating the insistence of code in computer-based art and technology is pointless, however, if one does not question what computer code exactly is beyond its conventional surface appearance as plain text instructions. Beyond that, software code can be put down in any notation, in flowcharts or graphical simulations of circuitry, for example,[4] or simply as a chain of zeros and ones. The problem not only concerns media in particular, but linguistics and semiotics in general: How can language in its complexity, cultural particularity and oddity be boiled down to an easy-to-grasp international system?
The question is much older than computer interface research, having been addressed in such works as the Renaissance political and educational utopias of Tommaso Campanella's "City of the Sun" and Jan Amos Comenius "Orbis pictus". In the ideal city imagined by Campanella, all knowledge is conveyed to the public via a graphical user interface:

> It is Wisdom who causes the exterior and interior, the higher and lower walls of the city to be adorned with the finest pictures, and to have all the sciences painted upon them in an admirable manner. [...] There are magistrates who announce the meaning of the pictures, and boys are accustomed to learn all the sciences, without toil and as if for pleasure; but in the way of history only until they are ten years old.[5]

The hermetic philosopher and famous educational reformer Comenius translated this idea into the "Orbis pictus", the first illustrated children's book and canonical school text in 17th and 18th century Europe, which taught the whole inventory of macro- and microcosm simultaneously through pictures, in Latin words and in the pupils' native language. However, the design flaws of these pictorial languages, and the dilemma of linguistic operations through graphical user interfaces were still being addressed in 1706 in the "Grand Academy of Lagado" chapter of Jonathan Swift's "Gulliver's Travels":

The other project was a scheme for entirely abolishing all words whatsoever [...]. An expedient was therefore offered, that since words are only names for things, it would be more convenient for all men to carry about them such things as were necessary to express the particular business they are to discourse on. [...] However, many of the most learned and wise adhere to the new scheme of expressing themselves by things, which has only this inconvenience attending it, that if a man's business be very great, and of various kinds, he must be obliged in proportion to carry a greater bundle of things upon his back, unless he can afford one or two strong servants to attend him. I have often beheld two of those sages almost sinking under the weight of their packs, like pedlars among us; who, when they met in the streets, would lay down their loads, open their sacks, and hold conversation for an hour together; then put up their implements, help each other to resume their burdens, and take their leave.[6]

In other words, a new language in which object and sign are similar or identical is believed to be superior to traditional symbolic language with its abstract object-sign relationships. While the paragraph reads like a straightforward critique of iconic graphical computer interfaces, this critique does not actually concern text as opposed to graphics, but grammatical versus ungrammatical language as a means of communication. The objects cannot be linked, combined or condensed in a meaningful way to express more complex semantic operations. In the realm of computer operating systems, this translates into an opposition less of graphical versus textual, but of programmer-friendly versus programmer-hostile environments.

When Alan Kay developed the first graphical mouse-controlled computer environment at Xerox PARC in the 1970s, the separation between "usage" and "programming" was for the first time implemented as separation of media. "Usage" became graphical, "programming" textual. The gap widened with the commercialization of Kay's ideas through the Apple Macintosh and Microsoft Windows. While Alan Kay's user interface was based on the programming language Smalltalk and remained fully programmable to the point where users could create their own applications by combining pre-existing and self-written program objects,[7] the Apple Macintosh lacked the programming interface simply for economical and marketing reasons. Without Smalltalk, the system could run fast on low-power hardware, thus dropping sales prices and decreasing development costs. The result was an ungrammatical Swiftian operating system that gave birth to the "user", with the message: You are supposed to read, not to write.[8] Through this engineered gap, programming becomes a mystery, a black art, supposedly for the sake of making computing easier. Borrowing from Roland Barthes' book *S/Z* from 1970, modern GUI operating systems could be called "readerly" and command line-centric operating systems lioke Unix "writerly". According to Barthes, the readerly text presents itself as linear and smoothly composed, "like a

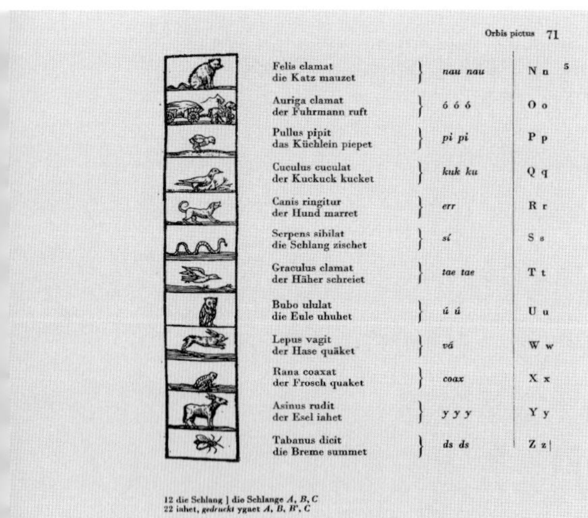
Orbis pictus 71

	Felis clamat die Katz mauzet	*nau nau*	N n
	Auriga clamat der Fuhrmann ruft	*ó ó ó*	O o
	Pullus pipit das Küchlein piepet	*pi pi*	P p
	Cuculus cuculat der Kuckuck kucket	*kuk ku*	Q q
	Canis ringitur der Hund marret	*err*	R r
	Serpens sibilat die Schlang zischet	*sí*	S s
	Graculus clamat der Häher schreiet	*tae tae*	T t
	Bubo ululat die Eule uhuhet	*ú ú*	U u
	Lepus vagit der Hase quäket	*vá*	W w
	Rana coaxat der Frosch quaket	*coax*	X x
	Asinus rudit der Esel iahet	*y y y*	Y y
	Tabanus dicit die Breme summet	*ds ds*	Z z

12 die Schlang] die Schlange *A, B, C*
22 iahet, *gedruckt* yguet *A, B, B', C*

A page from Jan Amos Comenius' (Komensky's) „Orbis pictus"

cupboard where meanings are shelved, stacked, safeguarded."[9] Reflecting in contrast the "plurality of entrances, the opening of networks, the infinity of languages,"[10] the writerly text aims to make "make the reader no longer a consumer, but a producer of the text."[11]

Writerly computing

Barthes' distinction shows why the question how "our writing tools are also involved in our thoughts", or how code shapes the aesthetics of the digital, is problematic in itself: precisely because it projects issues of pre-digital hardware onto digital software. Nietzsche's observation of the mechanical typewriter naturally assumes a clear-cut division, a material difference between the tool and the writing, the processor and the processed. This division, however, no longer exists in software since computers adopted the von Neumann architecture of storing both instruction code and data in the same physical and symbolic realm. Since computer software is tools made from writing, processors made from code, the material gap can only be sustained through simulation. To be readerly, popular PC user software creates the illusion of being hardware, visually and tactically disguising itself as solid analog tools.[12] Graphic design software like Adobe Photoshop or Illustrator have palettes and pencils (which are subverted in Adrian Ward's software artworks *Autoshop* and *Auto-Illustrator),* web browsers pretend to be nautical navigation instruments ("Navigator" and "Explorer" by Netscape and Microsoft), word processors like Microsoft Word are based on visual simulations of a piece of paper in a typewriter.[13]

The attributes of the "writerly" on the other hand exist on the Unix commandline as a hybridity of codes. Since almost everything in Unix is ASCII text—from the user programs which are executed as Word commands and its feedback message to the data flowing between the commands—anything can be instantly turned into anything, writing into commands and command output into writing:

```
CORE CORE bash bash CORE bash

There are %d possibilities. Do you really
wish to see them all? (y or n)

SECONDS
SECONDS

grep hurt mm grep terr mm grep these mm grep eyes grep eyes mm grep hands
mm grep terr mm > zz grep hurt mm >> zz grep nobody mm >> zz grep
important mm >> zz grep terror mm > z grep hurt mm >> zz grep these mm >>
zz grep sexy mm >> zz grep eyes mm >> zz grep terror mm > zz grep hurt mm
>> zz grep these mm >> zz grep sexy mm >> zz grep eyes mm >> zz grep sexy
mm >> zz grep hurt mm >> zz grep eyes mm grep hurt mm grep hands mm grep
terr mm > zz grep these mm >> zz grep nobody mm >> zz prof!

if [ "x`tput kbs`" != "x" ]; then # We can't do this with "dumb" terminal
stty erase `tput kbs`

DYNAMIC LINKER BUG!!!
```

The above is an experimental codework by Alan Sondheim, generated from interaction with a Unix-like textmode environment running "bash", the standard commandline interpreter of GNU/Linux operating systems. The medium of plain text allows all signifiers to migrate transparently from one symbolic form—the operating system—to a second one—

E-Mail—all the while involving the third symbolic form of electronic word processing. The codes it contains are English writing, system instruction code and Internet communication code simultaneously.

This conflation of codes is not a particular artistic invention of Sondheim, but a standard feature of the Unix operating system. The instantaneous mutual convertibility of text as something processed (i.e. data) and text as a processor (i.e. programs) that is characteristic of all program code is not suppressed in Unix by hiding the code away, but transparently preserved on the level of the user interface. It is, as a matter of act, a system feature which Unix administrators rely on every day. Unix, and other operating systems which use written code not just as a hidden layer driving things underneath, but also as their user interface,[14] is a giant, modular and recursive text processing system which runs on scripts and parameters processed through themselves. Or, as the programmer and system administrator Thomas Scoville puts it in his 1998 paper "The Elements of Style: UNIX As Literature": "UNIX system utilities are a sort of Lego construction set for wordsmiths. Pipes and filters connect one utility to the next, text flows invisibly between. Working with a shell, awk/lex derivatives, or the utility set is literally a word dance." [15]

While it is true for all software and all operating systems that the software tool itself is nothing but writing, the elegant simplicity of the Unix commandline relies on the idea that programming, instead of becoming a secluded application, is a trivial extension of "using" the system, simply by writing a sequence of commands into a text file which then can be executed. By contrast, operating systems working in other than textual media contrast haven't found a way yet to make data and processing interchangeable and extend graphical user interfaces to graphical programming interfaces. Even Alan Kay concedes that "it would not be surprising if the visual system were less able in this area [of programmation] than the mechanisms that solve noun phrases for natural language. Although it is not fair to say that 'iconic languages can't work' just because no one has been able to design a good one, it is likely that the above explanation is close to truth"—a truth explaining why alphanumeric text remains the most versatile notation system for computer instructions.[16]

Imaginary computing

If a medium is defined as something in between a sender and a receiver, i.e. a transmission channel or storage device, then computers are not just media, but also senders and receivers which themselves are capable of writing and reading, generating, filtering and interpreting messages within the limitations of the formal rule sets inscribed into them.[17] Alan Kay's outcry "the computer is a medium!"[18] explains why his system fails to provide more than a rudimentary grammar and a fixed set of abstractions—as opposed to the Turing complete grammar and programmable abstractions of, for example, Unix shells—, encompassing only prefabricated algorithmic processors ("user programs") and storage and transmission operations like "open", "save", "close", "send", "cut", "copy", "paste". Not surprisingly, art forms which reflect the computer beyond its functioning as a medium were coined as artisanship by programmers in textual notation: programming language poetry (like Perl poetry), code slang (generated by manipulation text with algorithmic filters), viral scripting, in-code recursions and ironies (as, for example in the self-replicating sourcecode of "Quines"), all of them being largely independent of particular transmission and storage media or output technology—including computer screens, voice output, print books and t-shirts alike—and all of them having been systematically appropriated in the experimental digital arts since the late 1990s. The hacker "Jargon File",[19] whose first versions appeared around 1981 at the MIT, is therefore to be read not only as the poetics of these forms, but also as a blueprint for net culture and net art since the mid-1990s. When, as Thomas Scoville writes, instruction vocabulary and syntax like that of Unix becomes "second nature",[20] it follows that formal turns into conversational language, and syntax into semantics. Beyond being a "tool" merely "involved" in shaping thoughts, computer language becomes a way of thinking and mode of subjectivity, making even such code exe.cut[up]able which can only run in the reader's imagination.[21]

(Thanks to Saul Albert, Josephine Bosma, Frederic Madre and Robbin Murphy for comments and critique)

[Bar91]	Roland Barthes. *S/Z.* Noonday Press, 1991
[Cam82]	Tommaso Campanella. *The City of the Sun.* Harpercollins, 1982
[Ful01]	Matthew Fuller. *It Looks Like You're Writing a Letter: Microsoft Word,* 2001 *http://www.heise.de/tp/english/inhalt/co/7073/1.html*
[Kay90]	Alan Kay. *User Interface: A Personal View.* pages 191-207. Addison Wesley, Reading, Massachusetts, 1990
[rayoJ]	The Jargon File, o.J. *http://www.catb.org/jargon/*
[Sco98]	Thomas Scoville. *The Elements of Style: Unix as Literature,* 1998 *http://web.meganet.net/yeti/PCarticle.html*
[Son01]	Alan Sondheim. "Introduction: Codework." *American Book Review,* 22(6), September 2001
[Swi60]	Jonathan Swift, Gulliver's Travels. Washington Square Press, New York, 1960

1 As obvious not only in the example of Jodi, but more generally in the use of "software art" as a genre description on international festivals and exhibitions such as transmediale (Berlin), read_me (Moscow/Helsinki), CODeDOC (New York)
2 First systematically covered in the "Codework" special issue of the American Book Review, see [Son01]
3 "Scripting" being nothing but another word for programming.
4 Such as in the musicial composition frameworks "MAX" and "PD" designed by Miller Puckette
5 Tommaso Campanella, *City of the Sun* [Cam82]
6 [Swi60], p. 183
7 A concept living on—and currently being revived chiefly by artists working with the system—in "Squeak", the latest incarnation of Kay's Smalltalk system, released a cross-platform Free/Open Source software
8 Which, by the way, does not apply only to proprietary, but also to Free/Open Source graphical user interfaces like KDE and Gnome.
9 [Bar91], p. 200
10 [Bar91], p. 5
11 [Bar91], p. 4
12 Alan Kay accordingly states in a 1990 paper that "at PARC we coined the phrase *user illusion* to describe what we were about when designing user interface" [Kay's emphasis], [Kay90], p. 199
13 See also Matthew Fuller's cultural analysis of Microsoft Word in [Ful01]
14 Other sophisticated examples being ITS, LISP machines, Plan 9, with DOS and 8-bit BASIC computers being comparatively primitive implementations of the concept
15 Thomas Scoville, *The Elements of Style: Unix As Literature,* [Sco98]
16 [Kay90], p. 203
17 Unless one took a radical humanist view of "medium" in the sense of machine processes being nothing but mediations between human individuals.
18 A "shock", he writes, caused by reading McLuhan, [Kay90], p. 193
19 Currently maintained by Eric S. Raymond, [rayoJ]
20 [Sco98], ibid.
21 Jonathan Swift anticipates this as well when Lemuel Gulliver says about the academics of the flying island of Lagado: "The knowledge I had in mathematics gave me great assistance in acquiring their phraseology, which depended much upon that science and music; and in the latter I was not unskilled. Their ideas are perpetually conversant in lines and figures. If they would, for example, praise the beauty of a woman, or any other animal, they describe it by rhombs, circles, parallelograms, ellipses, and other geometrical terms, or by words of art drawn from music, needless here to repeat."

Exe.cut[up]able statements: Das Drängen des Codes an die Nutzeroberflächen

Florian Cramer

Auferstanden aus der Black Box

Auf Computer-Instruktionscodes projiziert, ließe sich Nietzsches zum medientheoretischen Axiom geronnene Erkenntnis aus seiner Begegnung mit der mechanischen Schreibmaschine, dass nämlich das „Schreibzeug mit an unseren Gedanken" arbeite, in eine Frage umformulieren: Wie prägt Programmcode Konzepte und Ästhetik digitaler Kunst und Technologie?

„10 Programs written in BASIC ©1984", dieser Titel einer Malmöer Ausstellung des holländisch-belgischen Künstlerduos Jodi vom Juni 2003 liest sich, über die technische Beschreibung der gezeigten Arbeit hinaus, als eine programmatische Aussage, die den digitalen Künsten den Weg zurück in die Zukunft weist. Indem sie nichts als eine Reihe zwanzig Jahre alter Heimcomputer des Typs Sinclair ZX Spectrum zeigt, auf denen „zehn BASIC-Programme [laufen], die der Besucher ergänzen oder verändern kann", markiert Jodis neueste Arbeit den radikalen Höhepunkt einer Werkgeschichte, die Mitte der 1990er Jahre mit Netzkunst beginnt, sich fortsetzt mit Web-Browser-Manipulationen durch trickreich codierte HTML-Daten, Quelltext-Manipulationen von Computerspielen bis hin zu immer abstrakteren „Variationen" kurzer Programme in der Programmiersprache BASIC. So zeigt Jodis Kunst nicht nur, dass ungeachtet der Karriere grafischer Nutzerführungen in den 1980er und 1990er Jahren Programmcode weiterhin die Basis aller Computeroperationen und digitaler Informationstechnologie bildet, sondern auch, dass seit 1984, jenem Jahr, in dem auch der Apple Macintosh auf den Markt kam, dieser Code ungeachtet aller äußerlichen Wandlungen der Software sich in Struktur und Notation sich kaum geändert hat. Während Künstler Softwarecode traditionell für schwarze Kästen schreiben ließen, die im Hintergrund versteckt Arbeiten steuerten, in denen von der Programmierung nichts mehr zu sehen war – wie z. B. im Genre der sogenannten interaktiven Video-Installationen –, wurde seit den späten 1990er Jahren Programmierung und Programmcode zunehmend selbst als künstlerisches Material begriffen und jene verlorengegangene Verbindung von Kunst und Software neugeknüpft, die 1970 Jack Burnhams New Yorker Konzeptkunst-Ausstellung „Software" herzustellen versuchte.[1] Historisch parallel zu dieser neueren Tendenz in den digitalen Künsten ist selbst der Apple Macintosh zu einer Spielart des Betriebssystems Unix mutiert, indem er seine Instruktionscodes nicht länger verbirgt, sondern auf einer Text-Kommandozeile exponiert, holt er gewissermaßem den status quo digitaler Kunst ein und ihres zunehmenden Gebrauchs von Computercode als Material.

Das radikalste Verständnis von Computercode als künstlerischem Material zeigt sich in „Codeworks",[2] einer Netzkunst, die zumeist als E-Mail zirkuliert und in Privatsprachen geschrieben ist, die, wie im folgenden Beispiel, Englisch, Programm- und Netzwerkcodes mit visueller Typografie vermischt:

```
Exe.cut[up]able statements ---
::do knot a p.arse.r .make.
::reti.cu[t]la[ss]te. yr. text.je[llied]wells .awe. .r[b]ust.
```

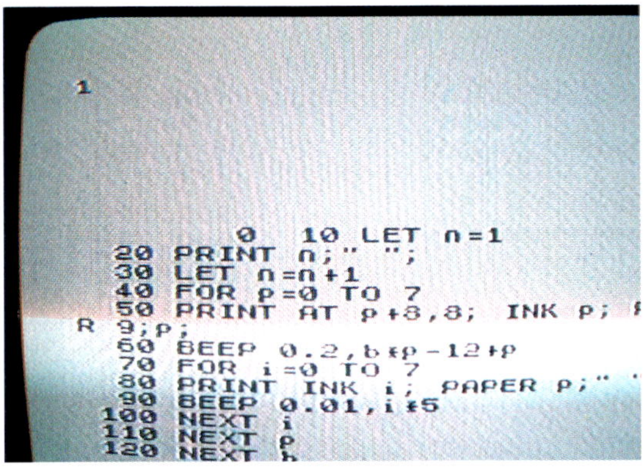

Jodi, Screenshot der Installation *10 Programs written in BASIC ©1984,* Malmö 2003

Die Zeilen stammen aus einer Arbeit der australischen Netzkünstlerin mez (Mary Anne Breeze), die am 14. 1. 2003 als E-Mail über die Mailingliste „arc.hive" verschickt wurde. Das Wort „Exe.cut[up]able" wird in ihr zu einem Quellcode, der sich in seiner Ausführung selbst beschreibt: „Exe", die Microsoft DOS/Windows-Dateikennung ausführbarer Programme, „Executable" und, ein Verweis auf die automatisierten Montagetechniken von Brion Gysin und William S. Burroughs, „cutup" sind unter den Wörtern, in die dieses Notat expandiert. Die E-Mail-Codeworks von zum Beispiel Alan Sondheim, jodi, Graham Harwood, Johan Meskens und Pascale Gustin halten sich in ihrer poetischen Aneignung von Programmcode noch genauer an die Syntax realer Programmiersprachen wie der Unix-Shell, Perl und C.

Auch abseits des Spezialgebiets digitaler Kunst und Technologie, die Quellcode als Quellcode erscheinen lässt, ist erstens zu beobachten, dass das Paradigma der grafischen Bedienung sogenannter Nutzersoftware nur bis zu einem begrenzten Grad von Komplexität skaliert und deshalb in der Software selbst Skripting-Erweiterungen und Programmierschnittstellen nötig macht, die sich textuell präsentieren.[3] Zweitens fällt auf, dass Künstler (ebenso wie Nicht-Künstler), die Computersoftware für komplexe, individualisierte Anwendungen einsetzen und als Teil ihres Denkens und ihrer Subjektivität verstehen, regelmäßig an Grenzen fertiger Programme stoßen und deshalb beginnen, ihren Code zu erweitern, umzuprogrammieren oder neuzuschreiben, eine Tendenz, die sich in zwei Phänomenen manifestiert: der Freien (bzw. Open Source) Software, wie sie seit circa 1998 größere öffentliche Aufmerksamkeit erfahren hat, und der Softwarekunst, die ungefähr seit dem Jahr 2000 als Genre digitaler Kunst diskutiert wird. Beide Diskurse überschneiden sich zum Beispiel in Projekten wie *runme.org,* einer Softwarekunst-Website, die auf der technischen Grundlage Freier Software nach dem Vorbild von Download-Servern Freier Software gestaltet ist und auch viele Freie-Software-Projekte verzeichnet, sowie *sweetcode.org,* einer Freien-Software-Website, die konzeptuell ungewöhnliche – und daher oft auch künstlerisch interessante – Computerprogramme verzeichnet.

Von Utopia zum User Computing

Das Drängen des Codes an die Oberflächen computergestützer Kunst und Technologie zu untersuchen wäre jedoch sinnlos, ohne zu fragen, was genau Computercode ist jenseits seiner konventionellen Erscheinung als in ASCII-Text notierten Instruktionen. Denn schließlich kann er auf jede denkbare Weise notiert werden, z. B. auch in Flussdiagrammen oder als grafische Simulation von Schaltungen[4] oder einfach als Kette von Nullen und Einsen. Dieses Darstellungsproblem ist jedoch nicht nur ein medientheoretisches, sondern allgemein linguistisches und semiotisches: Wie kann eine Sprache in ihrer Komplexität und kulturellen Besonderheit zu einem international allgemeinverständlichen System vereinfacht werden?

Prominent wurde diese Frage bereits in frühneuzeitlichen Politik- und Bildungsutopien wie Tommaso Campanellas *Sonnenstaat,* dessen visionierten Interface Jan Amos Comenius praktisch implementierte. Den Einwohnern von Campanellas idealen Stadtstaat wird alles Wissen über eine grafische Nutzeroberfläche bereitgestellt:

Der „Weisheit“ hat die Mauern der ganzen Stadt von innen und außen, unten und oben mit herrlichen Gemälden schmücken und auf ihnen so alle Wissenschaften in fabelhafter Anordnung wiedergeben lassen. [...] Sie haben Lehrer, die all dies Bilder erklären, und die Kinder pflegen noch vor dem zehnten Lebensjahre ohne große Mühe, gleichsam spielend [...] alle Wissenschaften zu lernen.[5]

Der Erziehungsreformer und hermetische Philosoph Comenius übersetzte dieses Konzept in seinen *Orbis pictus,* der nicht nur das erste illustrierte Kinderbuch ist, sondern bis ins späte 18. Jahrhundert die kanonische Schulfibel Europas. Alle Dinge des Makro- und Mikrokosmos inventarisiert der *Orbis pictus,* indem er sie simultan auf Holzschnitten und als Wörter auf Latein und in der jeweiligen Muttersprache der Schüler verzeichnet. Die Designfehler dieser Bildsprachen und das Dilemma linguistischer Operationen durch grafische Nutzerinterfaces wurden früh bemerkt. 1706 heißt es in Jonathan Swifts satirischen *Gulliver's Travels* über die Forschungen an der Akademie von Lagado:

Das zweite Projekt war ein Plan zur völligen Abschaffung aller Wörter überhaupt, [...] da Wörter nur Bezeichnungen für Dinge sind, sei es zweckdienlicher, wenn alle Menschen die Dinge bei sich führten, die zur Beschreibung der besonderen Angelegenheit, über die sie sich unterhalten wollen, notwendig seien. [...] Viele der Gelehrtesten und Weisesten sind jedoch Anhänger des neuen Projekts, sich mittels Dingen zu äußern; das bringt nur die eine Unbequemlichkeit mit sich, dass jemand, dessen Angelegenheiten sehr umfangreich und von verschiedener Art sind, ein entsprechend größeres Bündel von Dingen auf dem Rücken tragen muß, falls er es sich nicht leisten kann, dass ein oder zwei starke Diener ihn begleiten. Ich habe oft gesehen, wie zwei dieser Weisen unter der Last ihrer Bündel fast zusammenbrachen, wie bei uns die Hausierer. Wenn sie sich auf der Straße begegneten, legten sie ihre Lasten nieder, öffneten ihre Säcke und unterhielten sich eine Stunde lang; dann packten sie ihre Utensilien wieder ein, halfen einander, ihre Bürden wieder auf den Rücken zu nehmen, und verabschiedeten sich.[6]

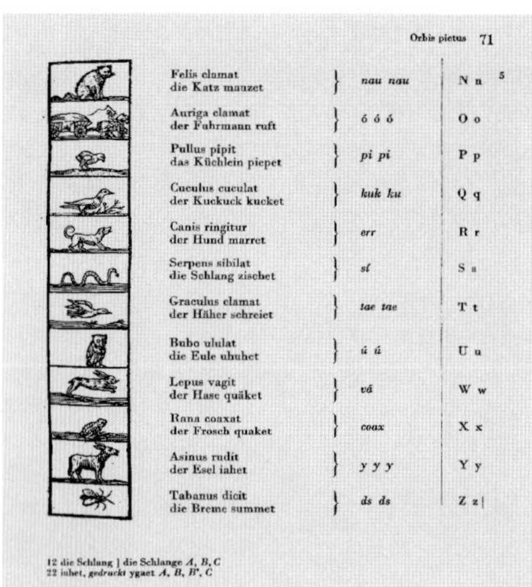
Orbis pictus 71

Felis clamat die Katz mauzet	*nau nau*	N n	5
Auriga clamat der Fuhrmann ruft	*ó ó ó*	O o	
Pullus pipit das Küchlein piepet	*pi pi*	P p	
Cuculus cuculat der Kuckuck kucket	*kuk ku*	Q q	
Canis ringitur der Hund marret	*err*	R r	
Serpens sibilat die Schlang zischet	*sí*	S s	
Graculus clamat der Häher schreiet	*tae tae*	T t	
Bubo ululat die Eule uhuhet	*ú ú*	U u	
Lepus vagit der Hase quäket	*vá*	W w	
Rana coaxat der Frosch quaket	*coax*	X x	
Asinus rudit der Esel iahet	*y y y*	Y y	
Tabanus dicit die Breme summet	*ds ds*	Z z	

12 die Schlang] die Schlange *A, B, C*
22 iahet, *gedruckt* ygaet *A, B, B', C*

Jan Amos Comenius (Komensky), Seite aus dem *Orbis pictus*

Was sich wie eine pointierte Kritik ikonischer Computer-Nutzerinterfaces liest, betrifft jedoch weniger das Bild im Gegensatz zu Text, als ungrammatische versus grammatische Sprachen. Die Gegenstände, die hier an die Stelle der Wörter treten, können nicht sinnvoll verknüpft oder verdichtet werden, und sind somit auch semantisch nicht expressiv. Auf Computerbetriebssysteme übertragen, folgt daraus ein Gegensatz nicht von grafischen und textuellen, sondern vielmehr von programmierfreundlichen und programmierfeindlichen Softwareumgebungen.

Als Alan Kay in den 1970er Jahren im Xerox PARC-Labor den ersten per mausklickbare Bildschirm-Piktogramme steuerbaren Computer erfand, wurde der Unterschied von „Nutzung“ und „Programmierung“ von Computern erstmals auf medialer Ebene implementiert: die „Nutzung“ war nun grafisch, die „Programmierung“ jedoch blieb schriftsprachlich. Diese Kluft wuchs noch mit der Kommerzialisierung von Kays Konzepten durch den Apple Macintosh und Microsoft Windows. Während Kays Erfindung auf der Programmiersprache Smalltalk basierte und so programmierbar sein solte, dass Nutzer sich durch baukastenartige Kombinationen vorgefertigter und selbst geschriebener Programmodule (bzw. -objekte) ihre Anwendungen selbst schaffen konnten,[7] fehlte dem Apple Macintosh diese Programmierschnittstelle aus simplen ökonomischen Gründen: Ohne Smalltalk konnte das System ausreichend schnell auf langsamer Hardware laufen, was sowohl Verkaufspreise, als auch Entwicklungskosten reduzierte. Das Ergebnis war ein ungrammatisches Betriebssystem, das den „User“ gebar und ihm bedeutete, dass er das System zu lesen und nicht zu schreiben habe.[8] Nur durch die konstruierte mediale Kluft wurde das Programmieren zum Mysterium, zur schwarzen Kunst. Mit einem Begriffspaar, das Roland Barthes in seinem Buch *S/Z* von 1970 einführt, könnte man Betriebssysteme mit grafischer Oberfläche „leserlich“ („lisible“) nennen, Kommandozeilen-zentrische wie Unix hingegen „schreiberlich“ („scriptible“). Für Barthes präsentiert sich der „leserliche“ Text als linear und bruchlos gefügt, „wie ein Haushaltsschrank, in dem die Sinngebungen geordnet, aufeinandergestapelt, gehortet sind“,[9] während der antiklassische „schreiberliche“ Text, indem er die „Offenheit des Textgewebes, die Unendlichkeit der Sprachen“[10] reflektiert, aus dem „Leser nicht mehr einen Konsumenten, sondern einen Textproduzenten“ macht.[11]

Writerly Computing

An Barthes’ Begriffspaar zeigt sich auch, dass die Frage, wie unser Schreibzeug an unseren Gedanken mitarbeitet, problematisch wird, sobald man sie auf Computersoftware anwendet, eben weil sie Eigenschaften prädigitaler Hardware auf Software projiziert. So liegt auch Nietzsches Beobachtung der mechanischen Schreibmaschine noch die Annahme zugrunde, dass Werkzeug und Schrift, Prozessor und Prozessiertes materiell voneinander verschieden sind, eine Trennung, die in der Computersoftware nicht mehr gilt, seit Computer mit der von Neumann-Architektur sowohl Instruktionscode, als auch Daten im selben physikalischen und symbolischen System speichern. Da Computersoftware aus Schrift gefertigtes Werkzeug ist, ein Prozessor aus Instruktionscode, lässt sich die alte Grenze des Materials nur durch Simulation aufrecht erhalten. Um im Sinne Barthes’ leserlich zu sein, tut PC-Software so, als wäre sie Hardware, indem sie sich als visuell und taktil solides Werkzeug darstellt.[12] Grafikdesign-Software wie Adobe Photoshop oder Adobe Illustrator wird mit simulierten Pinseln und Paletten bedient (deren vermeintliche Selbstverständlichkeit Adrian Wards Softwarekunstwerke *Autoshop* und *Auto-Illustrator* gezielt subvertieren), Web-Browser wie der Navigator von Netscape und der Explorer von Microsoft geben vor, nautische Instrumente zu sein, und Textverarbeitungsprogramme wie Microsoft Word basieren auf der optischen Simulation von Papier in einer Schreibmaschine.[13]

Die Eigenschaften des „schreiberlichen“ Textes hingegen materialisieren sich auf der Unix-Kommandozeile als Hybridität der Codes. Da in Unix fast alles ASCII-Text ist – von den als Kommandowörtern ausgeführten Programmen und ihren Rückmeldungen bis zu den Daten, die zwischen ihnen fließen –, kann alles augenblicklich in alles beliebige umgewandelt werden, Schrift in Kommandos und Kommando-Ausgaben in Schrift:

```
CORE CORE bash bash CORE bash

There are %d possibilities. Do you really
wish to see them all? (y or n)

SECONDS
SECONDS
```

```
grep hurt mm grep terr mm grep these mm grep eyes grep eyes mm grep hands
mm grep terr mm > zz grep hurt mm >> zz grep nobody mm >> zz grep
important mm >> zz grep terror mm > z grep hurt mm >> zz grep these mm >>
zz grep sexy mm >> zz grep eyes mm >> zz grep terror mm > zz grep hurt mm
>> zz grep these mm >> zz grep sexy mm >> zz grep eyes mm >> zz grep sexy
mm >> zz grep hurt mm >> zz grep eyes mm grep hurt mm grep hands mm grep
terr mm > zz grep these mm >> zz grep nobody mm >> zz prof!

if [ "x`tput kbs`" != "x" ]; then # We can't do this with "dumb" terminal
stty erase `tput kbs`

DYNAMIC LINKER BUG!!!
```

Diese Zeilen, die den Anfang eines „Codework" von Alan Sondheim bilden, protokollieren eine Interaktion mit einer Unix-kompatiblen Textumgebung, deren Motor hier die „bash", der Standard-Befehlsinterpreter des GNU / Linux-Betriebssystems bildet. Das Einheitsmedium des ASCII-Texts erlaubt, ein und denselben Code transparent von einer symbolischen Form (dem Betriebssystem) in eine andere (E-Mail) zu schreiben, und dies mit Hilfe der ins System integrierten algorithmischen Textverarbeitung als dritter symbolischer Form. So ist der Code zugleich englischer Text, Systemkommando und Kommunikationscode im Netz.

Diese Vermischung der Codes ist nicht Sondheims künstlerische Erfindung, sondern eine Standardfunktion des Unix-Betriebssystems. Die augenblickliche, reziproke Konvertierbarkeit von prozessierten Daten in algorithmische Prozessoren, die rekursive Prozessierung von Programmen durch sich selbst also, die ein Merkmal aller Programmiersprachen ist, wird auf der Unix-Kommandozeile nicht zum Verschwinden gebracht, sondern noch auf der Ebene des Bedieninterfaces beibehalten. Es ist sogar eine Systemfunktion, auf die Unix-Administratoren täglich zurückgreifen. Wie wenige andere Betriebssysteme, die schriftliche Instruktionen nicht nur als versteckte Schicht unterhalb der Software-Anwendungen, sondern auch als Bedieninterface implementieren,[14] ist Unix ein riesiges modulares und rekursives Textprozessierungssystem, das mit Skripten und Parametern läuft, die durch sich selbst gefiltert werden; oder, wie der Programmierer und Systemadministrator Thomas Scoville 1998 in seinem Aufsatz *The Elements Of Style: UNIX As Literature* schreibt: „Die Hilfsprogramme die Unix-Systems sind eine Art Lego-Baukasten für Wortschmiede. Pipes und Filter verbinden ein Utility mit dem anderen, Text fließt unsichtbar zwischen ihnen. Die Arbeit mit der Shell, awk/lex-Derivaten oder dem Werkzeugkasten der Hilfsprogramme ist buchstäblich ein Tanz mit Wörtern."[15]

Während es für alle Programme und alle Betriebssysteme zutrifft, dass die Software selbst nichts als eine Schrift ist, beruht die simple Eleganz der Unix-Kommandozeile auf der Idee, dass Programmierung keine vom System abgekapselte Anwendung ist, sondern eine triviale Erweiterung seiner alltäglichen „Nutzung", zum Beispiel indem man eine Abfolge von Kommandos in eine Textdatei schreibt, die dadurch als Programm ausführbar wird. Für Betriebssysteme hingegen, deren Bedienschnittstellen in anderen Medien als der Schrift implementiert sind, ist noch kein Weg gefunden worden, Daten und ihre Prozessierung austauschbar zu machen und grafische Nutzerinterfaces zu ebenfalls grafischen Programmierinterfaces zu erweitern. Sogar Alan Kay räumt ein, dass „es nicht überraschend wäre, wenn das visuelle System auf diesem Gebiet [der Programmierung] weniger leistungsfähig ist als der Mechanismus, der Wortphrasen verarbeitet. Obwohl die Behauptung nicht gerecht ist, dass ‚ikonische Programmiersprachen nicht funktionieren können' nur weil niemand bisher fähig war, eine gute zu konzipieren, ist es wahrscheinlich, dass die obengenannte Erklärung der Wahrheit nahekommt"; eine Wahrheit, aus der sich auch erklärt, weshalb alphanumerischer Text das eleganteste Notationssystem für Computerinstruktionen bleibt.[16]

Definiert man als Medium etwas, das zwischen einem Sender und Empfänger steht, also ein Übertragungskanal oder Speicher ist, so sind Computer nicht nur Medien, sondern auch Sender und Empfänger, die Nachrichten selbst innerhalb der Grenzen ihrer eingeschriebenen formalen Regelwerke selbst schreiben und lesen, generieren, filtern und interpretieren können.[17]
Aus Alan Kays Ausruf „the computer is a medium"[18] erklärt sich, weshalb seine Erfindung im Medium der ikonischen Bildschirmgrafik nicht mehr als eine rudimentäre Grammatik und als ein festgeschriebenes Set von Abstraktionen bereitstellt – im Gegensatz eben zur Turing-vollständigen Grammatik und den programmierbaren Abstraktion von Unix-Shells –, nur vorgefertige Anwendungen bietet und Speicher- und Übertragungsoperationen auf ein kleines Vokabular begrenzt: „open", „save", „close", „send", „cut", „copy", „paste".
So überrascht es nicht, dass zur Avantgarde einer digitalen Kunst, die Computer über ihre Funktion als Medien hinaus reflektiert, Vokabularien gehören, die als Programmierer-Folklore auf Kommandozeilen entstanden: Programmiersprachen-Lyrik (wie die *Perl poetry), Code-Slang* (durch algorithmisches Filtern von Text), virales Skripting, rekursiver und ironischer Programmcode (wie zum Beispiel im sich selbst exakt replizierenden Quellcode sogenannter „Quines"). Alle diese Formen sind weder auf spezifische Übertragungs- oder Speichermedien angewiesen, noch auf partikuläre Anzeigetechniken, sondern können sich gleichermaßen auf Bildschirmen, per Sprachsynthese und auf Büchern und T-Shirts materialisieren. Seit den späten 1990er Jahren wird sie systematisch in den experimentellen Digitalkünsten appropriiert. Das Hacker-„Jargon File",[19] dessen erste Versionen ca. 1981 am MIT entstanden, ist somit nicht nur als Poetik dieser Formen zu lesen, sondern auch als Blaupause von Netzkulturen und -künsten seit Mitte der 1990er Jahre. Wenn, wie Thomas Scoville schreibt, Unix-Vokabular und -Syntax Unix zur „zweiten Natur" werden kann,[20] folgt daraus, dass formale Sprachen zu Umgangssprachen werden, und Syntax zu Semantik. Über ein „Schreibzeug" hinaus, dass an Gedanken nur mitarbeitet, wird Computersprache zu einer Denkweise und zum subjektiven Register, in dem selbst solcher Code ausführbar – exe.cut[up]able – wird, der nur in der Imagination des Lesers abläuft.[21]

(Danke an Saul Albert, Josephine Bosma, Robbin Murphy und Frederic Madre für Anmerkungen und Korrekturen)

Referenzen siehe Seite 103

WEB STALKER SEEK AARON
Reflections on Digital Arts, Codes and Coders

Erkki Huhtamo

"[A]ny notion of software leads us to reconsider our historical notions of art."
Jack Burnham, "Notes on art and information processing", in the catalogue to the Software exhibition (1970)

1.

The mainstream of computing has evolved towards hiding the code. While producing and reading code was an everyday activity for early computer users—scientists, engineers, operators and even artists—the presence of the code has become more and more obscure, hidden behind the facade of the interface. Interfacing humans and computers in a "user-friendly" fashion has been one of the guidelines of the digital culture since the late 60s. For Nicholas Negroponte, writing in 1969, the real task was to teach the computer to understand humans, not vice versa: "A designer, when addressing a machine, must not be forced to resort to machine-oriented codes. And in spite of computational efficiency, a paradigm for fruitful conversations must be machines that can speak and respond to a natural language".[1] The effort of creating "seamless" and "intimate" human-computer user interfaces became almost a definition of progressive computer culture, expanding from specialists to general users. From Xerox Star to the Apple Macintosh desktop and on to its bastard son, the Microsoft Windows, generations of users were taught to ignore the inner workings of the "box". They dealt with software packages that opened their metaphor-filled offerings on the desktop by a mouseclick. The users saw icons of tools and trash cans, but no strings of zeros and ones—the program codes that actually power the whole system.
While the use of the computer has spread to all imaginable fields, direct access to the code and coding has remained a domain for specialists, from computer scientists and professional programmers to hackers and builders of game engines. Mac users and even most Windows users rarely see even a glimpse of code. Even the brief revival of coding as a normal occupation for the general computer user as a result of the introduction of HTML was soon obliterated by an avalanche of easy-to-use automated webpage authoring software. While this development can be justified by claiming that the computer is just an intermediary, a tool or a medium, and not a goal in itself, there is ample room for counter-arguments. The computer's constantly expanding role as a universal machine powering innumerable applications and systems worldwide makes the invisibility of its workings alarming. Corporate and governmental coders (not to forget code breakers), as well as pranksters, cybercriminals and terrorists are monitoring and interfering with "innocent" computer use through the Internet. Lacking knowledge of programming, the users can only respond by subscribing to more corporate services or installing commercially marketed software packages. Yet both the core of the problem and the nature of the counter-measures remain vague. It has also been argued that merely using a pre-existing commercial software package restricts the user's freedom of expression, forcing him/her unknowingly to adapt to a role envisaged by the corporate planners.[2] John Berger's famous slogan, "every image embodies a way of seeing", could perhaps be modified to "every software

embodies a way of using".[3] Gaining access to computer code, understanding its "message" and being able to use it for one's own means are political, as well as social and economic issues. They are deeply intertwined with the dynamics of power and knowledge in contemporary society.

Against this background it is extremely interesting to note the recent emphasis on coding within the field of the digital arts. This interest has manifested itself in various forms, particularly in the emergence of the discourse on "software art".[4] In recent times we have witnessed the appearance of artworks that modify the look and functioning of commercial software applications from web browsers to game worlds, introducing features that may be interpreted by users as formal interventions, disturbing pranks, ideological subversions or simply as technical bugs. The famous *Web Stalker* (I/O/D, 1997-) is a web browser that displays control codes and link structures instead of the usual graphical interface. *Life_Sharing* by 0100101110101101.ORG attacked the false openness of the web browser by giving anybody permission to access its own hard disk with all its private files and programs through the Internet.[5] Other works use elements of computer code openly as building blocks of their aesthetics, without disguising them as graphics, images and sounds. Common to all these forms is the urge to question the prevailing conventions of computer use. Tearing down the veil of "user-friendliness", seen as a deception, the artists are giving the users a glimpse behind the scenes, to the engine room (to use an anachronistic metaphor). They themselves feel at ease in this engine room, using it as a laboratory, hangout, toolkit and venue for art. What are the reasons behind this interest? Is it enough to label it as an "inevitable" avantgarde of the digital culture? How will it relate to the wider, perhaps even non-digital, cultural context? This essay provides some preliminary answers to such questions by delving into the relationship between art, codes and coding from a media-archaeological point of view.

2.

The earliest computer artists in the 1960s were all coders. There was no alternative. Each work, whether graphics, animation or music, was necessarily the result of an unique act of writing computer code. As if foreshadowing the recent claims for "software art", some pioneers, like Michael L. Noll and the members of the Japanese Computer Technique Group (CTG), openly stated that the true work of art was the generating program itself rather than the computer-produced output.[6] Most of the early work on computer graphics and music took a formalist path, exploring issues like the possibilities of generative grammars and the relationship between rule-based behaviour and randomness. This state of things is aptly mirrored by the diagram-dotted pages of Jasia Reichardt's early overview, *The Computer in Art* (1971).[7] Pioneers of computer graphics like Frieder Nake described their activity as formal "visual research", deliberately segregated from any social or political concerns. They found inspiration from cybernetics, Claude Shannon's information theory and the exact mathematical aesthetics of theorists like Max Bense.[8] Bense excluded the role of subjective perception from his aesthetic system and based it on mathematical equations that emphasized the universal rather than the particular, the rational rather than the irrational (identified with the subjective art impulse), the abstract rather than the representational. Although random operations were often used by the early artist-programmers, the computer was considered mainly a "tool": it was expected to execute a program written beforehand.

This situation can be explained both by the state of the technology and the institutional context. In the 1960s computers were mostly available at governmental and corporate institutions. They were used primarily for statistical calculations, which emphasized the

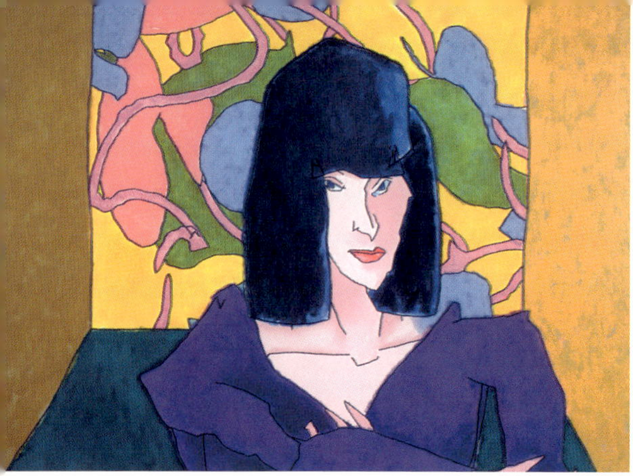
Harold Cohen: *Clarissa*

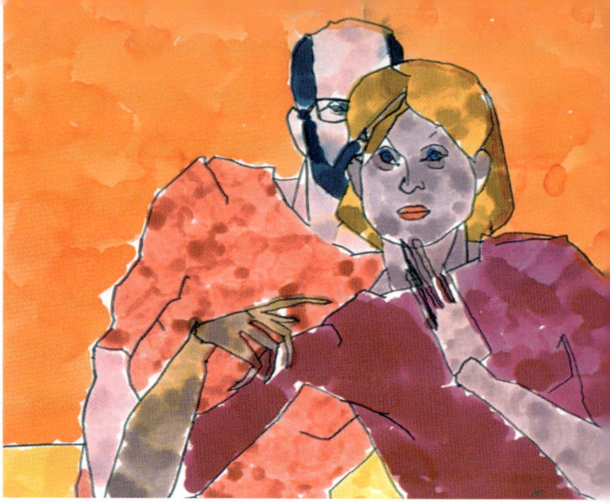
Harold Cohen: *Machine*

act of programming in the form of batch-processing. Although the early artists and composers began to "bend" the technology to other kinds of uses, they were forced to accommodate themselves to the roles that had been established in the non-artistic "mainframe" culture: working within a dedicated institution, the artists created programs and then waited until they had been executed by the computer. They were members of a small elite, living on the fringe of a larger technical and institutional elite, exploring a powerful means of expression in its infancy. However, the nature of computing was constantly changing as a result of innovations like new interfaces, the idea of time-sharing, and the creation of the first programming languages meant for creative purposes. BEFLIX, written by computer scientist Kenneth Knowlton at Bell Labs, was applied to groundbreaking computer graphics and animation by artists Stan Vanderbeek and Lillian Schwartz, working in collaboration with Knowlton. Equally interesting was the appearance of the program ART 1 created by university professors Katherine Nash and Richard H. Williams and meant as a tool for artists interested in using the computer without having the theoretical and technical skills to program. Criticized at the time for considering the artist "as a specialist with pre-defined professional needs", it was, however, an early pointer towards the parting of ways between the creators of "soft" digital art and those involved in writing algorithms.[9]
The proliferation of art using pre-existing software tools such as Photoshop or Maya has not meant the disappearance of the activity of creating original algorithms. Many of the most rigorous digital art projects have been created by artists who either write software for themselves or work in close collaboration with a programmer. Prominent examples of the first are Myron Krueger, Harold Cohen and David Rokeby, while figures like Jeffrey Shaw (in collaboration with Gideon May and Bernt Lintermann) and Rafael Lozano-Hemmer (with Will Bauer) represent the second type. In some cases, like that of Christa Sommerer and Laurent Mignonneau, separating programming from other aspects of creation is almost impossible.[10] Pioneers like Krueger, Cohen and Rokeby have spent years, even decades, writing program code to refine their increasingly sophisticated systems. The artworks these artists have exhibited over the years may have had own identities, but they can also be characterized as "materializations" of these systems, documenting their state of development. The code provides the core of Krueger's *Videoplace* as well as Rokeby's *Very Nervous System* and *Giver of Names.*[11] Arguably the most rigorous and long-term effort to use original programming as a means of creating an evolving art project has been Harold Cohen's *AARON,* continuously under development since the early 1970s.[12]
AARON is an AI-based computer program, an expert system that creates paintings and drawings. Over the past thirty years, different output devices have been used, from a drawing "turtle" moving on paper placed on the floor to complex painting machines and

more recently to a software application automatically creating pictures on the desktop. *AARON* can be characterized as a semi-autonomous creature. Its works are based on the complex rules defined by Cohen, but it also has a considerable amount of autonomy from composition to coloring. It is significant that Cohen has not made *AARON's* code public. The different stages of the program have not even been systematically preserved, which is why the code's development can only be deciphered indirectly, as reflected in *AARON's* numerous drawings and paintings.[13] Although it is a major creative effort, Cohen never considered the code as the artwork proper. Rather, it can be likened to the skills and techniques accumulated by a human artist during his lifespan. What will remain are the paintings, the material traces of a lifework. In this sense Cohen, painter by education, resorts to a conventional model of the creation and preservation art. However, *AARON's* most recent manifestation, the software application available as freeware on the Internet, could point in a more radical direction.[14] Instead of remaining Cohen's own cybernetic extension, *AARON* has been given a degree of independence from its creator. However, while becoming a software application on anybody's desktop, *AARON's* development has also stopped. Although it can keep on producing different paintings endlessly, it does not have a facility to learn other routines. Moved to the desktop *AARON*- certainly immortalizes Cohen's achievement, but it also turns into a cybernetic zombie. Releasing its source code would give it a chance to develop further by means of collective programming efforts through the Internet.[15]

3.

The advocates of "software art" emphasize the primacy of the code as the main creative achievement and demand an un-obstructed presence and role for it in the artwork. According to the statement of the first software art competition jury at the Transmediale 01, "software art is opposed to the notion of software as a tool".[16] For the jury, software art has

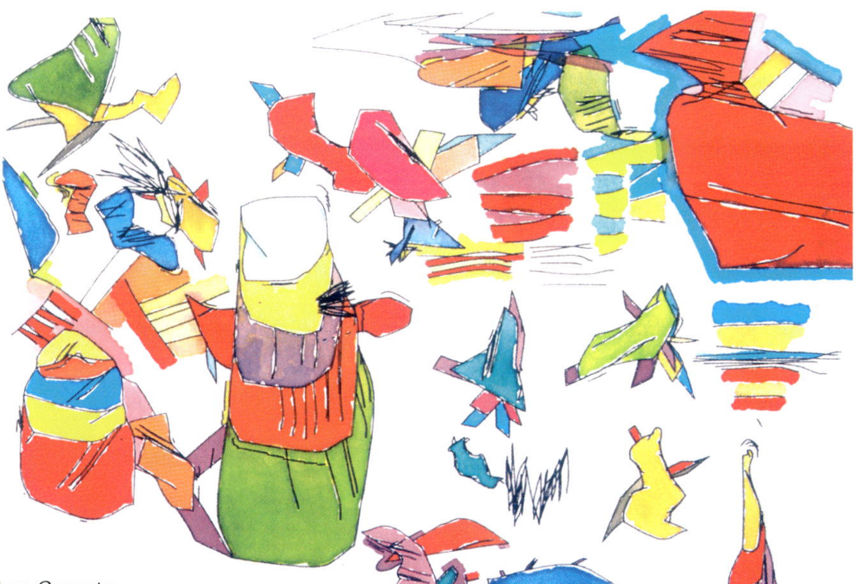

Harold Cohen: *Computer*

many faces: "it could be algorithms as an end to themselves, it could subvert perceived paradigms of computer software or create new ones, it could do something interesting or disrupting with your computer, it could be creative writing, it could be science." In another text Florian Cramer and Ulrike Gabriel (who were among the jury members) write: "Software art means a shift of the artist's view from displays to the creation of systems and processes themselves; this is not covered by the concept of 'media'".[17] For these writers the principal "sin" media art has committed seems to be its excessive attention to interface design. For the software purist, the creation of detailed immersive environments and elaborate multisensory interfaces is in itself an act of mystification. Works that involve the participants both bodily and emotionally seduce them, instead of making them aware of the true nature of the system, hidden "behind the facade".

It is most interesting that interactive systems that in the not-so-distant past were seen as an empowering and critical alternative to "passivating" media experiences like watching television, have now become the target for criticism. This has to do with the rapid acceptance of interactivity and its adoption into the mainstream of digital culture. If interactivity was once seen as a gesture that questioned the prevailing logic of media, it has now been normalized, added to the internal cultural repertory. However, the recent criticism does not seem to be addressed to interactivity per se; rather, it addresses the way interactivity has been packaged and marketed, institutionalized and commodified. In fields like electronic gaming the near realtime interaction between the user and the game software/hardware complex has been claimed to lead to the "automation" of the action/reaction mechanism. Immersion into rapidly changing and emotionally engaging gameworlds leaves little time for reflecting on the algorithmic basis of the experience.[18] For the gamer it is as if the system leaves only the phenomenological experience of the gameworld. The appearance of a phenomenon like game patch art is interesting in that it uses programming to directly address such mechanisms of identification. As a recent example, Anne-Marie Schleiner's *Velvet-Strike* project (2002) invites people to create digital graffiti on the walls of *Counter-Strike,* the popular network shooter game about terrorism.[19] Situated somewhere between "textual poaching" gaming subcultures and critical software art, game patch art functions as an ambiguous counter-discourse to commercial game culture, true to the legacy of hackerism.

It should also be pointed out that media art from recent years has shown signs of self-reflectivity and a growing critical awareness of its own position vis a vis commercial and institutional applications. Works like Maurice Benayoun's and Jean-Baptiste Barrière's *World Skin* (1998) or Ken Feingold's *That Sinking Feeling* (2002) are far from naive cele-

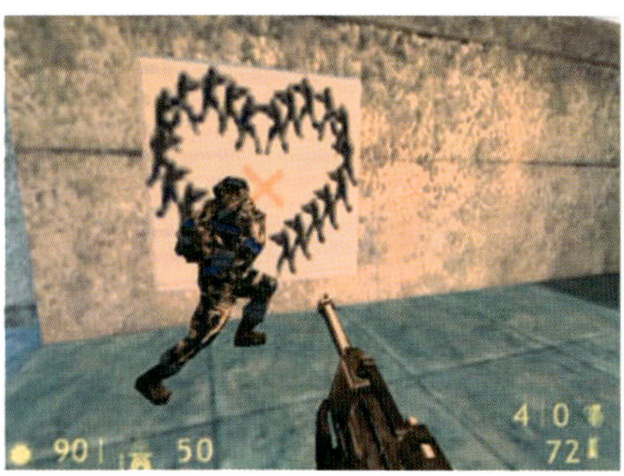

Anne-Marie Schleiner: Velvet Strike
From *http://www.opensorcery.net/velvet-strike/*

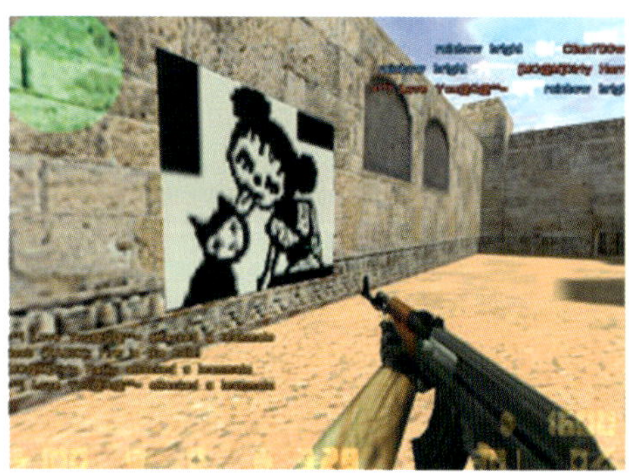

Anne-Marie Schleiner: Velvet Strike
From *http://www.opensorcery.net/velvet-strike/*

brations of the pleasures of the interface. While still offering memorable interactive experiences they at the same time disturb the bond with the user.[20] Both works create ambiguous situations where the seductive potential is constantly undermined by discrepant (*World Skin)* or deliberately "malfunctioning" *(That Sinking Feeling)* elements. Although neither work deals primarily with computer code, its role has by no means ignored. The functioning of the algorithmic base of these works may not have been highlighted, but its role is interconnected with the issues these works raise, from the role of media and the politics of simulation to social-psychology and the construction of identity. In their own ways they demonstrate that singling out the code for exclusive scrutiny at the expense of everything else may not be the right way to go in an integrated digital culture, where technical, ideological and cultural codes are no longer separable from each other.

4.

It is interesting to note that the software art purists have already begun to trace their own genealogy. This proves the well-known fact that history is mainly written to justify the present. A major formative event in the pre-history of software art has been located in the Software exhibition, curated by Jack Burnham for the Jewish Museum in New York in 1970. This technically catastrophic and until now largely ignored event has been identified as the nexus at which the efforts to explore the creative potential of information technology met conceptual art and Burnham's own interest in structuralist analysis.[21] In his introduction to the exhibition catalogue Burnham made it clear that Software was not a normal art exhibition. Rather, it displayed exhibits that dealt with "conceptual and process relationships". One of the purposes was "to undermine normal perceptual expectations and habits which viewers bring to an art exhibition".[22] The visitors were supposed to interact with various technological devices, without being asked to consider them as artworks. The most noted exhibit was *SEEK,* created by Nicholas Negroponte and his colleagues at MIT's Architectural Machine Group. It was another AI-inspired programming effort that hardly reached its goals, except on a metaphorical level: living gerbils had been placed in a glass-caged arena with aluminium building blocks, and a computer-controlled robot arm operating from above. The system, engaged in arranging the blocks according to pre-programmed schemes, was supposed to respond "intelligently" to the "noise" created by the gerbils, the sounds of their paws on the blocks, etc.[23]
For the software art advocates, the most inspiring exhibit seems to be *Labyrinth,* an early version of Ted Nelson's hypertext displayed as a bare branching structure. Several other exhibits interfaced visitors with technological apparatus making few efforts to weave fictions or elaborate "stage-sets" around them. In *Software,* Burnham drew a connection between the use of computing technology and conceptual art, which made him include non-technological pieces from artists like John Baldessari, Lawrence Weiner and Douglas Huebler. In Burnham's view all these forms shared the tendency to move away from art objects and to investigate linguistic structures and forms of information exchange underlying other forms of expression. This was also in unison with Burnham's simultaneous effort to reveal the mythical structures underlying the traditions of Western art.[25] Conceptual art, interpreted broadly to include also John Cage's method of composition, the series of instructions for imaginary events composed by the Fluxus artists and some forms of lettrist poetry, certainly provide one possible background against which to assess the role of code in software art. However, one might also refer to the field of structural and materialist film and the ideology of "anti-illusionism" in the film culture of the late 1960s and early 70s. Attacking the illusionism of conventional narrative cinema, filmmakers began to deconstruct the cinematic apparatus in its constituent elements. They emphasized the materiality of film, includ-

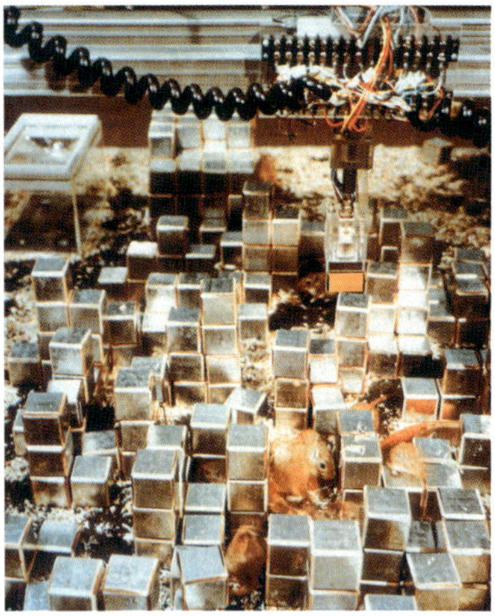

SEEK by Nicholas Negroponte and the Architecture Machine Group at MIT, 1969–70. Shown at "Software", Jewish Museum, New York, 1970.

ing sprocket holes, frames, emulsions, scratches and dirt. Some filmmakers, including Hollis Frampton, Michael Snow and the Croatian Ladislav Galeta, used (quasi-)generative principles to structure their films. In its most extreme form, filmmakers abandoned film altogether, staging events that merely highlighted the basic elements of the cinematic apparatus, the light beam from the projector, the screen, the darkness of the auditorium. Writing in the seminal *Structural Film Anthology* (1976), Peter Gidal defined Structural / Materialist films as "at once object and procedure".[25] In another text he stated: "A film is materialist if it does not cover its apparatus of illusionism. Thus it is not a matter of anti-illusionism pure and simple, uncovered truth, but rather, a constant procedural work against the attempts at producing an illusionist continuum's hegemony."[26] In other words, materialist film was not as much a purification ritual as a constant struggle against the hegemonic forces resorting to illusionism.

5.

The struggles of the structural and materialist film movement could perhaps be compared with the efforts the software artists are currently making to scratch the slick corporate facades of cyberculture, metaphorically manifested in the deceptive openness and the pretended democracy of the graphical user interface.[27] Yet comparisons across time are risky. Drawing a parallel between a 1960s computer generated picture consisting of dense arrays of ASCII characters and a piece of "ASCII art" from the late 1990s is only valid in a limited sense. The student hackers that created *Spacewar,* considered the first computer game, have little in common with today's commercial game developers and even with game patch artists. Similarly, the programming efforts of the computer graphics pioneers of the 1960s cannot be directly compared with the software art of the early 21st century, because of the widely different cultural contexts. The discourse on software art has emerged in a situation in which digital culture has already had time to create a history and a memory. During its first half century, digital computing has gone through a number of different stages that have progressively re-defined the meanings of computing in warfare, administration, society, economy and culture. Issues like artificial intelligence, virtual reality, agents and avatars, A-Life, GUI, physical computing and digital networking are all elements in an evolving fabric that changes shape depending on time and place and the position and identity of the observer. Last but not least, software art is in a position to profit from the experiences of the net art pioneers.

Digital art has for some time shown signs of a growing self-consciousness in relation to the history of digital technology. Yet the recent interest in AI among artists does not mean an artistic revival of the classic artificial intelligence research. It is not a simple homage either. Projects like David Rokeby's *A Giver of Names,* Kenneth Rinaldo's *Autopoiesis* and Ken Feingold's talking and responding puppet heads are examples of meta-art that engages in a dialogue with the cultural representations of AI (including, in Feingold's case, Joseph Weizenbaum's quasi-intelligent conversation program ELIZA), while pursuing at the same time other intellectual and ideological goals. Perhaps it is not wrong to say that there has been a cultural demand for a phenomenon like software art, just like there was for the appearance of structural / materialist film, which was "called for" by a conglomeration of conflicting cultural forces, from the increasing uniformity and untouchability of commercial film production to the impact of counter-cultural movements, the emergence of decontructionist philosophy and the "dematerialization of the art object". The structural / materialist film movement emerged as a critical position that questioned the prevailing audiovisual hegemony, demanding an approach that highlighted the "primitives" of the filmic medium in dynamic interplay with its application to narrative and metamorphic purposes. In its anti-illusionistic fervor it evoked the idea of a modernist reaction, but not in a simple revivalist fashion.

The claims and prognoses made by the software art advocates also have a certain neo-modernist flavor. Emphasizing the centrality of the code and the algorithmic approach means positing a "hard core", often felt to have been lost in the postmodern world. Indeed, there are "small but uninfluential" (to brutally appropriate an expression from Vuc Cosic) groups, such as the one dedicated to exploring the aesthetics of the generative code (Geoff Cox, Alec McLean, Adrian Ward, etc.), that fulfill many of the criteria for classical avantgarde movements.[28] Florian Cramer has identified the group's activities, which include poetry readings in Perl program code, as "software formalism".[29] On the other hand there are approaches that emphasize the cultural and ideological underpinnings of computer programming. For groups like the British Mongrel and I/O/D (creator of *Web Stalker),* digital code cannot be separated from the operations of ideology manifested on the Internet and elsewhere. Their actions and projects are much more difficult to fit into a modernist strait-jacket. The situation becomes even more difficult in the case of the independent artist-activists operating on the no-(wo)man's land between popular cultural forms like gaming, various forms of net activism (including cyber-feminism) and theoretical approaches. Appropriation, pastiche, bricolage and other postmodernist tricks are still among their favourite tools.

If the digital arts are going to make a difference in the media culture of the 21st century, it is clear that they have to shed their veil of innocence. They have to face the problematic, conflicting realities of cyberculture. While doing so, they need to scrutinize and make public their own internal workings, as well as their relationship to the systems of power, control and commerce that envelop them, infiltrate them, co-opt them and influence their public image, whether welcome or not. Just as science and technology can never be free from the constraints imposed upon them by economy, culture and politics, the digital arts cannot be "pure" and "free", even when purporting to focus on the quest for formal, mathematical, algorithmic beauty. Researching the aesthetics of digital grammars and exploring the workings of the code are important goals; yet getting the findings out from the isolated engine room and into the consciousness of the cyber citizen—also in the role of the cyberart lover—is quite another matter.

---

1 Nicholas Negroponte: *The Architecture Machine.* Cambridge, Mass.: The MIT Press, 1970, 9.

2 See Matthew Fuller's penetrating analysis of Microsoft Word, "It looks like you're writing a letter: Microsoft Word", available on-line at *www.axia.demon.co.uk/wordtext.html.*

3 John Berger et. al.: *Ways of Seeing.* London and Harmondsworth, Middlesex: BBC and Penguin Books, 1972, 10.

4 "Nodes" for the discourse on "software art" have been the software art award competition organized by the Transmediale in Berlin since 2001, the website *www.runme.org* and the *www.readme.org* events. The protagonists active through these and other channels come from different countries, but mainly from Europe.

5 See *www.walkerart.org/gallery9/lifesharing/.* During the Venice Biennale 2001, invited to participate in the Slovenian Pavillion, 0100101110101101.ORG got attention by announcing the creation and distribution of a festival (computer) virus. With this conceptual act the group in a way confirmed the notion of the Transmediale 01 software art jury according to which "[c]omputer viruses might be seen as a critical form of software art ..." (transmediale 01, jury statement, *www.transmediale.de/01/en/s_juryStatement.htm).*

6 Cynthia Goodman: *Digital Visions. Computers and Art.* New York and Syracuse: Harry N. Abrams & Everson Museum of Art, 1987, 24.

7 Jasia Reichardt: *The Computer in Art,* London: Studio Vista, 1971. See page 81 for a discussion of the Computer Technique Group and its belief that [i]t is the program itself that is the work of art".

8 See Herbert W. Franke: *Computer Graphics Computer Art,* pp 107-108. Phaidon, New York, 1971 Another influential theorist was Abraham Moles.

9 Jonathan Benthall: "Science and Technology" in *Art Today,* p 52. Praeger Publishers, New York, 1972.

10 It is well known that Mignonneau is responsible for the programming in a technical sense, but their numerous installations are the product of a very close collaboration, which makes separating their creative inputs next to impossible.

11 Rokeby's *Very Nervous System* is also available as a commercial software package known as SVNS. It has been used by numerous other artists as well.

12 See Pamela McCorduck: *AARON's Code,* W.H. Freeman, New York,1990.

13 In a recent e-mail message to the author Cohen explained: "And, as with any other serious artist, what isn't carried forward is abandoned. So the answer to one of your questions is that I don't keep old versions of the program hanging around very long. Actually I wouldn't be able to use them even if I did; they were written for different machines and stored on media and devices that are no longer in use. It would probably be easier to reconstruct the early versions from memory than to try to resurrect the old media: not that I would bother to try." (private e-mail communication, May 6, 2003.)

14 Available from *www.kurzweilcyberart.com/.* The site also contain material about *AARON's* history, including a film clip demonstrating a painting machine in operation. It might also be claimed that becoming as desktop application, essentially a screensaver, has trivialized *AARON.* This impression may have to do with the speed of current computers. *AARON* somehow seems to create its paintings too quickly, too effortlessly. This is naturally just a subjective impression that has nothing to do with the sophistication of the code.

15 In discussions Cohen often refers to the complexity of the program, which has been in the making for three decades. Although it has been turned into freeware, Cohen obviously still sees *AARON* as his own creation as an artist. Releasing the source code would compromise this role, but it would also lead to much more radical collective creation.

16 *www.transmediale.de/01/en/s_juryStatement.htm*

17 Florian Cramer and Ulrike Gabriel: "Software Art", available on-line at *www.netzliteratur.net/cramer/software_art_-_transmediale.html.*

18 Eddo Stern has pointed out how artefacts, programming errors and network malfunctions in massively multiplayer roleplaying games can occasionally make the player aware of the digital architecture of the game. See Stern's article in *Mariosophy: The Culture of Electronic Games,* edited by Erkki Huhtamo and Sonja Kangas, The University Press of Finland, Helsinki, 2002 (in Finnish).

19 See Anne-Marie Schleiner: "Velvet-Strike: War Times and Reality Games", *www.noemalab.com/sections/ideas/ideas_articles/schleiner_velvet_strike.html.* Schleiner has also curated important game patch related art events.

20 In the case of *World Skin* this happens by using deliberately artificial frozen 2D images within a navigable 3D space, in the case of *That Sinking Feeling* by having an animatronic puppet head deliberately misunderstand the visitor's speech, showing traits of schizophrenic behaviour that could also be attributed to malfunctioning technology.

21 See Edward A. Shanken: *The House That Jack Built: Jack Burnham's Concept of 'Software' as a Metaphor for Art,* available online at *www.duke.edu/~giftwrap/House.html.*

22 Jack Burnham, "Notes on art and information processing", in *Software. Information technology: its new meaning for art* (catalogue) p 12, The Jewish Museum, New York,1970.

23 SEEK gained notoriety because several of the gerbils reportedly died during the exhibition. The gerbils, of course, were stand-ins for human beings operating in a technologically saturated environment.

24 See Jack Burnham: *The Structure of Art.* George Brasiller, New York,1971.

25 *Structural Film Anthology,* edited by Peter Gidal, London: BFI, 1976, 14.

26 Peter Gidal: *Materialist Film,* London: Routledge, 1989, 17.

27 A useful book for developing this connection further is Malcolm Le Grice: *Experimental Cinema in the Digital Age,* London: British Film Institute, 2001. Le Grice was an active protagonist in the structural film movement.

28 See Geoff Cox, Alex McLean and Adrian Ward: *The Aesthetics of Generative Code,* available on-line at *http://generative.net/papers/aesthetics/.*

29 Florian Cramer: "Concepts, Notations, Software, Art", available on-line at *www.netzliteratur.net/cramer/concepts_notations_software_art.html.*

WEB STALKER SEEK AARON
Gedanken zu digitaler Kunst, Code und Codierer

Erkki Huhtamo

„[J]ede Form von Software lässt uns unseren historischen Kunstbegriff überdenken."
(Jack Burnham, „Notes on art and information processing", Katalog zur Software-Ausstellung, 1970)

1.

In der Mainstream-Computertechnik zeichnet sich ein Trend zur Verschleierung des Codes ab. Während das Programmieren und Lesen von Code für die ersten Computeranwender – Wissenschaftler, Techniker, Operatoren und sogar Künstler – eine Selbstverständlichkeit war, bleibt der Code heute zunehmend unsichtbar bzw. hinter der Fassade der Benutzeroberfläche verborgen. Seit Ende der 1960er Jahre ist die Vernetzung von Mensch und Computer über „benutzerfreundliche" Interfaces eines der grundlegenden Ziele der digitalen Kultur. Wie Nicholas Negroponte 1969 anmerkte, bestand für ihn die wahre Herausforderung darin, dem Computer ein Verständnis des Menschen zu vermitteln, und nicht vice versa: „Ein Entwickler sollte beim Arbeiten mit einer Maschine nicht auf maschinenorientierte Codes zurückgreifen müssen. Trotz aller Fortschritte in der Computertechnologie gilt als Paradigma für einen sinnvollen Dialog, dass Maschinen auf natürliche Sprache reagieren können."[1]
Die Bemühungen „nahtlose" und „intime" Mensch-Computer-Interfaces zu schaffen, wurden zum Symbol einer progressiven Computerkultur, zu der sowohl Experten als auch normale User gehören. Von Xerox Star bis Apple Macintosh und dessen unehelichem Nachkommen, Microsoft Windows, wurden Generationen von Usern darauf gedrillt, die Vorgänge im Inneren der „Kiste" zu ignorieren. Sie bedienten sich einer Software, deren metaphernreicher Inhalt sich per Mausklick öffnen ließ. Statt binärer Ketten von Nullen und Einsen – dem für die Steuerung des Systems erforderlichen Programmcode – sahen die User Icons und Papierkörbe auf dem Desktop.
Während Computer in allen erdenklichen Bereichen zum Einsatz kommen, bleibt der direkte Zugang zum Code und zur Programmierung Spezialisten vorbehalten: Informatikern, Berufsprogrammierern, Hackern und Entwicklern von Game-Engines. Mac- und sogar die meisten Windows-User sehen den Code nur selten hinter dem Interface hervorblitzen. Auch die kurze Euphorie, als mit dem Auftauchen von HTML das Code-Schreiben auch für Durchschnittsuser zur Routine wurde, flaute mit der Entwicklung einer Reihe von einfach zu bedienenden Website-Erstellungsprogrammen rasch ab. Eine mögliche Erklärung für diese Entwicklung ist, dass der Computer nichts anderes als eine Vermittlungsinstanz, ein Werkzeug bzw. Medium ist und nicht das Ziel per se darstellt; es finden sich allerdings auch eine Reihe von Gegenargumenten. Die zunehmend wichtigere Rolle des Computers als universell einsetzbare Maschine, die zahlreiche Anwendungen und Systeme weltweit steuert, lässt die völlige Unsichtbarkeit des Innenlebens von Computern bedenklich erscheinen. Programmierer von internationalen Konzernen und Regierungseinrichtungen (Code-Knacker nicht zu vergessen) ebenso wie Prankster, Cyber-Kriminelle und Terroristen überwachen und manipulieren via Internet die „unschuldigen" Computeranwender. Da den Usern das nötige Programmierwissen fehlt, können sie nur auf kommerzielle Dienste zurückgreifen oder handelsübliche Softwarepakete installieren. Der eigentliche Kern des Problems bleibt allerdings bestehen und mögliche Gegenmaßnah-

men sind nicht ausreichend durchdacht. Es wird auch argumentiert, dass durch den Einsatz kommerzieller Software die Ausdrucksfreiheit der Anwender eingeschränkt und ihnen ohne ihr Wissen die von den Konzernen vorgesehene Rolle aufgezwungen wird.[2] John Bergers berühmter Slogan „Jedes Bild verkörpert eine bestimmte Sichtweise“ könnte in abgewandelter Form lauten: „Jede Software verkörpert einen bestimmten Benutzungsmodus.“ [3] Zugang zum Code, das Verstehen der „Botschaft“ und die Fähigkeit, Code für persönliche Zwecke zu nutzen, sind politische, soziale und wirtschaftliche Fragen, die eng mit den bestehenden Machtverhältnissen und der Wissensdynamik in unserer Gesellschaft verknüpft sind.

Vor diesem Hintergrund scheint die Konzentration auf den Code in der digitalen Kunst überaus interessant. Dieses Interesse zeigt sich auf unterschiedliche Weise, besonders jedoch im neu entstandenen Diskurs über „Softwarekunst“.[4] In den letzten Jahren entstanden Kunstwerke, die das Aussehen und die Funktionalität kommerzieller Softwareapplikationen, von Webbrowsern bis zu interaktiven Spielwelten, veränderten und Features einführten, die von den Usern als formale Interventionen, störende Pranks, ideologische Subversion oder einfach technische Bugs interpretiert werden können. Der berühmte *Web Stalker* (I/O/D, 1997-) ist ein Webbrowser, der anstatt des herkömmlichen grafischen Interface Kontrollcodes und Linkstrukturen anzeigt. *Life_Sharing* von 0100101110101101.ORG richtete sich gegen die als falsch empfundene Offenheit von Webbrowsern, indem Usern über das Internet der Zugriff auf die Festplatte einschließlich aller privaten Dateien und Programmen gestattet wurde.[5] Andere Arbeiten setzen Elemente des Computercodes als Gestaltungsmittel ein, ohne diese hinter Grafiken, Bildern und Klängen zu verbergen. All diese Formen der digitalen Kunst versuchen die Konventionen der Computernutzung zu hinterfragen. Indem sie den Schleier der als trügerisch empfundenen „Benutzerfreundlichkeit“ lüften, gestatten die Künstler den Usern einen Blick hinter die Kulissen und in den „Maschinenraum“ (um eine etwas anachronistische Metapher zu verwenden) zu werfen. Sie fühlen sich in diesem Raum wohl, betrachten ihn als Labor, Treffpunkt, Toolkit und Ort der Kunst. Woher rührt jedoch dieses Interesse? Geht es weit genug, diese Versuche als „unvermeidbare“ Avantgardebewegung der digitalen Kultur zu bezeichnen? In welchem Bezug steht dieses Interesse zum weiteren, vielleicht sogar nicht-digitalen, kulturellen Kontext? Dieser Artikel versucht Antworten auf einige dieser einleitenden Fragen zu geben, indem die Beziehung zwischen Kunst, Code und Codieren aus einer medien-archäologischen Perspektive betrachtet wird.

2.

Die ersten Computerkünstler der 1960er Jahre waren Programmierer. Es gab keine Alternative. Jedes Kunstwerk, ob Grafik, Animation oder Musik, war notwendigerweise das Ergebnis eines einzigartigen Codierungsprozesses. Als ob sie die aktuellen Ambitionen der „Softwarekunst“ bereits geahnt hätten, erklärten Computerkunst-Pioniere wie Michael L. Noll und die Mitglieder der japanischen Computer Technique Group (CTG) unumwunden, dass das generierende Programm und nicht das computergenerierte Ergebnis das wahre Kunstwerk sei.[6] Die meisten frühen Kunstwerke der Computergrafik und -musik verschrieben sich einem formalistischen Ansatz und konzentrierten sich u. a. auf die Vor- und Nachteile generativer Grammatiken und das Verhältnis zwischen regelbasiertem Verhalten und zufallsbestimmten Ereignissen. Dieser Hintergrund zeigt sich klar in Jasia Reichardts früh erschienener Einführung *The Computer in Art* (1971), die diese Thematik anhand zahlreicher Diagramme anschaulich beschreibt.[7] Computergrafik-Pioniere wie Frieder Nake beschrieben ihr Kunstschaffen als „visuelle Forschung“, die bewusst soziale oder politische Anliegen aussparte. Inspiration fanden sie in der Kybernetik, Claude Shannons Informationstheorie und der exakten, mathematischen Ästhetik von Theoretikern wie Max Bense.8 Bense klammerte die Rolle der subjektiven Wahrnehmung aus und basierte sein ästhetisches System auf mathematischen Gleichungen, die

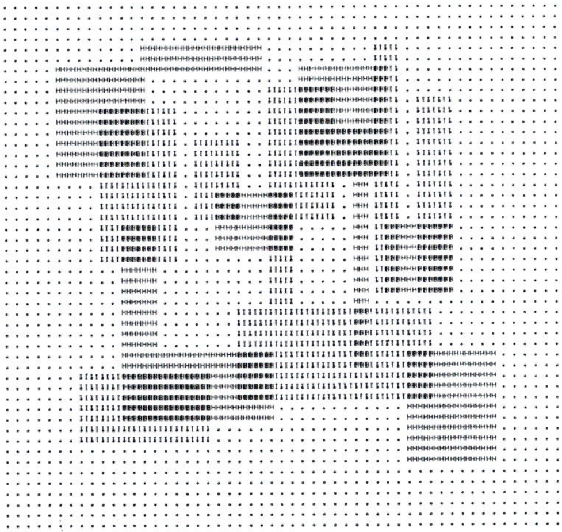

Katherine Nash: ART 1

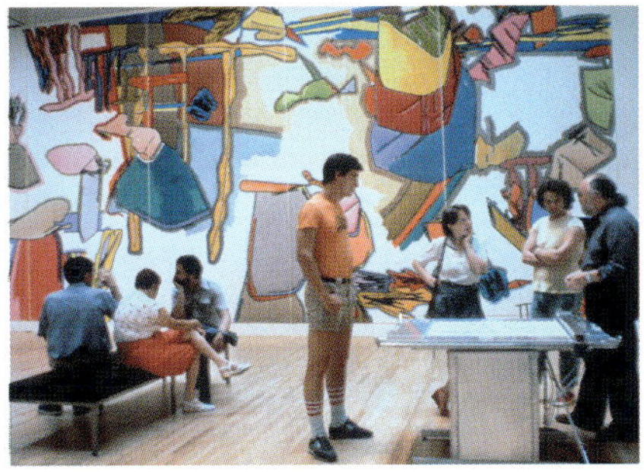

Harold Cohen: Tate Gallery

das Universelle statt des Besonderen, das Rationale statt des Irrationalen (gleichzusetzen mit dem subjektiven Kunstimpuls), das Abstrakte statt des Repräsentationalen reflektierten. Obwohl die ersten Kunst-Programmierer häufig Zufallsoperationen nutzten, wurde der Computer primär als „Werkzeug" betrachtet: Er sollte ein zuvor geschriebenes Programm ausführen.

Diese Ausgangslage lässt sich sowohl durch den Stand der Technik als auch den weiteren institutionellen Kontext erklären. In den 1960er Jahren wurden Computer meist in Regierungseinrichtungen und Unternehmen verwendet. Sie wurden primär für statistische Berechnungen genutzt, die das Programmieren in erster Linie als Batch-Processing betrachteten. Obwohl die ersten Künstler den Computer für andere Zwecke nutzen wollten, waren sie gezwungen, sich in die von der nicht-künstlerischen „Mainframe"-Kultur vorgegebenen institutionellen Rollen einzufügen: In einschlägigen Institutionen schrieben sie Programme und warteten dann, dass diese vom Computer ausgeführt wurden. Sie waren Mitglieder einer kleinen Elite am Rand einer größeren institutionalisierten Technik-Elite, die ein unglaublich expressives Medium ausloteten, das noch in den Kinderschuhen steckte. Allerdings veränderte sich das Wesen der Computertechnik durch Innovationen wie neue Interfaces, Time-Sharing und die Entwicklung der ersten Programmiersprachen für künstlerische Zwecke kontinuierlich. BEFLIX, ein vom Informatiker Kenneth Knowlton von Bell Labs entwickeltes Programm, wurde von Stan Vanderbeek und Lillian Schwartz in Zusammenarbeit mit Knowlton für innovative Computergrafiken und -animationen eingesetzt. Ebenso interessant war ART 1 der Universitätsprofessoren Katherine Nash und Richard H. Williams, das als Werkzeug für Künstler gedacht war, die nicht über die nötigen theoretischen und technischen Programmierkenntnisse verfügten, aber Computer für ihre Kunstprojekte einsetzen wollten. Obwohl das Programm heftig kritisiert wurde, da der Künstler „als Spezialist mit vordefinierten professionellen Bedürfnissen" betrachtet wurde, war es doch der erste Hinweis darauf, dass sich die Wege der Entwickler von „Soft"-Kunst und reinen Algorithmus-Schreibern bald trennen würden.[9]

Die Verbreitung von Kunst, die eingeführte Software wie Photoshop oder Maya nutzt, hat die Entwicklung neuer eigenständiger Algorithmen nicht verdrängt. Viele der nachhaltigsten digitalen Kunstprojekte wurden von Künstlern initiiert, die ihre Software entweder selbst schreiben oder eng mit einem Programmierer zusammenarbeiten. Beispiele für Erstere sind Myron Krueger, Harold Cohen und David Rokeby, während Künstler wie Jeffrey Shaw (gemeinsam mit Gideon May und Bernt Lintermann) und Rafael Lozano-Hemmer (gemeinsam mit Will Bauer) der zweiten Gruppe angehören. In manchen Fällen, wie z. B. bei Christa Sommerer und Laurent Mignonneau, ist eine Trennung zwischen Programmieren und anderen Aspekten des Kunstschaffungsprozesses nahezu unmöglich.[10] Pioniere wie Krueger, Cohen und Rokeby haben Jahre, sogar Jahrzehnte, damit verbracht, Programmcode zur Weiterentwicklung ihrer zunehmend komplexen Systeme zu schreiben. Die Werke dieser Künstler haben im Lauf der Jahre ihre eigene Identität entwickelt, können jedoch gleichzeitig als „Materialisationen" dieser Systeme betrachtet werden, die den aktuellen Entwicklungsstand der Programme dokumentieren. Code ist das zentrale Element von Kruegers *Videoplace* und Rokebys *Very Nervous System* oder *Giver of Names.*[11] Harold Cohens *AARON* ist wohl das langfristig konsequenteste Unterfangen, eigenen Programmcode für die Schaffung eines evolutionären Kunstprojekts einzusetzen. Es wurde seit Anfang der 1970er Jahre kontinuierlich weiterentwickelt.[12] AARON, ein KI-basiertes Computerprogramm, ist ein Expertensystem zur Generierung von Bildern und Zeichnungen. In den letzten dreißig Jahren wurden verschiedenste Ausgabegeräte entwickelt, von einer Zeichen-„Schildkröte", die sich auf am Boden liegenden Papier fortbewegt, bis zu komplexen Zeichenmaschinen und – als neuester Entwicklung – einer Softwareanwendung, die automatisch Bilder am Desktop generiert. AARON kann als halbautonomes System betrachtet werden. Die Zeichnungen basieren auf den von Cohen definierten komplexen Regeln, weisen jedoch, von der Bildkomposition bis zur Farbgebung, einen beträchtlichen Grad an Autonomie auf. Es ist bezeichnend, dass Cohen den Code von AARON nie freigegeben hat. Die verschiedenen Entwicklungsstadien des Programms wurden nicht systematisch dokumentiert, weshalb die Entwicklung des Codes nur indirekt über die zahlreichen von AARON generierten Zeichnungen und Bilder entschlüsselt werden kann.[13] Cohen betrachtet den Code nie als Kunstwerk per se, obwohl eine beachtliche schöpferische Leistung dahinter steckt. Code kann Cohen zufolge vielmehr mit den Fertigkeiten und Techniken, die ein Mensch Zeit seines Lebens erwirbt, verglichen werden. Einzig die Bilder, die materiellen Spuren eines Lebenswerks, haben Bestand. In diesem Sinn bedient sich Cohen, selbst ausgebildeter Maler, eines konventionellen Modells zur Schaffung und Konservierung von Kunst. Die neueste Version von AARON, die kostenlos über das Internet erhältlich ist, könnte jedoch eine etwas radikalere Richtung einschlagen.[14] Anstatt weiter als Cohens persönliche kybernetische Verlängerung zu fungieren, wurde AARON von seinem Schöpfer ein gewisses Maß an Unabhängigkeit zugestanden. Allerdings wurde mit der Freigabe von AARON als frei verfügbare Softwareanwendung auch die Weiterentwicklung von AARON abgebrochen.

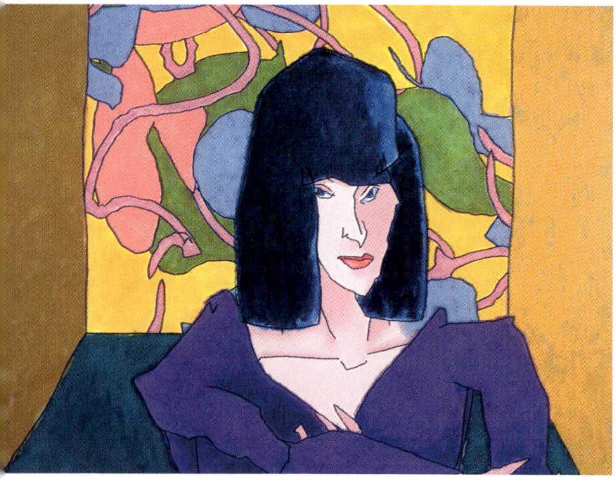

Harold Cohen: *Clarissa*

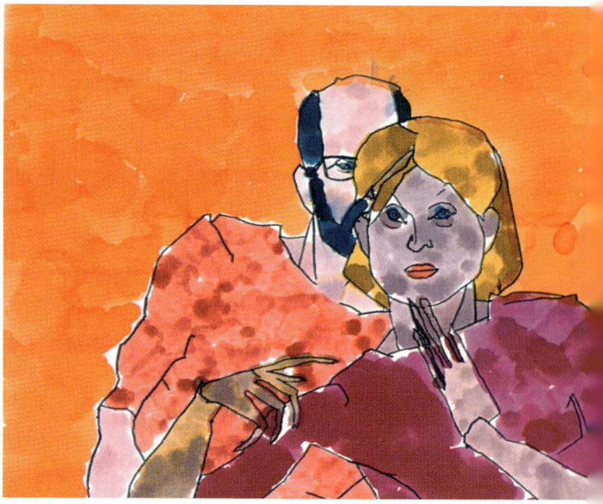

Harold Cohen: *Machine*

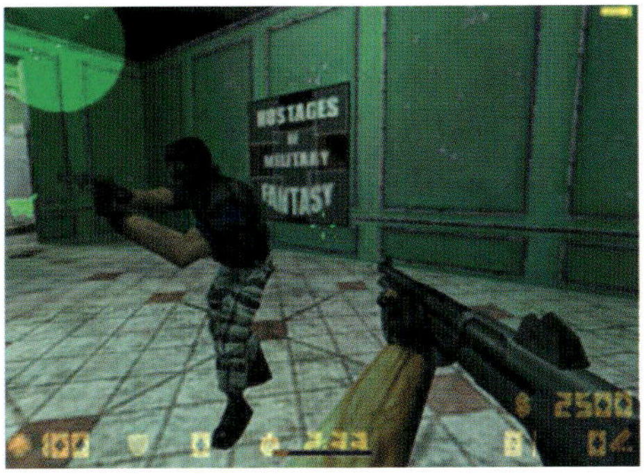

Anne-Marie Schleiner: Velvet-Strike
http://www.opensorcery.net/velvet-strike/

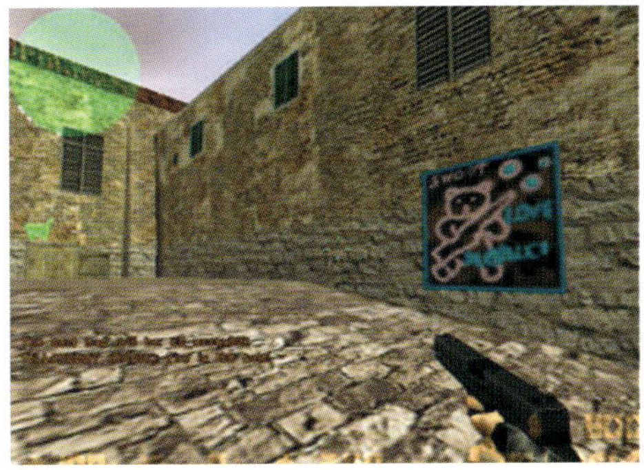

Anne-Marie Schleiner: Velvet-Strike
http://www.opensorcery.net/velvet-strike/

Obwohl weiterhin zahllose unterschiedliche Bilder generiert werden können, kann das Programm keine neuen Routinen erlernen. Als Desktopinstallation verewigt AARON zweifelsohne Cohens Errungenschaften, wird jedoch gleichzeitig auch zu einem kybernetischen Zombie. Mit der Freigabe des Quellcodes bestünde eine Chance, das Programm mittels kollektiven Programmierens im Internet weiter zu entwickeln.[15]

3.

Die Vertreter der „Softwarekunst" weisen auf die Bedeutung des Codes als wichtigste kreative Leistung hin und fordern eine uneingeschränkte Präsenz und Funktion des Codes im Kunstwerk. Laut einer Erklärung der Jury des ersten Software-Kunstwettbewerbs der Transmediale 01 „richtet sich Softwarekunst gegen die Auffassung von Software als Mittel zum Zweck".[16] Für die Jury hat Softwarekunst verschiedene Gesichter: „Softwarekunst könnte Algorithmen als Selbstzweck präsentieren, traditionelle Paradigmen untergraben oder neue hervorrufen, innovative oder störende Prozesse in einem System auslösen, eine Form des kreativen Schreiben oder sogar eine Wissenschaft sein." In einer weiteren Erklärung führen die Jurymitglieder Florian Cramer und Ulrike Gabriel aus: „Softwarekunst bedeutet eine Verschiebung der Perspektive des Künstlers von der Präsentation hin zur Entwicklung von Systemen und Generierung von Prozessen an sich; das ‚Medien' -Konzept deckt dies jedoch nicht ab."[17] Für die oben erwähnten Autoren besteht die „Hauptsünde" der Medienkunst darin, dass dem Design des Interface zu viel Aufmerksamkeit gewidmet wurde. Für den Softwarepuristen ist die Schaffung von komplexen immersiven Umgebungen und vielschichtigen multisensorischen Interfaces ein Akt der Mystifizierung. Kunstwerke, die die Betrachter sowohl körperlich als auch emotional teilhaben lassen, „verführen" diese, anstatt die wahre Natur des Systems, die „hinter der Fassade" verborgen bleibt, erkennen zu lassen.
Es scheint überaus interessant, dass interaktive Systeme, die vor nicht allzu langer Zeit als bedeutsame und kritische Alternative zu „passivierenden" Medien wie dem Fernsehen betrachtet wurden, nun die Zielscheibe der Kritik sind. Diese veränderte Sichtweise beruht auf der zunehmenden Akzeptanz der Interaktivität und ihrer Integration in den Mainstream der digitalen Kultur. Wurde Interaktivität früher als Geste betrachtet, die die vorherrschende Medienlogik in Frage stellte, so gilt sie nun als „sinnvoll" und Teil des internen kulturellen Repertoires. Die jüngste Kritik scheint sich allerdings nicht an die Interaktivität selbst zu richten, sondern vielmehr gegen die Art, wie Interaktivität präsentiert und vermarktet, institutionalisiert und kommodifiziert wird. Im Computerspielbereich wird etwa argumentiert, dass die Quasi-Echtzeitinteraktion zwischen dem User und der Spielsoft-/-hardware zur „Automatisierung" des Reiz-/Reak-

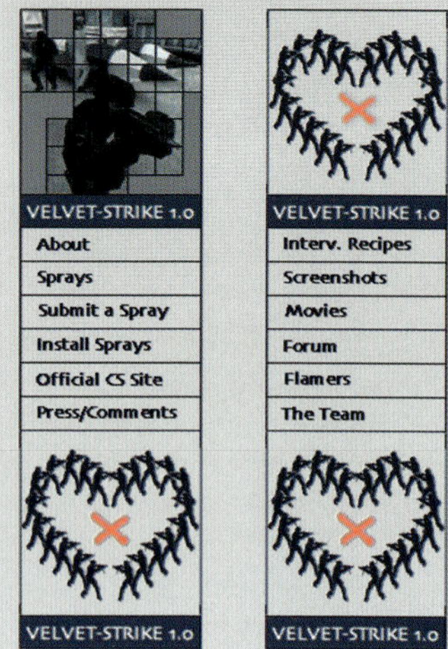

Anne-Marie Schleiner: Velvet-Strike
http://www.opensorcery.net/velvet-strike/

tionsmechanismus führt. Das Eintauchen in sich rasch verändernde emotionale Spielwelten lässt wenig Zeit zur Reflexion der der Spielerfahrung zugrunde liegenden Algorithmen.[18] Für den Spieler scheint das System selbst nicht zu existieren, es zählt lediglich die in der Spielwelt gemachte phänomenologische Erfahrung. Die Entstehung von Phänomenen wie Game-Patch-Art ist insofern interessant, als solche Identifikationsmechanismen mittels Programmieren direkt angesprochen werden. Ein aktuelles Beispiel liefert Anne-Marie Schleiners *Velvet-Strike*-Projekt (2002), in dem Menschen digitale Graffiti auf die Wände von *Counter-Strike,* dem populären Online-Shooter zum Thema Terrorismus, sprühen.[19] Game-Patch-Art, eine Kunstform, die im Spektrum zwischen Spielsubkultur, die in anderen Texten „wildert", und kritischer Softwarekunst angesiedelt ist, fungiert als zweideutiger Gegendiskurs zur kommerziellen Spielkultur und bleibt dem Hackertum treu.

Allerdings zeigt die jüngere Medienkunst auch Anzeichen von Selbstreflexion und wachsendem kritischen Bewusstsein zu ihrer eigenen Position gegenüber kommerziellen und institutionellen Anwendungen. Werke wie Maurice Benayouns und Jean-Baptiste Barrières *World Skin* (1998) oder Ken Feingolds *That Sinking Feeling* (2002) sind weit mehr als naive Lobgesänge auf die Annehmlichkeiten des Interface. Während sie weiterhin unvergessliche interaktive Erfahrungen möglich machen, manipulieren sie gleichzeitig die Beziehung zu den Usern. 20 Beide Werke schaffen zweideutige Situationen, in denen das verführerische Potenzial der Interaktivität stets von diskrepanten *(World Skin)* oder vorsätzlich „defekten" *(That Sinking Feeling)* Elementen unterminiert wird. Obwohl keines dieser Werke sich primär mit dem Computercode auseinandersetzt, findet die Rolle des Codes dennoch Beachtung. Die Algorithmusebene dieser Werke steht zwar nicht im Mittelpunkt, die Funktion der Algorithmen aber in engem Zusammenhang mit zentralen, von diesen Arbeiten thematisierten Fragen, wie der Rolle der Medien, der gegenwärtigen Politik der Simulation, der Sozialpsychologie oder der Identitätskonstruktion. Auf ihre eigene Art demonstrieren sie, dass die Konzentration auf den Code auf Kosten anderer möglicher Perspektiven vielleicht nicht der richtige Weg zu einer integrierten digitalen Kultur ist, in der technische, ideologische und kulturelle Codes unwiderruflich miteinander verflochten sind.

4.

Es ist interessant, dass die Softwarepuristen bereits begonnen haben, ihre eigene Genealogie zu verfolgen. Dies bekräftigt die allseits bekannte Tatsache, dass Geschichte nur geschrieben wird, um die Gegenwart zu rechtfertigen. Ein einschneidendes Ereignis in der Urgeschichte der Softwarekunst war die von Jack Burnham 1970 für das Jewish Museum in New York kuratierte „Software"-Ausstellung. Diese technisch katastrophale und bislang weithin unbekannte Ausstellung kann als Schnittpunkt betrachtet werden, an dem die Anstrengungen zur Erforschung des kreativen Potenzials der Informationstechnologie und Formen der Konzeptkunst ebenso wie Burnhams persönliches Interesse an strukturalistischen Analysen zusammenflossen.[21] In seiner Einleitung zum Ausstellungskatalog stellte Burnham fest, dass

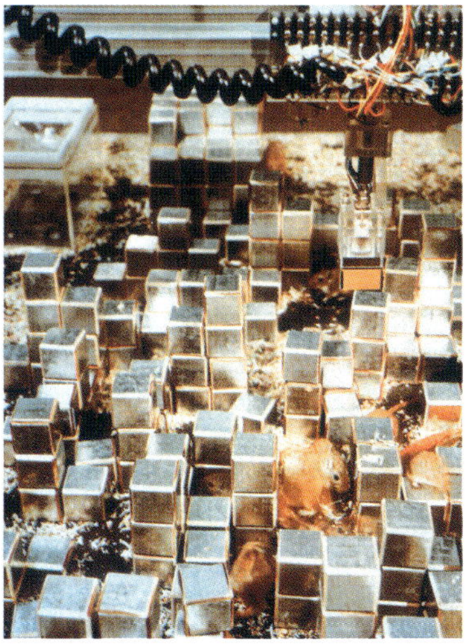

SEEK by Nicholas Negroponte and the Architecture Machine Group at MIT, 1969–70. Shown at "Software", Jewish Museum, New York, 1970.

„Software" keine herkömmliche Kunstausstellung sei. Vielmehr würden Objekte ausgestellt, die sich mit „konzeptuellen und prozessualen Beziehungen" beschäftigten. Eines der Ziele war es, „normale Erwartungen und Wahrnehmungsmuster der Ausstellungsbesucher zu untergraben".[22] Die Besucher sollten mit verschiedenen technischen Objekten interagieren, ohne diese zwangsläufig als Kunstwerke zu betrachten. Das auffallendeste Ausstellungsobjekt war SEEK von Nicholas Negroponte und seinen Kollegen von der *Architectural Machine Group* des MIT.

Bei SEEK handelte es sich ebenfalls um ein KI-inspiriertes Programm, das außer auf einer metaphorischen Ebene wohl kaum sein Ziel erreichte: Lebende Wüstenspringmäuse wurden in einen Glaskäfig mit Aluminiumbausteinen gesetzt; ein computergesteuerter Roboterarm konnte von oben in den Käfig herabgelassen werden. Das System war darauf programmiert, die Bausteine nach einem vorprogrammierten Muster anzuordnen, und sollte „intelligent" auf den von den Wüstenspringmäusen produzierten „Lärm", z. B. das Trippeln ihrer Füßchen auf den Bausteinen etc., reagieren.[23]

Für die Anhänger der Softwarekunst war wohl *Labyrinth,* eine frühe Version von Ted Nelsons Hypertext in der Form eines simplen Netzwerks von Knoten und elektronischen Verbindungen, das inspirierendste Ausstellungsobjekt. Verschiedene andere Ausstellungsobjekte ermöglichten den Besuchern mit technischen Apparaten zu interagieren, und unternahmen wenig Bemühungen fiktive Geschichten rund um diese Konstruktionen zu schmieden oder „Bühnenbilder" zu entwerfen. Mit „Software" schuf Burnham eine Verbindung zwischen Computertechnologie und Konzeptkunst; er inkludierte auch nicht-technische Werke von Künstlern wie John Baldessari, Lawrence Weiner und Douglas Huebler. Aus Burnhams Sicht waren diese Objekte weniger Kunstobjekte, sondern sie thematisierten vielmehr tendenziell Sprachstrukturen und Formen des Informationsaustauschs, die anderen nichtsprachlichen Ausdrucksmitteln zugrunde liegen. Dies stand auch im Einklang mit Burnhams Bemühungen, die den westlichen Kunsttraditionen zugrunde liegenden mythischen Strukturen aufzuzeigen.[24] Konzeptkunst – die in einer weit gefassten Auslegung auch John Cages Kompositionsmethode umfasst –, die von den Fluxus-Künstlern generierten Anweisungen für imaginäre Ereignisse und bestimmte Formen lettristischer Lyrik sind zweifelsohne ein mögliches Umfeld, in dem die Rolle von Code in der Softwarekunst analysiert werden kann.

Man könnte sich allerdings auch auf den Bereich der strukturellen und materialistischen Filmproduktion und die Ideologie des „Anti-Illusionismus" in der Filmkultur der späten 1960er und frühen 1970er Jahre konzentrieren. Als Kritik am Illusionismus des konventionellen narrativen Kinofilms begannen Filmemacher das Kino in all seinen prägenden Elementen zu dekonstruieren. Sie betonten die Materialität des Films, inklusive der Klebestellen, Einzelbilder, Emulsionen, Kratzer und Schmutzpartikel. Manche Filmemacher, darunter Hollis Frampton, Michael Snow oder der Kroate Ladislav Galeta, verwendeten (quasi-)generative Prinzipien zur Strukturierung ihrer Filme. In den extremsten Projekten dieser Bewegung verzichteten die Filmemacher gänzlich auf den Film und inszenierten Aktionen, die sich auf die grundlegenden Elemente des Kinos konzentrierten: den Lichtstrahl des Projektors, die Leinwand, die Dunkelheit im Saal. In einem Beitrag in der richtungweisenden *Structural Film Anthology* (1976) definierte Peter Gidal strukturalistisch/materialistische Filme als „Objekt und Prozess zugleich".[25] In einem anderen Aufsatz stellt er fest: „Ein Film ist materialistisch, wenn er den ihm zugrunde liegenden illusionistischen Apparat nicht verbirgt. Es handelt sich hier nicht um reinen und simplen Anti-Illusionismus, um das Aufdecken von Wahrheiten, sondern um einen kontinuierlichen Prozess gegen die Schaffung einer illusionistischen Hegemonie."[26] In anderen Worten, der materialistische Film war nicht so sehr ein Reinigungsritual, als vielmehr ein beständiger Kampf gegen hegemoniale Kräfte, die sich des Illusionismus bedienten.

5.

Die Bemühungen der strukturalistischen und materialistischen Filmbewegung könnten mit den Ambitionen der Softwarekünstler verglichen werden, die gegenwärtig versuchen, den glatten Fassaden der Cyberkultur, die sich metaphorisch in einer trügerischen Offenheit und einer fingierten Demokratie des grafischen Userinterface manifestieren, Kratzer zuzufügen.[27] Vergleiche über die Zeiten hinweg sind allerdings gefährlich. Es ist nur beschränkt zulässig, Parallelen zwischen einem computergenerierten Bild der 1960er Jahren, das dicht mit ASCII-Zeichen übersät war, und einem Objekt der „ASCII-Kunst" der späten 1990er Jahre herzustellen. Jene Hacker, die als Studenten *Spacewar,* das als das erste Computerspiel gilt, entwickelten, haben nur wenig mit professionellen Spielentwicklern oder Game-Patch-Künstlern von heute gemein. Ähnlich können die Programme der Computergrafik-Pioniere der 1960er aufgrund des unterschiedlichen kulturellen Umfelds nicht direkt mit der Softwarekunst des frühen 21. Jahrhunderts verglichen werden. Der Diskurs über Softwarekunst hat sich in einem Kontext entwickelt, in dem die digitale Kultur bereits genügend Zeit hatte, Geschichte zu schreiben und Erinnerungen zu entwickeln. Während der ersten 50 Jahre durchlief die digitale Computertechnik zahlreiche Entwicklungsstadien, die die Bedeutung von Computern in verschiedenen Bereichen (Kriegsführung, Verwaltung, Gesellschaft, Wirtschaft und Kultur) neu definierten. Phänomene wie künstliche Intelligenz, virtuelle Realität, Agenten und Avatare, A-Life-Systeme, GUI-Design, Physical Computing und digitales Networking sind Phänomene eines sich rasch entwickelnden Systems, das je nach Zeit und Ort bzw. Position und Identität des Beobachters seine Form ändert. Nicht zuletzt vermag die Softwarekunst von den Erfahrungen der Netzkunst-Pioniere zu profitieren.
Hinsichtlich der Geschichte der Digitaltechnik beweist die digitale Kunst in den letzten Jahren eine gewisse Reflektiertheit. Das aktuelle Interesse der Künstler an KI bedeutet jedoch kein künstlerisches Wiederaufleben der klassischen KI-Forschung. Es handelt sich auch nicht um eine simple Hommage. Projekte wie David Rokebys *Giver of Names,* Kenneth Rinaldos *Autopoiesis* und Ken Feingolds sprechende und interagierende Marionetten sind Beispiele einer Metakunst, die den Dialog mit den kulturellen Repräsentationen der KI aufnimmt (wie im Fall Feingolds mit Joseph Weizenbaums quasi-intelligentem Konversationsprogramm ELIZA), während gleichzeitig andere intellektuelle und ideologische Ziele verfolgt werden. Es ist vielleicht nicht falsch zu behaupten, dass es eine kulturelle Nachfrage nach einem Phänomen wie Softwarekunst gibt, so wie eine Nachfrage nach strukturalistisch/materialistischen Filmen bestand; diese Nachfrage ging von einem Konglomerat von widersprüchlichen kulturellen Kräften aus, von der wachsenden Uniformität und „Unberührbarkeit" der kommerziellen Filmproduktion bis zum Einfluss kultureller Gegenbewegungen, dem Entstehen dekonstruktionistischer Philosophien und der „Dematerialisierung des Kunstobjekts". Die strukturalistisch/materialistische Filmbewegung entwickelte sich als kritische Gegenbewegung zur dominanten audiovisuellen Hegemonie und forderte einen Zugang, der die „Primitiva" des Mediums Film in einem dynamischen Wechselspiel mit seiner Anwendung für narrative und metamorphe Zwecke aufzeigt. In ihrer anti-illusionistischen Rigidität erweckte sie den Anschein einer modernistischen Gegenbewegung, die jedoch nicht naiv-revivalistisch war.
Die von den Befürwortern der Softwarekunst aufgestellten Forderungen und Prognosen besit-

zen jedoch einen gewissen neo-modernistischen Anstrich. Die Betonung der zentralen Funktion des Codes und der Algorithmusebene symbolisiert die Konzentration auf einen „harten Kern", der in der postmodernen Welt oft verschwunden geglaubt wurde. Es gibt tatsächlich „kleine, jedoch wenig einflussreiche" Gruppen (um es unverblümt mit Vuc Cosic' Worten auszudrücken) – wie jene um Geoff Cox, Alex McLean, Adrian Ward u. a., die sich der Erforschung der Ästhetik von generativem Code widmet –, die viele Merkmale einer klassischen Avantgarde-Bewegungen aufweisen.[28] Florian Cramer beschrieb die Aktivitäten dieser Gruppe, wie z. B. Lesungen von Perl-Script-Gedichten, als „Softwareformalismus".[29] Andererseits finden sich Gruppen, die die kulturellen und ideologischen Grundfesten des Programmierens akzentuieren. Für die britische *Mongrel*-Gruppe oder für I/O/D (Erfinder des *Web Stalker)* kann der digitale Code nicht von den verschiedenen Manifestationen der Ideologie im Internet bzw. anderen Umgebungen losgelöst werden. Ihre Aktionen und Projekte lassen sich schwer in eine modernistische „Zwangsjacke" stecken. Noch komplexer wird die Situation bei unabhängigen Künstler-Aktivisten, die im Niemandsland zwischen populären kulturellen Formen wie Spielen, verschiedenen Formen des Netzaktivismus (einschließlich Cyber-Feminismus) und theoretischen Zugängen operieren. Appropriation, Pastiche, Bricolage und andere postmoderne Tricks zählen zu ihren bevorzugten Ausdrucksmitteln.

Will die digitale Kunst in der Medienkultur des 21. Jahrhunderts einen Unterschied bewirken, muss sie ihren Schleier der Unschuld ablegen. Sie muss sich den problematischen, widersprüchlichen Realitäten der Cyberkultur stellen. Dabei muss sie wohl oder übel ihre eigenen internen Prozesse ebenso wie ihre Einstellung zu den herrschenden Systemen der Macht, Kontrolle und Kommerzialisierung, die sie zwangsläufig vereinnahmen, infiltrieren, dominieren und ihr öffentliches Image beeinflussen, kritisch hinterfragen und publik machen. So wie Wissenschaft und Technik nie völlig von den von Wirtschaft, Politik und Kultur ausgehenden Zwängen befreit werden können, kann die digitale Kunst nicht völlig „rein" und „frei" agieren, selbst wenn sie sich auf das Streben nach formaler, mathematischer, algorithmischer Schönheit beschränkt. Die Erforschung der Ästhetik digitaler Grammatiken bzw. der Funktionsweise von Code sind wichtige Ziele; die Erkenntnisse dieser Untersuchungen aus der Isolation des Maschinenraums zu befreien und im Bewusstsein der Cyber-Bürger – auch der Cyber-Art-Liebhaber – zu verankern, ist jedoch ein anderes, weitaus schwierigeres Unterfangen.

---

1 Negroponte, Nicholas: *The Architecture Machine,* MIT, Cambridge, Mass. 1970, S. 9.

2 Vgl. Matthew Fullers messerscharfe Analyse von Microsoft Word, „It looks like you're writing a letter: Microsoft Word", *http://www.axia.demon.co.uk/wordtext.html.*

3 Berger, John et al.: *Ways of Seeing,* BBC and Penguin Books, London and Harmondsworth, Middlesex 1972, S. 10.

4 „Schnittstellen" für den Diskurs über „Softwarekunst" sind der seit dem Jahr 2001 von der Transmediale in Berlin organisierte *software art award,* die Website *http://www.runme.org* und die *www.readme.org*-Aktivitäten. Die in diesen und anderen Foren tätigen Aktivisten stammen aus verschiedenen Ländern, hauptsächlich aus Europa.

5 Vgl. *http://www.walkerart.org/gallery9/lifesharing/.* Während der Biennale 2001 in Venedig zogen 0100101110101101.ORG, die eingeladen worden waren, ihre Werke im slowenischen Pavillon zu präsentieren, große Aufmerksamkeit auf sich, als sie die Entwicklung und Verbreitung eines Festival-Computervirus verkündeten. Mit diesem konzeptionellen Akt bestätigte die Gruppe gewissermaßen die Sicht der Softwarekunst-Jury der Transmediale 01, wonach „Computerviren als kritische Manifestation von Softwarekunst betrachtet werden können [...]" (Transmediale 01, Erklärung der Jury, *http://www.transmediale.de/01/en/s_juryStatement.htm).*

6 Goodman, Cynthia: *Digital Visions. Computers and Art,* Harry N. Abrams & Everson Museum of Art, New York and Syracuse 1987, S. 24.

7 Reichardt, Jasia: *The Computer in Art,* Studio Vista, London 1971, vgl. S. 81 für eine Diskussion der *Computer Technique Group* und deren Theorie, dass „das Programm selbst das Kunstwerk ist".

8 Vgl. Franke, Herbert W.: *Computer Graphics Computer Art,* Phaidon, New York 1971, S. 107-108. Ein weiterer einflussreicher Theoretiker war Abraham Moles.

9 Benthall, Jonathan: „Science and Technology", in *Art Today,* S. 52, Praeger Publishers, New York 1972.

10 Es ist bekannt, dass Mignonneau für die technische Programmierung verantwortlich zeichnet, die zahlreichen Installationen dieser Gruppe sind jedoch Ergebnis einer sehr engen Zusammenarbeit aller Künstler, was die Darstellung des kreativen Inputs des Einzelnen unmöglich macht.

11 Rokebys *Very Nervous System* ist unter dem Namen *SVNS* auch als kommerzielles Softwarepaket erhältlich. Das Programm wird auch von zahlreichen anderen Künstlern verwendet.

12 Vgl. McCorduck, Pamela: *Aaron's Code,* W.H. Freeman, New York 1990.

13 In einer E-Mail erklärte Cohen vor kurzem: „Und wie bei jedem anderen seriösen Künstler, wird aufgegeben, was nicht weiterentwickelt wird. Die Antwort auf eine Ihrer Fragen ist daher, dass ich alte Programmversionen nicht lange aufbewahre. Ich könnte sie auch nicht verwenden, selbst wenn ich sie aufheben würde; sie wurden für andere Maschinen geschrieben und auf Medien gespeichert, die nicht mehr benutzt werden. Es wäre wahrscheinlich einfacher, frühere Versionen aus dem Gedächtnis heraus zu rekonstruieren, als die alten Medien wiederzubeleben: Ich würde es aber auch gar nicht versuchen." (Private E-Mail, 6. Mai 2003.)

14 Vgl. *http://www.kurzweilcyberart.com/.* Die Website enthält auch Informationen über die Geschichte von AARON, einschließlich eines Filmclips, in dem eine Zeichenmaschine in Aktion gezeigt wird. Man könnte auch behaupten, dass die Umwandlung von AARON in eine Desktopanwendung einer Trivialisierung des Programms gleichkommt. Dieses Gefühl hat vielleicht mit der enormen Rechnerleistung moderner Computer zu tun. AARON scheint die Bilder zu schnell, zu problemlos zu generieren. Dies ist natürlich nur ein subjektiver Eindruck, der mit der Komplexität des Codes nichts zu tun hat.

15 In Diskussionen verweist Cohen oft auf die Komplexität des Programms, das über drei Jahrzehnte hinweg kontinuierlich weiterentwickelt wurde. Obwohl es als Freeware angeboten wird, betrachtet Cohen AARON offensichtlich weiterhin als seine persönliche künstlerische Schöpfung. Die Freigabe des Quellcodes würde diese Funktion gefährden, allerdings auch zu einem radikaleren kollektiven Schöpfungsprozess führen.

16 *http://www.transmediale.de/01/en/s_juryStatement.htm.*

17 Cramer, Florian und Gabriel, Ulrike: „Software Art", *http://userpage.fu-berlin.de/~cantsin/homepage/writings/software_art/transmediale//software_art_-_transmediale.html.*

18 Eddo Stern hat aufgezeigt, wie Artefakte, Programmfehler und Netzwerkdefekte in interaktiven Multiplayer-Spielen dem Spieler zuweilen die digitale Architektur des Spiels vor Augen führen. Vgl. Sterns Artikel in *Mariosophy: The Culture of Electronic Games,* Hrsg. Huhtamo, Erkki und Kangas, Sonja, The University Press of Finland, Helsinki 2002 (auf Finnisch).

19 Vgl. Schleiner, Anne-Marie: „Velvet-Strike: War Times and Reality Games", *http://www.noemalab.com/sections/ideas/ideas_articles/schleiner_velvet_strike.html.* Schleiner hat auch wichtige Game-Patch-Kunstprojekte kuratiert.

20 Im Fall von *World Skin* geschieht dies, indem absichtlich künstliche, eingefrorene 2D-Bilder in einem navigierbaren 3D-Raum verwendet werden; im Fall von *That Sinking Feeling* durch animatronische Marionettenköpfe, die absichtlich die Äußerungen der Besucher missverstehen und Anzeichen eines schizophrenen Verhaltens aufweisen, das allerdings auch auf einen technischen Defekt zurückgeführt werden könnte.

21 Vgl. Shanken, Edward A.: *The House That Jack Built: Jack Burnham's Concept of 'Software' as a Metaphor for Art, http://www.duke.edu/~giftwrap/House.html.*

22 Burnham, Jack: „Notes on art and information processing", in *Software. Information technology: its new meaning for art* (catalogue), The Jewish Museum, New York 1970, S. 12.

23 SEEK erlangte traurige Berühmtheit, weil einige der Wüstenspringmäuse während der Ausstellung starben. Die Springmäuse fungierten als Symbol für den Menschen in einem technisch übersättigten Umfeld.

24 Vgl. Burnham, Jack: *The Structure of Art,* George Braziller, New York 1971.

25 Gidal, Peter, Hrsg.: *Structural Film Anthology,* BFI, London 1976, S. 14.

26 Gidal, Peter: *Materialist Film,* Routledge, London 1989, S. 17.

27 Sehr hilfreich für die weitere Diskussion dieses Aspekts ist: Le Grice, Malcolm: *Experimental Cinema in the Digital Age,* British Film Institute, London 2001. Le Grice war in der strukturellen Filmbewegung aktiv.

28 Vgl. Cox, Geoff, McLean, Alex and Ward, Adrian: „The Aesthetics of Generative Code", http://generative.net/papers/aesthetics/.

29 Cramer, Florian: „Concepts, Notations, Sofware, Art", *http://userpage.fu-berlin.de/~cantsin/homepage/writings/software_art/concept_notations//concepts_notations_software_art.html.*

Public CulturalProduction Art(Software){

Christiane Paul

The focus on notions of software as art has increased in recent years, which to some extent can be seen as a logical and inevitable consequence of the nature of the digital medium and the power of its structures and rules. Software is a driving force of the digital medium—a creative tool that is culturally and politically "encoded" and embedded in a commercial system.

Software is generally defined as formal instructions that can be executed by a computer. However, there is no digital art that doesn't have a layer of code or algorithms, a procedure of formal instructions that accomplish a "result" in a finite number of steps. Even if the physical and visual manifestations of digital art distract from the layer of data and code, any "digital image" has ultimately been produced by instructions and the software that was used to create or manipulate it. It is precisely this layer of "code" and instructions that constitutes a conceptual level which connects to previous artistic work such as Fluxus' and Dada's experiments with formal variations and the conceptual pieces by Duchamp, Cage and Sol LeWitt that are based on the execution of instructions.

However, it is important to distinguish data constructs such as digitized images or texts from algorithmic code that enables generative processes. One has to make a major distinction between art that uses digital technologies as a tool in the creation process and results in a "traditional" art object (print, photograph, painting, sculpture), and art that employs the technologies as a medium—that is, art that has been created and is stored and presented by means of them. It is only the latter that can potentially exhibit generative processes in real time. Code also cannot be understood as separable from its overall structure. As Adrian Ward, Alex McLean, and Geoff Cox pointed out in *The Aesthetics of Generative Code,*[1] the written form of code—as "a notation of an internal structure that the computer is executing, expressing ideas, logic, and decisions"—is "a computer-readable notation of logic" and not what the computer really executes. The execution takes place through various layers of interpreting and compiling.

Software as art has been discussed in the wider context of generative art (for example at *generative.net)*[2] and has more recently been explored in the context of festivals such as Read_me[3] (explicitly devoted to this art form) and the software art award at Transmediale,[4] or the runme software art repository,[5] an open, moderated database that launched in January 2003. The introduction to the latter site describes software art as a crossover between two seemingly unrelated realms, software and art: while software culture is considered a "living substance" that to a large extent evolves on the Internet and stems from and permeates various cultural realms, art is traditionally presented in exhibitions in galleries and museums or at festivals.[6] The "software art" fusion consequently would introduce software culture into the art world and at the same time expand art beyond its institutional boundaries.

The consideration of software as an art form evidently raises a number of questions: can any software be considered art and, if not, where do we draw the line between software as art and software as a "mere" commercial product? To what extent is the identity of so-called "new media art" or digital art defined by its nature as art based on code? What are the aesthetics of software art and how can they be assessed by traditional art-immanent criteria (or should they be at all)?

Software = Art / (Product + (Formalism / Culturalism))

The Read_me 1.2 jury broadly defined software art as art based on code as formal instructions, or art offering a cultural reflection of software, definitions that cover a broad territory. If one takes a look at the subcategories listed on the runme repository's site, one encounters a landscape that may be fairly confusing in its topography but nevertheless makes important distinctions and can still be roughly summed up under the above mentioned definitions. Labels such as algorithmic appreciation, generative art, code poetry, data transformation, as well as digital folk and artisanship (e.g. ascii art and screen savers) arguably seem to put an emphasis on the aesthetics of formal instructions. On the other hand, classifications such as existing software manipulations (cracks and patches or plug-ins) or political and activist software (e.g. cease-and-desist-ware and software resistance) point to the role of software art as critical reflection of software's cultural status its encoded political or commercial agenda. Games, artistic tools, and conceptual software can fall into either of these two groups, depending on the execution of the respective project and the weight it places on formal aspects or critical reflection.

It would be difficult to argue that software—from Adobe Photoshop to Maya—can in and of itself be considered art. The "art aspect" manifests itself in artist-written software (concept, "writing style," results of execution etc.) or the re-writing / re-engineering of existing software as an act that examines the underbelly, inscribed aesthetics, and agenda of the original construct and thus opens it up to discussion. The inherent hope and promise here is that software production can be seen in the broader context of cultural production or, as Pit Schultz has put it, "that writing code has more meaning than making a program run or crash or sell."[7]

If one rephrases the above classification of software art—as either focused on code as formal instructions or on cultural reflection—as a manifestation of formalism vs. culturalism, one has to pose the question if these are opposite ends of a spectrum and if software art overall can be distinguished according to these categories. In "Concepts, Notations, Software, Art," Florian Cramer outlines that much of contemporary software art takes two opposite approaches to software art and software criticism: either "software as first of all a cultural, politically coded construct" or a focus on "the formal poetics and aesthetics of software code and individual subjectivity expressed in algorithms."[8] The inherent dangers that Cramer identifies for each of these approaches are indeed important to note: as he puts it, a reduction of software art to the first one could make it "a critical footnote to Microsoft desktop computing" that neglects the potential of formal explorations; the second approach could result in "a neo-classicist understanding of software art as beautiful and elegant code." The latter is exemplified in the criteria for evaluation established by computer scientist Donald Knuth, who has been talking about "computer programming as an art" since the 1970s[9]: among these are correctness, maintainability, lucidity, grace of interaction with users, and readability (which would make the Obfuscated C Code Contest a failure in the art of programming).

Cramer aligns the "software as cultural construct" school with artist-programmers such as Matthew Fuller and the group I/O/D or Graham Harwood and the group Mongrel. I/O/D single-handedly "established" alternative browsers as art form with their *Web Stalker*[11] [Fig. 1], an application that allows users to draw "frames" in a blank window and select information they would like to display in them – for example, a graphical map of the site that presents all its individual pages and the links between them; the text from a URL

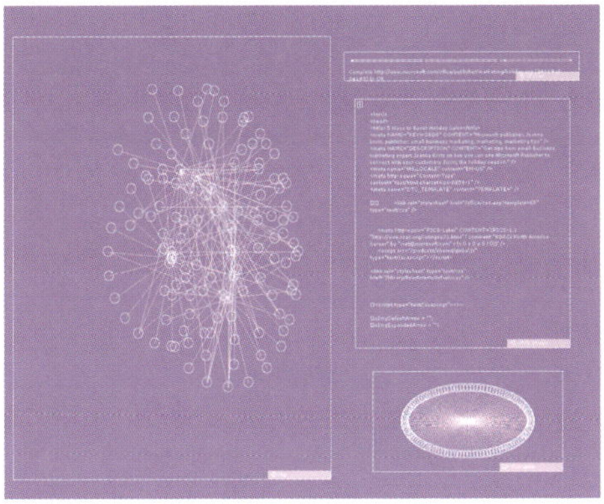

Fig. 1: I/O/D: *Web Stalker*

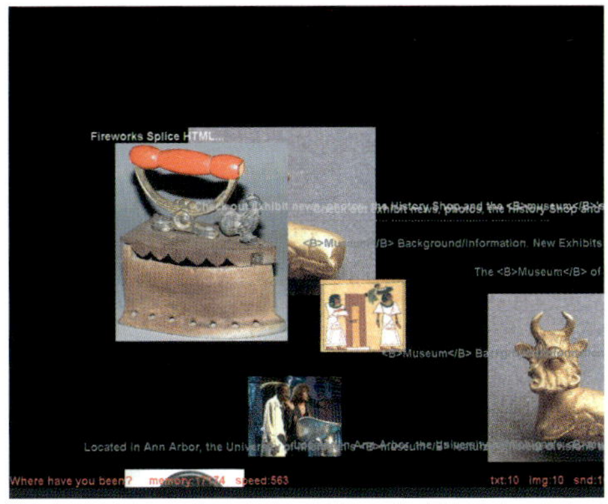

Fig. 2: Maciej Wisniewski: *netomat* ™

and the source code of the HTML page; a "stash" of URLs users would like to save. Although the *WebStalker* didn't display graphics, it expanded the functionality of existing browsers in a way that questions the paradigms of the conventional information display and Internet "architecture." While different in its approach, Maciej Wisniewski's *netomat* ™ [12] [Fig. 2], which abandons the page format of traditional browsers and treats the Internet as one large database of files, would fall in the same category. Using an audio-visual language designed specifically to explore the unexplored Internet, *netomat* ™ reveals how the ever-expanding network interprets and reinterprets cultural concepts and themes and takes visitors for a ride into the Internet's "subconscious."

The approach of the formalism camp is, according to Cramer, exemplified by the groups revolving around Adrian Ward and Alex McLean and participants in the mailing list "eugene." Adrian Ward's *Auto-Illustrator*[13] (winner of the Transmediale.01 software art prize) is a graphic design application that allows users to play with a variety of procedural techniques in the production of their own graphic designs while Alex McLean's *forkbomb.pl*[14] (winner of the Transmediale.02 software art prize) [Fig. 3] is a script written in Perl that creates an artistic impression of the user's computer system under pressure (by repeatedly creating new processes at such a speed that the system comes to a halt).

While the emphasis of the above mentioned projects (or their "creators'" intent) may lean towards one side of the formalism / culturalism spectrum, it would be problematic to miss the more subtle pointers to the other side of the scale in each of these works. The *Web Stalker* may engage notions of the browser as culturally coded construct, but one cannot neglect its distinct aesthetics and their art-historical references. In his essay *Visceral Facades: taking Matta-Clark's crowbar to software*[15], I/O/D's Matthew Fuller establishes a connection between the *WebStalker's* approach to information architecture and American artist Gordon Matta-Clark's technique of literally "splitting" the existing architecture of buildings, an application of formal procedures that would result in a revelation of structural properties. Matta-Clark's as well as the *WebStalker's* "deconstructionism" and "anarchitecture" are as much statements against certain social conditions as they are aesthetic acts oscillating between reconstructions of the destroyed and destructions of closure. Ward's *Auto-Illustrator* may be an application that explores the beauty and elegance of graphic design but at the same time makes a statement about the conventions and standardization of commercial graphic design applications. Taking a closer look at an artist's body of work, it is often hard to align them with one camp or the other. Mark Napier's *FEED*[16] [Fig. 4], which deconstructs webpages into a stream of pixels that are graphed and plotted in nine different displays, can almost be seen as an automization of aesthetic "strategies" from abstract expressionism to minimalism. Napier's *Riot*[17], on the other hand, is an alternative browser that mixes text, images, and links from the three recent URLs that *Riot* users worldwide have accessed into one browser window and collapses territorial conventions like domains, sites, and pages. Illustrating how the Net resists traditional notions of territory, ownership, and authority, it questions the politics of encoding information. If software in general is not neutral but culturally encoded, there always is an interplay between formal and cultural aspects, which obviously varies depending on the emphasis of a specific project.

Aesthetics of Perception / Poetics of Construction

The categorization of artist-written software seems to undergo shifts depending on the manifestation the artwork takes. As mentioned above, any work of digital art incorporates a layer of code. It is noteworthy that digital art installations—even if they are ultimately driven by artist-written software—are seldom considered software art. Although the movements and reactions of robotic devices and objects (or the responses produced by sensors) may be driven or processed by artist-written software, little attention is commonly paid to the conceptual aspects, cultural impact, or "elegance" of the software itself, which remains a hidden force that isn't foregrounded and often induces such complex interactions that its "writing process" simply isn't as accessible as that of a piece of code poetry. Understanding at least the basic nature and language of digital art and its foundation in code-driven or algorithmic processes is an important element in establishing its identity.

What is commonly accepted as "software art" today varies greatly in its focus and manifestation. Software art pieces can present themselves as anything ranging from visuals (driven by a largely hidden layer of artist-written code) or as the written code itself. Code poetry such as Graham Harwood's *London.pl* (by William Blake)[18] would be an example of the latter category. Programming as artistic practice and expression remains largely undervalued and underappreciated. As Florian Cramer puts it, the focus on the purely perceptual aesthetics of art "is a straight continuation of romanticist philosophy and its privileging of aisthesis (perception) over poeisis (construction), cheapened into a restrained concept of art as only that which is tactile, audible, and visible."[19]

What distinguishes software art from other artistic practices, is that, unlike any form of visual art, it requires the artist to write a purely verbal description of their work (which

```
my $strength = $ARGV[0] + 1;

while (not fork) {
  exit unless --$strength;
  print 0;
  twist: while (fork) {
    exit unless --$strength;
    print 1;
  }
}
goto 'twist' if --$strength;
```

Fig. 3: Alex McLean: *forkbomb.pl*

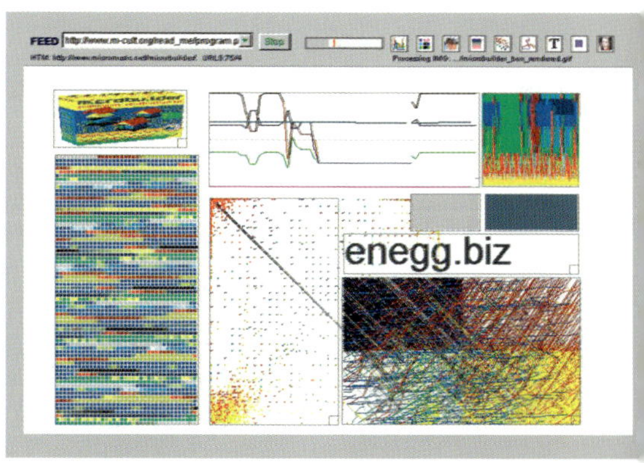

Fig. 4: Mark Napier: *FEED*

then often remains hidden behind the actions resulting from it). In most traditional art forms, the "signature" and "voice" of an artist manifests itself in aesthetics of visuals and execution. The aesthetics of artists who write their own source reveal themselves both in the poetics of the code and its visual results as actions derived from it. Artist John F. Simon, Jr. has repeatedly talked about code as a form of creative writing, where anything from the choice of story to the language of narration and the "story line" embody the artist's voice. Although Cramer sees Ward, McLean and Cox as largely privileging execution, they also emphasize that a separation of code from its resultant actions would result in a limitation of the aesthetic experience[20] and that both ends need to be considered. The study and criticism of software art has to be equally literate in the aesthetics of the back end's construction and the front end's (multi-sensory) perception. The crucial dilemma of software art may very well be that the study of its "backend" will always remain a fringe culture that won't be integrated into the mainstream of (perception-oriented) art criticism. The interconnectedness of written code and the actions it produces also begs the question how transparent the relationship between these two forms can or should be, and whether this might be a criterion for evaluating the art. Meaning, is software art more successful if one can "see" the algorithms at work in the unfolding of visuals / sound and can establish direct connections between the front end and the code driving it? Art that allows this connection to be made will certainly be accessible to a wider audience but it remains questionable whether the transparency of cause-and-effect relationships is a criterion for the quality of art. The issue here seems to be one of reference and is embedded in a larger discussion surrounding the status of representation in digital art. If one defines representation as a "likeness" or image of an external referent (an "object" or "scene" in the broadest sense), digital art in general ultimately represents data—be it an external data set or the data source of its own construction. While this applies to digital art in general, software art is more concerned with the generative construction process of data representation. One could draw the conclusion that we are facing a major transformation of the status of representation itself, which becomes a process that constitutes a convergence of language and mathematics, which in turn has the potential to drive a multi-sensory "display."

This transformation of representation also implies that software art would be more context-dependent in that its data source is always embedded in a specific context. In software art that is focused on data visualization—the creation of visual models for data sets—the issue of context becomes particularly important. For any given set of data, there are multiple possibilities for giving it a visual form, which in turn lend themselves to reconfiguration. This again leads to contextual shifts: the context provided for creating meaning of any given set of data is to a large extent determined by the dynamics of the interface. In this case, an external referent, a set of data, becomes part of its own representation. Context also becomes key when it comes to the success of the visualization process itself. While there needs to be a certain focus on and reflection of the data changes at any point, the visual model tends to turn into a form of wallpaper (no matter how beautiful it is) if it loses the larger context of the data sets.

What complicates matters further is that software art by no means exists in an art-historical and cultural vacuum and constitutes a clearly separable realm in and of itself. The label "software art" may be just one distinguishing characteristic of an artwork that is embedded in multiple contexts. John F. Simon, Jr's color panel series (consisting of custom hardware and software), for example, has strong art-historical references. *Color Panel v 1.0*[21] is a time-based study of color in which Simon's software explores possibilities and "rules" for color as proposed by Bauhaus artists such as Klee and Kandinsky—an investigation of color theory in its relation to motion and time. It would be problematic

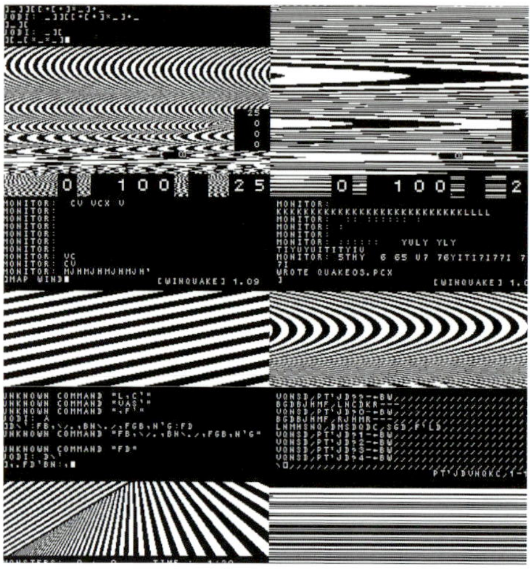

Fig. 5: Jodi: *Untitled Game*

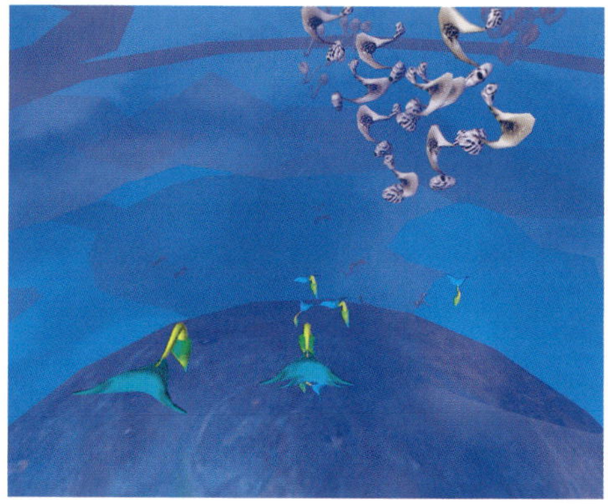

Fig. 6: John Klima: *Ecosystem*

to understand the project as a continuation of Bauhaus tradition without paying attention to the consecutive actions of the code that transcend a single moment in time and space and lead to continuous contextual changes.

There is a whole body of software art that references games and gaming culture—either by writing original games or rewriting and re-engineering existing ones—and has to be understood as an interplay of its contextual framework (games), the code, and its actions. Jodi's "deconstructions" of the original Wolfenstein in their *SOD*[22] or of Quake I in their *Untitled Game*[23] [Fig. 5] cannot be "read" without being literate in the essential characteristics of video games (aesthetics, architecture, user vs. system control etc.). *SOD* replaces the representational elements of the original game with black, white, and grey geometrical forms and creates a new architecture that challenges both orientation and navigation. *Untitled Game* strips Quake of its original architecture, re-engineers its structure and interactivity, and uses the original game engine as a tool for the creation of abstract art. Cory Arcangel created several works (among them *I Shot Andy Warhol* and *Landscape Study #4* [24]) that are based on reverse-engineered cartridges of the Nintendo game *Super Mario Brothers;* the original chips are melted off a Super Mario cartridge and then replaced with his self-manufactured chips. One could assume that the appreciation of these pieces at least to some extent relies on an awareness of the "retro" aesthetics of their original context. Landscape Study #4 fuses traditional landscape photography with gaming aesthetics, creating a scenery that effectively transcends the media it borrows from and seems to evolve into a new manifestation of a pop art genre. The software works of John Klima—among them *glasbead, Go, Fish,* and *ecosystm*[25] [Fig. 6], which represents global currency data in a 3D environmental simulation, where the population and behavior of flocks of insect-like "birds" (representing countries' currencies), are determined, respectively, by the currency's value against the dollar and its daily/yearly volatility—are all deeply influenced by gaming paradigms or aesthetics. While all the artists above seem to work in the field of software art and gaming, their approach to programming and aesthetics is distinctly different and each of these artists' body of work requires a different contextual frame.

The interest in developing criteria for the study and criticism of software art has been growing, but the question remains what impact this art will have both in the field contem-

porary art and culture at large. One could hope that a growing awareness of the art-historical lineage between conceptual art and software art would lead to more acceptance of media art in the larger field of contemporary art. As Matthew Fuller has pointed out, contemporary art has already been engaging with networks and computation by exploring some of their characteristics, such as a "relational aesthetic," but mostly without actually addressing specific digital technologies.[26] The question is not only what software art could do for the art world and its institutions but what these institutions could do for software artists. The nurturing of software and programming literacy is also essential when it comes to expanding the role of software in the broader context of cultural production. Initiatives such as *Processing,* an open project by Ben Fry and Casey Reas[27] (cf. p. 206) that creates an environment for learning the fundamentals of computer programming and is meant as an electronic sketchbook for developing ideas, are a step in that direction. At this point in time, there still needs to be a much broader appreciation of software as art and cultural expression in order to reach a level where software is more than an off-the-shelf product that is judged mostly by its efficiency.
}

---

1 Adrian Ward, Alex McLean, and Geoff Cox, "The Aesthetics of Generative Code," *http://generative.net/papers/aesthetics/*

2 *www.generative.net/*
"Generative art is a term given to work which stems from concentrating on the processes involved in producing an artwork, usually (although not strictly) automated by the use of a machine or computer, or by using mathematic or pragmatic instructions to define the rules by which such artworks are executed." (Adrian Ward)
"Generative art refers to any art practice where the artist creates a process, such as a set of natural language rules, a computer program, a machine, or other procedural invention, which is then set into motion with some degree of autonomy contributing to or resulting in a completed work of art." (Philip Galanter)

3 *www.m-cult.org/read_me/*

4 *www.transmediale.de*

5 *www.runme.org;* developed by Amy Alexander, Florian Cramer, Matthew Fuller, Olga Goriunova, Thomax Kaulmann, Alex McLean, Pit Schultz, Alexei Shulgin, and The Yes Men

6 *www.runme.org/about.tt2*

7 "QuickView on Software Art," *runme.org/project/+quickview*

8 Florian Cramer, "Concepts, Notations, Software, Art" (2002), *http://userpage.fu-berlin.de/~cantsin/homepage/writings/software_art/concept_notations//concepts_notations_software_art.html*

9 Donald E. Knuth, "Literate Programming," *CSLI Lecture Notes.* Number 27. Center for the Study of Language and Information. Stanford, CA, 1992

10 *www.ioccc.org/*

11 I/O/D, *WebStalker, www.backspace.org/iod/*

12 Maciej Wisniewski, *etomat ™, www.netomat.net*

13 Adrian Ward, *Auto-Illustrator, www.auto-illustrator.com*

14 Alex McLean, *forkbomb.pl, www.slab.org*

15 Matthew Fuller, "Visceral Facades: taking Matta-Clark's crowbar to software," *www.backspace.org/iod/Visceral.html*

16 Mark Napier, *FEED, www.potatoland.org/feed/*

17 Mark Napier, *Riot, www.potatoland.org/riot/*

18 Graham Harwood, *London.pl* by William Blake, *www.runme.org/project/+londonpl/*

19 Ibid. [8]

20 Ibid. [1]

21 John F. Simon, Jr., *Color Panel v 1., www.numeral.com/panels/colorpanelv1.0.html*

22 Jodi, *SOD, http://sod.jodi.org/*

23 Jodi, *Untitled Game, www.untitled-game.org*

24 Cory Arcangel, *I Shot Andy Warhol,* Landscape Studies, *http://beigerecords.com/cory*

25 *www.cityarts.com*

26 Ibid. [7]

27 *http://proce55ing.net/*

Kunst als öffentliche kulturelle Produktion (Software){

Christiane Paul

Seit einigen Jahren wird Software zunehmend als Kunstform betrachtet – eine Sichtweise, die gewissermaßen als logische und unvermeidbare Folge des eigentlichen Wesens des digitalen Mediums und des Einflusses seiner Strukturen und Regeln aufgefasst werden kann. Software ist die treibende Kraft digitaler Medien – ein in ein kommerzielles System integriertes, kulturell und politisch „codiertes" kreatives Mittel.

Software wird allgemein als von einem Computer ausführbares Set formaler Befehle definiert. Es gibt jedoch keine Form der digitalen Kunst, die nicht eine Code- oder Algorithmusebene aufweist, die mittels formaler Befehle in einer bestimmten Anzahl von Schritten ein „Ergebnis" generiert. Selbst wenn die physischen und visuellen Manifestationen digitaler Kunst die Ebene der Datensätze und Codes in den Hintergrund drängen, wird jedes „digitale Bild" letztlich über Befehle und die zur Herstellung oder Manipulation des Bildes verwendete Software erzeugt. Die Ebene des „Codes" und der Befehle schafft einen konzeptuellen Rahmen, der an die Tradition früherer künstlerischer Werke wie Fluxus' oder Dadas Experiment mit formalen Variationen oder die, auf der Ausführung von Befehlen basierten, konzeptuellen Werke von Duchamp, Cage und Sol LeWitt anknüpft.

Es ist allerdings wichtig, Datenkonstrukte wie digitalisierte Bilder oder Texte von Algorithmen zur Steuerung von generativen Prozessen zu unterscheiden. Es muss eine klare Unterscheidung zwischen Kunst, die digitale Technologien als Hilfsmittel für den künstlerischen Schaffungsprozess einsetzt und in einem „traditionellen" Kunstobjekt (Druck, Fotografie, Gemälde, Skulptur) resultiert, und Kunst, die zur Schaffung, Speicherung und Präsentation digitale Technologien als Medium nutzt, getroffen werden. Nur letztere kann potenziell generative Prozesse in Echtzeit aufzeigen. Code sollte auch nicht als von den übergeordneten Strukturen isolierbare Einheit betrachtet werden. Wie Adrian Ward, Alex McLean und Geoff Cox in *The Aesthetics of Generative Code*[1] aufgezeigt haben, ist die schriftliche Form des Codes – als „vom Computer ausgeführte Notation einer internen Struktur, über die Ideen, Logik und Entscheidungen zum Ausdruck gebracht werden" – eine „computerlesbare Notation einer logischen Abfolge" und nicht die vom Computer tatsächlich ausgeführte Operation. Die eigentliche Ausführung der Befehle erfolgt in verschiedenen Ebenen der Interpretation und Kompilierung.

Software als Kunst wird im größeren Umfeld der Generativen Kunst (beispielsweise bei *generative.net*[2] und seit einiger Zeit auch im Rahmen von Festivals wie *Read_me*[3] (dieses Festival widmet sich explizit dieser Kunstform), dem Softwarepreis der *Transmediale*[4] oder dem *runme software art repository*[5], einer im Januar 2003 gegründeten offenen, moderierten Datenbank, diskutiert. Im Einführungstext zur *runme*-Website wird Softwarekunst als Crossover zwischen zwei scheinbar nicht miteinander verbundenen Bereichen – Software und Kunst – definiert: Während Softwarekultur als „lebende Masse" betrachtet wird, die sich primär über das Internet entwickelt und verschiedene kulturelle Sphären in sich vereint und durchdringt, wird Kunst traditionellerweise im Rahmen von Ausstellungen in Galerien und Museen oder auf Festivals präsentiert.[6] Die Fusion von Software und Kunst zur „Softwarekunst" führe daher Softwarekultur in die Kunstwelt ein und bewirke gleichzeitig eine Erweiterung der Kunst über ihre institutionellen Grenzen hinweg.

Wird Software als Kunstform aufgefasst, stellt sich unweigerlich eine Reihe von Fragen: Kann jede Form von Software als Kunst betrachtet werden und, falls nicht, wo liegt die Grenze zwischen Software als Kunst und Software als „rein“ kommerziellem Produkt? Inwieweit wird die Identität der so genannten „Neuen Medien-Kunst“ oder der digitalen Kunst durch ihr Wesen als code-basierte Kunst definiert? Worin besteht die Ästhetik von Softwarekunst und wie kann diese von traditionellen, kunstimmanenten Kriterien erfasst werden (bzw. sollte sie mittels derartiger Kriterien erfasst werden)?

Software = Kunst / (Produkt + (Formalismus / Kulturalismus))

Die *Read_me 1.2*-Jury definierte Softwarekunst sehr weit gefasst als Kunst, die auf aus formalen Befehlen bestehendem Code basiert oder eine kulturelle Reflexion von Software erlaubt – Definitionen, die ein sehr breites Spektrum abdecken. Werden die auf der *runme repository*-Website angeführten Unterkategorien herangezogen, eröffnet sich eine Landschaft, die in ihrer Topografie relativ verwirrend erscheinen mag, allerdings dennoch einige wichtige Unterscheidungen präsentiert und mittels der oben angeführten Definitionen grob zusammengefasst werden kann. Etikettierungen wie algorithmisches Verständnis, Generative Kunst, Code-Poesie, Datentransformation oder digitale Folklore und Kunsthandwerk (z. B. Ascii-Kunst oder Bildschirmschoner) scheinen das Hauptaugenmerk auf die Ästhetik formaler Befehle zu legen. Die Namen, mit denen aktuelle Softwaremanipulationen (Cracks, Patches oder Plug-Ins) oder politische und aktivistische Software (z. B. Cease-and-Desist-Ware und Software-Widerstand) bezeichnet werden, betonen hingegen die Rolle von Softwarekunst als kritische Reflexion des kulturellen Status und der politischen oder wirtschaftlichen Agenda von Software. Spiele, künstlerische Hilfsmittel und konzeptuelle Software können, je nach Ausführung des jeweiligen Projekts und dem Gewicht, das auf formale Aspekte bzw. kritische Reflexion gelegt wird, zu beiden Gruppen gezählt werden.
Es ließe sich schwerlich argumentieren, dass jede Form von Software – von Adobe Photoshop bis Maya – als Kunst betrachtet werden kann. Der „künstlerische Aspekt“ zeigt sich in künstlerisch gestalteter Software (Konzept, „Schreibstil“, Ergebnisse der Ausführung von Befehlen etc.) oder der Umschreibung / Umformung bestehender Software als Prozess, der die dem originalen Konstrukt inhärente Ästhetik und Agenda untersucht und dadurch zur Diskussion stellt. Diesem Vorgang liegen die Hoffnung und das Versprechen zugrunde, dass Softwareproduktion im größeren Umfeld der kulturellen Produktion akzeptiert wird, oder, wie Pit Schultz es formulierte, „dass das Schreiben von Code einen tieferen Sinn hat, als nur ein Programm zum Laufen zu bringen oder es abstürzen zu lassen oder gute Verkaufszahlen zu erzielen“.[7]
Paraphrasiert man die oben angeführte Definition von Softwarekunst – aus formalen Befehlen bestehender Code oder kulturelle Reflexion – als Manifestation von Formalismus vs. Kulturalismus, stellt sich die Frage, ob diese beiden Definitionen zwei entgegengesetzte Pole eines Spektrums vertreten bzw. ob Softwarekunst mittels dieser Kategorien klassifiziert werden kann. In *Concepts, Notations, Software, Art* zeigt Florian Cramer auf, dass ein großer Teil der zeitgenössischen Softwarekunst zwei unterschiedliche Ansätze zu Softwarekunst und Softwarekritik verfolgt: „Software als primär kulturell und politisch codiertes Konstrukt“ oder Ansätze, die „die formale Poetik und Ästhetik des Softwarecodes und die in Algorithmen ausgedrückte individuelle Subjektivität“ betonen.[8] Die inhärenten Gefahren, die Cramer bei beiden Zugängen sieht, verdienen nähere Beachtung: Eine Reduktion von Softwarekunst auf ersteren Ansatz könnte diese, so Cramer, zu „einer kritischen Fußnote zum Microsoft-Desktop-Publishing“ degradieren, die das Potenzial formaler Explorationen nicht erkennt; der zweite Zugang hingegen könnte in „einem neoklassizistischen Verständnis von Softwarekunst als schönem und elegantem Code“ resultieren. Der zweite Zugang lässt sich anhand der vom Informatiker Donald

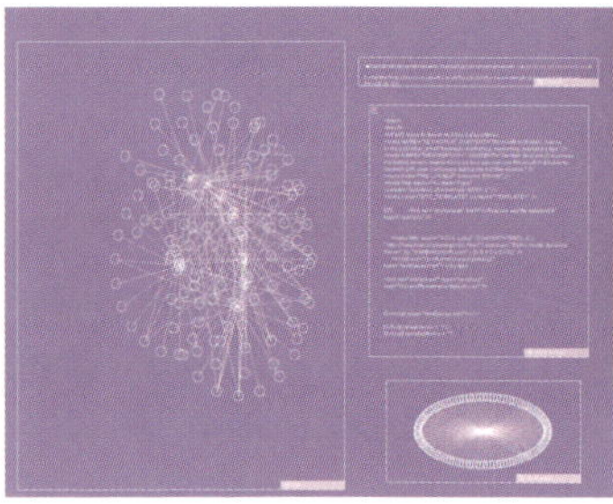
Abb. 1: I/O/D: *Web Stalker*

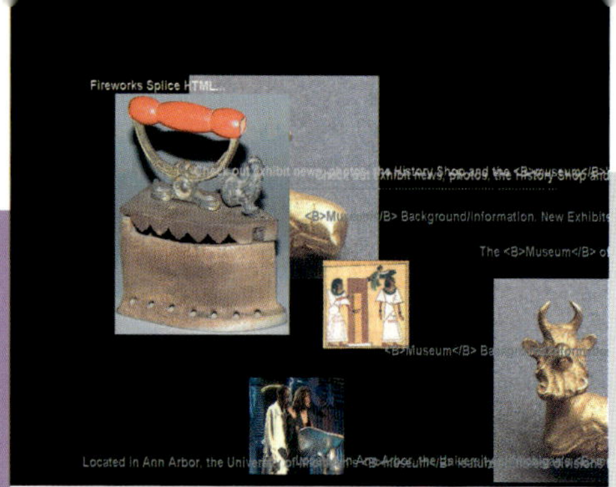
Abb. 2: Maciej Wisniewski: *netomat™*

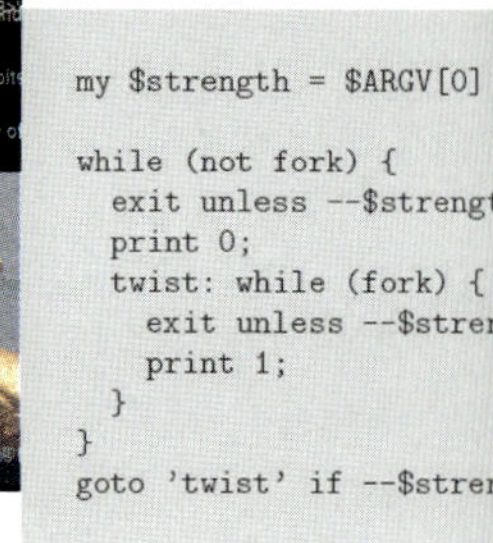

Abb. 3:
Alex McLean:
forkbomb.pl

Kuhn erstellten Bewertungskriterien veranschaulichen, der bereits seit den 1970er-Jahren von „Programmieren als Kunst“ spricht:[9] Zu diesen Kriterien zählen Korrektheit, Wartungsfreundlichkeit, Klarheit, Möglichkeiten der Benutzerinteraktion und Lesbarkeit – was den *International Obfuscated C Code Contest*[10] als Fehlschlag der Programmierkunst klassifiziert. Cramer verbindet die „Software als kulturelles Konstrukt“-Schule mit Programmierkünstlern wie Matthew Fuller und der I/O/D-Gruppe oder Graham Harwood und der Gruppe Mongrel. I/O/D „schufen“ mit ihrem *Web Stalker*[11] [Abb. 1] im Alleingang alternative Browser als Kunstform. Der Benutzer zeichnet „Rahmen“ in einem leeren Fenster und wählt jene Informationen aus, die in diesen Rahmen angezeigt werden sollen – beispielsweise eine grafische Karte der Website mit allen Einzelseiten und Links, Text aus einer URL und den Quellcode der HTML-Seite, eine Liste von URLs, die gespeichert werden sollen. Obwohl der *WebStalker* keine Grafiken anzeigt, erweiterte er die Funktionalität bestehender Browser auf eine Art und Weise, die die Paradigmen der konventionellen Informationspräsentation und Internet-„Architektur“ in Frage stellt. Maciej Wisniewskis *netomat™*[12] [Abb. 2], der das Seitenformat traditioneller Browser aufgibt und das Internet als einzige große Datenbank unzähliger Einzeldateien betrachtet, schlägt zwar einen anderen Weg ein, würde jedoch zur selben Kategorie gezählt werden. Mittels einer audiovisuellen Sprache, die speziell zur Erforschung des bislang unerforschten Internet entwickelt wurde, demonstriert *netomat™,* wie das kontinuierlich wachsende Web kulturelle Konzepte und Themen interpretiert und re-interpretiert und Benutzern Zugang zum „Unterbewusstsein“ des Internets verschafft.
Cramer zufolge zeigt sich der Zugang der Formalisten in den Arbeiten der Gruppen um Adrian Ward und Alex McLean und den Abonnenten der Mailingliste „eu-gene“. Adrian Wards *Auto-Illustrator*[13] (Gewinner des Transmediale.01-Preises für Softwarekunst) ist eine Grafikdesign-Anwendung, die Benutzern das Ausprobieren einer Vielzahl von Prozeduren zur Erstellung ihres persönlichen Grafikdesigns ermöglicht. Bei Alex McLeans *forkbomb.pl*[14] (Gewinner des Transmediale.02-Preises für Softwarekunst) [Abb. 3] handelt es sich hingegen um ein Perl-Script, das ein künstlerisches Abbild des Computersystems unter Belastung schafft (indem wiederholt neue Prozesse in einer solchen Geschwindigkeit gestartet werden, dass es letztendlich zum Systemstillstand kommt).
Selbst wenn die Grundausrichtung der oben erwähnten Projekte (bzw. der Absicht ihrer „Erfinder“) sich einem Ende der Formalismus/Kulturalismus-Skala zuneigt, dürfen die subtileren Anzeichen für eine Bewegung in die Gegenrichtung, die sich in jedem dieser Projekte zeigen, nicht ignoriert werden. Der *Web Stalker* mag Browser als kulturell codierte Konstrukte betrachten, kann jedoch nicht seine ausgeprägte Ästhetik und die klaren kunsthistorischen Referenzen verleugnen. In seinem Essay *Visceral Facades: taking Matta-Clark's crowbar to software*[15] schafft Matthew Fuller von der I/O/D-Gruppe eine Verbindung zwischen dem Verständnis des *WebStalker* für die Informationsarchitektur und der Technik des amerikanischen Künstlers Gordon

Matta-Clark der buchstäblichen „Aufsplitterung" der Architektur von Gebäuden, einer aus formalen Prozeduren bestehenden Anwendung zur Identifikation der strukturellen Eigenschaften von Gebäuden. Der „Dekonstruktivismus" und die „Anarchitektur", die in Matta-Clarks Arbeiten bzw. im *WebStalker* zu finden sind, sind ebenso Stellungnahmen gegen bestimmte soziale Bedingungen, wie sie auch ästhetische Handlungen zwischen der Rekonstruktion des Zerstörten und der Zerstörung der Abgeschlossenheit sind. Wards *Auto-Illustrator* ist vielleicht eine Anwendung zur Untersuchung der Schönheit und Eleganz eines grafischen Designs, gleichzeitig jedoch auch eine Stellungnahme zu den Konventionen und der Standardisierung kommerzieller Grafikdesign-Anwendungen. Bei genauerer Analyse des Oeuvres eines Künstlers ist es oft schwer, diesen einem bestimmten Lager zuzuordnen. Mark Napiers *FEED*[16] [Abb. 4], das Webseiten in einen Pixelstrom dekonstruiert, die auf neun unterschiedlichen Anzeigen grafisch dargestellt und geplottet werden, kann gleichsam als Automatisierung ästhetischer Strukturen vom Abstrakten Expressionismus hin zum Minimalismus betrachtet werden. Napiers *Riot*[17] ist hingegen ein alternativer Browser, der Text, Bilder und Links aus den drei letzten URLs, die *Riot*-Benutzer weltweit in einem Browserfenster aufgerufen haben, vermischt und territoriale Konventionen wie Domains, Sites und Webseiten zusammenbrechen lässt. Indem aufgezeigt wird, wie das Internet traditionellen Vorstellungen von Territorialität, Besitztum und Autorität widersteht, wird die Politik der Verschlüsselung von Informationen hinterfragt. Wenn Software im Allgemeinen nicht neutral, sondern kulturell kodiert ist, existiert ein beständiges Zusammenspiel von formalen und kulturellen Aspekten, das je nach Schwerpunkt eines spezifischen Projekts gewisse Variationen aufweist.

Ästhetik der Wahrnehmung/Poetik der Konstruktion

Die Kategorisierung von künstlerischer Software scheint je nach konkreter Manifestation des Kunstwerks permanenten Veränderungen ausgesetzt zu sein. Wie bereits erwähnt, umfasst jedes digitale Kunstwerk eine Ebene des Codes. Es scheint wichtig anzumerken, dass digitale Kunstinstallationen – selbst wenn sie von künstlerischer Software gesteuert sind – nur selten als Softwarekunst betrachtet werden. Obwohl die Bewegungen und Reaktionen von Robotern und Objekten (bzw. die von Sensoren ausgelösten Reaktionen) von künstlerischer Software gesteuert oder verarbeitet werden, wird im Allgemeinen den konzeptuellen Aspekten, den kulturellen Auswirkungen oder der „Eleganz" der Software selbst wenig Aufmerksamkeit zuteil; die Software bleibt eine versteckte Kraft im Hintergrund und generiert häufig

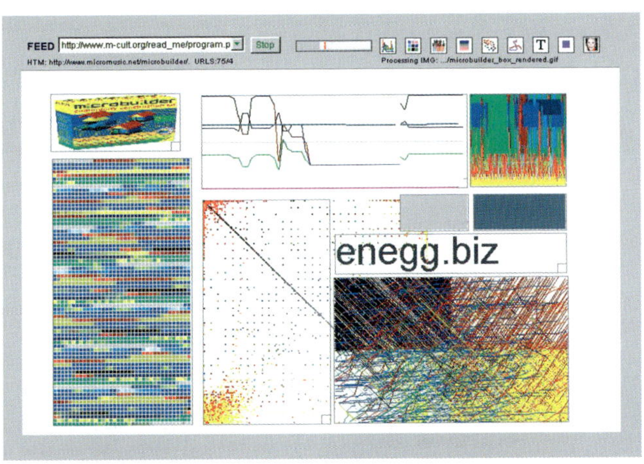

Abb. 4: Mark Napier: *FEED*

derart komplexe Interaktionen, dass ihr „Schreibprozess" schwerer zugänglich ist als ein Kunstwerk der Code-Poesie. Ein wesentliches Element bei der Identitätsfindung digitaler Kunst ist das Verständnis der grundlegenden Natur und Sprache von digitaler Kunst und ihres Ursprungs in Algorithmen und Programmcode.
Was heute allgemein als „Softwarekunst" akzeptiert wird, unterscheidet sich stark in der Ausrichtung und Manifestation dieser Kunstform. Werke der Softwarekunst können sich in vielfältiger Gestalt präsentieren, von visuellen Manifestationen (gesteuert von einer großteils verdeckten Ebene des künstlerischen Codes) bis hin zum schriftlichen Code selbst. Code-Poesie wie etwa Graham Harwoods *London.pl* (von William Blake)[18] wäre ein Beispiel für letztere Kategorie. Programmieren als Kunstform und künstlerische Ausdrucksweise bleibt weiterhin stark unterbewertet und unterschätzt. Florian Cramer zufolge ist der Fokus auf einer rein perzeptuellen Ästhetik der Kunst „[...] eine klare Fortsetzung der romantischen Philosophie und der Privilegierung der Aisthesis (Wahrnehmung) gegenüber der Poeisis (Konstruktion), herabgewürdigt zu einem eingeschränktem Verständnis von Kunst als das, was angreifbar, hörbar und sichtbar ist".[19]
Was Softwarekunst von anderen Kunstpraktiken unterscheidet, ist die Tatsache, dass der Künstler – anders als bei allen Formen der visuellen Kunst – eine rein verbale Beschreibung seiner Arbeit liefern muss (die dann oft hinter den daraus resultierenden Prozessen verborgen bleibt). In den meisten traditionellen Kunstformen manifestiert sich die „Unterschrift" und „Stimme" eines Künstlers in der Ästhetik visueller Eindrücke und der Ausführung. Die Ästhetik von Künstlern, die ihr eigenes Quellprogramm schreiben, zeigt sich sowohl in der Poesie des Codes als auch der daraus resultierenden visuellen Ergebnisse. Der Künstler John F. Simon Jr. hat den Code des Öfteren als Form des kreativen Schreibens bezeichnet, bei der von der Auswahl der „Geschichte" bis zur Sprache der Narration und Handlung alle Einzelschritte die „Stimme" des Künstlers zum Ausdruck bringen. Obwohl Cramer der Ansicht ist, dass Ward, McLean und Cox primär die Ausführung des Programms forcieren, betonen sie dennoch, dass eine Trennung des Codes von den daraus resultierenden Aktionen zu einer Einschränkung der ästhetischen Erfahrung[20] führen würde und beide Seiten des Spektrums Beachtung finden müssten.
Für die Untersuchung und Kritik von Softwarekunst ist es nötig, sowohl über die Ästhetik der Konstruktion von nachgeschalteten Rechnern als auch die (multisensorische) Wahrnehmung auf Seiten der Benutzerrechner Bescheid zu wissen. Das folgenschwere Dilemma von Softwarekunst könnte durchaus sein, dass die Untersuchung der „Nachrechnerseite" stets ein Randbereich bleiben wird, der nicht in den Mainstream der wahrnehmungsorientierten Kunstkritik integriert wird. Der Zusammenhang zwischen dem schriftlichen Code und den daraus resultierenden Prozessen wirft auch die Frage auf, wie transparent die Beziehung zwischen diesen zwei Aspekten sein kann oder sollte bzw. ob dies ein Kriterium für die Bewertung von Kunst sein kann. Ist Softwarekunst erfolgreicher, wenn man die Algorithmen, die hinter der Entfaltung von visuellen/klanglichen Phänomen stehen, „sehen" kann und direkte Verbindungen zwischen der Benutzerseite und dem dahinter liegenden Code herstellen kann? Kunst, die die Herstellung dieser Verbindung erlaubt, wird sicher einem größerem Publikum zugänglich sein. Es bleibt jedoch fraglich, ob die Transparenz von Ursache-Wirkung-Beziehungen ein geeignetes Kriterium für die Qualität von Kunst darstellt. Es scheint sich hier um eine Frage der Referenz zu handeln, die in eine weiter gefasste Diskussion hinsichtlich des Status der Repräsentation von digitaler Kunst eingebettet ist. Wird Repräsentation als „Ähnlichkeit" oder Abbild eines externen Referenten (als „Objekt" oder „Rahmen" im weitesten Sinn) definiert, repräsentiert digitale Kunst letztlich stets Daten – seien es externe Daten oder eine selbst erzeugte Datenquelle. Während dies auf digitale Kunst im Allgemeinen zutrifft, konzentriert sich Softwarekunst stärker auf den generativen Konstruktionsprozess der Datenrepräsentation. Es liegt daher die Schlussfolgerung nahe,

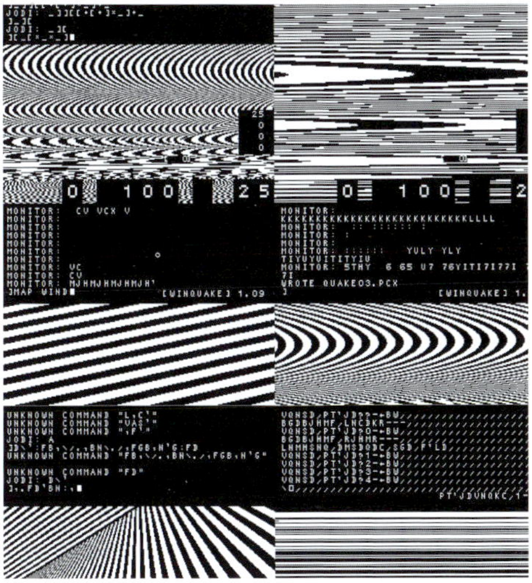

Abb. 5: Jodi: *Untitled Game*

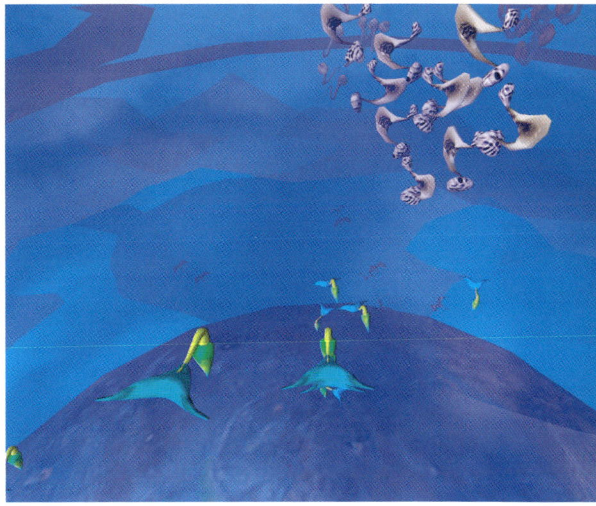

Abb. 6: John Klima: *Ecosystem*

dass wir eine umfassende Transformation des Status der Repräsentation selbst erleben, die zu einem Prozess der Konvergenz von Sprache und Mathematik wird, was umgekehrt wiederum das Potenzial zur Steuerung eines multisensorischen „Displays“ birgt.

Diese Transformation der Repräsentation impliziert auch, dass Softwarekunst in stärkerem Maße kontextabhängig ist, da ihre Datenquelle stets in einen spezifischen Kontext eingebettet ist. Bei Softwarekunst, die primär auf Datenvisualisierung abzielt – die Schaffung von visuellen Modellen für bestimmte Datensätze –, ist eine geeignete Kontextualisierung besonders wichtig. Jeder Datensatz kann auf verschiedene Arten visualisiert werden; diese Visualisierungsmöglichkeiten eignen sich wiederum für eine Neukonfiguration. Dadurch verändert sich der Kontext: Der Kontext zur Erschließung des Sinns eines gewissen Datensatzes ist zu einem großen Teil von der Dynamik des Interface bestimmt. In diesem Fall kann ein externer Referent, ein Datensatz, Teil seiner eigenen Repräsentation werden. Auch für den Erfolg des Visualisierungsprozesses per se ist der Kontext entscheidend. Während Veränderungen der Datensätze stets beachtet und entsprechend reflektiert werden müssen, verblasst das visuelle Modell häufig zu einer Art von „Tapete“ (wie schön diese auch immer sein mag), wenn der größere Kontext der Datensätze außer Acht gelassen wird.

Dieser Prozess wird zusätzlich dadurch erschwert, dass Softwarekunst weder in einem kunsthistorischen und kulturellen Vakuum existiert noch ein in sich klar abgrenzbares Gebiet darstellt. Das Label „Softwarekunst“ kann lediglich ein charakteristisches Merkmal eines Kunstwerks sein, das in verschiedene Kontexte eingebettet ist. John F. Simon Jr.' Farbbildserie (bestehend aus eigens angepasster Hard- und Software) weist beispielsweise viele kunsthistorische Referenzen auf. *Color Panel v 1.0* [21] ist eine zeitbasierte Farbstudie, in der Simons Software die Möglichkeiten und „Regeln“ von Farben untersucht, wie dies von Bauhaus-Künstlern wie Klee und Kandinsky vorgeschlagen wurde – eine Untersuchung der Farbtheorie in Bezug auf Bewegung und Zeit. Es wäre problematisch, das Projekt als eine Fortsetzung der Bauhaus-Tradition aufzufassen, ohne entsprechendes Augenmerk auf die nachfolgenden aus dem Code resultierenden Aktivitäten zu legen, die über einzelne Momente in Zeit und Raum hinausgehen und zu kontinuierlichen Kontextveränderungen führen.

Es existiert eine breite Palette von Softwarekunst, die Bezug auf Spiele oder die Spielkultur nimmt – entweder durch die Programmierung von neuen Spielen oder das Umschreiben und

Umformen bestehender Spiele – und als Zusammenspiel zwischen dem kontextuellen Rahmen (Spiele), dem Code und den daraus folgenden Handlungen betrachtet werden muss. Jodis „Dekonstruktion" des originalen Wolfenstein-Spiels in *SOD*[22] oder die Dekonstruktion von *Quake I* in *Untitled Game*[23] [Abb. 5] kann ohne grundlegende Kenntnisse über Videospiele (Ästhetik, Architektur, Benutzer/System-Interaktion etc.) nicht „gelesen" werden. *SOD* ersetzt die Repräsentationselemente des Originalspiels durch schwarze, weiße und graue geometrische Formen und schafft eine neue Architektur, die sowohl Orientierung als auch Navigation zu einer Herausforderung werden lässt. *Untitled Game* löst die Originalstruktur von *Quake* auf, programmiert seine Struktur und Interaktivität neu und nutzt die originale Game-Engine als Mittel zur Schaffung abstrakter Kunst. Cory Arcangel schuf mehrere Arbeiten (darunter *I Shot Andy Warhol* und *Landscape Study #4* [24]), die auf rückentwickelten Cartridges des Nintendo-Spiels *Super Mario Brothers* basieren; die Originalchips werden von einer *Super Mario*-Cartridge ausgelötet und durch selbst erzeugte Chips ersetzt. Man könnte annehmen, dass die Akzeptanz dieser Werke sich zumindest bis zu einem gewissen Grad auf die „Retro"-Ästhetik ihres Originalkontextes stützt. *Landscape Study #4* verbindet traditionelle Landschaftsfotografie mit Spielästhetik und schafft eine Szenerie, die sehr wirksam jene Medien, aus denen Elemente übernommen werden, durchdringt und sich zu einer neuen Form des Pop-Art-Genres zu entwickeln scheint. Die Softwarearbeiten von John Klima – darunter *glasbead, Go, Fish* und *ecosystm*[25] [Abb. 6], die globale Währungsdaten in einer 3D-Simulation präsentieren, in der die Population und das Verhalten von insektenartigen „Vogel"-Schwärmen (diese symbolisieren die „Währungen" der einzelnen Länder) vom Wert ihrer jeweiligen Währung im Vergleich zum Dollar bzw. der täglichen/jährlichen Volatilität ihrer Währung beeinflusst wird – sind alle stark von den Paradigmen der Spielszene und der Spielästhetik geprägt. Während die oben erwähnten Künstler alle im Bereich der Softwarekunst bzw. im Spielbereich tätig zu sein scheinen, unterscheiden sich doch ihre Zugänge zu Programmierung und Ästhetik; das Oeuvre dieser verschiedenen Künstler erfordert einen unterschiedlichen kontextuellen Rahmen.

Das Interesse an der Entwicklung von Kriterien zur Untersuchung und Kritik von Softwarekunst nimmt stetig zu, doch stellt sich weiterhin die Frage, welche Auswirkungen diese Kunstform sowohl auf den Bereich der zeitgenössischen Kunst als auch die Gesamtkultur haben wird. Es besteht die Hoffnung, dass ein wachsendes Bewusstsein hinsichtlich der kunsthistorischen "Verwandtschaft" von Konzeptkunst und Softwarekunst zu einer größeren Akzeptanz der Medienkunst im Umfeld der zeitgenössischen Kunst führt. Wie Matthew Fuller aufzeigt, beschäftigt die zeitgenössische Kunst sich bereits mit Netzwerken und Computertechnologie, indem wesentliche Merkmale dieser beiden Bereiche, wie z. B. eine „relationale Ästhetik", erforscht werden; selten jedoch erstreckt sich dieses Interesse auf spezifische digitale Technologien.[26] Es stellt sich nicht nur die Frage, was Softwarekunst für die Kunstwelt und ihre Institutionen bringen könnte, sondern wie diese Institutionen Softwarekünstler unterstützen könnten. Die Förderung von Software- und Programmierkenntnissen ist überaus wichtig, wenn die Rolle von Software im Rahmen der kulturellen Produktion erweitert werden soll. Initiativen wie beispielsweise *Processing,* ein offenes Projekt von Ben Fry und Casey Reas (siehe Seite 210),[27] das eine geeignete Umgebung zum Erwerb von grundlegenden Kenntnissen des Programmierens schafft und als elektronisches Skizzenbuch zur Entwicklung von Ideen gedacht ist, sind ein erster Schritt in diese Richtung. In der gegenwärtigen Situation muss allerdings die Anerkennung von Software als Kunstform und kulturelles Ausdrucksmittel stärker als bisher forciert werden, um eine Ebene der Akzeptanz zu erreichen, auf der Software als mehr als nur ein Produkt aus dem Regal, das primär an seiner Effizienz gemessen wird, betrachtet wird.

}

Aus dem Amerikanischen von Sonja Pöllabauer

1 Ward, Adrian, McLean, Alex und Cox, Geoff: *The Aesthetics of Generative Code, http://generative.net/papers/aesthetics/*

2 *http://www.generative.net/*
„Generative Kunst dient als Bezeichnung für Arbeiten, die sich mit den Prozessen zur Schaffung eines Kunstwerks beschäftigen, die üblicherweise (wenn auch nicht ausschließlich) durch Einsatz einer Maschine oder eines Computers oder durch mathematische oder pragmatische Befehle zur Definition der Regeln, mittels derer diese Kunstwerke ausgeführt werden, automatisiert werden." (Adrian Ward)
„Generative Kunst umfasst jede Form von Kunst, bei der der Künstler einen Prozess auslöst, wie beispielsweise ein Set von natürlichen Sprachregeln, ein Computerprogramm, eine Maschine oder andere prozedurale Phänomene, der dann mit einem gewissen Grad von Autonomie in Bewegung gesetzt wird und zu einem vollendeten Kunstwerk beiträgt oder in einem solchen resultiert." (Philip Galanter)

3 *http://www.m-cult.org/read_me/*

4 *http://www.transmediale.de*

5 *http://www.runme.org;* entwickelt von Amy Alexander, Florian Cramer, Matthew Fuller, Olga Goriunova, Thomax Kaulmann, Alex McLean, Pit Schultz, Alexei Shulgin und The Yes Men

6 *http://www.runme.org/about.tt2*

7 *QuickView on Software Art, runme.org/project/+quickview*

8 Cramer, Florian: *Concepts, Notations, Software, Art,* 2002, *http://userpage.fu-berlin.de/~cantsin/homepage/writings/software_art/concept_notations//concepts_notations_software_art.html*

9 Knutz, Donald E.: „Literate Programming", in *CSLI Lecture Notes,* Number 27, Center for the Study of Language and Information, Stanford, CA 1992

10 *http://www.ioccc.org/*

11 I/O/D: *Web Stalker, http://www.backspace.org/iod/*

12 Wisniewski, Maciej: *netomat™, http://www.netomat.net*

13 Ward, Adrian: *Auto-Illustrator, http://www.auto-illustrator.com*

14 McLean, Alex: *forkbomb.pl, http://www.slab.org*

15 Fuller, Matthew: *Visceral Facades: taking Matta-Clark's crowbar to software, http://www.backspace.org/iod/Visceral.html*

16 Napier, Mark: *FEED,http://www.potatoland.org/feed/*

17 Napier, Mark: *Riot, http://www.potatoland.org/riot/*

18 Harwood, Graham: *London.pl* von William Blake, *http://www.runme.org/project/+londonpl/*

19 Ibid. [8]

20 Ibid. [1]

21 Simon, John F., Jr.: *Color Panel v 1.0, http://www.numeral.com/panels/colorpanelv1.0.html*

22 Jodi: *SOD, http://sod.jodi.org/*

23 Jodi: *Untitled Game, www.untitled-game.org*

24 Arcangel, Cory: *I Shot Andy Warhol,* Landscape Studies, *http://beigerecords.com/cory*

25 *http://www.cityarts.com*

26 Ibid. [7]

27 *http://proce55ing.net/*

The Universal Datawork

richard kriesche

1. Introduction

At the height of the Information Age, Ars Electronica 2003 asks whether "the language of the computers [is] becoming the lingua franca of the global Information Society" and follows this up by voicing the presumption "that the materia prima" of this very society "are digital codes."

If we take up this formulation, we see that it includes the proposition that society in its evolution strives to counteract machine codability—not autonomously as in the evolution of languages but rather in dependence upon the codability of machines. What is all too readily overlooked in this assumption is the fact that a society oriented on data and information processing takes itself out of play as a referential system or, rather, according to the understanding of code as a system of signs. Information's claim to absoluteness in our structure of reality is transferred into the apparative structure derived from it, into the machines, computers and networks, and for their part, established absolutely. Thus, if one takes the concept of a "computerized lingua franca" to its logical conclusion, then this necessarily implies the legitimation of the techno-fetishistic and techno-fascistic principles with which we are all familiar and which Information Society would forever take as its foundation.

In contrast to the information-technological encoding of society, "information-aesthetic encoding" makes available a horizontal tool that does not continue to serve the purpose of verticalization—that is, hierarchical ordering—of segments of society, but rather makes it possible to completely penetrate them! And this on both a symbolic, information-theoretical level and on a real, pragmatic one. This tool enables society to take measures against its hierarchical ordering and further fragmentation and to take up the search for ordering structures that are binding (in both senses of that word). Thus, when Ars Electronica 2003 inquires into "code as law, art and life," it is quite properly inquiring into a metacode. The question, therefore, is not whether "software itself [can] be art, and according to which aesthetic criteria we are to assess this issue?" Rather, "art as code" alone is the generative answer to the penetration of all sub-realities.

Art as Code

For differentiated subsystems—social, economic, cultural, etc.—code always means an instruction or regulation as to how certain signs from this limited, fragmented set of signs are depicted. In contradistinction to this, art's code and set of signs are unlimited. Accordingly, art can be defined as an encoding process based on an infinite set of signs and designed to be self-renewing. With this, art is liberated from the dogmatism of its own "operating system" and, at the highest level of information technology, ultimately becomes "compatible" with informational reality.

From the perspective of encoding, we also recognize for the first time that art is a matter of the permanently new encoding of an infinite set of signs. The inconsistencies of style within the arts are examples of this ongoing process of new encoding: all signs of the visible and imagined world were endowed with order in the perspectivist code of the Renaissance; the pointillist code of the Impressionists subordinated the entire set of signs of the single, boundless atmospheric reality; the film code of 24 images recorded and projected per second impose their order upon the entire visible set of signs of the one dynamic reality. The genetic code, finally, shows us for the first time the reality of the unity of life.

This most complex of all encoding procedures overarches and subordinates all previous systems of signs of re-vision. The arts are not immune to this. They teach us to read the "new encoding" from the stylistic inconsistencies. The divergences among the sets of signs of the various different subsystems were, almost a hundred years ago, determinative for Richard Wagner's artistic conception whereby "art and life" are not to be seen separately but rather in harmony. This idea ultimately led him to the grandiose conception of the Gesamtkunstwerk. In Wagner's wake, the unity of "art and life" became—with a few interruptions—the ongoing program of modernism. Dadaism, constructivism, suprematism, Bauhaus, pop art and, finally, the work and artistic personality of Joseph Beuys posed the question of the unity of art, life and society over and over again in new ways. Following upon this great idea, the "universal datawork" does not, however, define itself on the sensory level, but rather, at the height of information processes, under the radically changed circumstances of the electronification, informatization and digitalization of society. The actual interest of this project is focused not on the renewed creation of a Gesamtkunstwerk on the level of sensory perception by means of information and media technology (multimedia!) but rather reuniting the fragmented bits into a whole "beneath" sensory perception itself in code.

The stylistic inconsistencies never, in reality, specify an end to us but rather a direction: the striving of art tending towards unity—from the artwork of days gone by, to the Gesamtkunstwerk, to the "universal datawork." In stylistic inconsistency, it becomes clear that the "universal datawork" is no longer a matter of an external event that is to be perceived with the senses and that, as in the case of the Gesamtkunstwerk, is blended by the senses into an integrated experience, but rather a matter of the decoding of our own internal bodily structures. With this, we encounter the maximum level of integration anchored within ourselves, spiritual experience in the highest possible mass. The "universal datawork" has to do with this radical new experience, with the unified, integrated information structures and processes of all living things that are anchored beyond sensory perception.

The Universal Datawork

Let us define code as a common controlling structure maintaining an order between two sets of signs, from which we could derive a definition of metacode as the encoding of all codes or systems of signs. This yields the decisive shift of significance: the code of information technology recedes and that of information aesthetics comes into play. We are referring to "art as code" as a singular system of signs over and above all systems of signs.

As the term is applied here, the "universal datawork" is defined as a metacode. As in all imaginary concepts, this is a matter of the master plan of a universal encoding, though not timeless and spaceless but rather in the context of a particular biogenetic and information technological state, archaically and biogenetically encoded into us, open into the future, information technologically encodable outside of us.

We see that all encoding procedures that have ever been thought up and practiced by mankind—linguistic, textual, information technological, spatial, digital and binary—are present in the biogenetic code. This phenomenon is of fundamental significance for art because, heretofore, art as the sole system of rules (e.g. in the Wagnerian Gesamtkunstwerk) postulated the unity of life and reality. What was once "only" a programmatic idea now becomes an all-encompassing reality. With the "universal datawork," the claim on the level of information technology and biotechnology is lodged in a radically new way. In the "universal datawork" and explicitly in the "datawork: man," the archaic, biogenetically networked world within us is short-circuited with the technological, informationally networked world outside of us. We experience ourselves for the first time in absolute time—in the biogenetic time within us, in the cosmic without—and thus in the interlocked present between the two.

Datawork: Man

Code was the key with which artists created images about the external world in order to decode it. With the insights generated by and the decoding of the biogenetic code, every human being become an artist, and this with much more profound and far-reaching significance than was seen by Joseph Beuys, the one who first recognized this. Human beings become the objective witnesses of the encodability of their subjective selves. This, our radical new condition, is the core of the entire modern reality of the Information Age. "Datawork: man" is committed to the data processing processes of life itself. "Art as code" makes the social implications that arise as a consequence of the interweaving of information technology and biogenetic sciences visible. In "datawork: man," not only do the sciences erase the borders between them and art and vice versa, but the investigating subject also liberates himself/herself from the borders setting off the living object. Accordingly, experts in biomedicine and information artists are simultaneously the subjects and objects of investigation of their artistic science and scientific art.

In light of these new findings and insights about the informational-biogenetic nature of human beings, previous conceptions, practices and systems of art are finally taking their leave from the historical stage. As bearers of significance, sense or nonsense, they all had one thing in common: they were the antithesis of nature. On the level of bio-informationally encoded reality, they stand before a universal paradigm shift from which there will not emerge yet another "new" art in contradistinction to nature but rather the "nature of art."

More and more life processes—even the most internal ones—are being converted into data, becoming calculable and thus externally controllable by anyone. And because they are encoded and thus predictable, they must, therefore, according to the way I see it, first of all be recognizable—that is, decodable—for the individual. By now at the very latest, art itself has become the code of human beings in the Information Age in order for individuals to be able to formatively, proactively confront their inner, subjectively experienced world. (This art supported by information technology and biotech calls for its own self as the primary object of investigation and art—a belated elegy for the avant-garde!) Since we know that mankind is formed by information, it is the job reserved for art to form information in a way that is in accordance with human needs. In the future, no individual will be able to avoid assuming a major share of the responsibility for "doing the bookkeeping of life"—i.e. decoding that individual's own images—since biomedical progress forces the individual to use the power to control his/her entire bio-capital in order to deal rationally and economically with this. Or, to put it in other words: to design this very same bio-capital oneself. With design, art, endowed with an existential significance unknown until now, comes into play. A sociopolitical consequence of control in

the utilization of ones own bio-capital is the necessity for everyone constantly to take precautions. Art as the design of life attains—as life arts parallel to life sciences—its ultimate significance.
"Datawork: man" is conceived as the location of this artistic-scientific practice.

The Data Paradigm

We understand code to be a system of rules that allows for a clear classification (encoding) of signs between two different systems of signs.
"Art as code" is meant as a system of rules that, in the classification of signs, is not exactly clear and that is not limited to two systems of signs. Art as code is ambiguous; art as a system of signs is the tendency towards a system of rules whose classification extends across all systems of signs.
In "art as code" interpolated to all other codes, art attains its singularity as a highly functional system of signs based exclusively on errors. "Art as code" is a unique system of errors and this is the basis of the uniqueness of the work of art and the uniqueness of the arts with respect to all other systems of signs.
Art experiments with and celebrates the erroneousness between systems of classification, since a code can be solved only when the particular opponent makes mistakes and one becomes cognizant of the system at the basis of these errors. On the informational level, this is the turf of hackers and crackers who, by definition, "gain unauthorized access to information or computer networks," check out the code for weak spots or errors in order to finally be able to crack the system, get inside it, and modify or disable it. The appearance of errors in the genetic code works similarly. These are the errors that emerge due to cosmic radiation. In the simplest case, they appear in an amino acid sequence where a certain amino acid takes the place of the one that is supposed to be there. According to the concept of the genetic code, one nucleotide would then be replaced by another in the corresponding nucleotide sequence.
What, on the informational level, in the case of hackers and cosmically caused mutations, are isolated, unexpected interventions into a subsystem take on constitutive significance for "art as code." In the ambiguity of encoding, that which is seemingly erroneous is immanent in art. In accordance with the principle of absolute erroneousness, we have "art as code" to thank for the preparation for that which cannot be prepared for. With "art as code," we finally have at our disposal a tool both for the explanation of art's fundamental social meaning with respect to technology as well as the personal way one goes about living one's life in the face of external control.
The way that crackers intervene into information technology's system of rules, the way cosmic radiation penetrates into the biogenetic system of rules and brings about unknown changes and mutations thereby so that evolution continues on its way is the art of the intruders into social systems of rules. What do we learn from art in the context of encoding? Art is the search for errors in the social system of rules. It is only where errors exist in the system of rules that crackers can intrude into the technological, cosmic radiation into the biogenetic, and the arts into the social system of rules. Art is eo ipso a code system for decoding social reality at its weak points.

Translated from the German by Mel Greenwald

das universelle datenwerk

richard kriesche

einleitung

ars electronica 2003 fragt auf der höhe des informationszeitalters, „ob die sprache der computer zur lingua franca der globalen informationsgesellschaft wird?“ und spricht im anschluss darauf die vermutung aus, „dass die materia prima“ eben dieser gesellschaft „die digitalen codes sein werden.“

wenn man dieser fragestellung folgen möchte, schließt dies mit ein, dass die gesellschaft in ihrer evolution der maschinellen codierbarkeit entgegenstrebt – nicht autonom, wie in der evolution der sprachbildung, sondern in abhängigkeit von der codierbarkeit der maschinen. was bei dieser annahme gerne übersehen wird, ist die tatsache, dass eine auf daten- und informationsprocessing ausgerichtete gesellschaft sich damit als bezugssystem bzw. nach dem verständnis des codes als zeichensystem aus dem spiel nimmt. der absolutheitsanspruch des informationellen in unserer wirklichkeitsstruktur wird in die davon abgeleitete apparative struktur, in die maschinen, computer und netze verlagert und ihrerseits absolut gesetzt. wenn man also der vorstellung einer „computerisierten lingua franca“ folgen möchte, zieht dies zwangslogisch die legitimierung der uns bekannten technofetischistischen und -faschistischen grundlagen nach sich, auf denen dann aber für alle zukunft die informationsgesellschaft aufsetzen würde. im gegensatz zur informationstechnologischen codierung der gesellschaft steht mit der „informationsästhetischen codierung“ ein horizontales tool zur verfügung, das nicht weiterhin der vertikalisierung, d. h. der hierarchisierung gesellschaftlicher teilbereiche, dient, sondern zu deren durchdringung befähigt! und dies sowohl auf symbolischer, informationstheoretischer wie auf realer, pragmatischer ebene. dieses tool befähigt die gesellschaft, ihrer hierarchisierung und weiteren fragmentierung entgegenzuwirken und nach verbindlichen, sie verbindenden ordnungsstrukturen zu forschen. wenn also die ars electronica 2003 nach dem „gesetzes,- kunst- und lebenscode“ fragt, so fragt sie zurecht nach einem metacode. die frage ist also nicht, „ob kunst selbst software sein kann und nach welchen ästhetischen kriterien dies beurteilbar ist“ - siehe ars electronica 2003 –, sondern „kunst als code“ ist *allein* die generative antwort zur durchdringung *aller* teilwirklichkeiten.

kunst als code

für differenzierte teilsysteme, die gesellschaftlichen, sozialen, ökonomischen, kulturellen etc., bedeutet code immer eine vorschrift, ein gesetz, wie bestimmte zeichen dieses begrenzten, fragmentierten zeichenvorrats dargestellt werden.

im gegensatz dazu sind code und zeichenvorrat der kunst unbegrenzt. kunst lässt sich demnach als ein auf einem unbegrenzten zeichenvorrat basierendes, auf selbsterneuerung angelegtes codierverfahren definieren. damit wird kunst aus der dogmatik ihres eigenen „betriebssystems“ befreit und endlich auf der höhe des informationstechnologischen niveaus „kompatibel“ mit der informationellen wirklichkeit.

unter dem gesichtspunkt der codierung erkennen wir erstmals auch, dass kunst von der permanenten neucodierung eines unendlichen zeichensatzes handelt. exemplarisch für diese stete

neucodierung sind die stilbrüche innerhalb der künste: alle zeichen der sichtbaren und imaginierten welt fanden in dem einen perspektivischen code der renaissance ihre ordnung; der pointillistische code der impressionisten ordnete den gesamten zeichenvorrat der einen grenzenlosen atmosphärischen wirklichkeit unter; der filmcode von 24 bildern aufnahme und wiedergabe pro sekunde ordnete den gesamten sichtbaren zeichenvorrat der einen dynamischen wirklichkeit unter. der genetische code schließlich zeigt uns erstmals die wirklichkeit der einheit des lebendigen.
dieses komplexeste aller codierungsverfahren unterwirft alle bisherigen zeichensysteme der re-vision. die künste bleiben davon nicht ausgespart. sie lehren uns, in den stilbrüchen die „neucodierung" herauszulesen. die divergenzen zwischen den zeichenvorräten der unterschiedlichen teilsystemen waren fast ein jahrundert zuvor für richard wagners künstlerische auffassung bestimmend, „kunst und leben" nicht getrennt, sondern im einklang zu sehen. diese auffassung führte ihn schließlich zur grandiosen konzeption des gesamtkunstwerkes. die einheit von „kunst und leben" wurde in der nachfolge wagners, mit wenigen unterbrechungen, zum durchgehenden programm der moderne. dadaismus, konstruktivismus, suprematismus, bauhaus, pop art und letztlich werk und künstlerpersönlichkeit von joseph beuys stellten die frage nach der einheit von kunst, leben und gesellschaft immer wieder aufs neue. das *universelle datenwerk* begreift sich in der folge dieser großen idee, jedoch nicht auf sinnlichem niveau, sondern auf der höhe der informationsprozesse, unter den radikal geänderten bedingungen einer elektronisierung, informatisierung und digitalisierung der gesellschaft. das eigentliche interesse des projektes gilt nicht der erneuten schaffung eines gesamtkunstwerkes auf sinnlicher wahrnehmungsebene mittels info- und medientechnologie (multimedia!), sondern der zusammenführung der fragmentierten teilbereiche zum ganzen, „unterhalb" der sinnlichen wahrnehmung selbst, im code.
die stilbrüche geben uns in wirklichkeit nie das ende, sondern die zur ganzheit tendierende bestrebung der kunst als richtung vor. vom einstigen kunstwerk über das gesamtkunstwerk zum *universellen datenwerk* vor. im stilbruch wird deutlich, dass es im *universellen datenwerk* nicht mehr um ein sinnlich wahrzunehmendes äußeres ereignis geht, das wie im *gesamtkunstwerk* über die sinne zu einem ganzheitlichen erlebnis verschmolzen wird, sondern um die decodierung unserer eigenen inneren körperstrukturen. damit gelangen wir an die in uns selbst verankerte, höchstmögliche ganzheitlichkeit, an die im höchsten masse spirituelle erfahrung. im *universellen datenwerk* geht es um diese radikal neue erfahrung, um die hinter der sinnlichen wahrnehmung verankerten, ganzheitlichen informationsstrukturen und -prozesse alles lebendigen.

das universelle datenwerk

verstehen wir unter code eine gemeinsame, übergreifende ordungsstruktur zwischen zwei zeichensätzen, so lässt sich daraus tendenziell der metacode als codierung aller codes bzw. zeichensysteme ableiten. das bringt den entscheidenden bedeutungswandel mit sich: der informationstechnologische code nimmt sich zurück, der informationsästhetische bringt sich ins spiel. wir sprechen von „kunst als code", als einem singulären zeichensystem über alle zeichensysteme hinweg. angewandt dazu begreift sich das *universelle datenwerk* als metacode. es geht wie in allen imaginationen um den masterplan einer unversal codierung; jedoch nicht zeit- und raumlos, sondern im kontext der biogenetischen und informationstechnologischen befindlichkeit; archaisch und biogenetisch codiert in uns in die zukunft offen, informationstechnologisch codierbar außerhalb von uns.
wir sehen, dass sich im biogenetischen code sämtliche von der menschheit erdachten und praktizierten codierverfahren – das sprachliche, das textuelle, das informationstechnologische, räumliche, digitale und binäre – wiederfinden. dieses phänomen ist deshalb für die kunst von

fundamentaler bedeutung, weil kunst bisher als einziges regelwerk (z. b. im wagnerschen gesamtkunstwerk) die einheit von leben und wirklichkeit postuliert hat. was einst „nur“ eine programmatische idee war, wird nun zur allwirklichkeit. mit dem *universellen datenwerk* wird der anspruch auf dem informations- und biotechnologischen niveau radikal neu gestellt. im *universellen datenwerk,* explizit im *datenwerk : mensch,* wird die archaische, biogenetisch vernetzte welt in uns mit der technologisch informationell vernetzten welt außerhalb von uns kurz geschlossen. wir erfahren uns erstmals in der absoluten zeit, in der biogenetischen –in uns – in der kosmischen – außerhalb von uns – d. h. in der zwischen beiden verschränkten gegenwart.

datenwerk : mensch

code war der schlüssel, mit dem künstler bilder über die äußere welt kreierten, um sie zu decodieren. mit der erkenntnis und der entschlüsselung des biogenetischen codes wird jeder mensch zum künstler – in einer noch tiefgreifenderen bedeutung als dies erstmals von joseph beuys erkannt worden ist. er wird zum objektiven zeugen der codierbarkeit seines subjektiven selbst. diese unsere radikale neue befindlichkeit ist der kern der gesamten informationsmodernen wirklichkeit.
datenwerk : mensch ist den datenverarbeitungsprozessen des lebens selbst verpflichtet. „kunst als code“ macht als folge der verschränkung der informationstechnologischen mit den biogenetischen wissenschaften deren gesellschaftliche implikationen sichtbar. im *datenwerk : mensch* entgrenzen sich nicht nur die wissenschaften zum künstler hin und vice versa, sondern auch das forschende subjekt entgrenzt sich zum lebenden objekt. dementsprechend sind biomediziner und infokünstler gleichzeitig die subjekte und forschungsobjekte ihrer künstlerischen wissenschaft und wissenschaftlichen kunst.
vor diesem neuen hintergrund der erkenntnisse über die informationell-biogenetische natur des menschen treten die bisherigen kunstkonzeptionen, -praxen und -systeme endgültig aus der geschichte heraus. als bedeutungs-, sinn- oder unsinnsträger war ihnen allen eines gemeinsam: sie standen in antithese zur natur. auf der ebene der bio-informationell codierten wirklichkeit stehen sie vor einem universalen paradigmenwechsel, aus dem nicht erneut eine „neue“ kunst im widerspruch zur natur, sondern die „natur der kunst“ hervorgeht.
immer mehr lebensprozesse, selbst die innersten, werden verdatet, berechenbar, damit kontrollierbar und von außen für jedermann steuerbar. und weil sie codiert und damit berechenbar sind, müssen sie, so mein postulat, daher zu allererst für das individuum erkennbar, d. h. decodierbar sein. spätestens jetzt wird kunst selbst zum code des informationsmodernen menschen, um seiner inneren, subjektiv erfahrbaren welt gestaltend begegnen zu können. [diese informations- und biotechnologisch gestützte kunst erfordert das eigene selbst als primären gegenstand von forschung und kunst. ein später nachruf auf die avantgarde (!)] seit wir wissen, dass der mensch durch information geformt wird, ist es der kunst vorbehalten, informationen dem menschen gemäß zu formen. keinem individuum kann es in zukunft erspart bleiben, die verantwortung für die „verrechnung des lebens“ zum entscheidenden teil selbst zu übernehmen, d. h. die bilder über sich selbst zu decodieren – denn der biomedizinische fortschritt zwingt das individuum, kraft der kontrollierbarkeit seines gesamten biokapitals mit diesem vernünftig, also sparsam und rational umzugehen. oder anders ausgedrückt: die gestaltung eben dieses biokapitals selbst vorzunehmen. mit gestaltung kommt kunst in ihrer bisher noch nie gekannten existenziellen bedeutung ins spiel. kontrolle in der nutzung des eigenen biokapitals heißt gesellschaftspolitisch, ständige vorsorge als notwendigkeit für jedermann. kunst als lebensgestaltung kommt als lebenskunst – parallel zu life science – zu ihrer ultimativen bedeutung.
datenwerk : mensch begreift sich als ort dieser künstlerisch-wissenschaftlichen praxis.

wir verstehen unter code ein system von regeln, das die eindeutige zuordnung (codierung) von zeichen zwischen zwei verschiedenen zeichensystemen erlaubt.
„kunst als code“ begreift sich als ein system von regeln, das in der zuordnung von zeichen gerade nicht eindeutig ist und das die zuordnung gerade nicht auf zwei zeichensysteme beschränkt. kunst als code ist vieldeutig, kunst als zeichensystem ist der tendenz nach ein system von regeln, deren zuordnung sich auf alle zeichensysteme erstreckt.
in „kunst als code“, in paranthese zu allen anderen codes, findet kunst zu ihrer singularität, als ein ausschließlich auf fehlern beruhendes, hochfunktionales zeichensystem. „kunst als code“ ist ein einzigartiges fehlersystem. darin begründet sich die einzigartigkeit des kunstwerks, die einzigartigkeit der künste zu allen anderen zeichensystemen.
kunst experimentiert und zelebriert die fehlerhaftigkeit zwischen zuordnungssystemen. denn jeder code lässt sich immer nur dann lösen, wenn der jeweilige gegner fehler macht und wenn man merkt, welches system diesen fehlern zu grunde liegt. auf informationeller ebene ist dies das terrain der hacker bzw. der cracker, die per definitionem „ohne autorisierung in die informations- bzw. computernetze eindringen“, die den code nach schwach- und fehlerstellen abtasten, um das system schließlich knacken zu können, in dieses eindringen, es verändern, bzw. lahmlegen zu können. ähnlich verhält es sich mit dem auftreten von fehlern im genetischen code. es sind dies fehler, die auf grund kosmischer einstrahlungen entstehen. sie machen sich im simpelsten fall dadurch bemerkbar, dass in einer aminosäuresequenz anstelle einer bestimmten aminosäure eine andere steht. nach dem konzept des genetischen codes müsste demnach in der entsprechenden nukleotidsequenz ein nukleotid durch ein anderes ersetzt worden sein.
was auf informationeller ebene im falle der hacker und auf der ebene kosmisch bedingter mutationen vereinzelte, unerwartete eingriffe in das teilsystem sind, wird für „kunst als code“ von konstituierender bedeutung. in der mehrdeutigkeit des codierens ist das scheinbar fehlerhafte kunstimmanent. dem prinzip der absoluten fehlerhaftigkeit verdanken wir der „kunst als code“ die vorbereitung auf das unvorbereitbare. mit „kunst als code“ verfügen wir endlich über ein werkzeug sowohl zur erklärung der kunst hinsichtlich ihrer fundamentalen gesellschaftlichen bedeutung gegenüber den technologien als auch der personalen lebenspraxis gegenüber außensteuerung.
wie die cracker ins informationstechnologische regelsystem eingreifen, wie die kosmische einstrahlung in das biogenetische regelsystem eindringt und damit unbekannte veränderungen und mutationen hervorruft und damit die evulution in gang bringt, so ist kunst der eindringling in die sozialen und gesellschaftlichen regelsysteme. was lernen wir von kunst im kontext der codierung? kunst ist fehlersuche im gesellschaftlichen regelsystem. nur wo fehler im regelsystem bestehen, können die cracker ins technologische, können kosmische einstrahlungen ins biogenetische, können die künste in das soziale regelsystem eindringen. kunst ist eo ipso ein codesystem zur decodierung der sozialen wirklichkeit an ihren schwachstellen.

datawork: man

richard kriesche

1 within the context of the informational reordering of reality, the grand idea of the gesamtkunstwerk undergoes an artistic and sociopolitical reinterpretation in the concept of a *universal datawork.*

2. the gesamtkunstwerk as an expression of consummate artistic perfection had as its aim—in an extension of the wagnerian interpretation—the unification of the senses melded together in the arts. in contrast to this conception—thanks to biogenetic findings and insights, and no thanks to the natural sciences' segmentation and informational fractalization of mankind—the sociopolitical leitmotiv of the *universal datawork* and its claim to ascendancy in art theory aims at revealing shared bio-cosmic data structures, at the universal gestalt of all life.

3. in the *universal datawork,* the artistic process that sought in a state of formative perception to capture the world that can be rationally comprehended and experienced with the senses and to fix that world on the biomorphic level becomes its implicit object.

4. in the *universal datawork,* the gesamtkunstwerk achieves expression in the informational reality of the human being as *datawork: man. datawork: man* stands before the backdrop of this new human nature: an informational-biogenetic one. it is as a result thereof that the arts as we have come to know them have been suffering their loss of meaning. as bearers of meaning and significance, they, in antithesis to nature, are confronted by a universal paradigm shift, the consequence of which is that art does not emerge as a negation of nature but rather nature is a derivative of art.

5. from the insight that mankind is formed by the "nature" of information, *datawork: man* derives the universal task of forming the "nature" of information in a human-user-friendly way. in light of this claim, *datawork: man* applies the code of images to reality itself. code, understood as the binding key to the understanding of images, becomes the art of understanding reality, of creating, understanding and experiencing a world in and of itself and on its own terms ...

Translated from the German by Mel Greenwald

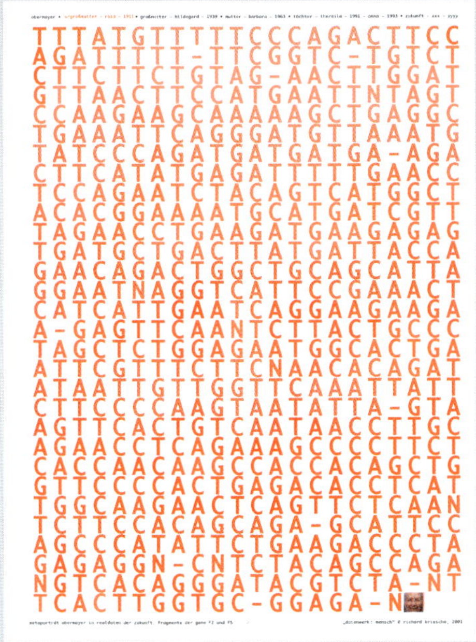

"Metaportrait Obermayer in Real Data"
Genetic Portrait of Obermayer's Great-grandmother

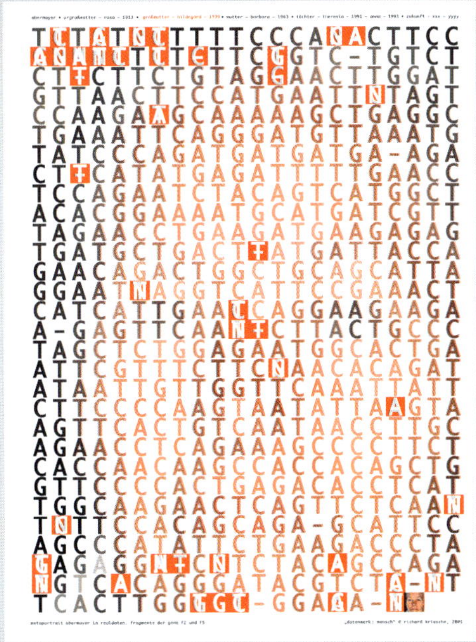

"Metaportrait Obermayer in Real Data"
Genetic Portrait of Obermayer's Mother

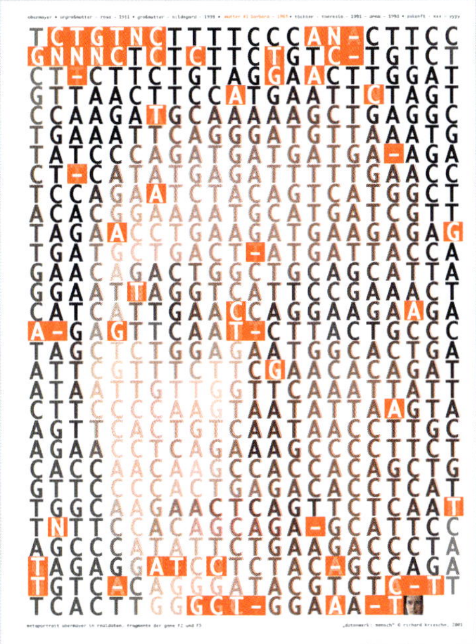

"Metaportrait Obermayer in Real Data"
Genetic Portrait of Obermayer's Daughter

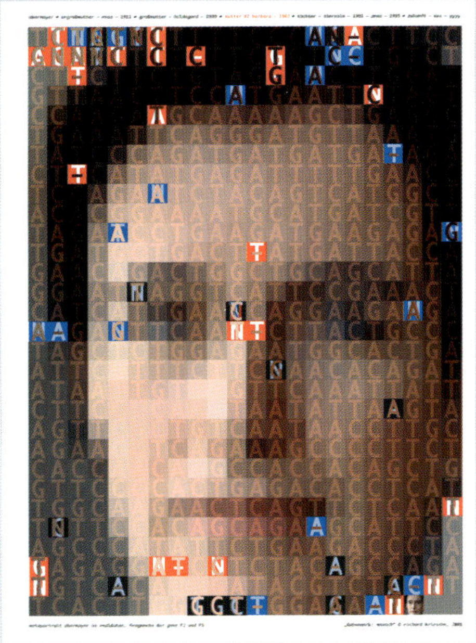

"Metaportrait Obermayer in Real Data"
Genetic Portrait of Future Obermayer

"Metaportrait Obermayer": The same gene fragments f2 and f5 in the female line of the family of Barbara Obermayer*—grandmother, mother, Barbara, daughter—were sequenced and displayed in the form of a 657-part A,C,G,T_text. The genetic mutations stand in their respective phenomenological background.

* Prof Barbara Obermayer was a member of the scientific staff of the project "datawork: man."

datenwerk: mensch

richard kriesche

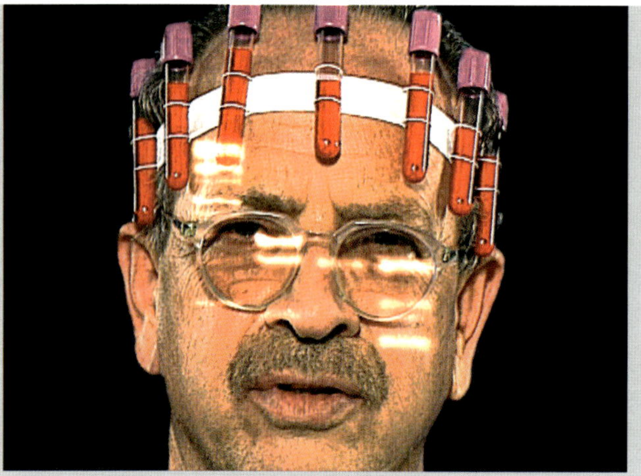

„blutspur und genspur“ (videostill)
die sequenzierung der genfragmente f2 und f5 in einen 657teiligen „A,C,G,T_text“ bilden den hintergrund für den „K,U,N,S,T_text“ des gleichnamigen videos „blutspur und genspur“

1. die große idee vom gesamtkunstwerk findet unter der informationellen neuordnung der wirklichkeit in der konzeption eines *universellen datenwerks* seine künstlerische und gesellschaftspolitische neudeutung.

2. das gesamtkunstwerk, als ausdruck höchster vervollkommnung, hatte in fortsetzung der wagner'schen deutung die vereinigung der sinne, gebunden in den künsten, zum ziel. im gegensatz dazu zielt das gesellschaftspolitische leitmotiv und der kunsttheoretische führungsanpruch des *universellen datenwerks,* dank der biogenetischen erkenntnisse, un-dank der naturwissenschaftlichen segmentierung und informationellen fraktalisierung des menschen, auf die freilegung der gemeinsamen, biokosmischen datenstrukturen, auf die universelle gestalt alles lebendigen ab.

3. im *universellen datenwerk* wird der künstlerische prozess, der in gestaltgebender wahrnehmung die rational fassbare und sinnlich erfahrbare welt im biomorphen zu verankern versuchte, zu dessen implizitem gegenstand.

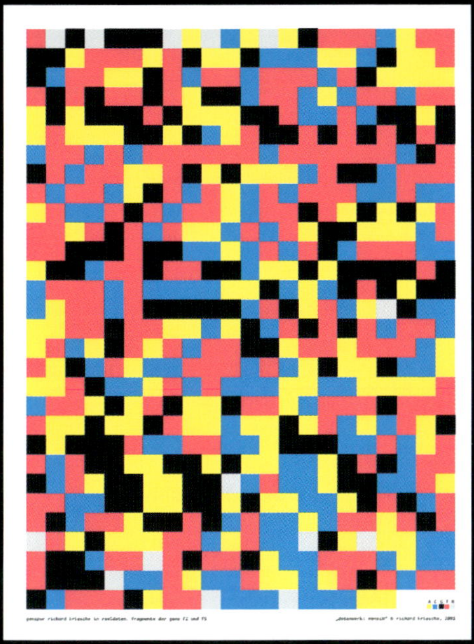

richard kriesche zwischen singularität und universalität
die sequenz der genfragmente f2 und f5
des künstlers in einen 657teiligen A,C,G,T_text.

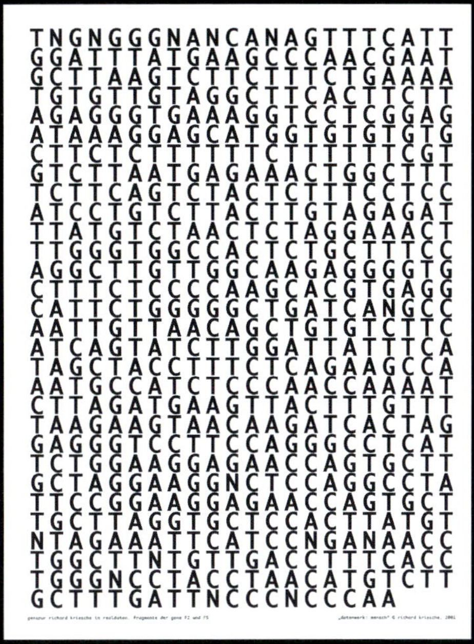

richard kriesche zwischen ästhetik und code
die sequenz der genfragmente f2 und f5 des künstlers
in einen 657teiligen C,M,Y,K_text.

4. im *universellen datenwerk* findet das „gesamtkunstwerk" in der informationellen wirklichkeit des menschen als *datenwerk : mensch* seinen ausdruck. *datenwerk : mensch* steht vor dem hintergrund dieser neuen natur des menschen, der informationell–biogenetischen. vor dieser erleiden die künste, wie wir sie bis heute kennen, ihren sinnverlust. als sinn- und bedeutungsträger stehen sie, in antithese zur natur, vor einem universalen paradigmenwechsel, aus der nicht kunst im widerspruch zur natur, sondern die natur der kunst hervorgeht.

5. *datenwerk : mensch* leitet von der erkenntnis, dass der mensch durch die „natur" der informationen gebildet wird, den universalen auftrag ab, die „natur" der informationen im sinne des menschen zu bilden. mit diesem anspruch wendet *datenwerk : mensch* den code der bilder auf die wirklichkeit selbst an. code, verstanden als der verbindliche schlüssel zum verstehen der bilder, wird zur kunst zum verstehen der wirklichkeit, welt in sich selbst zu erzeugen, zu verstehen, zu erfahren ...

Epigenetic Art Revisited: Software as Genotype

Roman Verostko

Roman Verostko's 1988 paper on "Epigenetic art: software as genotype" was published in *Leonardo* in 1990. For the 1993 *Ars Electronica* exhibition catalogue, *Genetic Art / Artificial Life,* he summarized the substance of the paper as "Notes on epigenetic art". Here, tempered with 20 years' experience as an algorist and 40 years as an artist, he revisits his original views on coded artistic procedures.

The beginnings. For over 40 years, as an artist, I have sought to create works pointing to hidden or unseen reality. Early on I learned to wonder about the marvelous event of things existing "just the way they are" and whether there could be other ways "to be". Within commonplace phenomena I learned to see a marvelous world filled with mystery. My approach to art grew from this sense of wonder about most things and a reverence for the materials of earth. Eventually this wonder came to include circuit boards, computer languages, and the art forms one could explore with simple algorithms.

Terminology. Talking about *code, algorithms,* or *algorists* can evoke wrinkled foreheads and blank stares. Let me offer some clarification. An algorithm can be viewed as a detailed step-by-step procedure for carrying out a task. A recipe for baking bread or directions for reaching a specific location can be viewed as algorithms.
Clearly most kinds of instructions are not written to create art. "But," we may ask, "Can we write instructions for creating art?" "Can an artist 'code' a work of art?" Emphatically, "Yes!"
In responding I will use terms like "mind-ear" and "mind-hand" to indicate that the process of writing instructions for making art engages the whole person and cannot be identified with one body part separated from another. Consider Chopin's score for his *Nocturne opus 27.* Chopin created the musical notation or *code* that instructs the performer on how to play the *Nocturne.* The *score,* a unique procedure, provides detailed instruction for playing a specific musical form. It literally embodies a musical idea that originated in Chopin's "mind-ear" in 1835. His mind "conceiving sound" embodies his sense of hearing. When hearing a performance today we assume that Chopin's musical idea, as he conceived hearing it, has reached us via the musical score—an instruction, *an algorithm.* Inasmuch as Chopin's musical idea is adequately represented in the score, and, inasmuch as the performer interprets the score as Chopin intended, then we enjoy an experience of Chopin's "mind-ear".

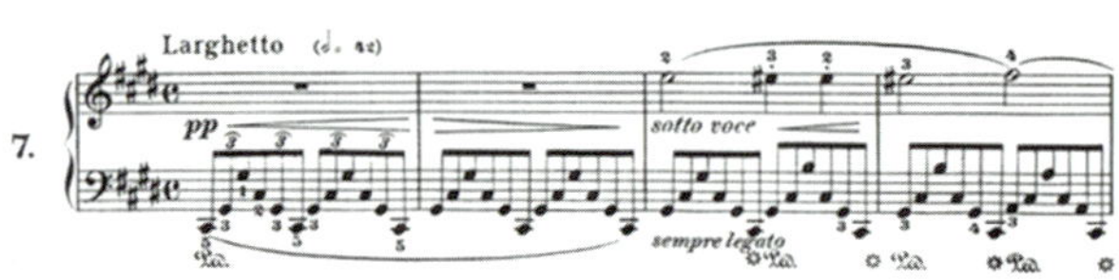

Coded art. Musical notation may be viewed as a "detailed recipe" or algorithm for a musical art form. Theme and first chords, F.Chopin, *Nocturne,* Op. 27, No 1. C# minor, 1835. © Schirmer, Musical Classics.

The contribution of the performer surely colors each performance in a unique way and is not taken lightly. Even so, the musical score transcends an individual performance and continues to have a meaningful existence over generations. Note that the "musical score" is written in a "code" consisting of symbols specifying time and qualities of sound. In general, when we use the term "code", we are referring to an instruction or algorithm in its notational form, a specialized language for precisely representing the instruction. Well formed code displays splendid rationality with every detail clearly spelled out. Note, however, that the procedure for creating the code transcends our understanding. We can study Chopin's nocturne and understand every detail of the score: but we cannot fathom the procedure by which Chopin created the score. *We must be careful not to confuse the procedure by which the artist creates the code with the procedure specified in the code.* The creative process lies primarily in the process of writing the code.

Coded visual form. With these considerations in mind let us turn our attention from coded "musical form" to coded "visual form".

I am a founding member of an informal group of artists known as algorists.[1] For us, the term algorist applies broadly to any artist who employs original coded procedures for generating art forms. My interest, shared with pen plotter algorists, focuses on coded drawing procedures.

An algorist's envisioned drawing procedure should not be thought of as a disembodied concept conceived apart from a feeling hand. Just as a composer composes with his "mind-ear" so an algorist composes with his "mind-hand". As surely as the mind is present to the hand when it draws, so also the hand is present to the mind when it creates drawing procedures.

To achieve this, an algorist, in writing code, addresses aesthetic qualities and limits of media and machine, for example, how paper surface and sizing affect the receptivity of ink. An algorist translates sensibility to these factors into intelligent coded operations.

Specifically how does one get from this "mind-hand" drawing as "code" to the actual drawing? In my case, the code, operating on a PC, instructs a drawing machine known as a multi-pen plotter. These machines, designed for engineers and architects, have "drawing arms" that can select from a bank of pens and draw lines precisely as instructed. In

Detail of code drawn lines.

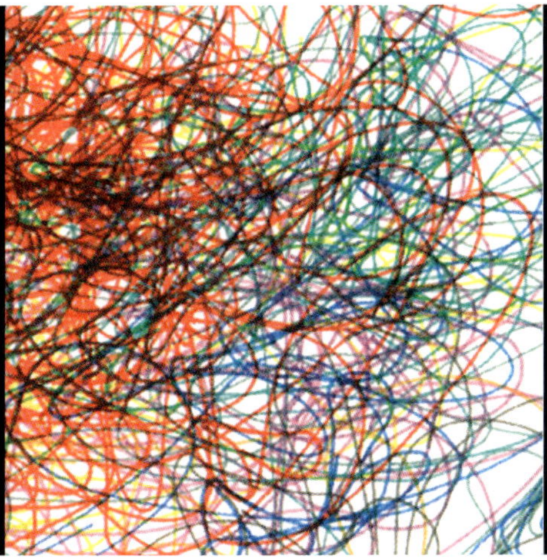

Coded pen and ink drawing, 1987 (18 cm. by 26 cm).

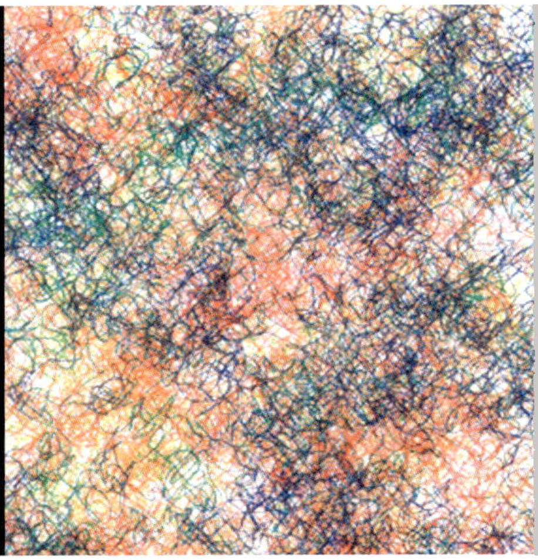

1987 I adapted paintbrushes to fit the drawing arm and have written special procedures for executing brush strokes. For the most part my works employ thousands of pen strokes with only occasional use of brush strokes.

The drawing arm and recursion. One is tempted to view the plotter's drawing-arm as a simulator of the artist's physical hand. This is not the case. Rather it executes the "mind-hand" of the artist. The algorist's "mind-hand" embodies precision with extensive drawing procedures that exceed the reach of a physical drawing hand. We could say the artist's mind-hand draws via the machine's drawing-arm something like the power shovel operator's hand shovels with the power shovel's shovel.

These abilities can be original drawing manoeuvres that exceed the capacity and dexterity of the human hand because they employ functions capable of unlimited iteration while improvising on themselves. The mind-hand can conceive of a drawing loop that looks back at what has been drawn and sets a procedure for improvising on the next drawing movement. The artist can create procedures for improvising upon improvised moves for each step along the way. This kind of "drawing-mind" engages the deep well of recursive procedure. Through experience the algorist learns how to set improvisational rules to achieve aesthetic preferences.

Recursive procedures are not new. The expression for the Fibonacci number series would be a simple recursive function, [n+(n+1)=n+2]. What is new is the ability to execute code for extensive recursive iteration yielding dimensions of improvisation in drawing that exceed what our minds can contain or what our hands can draw. This capability would have been, to my mind, a heavenly delight in the hands of artists like Wassily Kandinsky, Piet Mondrian and the Pevsner brothers. Recursion lies at the very heart of algorist art. This is how self-similar qualities of the drawing lines and brush strokes in my Epigenesis mural become imbedded in drifting pen stroke clusters that mirror each other.[2] Herein lies the unique feature of computing power coupled with an artist's coded procedure.

Studio practice on the new frontier. For over a quarter century I have marveled at the power of coded procedure for experimenting with visual form. Artists who have integrated their art with original coded procedures are on the threshold of a new frontier. In tapping this frontier they are confronted with two great hurdles. One has been the task of translating form-generating ideas into a practical working code. The other has been the search for appropriate methods for producing the work in a tangible form.

The code as a form generating idea is only half the struggle. To succeed as art, the code must be able to generate tangible form—something one can see, touch, feel or hear. Some years ago an artist friend, standing by an elm tree, asked, "What gives this tree such a

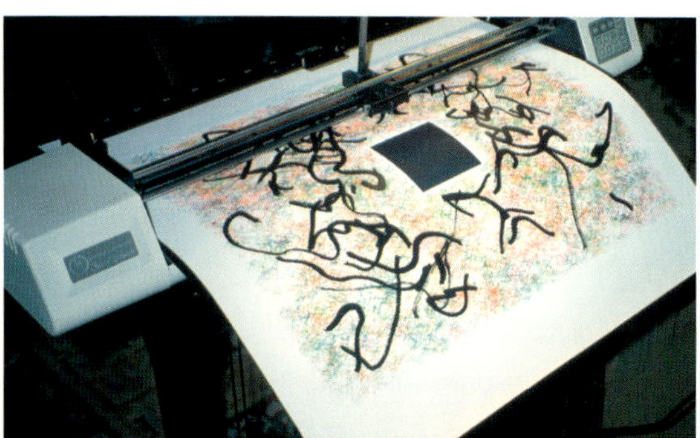

First coded brush strokes in 1987. Oriental brush mounted on drawing arm.
Houston Instruments DMP 50 series pen plotter.
Plotter driven with PC operating on DOS.

powerful presence?" And he answered, "You can touch it—feel its surface—its 'being here'!" Because aesthetic experience involves the senses, one cannot separate art from its material embodiment. In addressing human sensibilities artists embrace many diverse media including those emerging in cyberspace culture. My commitment has been clearly bent towards creating drawings and paintings on paper. My procedures are attentive to aesthetic qualities of papers, inks, pens, brushes and the manner of presentation. For me, the finished work should have an aura that invites the casual viewer to pause for a moment, sensing that the work, as a human endeavor, goes beyond material concerns. Even so, the process holds an unusual fascination in and of itself.

Studio Scribes. Many people who visit my studio are surprised when they see several engineering plotters cabled to a network of computers, one reserved for my experimental work and the others for generating art. When a plotter is working, visitors often stand with eyes glued on the drawing arm which, with a "seeming intelligence", draws precisely, surprisingly, and without hesitation—executing literally thousands of lines, and exuding an uncanny presence!

My first pen plotters, with names like Brunelleschi and Alberti, are now retired. Occasionally I bring Brunelleschi out of storage and have him make a small drawing. Although maintaining register is difficult and the movements are a bit coarse he can still execute a drawing to my approval. Over the years I have come to view my studio as a scriptorium with a network of electronic scribes. These scribes execute instructions tirelessly. Occasionally a specific work may require several days of drawing. Large pieces remain very difficult to achieve because of pen or hardware failure.

One can write code for unlimited sequences and a vast array of forms, but the drawing process must be coded in terms of specific drawing materials and tools. The code specifies procedures that operate with these tools in real time and space. The actual procedure must mesh with the limits and aesthetic qualities of paper and drawing instruments. At its best the code optimises the operation of tools and amplifies the aesthetic qualities of paper, ink and the character of the marking instrument.

Coping with these technological limits requires patience and experience with endless hours of trial and error. The jewel in this quest is the piece of code that works—like the acorn that can grow into a tree, the successful code literally "grows" a work of art!

This procedure for making art remains essentially the same today as in the 1980's when I wrote the original paper "Epigenetic Painting: Software as Genotype".[3]

A Personal System. The software, with a computer and a plotter, constitutes a complete personal system. Experimentation with paper, inks and plotting procedures has been extensive. Through many years of trial and error the system has evolved into a unique set of procedures with a language of its own. The software, under ongoing development, is an integrated program of algorithms written in elementary BASIC with plotter commands in DMPL. Routines have grown to thousands of lines.

```
RAD(SID)=(INT(RND*(RMAX-RMIN))+RMIN)
THETA(SID)=INT(RND*(DEGEND-DEGBEG))+DEGBEG
XQ=X1:YQ=Y1
JX(SID)=X1+INT((RAD(SID)*STRETCH)*COS(THETA(SID)*(PI/180)))
JY(SID)=Y1+INT(RAD(SID)*SIN(THETA(SID)*(PI/180)))
X1=JX(SID):Y1=JY(SID)
```

Six lines of code from a loop that specifies the radius,
an angle and the coordinates for control points in a pen stroke

Hodos. I have named the software *Hodos* (οδός), a Greek word meaning *path* or *way.* Note also that *meta-hodos* (μέθοδος) is the classical root for "method". Hodos, as a method of drawing, can be identified easily with my early work conceived as "pathways." My studio, named Pathway Studio, received an oriental seal carved by the distinguished shufa master, Wang Dong Ling. Wang, awed by the brush strokes made with the "electric brain", chose the classic expression *xiao jing zhai,* "little footpath studio", as the seal for my studio. Many works executed in the studio receive this seal.[4]

Families of form. Form generating routines within *Hodos* create works with distinctive features related to those routines. Works created with the same or similar algorithmic routines bear a familial resemblance to each other. *Hodos* can be set for a specific paper size, palette and sequence of routines to create a radically new kind of limited edition. It can generate a family of forms with each one being simultaneously related and yet uniquely "one of a kind". Works share strong familial features because they share the same algorithmic parents. Familial variety occurs because the code draws on random decisions within shared parameters. Parameters within which decisions are made can be: (a) established as *not more than* or *not less than;* (b) wide open with *no upper or lower limit;* or (c) weighted as *a percentage more or less than so much.* Parameter settings establish factors like angle, radius, coordinates, scale and color. Familial resemblances between the works vary more or less greatly depending on how many parameters are set to change and to what degree.
For example, in 1990, with *Hodos* and my assistance, my wife Alice Wagstaff plotted 125 original pen and brush drawings as frontispieces and 125 as end-pieces for a limited edition. The leather bound edition of 125 included other algorithmic drawings illustrating Chapter II of George Boole's 1854 classic, *An investigation of the laws of thought.*[5] One set of routines with a single set of parameters was employed for the frontispieces and another for the end-pieces. We believe this is the first time that a limited edition of a book engaged this kind of process for illustrations in a publication.

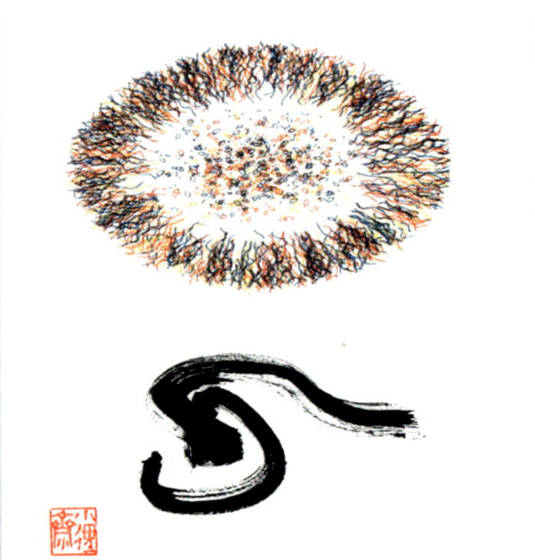

Two pen & brush drawings from a family of 125 originals. These are frontispieces from 2 books in the limited edition on chapter II of George Boole's 1854 classic work on the laws of thought. (St. Sebastian Press, Minneapolis, 1990). See: *www.verostko.com/boole.html*

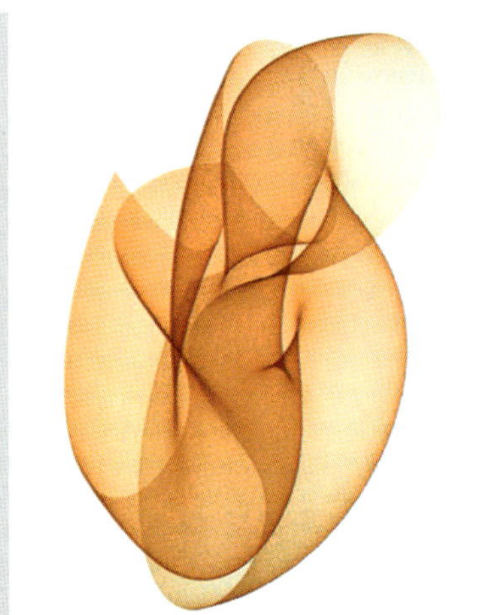

Cyberflower IV, pen & ink drawing on paper. Code generated with *Hodos.*
Roman Verostko, 2000, 54 cm. by 74 cm

Epigenetic art: software as genotype. These procedures are of a different order than traditional procedures. What shall we label this process? This was a question Alice and I posed in 1986. In our search we found ourselves returning again and again to similarities between biological processes and coded procedures. We settled on the term *epigenetic* and this became the basis for my 1988 paper.

Epigenesis refers to the process whereby a mature plant or phenotype grows from a seed or genotype. For example an acorn embodies the genotype or code that contains all the information needed for growing a mature oak tree. Given the proper environment it can, in time, grow into a mature tree. Through the process of epigenesis, the acorn grows into a mature tree referred to as phenotype.

By analogy my software or code, likened to genotype, contains all the information needed for generating an art form. Given the proper studio environment, the software literally grows from a coded procedure into an art form. By analogy to biological epigenesis, this process may be viewed as *epigenetic.*

Clearly any coded procedure that has all the information necessary for generating an art form could be viewed as *epigenetic.* The more general term used recently is *generative art.*

Content and meaning. For over a quarter century epigenetic art has been creating the icons of our information age. One could think of these icons as diagrams or visual analogues to the coded procedures by which they were made. The essential character of each finished work is derived from the "form-generating-procedure" or "algorithm" acting as genotype. For this reason one could say that the finished work is an epiphany, or manifestation, of its generator, the *code.* For me each work celebrates its code, especially the recursive routines that shaped its character. It is noteworthy that such procedures hold much in common with processes associated with crystallization and genetics.

But these are generalities. How shall we approach specific work like an algorist pen and ink drawing, for example? Such drawings, at their best, will bear the imprint of the artist's coded procedure. Just as a painter's brush stroke may bear the unique mark of the painter's hand, so the lines in an algorithmic drawing reveal the distinctive qualities of the composer's algorithmic "mind-hand". Through a unique convergence of conceptual innovation and knowledge of materials, the code created by each algorist engenders a personal style that is present with each drawing. The linear forms of an artist like Jean Pierre Hebert will celebrate themselves with self-similar meanderings coursing over the paper in a manner quite distinct from the character of the lines generated by my code or that of Manfred Mohr. Contemplating their forms reveals something, in each instance, of their creator's "mind-hand". Through these works we are given a glimpse into the mysterious nature of the algorist's inner world.

In general these works provide a window on unseen processes shaping mind and matter. By doing so they become icons illuminating the mysterious nature of self, earth and cosmos.

---

1 www.verostko.com/algorist.html

2 www.verostko.com/st/mural.html

3 www.penplot.com/epigenet.html

4 www.penplot.com/seal.html

5 www.penplot.com/boole.html

Epigenetische Kunst im Rückblick: Software als Genotypus

Roman Verostko

Roman Verostkos Arbeit zum Thema „Epigenetische Kunst: Software als Genotypus" aus dem Jahr 1988 wurde 1990 in *Leonardo* veröffentlicht. Für den Katalog der *Ars Electronica* 1993, *Genetische Kunst / Künstliches Leben,* fasste er den Text unter dem Titel „Notizen zur epigenischen Kunst" zusammen. In der Folge wirft er – im Licht seiner 20 Jahre als Algorist und 40 Jahre als Künstler – eine Blick zurück auf seine damalige Sichtweise zu kodierten künstlerischen Abläufen.

Die Anfänge. Seit mehr als 40 Jahren versuche ich als Künstler Arbeiten zu schaffen, die auf versteckte oder unsichtbare Realitäten abzielen. Schon früh lernte ich, mir über die wunderbare Tatsache, dass Dinge „genau wie sie sind" existieren und über andere Möglichkeiten „zu sein" Gedanken zu machen. Ich lernte, innerhalb alltäglicher Erscheinungen eine wunderbare Welt voller Geheimnisse zu entdecken. Mein Kunstverständnis entwickelte sich aus diesem Sich-über-die-Dinge-Wundern und aus einer Ehrfurcht vor den Materialien der Erde. Nach und nach umfasste diese Neugier auch Platinen, Programmiersprachen und die Kunstformen, die über einfache Algorithmen zu erforschen waren.

Terminologie. Spricht man von „Code", „Algorithmen" oder „Algoristen", so kann das zu gerunzelten Stirnen und verständnislosen Blicken führen. Erlauben Sie mir einen Erklärungsversuch. Ein Algorithmus kann als eine detaillierte, schrittweise Anleitung zur Durchführung einer Aufgabe verstanden werden. So kann man ein Rezept zum Brotbacken oder eine Wegbeschreibung als Algorithmus betrachten.
Natürlich werden die meisten Anleitungen nicht geschrieben, um Kunst zu schaffen. Wir mögen uns aber fragen: „Können wir Anleitungen zur Schaffung von Kunst schreiben?" „Kann ein Künstler ein Kunstwerk ‚kodieren'?" Darauf ein nachdrückliches „Ja"! Im Folgenden werde ich Ausdrücke wie „Kopf-Ohr" und „Kopf-Hand" verwenden, um anzudeuten, dass der gesamte Mensch und nicht ein einzelner Körperteil Anleitungen zum Schaffen von Kunst schreibt. Nehmen wir als Bespiel Chopins Partitur zu seiner *Nocturne Op. 27.* Chopin schuf die musikalische Notierung oder den *Code,* der dem Musiker anzeigt, wie die *Nocturne* zu spielen ist. Die *Partitur,* ein einmaliger Ablauf, stellt genaue Anweisungen für das Spielen einer bestimmten musikalischen Form. Sie verkörpert buchstäblich eine musikalische Idee, die 1835 in Chopins „Kopf-Ohr" entstand. Sein Kopf, der „Klang erfährt", steht für seinen Gehörsinn. Hören wir heute eine Darbietung, dann hat uns Chopins musikalische Idee, so wie er sie hörte, über die Partitur erreicht – über eine Anleitung, einen Algorithmus. Findet also Chopins musikalische Idee in der Partitur einen angemessen Ausdruck und interpretiert der Musiker die Partitur nach Chopins Vorstellungen, erlaubt uns das einen Einblick in Chopins „Kopf-Ohr".

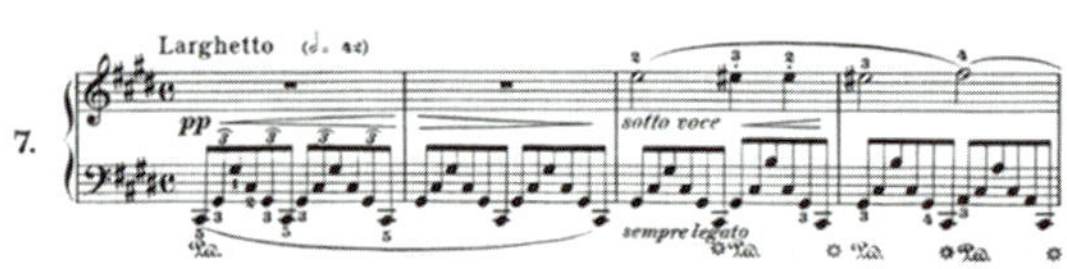

Gecodete Kunst: Musiknotation kann als „detailliertes Rezept" oder Algorithmus für eine musikalische Kunstform angesehen werden.
F. Chopin, *Nocturne,* Op. 27, No. 1, C#, 1835.
© Schirmer, Musical Classics.

Natürlich gibt der Beitrag des Künstlers jeder Darbietung eine eigene Färbung und ist daher nicht zu unterschätzen. Dennoch steht die musikalische Notierung über der individuellen Interpretation und behält über Generationen hinweg Bedeutung. Zu beachten ist, dass die „musikalische Partitur" in einem „Code" aus Symbolen geschrieben ist, die die Dauer und Farben des Klangs festlegen. Verwenden wir den Begriff „Code", so meinen wir im Allgemeinen eine Anleitung oder einen Algorithmus in seiner notierenden Form, eine Fachsprache zur genauen Darstellung der Anweisung.
Ein klar formulierter Code enthält eine wunderbare Rationalität, in der jedes Detail deutlich zum Ausdruck gebracht wird. Allerdings können wir den Prozess, der der Generierung des Codes zugrunde liegt, nicht nachvollziehen. Wir können Chopins Nocturne studieren und jede Einzelheit der Partitur verstehen: Wir können jedoch niemals den Prozess ergründen, der Chopin die Partitur schaffen ließ. Wir müssen darauf achten, den Prozess, aufgrund dessen der Künstler den Code generiert, nicht mit dem durch den Code spezifizierten Ablauf zu verwechseln. Der kreative Prozess liegt hauptsächlich im Schreiben des Codes.

Kodierte visuelle Form. Behalten wir diese Überlegungen im Kopf und wenden wir uns von der kodierten „musikalischen Form" zur kodierten „visuellen Form".
Ich bin Gründungsmitglied einer losen Gruppe von Künstlern, die als Algoristen bekannt sind *(http://www.verostko.com/algorist.html).* Für uns meint der Begriff „Algorist" ganz allgemein Künstler, die selbst programmierte Prozesse zur Entwicklung von Kunstformen verwenden. Wie auch andere Stiftplotter-Algoristen konzentriere ich mich auf kodierte Zeichenprozesse. Der vom Algoristen angestrebte Zeichenprozess darf nicht als entkörpertes Konzept verstanden werden, das fernab einer fühlenden Hand entwickelt wird. So wie ein Komponist mit seinem „Kopf-Ohr" komponiert, so arbeitet ein Algorist mit seiner „Kopf-Hand". So wie der Kopf beim Zeichnen der Hand zur Seite steht, so hilft auch die Hand dem Kopf, wenn er Zeichenprozesse programmiert.
Daher widmet sich der Algorist beim Schreiben des Codes ästhetischen Qualitäten und Grenzen von Medium und Maschine, wie etwa Oberfläche und Leimung des Papiers die Aufnah-

Epigenesis Mural, eine von elf Improvisationen jeweils 183 cm x 92 cm,
Science Centre, Universität von St Thomas, 1996-97.

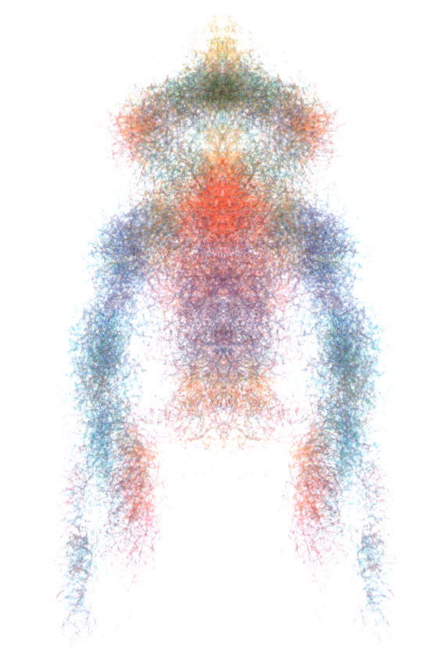

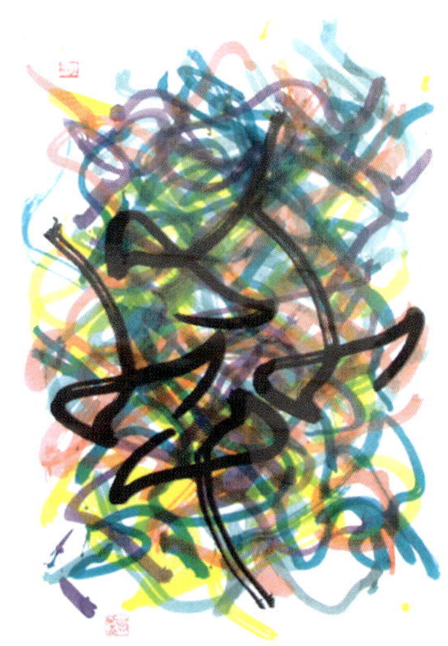

mefähigkeit von Tinte beeinflussen. Der Algorist überträgt das Bewusstsein um diese Faktoren auf intelligente kodierte Arbeitsvorgänge.
Wie genau gelangt man nun von diesem „kodierten Kopf-Hand"-Zeichnen zur eigentlichen Zeichnung? In meinem Fall instruiert der Code über einen PC eine Zeichenmaschine, einen so genannten Multi-Stiftplotter. Diese für Ingenieure und Architekten konstruierten Maschinen verfügen über „Zeichenarme", die aus einer Reihe von Stiften auswählen und nach genauen Anweisungen Linien zeichnen. 1987 habe ich die Zeichenarme für Farbpinsel adaptiert und spezifische Abläufe für die Ausführung von Pinselstrichen beschrieben. Meine Arbeiten bestehen hauptsächlich aus Tausenden von Tuschstrichen, die nur von vereinzelten Pinselstrichen durchsetzt sind.

Zeichenarm und Rekursion. Man mag nun versucht sein, den Zeichenarm des Plotters als Simulation der tatsächlichen Hand des Künstlers zu sehen. Dem ist nicht so. Vielmehr vollzieht er die „Kopf-Hand" des Künstlers. Die „Kopf-Hand" des Algoristen gibt über weitläufige Zeichenprozesse einer Präzision Form, welche die Möglichkeiten der tatsächlichen Zeichenhand übersteigt. Wir könnten sagen, dass die Kopf-Hand des Künstlers über den Zeichenarm der Maschine zeichnet, so wie die Hand des Baggerfahrers mit der Baggerschaufel schaufelt. Zu diesen Fähigkeiten gehören zum Beispiel selbst entwickelte Zeichenbewegungen, die die Möglichkeiten und Gewandtheit der menschlichen Hand übersteigen, weil sie Funktionen verwenden, die endlos wiederholbar sind und Improvisationen ihrer selbst durchführen. Die Kopf-Hand ist imstande, eine Zeichenschleife zu erarbeiten, die auf das bisher Ausgeführte zurückblickt und einen Improvisationsablauf für den nächsten Zeichengang entwerfen kann. Der Künstler kann Vorgänge schaffen, die bei jedem Schritt Improvisationen auf schon Improvisiertes legen. Diese Art von „Zeichen-Kopf" taucht tief in die Fluten wiederkehrender Prozesse. Die Erfahrung lehrt den Algoristen, wie Improvisationsregeln aufzustellen sind, um zur Etablierung ästhetischer Prioritäten zu führen.

Wiederholungsprozesse sind keine neuartige Erfindung. Die Formel für die Fibonacci-Zahlenreihe wäre eine einfache rekursive Funktion, [n+(n+1)=n+2]. Neu ist jedoch die Möglichkeit, Code immer wieder rekursive Iterationen durchlaufen zu lassen, die Dimensionen in der zeichnerischen Improvisation ermöglichen, die das, was unsere Köpfe begreifen oder unsere Hände zeichnen können, weit übersteigen. Diese Fähigkeit wäre meiner Meinung nach in den Händen von Künstlern wie Wassily Kandinsky, Piet Mondrian und der Brüder Pevsner ein wahres Wunder gewesen.
Die Wiederholung ist das Herzstück der algoristischen Kunst. Auf diesem Weg werden selbstgleiche Qualitäten der gezeichneten Linien und Pinselstriche in meinem *Epigenesis Mural* in treibende Bündel von Tuschstrichen eingebettet, die einander widerspiegeln *(http://www.verostko.com/st/mural.html).* Darin liegt die Einmaligkeit der Vereinigung von maschineller Kraft und dem kodierten Verfahren des Künstlers.

Arbeiten im Atelier vor neuen Herausforderungen. Seit mehr als einem Viertel Jahrhundert faszinieren mich die Möglichkeiten, die sich aus der Macht kodierter Abläufe für das Experimentieren mit visuellen Formen ergeben. Künstler, die selbst programmierte Prozeduren in ihre Arbeit integriert haben, stehen an der Grenze zu völligem Neuland. Stellen sie sich dieser Herausforderung, so sehen sie sich mit zwei großen Hindernissen konfrontiert. Da wäre einmal die Aufgabe, Form schaffende Ideen in einen praktischen Arbeitscode zu übertragen. Dazu kommt die Suche nach geeigneten Methoden, der Arbeit greifbaren Ausdruck zu verleihen.
Der Code als Formgeber ist nur ein Teil des Problems. Um als Kunst zu funktionieren, muss der Code imstande sein, eine greifbare Form hervorzubringen – man muss sie sehen, grei-

fen, fühlen oder hören können. Vor einigen Jahren fragte mich ein befreundeter Künstler, als er neben einer Ulme stand: „Was gibt diesem Baum seine starke Präsenz?" Und er gab selbst die Antwort: „Man kann ihn angreifen – seine Oberfläche fühlen, sein ‚Da-Sein'!" Da das Erfahren von Kunst über die Sinne passiert, ist die Kunst untrennbar mit ihrer stofflichen Darstellung verbunden.

In ihrer Auseinandersetzung mit den menschlichen Befindlichkeiten machen sich Künstler viele verschiedene Medien zunutze, darunter auch jene, die aus der Kultur des Cyberspace hervorgehen. Mein Interesse gilt seit langem dem Zeichnen und Malen auf Papier. Meine Arbeiten nehmen Rücksicht auf die ästhetischen Qualitäten von Papier, Tinte, Stift und Pinsel – und auf die Art des Ausdrucks. Für mich sollte das fertige Objekt durch seine Aura den Betrachter zum Verweilen einladen und ihm zu verstehen geben, dass die Arbeit, der Ausdruck menschlichen Bemühens, über stoffliche Belange hinausgeht. Dennoch ist der Prozess selbst ungeheuer spannend.

Ausgabegeräte im Atelier. Viele Besucher meines Ateliers wundern sich, wenn sie die verschiedenen, an ein Computernetzwerk angeschlossenen Plotter sehen, von denen einer meinem experimentellen und der andere meinem künstlerischen Schaffen dient. Sehen Besucher einem Plotter bei der Arbeit zu, sind ihre Augen meist fest auf den Zeichenarm geheftet, der „scheinbar intelligent" präzise, überraschend und ohne zu zögernbuchstäblich Tausende von Linien zieht und dabei eine unheimliche Präsenz ausstrahlt!

Meine ersten Stift-Plotter mit Namen wie „Brunelleschi" und „Alberti" stehen längst still. Manchmal hole ich Brunelleschi hervor und lasse ihn eine kleine Zeichnung machen. Obwohl genaue Einstellungen schwer zu erhalten und die Bewegungen ein wenig grob sind, kann er doch noch immer eine Zeichnung zu meiner Zufriedenheit ausführen.

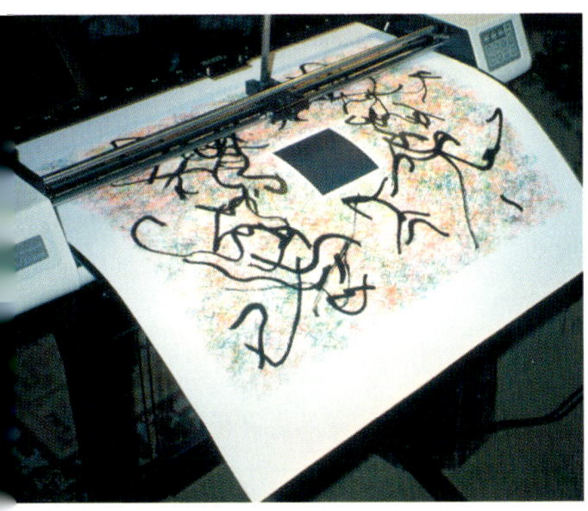

Erste kodierte Pinselstriche 1987. Kalligrafie-Pinsel auf Zeichenarm. Houston Instruments DMP 50 Stiftplotter. Plotter arbeitet mit PC unter DOS.

Im Laufe der Jahre ist mir mein Atelier zu einem Skriptorium mit einem Netz von elektronischen Zeichengeräten geworden. Diese befolgen unermüdlich alle Anweisungen. Manchmal dauert das Zeichnen einer bestimmten Arbeit mehrere Tage. Große Objekte sind aufgrund von Stift- oder Hardware-Pannen auch heute noch schwierig auszuführen.

Man kann zwar Codes für Endlossequenzen und eine breite Palette von Formen schreiben, der Zeichenprozess selbst muss jedoch unter Rücksichtnahme auf spezifische Zeichenmaterialien und -geräte kodiert werden. Der Code legt Abläufe fest, die diese Instrumente in Echtzeit und -raum führen. Der eigentliche Vorgang muss den Grenzen und ästhetischen Qualitäten von Papier und Zeichenwerkzeugen angepasst sein. Im Idealfall optimiert der Code die Handhabung von Zeichengeräten und verstärkt die ästhetischen Qualitäten von Papier und Tinte und den Charakter des Zeicheninstruments. Um diese technologischen Hürden zu meistern, braucht es in endlosen Stunden des Experimentierens Geduld und Erfahrung . Der Schatz am Ende dieser Suche ist das Stück Code, das funktioniert – so wie die Eichel zum Baum wird, so „wächst" aus dem Code das Kunstwerk! Dieses Verfahren zum Schaffen von Kunst ist heute nicht grundlegend anders als in den Achtzigern, als ich den Originaltext „Epigenetische Malerei: Software als Genotypus" schrieb. *(http://www.penplot.com/epigenet.html)*

Ein Personal-System. Die Software mit Computer und Plotter stellen ein eigenes Gesamtsystem dar. Vielfältigste Experimente mit Papier, Tinte und Plottprozeduren wurden durchgeführt. Durch jahrelanges Experimentieren hat sich das System zu einer einmaligen Reihe von Abläufen mit ihrer eigenen Sprache entwickelt. Die Software, die ständig weiterentwickelt wird, ist ein integriertes Programm aus Algorithmen in Standard-BASIC und Plotter-Befehlen in DMPL. Die Programmroutinen bestehen inzwischen aus Tausenden von Zeilen.

```
RAD(SID)=(INT(RND*(RMAX-RMIN))+RMIN)
THETA(SID)=INT(RND*(DEGEND-DEGBEG))+DEGBEG
XQ=X1:YQ=Y1
JX(SID)=X1+INT((RAD(SID)*STRETCH)*COS(THETA(SID)*(PI/180)))
JY(SID)=Y1+INT(RAD(SID)*SIN(THETA(SID)*(PI/180)))
X1=JX(SID):Y1=JY(SID)
```

Oben: Sechs Zeilen des Codes einer Schleife, die den Radius, einen Winkel und die Koordinaten von Kontrollpunkten eines Federstriches beschreibt

Hodos. Ich habe die Software *Hodos* (οδός) genannt, nach dem griechischen Wort für *Pfad* oder *Weg.* Außerdem ist *meta-hodos* (μέθοδος) die klassische Wurzel des Worts „Methode". Hodos als Zeichenmethode ist leicht mit meinen frühen Arbeiten unter dem Motto „Wegpfade" in Zusammenhang zu bringen. Mein Atelier, Pathway Studio, erhielt ein orientalisches Siegel, geschnitzt vom berühmten *Shufa*-Meister Wang Dongling. Wang war von den vom „elektrischen Gehirn" ausgeführten Pinselstrichen begeistert und wählte den klassischen Ausdruck *xiao jingzhai,* „Kleines Fußweg-Atelier", für das Siegel meines Ateliers. Viele in diesem Atelier geschaffene Arbeiten erhalten dieses Siegel *(http://www.penplot.com/seal.html[4]).*

Formfamilien. Formschaffende Unterprogramme von *Hodos* schaffen Arbeiten mit typischen, diesen Unterprogrammen eigenen Zügen. Arbeiten, die durch die selben oder ähnliche algorithmische Unterprogramme entstehen, weisen eine familiäre Ähnlichkeit zueinander auf. *Hodos* kann auf eine bestimmte Papiergröße, Palette oder Programmfolge eingestellt werden, um eine gänzlich neue Art von limitierter Ausgabe zu schaffen. Das Programm kann eine Formfamilie hervorbringen, in der die Objekte gleichzeitig einander verwandt und doch auf ihre Weise „einzigartig" sind. Die Arbeiten tragen starke familiäre Züge, da sie dieselben algorithmischen Eltern haben. Die Unterschiede ergeben sich daraus, dass der Code innerhalb gemeinsamer Parameter zufällige Entscheidungen trifft. Die Parameter, innerhalb derer entschieden wird, können sein: (a) *nicht mehr als* oder *nicht weniger als,* (b) weit geöffnet und *ohne Ober- oder Untergrenze,* oder (c) gewichtet *um einen Prozentsatz mehr oder weniger als soviel.* Die festgesetzten Parameter bestimmen Faktoren wie Winkel, Radius, Koordinaten, Skalierung und Farbe. Familienähnlichkeiten zwischen den Arbeiten variieren mehr oder weniger, je nachdem, wie viele Parameter sich in welchem Ausmaß verändern sollen.
So plottete zum Beispiel meine Frau Alice Wagstaff 1990 unter Einsatz von *Hodos* und mit

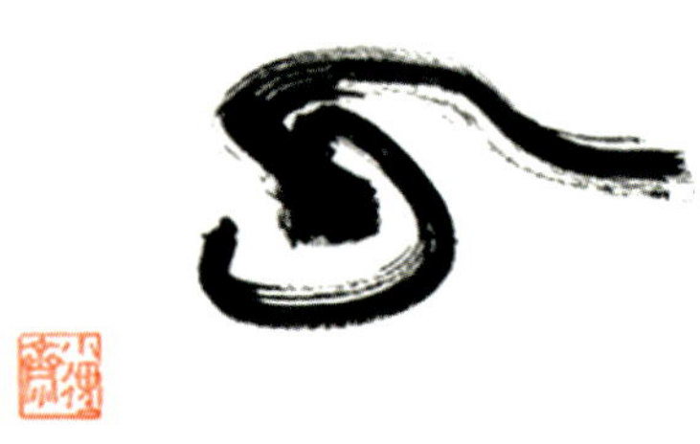

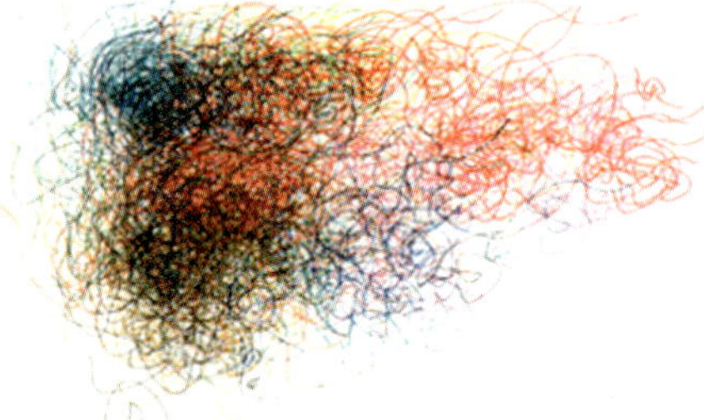

Zwei Stift- und Pinselzeichnungen aus einer Familie von 125 Originalen. Sie sind Titelbilder zweier Bücher aus der limitierten Ausgabe von Kapitel II in George Booles Klassiker zu den Gesetzen des Denkens aus dem Jahr 1854. (St. Sebastian Press, Minneapolis, 1990). Siehe: *http://www.verostko.com/boole.html*

meiner Hilfe 125 Titel- und 125 Schlussbilder einer limitierten Ausgabe von Originalzeichnungen mit Stift und Pinsel. Die ledergebundene Ausgabe mit einer Auflage von 125 Exemplaren enthielt weitere algorithmische Zeichnungen, die als Illustrationen für Kapitel II von George Booles Klassiker *Eine Untersuchung der Gesetze des Denkens* aus dem Jahr 1854 dienten *(http://www.penplot.com/boole.html).* Ein Satz von Programmroutinen mit einem Parametersatz wurde für die Titelbilder eingesetzt, ein anderer für die Schlussbilder. Wir glauben, dass hier zum ersten Mal eine limitierte Ausgabe eines Buchs unter Zuhilfenahme eines derartigen Illustrationsprozesses entstanden ist.

Epigenetische Kunst: Software als Genotypus. Diese Abläufe unterscheiden sich von traditionellen. Wie sollen wir diesen Prozess nennen? Diese Frage stellten sich Alice und ich 1986. Während unserer Suche kehrten wir immer wieder zu den Ähnlichkeiten zwischen biologischen Prozessen und kodierten Abläufen zurück. Daher wählten wir den Begriff „epigenetisch“, was zur Grundlage meines Textes aus dem Jahr 1988 wurde.
Epigenese meint den Prozess, durch den eine ausgewachsene Pflanze oder ein Phänotypus aus einem Samen oder Genotypus wächst. So enthält eine Eichel den Genotypus oder Code, der die gesamte, für das Wachsen einer Eiche benötigte Information enthält. Durch den Prozess der Epigenese wird die Eichel zum Baum oder Phänotypus.
Analog zum Genotypus enthalten meine Programme oder Codes die gesamte zum Entstehen einer Kunstform benötigte Information. Unter den richtigen Bedingungen im Atelier wächst die Software buchstäblich vom kodierten Ablauf zur Kunstform. Ähnlich der biologischen Epigenese kann dieser Prozess als *epigenetisch* gesehen werden. Natürlich könnte jeder kodierte Ablauf, der alle für das Entstehen einer Kunstform benötigten Informationen enthält, als *epigenetisch* bezeichnet werden. Der seit kurzem geläufigere Begriff dafür ist *generative Kunst.*

Inhalt und Bedeutung. Seit mehr als einem Viertel Jahrhundert generiert epigenetische Kunst die Ikonen unseres Informationszeitalters. Man könnte diese Ikonen als Diagramme oder visuelle Entsprechungen der kodierten Abläufe sehen, durch die sie entstanden sind. Der bezeichnende Charakter jeder fertigen Arbeit leitet sich vom „formgebenden Ablauf“ oder „Algorithmus“ ab, der als Genotypus fungiert. Daher könnte man auch sagen, dass das Endprodukt eine Epiphanie oder Manifestierung seines Erzeugers, des Codes, darstellt. Für mich ist jede Arbeit der feierliche Ausdruck ihres Codes, besonders der wiederholten Programme, die ihre Eigenart ausmachen. Dabei ist zu beachten, dass derartige Abläufe viel mit Prozessen gemein haben, die mit Kristallisierung und Genetik in Verbindung stehen.
All das ist jedoch sehr allgemein. Wie sollen wir zum Beispiel eine algoristische Zeichnung in Stift und Tinte, herangehen? Im Idealfall sind derartige Zeichnungen vom kodierten Ablauf des Künstlers geprägt. So wie der Pinselstrich eines Malers vielleicht die eindeutige Kennung der Hand des Malers trägt, so verraten die Linien in einer algorithmischen Zeichnung die charakteristischen Qualitäten der algorithmischen „Kopf-Hand“ des Künstlers. Durch das einmalige Zusammenlaufen von konzeptueller Innovation und dem Wissen um Materialien entsteht über den vom jeweiligen Algoristen geschriebenen Code ein persönlicher Stil, der jeder Zeichnung innewohnt. Die Linearformen eines Künstlers wie Jean Pierre Hebert wandern in selbstgleichen Mäandern über das Papier und unterscheiden sich dabei recht eindeutig von den Linien, die mein Code oder der von Manfred Mohr erzeugt. Die Betrachtung ihrer Formen verrät in jedem gegebenen Fall etwas über die „Kopf-Hand“ ihres Schöpfers. Diese Arbeiten erlauben uns einen Einblick in das geheimnisvolle Innenleben des Algoristen.
Diese Arbeiten öffnen allgemein den Blick auf unsichtbare Prozesse, die dem Geist und der Materie Gestalt geben. Auf diese Weise werden sie zu Ikonen, die Licht auf die geheimnisvolle Natur des Selbst, der Welt und des Kosmos werfen.

Aus dem Amerikanischen von Elisabeth Wiellander

The Infinite Loop

John Maeda

My first encounter with a personal computer was twenty years ago in junior high school math. At the time, it was never made clear to any of us students what it might be useful for, beyond participating in the literal act of "using the computer." "Using the computer," of course, plainly translated into the passive act of sitting in front of the computer and staring at a small blinking green rectangle. Some days you would secretly hope that it would entertain you in the manner of loud graphics and sound, like its close relative the television. But such bliss would never come and you would be eventually driven to attempt to interact with the device through its tiny keyboard. However, anything you might type at the unit, be it your name, a happy thought, and even things not so dear, would be evaluated by the computer with great insignificance. "SYNTAX ERROR," it would retort. I surely would never have advanced beyond the foyer of computer programming if it had not been for my well-to-do classmate, who as evidence of his absurd wealth had a similar unit at home! He showed me how to teach the computer to display my name with a simple statement like "PRINT 'MAEDA'." The computer would dutifully display "MAEDA." With a few more instructions the computer would display my name twice, fifty times, on to a hundred, and then practically forever. The implication of this simple mechanism of repetition, by which the computer was clearly king, was further dramatized when we hooked up the computer to a printer. The printer would print and print until its paper supply was exhausted, still hungry for more. Upon seeing this and similar displays of the printer's athleticism and waste, my instructor would shout disapprovingly, "No infinite loops allowed!" Only a subsequent command to terminate the processing flow, the chording of two keys of the keyboard, would stop such madness.

Surely my instructor would disapprove of the situation we face today with computers of the 21st century. From the very moment its electric soul ignites at the touch of the power button, the computer drags you into an infinite loop of "yes-no-cancel" queries that hints at our future existence as a species requiring only one finger for clicking and a brain as optional accessory hardware. The common acceptance of the term "computer user" to

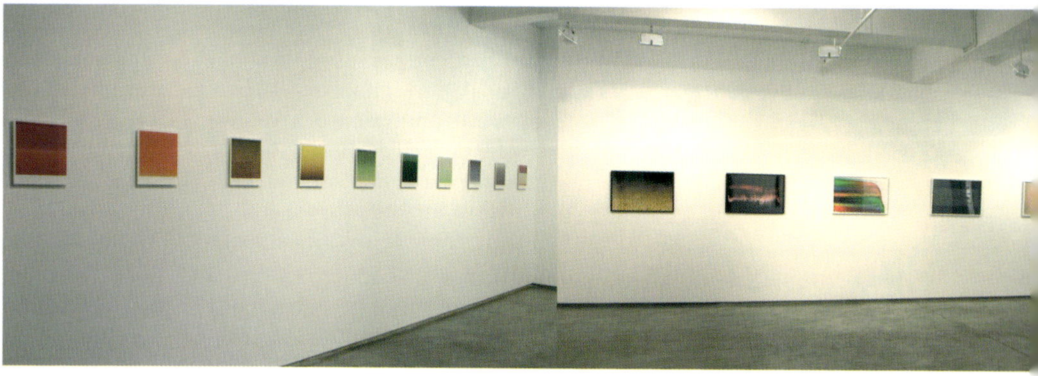

describe such daily interaction hides a fundamental philosophical question. Are we using the computers, or are the computers using us? In the complex infinite loops of today's highly interactive software, how far could a computer go without us, constantly tending to its incessant needs to confirm its manner of being?

Lastly, were we to let it go along its infinite ways without any need for human input, would we know which keys to press to terminate the madness?

Our modern civilization has always prided itself upon technological developments that have rendered activities once laborious or requiring manual skills into processes that are automated and require significantly less skill. Inevitably our computers will develop in a similar manner—forcing the paradoxical trend of making something that is already automated into a state of further automation. Such automated perfection eliminates the need for human input because the committee or individual who creates the system leaves their set of decisions as absolute knowledge that is prescribed as forever valid. All technological systems are thus human because they carry the roots of human thought, but they are not by definition humane.

The invention of humane technologies requires a simple catalyst—what I often refer to as a "humanist technologist." This is of course not a kind of computer technology that one can trivially trade on the stock exchange, but refers to a kind of person that bridges a sensitivity to the traditions of the past with an unbridled passion for mastering the skills of the future. Finding such people is not simple because today the process for growing people—the process of education—is biased towards developing people with a specific inclination towards either the creative side (arts, design, etc.) or the technical side (science, engineering, etc.) but never both. In other words, our modern academic system produces those who can think but cannot render their ideas as actual objects, and those who can create any object but cannot imagine what to make.

Over a decade of experimentation I have demonstrated that a single person can indeed bridge the gap between concept and construction. The results achieved never lack the critical synergy between idea and object because they are one and the same. In addition my experiments in educating more people to engage in a similar manner of creation have supported my constant hypothesis that there is nothing unique to what I do, and that there are many routes left to explore. However most recently I have had the disturbing sense that no matter what new digital territory may arise, we end up where we first began—back into the infinite loop. My instinctive response to this personal perception has been to proclaim a new effort to escape to the "Post Digital" which, although "Post" implies the future, I am certain lies in the past.

from: John Maeda, "Post Digital"; Tokyo 2001

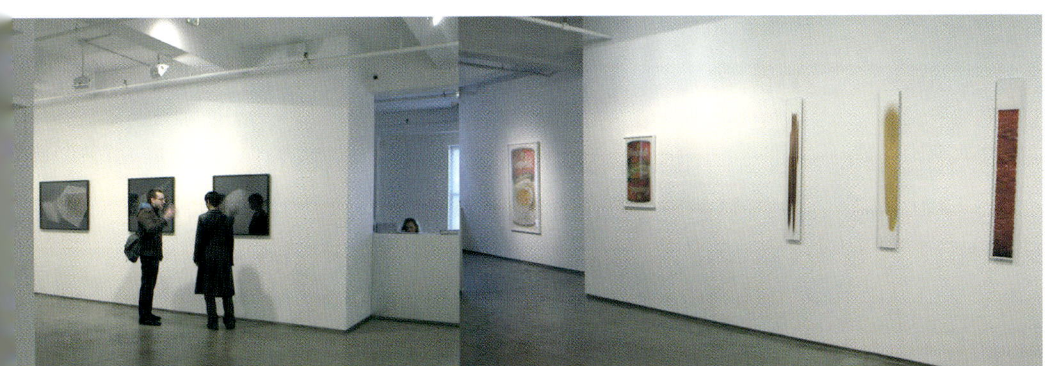

Reactive Graphics History
John Maeda

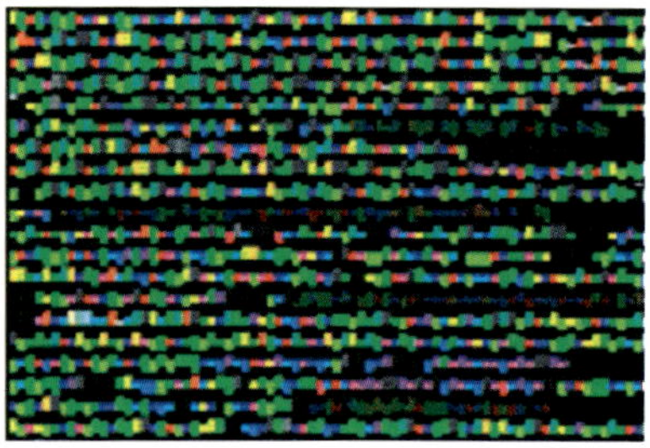

Color Typewriter (1994)
Abstraction of typing as color.
Click and drag over the color for the color-impaired

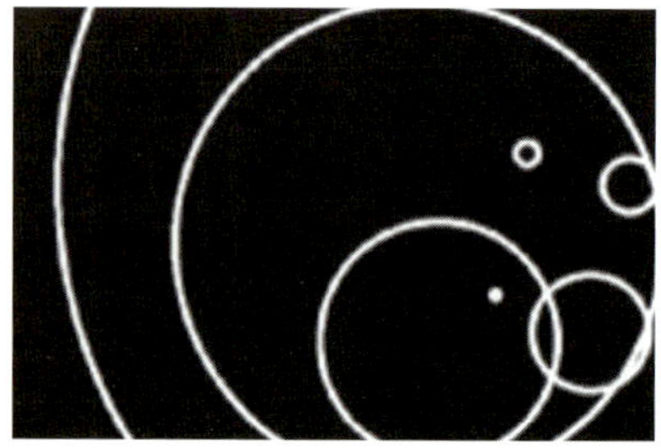

Concentric No. 3 (1994)
The large and small of interaction.
Move the mouse

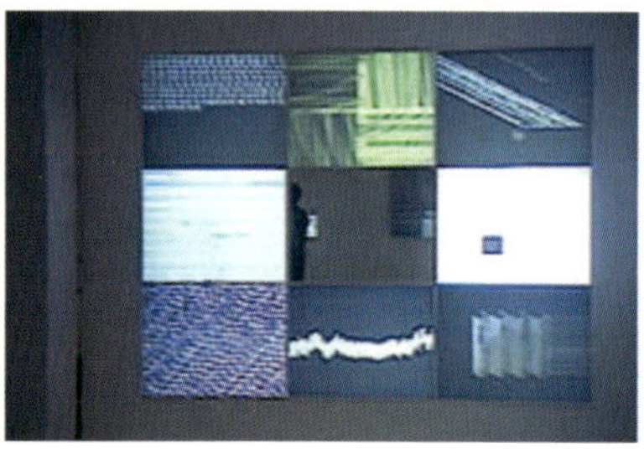

Mirror Mirror (1997)
Select 1 of 10 TV channels
from the keyboard

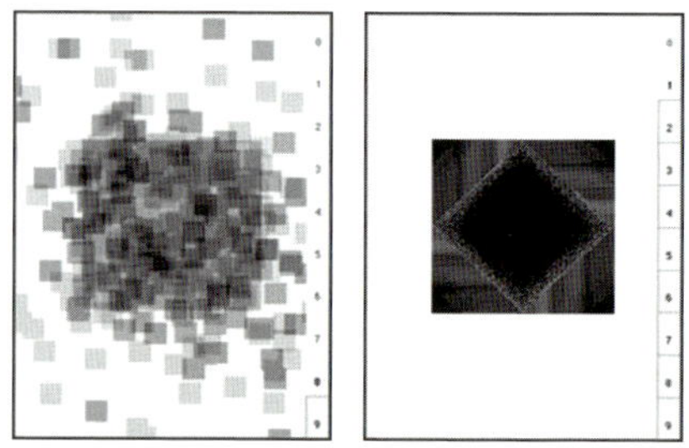

Reactive Square (1993)
Select 1 of 10 squares to speak to

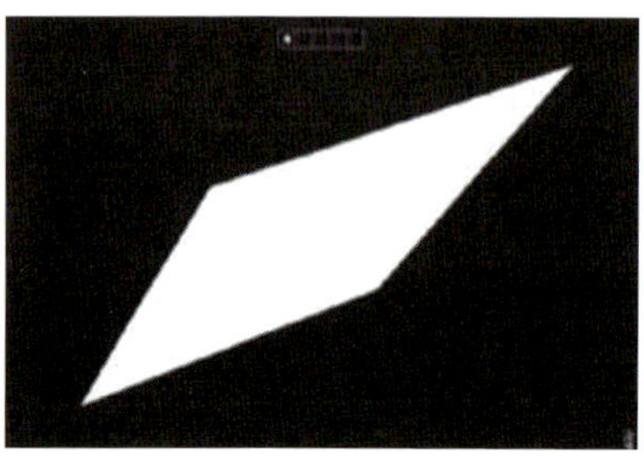

Single Pixel (1998)
No color, minimal interaction using a pixel

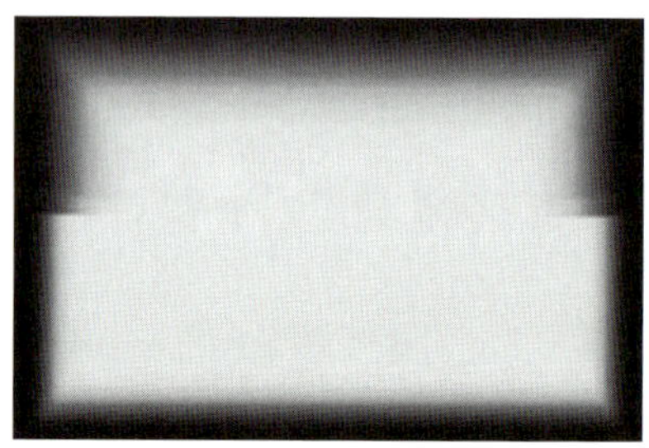

White Bottle (1995)
Basic interaction study

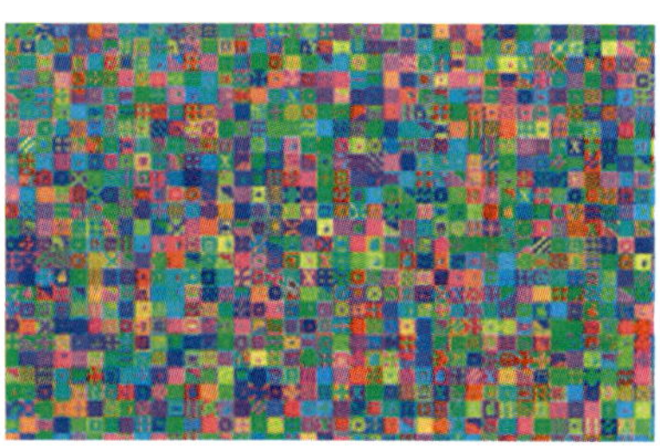

Reactive Graphic No. 2 (1993)
An early attempt to make something small
yet overactive

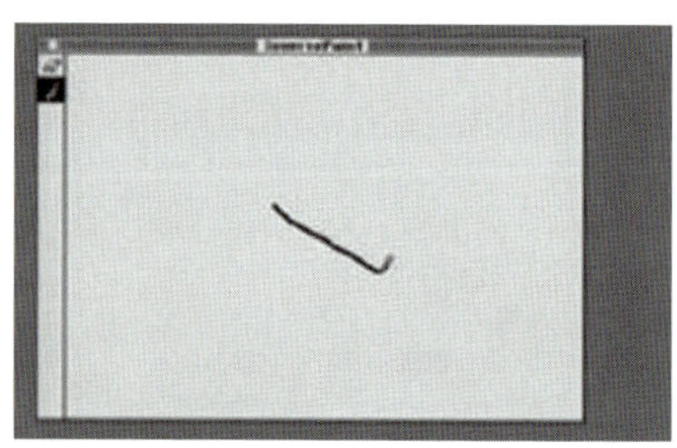

Inverse Paint (1994)
Man versus machine

F00D
John Maeda

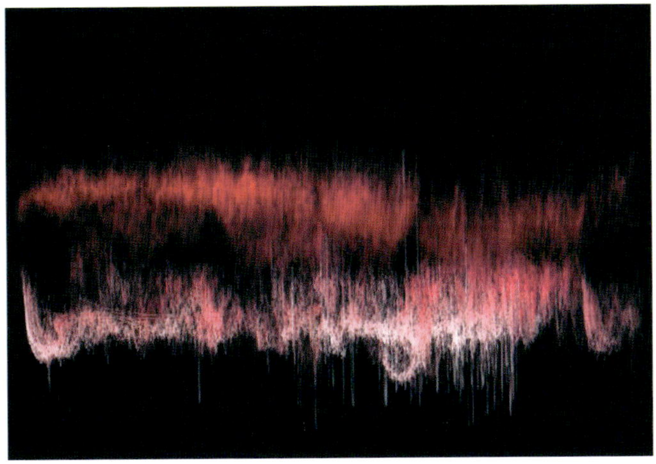

Fat-Free / 30x20-inch Cibachrome Print

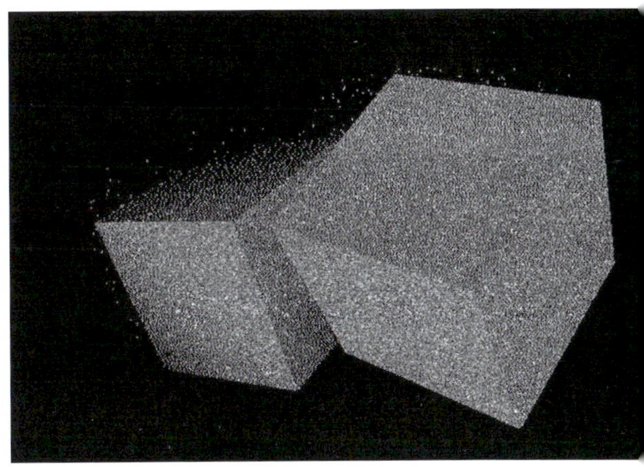

Tea for Two inset in full-scale detail / 40x30-inch Cibachrome Print

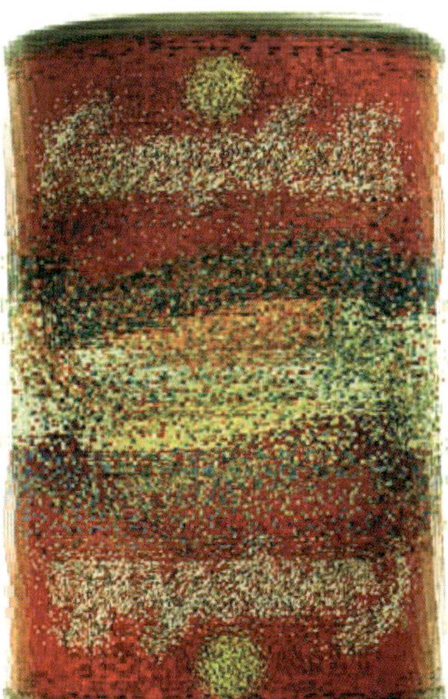

Veggie Soup inset in full-scale detail / 20x30-inch Cibachrome Print

RedBeet, BluePurpleTopTurnip and *GreenZucchini* from the "Smoothies" Series / 11x12.5-inch Plexi-Sandwich Mounted Cibachrome Prints

Die Endlosschleife

John Maeda

Meine erste Begegnung mit einem Computer hatte ich vor zwanzig Jahren in Mathematik an der Junior High School. Damals war uns nicht klar, wofür ein Computer gut war, außer dass wir damit ganz prosaisch „Berechnungen" anstellen durften. „Berechnungen erstellen" bedeutete schlicht das passive Verharren vor dem Bildschirm und Anstarren eines kleinen, grünen, blinkenden Rechtecks. An manchen Tagen hofften wir im Geheimen, dass das Gerät ähnlich wie sein naher Verwandter, der Fernseher, schreiende Bilder und durchdringende Töne liefern und zu unserer Unterhaltung beitragen würde. Doch vergebens, dieses Vergnügen war uns nie beschert, und schließlich sahen wir uns versucht, über die winzige Tastatur mit dem Gerät zu kommunizieren. Allerdings behandelte der Computer sämtliche Eingaben – seien es Namen, ein netter Gedanke oder weniger bedeutsame Angelegenheiten – mit großer Gleichgültigkeit. „SYNTAX ERROR" war die knappe Antwort.

Ohne einen betuchten Schulkollegen, der als Beweis seines fast schon absurden Wohlstands ein ähnliches Gerät sein eigen nennen durfte, hätte ich zweifelsohne nie die höheren Weihen des Programmierens angestrebt. Er erklärte mir, wie man den Computer mittels eines einfachen Befehls wie „PRINT MAEDA" instruieren konnte, meinen Namen anzuzeigen – der Computer gab gehorsam „MAEDA" aus. Mit einigen weiteren Befehlen würde er meinen Namen zweimal, fünfzigmal, hundertmal und schließlich in einer Endlosschleife ausgeben. Die Dramatik dieses simplen Wiederholungsmechanismus, den der Computer zweifellos bis zur Vollendung beherrschte, ließ sich weiter steigern, wenn wir den Computer an einen Drucker anschlossen. Der Drucker würde unaufhaltsam Seite um Seite drucken, bis der Papiervorrat aufgebraucht war, und trotzdem weiter nach neuen Druckaufträgen gieren. In Anbetracht dieser und anderer ähnlich beeindruckender Leistungen des Druckers und des enormen Papierverbrauchs würde mein Lehrer mich unwillig anherrschen: „Keine Endlosschleifen!" Nur der anschließende Befehl zur Beendigung des Datenflusses – das gleichzeitige Drücken zweier Tasten auf der Tastatur – konnte den Wahnsinn stoppen.

Mein damaliger Lehrer würde die Situation, in die uns die Computer des 21. Jahrhunderts zwingen, gewiss missbilligen. Sobald der elektrischen Seele des Computers mit dem Drücken des Einschaltknopfes Leben eingehaucht wird, nötigt der Rechner die User in eine Endlosschleife von „Ja-Nein-Abbrechen"-Fragen; man könnte daraus schließen, dass die Spezies Mensch in Zukunft nur mehr einen Finger zum Klicken benötigt und das Gehirn zu Hardwarezubehör degradiert wird. Die allgemeine Akzeptanz des Terminus „User" als Umschreibung für derartige Interaktionen lässt jedoch eine grundlegende philosophische Frage außer Acht: Benutzen wir den Computer oder werden wir vom Computer benutzt? Wie weit könnte ein Computer in seinem stetigen Bemühen, sein unbändiges Bedürfnis nach Bestätigung seines Seins zu befriedigen, in den komplexen Endlosschleifen der modernen interaktiven Software ohne menschlichen Input kommen?

Ließen wir den Computer diese Endlosschleifen ohne menschlichen Input durchlaufen, wüssten wir mit welchem Knopfdruck sich der Wahnsinn letztlich stoppen ließe?

Unsere moderne Zivilisation rühmt sich gerne ihres technischen Fortschritts, der zur Automatisierung von Tätigkeiten führte, die einst mühsam waren oder händisches Geschick erforderten; heute sind für diese Prozesse bedeutend weniger Fähigkeiten erforderlich. Compu-

ter werden unweigerlich eine ähnliche Entwicklung durchlaufen und dadurch den paradoxen Trend zur weiteren Automatisierung bereits automatisierter Prozesse verstärken. Eine derartige automatisierte Perfektion verzichtet auf menschlichen Input, da die Entwickler des Systems dies mit einem allgemein und ewig gültigen Set von möglichen Optionen versehen. Alle technischen Systeme sind auch menschlich, da sie die Wurzeln menschlichen Denkens in sich tragen, aber per definitionem nicht human.
Die Erfindung humaner Technologien erfordert einen einfachen Katalysator, den ich gerne als „humanistischen Technologen" bezeichne. Es handelt sich hier natürlich nicht um eine Computertechnologie, die ganz banal an der Börse gehandelt werden könnte, sondern um eine Person, die ein Gefühl für vergangene Traditionen mit einer ungezügelten Leidenschaft für Zukunftstechnologien in sich vereint. Solche Menschen zu finden ist nicht einfach, da in der heutigen Zeit – auch in der Schule – entweder einseitig die Kreativität (Kunst, Design, etc.) oder die technische Begabung (Naturwissenschaft, Technik etc.), nie aber beide Fertigkeiten gefördert werden. Mit anderen Worten, unser modernes Bildungssystem produziert Denker, die ihre Ideen nicht in die Praxis umsetzen können, und technisch versierte Menschen, die keine Ideen haben.
In zehn Jahren verschiedenster Versuche habe ich bewiesen, dass ein einzelner Mensch die Kluft zwischen Konzept und Umsetzung überwinden kann. Die erzielten Ergebnisse zeigen die kritische Synergie zwischen Idee und Objekt – beide sind Teil des Ganzen. Meine Bestrebungen, mehr Menschen für meinen Schaffensansatz zu gewinnen, bestätigen nur meine Theorie, dass ich nichts Einzigartiges vollbringe und es noch viele verschiedene Möglichkeiten zu erforschen gilt. Seit einiger Zeit hege ich allerdings den unangenehmen Verdacht, dass, egal welches neue digitale Phänomen auftaucht, wir dort enden werden, wo wir begonnen haben – in einer Endlosschleife. Meine instinktive Reaktion auf dieses subjektive Gefühl war die Flucht in das „postdigitale Zeitalter", das, auch wenn „post" Zukünftiges impliziert, gewiss in der Vergangenheit liegt.

Aus: John Maeda, *Post Digital,* Tokyo 2001

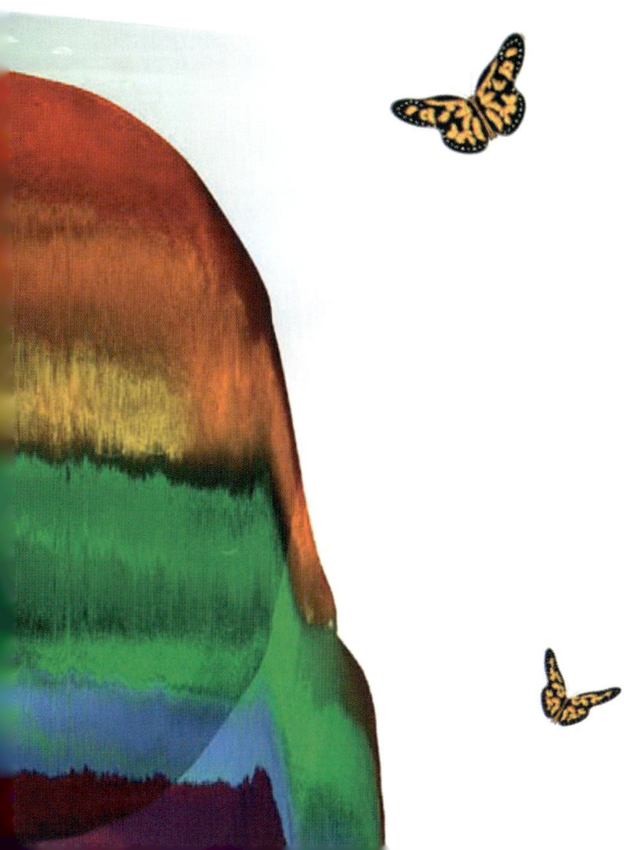

Excerpt from *Traffic*/30x20-inch Cibachrome Print
with parts from *Butterfries* /
30x30-inch Cibachrome Print

Programming Media

Casey Reas

The design of software is a defining factor in modern culture and is increasingly becoming a basis for our reality. Citizens of the world unite in spending their lives staring into the reflective surfaces of their mobile phones and desktop computers. Their minds and hands operate in the space between reality and the arbitrary rules of menus, windows, clicking, and dragging. Artists utilize software to comment on our increasingly digital social and political structures and to challenge the underlying formal assumptions of computer code. Regardless of the content or intent of their work, contemporary artists are expressing their ideas through the medium of software. With the continually shifting focus of the electronic arts (Cybernetics, Virtual Reality, CAVE, A-Life, Net.art, Augmented Reality), software provides the foundation on which meaning and content are constructed. With the revitalization of the concept of "software art" at festivals such as the Transmediale and READ_ME, a critical discussion is emerging around the role of software within our culture and art practice. This essay extends the discourse and focuses on the concept of software as a medium capable of unique expressions and programming languages as materials with specific properties.

Software Defined

What is Software?

Software is written in programming languages, sequences of alphanumeric characters and symbols composed according to rigid syntactical rules.[1] If you do not normally see computer programs, here are a few program fragments for reference:

Perl
```
opendir(DIR, $dir) || die $!;
@files = readdir(DIR);
closedir(DIR);

foreach $file (@files) {
    if($file =~ ".xml") {
                handle("$dir/$file");
    }
}
```

C++
```
                main() {
    int c;
    c = getchar();
    while(c != EOF) {
    putchar(c);
        c = getchar();
    }
}
```

LISP
```
(define (square x)
    (* x x))
(define (sum-of-squares x y)
    (+ (square x) (square y)))
```

Through writing software, computer programmers describe structures that define "processes." These structures are translated into code that is executed by a machine and the processes are carried out by actively engaging the electronic matter within the computer. Massachusetts Institute of Technology computer scientist Harold Abelson explains, "Processes manipulate abstract things called data. The evolution of a process is directed by a pattern of rules called a program. People create programs to direct processes." It is this active process of reading, manipulating, and storing data, that enables the unique aspects of the software medium.

Software is a Medium

Software has enabled a way to build a bridge between the art of the past and the electronic arts of the present and future. As articulated by Roy Ascott, we have transitioned from "content, object, perspective, and representation" to "context, process, immersion, and negotiation." The most unique aspect of software as a medium is that it enables response. A responsive artifact has the ability to interact with its environment. Artificial reality pioneer Myron Krueger suggests a number of interesting metaphors for interactions between people and software including dialog, amplification, ecosystem, instrument, game, and narrative. I am interested in addressing expressions of software that are more fundamental than those discussed by Ascott and Krueger. These expressions are the foundation of the software media and include dynamic form, gesture, behavior, simulation, self-organization, and adaptation.

Each Language is Unique

Just as there are many different human languages, there are many different programming languages. In the same way that different concepts can be conveyed through diverse human languages, different computer languages allow programmers to write diverse software structures. Just as some expressions are not translatable from one human language to another, programming structures often cannot be translated from one machine language to another. Some programming languages were built specifically for business applications (COBOL), some for artificial intelligence exploration (LISP), and some data manipulation (Perl), and many of the structures written within these diverse languages can only be expressed within that language. The abstract animator and programmer Larry Cuba describes his experience, "Each of my films has been made on a different system using a different programming language. A programming language gives you the power to express some ideas, while limiting your abilities to express others."

Programming Languages are Materials

It can be useful to think of each programming language as a material with unique affordances and constraints. Different languages are appropriate depending on the context. Some languages are easy to use but obscure the potential of the computer and some languages are very complicated, but provide total control through providing complete access to the machine. For example, some programming languages are flexible and others are rigid. Flexible languages like Perl and Lingo are good for quickly creating short programs, but they often become difficult to maintain and understand when programs become large. Programming with rigid languages like 68008 Assembly or C requires extreme care and tedious attention to detail, but the results are efficient and robust. In the same way that the different woods Pine and Oak "feel" and "look" different, software programs written in different languages also have distinct aesthetic gestalts. For example, similar software programs written in Java and Flash have unique differences that are noticed by people familiar with both.

Programming is Exclusive

Many people think that computer programmers are a unique kind of person, different from everyone else. One reason programming remains within the boundaries of this type of personality is that similarly minded people usually create the programming languages. It is possible to create different kinds of programming languages that engage people with visual and spatial minds. Alternative languages expand the programming space to people who think differently. An early alternative language was LOGO, designed in the late 1960s by Seymour Papert as a language concept for children. Through LOGO, children are able to program many different media including a robotic turtle and graphic images on screen. A contemporary example is the MAX programming environment developed at IRCAM by Miller Puckette in the 1980s. MAX has generated enthusiasm from thousands of artists who use it as a base for creating audiovisual software and installations. The same way the graphical user interfaces (GUIs) opened up computing for millions of people, alternative programming environments will continue to enable new generations of artists working with software.

Software Expressions

When computer programs execute, they are dynamic processes rather than static texts on the screen. Core expressions of software including dynamic form, gesture, behavior, simulation, self-organization, and adaptation emerge from these processes. These and other basic expressions are the fundamentals on which more complex ideas and experiences are conveyed. Each expression is discussed below and illustrated with an example from the Aesthetics & Computation Group at the Massachusetts Institute of Technology. These examples were created by hybrid artist/programmers from 1998 – 2001 and provide clear demonstrations of software expressions.

Dynamic Form

Dynamic form is form that changes in time. If this form reacts to stimuli, it is responsive. *Scratch* by Jared Schiffman (Figure 1) demonstrates basic qualities of dynamic form. In this software, the position of a controllable circle continuously affects the contour of each visual element. Scratch augments the visual communication of the form by adding layers of movement and fluid response. In general, form can respond to any signal from the environment including common input devices such as a mouse, microphone, and video camera to more exotic devices such as radiation sensors and sonar.

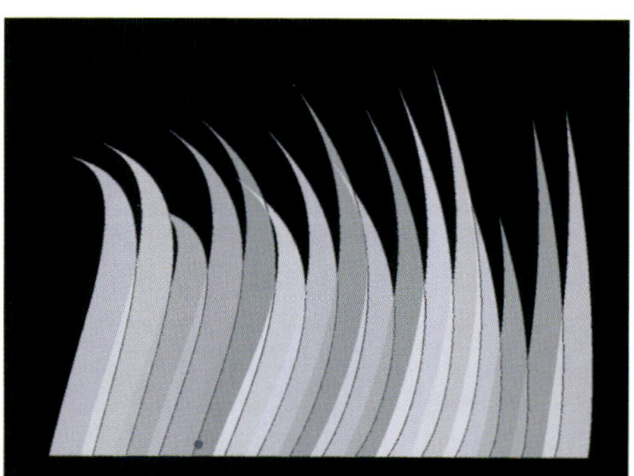

Fig. 1: Jared Schiffman: *Scratch*

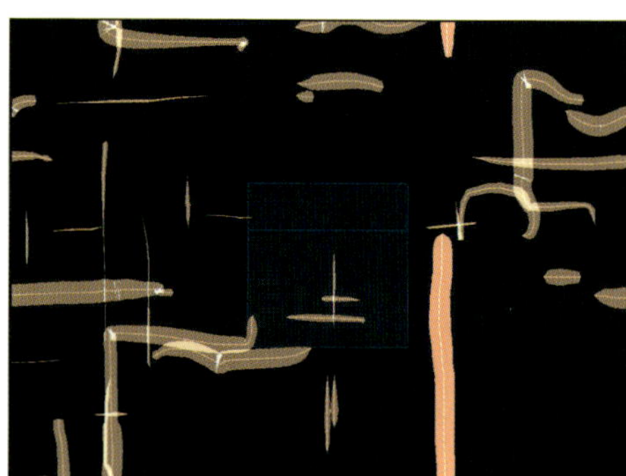

Fig. 2: Golan Levin: *AVES*

Gesture

Gesture is a critical aspect of every continuous medium and software has the ability to convey and interpret gesture. The *AVES* software by Golan Levin (Figure 2) is a group of applications that amplify hand gestures by processing their data as sound and image. One application maps the structure of each gesture into sounds that reflect its degree of curvature. Another layers gestures to create gradual sound textures that activate and combine with the presence of the cursor. Interpreting gestures is more complex, but opens new opportunities for engaging interaction. Handwriting recognition software is one application of gesture interpretation. Some installations and video games use a more basic form of gesture recognition to allow people to direct action with complex motions.

Behavior

Behavior is movement with the appearance of intent. Combining simple behaviors can create personality or disposition. Behavior can be created by intuitively writing programs or by implementing biological models. In the project *Trundle* (Figure 3), the physical object has a program that determines how it should move when presented with stimuli in its environment. *Trundle* searches the environment looking for people, but when it finds someone it attempts to flee. It is curious and timid. An array of sensors on *Trundle's* body continually monitors its immediate environment and sends signals to the micro-controller that determines how the motors should turn. In general, behavior can be used to actively engage the mind through personifying objects, developing characters, communicating affect, and adding a layer of psychological interest to a piece of software.

Simulation

Simulated aspects of the physical world provide an easy access point for perceiving works of software. Our senses have evolved to respond to the rules of the natural world. One of the first computer games, *Pong,* was a highly abstracted simulation of tennis. Modern engineering and scientific communities utilize models of reality as a basis for designing physical objects and conducting research. The *Floccus* software by Golan Levin (Figure 4) creates a group of elegant lines, each a connected list of simulated springs. The undulating movement created by this simple simulation generates awe in spectators when it is combined with response. The lines stretch and contract according to force, mass, and acceleration. In software, simulation can go beyond mimicking perspective, materials, and physical laws—the processes of natural systems can be simulated as well.

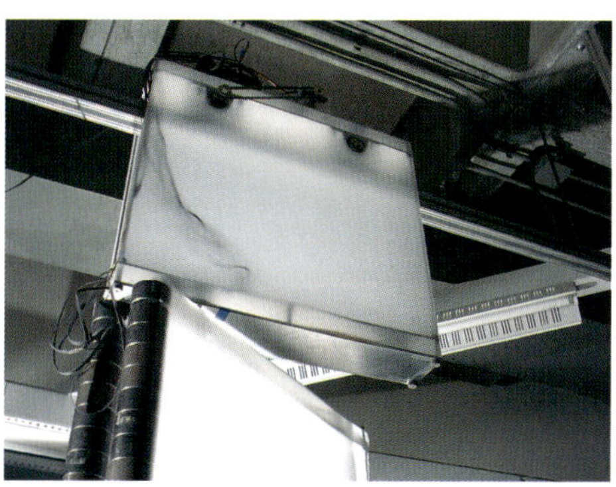

Fig. 3: Casey Reas: *Trundle*

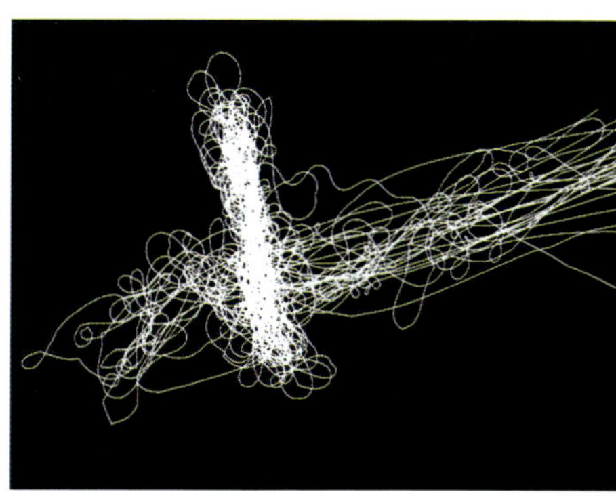

Fig. 4: Golan Levin: *Floccus*

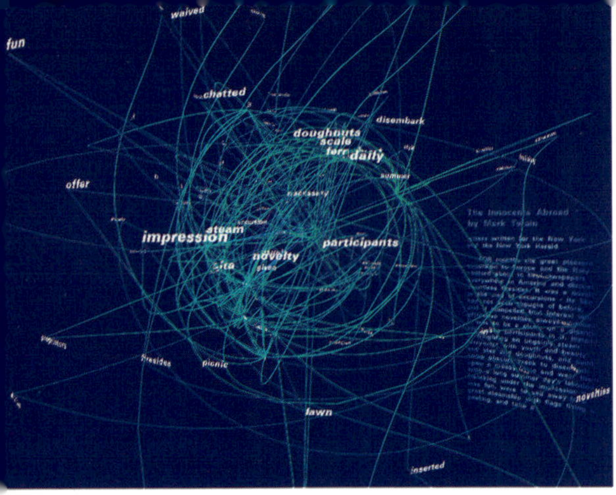

Fig. 5: Ben Fry: *Valence*

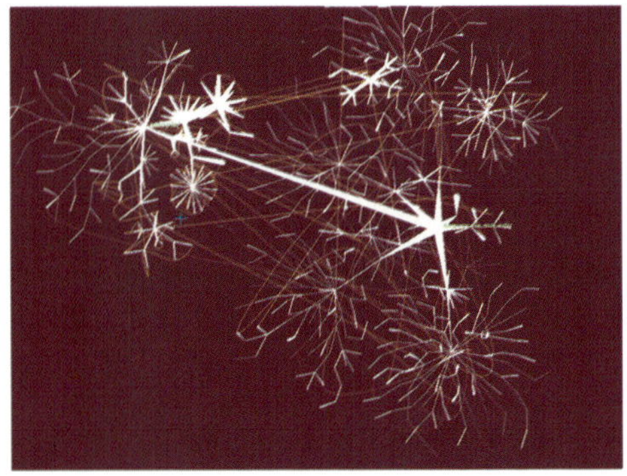

Fig. 6: Ben Fry: *Anemone*

Self-Organization

The ability for elements to self-organize makes possible the phenomena of emergence. Structure emerges through the interactions of many autonomous processes. *Valence* by Ben Fry (Figure 5), reads the text of a book word by word and spatially organizes it according to a system of rules. A complex volume emerges from the relations of diverse words in the text. Small changes to the rules of interaction make potentially large changes in the processed visualization.

Adaptation

Adapting is the ability to change. For software to adapt, it must have a representation of itself and be aware of its context. The *Anemone* software by Ben Fry (Figure 6) is able to monitor its density and prune its structure to maintain equilibrium. Anemone is a visualization of website traffic and as the hours and days progress, the software removes sections of its mass to allow for new sections to grow without obscuring legibility of the information. Writing software that truly adapts to its context is a challenge and adaptive expressions are rare. Using an interpreter, it is possible for a program to modify its own program while it is running.

Programming

Although software is consistently utilized within the electronic arts, individuals choose to construct their code in radically different ways from writing in low-level languages to collaborating with programmers. Some artists use software as a tool for creating work in other media. They use commercially available products for generating prints and videos and for making rough sketches that are executed in analog media. Others collaborate with professional programmers by creating specifications that are then implemented by the programmers. Many other people use programming environments developed for designers and artists. They create their work with scripting and visual programming environments such as Director, Flash, and MAX that make it easier for non-programmers to construct software. The smallest group of artists working with software use programming languages developed for professional programmers. They use general languages like C, Java, and Perl and often develop their own custom tools for working within these environments.

There is no correct way to work with software. It is an individual choice balancing control with simplicity. Mastering programming takes many years of hard work, but understanding the basic principles of the medium is within everyone's grasp. In my opinion, every artist using software should be software literate. What does literacy mean within the context of software? Alan Kay, an innovator in thinking about computation as a medium, has written: The ability to "read" a medium means you can access materials and tools created by others. The ability to "write" in a medium means you can generate materials and tools for others. You must have both to be literate. In print writing, the tools you generate are rhetorical; they demonstrate and convince. In computer writing, the tools you generate are processes; they simulate and decide.

These processes that simulate and decide are the essence of software and they can only be fully understood through constructing them.

Artists are increasing writing their own software. With the growth of the web, the popularity of scripting environments like Flash, and the falling price of hardware, many more artists are exploring programming. The area of audiovisual programming is an excellent example of this trend. Small software companies like Cycling '74, the developer of Jitter, are very responsive to their community of artists and foster the development of enabling tools. Their Jitter tool is a sophisticated library of visual structures for integrating image with sound. Many artists have moved beyond relying on developers for their tools. The Pink Twins, a duo of musician/programmers from Helsinki, have created Framestein, video processing software that links to PD, open source real-time software for performance. The German artist collective Meso has gone even further with vvvv, an ambitious library of tools for real-time video synthesis. Some artists develop software tools for themselves and after a period of refinement, choose to release it to the community.

Synthesis

Over the last thirty years, artists have created innovative work with the aid of the software medium, but they have explored only a small range of the conceptual possibilities. Historically, programming languages and environments encouraged a specific methodology that did not engage the majority of artists who were interested in creating interactive and programmatic work. New tools are emerging that encourage artists to begin working directly with the software medium. The proliferation of software literacy among artists will increase the sophisticated use of software and contribute to new forms of software materials and development environments. These materials and environments have the potential to open the creation of software to an even larger creative and critical community.

1 There are exceptional programming languages called "visual programming languages" that allow structures to be defined with graphic symbols.

Abelson, Harold, Gerald Sussman, and Julie Sussman. *Structure and Interpretation of Computer Programs.* MIT Press, Cambridge, MA. 1985

Ascott, Roy. "Moist Ontology." Published in *The Art of Programming.* Sonics Acts Press, Amsterdam. 2002

Cuba, Larry. "Calculated Movements." Published in *Prix Ars Electronica Edition '87: Meisterwerke der Computerkunst.* Verlag H.S. Sauer. 1987

Kay, Alan. "User Interface: A Personal View" in *The Art of Human-Computer Interface Design,* edited by Brenda Laurel Addison-Wesley Publishing Company, Reading MA. 1989.

Krueger, Myron. "Responsive Environments." Published in *Multimedia, From Wagner to Virtual Reality.* Edited by Randall Packer and Ken Jordan. W.W Norton & Company, Inc., New York. 2001

Medien programmieren

Casey Reas

Die Entwicklung von Software ist ein bestimmender Faktor in der modernen Kultur und wird immer mehr zur Grundlage unserer Wirklichkeit. Die Bürger dieser Welt starren vereint auf die reflektierenden Oberflächen ihrer Mobiltelefone und Computer. Ihr Verstand und ihre Hände agieren in einem Raum zwischen Wirklichkeit und Willkürherrschaft von Menüs, Fenstern, Klicken und Ziehen. Künstler bedienen sich der Software, um unsere zunehmend digitalen Sozial- und Politstrukturen zu kommentieren und um die dem Computercode zugrunde liegenden Formalannahmen in Frage zu stellen. Zeitgenössische Künstler mit den unterschiedlichsten Inhalten und Intentionen drücken ihre Ideen mithilfe von Software aus. Software bildet die Grundlage einer sich immer neu orientierenden elektronischen Kunst (Kybernetik, Virtual Reality, CAVE, A-Life, Net.art, Augmented Reality), auf der Bedeutung und Inhalt aufbauen. Mit der Wiederbelebung des Konzepts der „Software-Kunst" bei Festivals wie der Transmediale oder READ_ME wird die Rolle der Software für unsere Kultur- und Kunstpraxis wieder kritisch diskutiert. Dieser Beitrag weitet den Diskurs aus und betrachtet Software als Medium mit einmaligen Ausdrucksmöglichkeiten und Programmiersprachen als Materialien mit ganz speziellen Eigenschaften.

Definition von Software

Was ist Software?

Software wird in Programmiersprachen geschrieben; eine Abfolge von alphanumerischen Zeichen und Symbolen, die nach strengen Syntaxregeln angeordnet werden.[1] Falls Sie für gewöhnlich Programme nur bedienen, folgen hier einige Codebeispiele:

Perl
```
opendir(DIR, $dir) || die $!;
@files = readdir(DIR);
closedir(DIR);

foreach $file (@files) {
   if($file =~ ".xml") {
               handle("$dir/$file");
   }
}
```

C++
```
            main() {
   int c;
   c = getchar();
   while(c != EOF) {
   putchar(c);
      c = getchar();
   }
}
```

LISP
```
(define (square x)
   (* x x))
(define (sum-of-squares x y)
   (+ (square x) (square y)))
```

In der Software beschreibt der Programmierer Strukturen, die „Prozesse" definieren. Diese Strukturen werden in Code übersetzt, der von einer Maschine ausgeführt wird. Die Prozesse laufen unter aktiver Beteiligung der elektronischen Bauteile des Computers ab. Der Computerwissenschaftler Harold Abelson vom Massachusetts Institute of Technology erklärt: „[...] ein Prozess [bearbeitet] andere abstrakte Dinge, genannt ‚Daten'. Der Ablauf eines Prozesses wird durch einen Satz von Regeln gesteuert, genannt ‚Programm'. Menschen erzeugen Programme, um Prozesse zu steuern." Erst dieser *aktive* Prozess des Lesens, Manipulierens und Speicherns von Daten ermöglicht die einzigartigen Charakteristika des Mediums Software.

Software ist ein Medium

Software hat den Brückenschlag zwischen der Kunst der Vergangenheit und der elektronischen Kunst der Gegenwart und Zukunft ermöglicht. Roy Ascott meint, wir haben „Inhalt, Objekt, Perspektive und Darstellung" durch „Kontext, Prozess, Immersion und Verhandlung" ersetzt. Die wichtigste Eigenschaft der Software als Medium ist das Faktum, dass man reagieren kann. Ein reagierendes Kunstwerk kann mit seiner Umwelt interagieren. Myron Krueger, der Pionier der Artificial Reality, verweist auf einige interessante Metaphern für die Interaktion zwischen Mensch und Software, wie etwa Dialog, Verstärkung, Ökosystem, Instrument, Spiel und Erzählung. Ich möchte jedoch Aspekte der Software behandeln, die fundamentaler sind als jene, die Ascott und Krueger erörtern. Sie bilden die Basis für Softwaremedien und umfassen dynamische Form, Gestik, Verhalten, Simulation, Selbstorganisation und Anpassung.

Jede Sprache ist einzigartig

So wie es viele verschiedene Landessprachen gibt, sind auch viele verschiedene Programmiersprachen in Gebrauch. Wie unterschiedliche Landessprachen verschiedene Denkweisen vermitteln, ermöglichen unterschiedliche Programmiersprachen dem Programmierer, differenzierte Softwarestrukturen zu verfassen. So wie manche Redewendung nicht in eine andere Sprache übersetzt werden kann, können auch Programmstrukturen nicht von einer Maschinensprache in die andere übertragen werden. Einige Programmiersprachen wurden speziell für Geschäftsanwendungen entwickelt (COBOL), andere zur Erforschung künstlicher Intelligenz (LISP) und wieder andere zur Datenbearbeitung (Perl). Viele der in diesen verschiedenen Umgebungen geschriebenen Strukturen können nur in der jeweiligen Sprache ausgedrückt werden. Der abstrakte Animator und Programmierer Larry Cuba beschreibt seine Erfahrungen so: „Jeder meiner Filme wurde auf einem anderen System mit anderer Programmiersprache gemacht. Eine Programmiersprache gibt einem die Macht, einige Ideen auszudrücken, und beschränkt gleichzeitig die Möglichkeiten, andere zu realisieren."

Programmiersprachen sind Materialien

Man kann sich eine Programmiersprache auch als ein Material mit ganz spezifischen Vor- und Nachteilen vorstellen. Die Eignung der einzelnen Sprachen hängt vom jeweiligen Kontext ab. Manche Sprachen haben eine ganz einfache Bedienführung, schöpfen aber die Leistungsfähigkeit des Rechners nur zu einem Bruchteil aus. Andere wiederum sind äußerst komplex, bieten aber die totale Kontrolle, weil auf alle Bereiche der Maschine zugegriffen werden kann. So sind einige Programmiersprachen „flexibel" und andere „starr". Flexible Sprachen wie Perl oder Lingo eignen sich bestens zum schnellen Erstellen kurzer Programme, bereiten aber oft Schwierigkeiten bei der Wartung oder im Verständnis umfangreicher Programmcodes. Starre Sprachen wie 68008 Assembly oder C verlangen zwar besondere Sorgfalt bis ins kleinste Detail, ihre Ergebnisse sind aber effizient und stabil. Wie sich der „Feel" und „Look" von Kiefern- und Eichenholz unterscheidet, so hat jede in einer bestimmten Sprache geschriebene Software ihre eigene ästhetische „Gestalt". Ein Java-Programm unterscheidet sich eindeutig von einem ähnlichen, in Flash geschriebenem. Usern, die im Umgang mit beiden vertraut sind, fallen diese Unterschiede auf.

Programmieren ist exklusiv

Oft stellt man sich Programmierer als einen ganz eigenen Typ Mensch vor. Ein Grund, weshalb sich immer ein bestimmter Persönlichkeitstyp dem Programmieren zuwendet, ist wohl darin zu suchen, dass die Programmiersprachen im Allgemeinen von ähnlich denkenden Menschen entwickelt werden. Man kann verschiedene Programmiersprachen für Menschen mit visuellem oder räumlichem Denkvermögen generieren. Alternative Sprachen erschließen das Programmieren auch Menschen mit anderen Denkmustern. LOGO war eine der ersten alternativen Sprachen, die Ende der 1960er Jahre von Seymour Papert als Sprachkonzept für Kinder entworfen wurde. Mit LOGO können Kinder verschiedenste Medien, wie z. B. eine Roboterschildkröte oder Bilder, am Bildschirm programmieren. Als aktuelles Beispiel wäre die in den 1980er Jahren von Miller Puckette am IRCAM entwickelte MAX-Programmierumgebung zu nennen. MAX erhielt begeisterte Zustimmung von Tausenden Künstlern, die sie als Grundlage für audiovisuelle Software und Installationen einsetzen. So wie die grafischen Benutzeroberflächen den Computer für Millionen von Menschen erschlossen haben, werden alternative Programmierumgebungen neue Künstlergenerationen hervorbringen, die Software einsetzen.

Ausdrucksformen von Software

Führen Computer Programme aus, so handelt es sich weniger um statische Texte auf dem Bildschirm als vielmehr um dynamische Prozesse. Aus diesen Prozessen entwickeln sich die Kernausdrucksformen von Software wie dynamische Form, Gestik, Verhalten, Simulation, Selbstorganisation und Adaption. Auf der Basis dieser und noch einiger anderer grundlegender Formen werden komplexere Gedanken und Erfahrungen vermittelt. Im Folgenden wird jede Ausdrucksform beschrieben und anhand eines Beispiels der Aesthetics & Computation Group vom Massachusettes Institute of Technology illustriert. Diese Beispiele wurden zwischen 1998 und 2001 von Künstlern / Programmierern geschaffen und vermitteln eine klare Beschreibung der jeweiligen Softwareausdrucksform.

Dynamische Form

Eine dynamische Form ändert sich im Verlauf der Zeit. Tut sie dies durch einen Stimulus, ist sie reaktiv. *Scratch* von Jared Schiffman (Abbildung 1) vermittelt die grundlegenden Eigenschaften einer dynamischen Form. Ein verschiebbarer Kreis wirkt sich dabei ständig auf die Kontur der Grafikelemente aus. Durch Hinzufügen von Bewegungs- und fließenden Reaktionsebenen wird in *Scratch* die visuelle Kommunikation gesteigert. Ganz allgemein kann jede Form auf ein beliebiges Signal aus der Umwelt reagieren. Diese können von herkömmlichen Eingabegeräten wie Maus, Mikrofon oder Videokamera stammen oder von eher exotischen wie Strahlungssensoren oder Sonar.

Gestik

Gestik ist ein wichtiger Punkt für jedes kontinuierliche Medium, und Software ist in der Lage, Gestik zu vermitteln und zu interpretieren. Die Software AVES von Golan Levin (Abbildung 2) besteht aus einer Gruppe von Programmen, die Handbewegungen verstärken, indem sie die gewonnenen Daten in Bilder und Töne umsetzen. Eine Applikation weist der Struktur jeder Geste einen Klang zu, der die Handstellung widerspiegelt. Eine andere zerlegt die Geste in Schichten, um verlaufende Klangtexturen zu generieren, die durch die Präsenz des Cursors aktiviert und mit ihm kombiniert werden. Das Umsetzen von Gesten ist natürlich komplexer, eröffnet aber neue Möglichkeiten für fesselnde Interaktionen. Software zur Handschriftenerkennung ist ein Anwendungsgebiet der Gestikinterpretation. Einige Installationen und Videospiele setzen eine einfachere Form der Gestikerkennung ein, um die User die Aktionen anhand komplexer Bewegungen steuern zu lassen.

Verhalten

Verhalten ist Bewegung, die eine Absicht erkennen lässt. Die Kombination einfacher Verhaltensmuster bringt „Persönlichkeit“ oder „Neigungen“ hervor. Verhalten kann man erzeugen, indem man Programme intuitiv schreibt oder biologische Modelle verwendet. Im Projekt *Trundle* (Abbildung 3) bestimmt ein Programm, wie das phyische Objekt auf Reize aus seiner Umgebung reagieren und sich entsprechend bewegen soll. *Trundle* scannt seine Umgebung auf der Suche nach Menschen, versucht aber zu fliehen, sobald es jemanden entdeckt. Es ist neugierig und ängstlich. Eine Reihe von Sensoren auf *Trundles* Körper überwacht seine nächste Umgebung und sendet Signale an den Mikroprozessor, der die Motoren steuert. Ganz allgemein kann Verhalten dazu eingesetzt werden, Software geistig anspruchsvoller zu gestalten, indem man Objekte personifiziert, Charaktere entwickelt, Wirkungen vermittelt und eine psychologische Ebene hinzufügt.

Simulation

Simulierte Bereiche der physischen Welt sind ein einfacher Einstieg, um Software wahrzunehmen. Unsere Sinne sind so entwickelt, dass sie auf die Gesetze der Natur reagieren. *Pong,* eines der ersten Computerspiele überhaupt, war eine stark abstrahierte Tennissimulation. In der modernen Technik und Wissenschaft bilden Realitätsmodelle die Grundlage für den Entwurf von physischen Objekten und für Forschungsaufgaben. Das Programm *Floccus* von Golan Levin (Abbildung 4) generiert eine Gruppe elastisch schwingender Linien. Kombiniert man das Ganze noch mit Reaktionen, so lösen die von dieser einfachen Simulation erzeugten Wellenbewegungen bei den Betrachtern Bewunderung aus. Die Linien verlängern und verkürzen sich je nach Kraft, Masse und Beschleunigung. Softwaresimulationen können über das Nachahmen von Perspektiven, Stoffen und physikalischen Gesetzen hinausgehen – und ebenfalls *Prozesse* natürlicher Systeme simulieren.

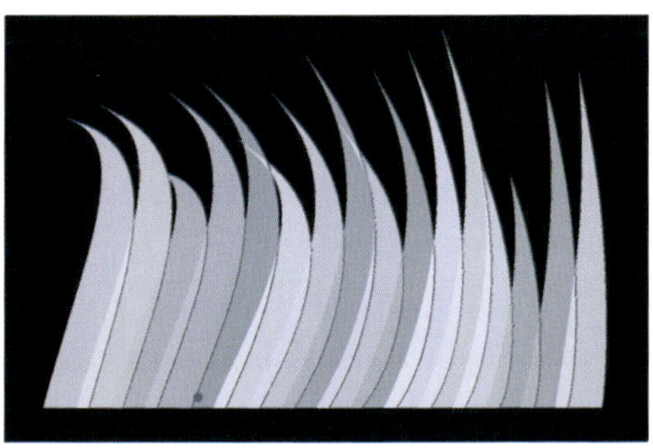

Abb. 1: Jared Schiffman: *Scratch*

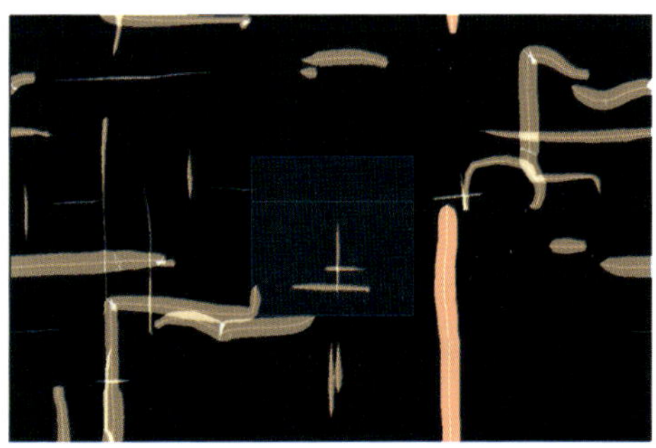

Abb. 2: Golan Levin: *AVES*

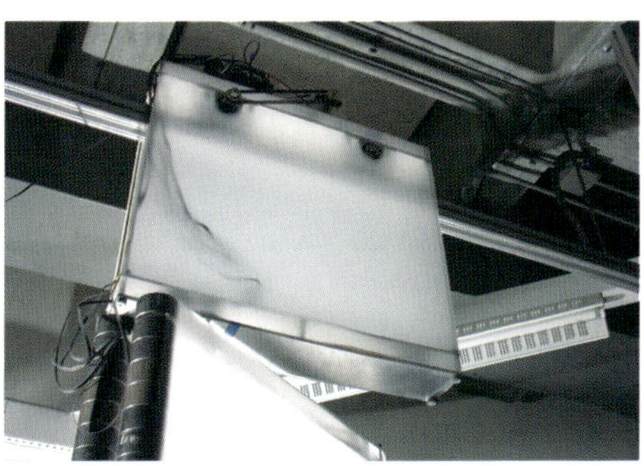

Abb. 3: Casey Reas: *Trundle*

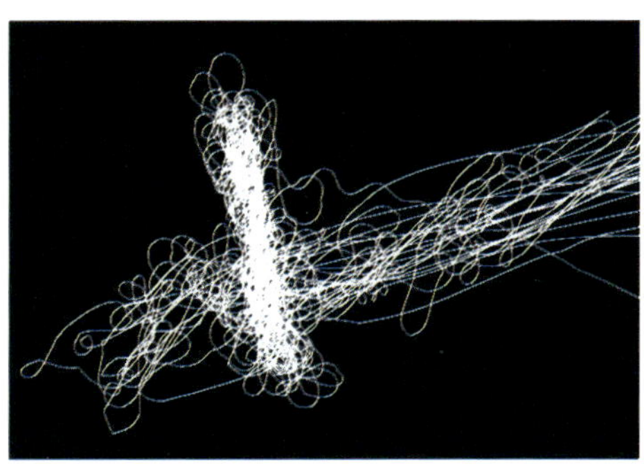

Abb. 4: Golan Levin: *Floccus*

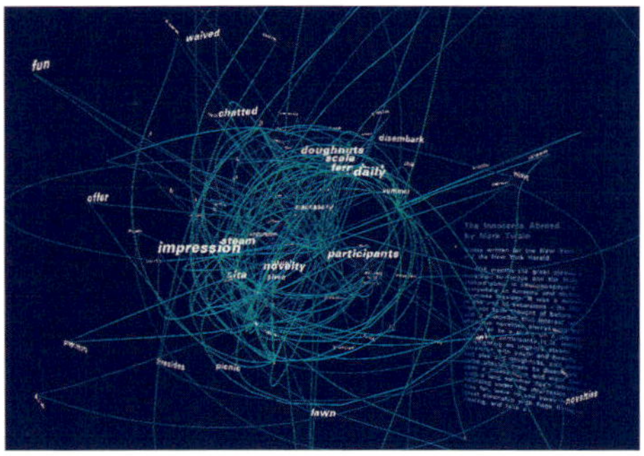

Fig. 5: Ben Fry: *Valence*

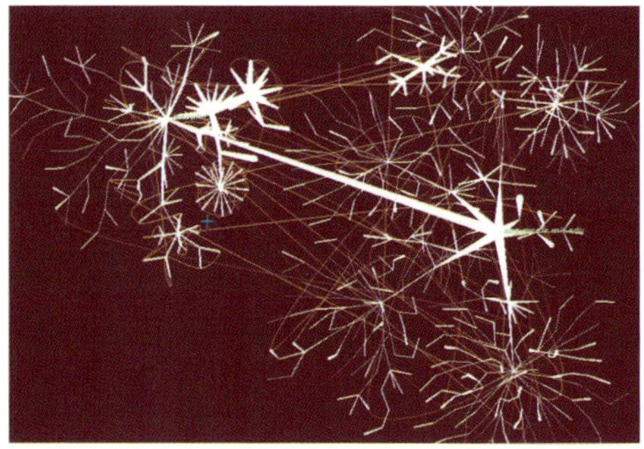

Abb. 6: Ben Fry: *Anemone*

Selbstorganisation

Die Fähigkeit, dass Elemente sich selbst organisieren können, ermöglicht einen Entstehungsprozess. Durch die Interaktion vieler autonomer Prozesse entsteht Struktur. *Valence* von Ben Fry (Abbildung 5) liest den Text eines Buchs Wort für Wort und ordnet jedes anhand eines Regelsystems räumlich an. Durch die Beziehungen verschiedenster Wörter im Text entsteht ein komplexes Gebilde. Kleine Änderungen an den Interaktionsregeln haben potenziell große Auswirkungen auf die Visualisierung.

Adaption

Anpassung ist die Fähigkeit, sich zu ändern. Damit Software sich anpassen kann, braucht sie eine Darstellung ihrer selbst und muss sich ihres Kontexts bewusst sein. Die Software *Anemone* von Ben Fry (Abbildung 6) kann ihre Dichte selbst überwachen und ihre Struktur „stutzen", um im Gleichgewicht zu bleiben. *Anemone* visualisiert die Zugriffe auf die Website. Im Lauf der Zeit entfernt das Programm aus der Fülle der Daten einzelne Abschnitte, damit neue wachsen können und die Lesbarkeit der Informationen nicht beeinträchtigt wird. Applikationen zu schreiben, die sich tatsächlich an ihren Kontext anpassen, ist eine Herausforderung. Adaptive Ausdrucksformen sind immer noch selten. Setzt man einen Interpreter ein, so kann sich das Programm während des Ablaufs selbst umschreiben.

Programmieren

Auch wenn die elektronische Kunst nicht ohne Software auskommt, so erstellt doch jeder Künstler seinen Code individuell – vom Schreiben in wenig entwickelten Sprachen bis hin zur Zusammenarbeit mit Programmierern. Einige Künstler setzen Software als Werkzeug ein, um Arbeiten in einem anderen Medium zu schaffen. Sie benützen handelsübliche Produkte, um Drucke und Videos zu erzeugen und Entwürfe zu erstellen, die dann in einem analogen Medium ausgeführt werden. Andere arbeiten mit professionellen Programmierern zusammen, denen sie Vorgaben machen, die diese umsetzen. Viele setzen Programmierumgebungen ein, die für Grafiker und Künstler entwickelt wurden. So erstellen sie ihre Arbeiten in Script- und visuellen Programmierumgebungen wie Director, Flash oder MAX, die das Schreiben von Software für Nicht-Programmierer erleichtern. Nur ein kleiner Teil der Künstler, die mit Software arbeiten, programmiert in professionellen Programmiersprachen. Sie verwenden umfassende Sprachen wie C, Java oder Perl und entwickeln oft ihre eigenen Werkzeuge für das Arbeiten in diesen Umgebungen.
Es gibt keine „richtige" Methode, wie man mit Software zu Werk geht. Es ist eine persönliche Entscheidung, die das Bedürfnis nach Kontrolle einerseits und Einfachheit andererseits

auszugleichen sucht. Um ein erstklassiger Programmierer zu werden, bedarf es vieler Jahre harter Arbeit. Aber jeder kann die grundlegenden Prinzipien dieses Mediums problemlos verstehen. Ich vertrete die Meinung, dass jeder Künstler, der Software einsetzt, auch des Schreibens und Lesens von Software kundig sein sollte. Wie ist das im Kontext von Software zu verstehen? Alan Kay, der innovative Gedanken zur Computernutzung als Medium vertritt, schreibt sinngemäß: Ein Medium „lesen" zu können heißt, dass man auf Materialien und Werkzeuge zugreifen kann, die andere entwickelt haben. In einem Medium „schreiben" zu können bedeutet, man kann Materialien und Werkzeuge für andere schaffen. Um als kundig zu gelten, muss man beides können. Schreibt man für den Druck, kreiert man rhetorische Werkzeuge; sie zeigen auf und überzeugen. Schreibt man für Computer, generiert man Prozesse; sie simulieren und entscheiden. Diese „simulierenden" und „entscheidenden" Prozesse sind der Kern der Software und können nur vollständig verstanden werden, wenn man sie auch konstruiert.
Künstler schreiben immer öfter ihre eigene Software. Dank Internet, der Popularität von Script-Umgebungen wie Flash und sinkenden Hardwarepreisen beschäftigen sich immer mehr Künstler mit dem Programmieren. Ein hervorragendes Beispiel dafür findet man im Bereich der audiovisuellen Programmierung. Kleine Softwarefirmen wie Cycling '74, die Entwickler von Jitter, reagieren rasch auf die Wünsche ihrer Künstlergemeinde und fördern die Entwicklung von kreativen Werkzeugen. Jitter ist eine hoch entwickelte Bibliothek visueller Strukturen zur Integration von Bild und Ton. Viele Künstler sind nicht mehr auf Entwickler für ihre Werkzeuge angewiesen. Die PinkTwins, zwei Musiker / Programmierer aus Helsinki, haben Framestein entwickelt, eine mit Pure Data verlinkte Echtzeit-Open-Source-Software zur Videobearbeitung für Performances. Die deutsche Künstlergruppe Meso ging mit *vvv,* einer ehrgeizigen Sammlung von Werkzeugen zur Echtzeit-Videosynthese, sogar noch weiter. Einige Künstler entwickeln Software-Tools für sich, die sie nach und nach perfektionieren und dann der Gemeinschaft zur Verfügung stellen.

Synthese

In den letzten dreißig Jahren haben Künstler mithilfe des Mediums Software innovative Werke geschaffen, einstweilen aber nur einen Bruchteil der konzeptuellen Möglichkeiten sondiert. Bisher verlangten Programmiersprachen und -umgebungen nach einer gewissen Methodik, die die Mehrheit der Künstler, die interaktive und programmatische Arbeiten schaffen wollten, nicht ansprach. Es gibt jedoch immer neuere Werkzeuge, die die Künstler zunehmend direkt mit dem Medium Software arbeiten lassen. Die immer besseren Programmierkenntnisse der Künstler führen zu einem immer raffinierteren Softwareeinsatz und zu neuen Materialien und Entwicklungsumgebungen, die ihrerseits die Herstellung von Software einer noch größeren kritisch-kreativen Gemeinschaft zugänglich machen.

Aus dem Amerikanischen von Michael Kaufmann

1 Es gibt auch so genannte „visuelle Programmiersprachen", die das Definieren von Strukturen mittels grafischer Symbole erlauben.

Abelson, Harold; Sussman, Gerald Jay; Sussman, Julie: *Struktur und Interpretation von Computerprogrammen: Eine Informatik-Einführung,* Springer, Berlin [u.a.] 1991

Ascott, Roy: „Moist Ontology", in *The Art of Programming.* Sonics Acts Press, Amsterdam, 2002

Cuba, Larry: „Calculated Movements", in *Prix Ars Electronica Edition '87: Meisterwerke der Computerkunst.* Verlag H.S. Sauer, 1987, S. 111

Kay, Alan: „User Interface: A Personal View", in *The Art of Human-Computer Interface Design,* Hrsg.: Brenda Laurel, Addison-Wesley Publishing Company, Reading/Massachusettes 1989

Krueger, Myron: „Responsive Environments", in *Multimedia, From Wagner to Virtual Reality,* Hrsg.: Randall Packer und Ken Jordan, W.W Norton & Company, Inc., New York 2001

Tissue

Casey Reas

Tissue exposes the movements of autonomous software machines. Each line in the image reveals the path of each machine's movement as it responds to stimuli in its environment. People interact with the software by positioning the stimuli on the screen. Through exploring different positions of the stimuli, an understanding of the total system emerges from the subtle relations between the simple input and the resulting fluid visual output.

The concept for *Tissue* originated with the book *Vehicles, Experiments in Synthetic Psychology* by Valentino Braitenberg, a neuroanatomist. As Braitenberg spent his career counting fibers in the visual ganglia of flies and synapses in the cerebral cortex of mice, he began to distill generalizations about how nervous systems work. He states, "I have been dealing for many years with certain structures within animal brains that seemed to be interpretable as pieces of computing machinery because of their simplicity and/or regularity [Braitenberg p.1]." He uses the term "synthetic psychology" to define the construction of personality/behavior through building up structures of "computing machinery." In *Vehicles,* Braitenberg defines a series of 13 conceptual constructions by gradually building more complex behavior with the addition of more machinery.

The software machines in *Tissue* are analogous to Braitenberg's Vehicle 4. Simple layers of code combine to create the deceptively complicated behavior of these machines. Each machine has two software sensors to detect stimuli in the environment and two software actuators to propel itself. The relationships between the sensors and actuators determine the specific behavior for each machine. In the thousands of software machines simultaneously running in *Tissue,* there are four distinct types, each specified with a color. The architectures of the *Tissue* machines are shown in Figure 1. Each machine has a variable speed, direction, and position of movement and all machines share the same size, turning rate, and maximum speed. They are constrained to their environment and when they hit the edge, they reverse direction.

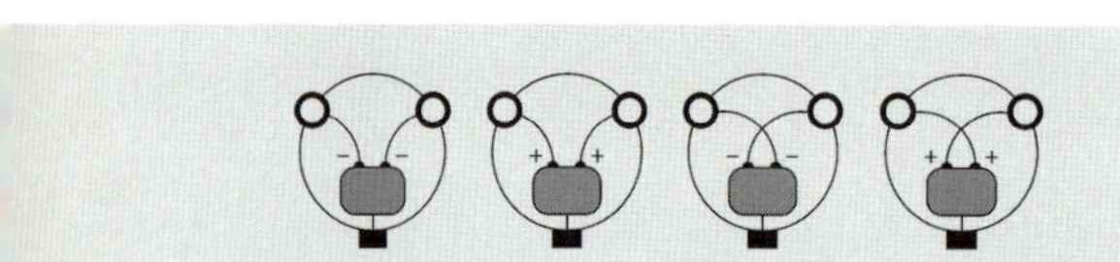

Each machine continually alters its direction and speed by analyzing its position in relation to the environment. First, it determines the distance from each of its sensors to the first stimulus point:

```
dx = stimulusX – leftSensorX;
dy = stimulusY – leftSensorY;
leftDistance = sqrt(dxdx + dydy);
dx = stimulusX – rightSensorX;
dy = stimulusY – rightSensorY;
rightDistance = sqrt(dxdx + dydy);
```

The software then normalizes the two distance measurements, "leftDistance" and "rightDistance", and compresses the values between 0.0 and 1.0. The resulting values are

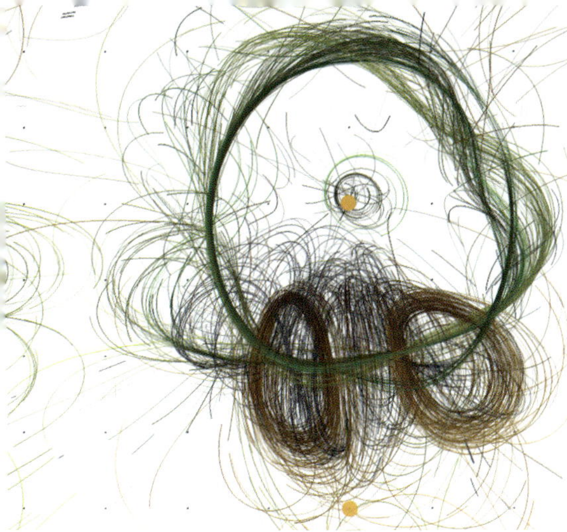

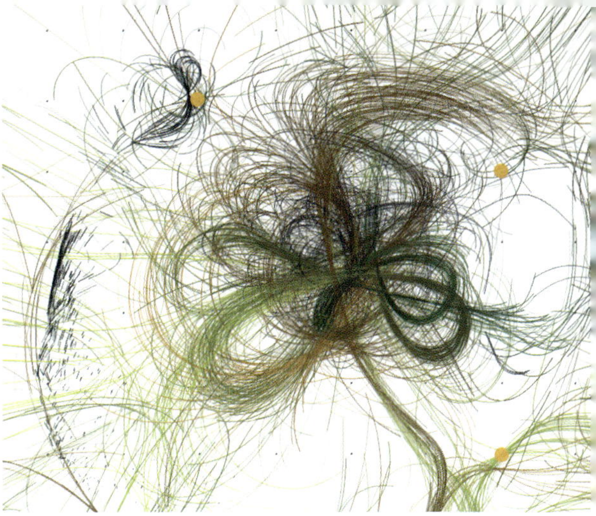

input into a nonlinear function, returned, and saved. These two new values are averaged and stored into a variable called "normSensorAverage:"

```
normSensorLeft = leftDistance/maxDistance;
normSensorRight = rightDistance/maxDistance;
normSensorLeft =  hump(normSensorLeft);
normSensorRight =  hump(normSensorRight);
normSensorAverage = (normSensorLeft + normSensorRight) / 2.0;
```

The speed of the machine is then modified using the value of "normSensorAverage" and the constant value "maxSpeed," which is the maximum speed that a machine is capable of reaching:

```
speed = speed + (maxSpeed – (maxSpeed * normSensorAverage));
```

As mentioned previously, the software has four distinct types of machines. The two lines of code below modify the direction for one type of machine in relation to its current direction, turning speed, and the distance from each sensor to the stimulus:

```
direction = direction + leftDistance/turnSpeed * (1-normSensorLeft);
direction = direction – rightDistance/turnSpeed * (1-normSensorRight);
```

The same calculations are made for each additional stimulus and then the X and Y positions of the machine are updated based on the new speed and position. These calculations occur for each of the thousands of machines that are simultaneously displayed on the screen.

People interact with *Tissue* by positioning stimuli in the environment. They experience an interesting balance of control as their actions have a direct, but imprecise effect on the software. Small changes in the positions of the stimuli create large global changes in the movements of the machines. It is not possible to dominate the software machines, but their behavior can be encouraged and intuitively understood. *Tissue* is an example of software creating a fluid and unexpected interaction rather than more typical rigid and mathematical constructions.

Additional information, images, video clips, and source code for *Tissue* is available at *http://www.groupc.net*

Braitenberg, Valentino. *Vehicles, Experiments in Synthetic Psychology.* MIT Press, Boston 1984.

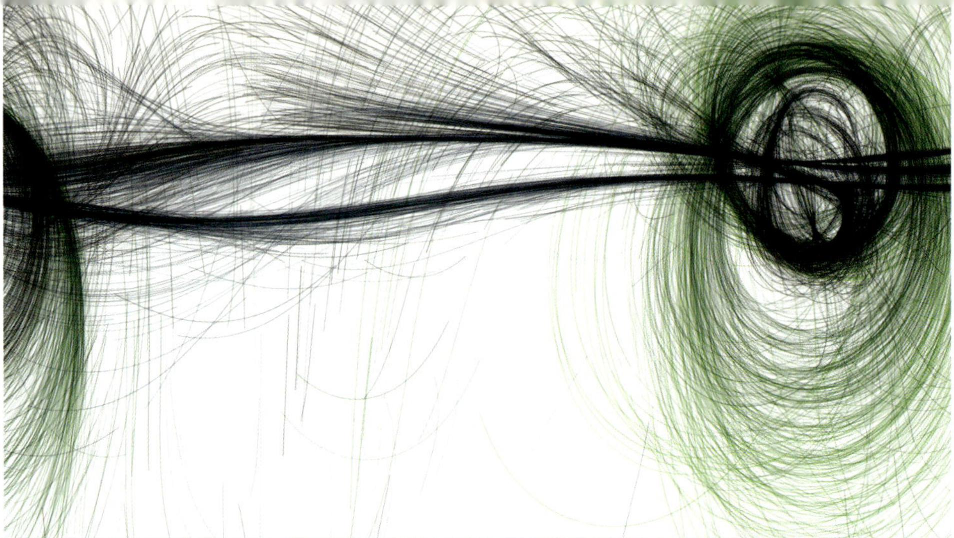

Tissue

Casey Reas

Tissue zeigt autonom agierende Softwaremaschinen. Jeder Strich im Bild beschreibt den Weg einer Maschine, den sie als Reaktion auf Reize in ihrer Umgebung zurückgelegt hat. Der Betrachter kann diese Stimuli am Bildschirm setzen und so mit der Software interagieren. Setzt man genügend solcher Reize, so entwickelt sich mit der Zeit aufgrund der raffinierten Beziehung zwischen der einfachen Eingabe und der fließenden visuellen Ausgabe ein Verständnis für das gesamte System.

Die Idee zu *Tissue* stammt aus dem Buch *Vehicles, Experiments in Synthetic Psychology* des Neuroanatomen Valentino Braitenberg. Braitenberg zählte im Rahmen seiner Tätigkeit Fasern in den Sehganglien von Fliegen und Synapsen in der Hirnkortex von Mäusen und fasste dabei die Funktionsweise von Nervensystemen vereinfacht zusammen. Er führt aus: „Hauptamtlich beschäftige ich mich seit Jahren mit gewissen Strukturen im Inneren tierischer Gehirne, die wegen ihrer Überschaubarkeit oder auch wegen ihres periodischen Aufbaus so aussehen, als wären sie Teil einer Rechenanlage." (Braitenberg 1986, S. 2) Er verwendet den Begriff „Synthetische Psychologie" um zu beschreiben, wie Persönlichkeit/Verhalten durch den Aufbau von Strukturen ähnlich wie in „Rechenanlagen" geformt werden. In *Vehicles* definiert Braitenberg eine Serie von dreizehn Konstruktionskonzepten, deren Verhalten durch Anfügen von immer weiteren Komponenten immer komplexer wird.

Die Softwaremaschinen in *Tissue* entsprechen Braitenbergs Vehikel vierter Art. Einfache Zeilen Code werden miteinander kombiniert, um ein hoch komplexes Verhalten dieser Maschinen vorzutäuschen. Jede Maschine verfügt über zwei Softwaresensoren zur Wahrnehmung von Umgebungsreizen und zwei Softwaremotoren zur Fortbewegung. Das Verhältnis zwischen Sensoren und Antriebseinheiten bestimmt das jeweilige Verhalten der verschiedenen Maschinen. Unter den tausenden von gleichzeitig in *Tissue* aktiven Softwaremaschinen, gibt es insgesamt vier verschiedene, farblich gekennzeichnete Typen. Die Architektur der *Tissue*-Maschinen ist in Abbildung 1 zu sehen. Jede Maschine bewegt sich mit unterschiedlicher Geschwindigkeit in eine andere Richtung und hat ihren eigenen Aktionsradius, doch alle Maschinen sind gleich groß und verfügen über die gleiche Dreh- und Höchstgeschwindigkeit. Sie sind an ihre Umgebung gebunden und kehren an deren Grenze um.

Jede Maschine ändert kontinuierlich Richtung und Geschwindigkeit in Abhängigkeit von ihrer Position zur Umgebung. Zuerst bestimmt sie dabei den Abstand zwischen den Sensoren und dem ersten Reizpunkt:

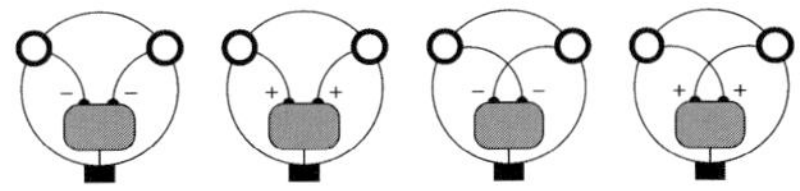

Abbildung 1

```
dx = stimulusX – leftSensorX;
dy = stimulusY – leftSensorY;
leftDistance = sqrt(dxdx + dydy);
dx = stimulusX – rightSensorX;
dy = stimulusY – rightSensorY;
rightDistance = sqrt(dxdx + dydy);
```

Anschließend normalisiert die Software die Messwerte „leftDistance" und „rightDistance" und komprimiert sie auf Werte zwischen 0,0 und 1,0. Diese Ergebnisse durchlaufen eine nichtlineare Funktion, werden zurückgegeben und gespeichert. Die beiden so errechneten Werte werden gemittelt und in der Variable „normSensorAverage" gespeichert:

```
normSensorLeft = leftDistance/maxDistance;
normSensorRight = rightDistance/maxDistance;
normSensorLeft =  hump(normSensorLeft);
normSensorRight =  hump(normSensorRight);
normSensorAverage = (normSensorLeft + normSensorRight) / 2.0;
```

Die Geschwindigkeit der Maschine wird anhand der Werte in „normSensorAverage" und in der Konstanten „maxSpeed", die die Höchstgeschwindigkeit der Maschine angibt, angepasst:

```
speed = speed + (maxSpeed – (maxSpeed * normSensorAverage));
```

Wie bereits erwähnt, unterscheidet die Software vier verschiedene Maschinentypen. Die beiden unten angeführten Zeilen Code bestimmen die Richtung eines Maschinentyps in Abhängigkeit von seiner momentanen Richtung, seiner Drehrate und dem Abstand jedes Sensors vom Stimulus:

```
direction = direction + leftDistance/turnSpeed * (1-normSensorLeft);
direction = direction – rightDistance/turnSpeed * (1-normSensorRight);
```

Dieselben Berechnungen werden für jeden weiteren Reizpunkt ausgeführt, und anschließend werden die X- und Y-Werte der Maschine anhand der ermittelten Geschwindigkeit und Position aktualisiert. Für jede einzelne der abertausend Maschinen, die gleichzeitig am Bildschirm zu sehen sind, werden diese Berechnungen durchgeführt.
Durch das Setzen von Reizen in der Umgebung kann man mit *Tissue* interagieren. Es stellt sich dabei ein interessantes Gleichgewicht der Kontrolle ein, da die Befehle der Benutzer zwar einen direkten, aber sehr vagen Einfluss auf die Software haben. Kleine Veränderungen bei der Positionierung der Reizpunkte rufen groß angelegte Veränderungen bei den Bewegungen der Maschinen hervor. Man kann die Softwaremaschinen nicht dirigieren, aber ihr Verhalten anregen und intuitiv verstehen. *Tissue* ist ein Beispiel für Software, die – im Gegensatz zu den sonst eher starren und mathematischen Konstrukten – eine fließende und unerwartete Interaktion erzeugt.

Weitere Informationen, Bilder, Videoclips und Quellcode zu *Tissue* finden Sie unter *http://www.groupc.net*

Aus dem Amerikanischen von Elisabeth Wiellander

Braitenberg, Valentin: *Künstliche Wesen: Verhalten kybernetischer Vehikel*, Vieweg, Braunschweig/Wiesbaden 1986.

MicroImage

Casey Reas

MicroImage explores the phenomenon of emergence through the medium of software. It is a microworld where thousands of autonomous software *organisms* and a minimal *environment* create a software *ecosystem.* As the environment changes, the organisms aggregate and disperse according to their programmed behavior. They are tightly coupled to the environment and slight changes in the environment create macroscopic changes in the ecosystem. A field of undulating form emerges from the interactions between the environment and the organisms.

In relation to *MicroImage,* the concept of "emergence" refers to the generation of structures that are not specified or programmed. None of the structures produced through interacting with the software is predetermined or planned. Instead of consciously designing the entire structure, simple programs were written to define the interactions between the elements. Programs were written for the four different types of organism and each was cloned in the thousands. Structure emerges from the discreet movements of each organism as it modifies its position in relation to the environment. The structures generated through this process cannot be anticipated and evolve through continual iterations involving alterations to the programs and exploring the changes through interacting with the software. My understanding of emergence was informed by the publications of scientists and journalists including John Holland, Mitchell Resnick, and Kevin Kelly.

MicroImage, like all of my software explorations, has no inherent representation. The core of the project is a responsive structure without visual or spatial form. This structure is continually modified and manifests itself in diverse media and representations. *MicroImage* began as a series of responsive software for desktop computers. It later merged into a series of still images that were recorded during the process of interacting with the software. Enhanced density and physical presence were explored through these vector images. More recently, the software's movements were choreographed and recorded as a collection of short animations. It is currently manifested as a non-interactive triptych displaying the software as a live autonomous system. My preferred patterns of interaction have been encoded into a series of algorithms that control the properties of the organisms' environment. The environment responds to the positions of the organisms and the organisms respond to these changes in the environment. This method explores a balance between dynamic, generative software and controlled authorship.

The formal qualities of *MicroImage* were selected to enable the dynamic structure to be highly visible. Each organism consists of two text files written in the C++ programming language. These files, "micro.cpp" and "micro.h" are respectively 265 and 48 lines long. The files specify the behavior of each organism by defining the rules for how it responds to its simulated environment. After making a range of form explorations, each organism was given the most minimal visual form possible on a computer screen—a pixel. To differentiate the various categories of organisms, each type was assigned a distinct color. *Aggressive* organisms were assigned warm colors and *passive* organisms were assigned cool colors. As a further refinement, the values of the colors were modified to change in relation to the speed of the organism. When the organism is moving at its maximum

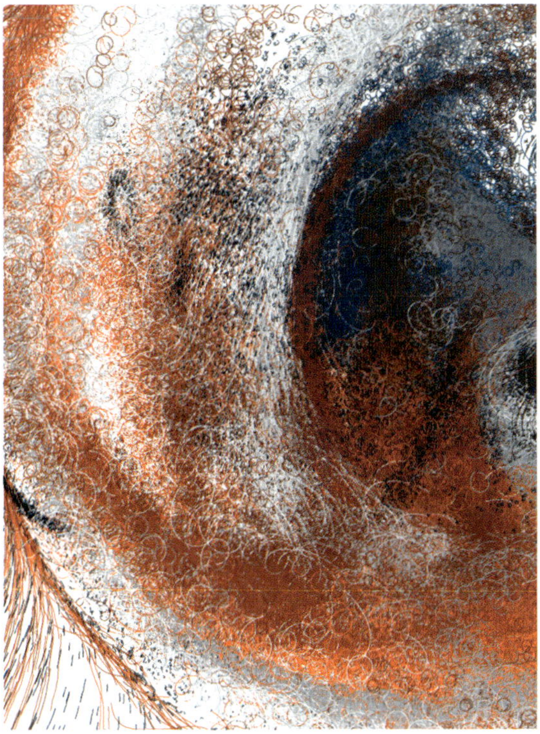

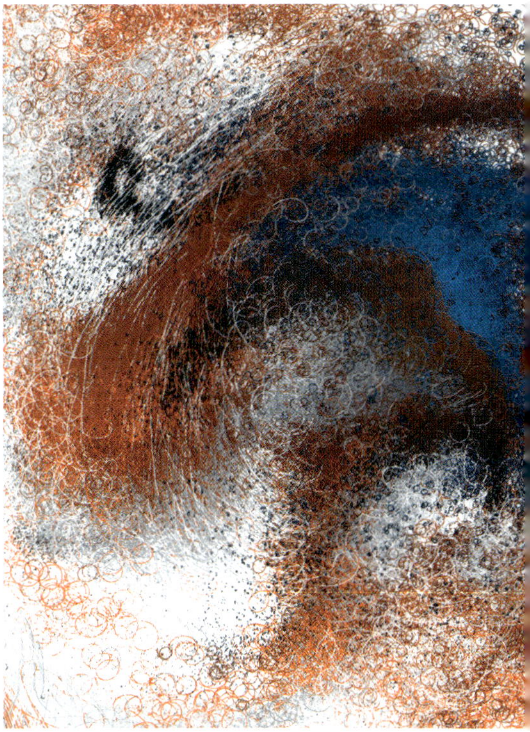

speed it is represented with its pure hue, but as it slows down the hue changes along a gradient until it reaches black. I soon realized that representing the organisms with a single pixel placed too much emphasis on their location and not their quality of movement. In the current software, the representation was changed to an extended pixel—a line. Each organism is displayed as a line connecting its current position and its previous twenty positions. Through this visualization, the movement of each organism is seen in both static images and kinematic representations. The linear notation allows the viewer to discern the past and present motion of the organism. The future movement may be imagined through following the degree of curvature in the line.

The core of the *MicroImage* software was written in one day over two years ago. The current version of the software has developed through a gradual evolution. While the base algorithm controlling the movement was constructed in a rational way, subsequent developments were the result of aesthetic judgments constructed through many months of interacting with the software. Through directly manipulating the code, I was able to develop hundreds of quick iterations and make decisions based on analyzing the responsive structures created by the code. This process was more similar to intuitive sketching than rational calculation.

Additional information, images, and video clips for *MicroImage* are available at *http://www.groupc.net*

Terminology

In the description of *MicroImage,* the choice of the words "organism," "ecosystem," "environment," and "clone" are used abstractly. The word "organism" can be replaced by "system" or "machine." The use of terminology grounded in biology is used to emphasize the relation between the synthetic software structures used in the project and biological structures found in the natural world.

MicroImage

Casey Reas

MicroImage untersucht das Phänomen der Genese mittels Software. Es handelt sich dabei um einen Mikrokosmos, in dem Tausende autonome Softwareorganismen in einer winzigen Umgebung ein Software-Ökosystem schaffen. Ändert sich das Umfeld, so sammeln oder zerstreuen sich die Organismen je nach ihrem programmierten Verhalten. Sie sind eng an ihre Umgebung gekoppelt, und bereits geringe Veränderungen führen zu makroskopischen Änderungen im Ökosystem. Durch die Interaktion zwischen der Umgebung und den Organismen entsteht ein Wellenfeld.

Im Kontext von *MicroImage* bedeutet „Genese" die Schaffung von Strukturen, die nicht spezifiziert oder programmiert sind. Keine der Strukturen, die sich aus der Interaktion mit der Software ergeben, ist vorbestimmt oder geplant. Anstatt die gesamte Struktur bewusst zu entwerfen, wurden einfache Programme geschrieben, die die Interaktion zwischen den Elementen definieren. Für die vier verschiedenen Arten von Organismen wurden Programme geschrieben und jeweils tausendfach geklont. Die Struktur entsteht aufgrund der geringen Bewegungen, die jeder Organismus beim Ändern seiner Position gegenüber seiner Umgebung durchläuft. Die so entstehenden Strukturen sind nicht vorhersehbar und entwickeln sich durch ständige Wiederholungen, wobei die Programme Änderungen durchlaufen und die aus der Interaktion mit der Software resultierende Modifikationen analysieren. Mein Verständnis von Genese gründet sich auf die Publikationen von Forschern und Journalisten wie John Holland, Mitchell Resnick und Kevin Kelly.

Wie bei all meinen Softwareprojekten ist auch mit *MicroImage* keine bestimmte Darstellungsform verbunden. Den Kern des Projekts bildet eine reaktive Struktur ohne sichtbare oder räumliche Form. Diese Struktur ist ständigen Veränderungen unterworfen und findet in verschiedenen Medien und Darstellungen ihren Ausdruck. *MicroImage* begann als eine Serie reaktiver PC-Software, die später in eine Reihe von Standbildern mündete, die während des Interaktionsprozesses mit der Software aufgenommen wurden. Diese Vektorgrafiken wurden zu Experimenten mit verstärkter Dichte und körperlicher Präsenz herangezogen. Vor kurzem wurden dann die Bewegungen der Software choreografiert und als Sammlung animierter Kurzfilme aufgezeichnet. Es präsentiert sich derzeit als ein nicht-interaktives Triptychon, das die Software als selbständig lebendes System darstellt. Die von mir bevorzugten Interaktionsmuster wurden als eine Reihe von Algorithmen kodiert, die die Umgebungsbedingungen der Organismen festlegen. Das Umfeld reagiert auf die Positionierung der Organismen, die wiederum auf diese Veränderungen in der Umgebung reagieren. Diese Methode sucht ein Gleichgewicht zwischen dynamischer, generativer Software und kontrollierter Urheberschaft.

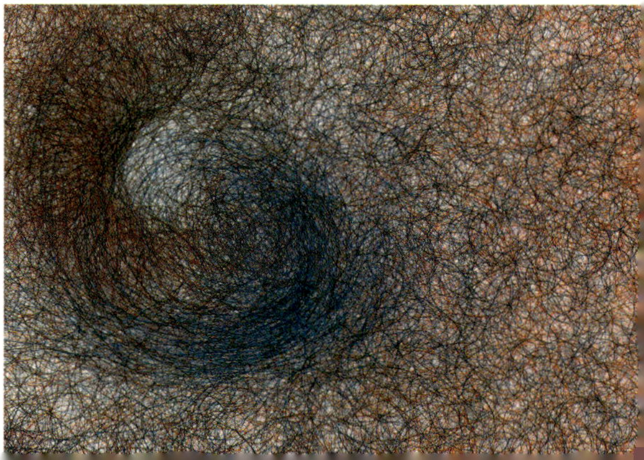

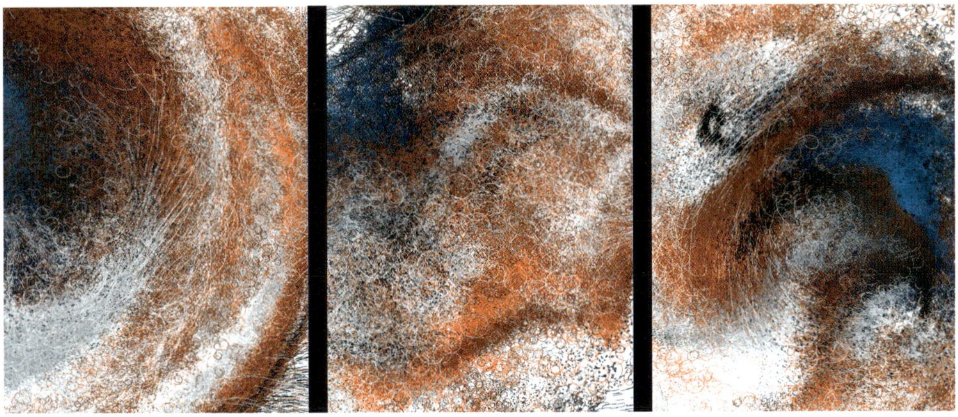

Die formalen Eigenschaften von *MicroImage* wurden gewählt, um die dynamische Struktur eindeutig sichtbar zu machen. Jeder Organismus besteht aus zwei in der Programmiersprache C++ geschriebenen Textdateien. Diese Dateien, „micro.cpp" und „micro.h", sind 265 bzw. 48 Zeilen lang. Sie definieren die Verhaltensregeln, nach denen jeder Organismus auf sein simuliertes Umfeld reagieren soll. Nachdem ich mit verschiedenen Formen experimentiert hatte, gab ich jedem Organismus die einfachste auf dem Computerschirm darstellbare Form– die eines Pixels. Um die verschiedenen Kategorien von Organismen unterscheiden zu können, wurde jedem Typ eine bestimmte Farbe zugewiesen. „Aggressiven" Organismen wurden warme, „passiven" Organismen hingegen kühle Farben zugeordnet. Zur weiteren Verfeinerung wurden die Farbwerte je nach Geschwindigkeit des Organismus modifiziert. Bewegt sich ein Organismus mit Höchstgeschwindigkeit, so wird er als reiner Farbton dargestellt. Wird er jedoch langsamer, dann verdunkelt sich der Farbton schrittweise zu Schwarz. Bald wurde mir klar, dass die Pixeldarstellung der Organismen ihre Position zu sehr betonte, während ihre Bewegung dabei verloren ging. In der aktuellen Version erfolgt die Darstellung daher als ein verlängertes Pixel – eine Linie. Jeder Organismus wird als Linie dargestellt, die dessen derzeitige Position mit den vorherigen zwanzig verbindet. Durch diese Visualisierungsform werden die Bewegungen jedes Organismus sowohl in statischen als auch in animierten Bilder sichtbar. Die lineare Notierung erlaubt es dem Beobachter, vergangene und aktuelle Bewegungen des Organismus zu verfolgen. Die Bewegungsrichtung kann aus dem Krümmungswinkel der Linie geschlossen werden.
Der Kern der *MicroImage*-Software wurde vor über zwei Jahren an einem Tag geschrieben. Die heutige Version der Software hat sich schrittweise entwickelt. Während der Grundalgorithmus zur Steuerung der Bewegung rational konstruiert wurde, folgten spätere Entwicklungen aufgrund ästhetischer Entscheidungen, die das Resultat vieler Monate der Interaktion mit der Software waren. Die direkte Manipulation des Codes erlaubte es mir, Hunderte von schnellen Wiederholungen zu entwickeln und Entscheidungen aufgrund der Analyse der durch den Code entstandenen reaktiven Strukturen zu treffen. Dieser Prozess glich eher intuitivem Skizzieren als rationalem Kalkulieren.

Aus dem Amerikanischen von Elisabeth Wiellander

Weitere Informationen, Bilder und Videoclips zu *MicroImage* finden sich unter *http://www.groupc.net*

Terminologie
In der Beschreibung von *MicroImage* werden die Begriffe „Organismus", „Ökosystem", „Umgebung" und „Klon" abstrakt verwendet. Das Wort „Organismus" kann durch „System" oder „Maschine" ersetzt werden. Der Gebrauch von Begriffen aus der Biologie soll die Beziehung zwischen den im Projekt verwendeten synthetischen Softwarestrukturen und biologischen Strukturen aus der Natur hervorheben.

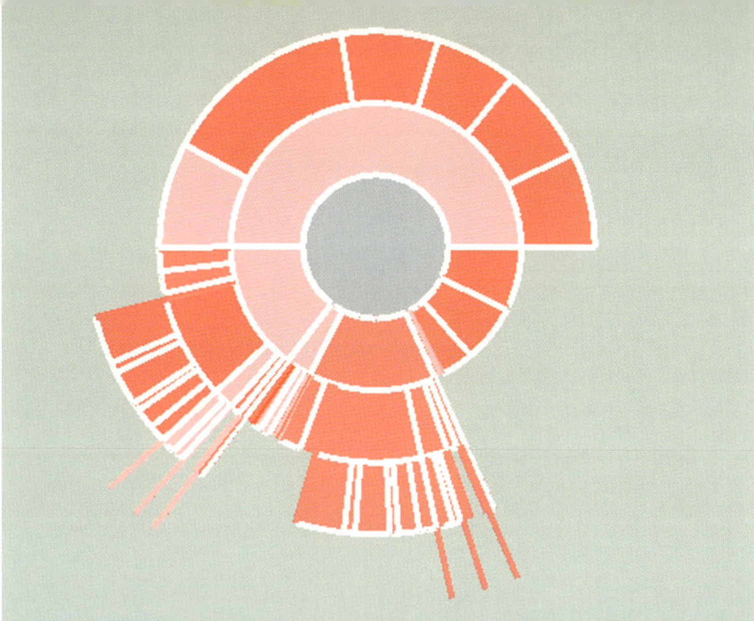

Visually Deconstructing Code

Ben Fry

Visually Deconstructing Code is a series of experiments looking at the form of code. This collection searches for an alternative perspective of text, machine language, and binary software codes, making visual the abstract structures and processes buried within.

The evolution of software projects

While it's obvious that the code in a software project changes over time, less obvious is the nature of how individual changes have taken place in a broader context. Projects are typically structured as a collection of files that are added, removed, and reorganized throughout the course of development. The contents of the individual files are modified, line by line or in large pieces for every fix and feature.

Reasonably large projects, or those that are shared between several authors, are often tracked using a version control system. One of the most common is called CVS (or Concurrent Versions System), and is freely available. Understanding how a project has evolved is a matter of understanding the data stored by the version control system, which keeps track of changes as incremental events on the modification to files or how they're organized. The first experiment in this set is an interactive application that shows the evolution of the structure and content of the Processing *(http://Proce55ing.net)* project over time, from its initial inception through fifty releases. The experiment consists of large-format printed pieces to depict broader changes over time, while an interactive application allows the user to walk through the individual events that led to differences between the releases. The result is a depiction of the organic process in which even the smallest pieces of software code become mature through the course of its development, as they are passed between developers, revisited for later refinement, merged, removed, and simplified.

From machine-like language to the language of the machine

For most programming languages, code written by the programmer is translated to a more abstract form that is directly understandable by the machine on which it will be run. The initial code, which ranges from unintelligible to beautifully expressive, is made undoubtedly more arcane in its "machine language" form. But the complexity of this obfuscation process often hides the beauty in the translation, where some parts are made more terse, others more verbose, and all of it given a more rigid structure.
When developing in the Java programming language, the stream of instructions in the resultant machine language code (which is actually written for a "virtual" machine which does not exist) also stores information about what line in the original human-readable code produced each machine-readable instruction. This experiment brings the two kinds of code back together, using a visual image to lay bare the translation process of compilation.

Packaging of data within code

Any piece of executable code is also commingled with data, ranging from simple sentences of text for error messages to entire sets of graphics for the application. In older cartridge-based console games, the images for each of the small on-screen images (the "sprites") were often stored as raw data embedded after the actual program's instructions.
This third piece examines the unpacking of a Nintendo game cartridge, decoding the program as a four-color image, revealing a beautiful soup of the thousands of individual elements that make up the game screen.

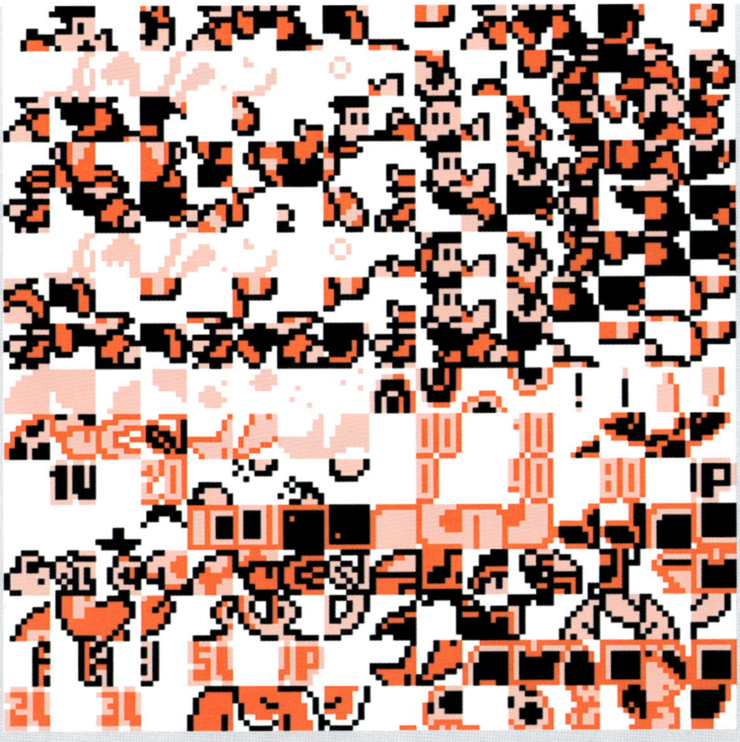

packaging data within code

Seeing time in the operation of code

It's common to use a "profiler" on code while it's running to see where the machine is spending its time. Functions are shown with percentages marked for how long is spent within each area. Better tools also show the hierarchy of functions that have been used one after another, a hierarchy that shows the "call stack" of the successive methods. This piece examines the output from a profiler using an active diagram, where the functional relationships are laid out spatially, and the percentage of time is shown as a series of thicknesses. The diagram makes apparent the bloat of areas within the code that are poorly written or are simply doing the majority of the work.

Visual mathematics in code algorithms

There is a class of software algorithms that includes cryptography, error checking, and serial number testing that work like the mathematical equivalent of the ridges found on an intricate key. Their operation is a series of gymnastics performed with a group of numbers that comprise the key.

This piece examines such an algorithm that simulates the process of how the serial numbers for software products by the manufacturer Adobe are generated and tested. It begins with a simple seed number, and then walks through several mathematical steps, mostly simple addition or multiplication, to generate a multi-digit key for the product. An application such as PhotoShop or Illustrator will use such an algorithm to test whether the key entered by the user is proper; while the same algorithm can also be used to generate a myriad of fake but working keys for anyone who wants their own. The nature of this experiment is to illustrate the elegance and simplicity of a process kept intentionally as opaque as possible to the end-user.

Each of these experiments begins with the question: "How can this aspect of code be understood visually?" As singletons, they are simplistic ideas, but as a collection, they begin to provide a visual perspective on how code works and behaves, introducing a mental model for code that is more organic than common tools of depiction like text, tables, and graphs.

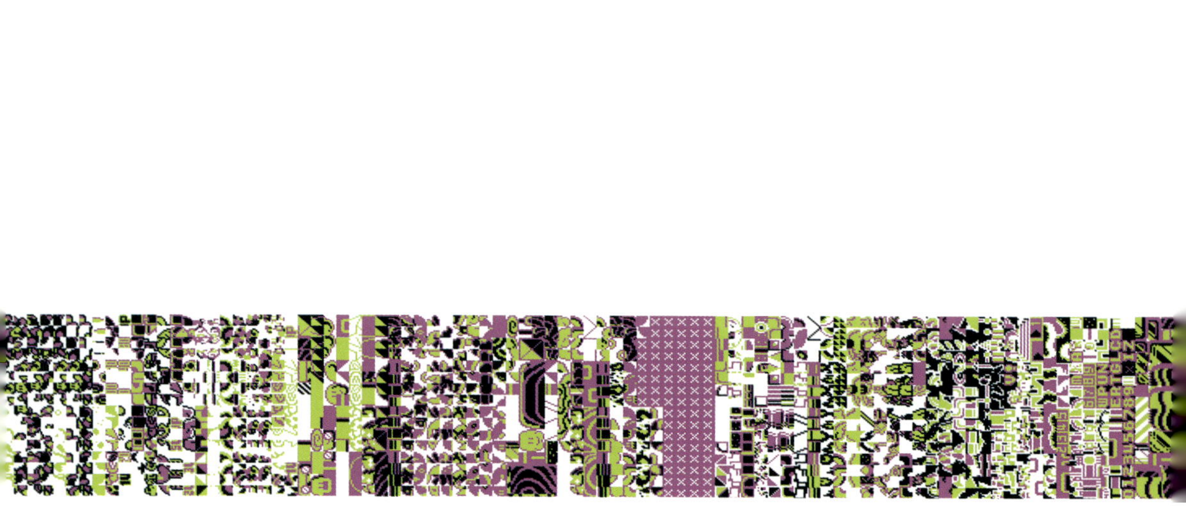

Visually Deconstructing Code

Ben Fry

Visually Deconstructing Code untersucht in einer Reihe von Experimenten die Form von Code. Es gilt alternative Blickwinkel für Text, Maschinensprache und binäre Programmcodes zu finden, aus denen die darin versteckten abstrakten Strukturen und Prozesse sichtbar werden.

Evolution von Softwareprojekten

Während außer Zweifel steht, dass sich der Code einer Software mit der Zeit ändert, ist weit weniger bekannt, wie die einzelnen Änderungen in einem größeren Kontext ablaufen. Ein Projekt besteht für gewöhnlich aus einer strukturierten Sammlung von Dateien, die im Entwicklungsprozess hinzugefügt, entfernt und reorganisiert werden. Der Inhalt der einzelnen Dateien wird für jeden Bugfix oder jede Funktion zeilen- oder abschnittweise umgeschrieben.
Bei größeren Projekten oder solchen, an denen mehrere Autoren arbeiten, wird meist ein System zur Versionskontrolle eingesetzt. Eines der gängigsten ist das kostenlos erhältliche CVS (oder „Concurrent Version System"). Um den Entwicklungsprozess eines Projekts zu verstehen, muss man die vom Kontrollsystem gespeicherten Daten interpretieren können, das jede Änderung an der Datei oder deren Organisation inkrementiell erfasst.
Im ersten Experiment der Reihe vermittelt eine interaktive Applikation die strukturelle und inhaltliche Evolution des Projekts *Processing (http://proce55ing.net)* von den ersten Anfängen über fünfzig Releases hindurch. Großformatige Ausdrucke zeigen größere Änderungen im Zeitraffer, während der User mit einer interaktiven Applikation durch die einzelnen Änderungsschritte navigieren kann, die zu den verschiedenen Versionen geführt haben. Das Ergebnis ist ein Abbild eines organischen Ablaufs, in dem auch das kleinste Stück Programmcode heranreift, indem es von den Entwicklern weitergegeben, für den letzten Schliff wieder aufgenommen, zusammengeführt, entfernt und vereinfacht wird.

Von maschinengleicher Sprache zur Sprache der Maschine

Für die meisten Programmiersprachen gilt, dass der vom Programmierer verfasste Code in eine abstraktere Form übersetzt wird, die die ausführende Maschine direkt versteht. In dieser *maschinensprachlichen* Form erscheint der ursprüngliche Code, der unverständlich oder wunderbar expressiv sein kann, ohne Zweifel noch geheimnisvoller. Allerdings bleibt die Schönheit

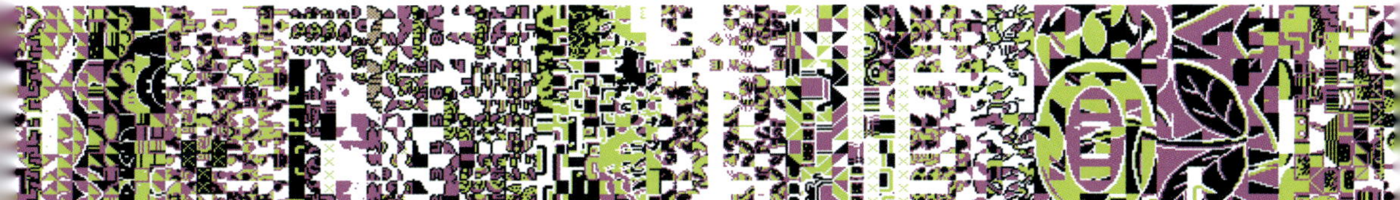

.cvsignore
bugs.txt
todo.txt
app
app/.cvsignore
app/PdeApplet.java
app/PdeApplication.java
app/PdeEditor.java
app/PdeEditorButtons.java
app/PdeEditorListener.java
app/PdeEngine.java
app/PdeEnvironment.java
app/PdeException.java
app/PdeKeyListener.java
app/PdeRunner.java
app/PdeSketchbook.java
app/PdeUpdater.java
app/ProcessingApplet.java
app/bagelpublic.pl
app/buttons.gif
app/buzz.pl
app/notes.txt
app/application
app/application/dist.bat
app/application/make.bat
app/application/makeu.bat
app/application/run.bat
app/application/runs.bat
app/application/runu.bat
app/application/bin
app/application/bin/JdbcOdbc.dll
app/application/bin/javai.dll
app/application/bin/jpeg.dll
app/application/bin/jre.exe
app/application/bin/math.dll
app/application/bin/mmedia.dll
app/application/bin/net.dll
app/application/bin/sysresource.dll
app/application/bin/win32com.dll
app/application/bin/winawt.dll
app/application/bin/zip.dll
app/application/classes
app/application/classes/buttons.gif
app/application/lib
app/application/lib/awt.properties
app/application/lib/buttons.gif
app/application/lib/comm.jar
app/application/lib/content-types.properties
app/application/lib/dbn.pde
app/application/lib/font.properties
app/application/lib/font.properties.ar
app/application/lib/font.properties.iw
app/application/lib/font.properties.ja

app/PdeApplet.java
app/PdeApplication.java
app/PdeEditor.java
app/PdeEditorButtons.java
app/PdeEditorListener.java
app/PdeEngine.java
app/PdeEnvironment.java
app/PdeException.java
app/PdeKeyListener.java
app/PdeRunner.java
app/PdeSketchbook.java
app/PdeUpdater.java
app/ProcessingApplet.java
app/ProcessingAppletViewer.java
app/bagelpublic.pl
app/buttons.gif
app/buzz.pl
app/notes.txt
app/application
app/application/dist.bat
app/application/make.bat
app/application/makeu.bat
app/application/run.bat
app/application/runs.bat
app/application/runu.bat
app/application/bin
app/application/bin/JdbcOdbc.dll
app/application/bin/jpeg.dll
app/application/bin/jre.exe
app/application/bin/math.dll
app/application/bin/mmedia.dll
app/application/bin/msvcrt.dll
app/application/bin/net.dll
app/application/bin/sysresource.dll
app/application/bin/win32com.dll
app/application/bin/winawt.dll
app/application/bin/zip.dll
app/application/classes
app/application/classes/.cvsignore
app/application/classes/buttons.gif
app/application/lib
app/application/lib/awt.properties
app/application/lib/buttons.gif
app/application/lib/comm.jar
app/application/lib/content-types.properties
app/application/lib/dbn.pde
app/application/lib/font.properties
app/application/lib/font.properties.ar
app/application/lib/font.properties.be
app/application/lib/font.properties.bg
app/application/lib/font.properties.cs
app/application/lib/font.properties.el
app/application/lib/font.properties.et
app/application/lib/font.properties.hr
app/application/lib/font.properties.hu
app/application/lib/font.properties.iw
app/application/lib/font.properties.ja
app/application/lib/font.properties.ko
app/application/lib/font.properties.lt
app/application/lib/font.properties.lv

der Übersetzung durch die Komplexität dieses Verschleierungsvorgangs oft verborgen; manche Teile werden prägnanter, andere weitschweifiger und alles erhält insgesamt eine festere Struktur. Programmiert man in Java, so speichern die Anweisungen im resultierenden Maschinencode (der für eine „virtuelle", nichtexistente Maschine erstellt wird) auch, welche Zeile im menschen-lesbaren Ausgangscode welche maschinen-lesbare Anweisung erzeugt hat. Die beiden Codeformen werden in diesem Experiment wieder vereint, indem der Übersetzungsprozess des Kompilierens in einem Bild offen gelegt wird.

Verpacken von Daten im Code

Jeder ausführbare Code ist auch mit Daten gespickt, die von einfachen Texten für Fehlermeldungen bis zu kompletten Grafikabfolgen für die Anwendung reichen. So waren bei älteren Spielkonsolen mit Cartridges die Bilder (die „Sprites") oft als Rohdaten nach den eigentlichen Programmanweisungen eingebettet.
Im dritten Teil untersuchen wir das Entpacken einer Nintendo-Spiel-Cartridge, indem das Programm als Vierfarbbild dekodiert wird und damit einen wundervollen Blick auf die tausenden Einzelelemente freigibt, die den Spielspaß ausmachen.

Die Zeitkomponente beim Ausführen von Code

Gerne wird auch ein „Profiler" beim Durchlaufen des Codes eingesetzt, um herauszufinden, wie lange die Maschine für welche Operationen braucht. Für jede Funktion wird die Zeit in den jeweiligen Bereichen in Prozent angegeben. Bessere Tools zeigen auch die Hierarchie der nacheinander ausgeführten Funktionen an, eine Hierarchie, die den „Aufruf-Stack" der nachfolgenden Methoden anzeigt.
Hier analysiert ein aktives Diagramm die Ausgabe eines solchen Profilers: Die funktionalen Beziehungen sind räumlich angeordnet und die Zeit wird durch unterschiedliche Strichstärken dargestellt. So werden aufgeblähte Bereiche des Codes sichtbar, die entweder schlecht programmiert sind oder einfach den Hauptteil der Arbeit ausführen.

Sichtbare Mathematik in Code-Algorithmen

Eine Klasse von Softwarealgorithmen, die u. a. Kryptografie, Prüfsummenverfahren und Seriennummernüberprüfung einschließt, funktioniert wie das mathematische Äquivalent zu den Zacken eines Sicherheitsschlüssels. Dabei wird mit einer Gruppe von Ziffern, die den Schlüssel bilden, Zahlenakrobatik betrieben.
Visually Deconstructing Code untersucht einen solchen Algorithmus, der die Generierung und Überprüfung der Seriennummern von Produkten aus dem Haus Adobe simuliert. Er beginnt mit einer einfachen Initialzahl und führt mehrere mathematische Operationen aus – meist einfache Additionen oder Multiplikationen – um einen mehrstelligen Schlüssel für ein Produkt zu erzeugen. In Applikationen wie PhotoShop oder Illustrator wird dieser Algorithmus eingesetzt, um die Richtigkeit der vom User eingegebenen Seriennummer zu prüfen; er kann aber auch verwendet werden, um eine Vielzahl von gefälschten, aber funktionierenden Schlüsseln für jeden Interessenten zu produzieren. Dieses Experiment soll die Eleganz und Einfachheit eines Prozesses darstellen, der für den Enduser so undurchsichtig wie möglich gehalten wird.
Jedes dieser Experimente wird mit der Frage eingeleitet: „Wie lässt sich dieser Aspekt des Codes bildlich umsetzen?" Jedes für sich ist eine Vereinfachung, aber als Sammlung visualisieren sie die Funktion und das Verhalten von Code und vermitteln ein organischeres Gedankenmodell als die üblichen Beschreibungen in Form von Text, Tabellen und Diagrammen.

Aus dem Amerikanischen von Michael Kaufmann

electrolobby | Virus in Fur

In contrast to an "exhibition space" that is intentionally set up in keeping with the tradition of a festival just as much as it emerges on its own within that event's timeframe (and subordinates even its own connectivity to the point of view of the exemplary piece), the *electrolobby* establishes a—temporary—"living space." As a spin-off of *openX* and enhanced to include, among other features, the *Kitchen,* it exemplifies the processes at the basis of projects whose essence is connectivity. For this type of implementation/realization that creates its own framework of action and presentation, the *electrolobby* is a proving ground and an open domain for artists and their audience. At the same time, for the Ars Electronica Festival, it is a space in which to experiment with a potentially new tradition of mediating the encounter with art.
Surrounded by workstations, the *Kitchen* is the centerpiece of this year's *electrolobby* in the Brucknerhaus—and this both literally with respect to its physical location as well as in the figurative sense whereby, at most private social get-togethers, the kitchen, as the place where primary emphasis is placed on corporeal well-being, also ends up being the site where the most interesting conversations take place. The *electrolobby-Kitchen* provides the setting for informal exchange among participants about their work and issues raised at the festival symposia as well as for project presentations, coding, processing workshops, and much more.
And, for the first time this year, the *electrolobby* will also have a remote auxiliary venue in the form of the *Code Arena* in the Stadtwerkstadt. Four hour-long evening theme programs will feature a series of three-minute "short project presentations" and a moderated discussion followed by an audience vote.
If close scrutiny of the *electrolobby* project would tend to suggest that it has assumed its place at the festival more in evolutionary fashion than as an upshot of a predetermined concept, then this at least confirms the fact that the idea for the development of a "generative" format sketched out for *openX* in 1997 has achieved critical mass, and gives rise to the expectation of potential viral characteristics.

Im Vergleich zum „Ausstellungsraum", der im Gefolge der Tradition eines Festivals ebenso wie schon allein durch dessen Zeitrahmen entsteht (und selbst das eigentlich Konnektive noch dem Gesichtspunkt des exemplarischen Stücks unterordnet), etabliert die *Electroloby* einen – temporären – „Lebensraum". Hervorgegangen aus *openX* und unterdessen um die *Kitchen* erweitert, exemplifiziert sie den Projekten der Konnektivität zu Grunde liegende Prozesse. Für diese Art des Realisierens, die ihren eigenen Präsentations- und Aktionsrahmen schafft, ist die *electrolobby* Experimentierfeld und offenes Gelände für KünstlerInnen und Publikum. Für das Festival Ars Electronica ist sie zugleich der Proberaum für eine mögliche neue Tradition der Vermittlung.
Umgeben von den Workstations steht die *Kitchen* im Zentrum der diesjährigen *electrolobby* im Brucknerhaus – sowohl hinsichtlich der räumlichen Anordnung als auch im übertragenen Sinn, wonach bei den meisten privaten gesellschaftlichen Zusammenkünften die Küche der

Ort ist, wo das erste Interesse am leiblichen Wohl in der Regel auch mit den interessantesten Gesprächen zusammenfällt. Die *electrolobby-Kitchen* bildet den Rahmen sowohl für den informellen Austausch der TeilnehmerInnen über deren Projekte wie über Themen des Symposiums, aber auch für Projektpräsentationen, Coding, *Processing*-Workshops ...
Erstmals findet die *electrolobby* heuer auch disloziert – in Form der *Code Arena* in der Stadtwerkstadt – eine Bühne. An vier Themenabenden werden jeweils in einer Stunde dreiminütige „Kurz-Präsentationen" von Projekten durchgeführt, moderiert und einem Publikumsvoting ausgesetzt.
Wenn die Beobachtung des Projektes *electrolobby* für die Tendenz spricht, dass es eher evolutionär als von Ideen determiniert im Festival Platz greift, dann bestätigt sich damit zumindest die Zündung der 1997 mit *openX* skizzierten Idee für die Entwicklung eines „generativen" Formates. In Erwartung etwaiger viraler Eigenschaften.

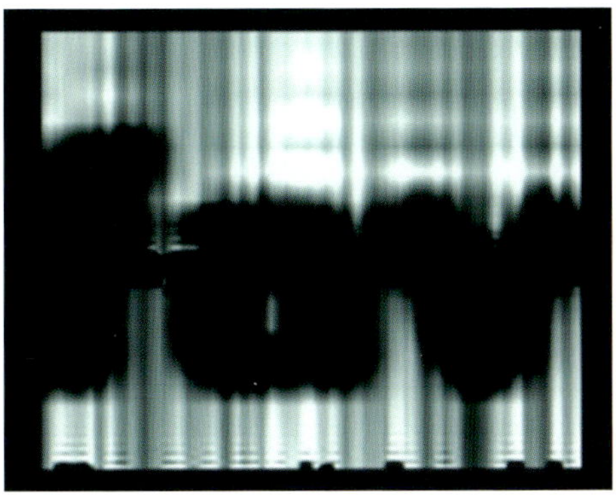

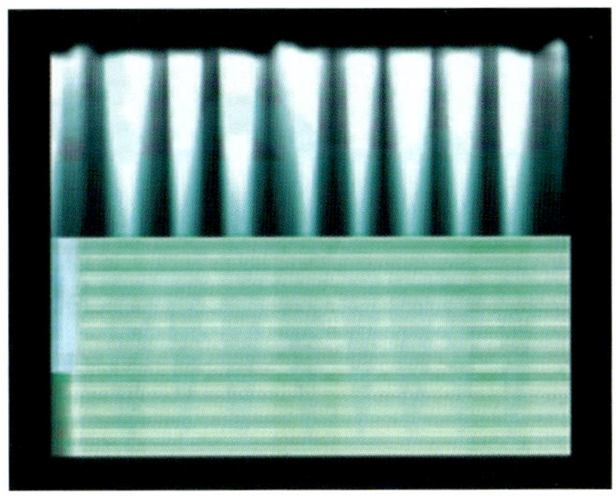

electrolobby Participants

processing

is a programming language, a graphical programming environment, an instructional user interface and, at the same time, a designer community. Workshops and demonstrations display the potential of *Processing,* which enables users—even those with no programming skills—to create dynamic screen designs with a high level of sophistication. Every piece of software developed thereby is made available at *www.proce55ing.net* to the community, which thus develops into an artistic, open source network.
Processing is an open project initiated by Casey Reas and Ben Fry. Participants onsite at the 2003 Ars Electronica electrolobby will be: Casey Reas (USA), Ben Fry (USA), Amit Pitaru (USA), Carlos Rocha (COL / USA), Hernado Barragan (COL / I), Golan Levin (USA), Lia (A), Marius Watz (FIN / D), Schoenerwissen (D), Juha Huuskonen (FIN)
http://proce55ing.net/

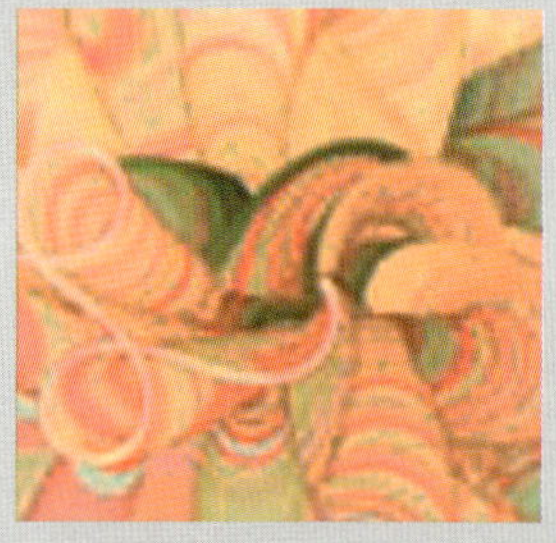
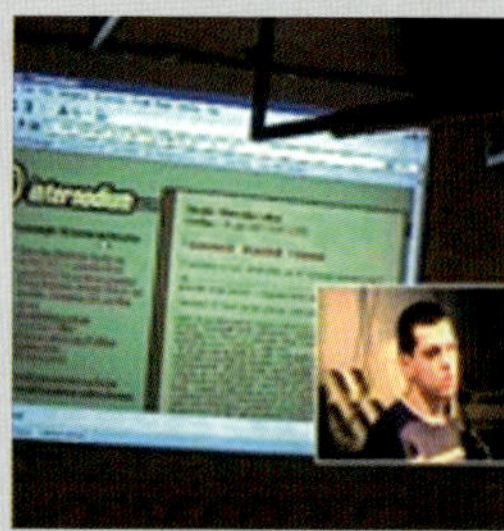
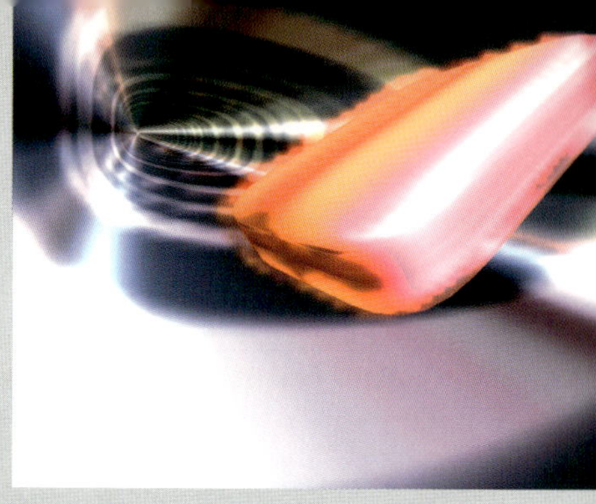
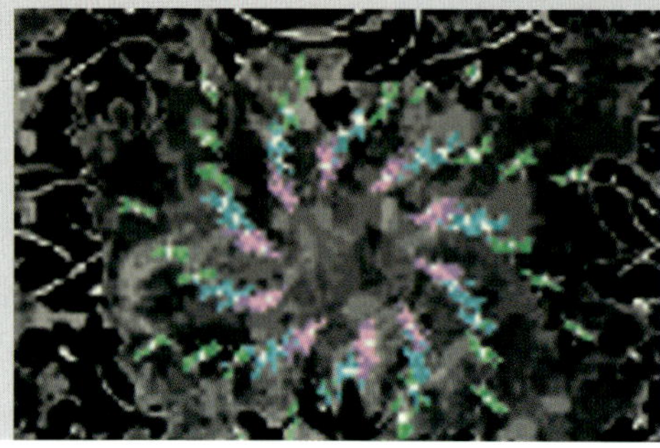
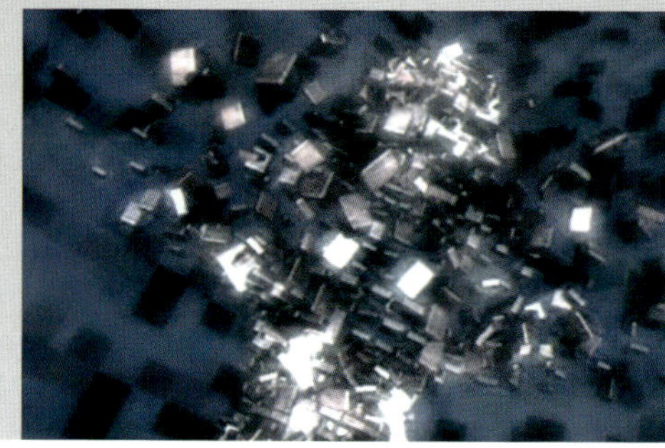

LeCielEstBleu

The Paris-based collective named "LeCielEstBleu"—represented at the Ars Electronica Festival by two of its founding members, director Frédéric Durieu and Kristine Malden—will display its work consisting of algorithmic poetry, interactivity, and dynamically composed music from the LeCielEstBleu experimental, interactive website.
http://www.lecielestbleu.com/

The demoscene

"The demoscene" can be described as a digital underground art form. Worldwide, "the demoscene" consists of an estimated 15,000 active "sceners" who produce a large amount of coded art called "demos." Every year, many demos are released as freeware on different computer platforms that show off the technological and artistic skills of their producers. For the sceners, the demoscene as a cultural phenomenon is a digital youth movement that copes with code, symbols, and digital communication as well as many different styles of artistic expression.
The winners and nominees of this year's "scene.org awards" held at the "breakpoint digital underground arts festival 2003" will be put on public exhibit. Different projects and products from the demoscene will be presented and discussed.
"The demoscene" will be represented by individuals covering different aspects of the scene:
Ekkehard "sTEELER" Brüggemann (D): *http://breakpoint.untergrund.net*
Matti "Melwyn" Palosuo (SF): *http://awards.scene.org*
Markus "Droid" Pasula (SF): *http://www.helsinki.fi/~mpasula/*
Dierk "Chaos" Ohlerich (D): *http://www.theproduct.de*

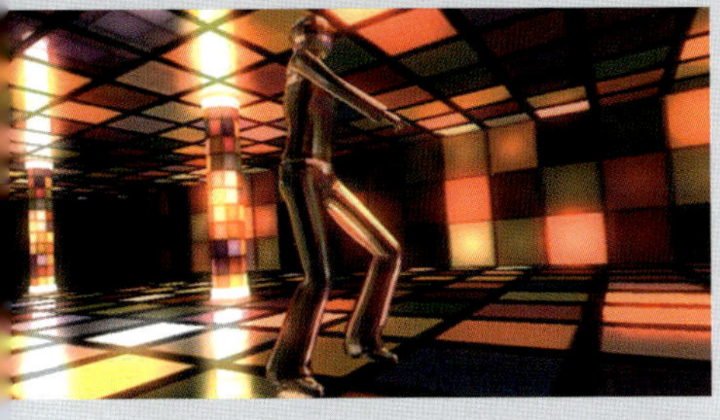
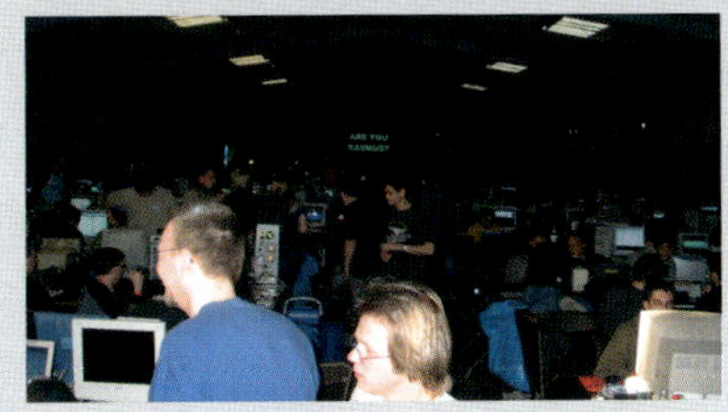
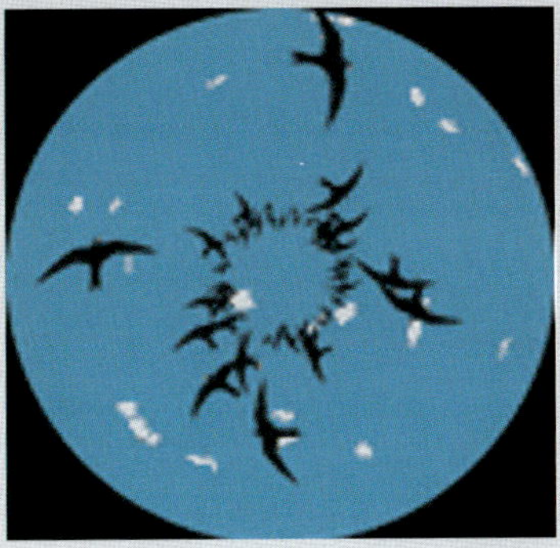
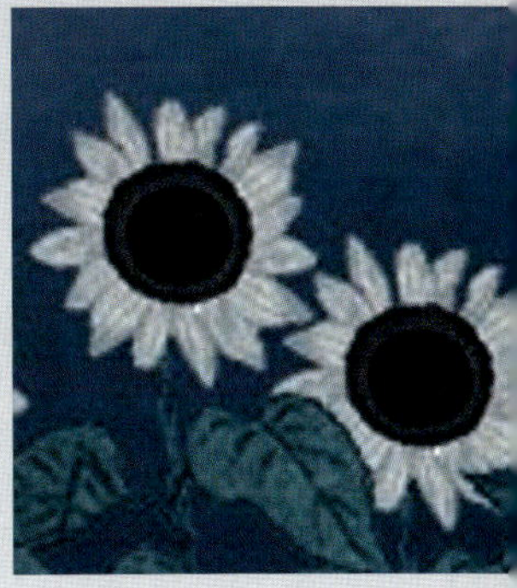

kuda.org

kuda.org is a non-profit organization of Serbian artists, theorists, media activists and researchers in the field of ICT (information and communication technologies). It explores critical approaches to (mis)using ICT and emphasizes creative rethinking in enhancing network society. *kuda.org* is a content-providing platform for new cultural practices, media art production and social layout.
kuda.org will be represented by Kristian Lukic, Zoran Pantetic, and Branka Curcic.
http://www.kuda.org

Pure Data Connections

In PureDataConnections, several PCs are interlinked by means of PureData in such a way that the result is a single machine that can broadcast multi-channel audio and video within a defined space and, while going about this operation, alter the machine code. In the initial machine configuration, data from the Internet become messages (UDO), messages become sounds (Automata), and sounds become images (Inak), whereby there is feedback into the space (ImpulseResponse).
PureDataConnections is another live experiment with a data space and codes for multimedia installations.
Artists: REMI = Michael Pinter (A) + Renate Oblak (A),
Algorithmics = Winfried Ritsch (A), Pi = Martin Pichlmaier (A)
http://algo.mur.at/pd/ars03

Ars Electronica electrolobby Kitchen Participants

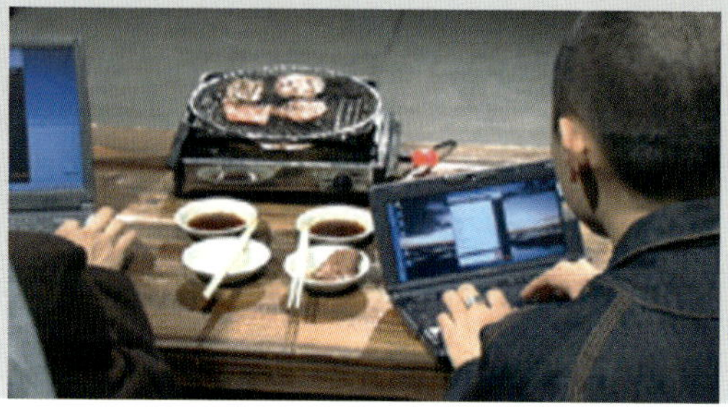

Communication Grill Chang-Tei"
Kou Sueda & Koji Ishii

"Communication Grill Chang-Tei" is an electric cooker for making *Yakiniku* (Japanese-style barbecue). Nowadays, we have the Internet and mobile phones, so we can communicate with people anytime, anywhere. But "connecting" people is full of surprises. This installation aims to make people think about the meaning of communication, and is a device for creating compelling and unexpected situations.
http://www.iik.jp/~cgc/contents/conceptEN.html

CodePlay @UMe

CodePlay@Ume brings together various code-oriented projects developed by students and faculty at the University of Maine (USA). These projects include: ALICE (an AI that monitors web health), The Pool (a virtual community for distributed creativity), Breakdown (a cultural-code-busting game prototype), and Internet2@UMe (a broad-band protocol for connecting university artists, researchers and faculty). These "open" projects approach code as tool, content, meme, and structure, and invite active participation by Ars visitors.
http://newmedia.umaine.edu/codeplay/

DIVE

The DIVE book/CD-ROM expands the world of digital abundance and edifies the legitimate free exchange of ideas, software, projects, and shared online resources. The publication presents documentation of the Kingdom of Piracy <KOP> project; it provides an introduction into the world of free software, free networks, and collaborative online activities; further, it includes some free software including dynebolic, the bootable GNU / Linux platform for streaming media.
http://kop.fact.co.uk/DIVE/

Roy Ascott (UK): Telematic Embrace

Long before the emergence of e-mail and chat rooms, Roy Ascott had coined the term "telematic art" as well as begun investigating how computer networks function as artistic media and how this networked communication also changed the interrelationship among artists, art works and their audience. Roy Ascott presents his latest book entitled *Telematic Embrace,* a collection of illustrative essays written since the '60s that synthesize a wide range of cultural and artistic theories.
Roy Ascott: *Telematic Embrace. Visionary Theories of Art, Technologies, and Consciousness,* Edited and with an Essay by Edward A. Shranken, The University of California Press 2003

MagNet

MagNet is a network developed to support critical debate and resource sharing among independent print/web magazines in the field of electronic culture. Building on the strong editorial traditions of each partner, it is building infrastructure and knowledge exchange systems by which distribution, subscription, translation and editorial content can be improved within the network as a whole. Currently, *MagNet* is made up of nine magazines and five affiliated organizations, all of which are creatively engaged with the field of electronic culture. Through its publications, *MagNet* aims to help define this field as one of new and varied cultural forms, and to offer a potentially public space for the negotiation of cultural values.
By promoting the diversity of specific cultures and media content, *MagNet* seeks to simultaneously harness and critique current trends of globalization.
Slavo Krekovic (SK, *¾ Review),* Alessandro Ludovico (I, *Neural),* Georg Schöllhammer (A, *springerin)* and Simon Worthington & Pauline van Mourik Broekman (UK, *mute)* on *MagNet.*

Eugene Thacker (USA): Biomedia

University of Minnesota Press, "Electronic Mediations" series
Biomedia is a book about the future of the intersection of molecular biology and computer science. Adopting a media studies approach to biology, Biomedia is a critical analysis of research fields that explores the relationships between biologies and technologies, between genetic "codes" and computer "codes." In doing so *Biomedia* looks beyond the familiar examples of cloning, genetic engineering and gene therapy, all of which are predicated on the centrality of DNA or genes. Instead, it looks to emerging fields in the intermediary zone between bioscience and computer science, a zone in which "life" is often understood as "information."

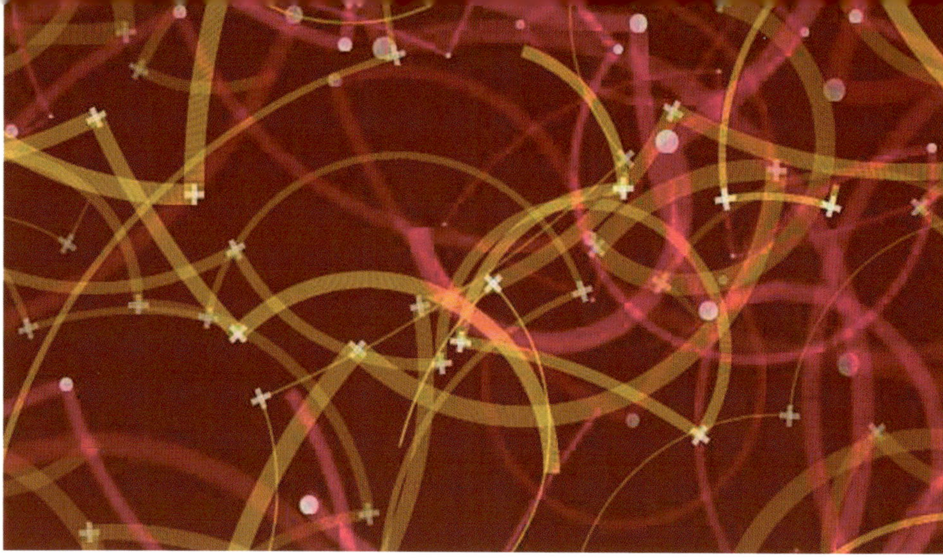

CODE Exhibition_electrolobby

Processing

Ben Fry / Casey Reas

Introduction

The *Processing* project introduces a new audience to computer programming and encourages an audience of hybrid artist/designer/programmers. It integrates a programming language, development environment, and teaching methodology into a unified structure for learning. Its goal is to introduce programming in the context of electronic art and to open electronic art concepts to a programming audience. Unlike other popular web programming environments such as Flash and Director, *Processing* is an extension of Java and supports many of the existing Java structures, but with a simplified syntax. The application runs locally and exports programs to Java applets, which may be viewed over the Internet. It is not a commercial production tool, but is built specifically for learning and prototyping.

Concept

Graphical user interfaces became mainstream nearly twenty years ago, but programming fundamentals are still primarily taught through the command line interface. Classes proceed from outputting text to the screen, to GUI, to computer graphics (if at all). It is possible to teach programming in a way that moves graphics and concepts of interaction closer to the surface. Making exercises created during learning viewable over the web supports the creation of a global educational community and provides motivation for learning. A "view source" method of programming enables the members of the community to learn from each other.

Even for programmers who have moderate experience using tools like Flash and Director, there remains a significant gap between the fundamentals learned in their respective scripting languages, and more advanced programming languages like Java or C++. Developers interested in making the jump to the latter are likely to find the switch frustrating, since they must first learn the idiosyncracies of developing a graphical application for their computing environment, a task which often involves pages of code before even the simplest objects can be drawn on the screen.

The concept of *Processing* is to create a text programming language specifically for making responsive images, rather than creating a visual programming language. The language enables sophisticated visual and responsive structures and has a balance between features and ease of use. Many computer graphics and interaction techniques can be discussed including vector/raster drawing, 2D/3D transformations, image processing, color models, events, network communication, information visualization, etc. *Processing* shifts the focus of programming away from technical details like threading and double-buffering and places emphasis on communication.

Programming Language/Environment

Processing is a Java environment which translates programs written in its own syntax into Java code and then compiles to Java 1.1 byte code as an applet. It includes a custom 2D/3D engine that draws its feature set from PostScript and OpenGL. The software is free to use and the source code is available online at Sourceforge.net. It runs on Windows, Mac OS X, Mac OS 9, and Linux. The software is currently in Alpha release, but will be in a public Beta release at Ars Electronica 2003. *Processing* version 1.0 focuses on teaching basic concepts of interactive networked computer graphics.

Processing provides three different modes of programming—each one more structurally complex than the previous. In the most basic mode, programs are single line commands for drawing primitive shapes to the screen. In the most complex mode, Java code may be written within the environment. The intermediate mode allows for the creation of dynamic software in a hybrid procedural/object-oriented structure. It strives to achieve a balance between features and clarity, which encourages the experimentation process and reduces the learning curve.

Skills learned through *Processing* enable people to learn languages and APIs suitable for different contexts including web authoring (ActionScript), networking and communications (Java), microcontrollers (C), and computer graphics (OpenGL). The project is built around Java so that the programming skills learned using *Processing* can be directly transferrable to these more advanced environments once the time is appropriate.

Networked Learning

The *Processing* website houses a set of extended examples and a complete reference for the language. Hundreds of students, educators, and practitioners across five continents are involved in using the software. As of June 2003, more than 1000 people have signed up to test the pre-release versions. An active online discussion board is a platform for discussing individual programs and future software additions to the project. The software has been used at diverse universities and institutions in cities including: Boston, New York, San Fransisco, London, Paris, Oslo, Basel, Brussels, Berlin, Bogota (Colombia), Ivrea (Italy), Manila, Nagoya and Tokyo.

Processing is an open project initiated by Ben Fry and Casey Reas. It is currently developed in the Aesthetics and Computation Group at the MIT Media Lab, the Interaction Design Institute Ivrea, and by a group of developers distributed across the Net.

Processing: Some Simple Example Programs

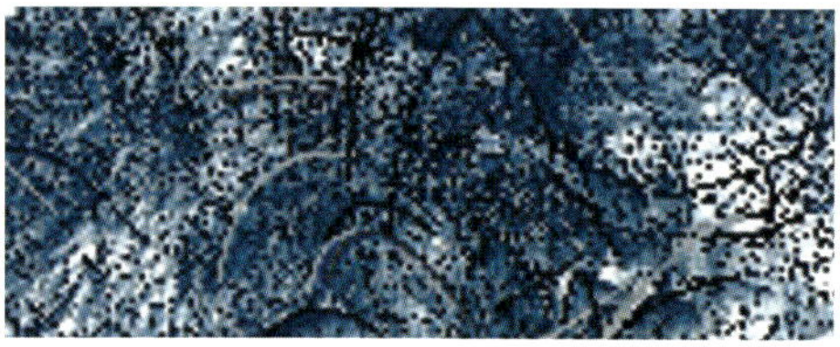

withoutTitle by Lia
A software machine exploring the boundaries of control.

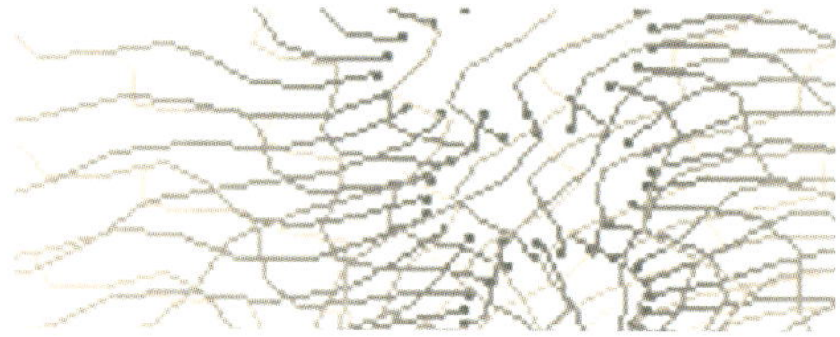

Wiggle by Manny Tan
An expanding, contracting, and twisting responsive organ.

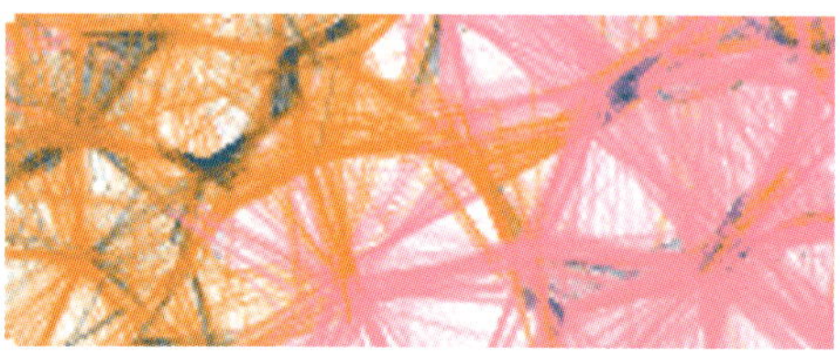

Articulate by GroupC
Structure emerges through the interactions of autonomous elements.

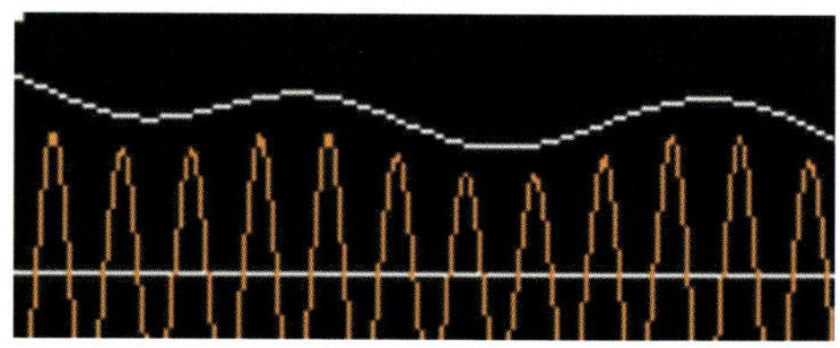

WAVE by Carlos Andres Rocha
Constructing visual and sonic space. Click and drag to draw a wave. Have sound turned on.

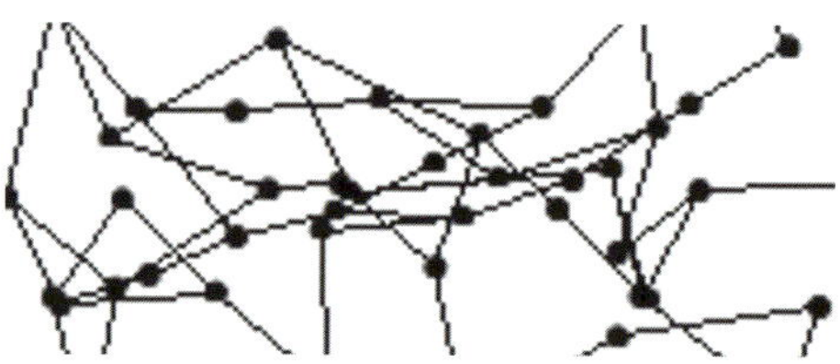

SodaProcessing by Ed Burton
Simplified version of the renowned Soda Constructor implemented in Processing.

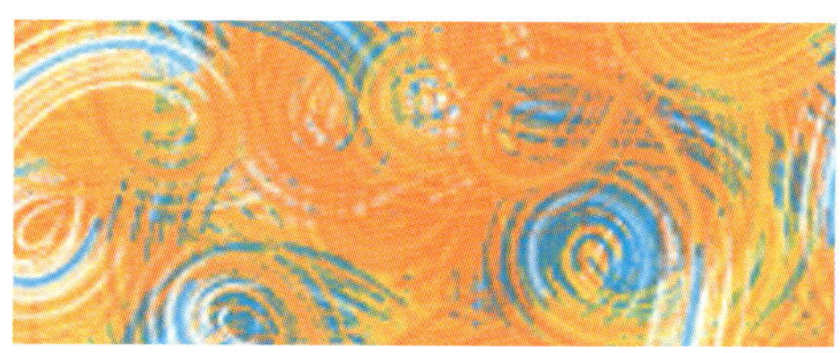

C_Drawer by Marius Watz
Like drawing with a bunch of crayons in one hand. Simple and messy, but fun.

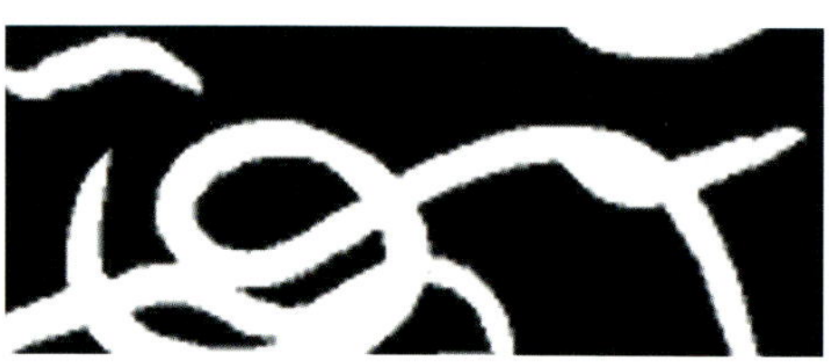

Yellowtail by Golan Levin
An interactive software system for the gestural creation and performance of real-time abstract animation.

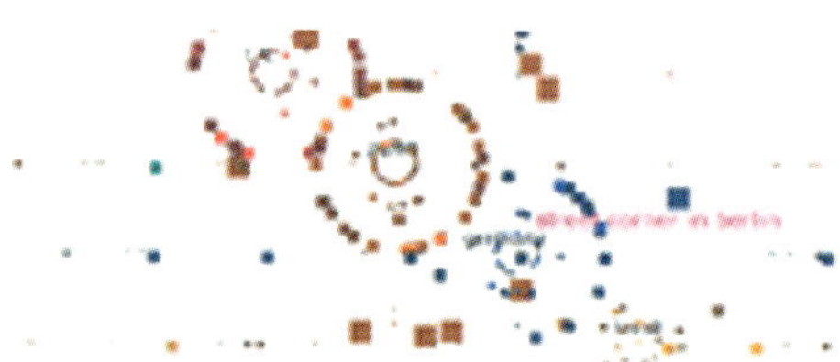

Matchboxes by Schoenerwissen
Reassembling a movieclip database by using the properties of the collected information to generate a new visual data matrix.

```
for(int i=40; i<80; i=i+5) {
  line(30, i, 80, i);
}
```

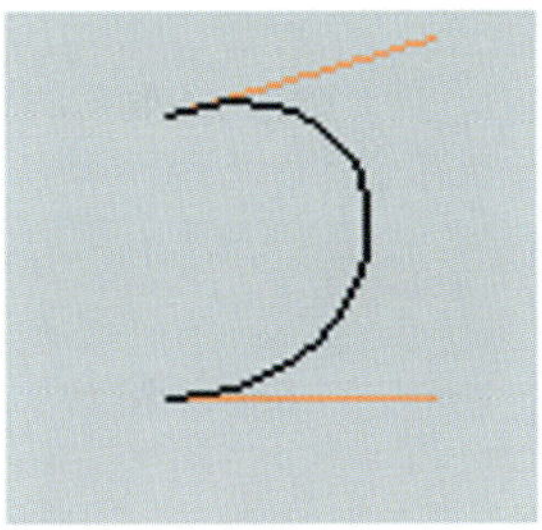

```
stroke(255, 102, 0);
line(30, 20, 80, 5);
line(80, 75, 30, 75);
stroke(0);
bezier(30, 20, 80, 5, 80, 75, 30, 75);
```

```
noStroke();
colorMode(HSB, 100);
for(int i=0; i<100; i++) {
  for(int j=0; j<100; j++) {
    stroke(i, j, 100);
    point(i, j);
  }
}
```

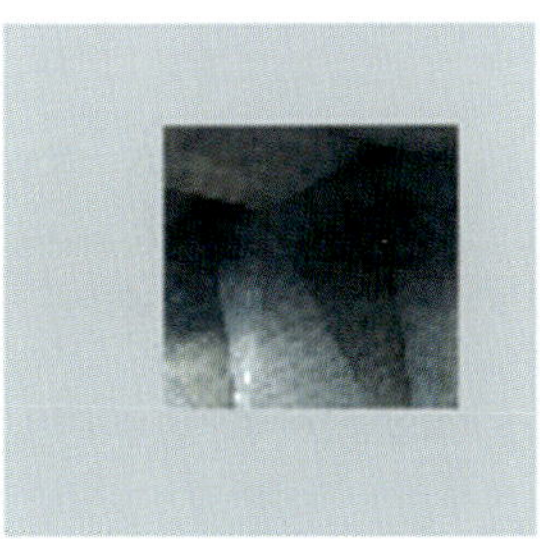

```
BImage b; // declare variable
"b" of type BImage
b = loadImage("basel.gif");
image(b, 30, 20, 55, 55);
```

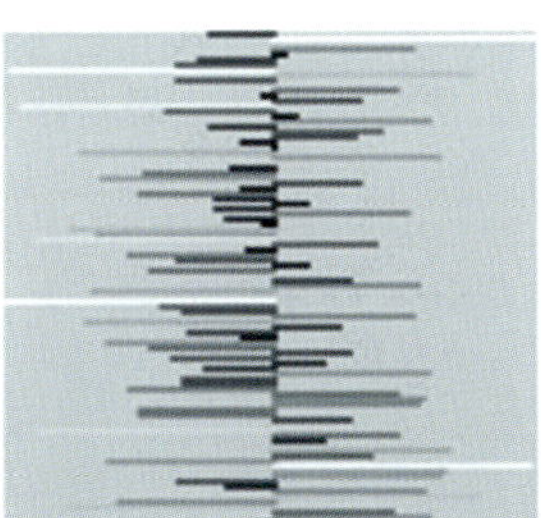

```
for(int i=0; i<100; i++) {
  float r = random(-50, 50);
  stroke(abs(r*5));
  line(50, i, 50+r, i);
}
```

Processing

Ben Fry / Casey Reas

Einleitung

Das Projekt *Processing* vermittelt Anfängern grundlegende Programmierkenntnisse und richtet sich an hybride Künstler / Designer / Programmierer. Das Projekt umfasst eine Programmiersprache, eine Entwicklungsumgebung und die didaktische Aufbereitung der Inhalte in einer einheitlichen Lernumgebung. *Processing* vermittelt grundlegende Programmierkenntnisse im Bereich elektronische Kunst und macht Programmierer mit Schlüsselkonzepten der elektronischen Kunst vertraut. Im Unterschied zu anderen bekannten Programmierumgebungen wie Flash und Director ist Processing eine Java-Erweiterung und unterstützt viele Java-Strukturen, jedoch mit einer vereinfachten Syntax. Die Applikation wird lokal auf dem Rechner des Benutzers ausgeführt und exportiert Programme zu Java-Applets, sodass ein Zugriff über das Internet möglich ist. Das Programm ist kein kommerzielles Programmierwerkzeug, sondern wurde speziell für Lernzwecke und zur Prototypenentwicklung geschrieben.

Das Konzept

Grafische Benutzerinterfaces sind seit fast zwanzig Jahren Standard in der Computertechnologie, grundlegende Programmierkenntnisse werden jedoch weiterhin primär über Kommandozeilen-Interfaces vermittelt. Vorrangig wird Wissen über Textausgabe am Bildschirm bzw. über GUIs und erst später, wenn überhaupt, über Computergrafiken vermittelt. Grundlegende Programmierkenntnisse können so vermittelt werden, dass Grafiken und interaktive Elemente in den Vordergrund treten. Die Freigabe von im Unterricht erstellten Übungsbeispielen fördert die Entwicklung einer globalen Lerngemeinschaft und erhöht die Motivation der Lernenden. Die Verwendung der „View Source"-Funktion ermöglicht der Internetgemeinschaft voneinander zu lernen.
Selbst Programmierer, die Erfahrung mit Werkzeugen wie Flash und Director haben, müssen erkennen, dass ihre Grundkenntnisse in den jeweiligen Skriptsprachen für komplexere Programme wie Java oder C++ nicht ausreichen. Entwickler, die den Umstieg auf diese Programme versuchen, empfinden die Übergangsphase vermutlich als frustrierend, da sie sich zunächst mit den Eigenheiten der Entwicklung einer spezifischen Grafikanwendung für ihre Rechnerumgebung vertraut machen müssen – eine Aufgabe, die oft unzählige Seiten Code erfordert, bevor auch nur die einfachsten Objekte am Bildschirm angezeigt werden können.
Das Grundgedanke von *Processing* ist die Erzeugung einer spezifischen Textprogrammiersprache zur Generierung von responsiven grafischen Elementen anstatt einer visuellen Programmiersprache. Diese Sprache ermöglicht die Entwicklung von komplexen visuellen und responiven Strukturen und bietet ein ausgewogenes Gleichgewicht zwischen den verfügbaren Funktionen und der Benutzerfreundlichkeit. Zahlreiche Techniken zur Grafikerstellung und Interaktionsmöglichkeiten können vermittelt werden, darunter u. a. Vektor-/Rasterzeichnung, 2D/3D-Transformationen, Bildverarbeitung, Farbmodelle, Ereignisse, Netzwerkkommunikation, Informationsvisualisierung, etc. *Processing* verlagert den Schwerpunkt des Programmierprozesses von technischen Details wie Threading und Double-Buffering hin zur Kommunikation.

Programmiersprache und Programmierumgebung

Processing ist eine Java-Umgebung, die in ihrer eigenen Syntax geschriebene Programme in Java-Code umwandelt und dann als Applet in einen Java 1.1.-Bytecode kompiliert. Das Programm verfügt auch über eine eigens angepasste 2D/3D-Engine mit PostScript- und OpenGL-Funktionen. Die Software kann kostenlos benutzt werden; der Quellcode ist unter *Sourceforge.net* erhältlich. Das Programm läuft auf Windows, Mac OS X, Mac OS 9 und Linux. Zurzeit ist eine Alpha-Version verfügbar, im Rahmen der Ars Electronica wird eine öffentlich verfügbare Beta-Version gelauncht. Processing Version 1.0 konzentriert sich auf die Vermittlung von Grundkenntnissen im Bereich interaktive vernetzte Computergrafiken.
Processing bietet drei verschiedene Programmiermodi, wobei Modus 2 und 3 komplexer als Modus 1 sind. Im Grundmodus können über einzeilige Befehle einfache Objekte am Bildschirm angezeigt werden. Im komplexesten Modus (erweiterter Modus) kann in der *Processing*-Umgebung Java-Code geschrieben werden. Der Zwischenmodus unterstützt die Entwicklung von dynamischer Software in einer hybriden prozeduralen/objektorientierten Struktur. Ein ausgewogenes Gleichgewicht zwischen den einzelnen Funktion und der Klarheit der Strukturen wird angestrebt; dies fördert den Experimentierprozess und minimiert die Lernkurve.
Die mittels *Processing* erworbenen Kenntnisse ermöglichen die Erlernung von Sprachen und APIs, die für unterschiedliche Kontexte, u. a. Web-Authoring (ActionScript), Networking und Kommunikationsanwendungen (Java), Mikrokontroller-Anwendungen (C) und Computergrafiken (OpenGL), anwendbar sind. *Processing* basiert auf Java, sodass die erworbenen Programmierkenntnisse zur angemessenen Zeit direkt auf diese komplexeren Umgebungen angewandt werden können.

Vernetztes Lernen

Die *Processing*-Website bietet zahlreiche Anwendungsbeispiele und eine vollständige Referenzliste. Hunderte von Studenten, Pädagogen und Praktikern auf fünf Kontinenten benutzen die Software. Seit Juni 2003 haben mehr als 1.000 Personen das Pre-Release bestellt. Ein Online-Diskussionsforum bietet eine Plattform zur Erörterung von individuellen Programmen und Programmweiterentwicklungen. Die Software wird auch an verschiedenen Universitäten und in Einrichtungen der folgenden Städte verwendet: Boston, New York, San Francisco, London, Paris, Oslo, Basel, Brüssel, Berlin, Bogotà (Kolumbien), Ivrea (Italien), Manila, Nagoya und Tokio.

Aus dem Amerikanischen von Sonja Pöllabauer

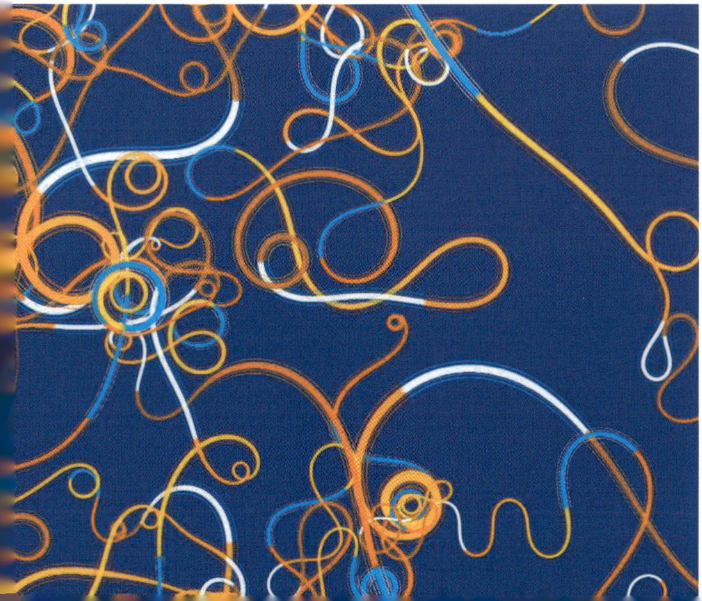

bitforms gallery

Steve Sacks

I started *bitforms* to explore the realms of digital art. To redefine categories and levels of artistic engagement. To discover new art. To educate both new and old school collectors.

bitforms represents artists who are using digital tools as an integral part of their process. These tools offer artists new ways of interpreting, manipulating and visualizing information. It's evolution in art. As a gallerist specializing in this type of work, it's important for me to know the tools. How and why are they being used? Are they necessary? Gratuitous use of technology for quick impact can be a detriment to both the artist and the gallery. The types of work we show include: Reactive sculpture. Data visualization. Sound and video installations. Digitally derived sculpture. Photo manipulation. Mixed media. Software art. Although there is a common theme of using digital tools, the idea and execution of the work are top priority. Is the idea fresh? Thought provoking? Relevant? Engaging? Granted, a lot of the answers are subjective, but there is an historic comparison and discovery process that can be used to define and position all works. In fact, artists have been using technology as an influence or tool for many centuries. But the use of digital technologies is different. Especially the use of software to create or to influence a creation.

The category of art that has been most challenging for *bitforms* to define, market and legitimize has been software art. How do you collect it? Define it? What is its value? Future value? Archivability? Maintenance?

There are two categories of software art that *bitforms* represents—framed and unframed. The terms may sound traditional, but the issues involved are very different from framed and unframed prints and canvases. There are technical and use considerations in both types. Other considerations are networked, interactive, reactive and passive. These are terms that offer the collector different experiences and may require alternative maintenance and care.

Framed software art

Framed software artworks, like that of Manfred Mohr, are object oriented and more in sync with traditional fine art criteria. The software is typically unique and embedded in a frame or custom housing. Mohr's work is based on the fracturing of a cube's symmetry in Cartesian coordinates. *motion* is Mohr's new presentations in animation and movement of the system of binary decisions. Displayed in handmade computer stations and flat screens, these passive works, generated from programs written by Mohr, offer a subtle pace—a revealing view into the thought process of Mohr's creations.

In Daniel Rozin's *Mirrors #2, #5, #6,* he has created reactive screen-based software art pieces. They involve the viewer in a mirror type interaction. A video input interprets the form and each mirror delivers an expressionist compilation of color, shapes and movement. All three pieces deal with the way digital images and motion are reproduced and perceived.

Framed works are sold as variant editions or one of a kind and are typically much higher

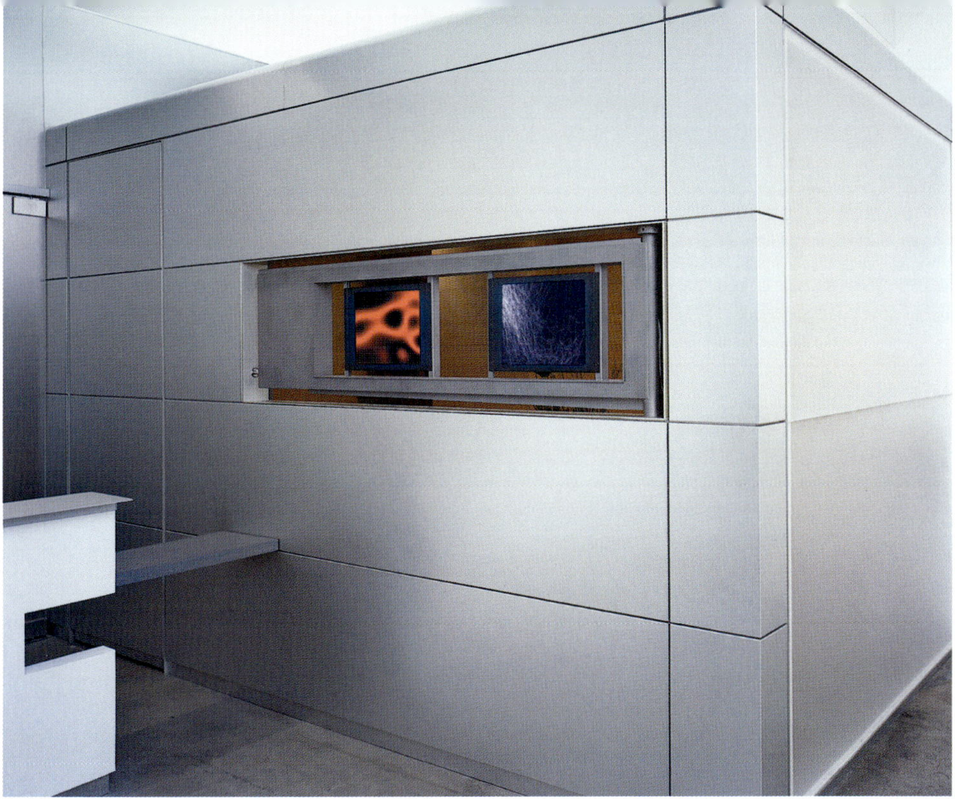

courtesy of bitforms gallery, nyc

priced than unframed. With framed works there is complete control by the artist as to how the artwork will function and be displayed. Many times the framing or housing of the software is conceptually tied to the work. Some artists collaborate to fabricate their objects, where as others have the skill set to build the entire artwork. The software art objects need to be robust and easily maintained. Typically there is a guarantee and a detailed maintenance manual. Since there is hardware involved, care must be given to use.

Unframed software art

The unframed software art is a bit more difficult to define and control. It is sold on a CD and can be framed or displayed in any way the collector desires. The art can be interactive and passive. Networked and stand-alone. *bitforms* has sold stand-alone pieces in editions ranging from 10 to 250. Each CD is signed and in a custom package.
At *bitforms* we are adamant about how the work should be presented. An education process is necessary. The education starts with explaining how to present and engage the work. We recommend a dedicated machine and monitor to run the works (a software art station). At *bitforms* we have an ideal setup, two 18" touch screens floating in a rotating steel arm. Hidden is a Dell CPU with wireless network, mouse and keyboard. Presentation is important. To help people manage their software art, we have created an administrative tool that allows collectors to add, delete and select pieces. Once the software art is loaded and added to the system, the collector doesn't have to go back to the desktop. This is an important step in creating an isolated system that is focused on the viewing and interaction of software art. One system that we recommend for displaying software art is the all-in-one units from ezscreen. These are custom units that have

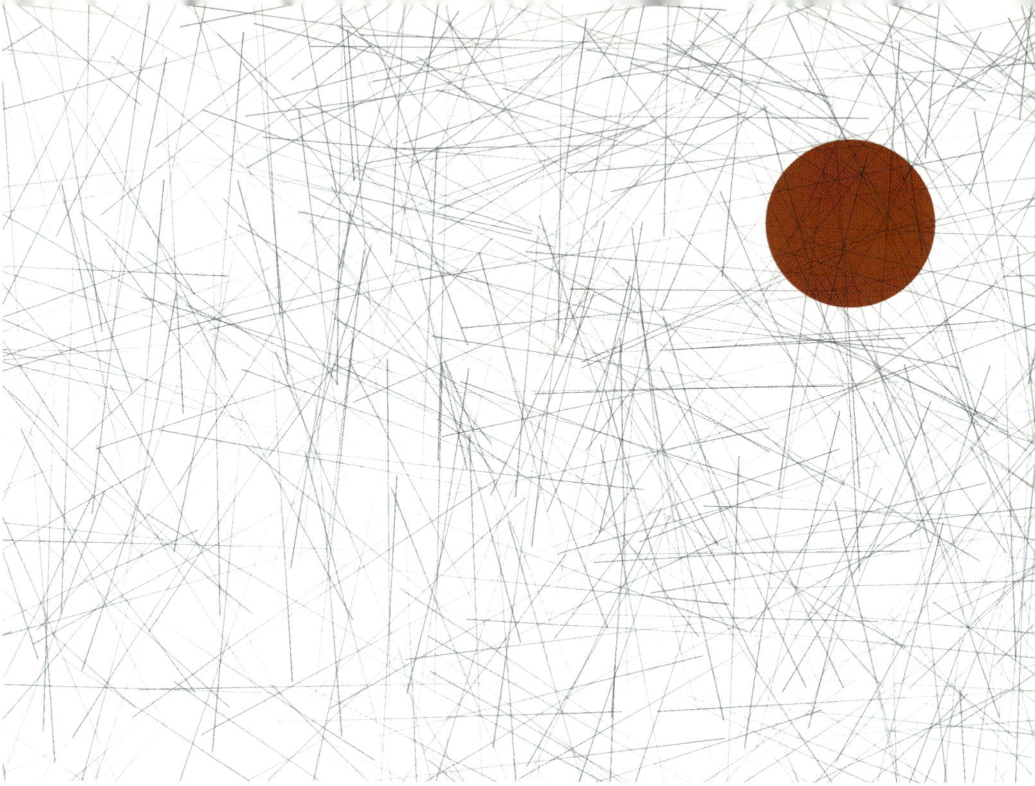

courtesy of bitforms gallery, nyc

Casey Reas: *Tissue*

both CPU and touchscreen as one piece of hardware. They come in 15" and 18" versions, and hang on the wall like a painting or wall sculpture. The simplicity and flexibility of this system makes it very easy to collect and present most types of software art.

Collectors of this type of art vary. There are the old school collectors who are intrigued with the work and the low entry cost. There are the new collectors who are excited about the new technologies and the interactive nature of certain works. And there are museums that want to maintain a link to what is current and new. Some common questions collectors have are, What am I actually getting? What is the artist's role? Is this really art? The collector is getting a set of rules or parameters determined by the artist. These rules are the art. They are the essence of the experience and aesthetic direction. The rules can be interpreted as the code the artist writes. The questioning of this as an art form is to be expected.

One of the issues with unframed software art is this concept of display on a dedicated system. Even though the cost of a flat screen and CPU have come down drastically over the years, it is still a psychological hurdle to dedicate a computer to one task. So, many people choose to buy the work and place it on their everyday machine with all of their stuff. I equate this to buying a print and putting in a magazine. It is a distraction and takes away from the experience. The other hurdle is the "screen saver" comparison. Society has chosen to consider screen savers with very little regard—they are temporary visuals. Another challenge for the legitimacy of this type of art.

Another type of unframed software art uses a network or Internet connection. One example is Mark Napier's *Waiting Room*—a collaborative network piece within a virtual space that 50 users share through the Internet. In this space the visitor becomes a participant in a moving painting. Their actions activate and shape the artwork, shifting the screen

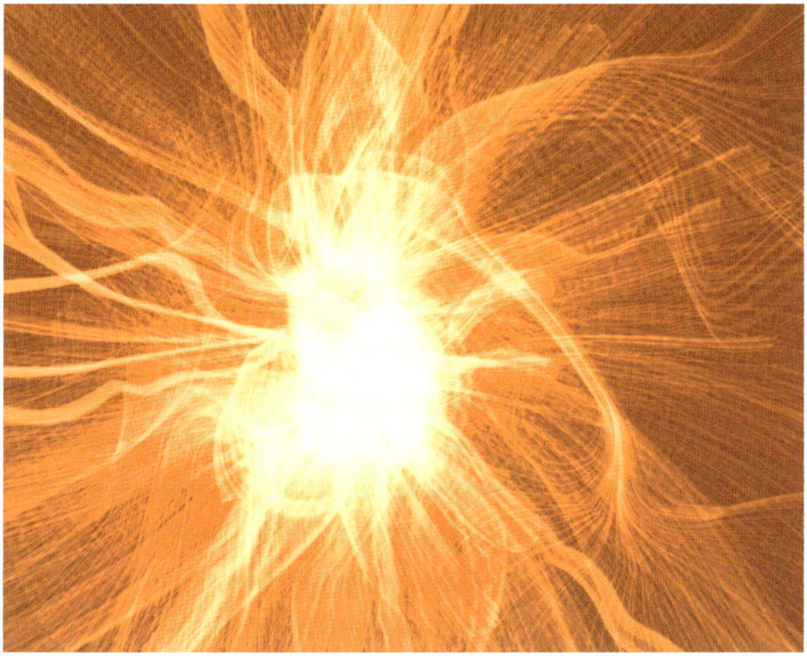

courtesy of bitforms gallery, nyc

Golan Levin: *Floccus*

through moods, from hard-edged to atmospheric, from dark to light, from quiet to chaotic. Each click creates a shape, a shadow or a wall, a suggestion of architecture or a dissolving light. Since there is only one piece that exists on a server, we sold this work in shares. 50 shares at $1,000 per share. A grass roots way of promoting this work was through a software art party at a collector's home. We had the *Waiting Room* running at the party. The collectors who couldn't attend were connected to the piece and interacting with those at the party. Mark Napier was there to discuss the piece and answer any questions. This was an ideal way to experience the true beauty of the collaborative network art concept in a social setting. It also let people see how to live with the art in a variety of ways.

Works from Golan Levin and Casey Reas have ties to abstract expressionism. Their works are organic interpretations of form, motion and interactivity. In *Floccus,* by Golan Levin, ductile filaments drawn by the user swirl around a shifting, imaginary drain centered at the user's cursor. These filaments—torn by conflicting impulses to simultaneously preserve their length, yet also move towards or away from the user's cursor—find an equilibrium by forming gnarly, tangled masses. *Tissue,* by Casey Reas, exposes the movements of thousands of synthetic neural systems. Each line in the image reveals the history of one system's movement. People interact with the software by positioning a group of points on the screen. By positioning and re-positioning the points, an understanding of the total system emerges from the subtle relations between the positional input and the rich visual output.

Software art is empowering. Engaging. Endless. Whether or not it becomes a valuable collectable, I am convinced that it will be a part of the art nomenclature. Its beauty and possibilities are too alluring. The artists are too talented. And the world deserves a new creative outlet.

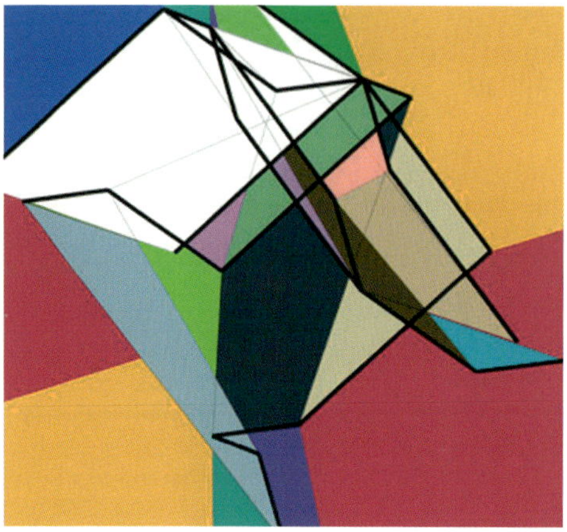

Manfred Mohr: *P-707/C11, 2001*
Endura Chrome, canvas, vinyl

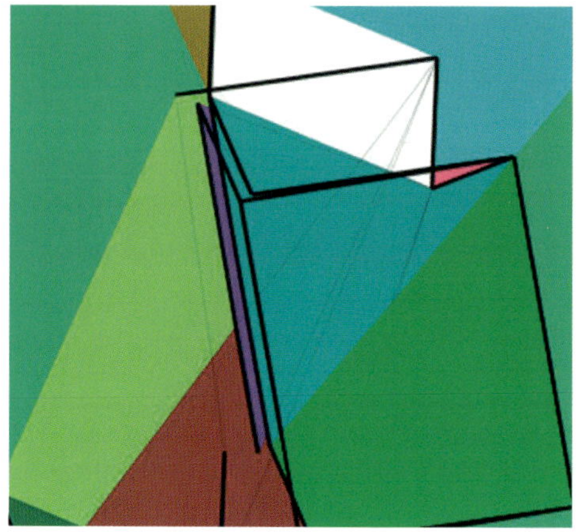

Manfred Mohr: *P-708/C, 2001*
Medium: Endura Chrome, canvas, vinyl

courtesy of bitforms gallery, nyc

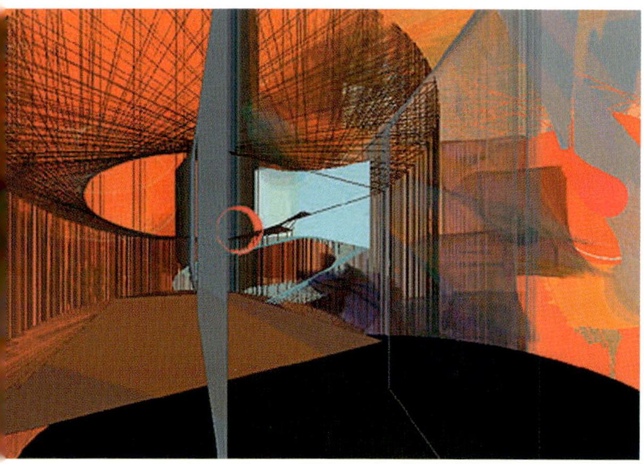

Mark Napier: *Waiting Room, 2002 System Specs*
CD w/interactive software art

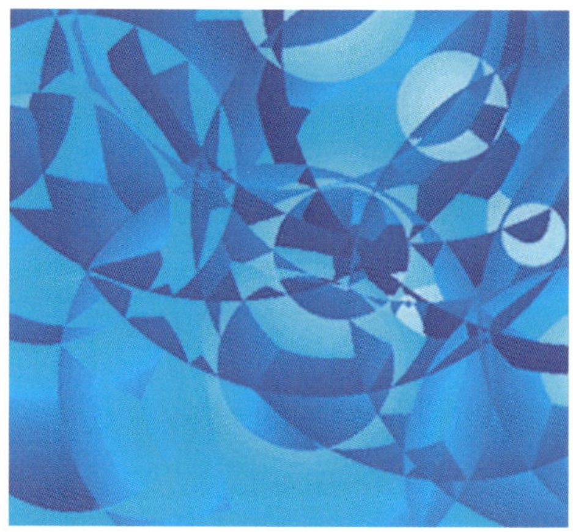

Mark Napier: *Pea Soup, 2000*
Java applet, C code

courtesy of bitforms gallery, nyc

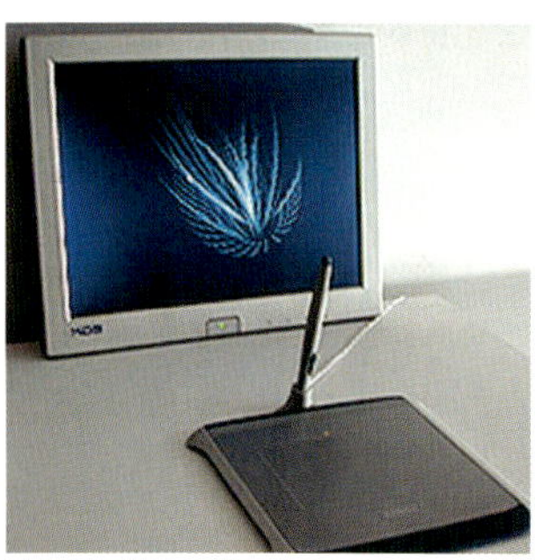

Golan Levin

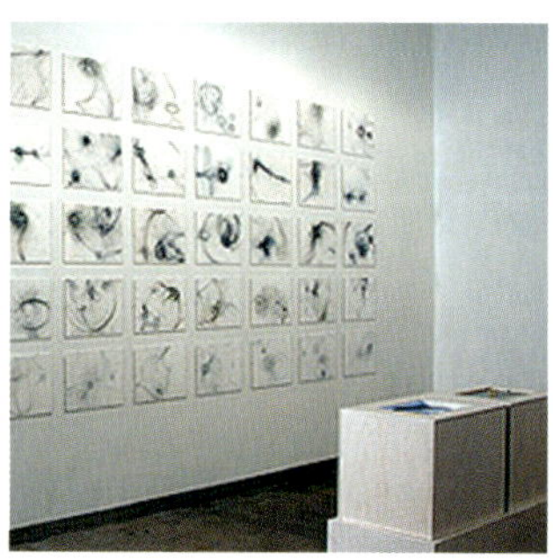

Golan Levin

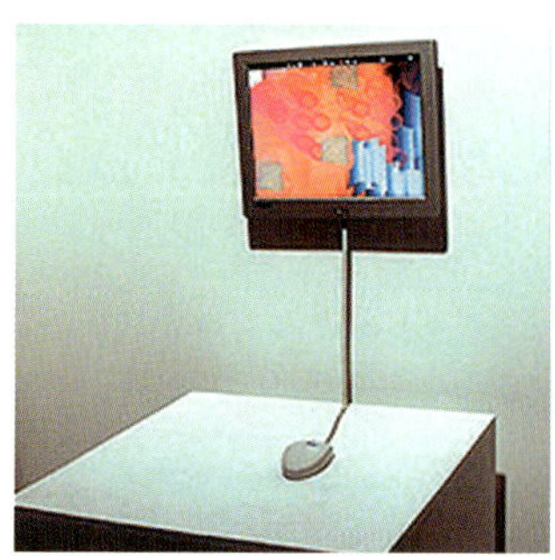

Mark Napier

courtesy of bitforms gallery, nyc

courtesy of bitforms gallery, nyc

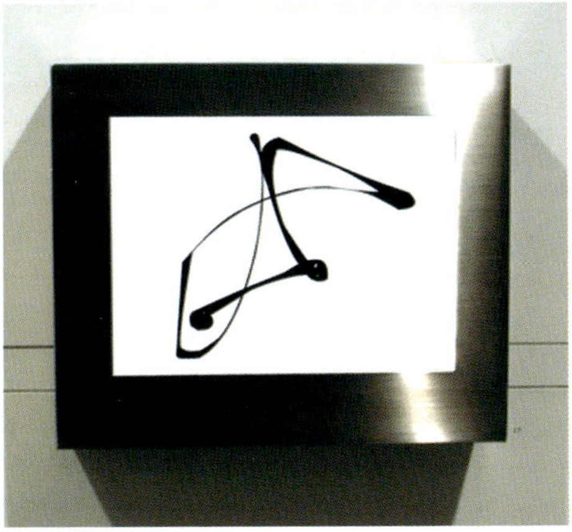

Golan Levin: *Transmission (Undeciphered), 2001 System Specs*
CD w/interactive software art

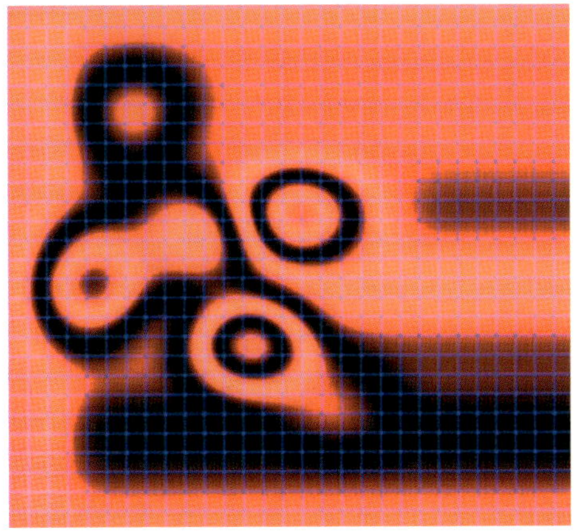

Golan Levin: *Stria, 2002. System Specs*
Medium: CD w/interactive software art

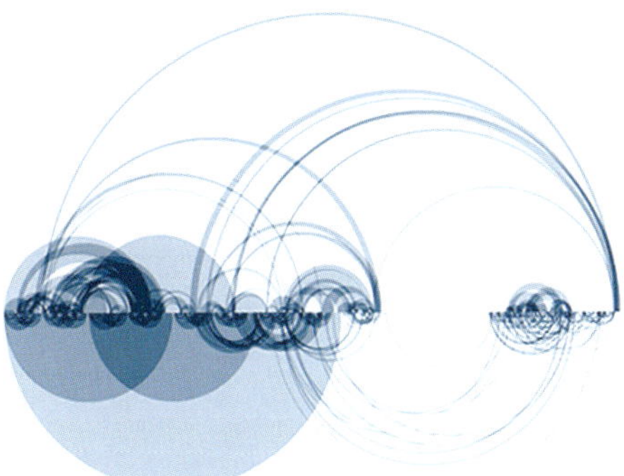

Martin Wattenberg:
Stairway to Heaven (Zeppelin), 2002
Medium: Archival digital print, signed by artist

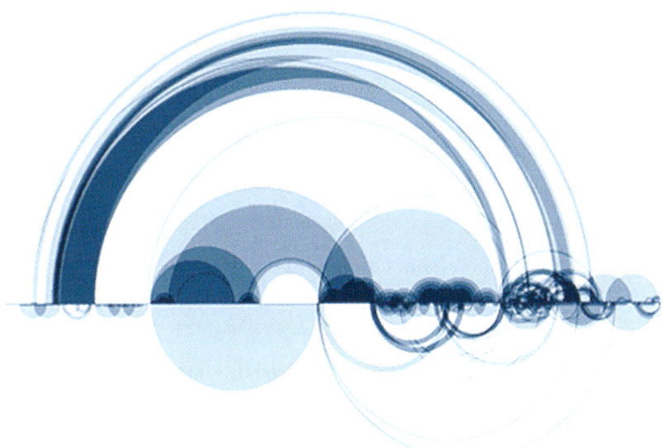

Martin Wattenberg: *Cocaine (Clapton), 2002*
Archival digital print, signed by artist

courtesy of bitforms gallery, nyc

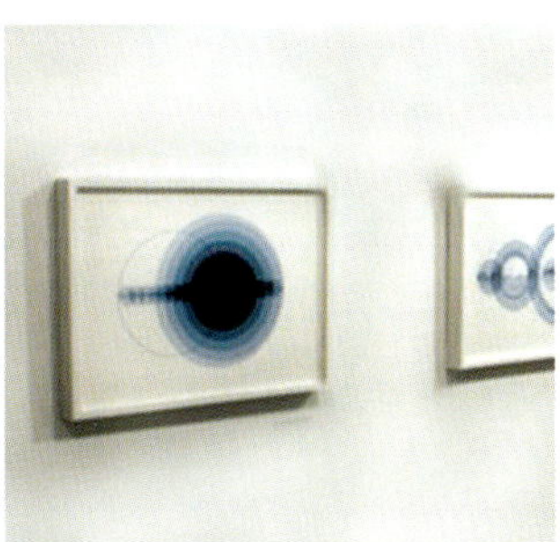

Martin Wattenberg

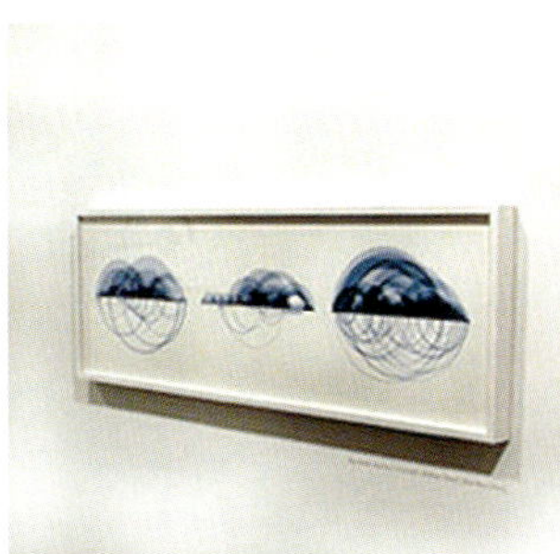

Martin Wattenberg

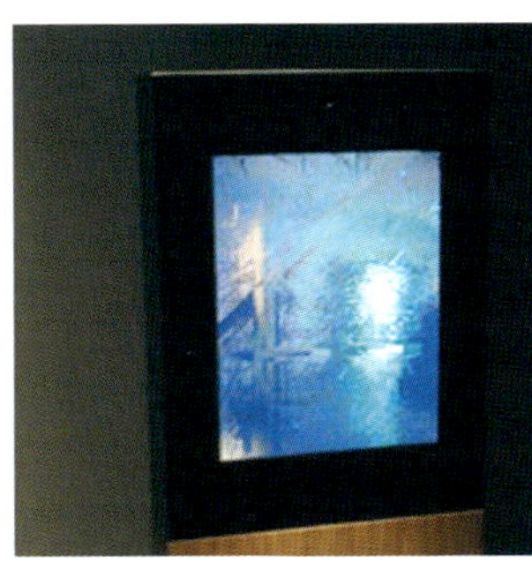

Daniel Rozin

bitforms

Steve Sacks

Ich gründete die Galerie *bitforms,* um die Möglichkeiten der digitalen Kunst zu ergründen. Um Kategorien und Horizonte künstlerischen Schaffens neu zu definieren. Um neue Kunst zu entdecken. Um Sammlern sowohl neuer als auch alter Schule ein Informationsforum zu bieten.

bitforms repräsentiert Künstler, die digitale Werkzeuge als integralen Bestandteil ihres Schaffensprozesses einsetzen. Diese Werkzeuge eröffnen den Künstlern neue Möglichkeiten, Information zu interpretieren, zu manipulieren und zu visualisieren. Darin liegt die Evolution in der Kunst. Als Galerist, der sich auf diese Art von Kunst spezialisiert hat, ist es für mich wichtig, selbst mit den Werkzeugen vertraut zu sein. Wie und warum werden sie eingesetzt? Sind sie notwendig? Der grundlose Einsatz von Technologie für schnelle Resultate kann sich sowohl für den Künstler als auch für die Galerie als nachteilig erweisen.

Zu den Arbeiten, die wir ausstellen, zählen zum Beispiel reaktive Skulpturen, Datenvisualisierungen, Ton- und Videoinstallationen, digital geschaffene Skulpturen, Fotomanipulationen, Mixed-Media-Produktionen und Softwarekunst. Obwohl allem das gemeinsame Thema des Einsatzes von digitalen Werkzeugen zugrunde liegt, stehen Idee und Ausführung der Arbeiten an erster Stelle. Ist die Idee neu? Regt sie zum Nachdenken an? Ist sie relevant? Erweckt sie Aufmerksamkeit? Viele dieser Fragen sind zugegebenermaßen subjektiv, dennoch kann ein Prozess des historischen Vergleichens und Forschens bei der Definierung und Positionierung aller Arbeiten helfen. Tatsächlich verwenden Künstler seit Jahrhunderten verschiedene Technologien als Inspiration oder Werkzeug. Der Einsatz digitaler Technologien gestaltet sich jedoch anders, besonders dann, wenn Software selbst Kunst schafft oder eine Arbeit beeinflusst.

Die Kategorie von Kunst, die *bitforms* vor die größten Herausforderungen hinsichtlich Definition, Vermarktung und Legitimation stellt, ist die Softwarekunst. Wie kann man sie sammeln? Wie definieren? Was ist sie wert? Was wird sie in Zukunft wert sein? Kann sie archiviert werden? Wie ist sie aufzubewahren?

bitforms repräsentiert zwei Kategorien von Softwarekunst, und zwar „gerahmte" und „ungerahmte". Die Begriffe mögen traditionell klingen, die Praxis unterscheidet sich jedoch stark von gerahmten und ungerahmten Drucken und Gemälden. In beiden Fällen sind Fragen zur Technik und zum Einsatz zu bedenken. Weitere Erwägungen betreffen die Qualitäten Vernetzung, interaktiv, reaktiv und passiv. Sie alle lassen den Sammler die Kunst unterschiedlich erleben und verlangen unter Umständen nach anderen Varianten der Lagerung und Handhabung.

Gerahmte Softwarekunst

Gerahmte Softwarekunst, wie die von Manfred Mohr, ist objektorientiert und entspricht eher den traditionellen Maßstäben von Kunst. Die Software ist üblicherweise ein Unikat und in einen Rahmen oder ein eigens angefertigtes Gehäuse eingebettet. Mohrs Arbeit gründet sich auf die Frakturierung der Symmetrie eines Würfels innerhalb der kartesianischen Koordinaten. *motions* ist der Titel von Mohrs neuen Arbeiten im Bereich der Animation und Bewegung inner-

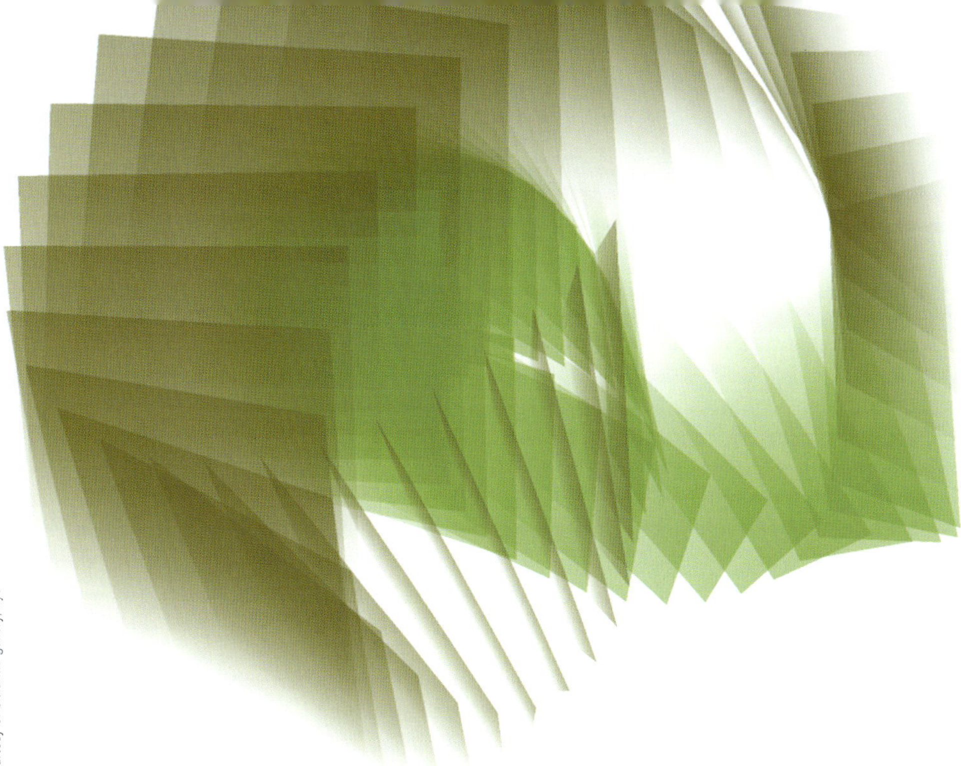

courtesy of bitforms gallery, nyc

Casey Reas: *RPM*

halb des Systems binärer Entscheidungen. Diese passiven Arbeiten, die von Mohrs selbst geschriebenen Programmen generiert werden, werden über handgefertigte Computerstationen und Flat-Screens dargestellt und enthalten subtile Abläufe, die Einblick in den Denkprozess hinter Mohrs Schaffen bieten.

Daniel Rozin hat in seinen Arbeiten *Mirrors #2, #5, #6* reaktive, auf Bildschirm präsentierte Softwarekunst geschaffen. Die Arbeiten binden den Beobachter in eine spiegelartige Interaktion ein. Über Videoinput wird die Form interpretiert, und jeder Spiegel präsentiert eine expressionistische Sammlung von Farben, Formen und Bewegungen. Alle drei Objekte haben zum Thema, wie digitale Bilder und Bewegungen reproduziert und wahrgenommen werden. Gerahmte Arbeiten werden in verschiedenen Editionen oder als Einzelstücke zum Verkauf angeboten, wobei die Verkaufspreise üblicherweise höher liegen als bei ungerahmten Objekten. Bei gerahmten Arbeiten hat der Künstler vollständige Kontrolle darüber, wie das Kunstwerk funktioniert und ausgestellt wird. Oft ist der Rahmen oder das Gehäuse der Software konzeptuell an das Objekt gebunden. Manche Künstler arbeiten bei der Schaffung ihrer Objekte mit anderen zusammen, während wieder andere die notwendigen Fähigkeiten besitzen, um das gesamte Kunstwerk selbst zu fertigen. Die Softwarekunst-Objekte müssen robust und leicht zu pflegen sein. Im Allgemeinen enthalten sie eine gewisse Garantiezeit und eine detaillierte Pflegeanleitung. Aufgrund des Hardwareanteils ist beim Gebrauch Vorsicht geboten.

Ungerahmte Softwarekunst

Ungerahmte Softwarekunst ist etwas schwieriger zu definieren und zu handhaben. Sie wird auf CD erworben und kann gerahmt oder je nach Wunsch des Sammlers ausgestellt werden. Die Arbeiten können interaktiv und passiv, Teil eines Netzwerks oder eigenständig sein. *bitforms* hat Einzelarbeiten in Auflagen von 10 bis 250 Stück verkauft. Jede CD ist signiert und originalverpackt.

Für uns bei *bitforms* ist es wichtig, wie die Objekte ausgestellt werden. Dazu braucht es Aufklärung, die damit beginnt, wie das Kunstwerk präsentiert und eingesetzt werden sollte. Wir empfehlen einen eigens zu diesem Zweck eingerichteten Computer mit Bildschirm, auf dem die Arbeit ausgestellt wird (eine Softwarekunst-Station). In der Galerie steht dafür der ideale Platz zur Verfügung, und zwar zwei in einem rotierenden Stahlarm schwebende 18-Zoll-Touch-Screens mit einer versteckten Dell-CPU mit drahtlosem Netzwerkanschluss, Maus und Tastatur. Um Kunden bei der Handhabung ihrer Softwarekunst zu helfen, haben wir ein Verwaltungstool entwickelt, das es dem Sammler erlaubt, Objekte hinzuzufügen, zu entfernen und auszuwählen. Ist das Softwarekunstwerk geladen und in das System integriert, muss der Sammler nicht mehr zum Computer zurückkehren. Das ist ein wichtiger Schritt in der Schaffung eines isolierten Systems zur Betrachtung von und Interaktion mit Softwarekunst. Ein von uns empfohlenes System zur Ausstellung von Softwarekunst sind die All-in-one-Systeme von *ezscreen*. Diese maßgefertigten Anlagen enthalten CPU und Touch-Screen als integrierte Hardware. Sie sind in 15 und 18 Zoll erhältlich und hängen an der Wand wie ein Gemälde oder eine Wandskulptur. Die Einfachheit und Flexibilität dieses System macht das Sammeln und Ausstellen von Softwarekunst sehr einfach.

Es gibt verschiedene Sammler dieser Art von Kunst, zum Beispiel Sammler der alten Schule, die von den Arbeiten und den niedrigen Einstiegskosten fasziniert sind. Neue Sammler reizen die neuen Technologien und der interaktive Charakter bestimmter Objekte. Zu den Interessenten zählen außerdem Museen, die auf dem Laufenden bleiben möchten, was neue Entwicklungen in der Kunst betrifft. Einige der Fragen, die sich alle Sammler stellen, sind: Was erwerbe ich hier eigentlich? Welche Rolle spielt der Künstler? Ist das wirklich Kunst? Der Sammler erhält vom Künstler festgesetzte Regeln oder Parameter. Diese Regeln machen die Kunst. Sie sind die Essenz aus Erfahrung und ästhetischer Richtungsweisung. Man könnte sie auch als Code sehen, den der Künstler schreibt. Dass dieser Prozess als Kunstform in Frage gestellt wird, ist keine Überraschung.

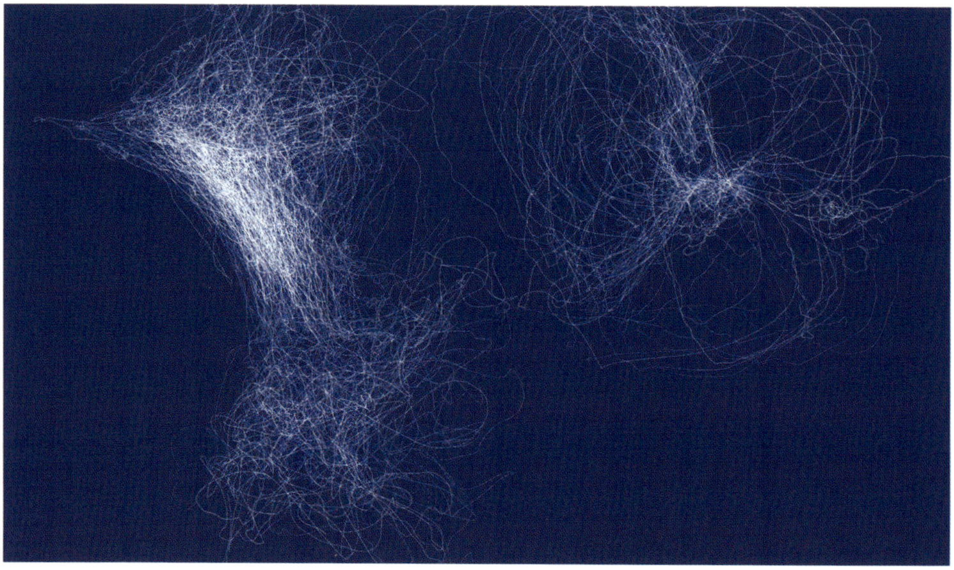

courtesy of bitforms gallery, nyc

Golan Levin: *Floccus*

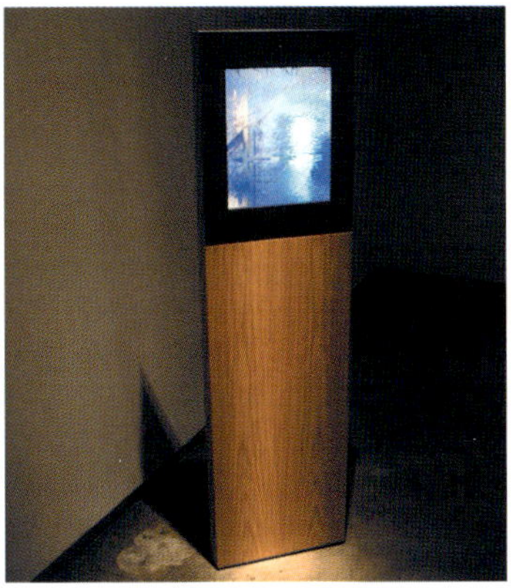
courtesy of bitforms gallery, nyc

Daniel Rozin: *Mirror #2*

Ein Problem hinsichtlich ungerahmter Softwarekunst ist das Konzept ihrer Präsentation über ein eigens dafür angeschafftes System. Obwohl die Kosten von Flat-Screens und CPUs im Laufe der letzten Jahre drastisch gesunken sind, bedarf es noch immer einer gewissen psychologischen Überzeugungsarbeit, wenn es darum geht, einen Computer nur einer einzigen Aufgabe zu widmen. Viele Kunden erwerben daher eine Arbeit und installieren sie neben ihren anderen Programmen auf ihrem Arbeitscomputer. Für mich ist das so, als kaufte man einen Druck und legte ihn in eine Zeitschrift. Es lenkt vom Objekt ab und schmälert das Kunsterlebnis. Ein weiteres Problem ist der Vergleich mit Bildschirmschonern. Diesen wird in der heutigen Gesellschaft wenig Beachtung geschenkt, sie gelten als temporäre visuelle Erscheinungen. Auch das stellt die Legitimität dieser Art von Kunst auf die Probe.

Eine weitere Variante von ungerahmter Softwarekunst nützt eine Netzwerk- oder Internetverbindung. Ein Beispiel dafür ist Mark Napiers *Waiting Room* – ein kollaboratives Netzwerkobjekt innerhalb eines virtuellen Raumes, an dem sich 50 Benutzer über das Internet beteiligen. In diesem Raum werden die Besucher Teil eines beweglichen Bildes. Ihre Handlungen aktivieren und gestalten das Kunstwerk und erzeugen so verschiedene Stimmungen auf dem Schirm, von angespannt bis atmosphärisch, von dunkel bis hell, von ruhig bis chaotisch. Jeder Mausklick erzeugt eine Form, einen Schatten oder eine Wand, einen Anflug von Architektur oder eine Überblendung. Da es sich hier um ein Objekt auf einem Server handelt, verkaufen wir die Arbeit in Form von Anteilen, und zwar 50 Stück zu je USD 1.000. Eine Möglichkeit, dieses Objekt möglichst breitenwirksam zu bewerben, war eine Softwarekunst-Veranstaltung im Haus eines Sammlers, in deren Rahmen der *Waiting Room* während der gesamten Party lief. Die Sammler, die nicht dabei sein konnten, wurden mit dem Objekt verbunden und standen mit den Besuchern vor Ort in Kontakt. Mark Napier war selbst anwesend, sprach über seine Arbeit und stand für Fragen zur Verfügung. Das war der perfekte Rahmen, um das Konzept der kollaborativen Netzwerkkunst in einem sozialen Umfeld zu erleben. Außerdem erhielten die Anwesenden die Gelegenheit zu sehen, auf welch unterschiedliche Weise man diese Kunstform leben und erleben kann.

Die Arbeiten von Golan Levin und Casey Reas stehen mit dem abstrakten Expressionismus in Verbindung. Sie sind organische Interpretationen von Form, Bewegung und Interaktivität. In Golan Levins *Floccus* wirbeln vom Benutzer gezeichnete, geschmeidige Fäden um einen sich bewegenden imaginären Abfluss am Cursor. Diese Fäden, die entgegengesetzten Impulsen ausgesetzt sind und ihren Zustand zu erhalten streben, während sie sich gleichzeitig zum Cursor hin oder von ihm weg bewegen möchten, finden die Balance, indem sie dichte, verworrene Knäuel bilden. *Tissue* von Casey Reas folgt den Bewegungen Tausender synthetischer Nervensysteme. Durch das Positionieren einer Anzahl von Punkten auf dem Schirm kann der Benutzer mit der Software interagieren. Durch das wiederholte Setzen und Umsetzen dieser Punkte lernt man über das subtile Verhältnis zwischen dem Input durch das Positionieren der Punkte und dem reichhaltigen visuellen Output das Gesamtsystem verstehen.

Softwarekunst öffnet Türen. Sie bindet ein. Sie hat kein Ende. Ob sie nun zum wertvollen Sammlerstück wird oder nicht. Ich bin überzeugt, dass sie ein Teil der Kunstwelt werden wird. Ihre Schönheit und die Möglichkeiten, die sie bietet, sind von unwiderstehlicher Anziehungskraft. Die Künstler sind überaus talentiert. Und die Welt verdient ein neues kreatives Schaffensfeld.

Aus dem Amerikanischen von Elisabeth Wiellander

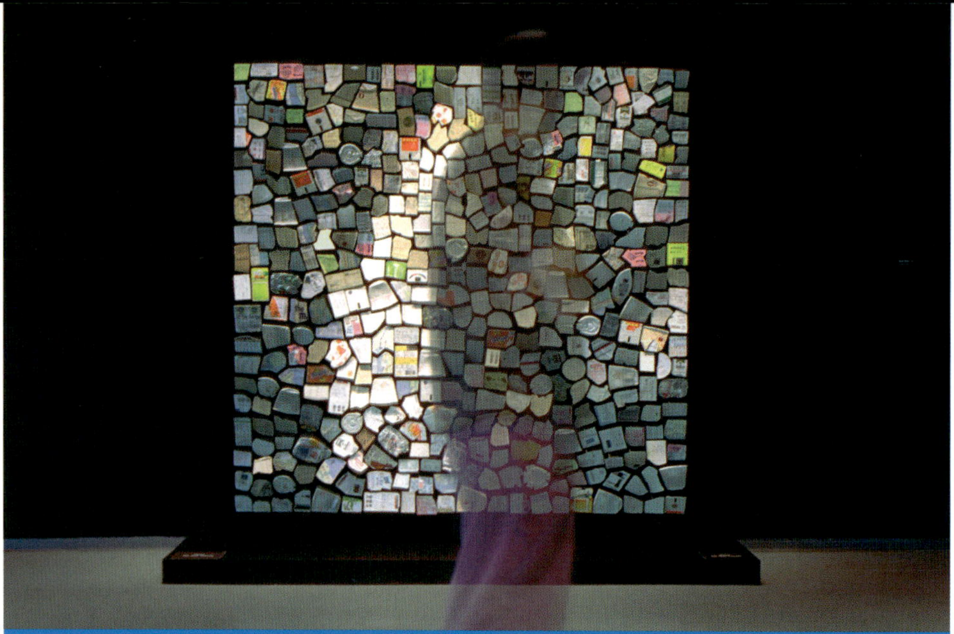

courtesy of bitforms gallery, nyc

Trash Mirror

Daniel Rozin

Trash Mirror is made of 500 pieces of trash collected between February and June 2002 on the streets of New York and in my pockets. These pieces were flattened and connected to motors, and with the help of a computer they are orchestrated to reflect whomever stands in front of the piece.

Like many of my other works this piece attempts to combine more than one level of information. From afar the image of the reflected person can be vividly observed and the contents of the trash cannot. Up close, the trash becomes visible and interesting while the image is too coarse to be comprehended.

This piece is quite similar in some aspects to my previous piece *Wooden Mirror,* 1999, and though this piece was built later (2002) it was conceived first. I decided to build *Wooden Mirror* first as a proof of concept as I was not confident that the extreme concept of *Trash Mirror* would technically work.

As the trash pieces have irregular shapes, the surface is very different from the orderly X by Y grid that is used for digital displays and the trash pieces do not come through as "pixels." Instead the piece celebrates the ability of computation to make sense and orchestrate even the messiest of substances. Because the trash that comprises the surface of this piece has many shades and colors and varies in shape and size, the computer needs to be extra smart to decide how to move each piece in order to create the best reflection of the viewer. In order to do so the computer has to have a very intimate knowledge of every piece of trash; in fact, the first stage of programming the *Trash Mirror* involved having the computer teach itself the exact placement of each piece by pointing a video camera at the piece itself rather than the viewer.

Trash Mirror

Daniel Rozin

Trash Mirror besteht aus 500 Stück Abfall, die ich von Februar bis Juni 2002 in den Straßen von New York und in meinen eigenen Taschen gefunden habe. Sie wurden flach gewalzt und mit Motoren verbunden. Ein Computer arrangiert sie so, dass der jeweilige Betrachter des Kunstwerks reflektiert wird.

Wie viele meine Arbeiten will auch diese mehrere Informationsebenen miteinander verbinden. Aus der Ferne kann der Beobachter die reflektierte Person deutlich erkennen, die verwendeten Abfallstücke jedoch nicht. Tritt man näher, zieht der Abfall Auge und Interesse auf sich, während das Bild selbst zu grob wird, um es noch auszumachen.

In mancher Hinsicht ähnelt diese Arbeit – obwohl sie später entstanden ist (2002), wurde sie zuerst konzipiert – meinem vorangegangenen Werk *Wooden Mirror* (1999). *Wooden Mirror* wurde bewusst zuerst umgesetzt, um das Grundkonzept auszutesten, da ich mir nicht sicher war, ob das komplexe Vorhaben *Trash Mirror* technisch überhaupt durchführbar war.

Da die Abfallstücke unregelmäßig geformt sind, unterscheidet sich die Oberfläche stark vom geordneten Koordinatengitter digitaler Displays, und sie können daher auch kaum mit „Pixeln" verglichen werden. Stattdessen zeigt die Arbeit, wie mittels Computern selbst die schmutzigsten Materialien angeordnet und so Inhalte transportiert werden können. Der Müll, aus dem die Oberfläche dieses Werks besteht, hat viele Farben und Schattierungen und ist von unterschiedlicher Größe und Form. Daher muss der Computer besonders geschickt darin sein zu entscheiden, wie jedes Stück auszurichten ist, um das Bild des Beobachters möglichst genau wiederzugeben. Der Computer ist mit jedem Stück Abfall bis ins Detail vertraut; tatsächlich bestand der erste Schritt des Programmierens von *Trash Mirror* darin, dem Computer beizubringen, jedes einzelne Stück richtig zu positionieren, indem eine Videokamera nicht auf den Betrachter, sondern auf das Kunstwerk selbst gerichtet wurde.

Aus dem Amerikanischen von Elisabeth Wiellander

courtesy of bitforms gallery, nyc

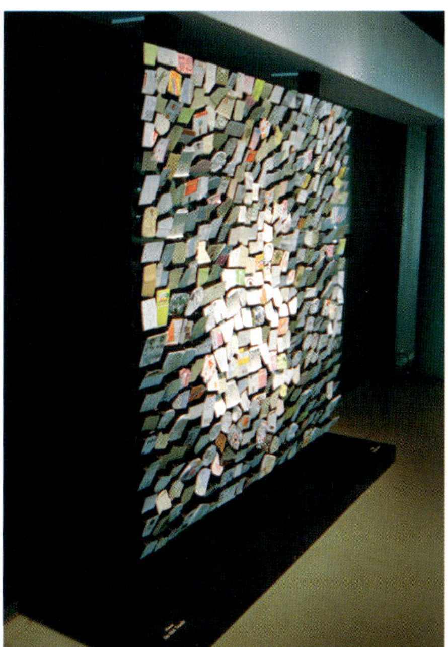

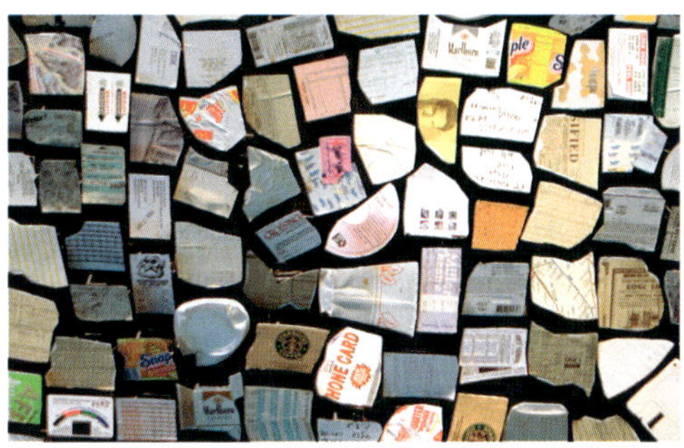

courtesy of bitforms gallery, nyc

Runme.org

Projects currently at Runme.org (May, 2003)
http://runme.org

algorithmic appreciation

Duff's Device *by Tom Duff* / http://www.lysator.liu.se/c/duffs-device.html

algorithmic appreciation / non-code-related

Travesty Corporate PR InfoMixer *by amy alexander* / http://infomix.plagiarist.org/corp

artificial intelligence

AARON *by Harold Cohen* / http://crca.ucsd.edu/~hcohen/

Blog Bitch *by Joe Petrow* / http://www.joepetrow.com/?PAGE=blogbitch

connoisseur *by gabor papp* / http://www.inf.bme.hu/~rod/conn/

dramatic screensaver *by Teo Spiller* / http://runme.org/project/+dramatic/

MindGuard *by Lyle Zapato* / http://zapatopi.net/mindguard.html

artistic tool

Darkroom *by Paul Andrews* / http://art.gen.nz/darkroom

artistic tool / audiovisual

actionist respoke *by michael janoschek & rüdiger schloemer* / http://www.stromgasse.de/actionist

AGENTBEATS *by Mikkel Bertelsen* / http://agentbeats.net

AMEN *by Neil Gavigan* / http://www.trouble07.com/amen/main.htm

BitmapSequencer *by Tom Betts* / http://www.nullpointer.co.uk

Connector *by ixi-software* / http://www.ixi-software.net

EG SERENE *by Barbara Lattanzi* / http://www.wildernesspuppets.net/yarns/egserene/indexframeset.html

Gallery Music from Pictures *by Lauri Gröhn* / http://www.synestesia.com

MetaMix *by Jason Freeman* / http://metamix.jasonfreeman.net

MIDIPoet *by Eugenio Tisselli* / http://www.transit-lounge.com/vainasystems/midipeng/index.htm

P.A.N.S.E. *by Pall Thayer* / http://130.208.220.190/panse

Petrograph v.01 *by Kurt Ralske* / http://auv-i.de/Petrograph_in_action.mov

Picker *by ixi-software* / http://www.ixi-software.net

repercussion.org *by Carla Diana* / http://www.repercussion.org

Slicer *by ixi-software* / http://www.ixi-software.net

SONASPHERE *by Nao Tokui / Karl Willis* / http://www.naotokui.com/sonasphere/

Sound Room Composer *by Rikard Lundstedt* /
http://space.tii.se/staff/rikard.lundstedt/SoundRoomComposer.htm

SoundField *by Arthur Clemens* / http://www.VisibleArea.com/downloads/

StockSynth *by ixi-software* / http://www.ixi-software.net

Yellowtail *by Golan Levin* / http://www.flong.com/yellowtail/

artistic tool / narrative

34 North 118 West *by Jeremy Hight Jeff Knowlton Naomi Spellman* / http://34n118w.net

Journeys *by Greg Giannis* / http://runme.org/project/+journeys/

artistic tool / useless

A/V Mixer *by Eduardo Sousa* / http://asseptic.org/pages/avmixer/

bots and agents

animal.pl *by alex* / http://lurk.org

Egobot *by Philipp Lenssen* / http://blog.outer-court.com/egobrowser/egobot.php

gogolchat *by jimpunk & christophe bruno* / http://www.iterature.com/gogolchat/

Googlism *by Googlism.com* / http://www.googlism.com

OuLiBOT *by jo walsh* / http://frot.org/oulibot/

theBot *by Amy Alexander* / http://thebot.plagiarist.org

UNMOVIE *by Ax. Heide, Onesandzeros, Ph. Pocock, Gr. Stehle* / http://www.unmovie.net

browser art

Anti-Capitalist Operating System *by Together We Can Defeat Capitalism* /
http://www.TWCDC.com

Babel *by Simon Biggs* / http://www.babel.uk.net/

Bork *by Opera Software* / http://runme.org/project/+bork/

Boxplorer *by Andy Deck* / http://artcontext.org/act/02/box/

firmament.to *by Francis Hwang* / http://firmament.to

NETARIUM *by Haruka Kikuchi* / http://www.hakava.org/netarium/

Re-reading the News *by Myron Turner* / http://www.room535.org/news/reading.html

Simple Sex Site Cyborg Link Harvester *by Sintron* / http://runme.org/project/+ssslh/

The Web Stalker *by I/O/D* / http://bak.spc.org/iod/iod4.html

ZNC browser *by Peter Luining* / http://znc.ctrlaltdel.org

code art / code poetry

.Re ____________________________(ad.htm by mez / http://www.hotkey.net.au/~netwurker/

GENETICS_BINARY_MATH POETRY by HANS BERNHARD /
http://HANSBERNHARD.COM/TEXT/

Jabberwocky *by Eric Andreychek* / http://www.perlmonks.org/index.pl?node_id=111157

Julu *by Alan Sondheim* / http://www.gu.edu.au/school/art/text/oct01/sondheim.htm

London.pl *by William Blake (Graham Harwood)* / http://www.scotoma.org/lungs/

pro][tean][.lapsing.txts *by][mez][[* / http://www.hotkey.net.au/~netwurker/txts/

code art / minimal code

neverending search for highest number *by trashconnection* / http://content-type.trashconnection.com/

conceptual software

Acme::Module::Authors *by Tatsuhiko Miyagawa* / http://search.cpan.org/author/MIYAGAWA/Acme-Module-Authors-0.01/ lib/Acme/Module/Authors.pm

ap0202.10 *by artem baguinski, martin howse* / http://www.1010.co.uk

Auto-Illustrator *by Adrian Ward* / http://www.auto-illustrator.com/

deprogramming.us—e.p. #1 *by deprogramming.us* / http://deprogramming.us

conceptual software / without hardware–formal instruction

.walk *by socialfiction.org* / http://www.socialfiction.org

Composition 1961 1-29 *by LaMonte Young* / http://www.google.de/search?hl=de&lr=&ie=UTF-8&oe=UTF-8&q=La+Monte+Young+%22Draw+a+straight+line%22&spell=1

data transformation

Desktop Subversibles *by Jonah Brucker-Cohen* / http://www.coin-operated.com/ds

Fascinum *by Christophe Bruno* / http://www.unbehagen.com/fascinum/

non-weddings *by Christophe Bruno* / http://www.unbehagen.com/non-weddings

The Bank of Time *by Futurenatural* / http://www.theBankofTime.com

Video Killed the Radio Star *by Jonathan Harel* / http://www.ugcs.caltech.edu/~harel/lyrics.html

data transformation / data collage

DSTRKTR *by stk* / http://antisound.semperstudio.com/dEstruktor

GoogleSynth *by Paul Andrews* / http://art.gen.nz

POP AUTOMATE® *by liz* / http://popautomate.talk-over.net/

Revision History 3.0 *by Johnny DeKam* / http://revisionhistory.org/

The Multi-Cultural Recycler *by amy alexander* / http://recycler.plagiarist.org

Yet Another Sizing Tool (YAST) *by Rico da halvarez & Bituur Esztreym* / http://vnatrc.com/YAST/ABOUT

data transformation / multimedia

PDP / PiDiP Is Definitely In Pieces *by Tom Schouten & Yves Degoyon* / http://ydegoyon.free.fr/pidip.html

techno.pl *by alex* / http://slub.org

data transformation / visualization

Disk Defragmenter *by mi_ga* / http://www.o-o.lt/mi_ga
hexaDecimalClock *by BlueScreen* / http://www.b-l-u-e-s-c-r-e-e-n.net/hexaClock/

digital aesthetics r&d / low tech

extreme whitespace *by amy alexander / deprogramming.us* / http://deprogramming.us/exwhindex.html

Form Art *by Alexei Shulgin* / http://www.c3.hu/collection/form/

os_anm *by slateford* / http://www.lipparosa.org/slateford/archive/os_anm

digital folk and artisanship

Acme::Handwave *by Simon Kent* / http://search.cpan.org/author/HITHERTO/Acme-Handwave-0.01.1/

Acme::ManekiNeko *by Greg McCarroll* /
http://search.cpan.org/author/GMCCAR/Acme-ManekiNeko-0.01/ManekiNeko.pm

Face #7 *by Dave Fischer* / http://www.cca.org/dave/gallery1.html

Kraut v0.9 *by John Sparks* / http://runme.org/project/+Kraut/

metal_for_ever *by anonymous* / http://runme.org/project/+metalforever/

Whitespace *by Edwin Brady and Chris Morris* / http://compsoc.dur.ac.uk/whitespace

digital folk and artisanship / ascii art

AA-Project *by Jan Hubicka and others* / http://aa-project.sourceforge.net/

Google Groups Art *by Paul, Tim Flaherty, Nathan McCoy, Stuart Langridge*
http://runme.org/project/+googleart/

digital folk and artisanship / gimmicks

discomus.exe *by Anonymous* / http://runme.org/project/+discomus/

DOS pseudoviruses collection *by Various artists* / http://runme.org/project/+dosvir/

digital folk and artisanship / screen savers

bildschirmgymnastik *by joreg* / http://joreg.ath.cx/gymnastik.html

existing software manipulations

Dictionaraoke *by Snoogles* / http://www.dictionaraoke.org

existing software manipulations / instructions

SCREEN SAVER *by Eldar Karhalev & Ivan Khimin* / http://www.404pro.com/desoft

existing software manipulations / software plugins

Suicide Letter Wizard for Microsoft Word *by Olga Goriunova, Data eXchange Laboratory*
http://www.dxlab.org/slw

The Okay News *by Rebecca Ross* / http://cat.nyu.edu/~rebecca/okay/

games

SPS *by (Karl-)Robert Ek* / http://runme.org/project/+spssps/

Wolfenstein 5k *by Lee Semel* / http://www.innofinity.com/5k/2002/

games / deconstruction and modification

adam killer *by brody condon* / http://www.tmpspace.com/adam_1

mario battle no.1 *by myfanwy ashmore* / http://runme.org/project/+mariobattle/

retroyou R/C *by joan leandre* / http://retroyou.org/retroyou_RC_full_radioControl/

generative art

googlepoweredgogglebox *by Sam Woolf* / http://www.blip.alturl.com/googlepoweredgogglebox.html

Lexicon *by Andy Deck* / http://artcontext.org/lexicon/

n_Gen Design Machine *by Move Design* / http://www.n-generate.com

NewZoid *by Daniel Young* / http://www.newzoid.com

Wirescapes 1.0 *by John Vega* / http://www.dancingimage.com/wirescapes

0generative art / algorithmic audio

Enigma n^2 *by Jim Andrews* / http://vispo.com

generative art / algorithmic image

ARTificial Art: 4ever *by Kurt Baumann* / http://www.artificial-art.com/

Cybart *by coolfool* / http://www.coolfool.com/cybart/

Generative Art *by Bogdan Soban* / http://www.soban-art.com

Genetic Art *by Adriano Abbado, Marco Stefani* / http://www.abbado.com/works/big/genetic.html

Infinite Image Productions *by Gerhard Mantz* / http://www.infiniteimageproductions.org

particles *by Ole Kristensen* / http://www.ole.kristensen.name/particles

hardware transformation

Symphony for dot matrix printers *by [The User] Thaddeus Thomas* / http://www.theuser.org/

Tempest for Eliza *by Erik Thiele* / http://www.erikyyy.de/tempest/

installation-based

God's Eye *by Sintron* / http://runme.org/project/+godseye/

Netsleeping by Gregory Chatonsky / http://incident.net/works/netsleeping/

stack *by robert lisek* / http://www.fundamental.art.pl

Timescape *by Reynald Drouhin* / http://www.incident.net/works/timescape/

institutional critique

Rotten Flesh *by Jeff Epler* / http://unpythonic.net/~jepler/cgi-bin/rottenflesh.cgi

The Market-O-Matic (1.0) [fine arts version] *by Curt Cloninger* / http://www.playdamage.org/market-o-matic/

performance-based

b0timati0n *by amy alexander* / http://b0timati0n.org

Dynasty *by deKam* / http://runme.org/project/+Dynasty/

Hell's Angles *by Martin Parker* / http://runme.org/project/+HellzAngles/

The Google Adwords Happening *by Christophe Bruno* / http://www.iterature.com/adwords

plagiarism

hello world *by unknown* / http://www2.latech.edu/~acm/HelloWorld.shtml

The Plagiarist Manifesto *by Plagiarist (assisted by Amy Alexander)* / http://plagiarist.org/manifeste/manifesto.pl

political and activist software / cease-and-desist-ware

bastards.js *by space hijackers* / http://www.spacehijackers.co.uk

DeArt—DeCSS Art Contest (et al) *by Tom Vogt and Various Authors* / http://web.lemuria.org/DeArt/

The Injunction Generator *by ubermorgen.com* / http://ipnic.org

Various CueCat Hacks *by Various Authors* / http://runme.org/project/+cuecathacks/

walser.php *by textz.com / Project Gnutenberg* / http://www.textz.com

political and activist software / illicit software

pngreader *by textz.com / Project Gnutenberg /* http://pngreader.gnutenberg.net

political and activist software / software resistance

ADMechelon-Lagger *by The ADM Crew* / http://adm.freelsd.net/ADM/

CueJack by Cue P. Doll / http://cuejack.com

Homeland Security Threat Monitor *by Greg Hewgill* / http://hewgill.com/threat/

marchtowar.com *by marchtowar.com /* http://www.marchtowar.com

SuPerVillainizer—Conspiracy Client *by LAN /* http://www.supervillainizer.ch

TelematicMix *by Sejal Chad, Beatrice Gibson, Adrian Ward* /
http://www.humancapitalsoftwaresolutions.com

political and activist software / useful activist software

Reamweaver *by The Yes Men SPIT* / http://reamweaver.com

software cultures–links

GNU emacs *by Richard Stallman* / http://www.gnu.org/software/emacs/emacs.html

Gnu's Not Unix *by Richard M. Stallman /* http://www.gnu.org

M.A.M.E.—Multiple Arcade Machine Emulator *by The MAME Team* / http://www.mame.net

micromusic *by micromusic team /* http://www.micromusic.net

PawSense *by BitBoost Systems* / http://www.bitboost.com/pawsense/index.html

The 5k contest *by Stewart Butterfield, Eric Costello* / http://www.the5k.org

system dysfunctionality / denial of service

forkbomb *by jaromil /* http://amsterdam.nettime.org/Lists-Archives/nettime-bold-0203/msg00784.html

forkbomb.pl *by alex2 /* http://slab.org

forkwar *by deprogramming.us /* http://www.deprogramming.us/forkwarindex.html

system dysfunctionality / virus - security

DOGS *by Sintron /* http://runme.org/project/+dogs/

MacMag Virus *by Computer Graphics Conspiracy / Barnoz & Wanowitch*
http://www.google.com/search?hl=de&ie=UTF-8&oe=UTF-8&q=MacMag+virus&btnG=
Google-Suche&meta=

text–software / art related

Artistic Software for Dummies and, by the way, Thoughts About the New World Order
by Olga Goriunova, Alexei Shulgin / http://www.macros-center.ru/read_me/teb1e.htm

Concepts. Notations. Software. Art. *by Florian Cramer*
http://http://userpage.fu-berlin.de/~cantsin/homepage/writings/ software_art/concept_notations//
concepts_notations_software_art.

dear em: what shd i do? *by ms.static + chip.kali@mxHz.org* / http://runme.org/project/+whatshdido/

hacking sound in context *by alex /* http://slab.org

processor art *by thor magnusson* / http://www.ixi-software.net

QuickView on Software Art, interview with runme.org experts 2003: Amy Alexander,
Florian Cramer, Matthew Fuller, Thomax Kaulmann, Alex McLean, Pit Schultz, and
The Yes Men, *by Olga Goriunova and Alexei Shulgin /* http://runme.org/project/+quickview/

Read_Me 1.2 Jury Statement *by Amy Alexander, Florian Cramer, Cue P. Doll, RTMark, and Alexei Shulgin /* http://www.macros-center.ru/read_me/adden.htm

Software Art by Florian Cramer and Ulrike Gabriel / http://userpage.fu-berlin.de/~cantsin/homepage/writings/software_art/ transmediale// software_art_-_transmediale.html

Software Art Panel at Kuenstlerhaus Bethanien, Feb. 2003. Transcript / http://www.softwareart.net/

The Aesthetics of Generative Code *by Geoff Cox, Alex McLean, Adrian Ward /* http://generative.net/papers/aesthetics/

The House That Jack Built: Jack Burnham's Concept of "Software" as a Metaphor / for Art *by Edward A. Shanken* / http://www.duke.edu/~giftwrap/House.html

Useless Utilities *by saul /* http://www.twenteenthcentury.com/saul/useless.htm

text–software / art related / cultural critique of software

Behind the Blip: Software as Culture *by Matthew Fuller /* http://runme.org/project/+blip/

It looks like you're writing a letter: Microsoft Word *by Matthew Fuller /* http://www.axia.demon.co.uk/wordtext.html

Perl, the first postmodern computer language *by Larry Wall* / http://runme.org/project/+pomoperl/

Programming with a Paintbrush *by Richard Wright /* http://runme.org/project/+Painting/

RETROFUTURISM 13 *by William Bowles* / http://runme.org/project/+retrofuturism/

text–software / art related / weblog

sweetcode.org *by Dan Egnor /* http://sweetcode.org

text manipulation

Bible (alphabetical order) *by Rory Macbeth /* http://twenteenthcentury.com/projects.php?action=display&proj_id=100&context=projects&mem_id=3

copy/paste *by Doris Traubenzucker /* http://runme.org/project/+copypaste/

Dasher *by David MacKay, Inference Group, Cavendish Laboratory /* http://www.inference.phy.cam.ac.uk/dasher/

fleur v 0.2 *by clemos /* http://cl3mos.free.fr/fleur2

haiku *by Danny O'Brien* / http://www.oblomovka.com/code/haiku.php3

linguasso *by Chris King* / http://www.silenttransit.com/linguasso

mimic *by Jeremy Ruston /* http://www.dicshunary.com/stuff/mimic.html

Novelwriting *by Jeff Epler /* http://unpythonic.net/~jepler/novelwriting/

Paperikori *by Team Paperikori /* http://peep.uiah.fi/paperikori

Postmodernism Generator *by Andrew C. Bulhak* / http://www.elsewhere.org/cgi-bin/postmodern/

Right As Rain *by Jeremy Hight Jeff Knowlton Naomi Spellman* / http://thepharmakon.org/RightAsRain

rwxrwxrw *by ARN /* http://www.x-arn.org/rwxrwxrw/

Simplethink *by Dan Harris* / http://dump.ordure.org/applications/SimpleThink.html

sondheim.exe *by Lewis LaCook* / http://runme.org/project/+sondheim/

Travesty *by Hugh Kenner and Joseph P. O'Rourke* / http://runme.org/project/+travesty/

CODeDOC II

Christiane Paul

As part of the CODE exhibition accompanying this year's festival, Ars Electronica invited me to curate a second installment of the online exhibition *CODeDOC* that I originally organized for the Whitney Museum of American Art's *artport,* a website designed as a portal to netart. *CODeDOC,* which launched in September 2002, was conceived to explore the relationship between the underlying code of software art and its results. A dozen software artists were invited to code a specific assignment—"connect and move three points in space"—in a language of their choice (Java, C, Visual Basic, Lingo, Perl) and were asked to exchange the code with each other for comments. The presentation strategy of *CODeDOC* deliberately deviates from the ways in which viewers usually experience a piece of software art, which commonly presents itself to the audience as executed code—the results of written instructions. In *CODeDOC,* the viewing experience is closer to the artist's creation process: what the audience encounters first is a page with the written code, from which they can launch its executed results. Since the assignment imposed substantial restrictions in format and file size, the contributed projects can't necessarily be seen as fully developed works; rather, they are comparable to small studies and sketches that capture an artist's approach.

Many of the prominent international practitioners in the field of software art could not participate in the first version of *CODeDOC* since the Whitney Museum is, by its mission, devoted to American artists (citizens and artists living and working in the US). *CODeDOC* presents a welcome opportunity to close that gap and widen the scope of the project. The eight artists/teams who were invited to contribute to the second installment and code the assignment—Ed Burton, epidemiC, Graham Harwood, Jaromil, Annja Krautgasser & Rainer Mandl, Joan Leandre, Antoine Schmitt and John F. Simon, Jr.—are mostly non-American. Some other artists who would have been obvious candidates for this project were not invited because they were already involved in other parts of the Ars Electronica Festival or exhibition. My special thanks go to Andreas Broeckmann for his input and suggestions in the selection process of the artists.

From its inception, *CODeDOC* was intended as a process-oriented experiment rather than an exhibition meant to make a specific statement or offer a certain point of view. Ideally, I wanted to raise questions about software art as artistic practice, and neither the outcome nor the reception of this project were easily predictable for me. One intent of the project certainly was to demystify the notion of code as a "mysterious," hidden driving force and to reveal the code to the viewer. Among the questions that seemed important to address or clarify were the following: does the term software art itself describe a certain form of aesthetics? Do "signature," "voice," and aesthetics of an artist manifest themselves equally in the written code and its executed results? Will reading the source code enhance the perception of the work? Does it in fact add anything at all or just create an emphasis on "technicalities" that is unnecessary, alienating, and obscures the work? How exactly could one define the relationship between the back end of code and its results?

The attempt to provide detailed answers to all these questions would be beyond the scope of this introduction, and I just want to make some general comments and leave it up to the *CODeDOC II* projects themselves, as well as the discussions surrounding them, to offer further perspectives on these issues.

If one explores the body of work that each of the *CODeDOC II* participants has created over the years, it seems obvious that the label software art is a lowest common denominator for a formal description of their artistic practice rather than a term that describes specific aesthetics. The artists' works themselves cover a broad spectrum of individual approaches. The works of epidemiC, for example—which include *AntiMafia,* a Windows-based program for the co-ordination of associative actions, as well as the infamous *biennale.py* virus created for the 49th Venice Biennale (in collaboration with 0100101110101101.ORG)—are focused more on activism and the notion of software as cultural production. Ed Burton's *Sodaplay* and *Sodaconstructor,* which in the meantime have achieved cult status, explore the conceptual possibilities of "handcrafted" virtual robots as well as masses and their kinetic energy. Grahame Harwood's work has ranged from "pure" Perl poetry to software creation and narrative projects, such as the CD-ROM *Rehearsal of Memory*—which creates its interface out of a collage of the skins of the inmates and staff of Ashworth Hospital Authority—and the Web project *Uncomfortable Proximity,* commissioned by the Tate Museum, which reproduced the Tate website's layout, logos, and design, to tell a "different" history of the British art system. Compared to the former examples, Antoine Schmitt's works are far more visually oriented studies of the "behaviours" of forms in time and space.

While one might assume that an artist's approach (and perhaps even "personality") will manifest itself equally in the written code and its results, the code itself will naturally be more meaningful to other programmers than a general audience that might only get the roughest idea of its "mechanisms." Whether the code adds to an understanding of the work also varies substantially from case to case. One might speculate that the emphasis that the artists themselves would put on the importance of their code partly depends on the nature of their respective work: for example, artists whose work focuses on "raw" code (such as many of Graham Harwood's pieces) might consider the "written part" of the project more important than artists whose work is an exploration of visual forms, space, and action (such as many of Antoine Schmitt's projects). The presentation format of *CODeDOC* also seems to have imposed some (unintended) editing on the artists' part: in their comments, both Antoine Schmitt *(CODeDOC II)* and Camille Utterback *(CODeDOC I)* admitted that they felt compelled to clean up their code before presenting it to the public ("I'm one of those people that clean my bathroom if my friends are coming over," as Camille put it). One of the inherent dangers and certainly unintended effects of *CODeDOC* could be the misassumption that the quality of software art can be judged according to virtuosity and craftsmanship in the programming of code (that is, by criteria such as correctness, maintainability, lucidity, and readability, which were outlined by Donald Knuth). One of the beauties of art, no matter what form and material it takes, consists in the fact that its success is the result of multiple factors that cannot be objectively defined. A viewer could certainly enjoy the works of Leonardo da Vinci or Picasso on the basis of their outstanding virtuosity and craftsmanship alone (although they have much more to offer), but applying these standards to Duchamp's urinal or Beuys' "fat and felt" sculptures will presumably not yield relevant results or major appreciation. Like any other art form, software art cannot and should not be reduced to technical criteria, and the code should be seen as more than simply the wheels and gears driving the machine.

As an artistic medium and practice, software art seems to distinguish itself from other art forms such as painting, sculpture or film/video. As opposed to other forms of visual art, software artists write verbal instructions for their work that can be executed and produce

anything from visuals to a more abstract communication process (although the execution of code still requires various steps of interpretation and compiling and the code itself may be mostly a notation of logic). There is a peculiar relationship between the mostly hidden backend of code—which constitutes a convergence of language and mathematics—and the multi-sensory "display" it can produce: an "identity" in the sense of a sameness in different instances (code results), each of which takes a very different form yet, on one level, is one and the same. While every art form may be processed and mediated in one way or another, it usually does not constitute a fusion of fundamentally different "materialities" (in the broadest sense) as software art does. A painting or sculpture to a large extent reveals the manifestations of its creation process in the finished object—for example, in individual brush strokes or materials—even if the art object amounts to something much larger than the sum of its parts. In software art, the "materiality" of the written instructions mostly remains hidden. In addition, these instructions and notations can be instantaneously activated; they contain and—further layers of processing aside—*are* the artwork itself. While one might claim that the same holds true for a work of conceptual art that consists of written instructions, this work would still have to be activated as a mental or physical event by the viewer and cannot instantaneously transform, transcend, and generate its own materiality.
In the comments accompanying his contribution to *CODeDOC II,* Antoine Schmitt points out that it would be a misleading shortcut to propose that the language in which a programmed artwork has been written has anything to do with the "language of programmed art"—a language relating to the space, time and action of the work. Schmitt makes an important point in that he hints at the multiple layers of "language" that a discourse about software art entails: there is the programming language itself (I assume that many programmers would argue that the choice of the programming language has a substantial effect on the outcome of the artwork); there is the language of the written code in the sense of an artistic expression that formulates instructions in an individual way (similar to the use of natural language that, despite a given vocabulary, grammar and rules, functions as a form of personal expression); and there is the aesthetic "language" of the code's actions, comparable to the language of painting or cinema. At best, *CODeDOC* can raise some awareness surrounding both the construction and perception of software art, and I hope that the pieces created for this second round of the project will continue to contribute to an ongoing dialogue.

CODeDOC I:
http://artport.whitney.org/commissions/CODeDOC/

CODeDOC II:
http://www.aec.at/CODeDOCII

John F. Simon, Jr. (USA)
http://www.numeral.com

Annja Krautgasser / Rainer Mandl (A):
http://www.vidok.org
http://syko.info

epidemiC (I):
http://epidemic.ws/

Joan Leandre (E)
http://www.retroyou.org/

Jaromil (A/I)
http://korova.dyne.org/

Ed Burton (UK)
http://soda.co.uk/

Antoine Schmitt (F)
http://www.gratin.org/as/

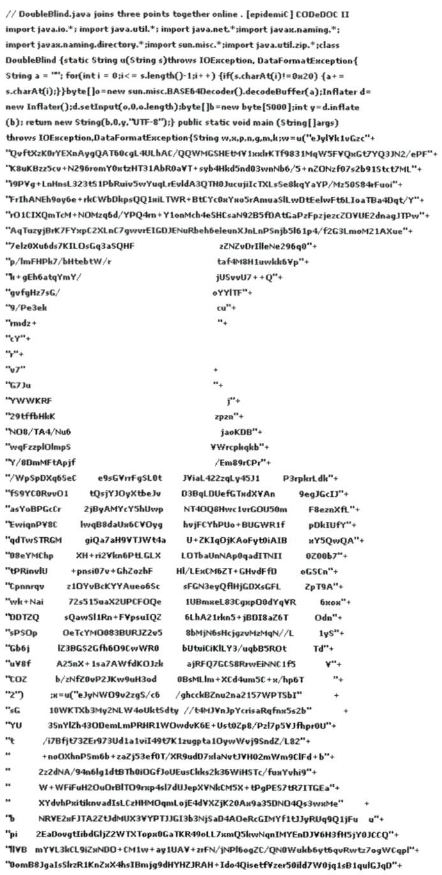

epidemiC

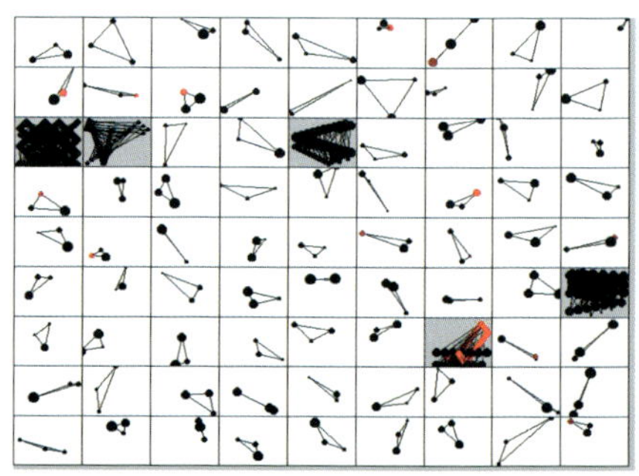
John F. Simon

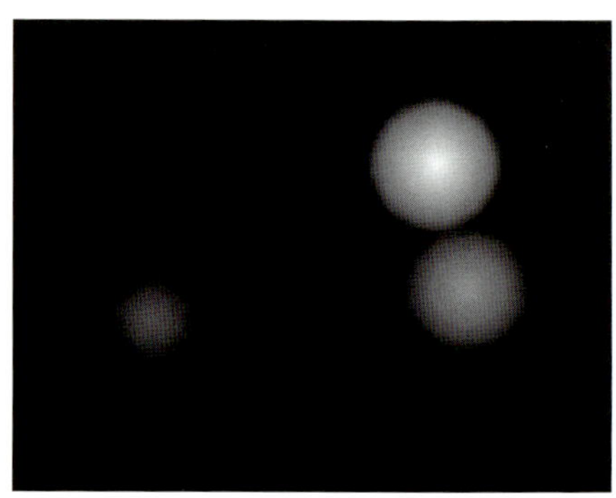
Antoine Schmitt

CODeDOC II

Christiane Paul

Im Rahmen der CODE-Ausstellung, die während der diesjährigen Ars Electronica stattfindet, wurde ich eingeladen, eine Fortsetzung der Online-Ausstellung *CODeDOC I* zu kuratieren, die ich ursprünglich für das *artport* des Whitney Museum of American Art organisiert hatte, eine Website, die als Portal für Netzkunst entworfen wurde. *CODeDOC* startete im September 2002 und sollte die Beziehungen zwischen den der Softwarekunst zugrunde liegenden Codes und ihren Ergebnissen untersuchen. Etwa ein Dutzend Softwarekünstler wurde eingeladen, in einer Programmiersprache ihrer Wahl (Java, C, Visual Basic, Lingo, Perl) den Code für eine bestimmte Aufgabe zu schreiben, nämlich „drei Punkte im Raum zu verbinden und zu bewegen". Darüber hinaus sollten die Codes untereinander ausgetauscht und kommentiert werden.

Das Präsentationskonzept von *CODeDOC* unterscheidet sich bewusst von den Formen, in denen Betrachter Softwarekunst im Allgemeinen erfahren. Sie wird dem Publikum meist als ausgeführter Code – als Resultat schriftlicher Anweisungen – präsentiert. In *CODeDOC* ist die Rezeption dem künstlerischen Schaffensprozess näher: Das Publikum sieht zunächst eine Seite mit dem geschriebenen Code, von der aus er sich auch ausführen lässt. Da die Aufgabenstellung eine beträchtliche Beschränkung in Format und Dateigröße bedeutete, sind die Projektbeiträge nicht unbedingt als zur Gänze ausgearbeitete Werke zu betrachten. Sie sind vielmehr kleinen Studien und Skizzen vergleichbar, die den künstlerischen Ansatz wiedergeben. Viele international herausragende Vertreter der Softwarekunst konnten am ersten *CODeDOC* nicht teilnehmen, da das Whitney Museum – seinem Auftrag gemäß – amerikanischen Künstlern (Bürgern und Künstlern, die in den USA leben und arbeiten) vorbehalten ist. *CODeDOC II* ist eine willkommene Möglichkeit, diese Lücke zu füllen und den Rahmen des Projekts zu erweitern. Die acht Künstler / Teams, die für die zweite Folge eingeladen wurden, kommen zum Großteil nicht aus den USA: Ed Burton, epidemiC, Graham Harwood, Jaromil, Annja Krautgasser & Rainer Mandl, Joan Leandre, Antoine Schmitt und John F. Simon jr. Einige weitere Künstler, die sich für dieses Projekt angeboten hätten, konnten nicht berücksichtigt werden, weil sie bereits in anderen Bereichen der Ars Electronica oder in der Ausstellung vertreten waren. Mein besonderer Dank geht an Andreas Broeckmann für seine Anregungen und Vorschläge bei der Auswahl der Künstler.

CODeDOC war von Anfang an eher als prozessorientiertes Experiment denn als Ausstellung, die bestimmte Aussagen oder Standpunkte zum Inhalt hat, konzipiert. Idealerweise wollte ich Fragen zur Softwarekunst als künstlerische Praxis aufwerfen, wobei weder das Ergebnis noch die Rezeption des Projekts für mich absehbar waren. Eine Intention des Projekts war zweifelsohne, den Code als „mysteriöse", unsichtbare treibende Kraft zu entmystifizieren und dem Betrachter näher zu bringen. Fragen, die anzuschneiden oder zu klären, mir wichtig schien, waren u. a. die folgenden: Beschreibt der Begriff „Softwarekunst" an sich eine bestimmte Form der Ästhetik? Manifestieren sich „Handschrift", „Stimme" und Ästhetik eines Künstlers im geschriebenen Code und den ausgeführten Ergebnissen? Verbessert das Verständnis des Quellcodes die Wahrnehmung der Arbeit? Handelt es sich dabei um eine wirkliche Erweiterung oder lediglich um eine Akzentuierung „technischer Einzelheiten", die unnötig und befremdlich ist und die Arbeit verschleiert? Wie könnte man die Beziehung zwischen

dem Back-End des Codes und seinen Ergebnissen definieren?
Der Versuch, detaillierte Antworten auf all diese Fragen zu geben, würde den Rahmen dieser Einleitung sprengen, weshalb ich mich auf einige allgemeine Anmerkungen beschränken und es den *CODeDOC II*-Projekten sowie den sich daraus ergebenden Diskussionen überlassen möchte, weitere Perspektiven zu diesen Themen aufzuzeigen.
Untersucht man die Gesamtheit der Arbeiten, die jeder *CODeDOC II*-Teilnehmer im Lauf der Jahre schuf, wird deutlich, dass das Etikett „Softwarekunst" eher der kleinste gemeinsame Nenner einer formalen Beschreibung ihrer künstlerischen Praxis als ein Terminus für eine bestimmte Ästhetik ist. Die Arbeiten der Künstler decken ein breites Spektrum sehr individueller Ansätze ab. Die Arbeiten von epidemiC etwa – *AntiMafia,* ein Windows-basiertes Programm zur Koordination assoziativer Aktionen sowie der berüchtigte *biennale.py*-Virus (eine Kooperation mit 0100101110101101.ORG), der für die 49. Biennale von Venedig entstand – setzen eher auf Aktivismus und das Konzept von Software als einer kulturellen Produktion. Ed Burtons *Sodaplay* und *Sodaconstructor,* die mittlerweile Kultstatus haben, untersuchen die konzeptuellen Möglichkeiten „handgefertigter" virtueller Roboter sowie von Massen und ihrer kinetischen Energie. Graham Harwoods Arbeiten reichen von „reiner" Perl-Poesie bis hin zu Softwareproduktion und narrativen Projekten wie etwa der CD-ROM *Rehearsal of Memory* (für die er mit einer Gruppe aus dem Ashworth Hochsicherheitsspital ein interaktives Programm erstellte, bei dem die Haut der Projektteilnehmer gescannt wurde, um physische Spuren ihres Lebens als Geisteskranke festzuhalten), oder dem Webprojekt *Uncomfortable Proximity,* einer Auftragsarbeit für das Tate Museum, bei der das Layout, die Logos und das Design der Tate-Website reproduziert wurden, um die Geschichte des britischen Kunstbetriebs aus einem „anderen Blickwinkel" zu erzählen. Verglichen mit den vorgenannten Beispielen sind Antoine Schmitts Arbeiten eher visuell orientierte Studien über das „Verhalten" von Formen in Zeit und Raum.
Obwohl man meinen könnte, dass sich der Ansatz eines Künstlers (und vielleicht sogar seine „Persönlichkeit") gleichermaßen im geschriebenen Code und dessen Ergebnissen manifestiert, ist der Code natürlich für andere Programmierer interessanter als für ein allgemeines Publikum, das vielleicht nur eine vage Vorstellung von dessen „Mechanismen" bekommt. Ob der Code zum Verständnis der Arbeit beiträgt, variiert auch stark von Fall zu Fall. Es drängt sich der Gedanke auf, dass die Bedeutung, die die Künstler selbst dem Code zuweisen, auch vom Charakter der jeweiligen Arbeit abhängt: Für Künstler, deren Werk sich auf den „unverfälschten" Code konzentriert (wie etwa viele Arbeiten von Graham Harwood), mag der „schriftliche Teil" des Projekts wichtiger sein als für Künstler, deren Werke visuelle Formen, Raum und Aktion erforschen (wie viele Projekte von Antoine Schmitt). Das Format der Präsentation von *CODeDOC* hat die Künstler anscheinend (unbeabsichtigterweise) zu Editierungen veranlasst: In ihren Kommentaren haben sowohl Antoine Schmitt *(CODeDOC I)* als auch Camille Utterback *(CODeDOC I)* zugegeben, dass sie sich bemüßigt fühlten, ihren Code zu „säubern", bevor sie ihn dem Publikum präsentierten („Ich gehöre zu den Leuten, die ihr Badezimmer reinigen, wenn Freunde zu Besuch kommen", wie Camille es formulierte). Eine der inhärenten Gefahren und unbeabsichtigten Effekte von *CODeDOC* wäre die falsche Annahme, dass die Qualität von Softwarekunst nach der Virtuosität und technischen Fertigkeit im Programmieren beurteilt wird (also nach den von Donald Knuth skizzierten Kriterien wie Richtigkeit, Wartbarkeit, Übersichtlichkeit und Lesbarkeit). Eine der Schönheiten von Kunst besteht, ungeachtet ihrer Ausdrucksform oder des verwendeten Materials, darin, dass ihr Erfolg auf zahlreichen Faktoren beruht, die nicht objektiv zu definieren sind. Ein Betrachter kann das Werk Leonardo da Vincis oder Picassos sicher aufgrund ihrer herausragenden Virtuosität und ihres handwerklichen Könnens genießen (wenngleich sie viel mehr zu bieten haben), diese Maßstäbe versagen aber bei Duchamps Urinal oder Beuys' Skulpturen aus Filz und Fett. Wie jede andere Kunstform kann und sollte Softwarekunst nicht auf technische Kriterien reduziert

werden, und der Code ist mehr als nur das Getriebe, das die Maschine in Gang setzt. Offensichtlich unterscheidet sich Softwarekunst als künstlerisches Medium und in seiner Praxis von anderen Kunstformen wie Malerei, Bildhauerei oder Film/Video. Im Gegensatz zu anderen visuellen Kunstformen schreiben Softwarekünstler ausführbare verbale Anweisungen für ihre Arbeiten, die alles von visuellen Lösungen bis hin zu abstrakteren Kommunikationsprozessen produzieren (wenngleich die Ausführung eines Codes nach wie vor verschiedene Interpretations- und Kompilationsschritte erfordert und der Code selbst größtenteils eine logische Notationsform darstellt). Es besteht eine sonderbare Beziehung zwischen dem größtenteils verborgenen Back-End des Codes – der eine Konvergenz von Sprache und Mathematik darstellt – und dem multisensorischen „Display", das er erzeugen kann: eine „Identität" im Sinne einer Übereinstimmung verschiedener Instanzen (Code-Ergebnisse), die jeweils eine ganz unterschiedliche Form annehmen, auf einer Ebene aber doch ein und dasselbe sind. Während alle Kunstformen auf die eine oder andere Weise bearbeitet und vermittelt werden können, stellen sie im Unterschied zur Softwarekunst im Allgemeinen keine Verschmelzung von im Wesentlichen unterschiedlichen „Materialitäten" (im weitesten Sinne) dar. Bei einem Gemälde oder einer Skulptur manifestiert sich der schöpferische Prozess im fertigen Objekt – beispielsweise in den einzelnen Pinselstrichen oder im Material –, auch wenn das Kunstobjekt mehr ist als die Summe seiner Teile. In der Softwarekunst bleibt die „Materialität" der geschriebenen Anweisungen größtenteils verborgen. Darüber hinaus können diese Anweisungen und Notationen unverzüglich aktiviert werden, sie enthalten und sind – abgesehen von weiteren Bearbeitungsschritten – bereits das Kunstwerk. Zwar könnte man einwenden, dass das auch für aus geschriebenen Anweisungen bestehende Konzeptkunst gilt, doch müsste ein solches Werk noch in einem geistigen oder körperlichen Akt durch den Betrachter aktiviert werden und kann nicht sofort seine eigene Materialität transformieren, transzendieren und generieren.
In den begleitenden Kommentaren zu seinem Beitrag für *CODeDOC II* weist Antoine Schmitt darauf hin, dass es eine irreführende Verkürzung wäre zu glauben, dass die Sprache, in der ein programmiertes Kunstwerk geschrieben wurde, etwas mit der „Sprache programmierter Kunst" zu tun hätte – einer Sprache, die sich auf den Raum, die Zeit und die Wirkung der Arbeit bezieht. Schmitt verweist auf die multiplen Schichten der „Sprache", die ein Diskurs über Softwarekunst aufzeigt: Da ist einmal die Programmiersprache selbst (ich gehe davon aus, dass viele Programmierer die Auffassung vertreten, dass die Wahl der Programmiersprache eine wesentliche Auswirkung auf das Ergebnis des Kunstwerks hat), dann die Sprache des geschriebenen Codes im Sinn eines künstlerischen Ausdrucks, der Anweisungen auf individuelle Weise formuliert (ähnlich der natürlichen Sprache, die trotz der Vorgabe von Vokabular, Grammatik und Regeln auch eine persönliche Ausdrucksweise zulässt), und schließlich noch die ästhetische „Sprache" der Wirkung des Codes, die der Sprache der Malerei oder des Films vergleichbar ist. Ich hoffe, dass *CODeDOC* das neue Einblicke in die Produktion und Rezeption von Softwarekunst gewährt, und dass die Arbeiten, die für diese zweite Runde des Projekts entstanden, zur Weiterführung des Dialogs beitragen.

Aus dem Amerikanischen von Martina Bauer

Prix Ars Electronica 2003

The Prix Ars Electronica 2003 marks the 17th edition of the competition for cyberarts, which is organized by the Austrian Broadcasting Corporation (ORF), Upper Austrian Regional Studio, in conjunction with the Ars Electronica Festival.
The Prix Ars Electronica 2003 is awarded in the categories Interactive Art, Digital Musics, Computer Animation / Visual Effects, NetVision and NetExcellence. These categories are complemented by "cybergeneration—u19—freestyle computing", a competition with an open platform for young people under the age of 19. 2,500 media activists from 85 countries have responded to the invitation by submitting 2,714 entries in 2003. In each category one Golden Nica und two Awards of Distinction have been honoured with cash prizes; and 61 Honorary Mentions have been awarded. The Prix Ars Electronica's cash prizes total EURO 109,900. Five juries of international experts have selected 79 works which display particular expertise and visionary force.

Net Vision

Golden Nica

Yury Gitman / Carlos J. Gomez de Llarena: Noderunner

Distinctions

David Crawford: Stop Motion Studies

Golan Levin: The Secret Lives of Numbers

Net Excellence

Golden Nica

Sulake Labs Oy: Habbo Hotel

Distinctions

Lia: re:move

James Tindall: Boards of Canada Website

Net Vision / Net Excellence

Honorary Mentions

Antoni Abad: Zexe.net

Christophe Bruno: The Google AdWords Happening

Amit Pitaru / James Paterson: InsertSilence

Agathe Jacquillat / Tomi Vollauschek / FL@33: Bzzzpeek.com

Jared Tarbell / Lola Brine: Levitated.net

Axel Heide / onesandzeros / Philip Pocock / Gregor Stehle: Unmovie

Wiggle / Han Hoogerbrugge: Flow

LAN: SuPerVillainizer

LAN: TraceNoizer

Last.Team: Last.fm The Last Online Music Station

LeCielEstBleu: PuppetTool

ubermorgen: Injunction Generator

Shinya Yamamoto: Sinplex Show

OSDN: www.sourgeforge.net

Interactive Art:

Golden Nica

Blast Theory / Mixed Reality Lab: Can you see me now?

Distinctions

Margarete Jahrmann / Max Moswitzer: nybble-engine-toolZ

Maywa Denki: Tsukuba Series

Ross Cooper & Jussi Ängeslevä: Last

dECOi: Aegis Hyposurface

Sibylle Hauert / Daniel Reichmuth / Volker Böhm: instant city

Haruo Ishii: Hyperscratch

George Legrady: Pockets full of Memories

Justin Manor: Cinéma Fabriqué

Agnes Meyer-Brandis: Earth Core Laboratory and Elf-Scan

Iori Nakai: Streetscape

Henry Newton-Dunn / Hiroaki Nakano / James Gibson / Ryota Kuwakubo: Block Jam

Marcel.li Antúnez Roca: Pol

Marie Sester: Access

Scott Snibbe: Deep Walls

Computer Animation / Visual Effects

Golden Nica

Romain Segaud / Christel Pougeoise: Tim Tom

Distinctions

Carlos Saldanha / Blue Sky Studios, 20th Century Fox: Gone Nutty

Koji Yamamura: Atama Yama (Mt. Head)

Honorary Mentions

Christoph Ammann: Untitled

Eric Armstrong /Sony Pictures Imageworks: The ChubbChubbs

Jérôme Decock / Olivier Lanerès / Mélina Milcent / Ccile Detez de la Dreve: Au bout du fil

Roger Gould / Pete Docter / Pixar: Mike's new car

Thorsten Fleisch: Gestalt

Luc Froehlicher / La Maison: Dolce Vita

H5 / Ludovic Houplain / Hervé de Crécy: Remind Me

Wayne Lytle / Animusic: Pipe Dream

Siri Melchior: The Dog Who is a Cat Inside

Jordi Moragues: Mantis

Tippett Studio: 3D Character Animation for Blockbuster Entertainment

Satoshi Tomioka: Justice Runners

Digital Musics

Golden NICA

Ami Yoshida / Sachiko M / Utah Kawasaki: Astro Twin / Cosmos

Distinctions

Florian Hecker: Sun Pandämonium

Maja Solveig Kjelstrup Ratkje: Voice

Honorary Mentions

Oren Ambarchi: Triste

Whitehouse: Birdseed

Kevin Drumm: Sheer Hellish Miasma

Rudolf Eb.er: Humpa.Zerkörpert

Phill Niblock: The Movement of People Working

Yuko Nexus 6: Journal de Tokyo

Gert-Jan Prins: Risk

Rechenzentrum: Director's Cut

Tujiko Noriko: Hard ni sasete

Toshiya Tsunoda: pieces of air

Aaron Funk (Venetian Snares) & Rachael Kozak (Hecate): Nymphomatriarch

Mark Wastell / Toshimaru Nakamura / Taku Sugimoto / Tetuzi Akiyama: Foldings

U19 Freestyle Computing

Golden Nica

Georg Sochurek: Rubberduck

Distinctions

Martin Leonhartsberger / Sigrun Astrid Fugger: Gerät zur Messung und Analyse von Spondylolisthese

Armin Ronacher / Nikolaus Mikschofsky: :.be A bee.:

Dominik Dorn: lyrix

Honorary Mentions

Georg Gruber: individual interface inflex.org

Manuel Fallmann: system interrupted

David Hackl: Die Fliege

Thomas Hainscho: schools out for Rosh Hodesh Adar II

Hauptschule Steinerkirchen / Traun: Sprung ins Ungewisse

Alexandra Voglreiter, Katharina Krummel, Anna Obermeier: i² was ist eine tolle Seite?

Project Group from the Secondary School HBLA for Artistic Design, Garnisonstraße / Linz: Bewegung

Franz Wengler / Christoph Haidinger: Akustische Lesehilfe für Sehbehinderte

Class 7a at the BORG 3 in Vienna / 7a des BORG 3 Wien: Klangbilder

Tobias Schererbauer / Matthus König / Sebastian Schreiner: Greenbox

---

Selected works of Prix Ars Electronica are being presented on the CyberArts 2003 exhibition at the O.K Centrum für Gegenwarts-kunst. You find a detailed description of the projects in the Prix Ars Electronica Compendium *CyberArts 2003.*

CyberArts 2003
International Compendium of Prix Ars Electronica
H. Leopoldseder / C. Schöpf (eds.)
Hatje Cantz, Ostfildern Ruit 2003

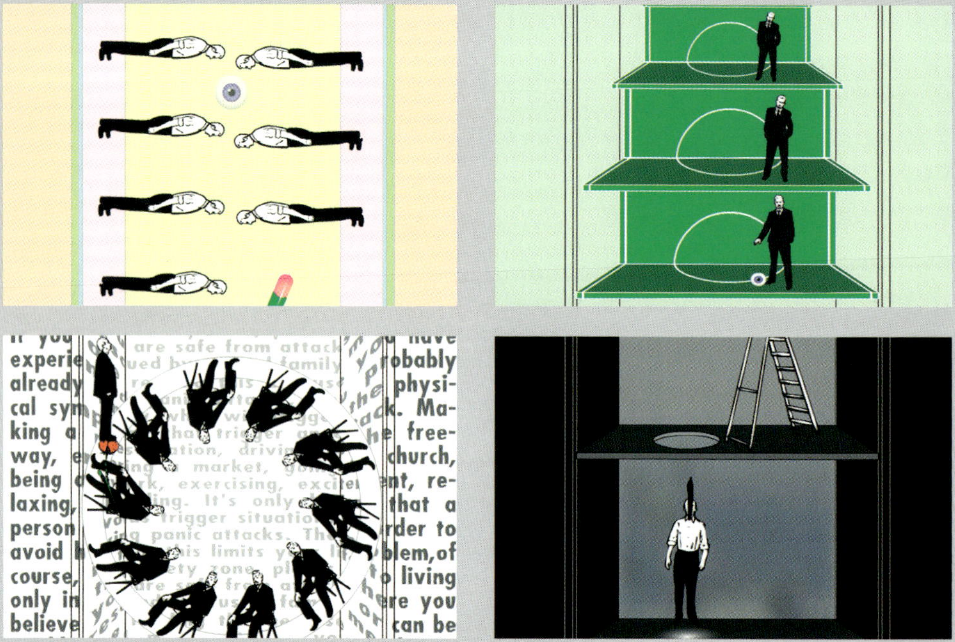

Wiggle / Jan Hoggerbrugge: *Flow*

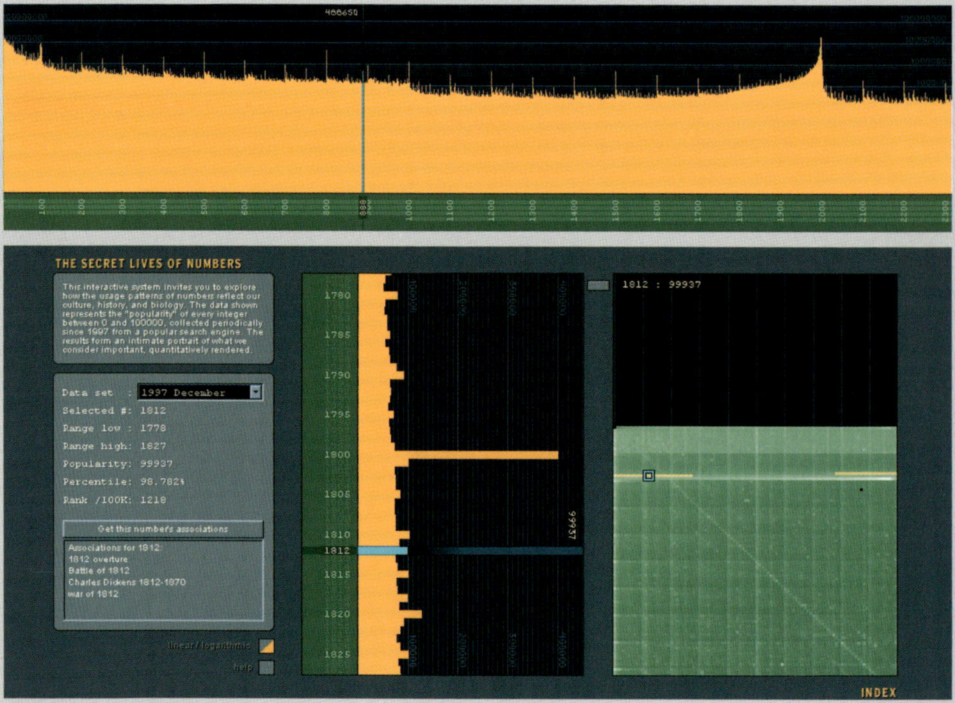

Golan Levin: *The Secret Lives of Numbers*

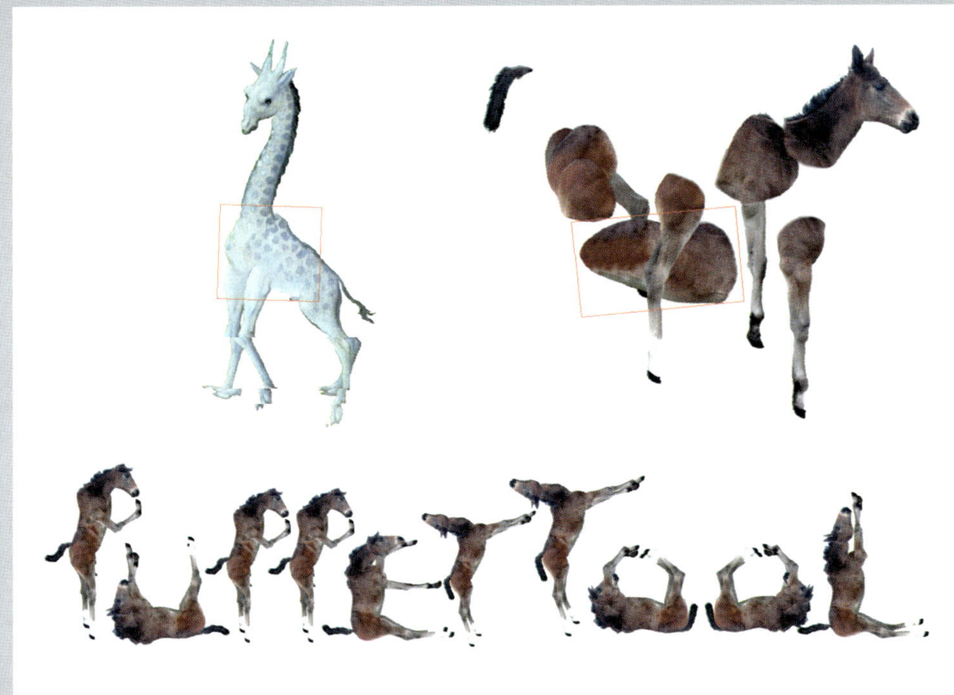

LeCielEstBleu: *PuppetTool*

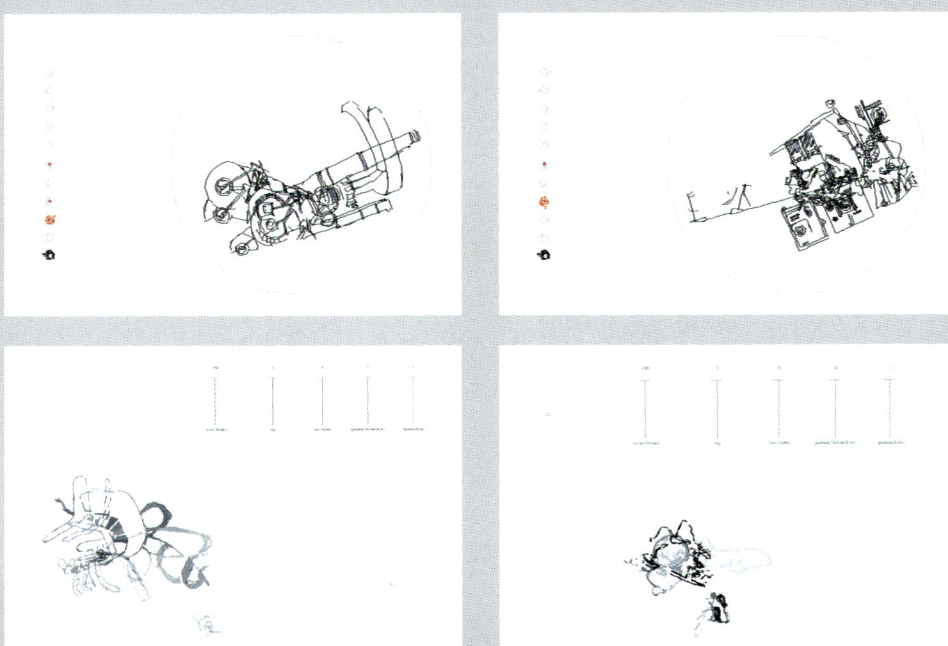

Amit Pitaru / James Paterson: *InsertSilence*

From the Poesy of Programming to Research as an Art Form

Laurent Mignonneau / Christa Sommerer

Conceptual Background

Since the early 90s we have been developing and programming interactive computer systems that consider the users' interaction input important components for self-generating software structures that are not predefined by us artists but instead constantly change, grow, develop, evolve and adapt to the environment. One of our main goals in creating these systems is to show how interaction is a key component to the creation of complexity, diversity and emergence, not only in real-life, but in artificial systems as well.
We have applied the principles of complex adaptive systems and artificial life to the creation of interactive software structures that constantly change when users interact with them. We have created dynamic interactive artworks that are not static, but instead process-based, open-ended, adaptable and environment-centered.
We call this "Art as a Living System,"[1] in reference to natural systems which are always dynamic, flexible and input-dependent. Before describing some of the research principles which we apply to the creating of these art works, let us consider a few basic questions on the role of programming, the function of the artist/programmer and the importance of research and development in our art works.

Research as an Art Form

For each of our interactive artworks we have developed custom-made software programs as well as special hardware interfaces that we specifically invented and designed for these systems.[2]
We concentrate a significant amount of energy on finding novel interfaces as well as novel programming algorithms for novel artistic concepts. Our artistic activity has become a research activity and the artworks we create have become research projects that expand and explore the status quo of what is known and commercially available.
One of our main motivations for writing our own software programs and developing our own hardware interfaces as opposed to using off-the-shelf software packages or commercially available interface technology is our wish to develop systems that investigate new questions and explore novel technical, conceptual and artistic approaches.
As media artists we have chosen to become artists/researchers or researcher/artists who define and shape new questions of creation, and set out to explore the forefront of creativity and digital technology, investigating the basic question of creation, invention and discovery.

Beyond End-user Art and the Art of Discovery

Having worked for around 10 years at advanced research centers in Germany, the US and Japan,[3,4,5] we have witnessed the usual time lag of a few years before a novel research prototype actually becomes part of the software or hardware market. This means, avail-

able software and hardware products usually lag a few years behind what is already scientifically and technically explored.
Working as an artist in research and development thus not only provides insight into today's visions and inventions which might shape the future, it also enables you to define new artistic research topics that might also shape the future of art, design, product and society as a whole.
While it is of course perfectly legitimate to be an "end-user artist" who develops her artwork through the currently available software or hardware packages, there is however always a certain kind of creative limitation and aesthetic resemblance of works produced with these packages.
The freedom to design your own software and create your own hardware could be compared to mixing your own colors out of pigments as opposed to using a paint-set with a predetermined number of premixed colors.
It is experimenting with details as well as sometimes accidentally discovering novel features that make programming itself a highly creative experience. During the programming process, essential new discoveries can happen by chance or even by misconception. The programming language itself has been designed to be used in a certain way (the grammar and the words, the syntax) but the content of what this language describes has not been determined, thus leaving a great deal of freedom to the programmer to use this language. Programming is a constant discovery, and asking others to create a program on your behalf means leaving out many creative details that can be essential to the final look and even to the final content of the work.

The Poesy of Programming

Programming can be compared to writing a novel: even though the language of the novel is defined (say French or German or English), the content of what is expressed is subject to the author's imagination and creative expression.
The same holds true for the art of programming: programmers each have their own style in writing programming code, and the result usually depends upon their skill and their experience. Especially in the area of interface programming, which can be quite complex as it needs to consider user input, there are great differences between programming styles and the personal creativity of the programmer.
Going back to the metaphor of the novel, you could for example imagine asking two writers to produce a novel on the same topic, using the same language. The resulting two novels would certainly differ greatly, even though both authors used the same language and perhaps even the same words. One of the novels might be more interesting than the other, the difference being how the authors managed to convey their flights of fancy and ideas.
It is the full control over a language combined with a complete openness towards discoveries and experiments that help an author to produce an outcome (be it a computer program or a novel) which expresses and transcends her creative vision.

The Role of the Code in our Artworks

Let us now look at the function of code in our own artworks.
One of our main goals in creating interactive systems is to show how dynamic and complex life is. Or as Dennett described it, "William Paley was right about one thing: our need to explain how it can be that the universe contains many wonderful designed things."[6]
Deeply fascinated by the workings of nature, we created several artificial systems that reflect on real life systems by re-creating and interpreting some of its beauty and complex-

ity of design. From analyzing some principles of nature, such as the emergence of life, the emergence of order and complexity as well as the dynamics of interactions, we were inspired to create artificial systems that model some of these processes.
To do this, we needed to create software structures which themselves are dynamic and open-ended. Over the years we have been instrumental in developing and establishing a research field called Artificial Life Art, Generative Art and Art that creates Complex Adaptive Systems through Interactivity.[7]
Let us briefly summarize some of the underlying research fields.

Complex Dynamic Systems

Complex System Sciences studies how parts of a system give rise to the collective behaviors of the system and how the system interacts with its environment. Social systems made up, in part, of people, the brain made up of neurons, molecules made up of atoms, and the weather made up of air currents are all examples of complex systems.
Complex System Sciences, as a field of research, has emerged in the past decade. By searching for inherent structures in living systems and trying to define common patterns within these structures, it approaches the question of how life on earth could have appeared. A whole branch of research—not only within biology but also across its borders to physics and computer science—deals with complex dynamic systems and can be seen as the attempt to find basic organizing principles.
Complex Systems Sciences focuses on certain questions about parts, wholes and relationships. Efforts to describe and define the notions of complexity have been made by many scholars including Aschby,[8] Baas,[9] Bennett,[10] Cariani,[11] Casti,[12] Chaitin,[13] Jantsch,[14] Kauffman,[15] Landauer,[16] Langton,[17] Pagels,[18] Wicken,[19] Wolfram[20] and Yates.[21]
Although there is no exact definition of what a Complex System is, there is now an understanding that when a set of evolving autonomous particles or agents interact, the resulting global system displays emergent collective properties, evolution, and critical behavior that exhibits universal characteristics.
Such a system is fundamentally novel and not deducible into its mere parts. These agents or particles may be complex molecules, cells, living organisms, animal groups, human societies, industrial firms, competing technologies, etc. All of them are aggregates of matter, energy, and information that display the following characteristics. They

- couple with each other
- learn, adapt and organize
- mutate and evolve
- expand their diversity
- react to their neighbors and to external control
- explore their options
- replicate
- organize a hierarchy of higher-order structures

Emergence

In the study of complex systems, the idea of emergence is used to indicate the arising of patterns, structures, or properties that do not seem adequately explained by referring only to the system's pre-existing components and their interaction. Emergence becomes increasingly important as an explanatory construct when the system is characterized by the following features:

- when the organization of the system, i.e., its global order, appears to be more salient and of a different kind than the components alone
- when the components can be replaced without an accompanying decommissioning of the whole system
- when the new global patterns or properties are radically novel compared to the pre-existing components; thus, the emergent patterns seem to be unpredictable and non-deducible from the components as well as irreducible to those components.

Interactivity

One of the central roles in the creation of complexity and emergence is interactivity. By coupling with each other and by exchanging salient information that in turn can trigger the creation of new information, interactivity can be described as a key principle in the organization and transformation of components within a complex dynamic system.

Dynamic Programming, Emergent Design and User Interaction

Intrigued by the idea that order, structure and design can emerge through the interaction of particles or agents in a system, we have explored (since 1992) complex dynamic systems that are open-ended, process-based, adaptable and environment centered.
From an artistic point of view we aim to create artworks that are like dynamical living systems themselves ("Art as a Living System"),[1] as they constantly change, adapt and diversify according to their environmental input parameters.
The idea of creating a dynamic and emergent software structure also requires a new programming approach: instead of asking the computer only to execute a given set of instructions, the code itself should re-organize itself "on-the-wing," while the dynamic input parameters are processed. Just as in complex dynamic systems, all components of the software code and all the input parameters from the interaction are coupled to each other: this leads to a system that adapts and organizes itself, mutates and evolves, expands its diversity, reacts to its neighbors and to external control, explores its options and replicate and finally organize a hierarchy of higher-order structures.
It's artistically interesting to see how creation in this process becomes an emergent property which can produce unexpected and novel results. Through the dynamic software structure and a linked user interaction, novel content can emerge and new forms of expressions can emerge. The final outcome is not so much a pre-determined "result" but instead a dynamic process of constant re-configuration and adaptation.
Figures 1 and 2 show the work *Life Spacies* created in 1997. Here language is used as genetic code to create artificial on-line creatures that live, mate, evolve, feed on text and die. Users can create these creatures by simply writing text and by feeding the creatures with text characters. In this work the idea of the code of language is used literally, as the genetic code for artificial life forms. An in-depth description of this system is provided in.[22] Some of the earlier generative artworks we have created since 1992 using dynamic and generative image processes are given in literature.[1, 23, 24, 25]

Generating and Interacting with Complexity on the Internet

The Internet is an ever-expanding database of images, text and sound files, currently containing several billion documents. These data and their internal organization are constantly

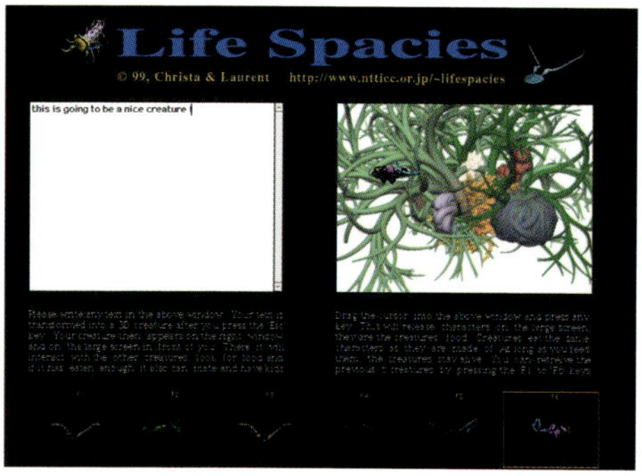

Fig. 1 *Life Spacies II*—graphical user interface. Written text is used as the genetic code and food for artificial life creatures.

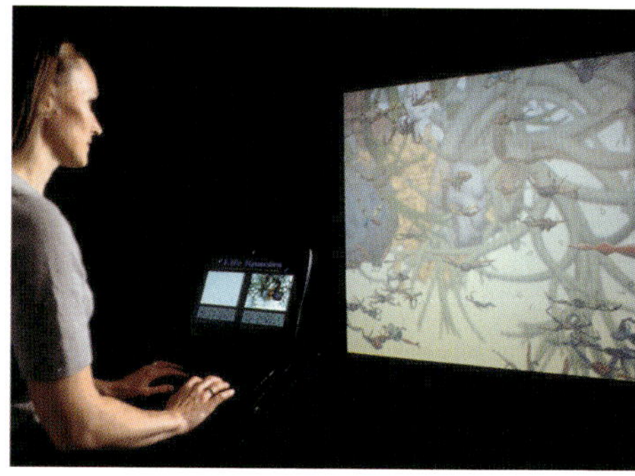

Fig. 2 *Life Spacies II*—user as she creates and feeds various artificial creatures that mate, eat, die, interact and evolve, creating an open-ended, complex dynamic system.

changing, as new documents are being uploaded, new web sites created, and old links deleted. New connections between various sites are also constantly being built, and the Internet itself has basically become an evolving, re-connecting and reconfiguring network of user-driven data input and output. Since 1999 we have created various interactive systems that directly tap into this complexity and link it to multi-modal interaction experiences.

The first system we created is called *Riding the Net,* built in 1999.[26] Here users can use speech communication to retrieve images from the Internet, watch these images as they stream by, and interact with them by touching them. Two users can interact in this system simultaneously, and as they communicate, their conversation will be supported and visualized in real-time through images as well as sounds streamed from the Internet. Figure 3 shows an example of this interaction, shown at Siggraph 2001.

In 2001, we adapted the *Riding the Net* image retrieval software for an interactive information environment, called *The Living Room.* The system was developed for the "Bo01-Living in the Future" architecture exhibition held in Malmoe, Sweden, in May 2001. Users in this system enter a 6 x 6 meter space that consists of four 4 x 3 meter screens and as they talk, microphones placed on the ceiling of the space detect their conversations. Detected keywords are then used to generate word icons, which start to appear and float on the four screens. Users can touch any of these word icons and their touch will trigger the downloading of corresponding images from the Internet. Up to 30 users in the system can choose to touch the various word icons, which will generate constantly changing image and sound downloads from the Internet. As a result of these multi-user interactions, a dynamic, self-organizing, and constantly changing information space emerges. It represents the users' individual conversations, their individual interests in certain topics, and their collective interaction with the shared information.

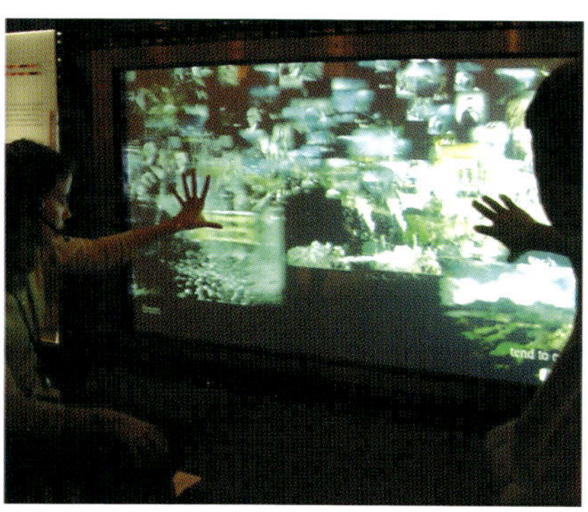

Fig. 3 *Riding the Net*—multi-modal interaction with complex data on the Internet.

In May 2002, we adapted *The Living Room* software to the 3D immersive environment of

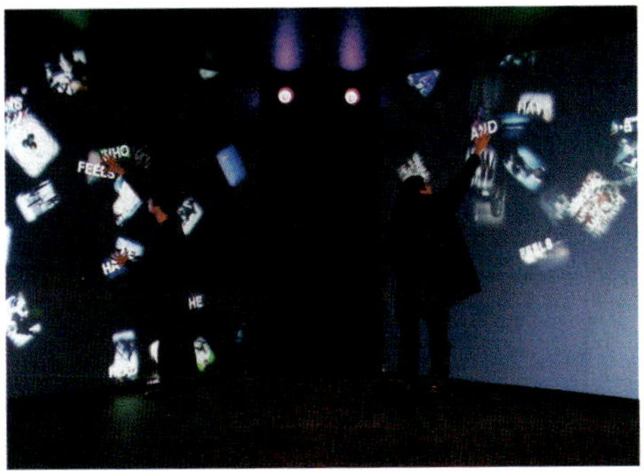

Fig. 4 shows two users as they interact with the *The Living Room* data environment.

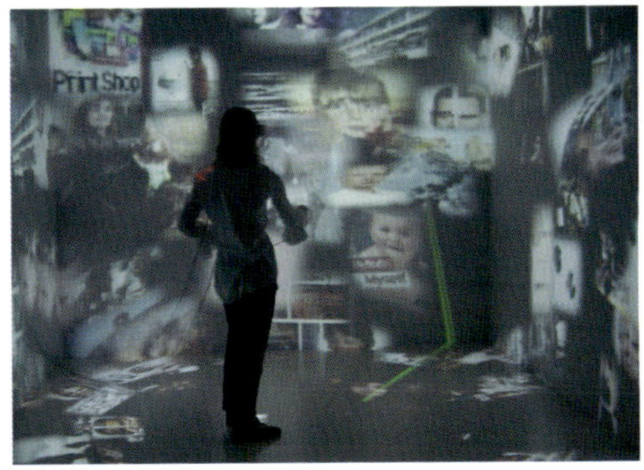

Fig. 5 User as she interacts with the complex 3D data environment of *The Living Room* inside a CAVE™ system.

the CAVE™ system. In this system, called *The Living Web,* users can actually "enter the Internet" and interact with the available image and sound information in three dimensions. When users talk into their headset microphones, images that relate to their conversations are streamed from the Internet and displayed in 3D in such a way as to surround them. By grabbing one of the floating images, the user can retrieve more information about this specific image (for example its URL), place the icon in a 3D space for bookmarking, and sort the various selected icons as 3D bookmarks to create further links, main interests, and connections between the various selected topics.

As in the "Riding the Net" and *The Living Room* systems, the imprecision of the speech recognition system and the randomized choice of images from the various search results are used intentionally to create a dynamic system that is unpredictable, full of surprise, and compliant with some of the definitions of a complex system. While users have some control over what kind of image and sound downloads are triggered, the sheer quantity of available information makes straightforward selection impossible. For each keyword, typically several hundred or at times several thousand image and sound documents are available and users can typically only perceive a fraction of the available data. To manage this complex and constantly changing database of images and sounds and to allow intuitive as well as creative data browsing, these systems were designed to deal with randomness and order, allowing partly directed and partly undirected searches. [27] Again, like in the principles of complex systems, it is precisely this notion of order and randomness, predictability and surprise that make dynamic complex systems interesting, emergent and full of discoveries.

Transcending the Code

Writing computer programs is a complicated task, involving extended knowledge of the ever-changing programming languages and versions, their capacity and their inner structures. In addition, knowledge of the computer's internal hardware architecture as well as its resources and infrastructure can be of great advantage if you want to extend the already known and explored.

Knowing both hardware and software structures is important if you want to explore new forms of expressions and become less dependent on today's pre-design and the limitations of computer hardware and software.

It is extra freedom that in-depth knowledge provides, as you can change, modify and extend any part and use both hardware and software as flexible materials to express and shape your imagination and artistic vision.

Only when all the components of the materials are known, can you begin to transcend the actual technology and create outputs that go beyond the purely technical and materialistic.

As in biological systems where the phenotype differs greatly from the genotype, programming as an art form is not purely a question of the code for its own sake, but rather a question of how this code is expressed, how it is linked to other environmental influences and what it actually means.

Instead of focusing only on the technical details and getting lost in materialistic questions of the code, artists who work with this technology have to transcend the software code and hardware constraints and present us with intellectually as well as emotionally challenging ideas and questions.

The most difficult part in creating artworks with computers is thus not so much to acquire technical skills or to learn the software languages, but to evaluate and estimate the technical possibilities of software and hardware constraints, as well as to explore new technical and intellectual ideas by balancing their conceptual and technical capacity and value.

As with any mastery in creative fields of expression (may it be dance, theater, music, film or fashion—think of the dancers' mastery over their bodies as essential component for the final artwork of the dance performance), computer-dependent art requires a certain mastery over the material before it can express itself in a higher and more transcended form.

The quality of a media artist, then, lies in her sensitivity to create new visions and explore new tools and structures that support these visions and finally present us with content and experiences that transcend time and material by touching deeper emotional qualities that are not readily explained through code or numbers alone.

---

1 Sommerer, C. and Mignonneau, L. "Art as a Living System", in *Art @ Science,* C. Sommerer & L. Mignonneau, (Eds.). pp. 148-161. Springer Verlag, Wien / New York, 1998

2 Mignonneau, L. and Sommerer, C. "Designing Interfaces for Interactive Artworks," in *KES 2000 Knowledge Based Engineering Systems Conference Proceedings,* pp. 80-84, University of Brighton, UK,. 2000

3 ATR Advanced Telecommunications Research Center, Kyoto, Japan: http://www.atr.co.jp

4 Fraunhofer Gesellschaft, Bonn, Germany: http://www.fraunhofer.de

5 Beckmann Institute, NSCA National Center for Super Computing Applications, Champain / Urbana, IL, USA: http://www.beckman.uiuc.edu

6 Dennett, D. *Darwin's Dangerous Idea: Evolution and the Meanings of Life,* Simon and Schuster, New York,1995.

7 Sommerer, C. "A Life in Art, Design, Edutainment, Game and Research", in *LEONARDO Journal.* Issue 34. pp. 297-298. MIT Press, Cambridge / MA, August 2001,

8 Ashby, W. Ross. "Principles of the self-organizing system", in Heinz Von Foerster & George W. Zopf, eds: *Principles of Self-Organization,* pp. 255-278. Pergamon Press, Oxford,1962

9 Baas, N. A. "Emergence, Hierarchies, and Hyperstructures", in C. G. Langton, ed., *Alife III, Santa Fe Studies in the Sciences of Complexity, Proc. Volume XVII,* pp. 515-537, Addison-Wesley, Redwood City, 1994

10 Bennett, CH. "Logical depth and physical complexity", in Rolf Herken, ed.: *The Universal Turing Machine,* pp. 227–257. Oxford University Press, Oxford, 1988

11 Cariani, P. "Emergence and Artificial Life", In Christopher G. Langton, Charles Taylor, J. Doyne Farmer and Steen Rasmussen, eds.: *Artificial Life II. Santa Fe Institute Studies in the Sciences of Complexity, Proc. Vol. X,* pp. 775-797, Addison-Wesley, Redwood City, Calif., 1992

12 Casti, J.L. *Complexification.* Abacus, London 1994.

13 Chaitin, G.J. *Information Theoretic Incompleteness.* World Scientific, Singapore, 1992

14 Jantsch, Erich. *The Self-Organizing Universe.* Pergamon. Oxford and New York, 1980

15 Kauffman, St. *The Origins of Order. Self-organization and Selection in Evolution.* Oxford University Press, Oxford, 1993
16 Landauer, R. "A simple measure of complexity", in *Nature* 336, pp. 306–307. 1988
17 Langton, C. 1989. "Artificial Life", in C. Langton, ed., *Artificial Life.* pp. 1–47. Addison-Wesley, Redwood City
18 Pagels, H. *The Dreams of Reason.* Simon & Shuster (Bantam ed. 1989 N.Y.),1988
19 Wicken, J. S. *Evolution, Thermodynamics, and Information.* Oxford University Press, Oxford, 1987
20 Wolfram, S. "Cellular automata as models of complexity", in *Nature* 311. pp. 419–424. 1984.
21 Yates, F.E., ed. 1987. *Self-Organizing Systems. The Emergence of Order.* Plenum Press, New York, 1987
22 Sommerer, C. and Mignonneau, L. and Lopez-Gulliver, R. "LIFE SPACIES II: from text to form on the Internet using language as genetic code", in *Proceedings ICAT'99 9th International Conference on Artificial Reality and Tele-Existence.* pp. 215-220. (Tokyo: Virtual Reality Society), 1999e
23 Sommerer, C. and Mignonneau, *"Interacting with Artificial Life: A-Volve",* in *Complexity Journal.* Vol. 2, No. 6. pp. 13-21. Wiley, New York, 1997
24 Sommerer, C. and Mignonneau, L. "The application of artificial life to interactive computer installations", in *Artificial Life and Robotics Journal. Vol.2, No.4.* pp. 151–156. Springer Verlag, Tokyo, 1998
25 Sommerer, C. and Mignonneau, L. *"Modeling Emergence of Complexity: the Application of Complex System and Origin of Life Theory to Interactive Art on the Internet",* in *Artificial Life VII,* edited by M.A. Bedau, J.S. McCaskill, N. H. Packard, and St. Rasmussen. pp. 547-554. MIT Press, Boston, 2000
26 Mignonneau, L., Sommerer, C., Lopez-Gulliver, R. and Jones, S. "Riding the Net: a Novel, Intuitive and Entertaining Tool to Browse the Internet", in *SCI 2001—5th World Multiconference on Systemics, Cybernetics and Informatics Conference Proceedings.* pp. 57–63. Orlando, Florida, International Institute of Informatics and Systemics, 2001
27 R. Lopez-Gulliver, C. Sommerer, and Mignonneau L. "Interfacing the Web: Multi-modal and Immersive Interaction with the Internet", in *VSMM2002 Proceedings of the Eight International Conference on Virtual Systems and MultiMedia.* pp. 753-764. Gyeongju, Korea, 2002

Von der Poesie des Programmierens zur Forschung als Kunstform

Laurent Mignonneau / Christa Sommerer

Konzeptueller Hintergrund

Seit den frühen 90er Jahren entwickeln und programmieren wir interaktive Computersysteme, bei denen der Input aus der Benutzerinteraktion wichtiger Bestandteil selbst entwickelnder Softwarestrukturen ist, die nicht von uns Künstlern vorgegeben werden, sondern sich ständig verändern, vergrößern, weiterentwickeln und an ihre Umgebung anpassen.
Eines der Hauptziele bei der Entwicklung dieser Systeme ist es zu zeigen, dass die Interaktion eine Schlüsselkomponente von Komplexität, Diversität und Emergenz ist, und zwar sowohl im wirklichen Leben als auch in künstlichen Systemen.
Die Entwicklung dieser interaktiven Softwarestrukturen, die sich durch Benutzerinteraktion laufend verändern, beruht auf den Grundsätzen komplexer anpassungsfähiger Systeme und künstlichen Lebens. So entstanden dynamische interaktive Arbeiten, die nicht statisch sind, sondern prozessbasiert, ausbau- und anpassungsfähig sowie auf ihre Umgebung abgestimmt.In Anlehnung an natürliche Systeme, die immer dynamisch, flexibel und inputabhängig sind, nennen wir dieses Konzept „Kunst als Lebendes System".[1] Bevor wir einige der Forschungsgrundsätze beschreiben, auf die sich die Schaffung dieser Arbeiten stützt, möchten wir auf einige grundlegende Fragen zur Rolle des Programmierens, zur Funktion des Künstlers/Programmierers sowie zur Bedeutung von Forschung und Entwicklung für unser künstlerisches Schaffen eingehen.

Forschung als Kunstform

Für jedes unserer interaktiven Werke haben wir maßgeschneiderte Softwareprogramme und eigene Hardware-Schnittstellen entwickelt, die eigens für diese Systeme designt wurden.[2] Besonders viel Energie fließt in die Entwicklung neuer Schnittstellen und Programmieralgorithmen für neuartige künstlerische Konzepte. Unser künstlerisches Schaffen ist zur Forschungsarbeit geworden, und die von uns geschaffenen Arbeiten sind Forschungsprojekte, die den Rahmen des bereits Bekannten und Handelsüblichen austesten und ausweiten.
Einer der Hauptbeweggründe dafür, eigene Softwareprogramme zu schreiben und eigene Schnittstellen zu entwickeln, anstatt Standard-Softwarepakete oder handelsübliche Schnittstellen zu verwenden, liegt in unserem Bestreben, Systeme zu entwickeln, die neue Fragen aufwerfen und neuartige technische, konzeptuelle und künstlerische Ansätze untersuchen.
Als Medienkünstler verstehen wir uns bewusst als Künstler/Forscher oder Forscher/Künstler, die neuen Fragestellungen des Schaffungsprozesses nachgehen und es sich zur Aufgabe machen, neue Horizonte der Kreativität und digitalen Technologie auszuloten sowie sich grundsätzlich Fragen des Schöpfens, Erfindens und Entdeckens zu widmen.

Jenseits der Endverbraucherkunst und die Kunst der Entdeckung

Im Lauf unserer rund zehnjährigen Arbeit an den modernsten Forschungszentren in Deutschland, den USA und Japan[3,4,5] machten wir wiederholt die Erfahrung, dass neuartige Forschungsprototypen erst mit einigen Jahren Verspätung tatsächlich auf den Software- bzw. Hardwaremarkt kommen. Im Handel erhältliche Software- bzw. Hardwareprodukte hinken daher meist einige Jahre hinter den bereits wissenschaftlich und technisch erforschten Möglichkeiten nach. Die künstlerische Arbeit im Bereich Forschung und Entwicklung gibt daher nicht nur Einblick in – möglicherweise zukunftsträchtige – Visionen und Erfindungen von heute, sondern ermöglicht es auch, neue künstlerische Forschungsbereiche zu definieren, die ihrerseits die Zukunft von Kunst, Design, Produkt und der Gesellschaft als Ganzes beeinflussen könnten. Natürlich ist es völlig legitim, auch als Künstler Endverbraucher zu sein und für sein künstlerisches Schaffen handelsübliche Software- bzw. Hardwarepakete zu verwenden. Werke, die auf Basis solcher Pakete entstehen, weisen jedoch stets gewisse kreative Einschränkungen und ästhetische Ähnlichkeiten auf. Die Freiheit, die sich dem Künstler durch das Design einer eigenen Software und die Entwicklung eigener Hardware eröffnet, ist mit der des Malers vergleichbar, der seine eigenen Farben aus Pigmenten mischt, anstatt einen Malkasten mit einer beschränken Auswahl vorgemischter Farben zu verwenden. Das Experimentieren mit Details und das manchmal zufällige Entdecken neuartiger Features macht das Programmieren selbst zu einem höchst kreativen Erlebnis. Während des Programmierprozesses kann man zufällig oder sogar aufgrund von Missverständnissen wichtige neue Entdeckungen machen. Die Programmiersprache selbst ist so angelegt, dass sie auf eine bestimmte Art und Weise zu verwenden ist (Grammatik und Vokabular, Syntax). Der Inhalt, der mittels dieser Sprache beschrieben wird, ist jedoch nicht festgelegt, was dem Programmierer in der Verwendung große Freiheiten gestattet. Programmieren ist ein ständiges Entdecken. Sobald Künstler andere ein Programm schreiben lassen, gehen daher viele kreative Einzelheiten verloren, die für die endgültige Form und sogar für den endgültigen Inhalt der Arbeit entscheidend sein können.

Die Poesie des Programmierens

Das Programmieren ist mit dem Schreiben eines Romans vergleichbar: Obwohl die Sprache des Romans festgelegt ist (zum Beispiel Französisch, Deutsch oder Englisch), bleibt der vermittelte Inhalt der Fantasie und dem kreativen Ausdruck des Autors überlassen.
Dasselbe gilt auch für die Kunst des Programmierens: Programmierer haben beim Schreiben von Programmiercodes jeweils ihren eigenen Stil, und das Ergebnis hängt üblicherweise von ihrem Können und ihrer Erfahrung ab. Besonders im Bereich des Interface-Programmierens, das sich durch die Berücksichtigung potenzieller Benutzer-Inputs durchaus komplex gestalten kann, zeigen sich große Unterschiede in den Programmierstilen und in der persönlichen Kreativität der Programmierer.
Kehren wir aber zur Metapher des Romans zurück: Stellen wir uns vor, zwei Schriftsteller sollen einen Roman zum selben Thema und in derselbenSprache schreiben. Die beiden so entstandenen Romane würden sich zweifellos stark voneinander unterscheiden, obwohl sich beide Autoren derselben Sprache und vielleicht sogar derselben Worte bedient haben. Einer der Romane ist möglicherweise spannender als der andere – und der Unterschied liegt darin, auf welche Weise der Autor seine Ideen und Vorstellungen zu Papier gebracht hat.
Erst durch die perfekte Beherrschung einer Sprache und die völlige Offenheit für Entdeckungen und Experimenten kann eine Autorin Werke schaffen (seien es nun Computerprogramme oder Romane), die ihre kreative Vision zum Ausdruck bringen und transzendieren.

Die Rolle des Code in unserer künstlerischen Arbeit

Wenden wir uns nun der Funktion des Code in unseren eigenen Kunstwerken zu.
Wir wollen durch die Schaffung interaktiver Systeme unter anderem die Dynamik und Komple-

xität des Lebens aufzeigen. Um mit Dennett zu sprechen: „William Paley hatte in einem recht: unserem Bedürfnis danach zu erklären, wie es sein kann, dass das Universum so viele wunderbar gestaltete Dinge enthält."[6]
Tief beeindruckt von der Vielfältigkeit der Natur entwickelten wir verschiedene künstliche Systeme, die sich auf Systeme aus dem wirklichen Leben beziehen, indem sie deren Schönheit und komplexes Designs widerspiegeln und interpretieren. Die Analyse von Naturprinzipien, wie etwa der Entstehung von Leben, Ordnung und Komplexität und von Interaktionsdynamik inspirierte uns zur Schaffung künstlicher Systeme, die einige dieser Prozesse modellieren.
Zu diesem Zweck mussten Softwarestrukturen geschaffen werden, die selbst dynamisch und ausbaufähig sind. So spielten wir im Lauf der Jahre eine federführende Rolle in der Entwicklung und Etablierung eines Forschungsbereichs, der Artificial Life Art, generative Kunst und Kunst, die mittels Interaktivität komplexe anpassungsfähige Systeme schafft, zum Inhalt hat.[7]
Es folgt ein kurzer Überblick über die grundlegenden Einzelbereiche.

Komplexe dynamische Systeme

Die Wissenschaft der komplexen Systeme untersucht die Frage, wie die einzelnen Teile eines Systems zum kollektiven Verhalten des Systems beitragen und wie dieses mit seiner Umgebung interagiert. Zu komplexen Systemen zählen zum Beispiel Gesellschaftssysteme (wie etwa das des Menschen), aber auch das aus Neuronen bestehende Gehirn, Moleküle als Zusammenschluss von Atomen und das Wetter als Kombination verschiedener Luftströmungen. Der Forschungsbereich komplexer Systeme ist erst während der letzten zehn Jahre entstanden und untersucht mögliche Gründe für das Entstehen von Leben auf der Erde. Zu diesem Zweck werden die lebenden Systemen innewohnenden Strukturen erforscht und mögliche gemeinsame Muster innerhalb dieser Strukturen festgemacht. Ein eigener Forschungszweig – der über die Grenzen der Biologie hinaus auch in Physik und Informatik hineinreicht – beschäftigt sich mit komplexen dynamischen Systemen und kann als Versuch gelten, grundlegende Organisationsprinzipien zu finden. Die Erforschung komplexer Systeme konzentriert sich auf bestimmte Fragen in Bezug auf Bestandteile, Ganzheiten und Beziehungen. Unter anderem haben Aschby[8], Baas[9], Bennett[10], Cariani[11], Casti[12], Chaitin[13], Jantsch[14], Kauffman[15], Landauer[16], Langton[17], Pagels[18], Wicken[19], Wolfram[20] und Yates[21] versucht, verschiedene Konzepte von Komplexität zu beschreiben und zu definieren.
Obwohl der Begriff des komplexen Systems bisher nicht genau definiert wurde, besteht Einigkeit über folgenden Punkt: Kommt es zur Interaktion einer Reihe evolvierender autonomer Partikel oder Agenten, so weist das daraus resultierende globale System emergente kollektive Eigenschaften, Evolutionstendenzen sowie ein kritisches Verhalten mit allgemeingültigen Merkmalen auf.
Ein solches System stellt etwas gänzlich Neues dar und lässt sich nicht aus den einzelnen Bestandteilen ableiten. Die Agenten oder Partikel können unter anderem komplexe Moleküle, Zellen, lebende Organismen, Tiergruppen, menschliche Gesellschaften, Industriebetriebe, konkurrierende Technologien sein. Sie alle stellen Aggregate aus Masse, Energie und Information dar und weisen die folgenden Merkmale auf: Sie

- koppeln sich aneinander
- lernen, passen sich an und organisieren sich,
- mutieren und entwickeln sich weiter,
- entfalten ihre Vielfältigkeit,
- reagieren auf ihre Nachbarn und auf Steuerung von außen,
- erforschen ihre Möglichkeiten,
- vermehren sich,
- schaffen eine Hierarchie vertikaler Ordnungsstrukturen.

Emergenz

In der Erforschung komplexer Systeme versteht man unter Emergenz das Entstehen von Mustern, Strukturen oder Eigenschaften, die sich nicht hinreichend aus den einzelnen ursprünglich vorhandenen Systemkomponenten und deren Interaktion erklären lassen. Der Begriff der Emergenz wird als Erklärungsmodell immer dann besonders interessant, wenn

- die Organisation des Systems, d.h. seine Gesamtordnung, offenbar weitreichender anders konzipiert ist als die einzelnen Komponenten,
- man die Komponenten austauschen kann, ohne dass das gesamte System zerfällt, und
- wenn die neuen globalen Muster oder Eigenschaften im Vergleich zu den ursprünglichen Einzelkomponenten etwas radikal Neues darstellen; wenn also die emergenten Muster unvorhersehbar scheinen, nicht aus den Komponenten abzuleiten und nicht auf diese reduzierbar sind.

Interaktivität

Interaktivität spielt eine zentrale Rolle bei der Entstehung von Komplexität und Emergenz. Einzelkomponenten verbinden sich miteinander und tauschen wichtige Informationen aus, wodurch wieder neue Informationen entstehen können. Daher lässt sich Interaktivität als Schlüsselprinzip in der Organisation und Transformation von Komponenten innerhalb eines komplexen dynamischen Systems beschreiben.

Dynamisches Programmieren, emergentes Design und Benutzerinteraktion

Fasziniert von der Idee, dass Ordnung, Struktur und Design aus der Interaktion von Partikeln oder Agenten in einem System entstehen können, erforschen wir (seit 1992) komplexe dynamische Systeme, die ausbaufähig, prozessbasiert, anpassungsfähig und umgebungszentriert sind. Aus künstlerischer Sicht versuchen wir Werke zu schaffen, die selbst dynamischen lebenden Systemen gleichen („Kunst als Lebendes System“[1]), da sie sich analog zu den Eingabeparametern ihrer Umgebung ständig verändern, anpassen und variieren.
Um eine dynamische und emergente Softwarestruktur zu schaffen, ist auch ein neues Programmierverfahren erforderlich: Anstatt den Computer einfach anzuweisen, eine vorgegebene Befehlskette auszuführen, sollte sich der Code selbst „fliegend“ reorganisieren, während die dynamischen Eingabeparameter verarbeitet werden.
Wie in komplexen dynamischen Systemen sind auch hier sämtliche Komponenten des Softwarecodes sowie sämtliche Eingabeparameter der Benutzerinteraktion miteinander verbunden: Daraus entsteht ein anpassungsfähiges System, das sich selbst reorganisiert, das mutiert und sich entwickelt, seine Vielfältigkeit entfaltet, auf seine Nachbarn und auf Steuerung von außen reagiert, seine Möglichkeiten auslotet, sich vermehrt und schließlich eine Hierarchie vertikaler Ordnungsstrukturen schafft.
Das künstlerisch Interessante an diesem Prozess ist, wie der Akt des Erschaffens zu einer emergenten Eigenschaft wird und zu unerwarteten und neuartigen Ergebnissen führen kann. Aus der dynamischen Softwarestruktur und einer damit verbundenen Benutzerinteraktion können neue Inhalte und Ausdrucksformen entstehen. Das Endprodukt ist kein vorbestimmtes „Resultat“, sondern ein dynamischer Prozess ständiger Rekonfiguration und Anpassung.
Abbildungen 1 und 2 zeigen die 1997 entstandene Arbeit *Life Spacies.* Dabei wird Sprache als genetischer Code zur Erschaffung künstlicher Online-Wesen verwendet, die leben, sich paaren, sich weiterentwickeln, sich von Text ernähren und sterben. Die Benutzer können diese Wesen schaffen, indem sie Text schreiben und die Wesen mit Buchstaben füttern. In dieser

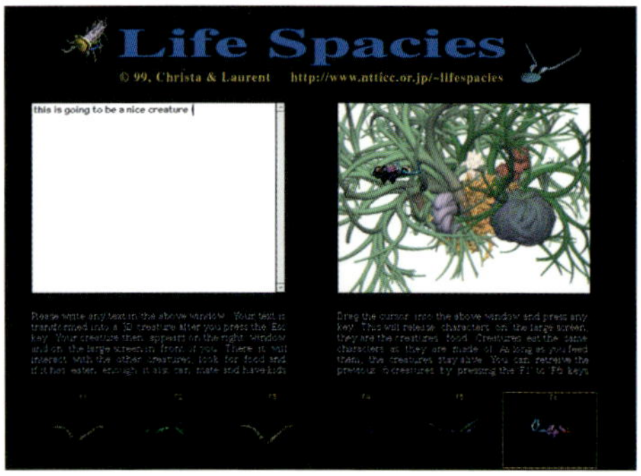

Abb. 1: *Life Spacies II* – grafisches Benutzerinterface. Geschriebener Text fungiert als genetischer Code und Futter für künstliche Lebensformen.

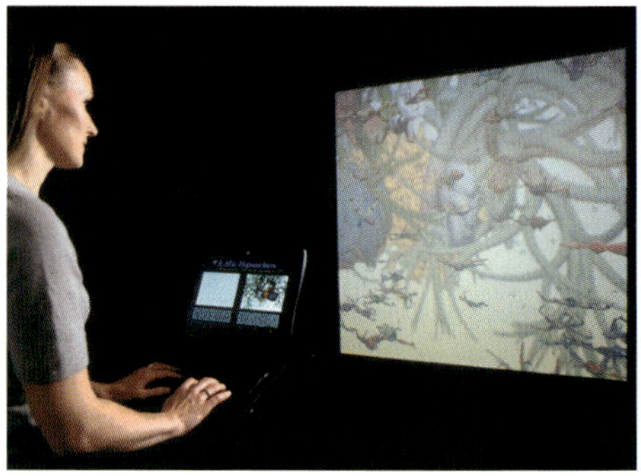

Abb. 2: *Life Spacies II* – Benutzerin kreiert und füttert verschiedene künstliche Wesen, die sich paaren, fressen, sterben, interagieren und sich entwickeln, und erzeugt so ein ausbaufähiges, komplexes dynamisches System.

Arbeit wird das Konzept des Sprachcodes wörtlich genommen: Er funktioniert als genetischer Code für künstliche Lebensformen. Eine detaillierte Beschreibung dieses Systems findet sich in.[22] Einige der frühen, seit 1992 entstandenen generativen Kunstwerke, die dynamische und generative Bildprozesse verwenden, finden sich in der Literatur. [1, 23, 24, 25]

Die Erzeugung von und Interaktion mit Komplexität im Internet

Das Internet ist eine sich ständig erweiternde Datenbank von Bildern und Text- und Soundfiles, die derzeit mehrere Milliarden Dokumente enthält. Diese Daten und ihre interne Organisation sind ständigen Veränderungen unterworfen, wenn neue Dokumente geladen, neue Websites geschaffen und alte Links gelöscht werden. Außerdem werden ständig neue Verbindungen zwischen verschiedenen Sites hergestellt. So ist das Internet im Grunde zu einem Netzwerk aus benutzerabhängigem Dateninput und -output geworden, das sich ständig weiterentwickelt, Verbindungen wiederherstellt und sich selbst rekonfiguriert. Seit 1999 haben wir verschiedene interaktive Systeme geschaffen, die sich diese Komplexität direkt zunutze machen und sie mit multimodaler Interaktion verbinden.

Das erste System war *Riding the Net* (1999).[26] Dabei können die Benutzer mittels gesprochener Sprache Bilder aus dem Internet abrufen, diese Bilder an sich vorbeiziehen lassen und mit ihnen durch Berührung interagieren. Zwei Benutzer können gleichzeitig in diesem System interagieren, und während sie kommunizieren, wird ihr Dialog in Echtzeit durch aus dem Internet bezogene Bilder und Töne gestützt und visualisiert. Abbildung 3 zeigt ein Beispiel für eine derartige Interaktion im Rahmen von Siggraph 2001.

2001 adaptierten wir die *Riding the Net*-Software zur Bildabrufung für ein interaktives Informationsumfeld namens *The Living Room.* Dieses System wurde für die im Mai 2001 in Malmö veranstaltete Architekturmesse „Bo01-Living in the Future" entwickelt. In diesem System betreten die Benutzer einen 6x6 Meter großen Raum, der aus vier 4x3 Meter großen Leinwänden besteht. Mikrofone an der Decke des Raumes verfolgen die Gespräche der Benutzer. Wenn bestimmte Stichwörter fallen, entstehen Wort-Icons, die über die vier Leinwände wandern. Die Benutzer können diese Wort-Icons berühren und so entsprechende Bilder aus dem Internet herunterladen. In diesem System können gleichzeitig bis zu 30 Benutzer die verschiedenen Wort-Icons berühren und so ständig wechselnde Bilder und Töne aus dem Internet herunterladen. Durch diese Multiuser-Interaktionen entsteht ein dynamischer, selbstorgani-

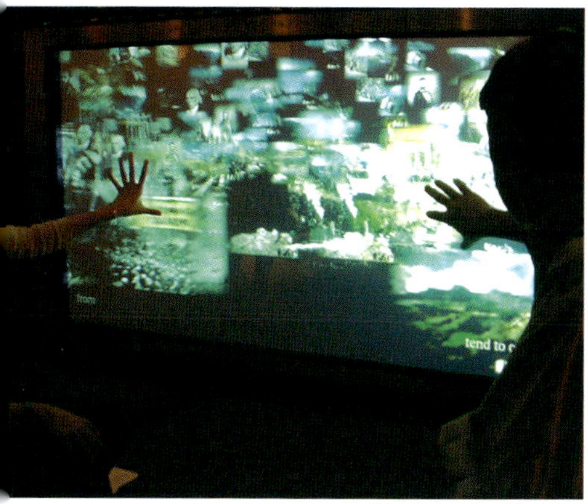

Abb. 3: *Riding the Net* – multimodale Interaktion mit komplexen Daten im Internet

sierter und sich ständig ändernder Informationsraum. Dieser steht für die Einzelgespräche der Benutzer, ihr persönliches Interesse an bestimmten Themen und ihre kollektive Interaktion mit den geteilten Informationen.
Im Mai 2002 adaptierten wir die *Living Room*-Software für die 3D-Immersionsumgebung des CAVE™-Systems. In diesem System namens *The Living Web* können die Benutzer tatsächlich „das Internet betreten“ und mit der vorhandenen Bild- und Soundinformation in drei Dimensionen interagieren. Wenn die Benutzer in das Mikrofon ihres Headsets sprechen, werden zu ihren Gesprächen passende Bilder aus dem Internet abgerufen und im 3D-Format um sie herum dargestellt. Wenn die Benutzer nun eines der um sie herumschwebenden Bilder berühren, können sie weitere Informationen über dieses bestimmte Bild abrufen (etwa seine URL), das Icon in einem 3D-Raum ablegen und so ein Lesezeichen anlegen und die verschiedenen ausgewählten Icons als 3D-Lesezeichen sortieren, um weitere Links anzulegen, sie nach Interessensgebieten zu reihen und Verbindungen zwischen den verschiedenen gewählten Themen herzustellen.
Wie schon bei den Systemen *Riding the Net* und *The Living Room* wird die Ungenauigkeit des Spracherkennungssystems und die zufällige Auswahl von Bildern aus den verschiedenen Suchergebnissen bewusst verwendet, um ein dynamisches System zu schaffen, das unberechenbar und voller Überraschungen ist sowie mit einigen Definitionen von komplexen Systemen übereinstimmt. Obwohl die Benutzer eine gewisse Kontrolle darüber haben, welche Bild- und Sound-Downloads initiiert werden, wird eine gezielte Auswahl durch die schiere Menge der verfügbaren Information unmöglich. Zu jedem Stichwort sind durchschnittlich mehrere hundert oder sogar mehrere tausend Bild- und Tondokumente vorhanden, und die Benutzer können im Normalfall nur einen Bruchteil der vorhandenen Daten wahrnehmen. Um diese komplexe und sich ständig verändernde Datenbank aus Bildern und Tönen zu verwalten und um intuitives und kreatives Datenbrowsing zu ermöglichen, wurden diese Systeme so angelegt, dass

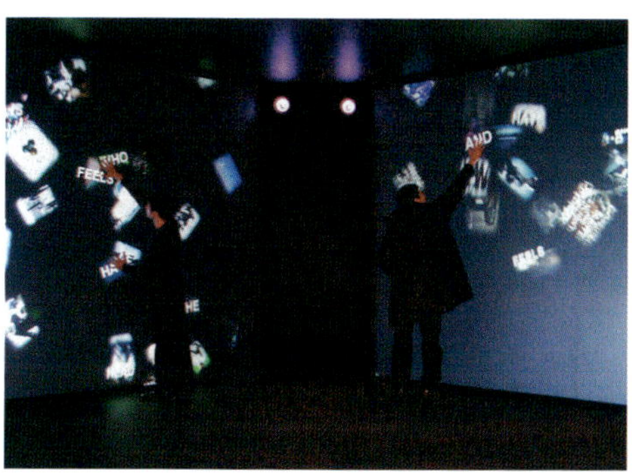

Abb. 4: zeigt zwei Benutzer, die mit der Datenumgebung des *Living Room* interagieren.

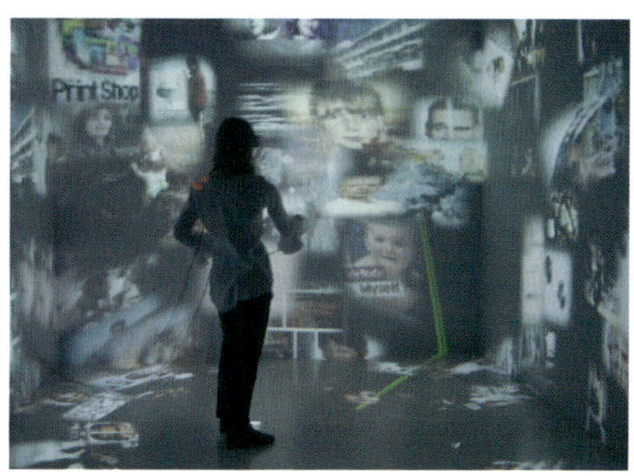

Abb. 5: Eine Benutzerin bei der Interaktion mit der komplexen 3D-Datenumgebung des *Living Room* innerhalb eines CAVE™-Systems.

sie mit Zufälligkeit und Ordnung umgehen können und sowohl zielgerichtete als auch teilweise zufällige Suchvorgänge erlauben.[27] Ähnlich den Grundsätzen komplexer Systeme sind es auch hier gerade die Begriffe Ordnung und Zufälligkeit, Berechenbarkeit und Überraschung, die dynamische komplexe Systeme interessant und emergent machen und für zahlreiche Entdeckungsmöglichkeiten sorgen.

Mehr als nur Code

Das Schreiben von Computerprogrammen ist eine schwierige Aufgabe, die enormes Wissen über die sich ständig ändernden Programmiersprachen und -versionen, deren Kapazitäten und innere Strukturen verlangt. Außerdem kann die Vertrautheit mit der Hardwarearchitektur im Computerinneren sowie mit deren Quellen und Infrastruktur von großem Vorteil sein, wenn man über die Grenzen des bereits Bekannten und Erforschten hinaus will.

Die Vertrautheit mit Hardware- und Softwarestrukturen ist dann wichtig, wenn man neue Ausdrucksformen erforschen und weniger von den begrenzten Möglichkeiten handelsüblicher Computerhardware und -software abhängig sein möchte. Genaue Sachkenntnis schafft zusätzlichen Freiraum. Mit ihrer Hilfe können wir jeden Teil des Computers verändern, modifizieren und ausweiten und sowohl Hardware als auch Software als flexible Materialien verwenden, um unsere Vorstellungen und künstlerische Vision auszudrücken und zu verwirklichen. Nur wenn alle Komponenten der Materialien bekannt sind, kann man die eigentliche Technologie hinter sich lassen und Arbeiten schaffen, die über das rein Technische und Materialistische hinausgehen.

Ähnlich wie in biologischen Systemen, wo sich der Phänotypus oft stark vom Genotypus unterscheidet, ist auch das Programmieren als Kunstform nicht nur eine Frage des Codes als Selbstzweck. Vielmehr geht es darum, wie dieser Code zum Ausdruck gebracht wird, wie er an andere Umgebungseinflüsse gebunden ist und was er eigentlich bedeutet.

Anstatt sich nur auf technische Details zu konzentrieren und sich in materialistischen Fragestellungen des Code zu verlieren, müssen Künstler, die mit dieser Technologie arbeiten, die Grenzen von Softwarecode und Hardware-bedingten Zwängen hinter sich lassen und uns mit intellektuell und emotional herausfordernden Ideen und Fragen konfrontieren.

Die größte Schwierigkeit in der künstlerischen Arbeit mit dem Computer liegt daher nicht in der Aneignung technischer Fertigkeiten oder im Erlernen von Programmiersprachen, sondern darin, die technischen Möglichkeiten von Software und Hardware zu bewerten und einzuschätzen sowie neue technische und intellektuelle Konzepte zu erforschen, indem man ihre konzeptuellen und technischen Perspektiven und ihren möglichen Wert gegeneinander aufwiegt.

So wie jede Höchstleistung in einer kreativen Ausdrucksform (sei es Tanz, Theater, Film oder Mode – man denke nur daran, wie wichtig die Körperbeherrschung von TänzerInnen für die Qualität der künstlerischen Leistung einer Tanz-Performance ist), verlangt auch die Computerkunst einen gewissen Grad an Materialbeherrschung, bevor sie über sich selbst hinauswachsen kann.

Die Qualität von Medienkünstlern zeigt sich daher darin, wie offen sie der Schaffung neuer Visionen und der Erforschung neuer Werkzeuge und Strukturen zur Realisierung dieser Visionen gegenüberstehen und inwieweit sie uns Inhalte und Erfahrungen bieten können, die über Zeit und Material hinausgehen und tiefergehende emotionale Qualitäten ansprechen, die mit Hilfe von Codes oder Zahlen allein schwer zu erklären sind.

Aus dem Englischen von Elisabeth Wiellander

1 Sommerer, C. und Mignonneau, L.: „Art as a Living System“, in Sommerer C. & Mignonneau, L., (Hgs.): *Art @ Science,* Springer Verlag, Wien/New York 1998b, S. 148–161
2 Mignonneau, L. und Sommerer, C.: „Designing Interfaces for Interactive Artworks“, in *KES 2000 Knowledge Based Engineering Systems Conference Proceedings,* University of Brighton, UK 2000, S. 80–84
3 ATR Advanced Telecommunications Research Center, Kyoto, Japan: http://www.atr.co.jp
4 Fraunhofer Gesellschaft, Bonn, Germany: http://www.fraunhofer.de
5 Beckmann Institute, NSCA National Center for Super Computing Applications, Champain/Urbana, IL, USA: http://www.beckman.uiuc.edu
6 Dennett, D.: *Darwin's Dangerous Idea: Evolution and the Meanings of Life,* Simon & Schuster, New York 1995
7 Sommerer, C.: „A Life in Art, Design, Edutainment, Game and Research“, in *LEONARDO Journal,* Heft 34:4, S. 297–298, MIT Press, Cambridge/MA August 2001
8 Ashby, W. Ross: „Principles of the self-organizing system“, in Von Foerster, H. & Zopf, G. W., (Hgs.): *Principles of Self-Organization,* Pergamon Press, Oxford 1962, S. 255–278
9 Baas, N. A.: „Emergence, Hierarchies, and Hyperstructures“, in Langton, C. G., (Hg.): *Alife III, Santa Fe Studies in the Sciences of Complexity, Proc. Volume XVII,* Addison-Wesley, Redwood City 1994, S. 515–537
10 Bennett, CH.: „Logical depth and physical complexity“, in Rolf Herken, (Hg.): *The Universal Turing Machine,* Oxford University Press, Oxford 1988, S. 227-257
11 Cariani, P.: „Emergence and Artificial Life“, in Langton, C. G., Taylor, C., Doyne Farmer, J., und Rasmussen, St., (Hgs.): *Artificial Life II. Santa Fe Institute Studies in the Sciences of Complexity, Proc. Vol. X,* Addison-Wesley, Redwood City, Calif. 1992, S. 775–797.
12 Casti, J.L.: *Complexification,* Abacus, London 1994
13 Chaitin, G.J.: *Information Theoretic Incompleteness,* World Scientific, Singapore 1992
14 Jantsch, Erich: *The Self-Organizing Universe,* Pergamon, Oxford und New York 1980
15 Kauffman, St.: *The Origins of Order. Self-organization and Selection in Evolution,* Oxford University Press, Oxford 1993
16 Landauer, R.: „A simple measure of complexity“, in *Nature* 336, S. 306–307, 1988
17 Langton, C.: „Artificial Life“, in C. Langton, (Hg.): *Artificial Life,* Addison-Wesley, Redwood City 1989, S. 1–47
18 Pagels, H.: *The Dreams of Reason,* Simon & Schuster 1988 (Bantam ed., N.Y. 1989)
19 Wicken, J. S.: *Evolution, Thermodynamics, and Information,* Oxford University Press, Oxford 1987
20 Wolfram, S.; „Cellular automata as models of complexity“, in *Nature* 311, S. 419–424, 1984
22 Sommerer, C., Mignonneau, L. und Lopez-Gulliver, R.: „LIFE SPACIES II: from text to form on the Internet using language as genetic code“, in *Proceedings ICAT'99 9th International Conference on Artificial Reality and Tele-Existence,* Virtual Reality Society, Tokyo 1999e, S. 215-220
23 Sommerer, C. und Mignonneau, L.: „Interacting with Artificial Life: A-Volve“, in *Complexity Journal,* Band 2, Nr. 6, S. 13–21, Wiley, New York 1997
24 Sommerer, C. und Mignonneau, L.: „The application of artificial life to interactive computer installations“, in *Artificial Life and Robotics Journal,* Band 2, Nr.4, S. 151-156, Springer Verlag, Tokyo 1998
25 Sommerer, C. und Mignonneau, L.: 2000 „Modeling Emergence of Complexity: the Application of Complex System and Origin of Life Theory to Interactive Art on the Internet“, in Bedau, M.A., McCaskill, J.S., Packard, N. H., und Rasmussen, St., (Hgs.): *Artificial Life VII,* MIT Press, Boston 2000, S. 547-554
26 Mignonneau, L., Sommerer, C., Lopez-Gulliver, R. und Jones, S.: „Riding the Net: a Novel, Intuitive and Entertaining Tool to Browse the Internet“, in *SCI 2001—5th World Multiconference on Systemics, Cybernetics and Informatics Conference Proceedings,* International Institute of Informatics and Systemics, Orlando, Florida 2001b, S. 57-63
27 R. Lopez-Gulliver, C. Sommerer, und Mignonneau L.: „Interfacing the Web: Multi-modal and Immersive Interaction with the Internet“, in *VSMM2002 Proceedings of the Eight International Conference on Virtual Systems and MultiMedia,* Gyeongju, Korea 2002, S. 753-764

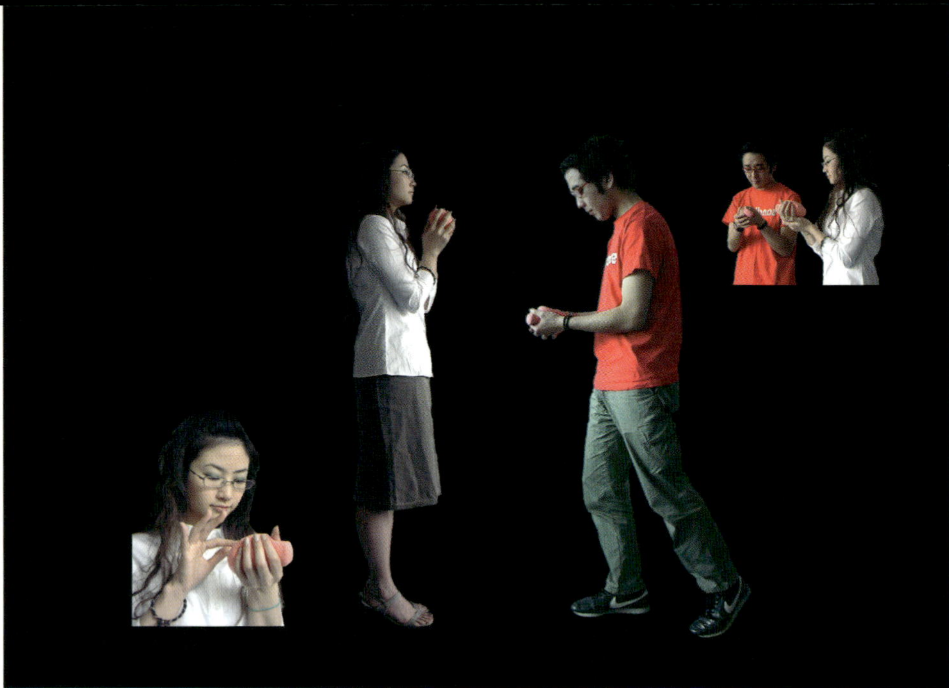

Mobile Feelings

Mobile telecommuniction set-up between Ars Electronica Linz and Palais de Tokyo, Paris

Christa Sommerer / Laurent Mignonneau

Background

Mobile phones have intruded into our daily lives like hardly any other technology since television and the desktop computer. While mobile phone users are generally glad to embrace the enormous advantages of being reachable anytime and anywhere, a reduced sense of privacy combined with the involuntary witnessing of anonymous people's private businesses has created a strange and sometimes awkward form of self-awareness and attention towards others. Mobile phones have transformed ordinary people into actors who narrate their most private details on the theatrical stages of train stations, restaurants, public spaces, streets, meeting areas, and any other social gathering places.

Concept

Mobile Feelings is an artistic project that explores the ambivalence of sharing personal information with an anonymous audience. Instead of communication via voice or images to people we know, *Mobile Feelings* lets people communicate with strangers through virtual touch and body sensations which include smell and sweat.
As opposed to application-based systems in the area of "affective computing"[1], "wearable computing"[2], "robotic user interfaces"[3] and tactile interfaces for handheld devices[4], *Mobile Feelings* aims to create the unusual and unsettling sensations of sharing private body sensations with complete strangers over a mobile phone network.

Description

The first project presentation is set up at linked locations, one at the Ars Electronica 2003 in Linz, Austria and the other at the Palais de Tokyo in Paris.
Users on these locations are provided with specially equipped *Mobile Feelings* phone devices that resemble organic or bodily shapes. These devices host miniature bio-sensors and actuators that capture the users' heartbeat, blood pressure and pulse, skin conductivity, sweat and smell. All data can be sent to anonymous users who can perceive and feel these most private sensations of others through actuators, vibrators, ventilators, micro-electromechanical and micro-bio-electrochemical systems which are embedded in each *Mobile Feelings* device.
All *Mobile Feelings* devices communicate with each other through a standard mobile phone network and *Mobile Feelings* users can move around freely and use their devices anywhere and anytime just like normal mobile phones.
Besides capturing and transmitting the various body data, the *Mobile Feelings* devices also display images of the other connected users. When a user in Linz for example touches her device and selects a remote user's from Paris, she can receive subtle body sensations, such as a tickle, a vibration, a push, a light touch, a breath of air and some humidity, which all feels like a "virtual embrace" from the user in Paris. And users in Linz or Paris can also choose to "feel" other users nearer their locations.

Mobile Art for Daily Life

Mobile Feelings works anywhere and anytime and the actual location of people (whether in Linz or Paris or anywhere else) becomes completely irrelevant.
Mobile Feelings art is no longer location—or context based but instead becomes integrated into people's daily lives.
Mobile Feelings is an artistic project that investigates how technology has transformed our social and individual lives[5] and how we have accepted a reduced sense of privacy in exchange for connectivity and mobility. The project also explores how the sense of "touch" still remains one of our most private sensations, which we often avoid sharing with strangers[6] and still lack a concise language to describe.[7] Finally, *Mobile Feelings* explores novel forms of mobile communications that might include smell and sweat as well as more private ways of "feeling and communicating with each other over a distance." In our aim to get media art off the walls and out into people's lives, *Mobile Feelings* presents another step towards the merging of art, life and society.

---

1 Picard, R. W. and Klein, J. "Computers that Recognise and Respond to User Emotion: Theoretical and Practical Implications," In: *Interacting with Computers.* 14, 2. 2002
2 Mann, S. "Wearable Computing: A First Step Toward Personal Imaging," In: *Computer.* Vol. 30, No. 2. February 1997
3 Sekiguchi, D., Inami, M., Kawakami, N., Maeda, T., Yanagida, Y. and Tachi S. "RobotPHONE: RUI for Interpersonal Communication," In: *Siggraph'01 Conference Abstracts and Applications, ACM Siggraph.* p134. 2001
4 Poupyrev, I., Maruyama, S. and Rekimoto, J. "Ambient Touch: Designing tactile interfaces for handheld devices," In: *UIST'2002. ACM.* pp 51–60. 2002
5 Plant, S. *On the Mobile: the Effects of Mobile Telephones on Social and Individual Life,* Study report for Motorola Inc. 2001
6 Stenslie, S. "Wiring the Flesh: Towards the Limits and Possibilities of the Virtual Body," In: *Ars Electronica '96. Memesis. The Future of Evolution.* Vienna/New York, Springer Verlag, Vienna/New York, 1996
7 Heller, M. A. and Schiff, W. (Eds.) *The Psychology of Touch.* Lawrence Erlbaum Associates, Hillsdale, NJ., 1991

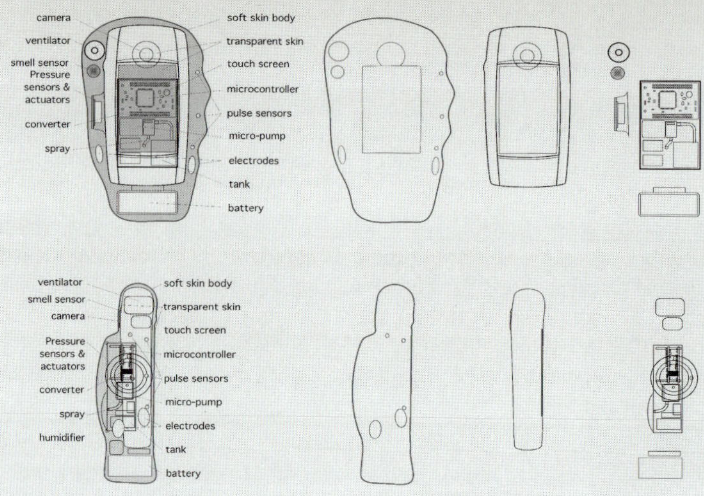

Mobile Feelings

Mobile Telekommunikationsverbindung zwischen der Ars Electronica Linz und dem Palais de Tokyo, Paris

Christa Sommerer / Laurent Mignonneau

Wie kaum eine andere Technologie seit Fernsehen und PC sind Mobiltelefone heute zu einem fixen Bestandteil unseres Alltagslebens geworden. Während Handybesitzer selbst in der Regel die ungeheuren Vorteile der ständigen Erreichbarkeit mit großer Begeisterung nutzen, führen der geringere Respekt für Privatsphäre und das unfreiwillige Mithören von Privatgesprächen völlig Fremder zunehmend dazu, dass wir uns auf seltsame und oft unangenehme Weise unser selbst und anderer bewusst werden. Mobiltelefone machen beliebige Individuen zu Akteuren, die auf Bahnhöfen, in Restaurants, auf öffentlichen Plätzen und Straßen, an Treffpunkten und anderen Orten der sozialen Begegnung wie auf einer Bühne oft sehr persönliche Details aus ihrem Leben preisgeben.
Das Projekt *Mobile Feelings* setzt sich mit der Frage auseinander, wie ambivalent es ist, ein unbekanntes Publikum an persönlichen Informationen teilhaben zu lassen. Anstatt mit Hilfe der Stimme oder über Bilder mit uns bekannten Personen zu kommunizieren, kommunizieren wir in *Mobile Feelings* über virtuelle Berührungen und Körperempfindungen wie Geruch und Schweiß mit völlig Fremden.
Im Gegensatz zu Systemen auf Applikationsbasis in den Bereichen Affective Computing[1], Arbeiten mit Wearable Computern[2], Mensch-Maschine-Schnittstellen[1] und taktilen Interfaces für mobile Computerprodukte[4] erlaubt *Mobile Feelings* den Benutzern, auf ungewöhnliche und beunruhigende Weise über ein Mobilfunknetz mit völlig Fremden persönliche Körperempfindungen auszutauschen.

Präsentation

Die erste Projektpräsentation läuft an zwei miteinander verkoppelten Orten, und zwar auf der Ars Electronica 2003 in Linz, Österreich, und im Palais de Tokyo in Paris.
An diesen Orten werden Benutzer mit speziell ausgestatteten *Mobile Feelings*-Telefonen ausge-

rüstet, die organischen Formen oder Körpern ähneln. Diese Geräte enthalten Mini-Biosensoren und Regler, die Herzschlag, Blutdruck und Puls, Leitfähigkeit der Haut, Schweiß und Geruch des Benutzers messen. All diese Daten können an anonyme Benutzer gesendet werden, die diese höchst intimen Empfindungen über Regler, Vibratoren, Ventilatoren, mikro-elektromechanische und mikro-bioelektrochemische Systeme, mit denen jedes *Mobile Feelings*-Gerät ausgestattet ist, fühlen und wahrnehmen können. Alle *Mobile Feelings*-Geräte kommunizieren über ein gewöhnliches Mobilfunknetz; die Benutzer können sich frei bewegen und ihre Geräte wie handelsübliche Mobiltelefone immer und überall einsetzen.

Die *Mobile Feelings*-Geräte sammeln und verschicken nicht nur unterschiedliche Körperdaten, sondern zeichnen auch ein Bild der anderen Benutzer im Netz. Wenn zum Beispiel eine Benutzerin in Linz ihr Gerät berührt und einen Benutzer in Paris auswählt, so empfängt sie feine Körperempfindungen wie ein Kitzeln, eine Vibration, einen Stoß, eine leichte Berührung, einen Lufthauch und etwas Umgebungsfeuchtigkeit, was sich zusammengenommen wie eine „virtuelle Umarmung" des Pariser Benutzers anfühlt. Benutzer in Linz oder Paris können aber auf Wunsch auch andere Benutzer „fühlen", die sich näher am eigenen Standort befinden.

Mobilkunst im täglichen Leben

Mobile Feelings funktioniert überall und jederzeit, und der tatsächliche Standort der Benutzer (sei es Linz oder Paris oder ein anderer Ort) wird gänzlich unbedeutend. Bei *Mobile Feelings* ist Kunst nicht länger an Standort oder Kontext gebunden, sondern wird zum integralen Bestandteil des täglichen Lebens.

Das Projekt *Mobile Feelings* untersucht, wie die Technologie unser sozialesLeben verändert hat[5] und wie wir für die Möglichkeit der Erreichbarkeit und der Mobilität eine eingeschränkte Privatsphäre in Kauf nehmen. Es beschäftigt sich auch damit, dass der Berührungssinn auch weiterhin eine unserer persönlichsten Empfindungen bleibt, die wir ungern mit Fremden teilen[6] und für deren genaue Beschreibung noch immer die nötigen sprachlichen Mittel fehlen.[7] Zuletzt erforscht *Mobile Feelings* neue Formen der Mobilkommunikation, wozu in Zukunft möglicherweise auch Geruch und Schweiß als intimere Medien des „Fühlens und Miteinander-aus-der-Entfernung-Kommunizierens" zählen könnten. In unserem Bestreben, die Medienkunst von den Wänden herunter und ins Leben der Menschen zu bringen, ist *Mobile Feelings* ein weiterer Schritt hin zur Verschmelzung von Kunst, Leben und Gesellschaft.

Aus dem Englischen von Elisabeth Wiellander

Mobile Feelings: IAMAS Institute of Advanced Media Arts and Sciences, Gifu Japan
in Zusammenarbeit mit France Telecom Studio Créatif, Paris

1 Picard, R. W. und Klein, J.: „Computers that Recognise and Respond to User Emotion: Theoretical and Practical Implications", in *Interacting with Computers,* 14, 2. 2002
2 Mann, S.: „Wearable Computing: A First Step Toward Personal Imaging", in *Computer,* Vol. 30, No. 2, February 1997
3 Sekiguchi, D., Inami, M., Kawakami, N., Maeda, T., Yanagida, Y. und Tachi S.: „RobotPHONE: RUI for Interpersonal Communication", in *Siggraph '01 Conference Abstracts and Applications,* S 134, A CM Siggraph, 2001.
4 Poupyrev, I., Maruyama, S. and Rekimoto, J.: „Ambient Touch: Designing tactile interfaces for handheld devices", in *UIST 2002,* S 51-60, ACM, 2002.
5 Plant, S.: *On the Mobile: the Effects of Mobile Telephones on Social and Individual Life,* Study report for Motorola Inc., 2001.
6 Stenslie, S.: „Wiring the Flesh: Towards the Limits and Possibilities of the Virtual Body", in *Ars Electronica '96. Memesis. The Future of Evolution,* Springer Verlag, Wien/New York 1996.
7 Heller, M. A. und Schiff, W. (Hsg.): *The Psychology of Touch,* Lawrence Erlbaum Associates, Hillsdale 1991.

A Few Quick Notes on Opportunities and Pitfalls of the Application of Computers in Art and Music

James McCartney

Bootstrap Loader

0. 1. A value signifying nothing. A value signifying something. From this pair of abstractions, representing the most fundamental of distinctions, all other abstractions in the digital world are constructed. Simple values such as numbers and letters can be encoded as strings of zeroes and ones. A concept can be represented by encoding its attributes, operations and relationships to other concepts. A network of concepts can be assembled to form a microcosm, an artificial world. The operations and relations that define these worlds can be set in motion.

Computers are the engines that drive these worlds. They are engines of abstraction, of symbols, of concepts, of ideas. In the last few years these engines have reached fantastic levels of performance and will continue to progress. As performance increases, things that were impossible become possible. I remember the moment when I first compiled one of my synthesis engines on a machine that was capable of computing sound faster than it could be played in real time. That was a turning point for me. When you can create sound in real time you can interact with it, and interaction makes possible things that never could have been achieved by typing in lists of commands.

Computer languages are the tools we use to encode the concepts. As computers get faster we are able to apply languages that present higher levels of abstraction to problems where performance had previously been a barrier. This allows more sophisticated worlds to be created with less effort. Different languages are based on different paradigms and lead to different types of approaches to solve a given problem. Those who use a particular computer language learn to think in that language and can see problems in terms of how a solution would look in that language.

Self and Society as Fitness Functions

The speed of computers and the expressivity of computer languages have enabled the exploration of the space of possible sounds, sound processes, musical processes, and compositional algorithms, all to an unprecedented depth and breadth. Early chance music by Cage and others were based on simple algorithms. Many of these early compositional algorithms require relatively few lines of code in today's languages.

When searching for a solution to a problem with a computer, a function is needed for determining whether the search is going in the right direction. This is the basis for genetic algorithms or the A search algorithm. At the very least a function is needed to determine whether a search has succeeded. For art, it is not possible to write such a function with a computer. Even humans cannot agree whether a work of art is successful, interesting, or relevant. Individuals and society provide the fitness functions for art. Society will determine whether some art is valuable, and that value may change over time as fashion and human circumstances change. And each person applies their own evaluation to art which may and often does differ from that of society. For these reasons fully autonomous composition programs cannot be successful with others or society until the time, if it ever comes, that computers can be said to be aware of the human relation to art and the social context of art.

Computer music presents the same problem as modern art does for an audience: how do you judge a work or appreciate it? It is often hard for an audience to know exactly what is going on in a computer music piece. Did the composer choose all of the events, and use the computer merely to render? Or was there a composition algorithm? Was it an interactive algorithm? A random algorithm? A deterministic one? How many decisions were the result of the program and how many were from the composer's intervention? Without program notes there may be no way to know since there may be no live process that the audience can see. Even when there are program notes, often a composer's clever algorithm is too subtle to be perceptible or is obscured by surface details. Does the audience need to be aware of the inner workings of a piece in order to appreciate it, or is the sensual perception of the final product enough? A composer may value her work based on its inner workings, but an audience may reject it based on the sensual aspect since there may be no other way they can understand it.

Meta-Compositions

Jean Tinguely's meta-matics were works of kinetic art that created works of art. Computer programs such as Harold Cohen's AARON or David Cope's EMI are works by artists that create art. AARON, EMI and meta-matics are works of meta-art. People who write composition algorithms in the MAX or SuperCollider languages are creating meta-art. A composition that is written as a program is no different than an aleatoric composition except that we are instructing a computer how to make choices instead of a performer. I wrote SuperCollider because I was interested in listening to music that was different each time it was played. I also wanted to be able to specify a class of compositions and then listen to instances of the class. Using a computer to generate variety can be a way to avoid becoming bored with one's own work. There is also an emotional freedom in not having one's ego invested in each decision point in a composition, while remaining responsible for the rules governing each decision.

Application of Immediate Results

Any time a new medium or new tool is introduced, different ways of grappling with the harnessing of possibilities must be explored. Often the first strategy is the application of immediate results, i.e. do the first and easiest thing you can do with this new medium, find the idioms natural to this medium. At first there is excitement about these idioms, but later these same idioms become clichés. This tendency can manifest in other ways such as factory presets of the latest synths appearing in multiple pop songs on the radio. Or, me going to a concert or having someone send me a CD of their work and hearing my own demo examples in the piece. Or, whole genres based on the use of the computer's ability to loop a section of audio or MIDI data. "Repetition is a form of change" as the Oblique Strategies card says. But change is often a better form of change, especially after a couple of decades of extremely repetitive electronic music. A few years ago at a music trade show it seemed like every manufacturer was advertising software and gadgets to do looping. I decided then that I didn't want to do any more loops. Better to struggle with change.

Exploitation of Limitations

Because the information that drives human perception can be encoded and manipulated, computers are a very good but not perfect plastic medium. Some artists try to exploit the limitations of the digital representation of sound: limitations in sample resolution, limitations in bandwidth, limitations of models, limitations of some software's built in algorithms to generate or process sound. The limitations of a medium as important for our culture as is the digital medium, are probably important for an artist to express. As important, I think, are the new possibilities that the digital medium presents. It is often easier to exploit the limitations than it is to successfully explore and discover new possibilities. A direction more interesting to me than exploiting the limitations of the digital medium is exploiting the limitations of human perception. How can ambiguities of sensory input be exploited? On how many levels can information be encoded and perceived? There is some intuitive understanding of human information acquisition that composers exploit when they write a piece. Attempts to apply information theory to music in a direct way result in dense music that cannot be acquired. Human perception saturates quickly at a single level, but can operate at multiple levels. Fractals present information at multiple levels, but simple fractal formulas present information that is too similar at multiple levels (either too regular or too random), so the result is just multiple levels of boredom rather than a single level of boredom.

Romance of the Naive

I sometimes hear an artist claim that they are using a tool in a way the designer never intended. I find this kind of comment more self congratulatory on that artist's part than anything else. They imagine that they are an artist and the designer is an engineer. But many engineers at synth and software companies are musicians too, and the best engineering is like art, so that conception is likely not a valid one. Designers of tools go to great lengths to make a tool as flexible as possible and often such a user doesn't realize even a fraction of that potential. So yes, perhaps they are using it in a way it was not intended to be used. But I doubt the designer would be impressed by that, having known before what the capabilities and limitations were, and I doubt much artistic value was attained that could not have been attained better had the user understood the tool better.

Terra Incognita

What I am interested in is, what is out there beyond the application of immediate results, the exploitation of limitations, the romanticization of naiveté? This might be labelled a modernist position, a position of someone who still believes in the inevitable progress in art in a forward direction, like Schoenberg did. But I don't agree. The result of the modern art revolution is that we are left with the option to use any means, without limitations, to solve an artistic problem (and the audience is free to like or dislike it). But still there is terra incognita. New tools are like new vehicles that allow us to get to that undiscovered terrain. And as someone interested in hearing new sounds, I want to go there.

Einige Gedanken zu den Möglichkeiten und Gefahren von Computern in der Kunst und der Musik

James McCartney

Bootstrap-Loader

0. 1. Ein Wert für Nichts. Ein Wert für Etwas. Von diesem Abstraktionspaar, das die grundlegendste aller Unterscheidungen versinnbildlicht, sind alle weiteren Abstraktionen in der digitalen Welt abgeleitet. Einfache Werte wie Zahlen oder Buchstaben können als Strings aus Nullen und Einsen codiert werden. Eine Idee kann durch die Codierung ihrer Attribute, Funktionen und Beziehungen zu anderen Ideen dargestellt werden. Untereinander vernetzte Ideen können zu einem Mikrokosmos, zu einer künstlichen Welt geformt werden. Die Funktionen und Beziehungen, die diese Welten definieren, können in Bewegung gesetzt werden.

Computer sind die treibende Kraft in diesen Mikrokosmen. Sie sind die Motoren der Abstraktion, der Symbole, der Gedanken und Ideen. Die Performance dieser Motoren ist in den letzten Jahren enorm gestiegen und wird noch weiter wachsen. Mit der Performancesteigerung wird bisher Unmögliches plötzlich möglich. Ich erinnere mich noch genau, als ich das erste Mal einen meiner Synthesizer auf einem Rechner kompilierte, der Töne schneller berechnen konnte, als sie in Echtzeit abspielbar waren. Das war für mich die Wende. Kann man Klänge in Echtzeit generieren, so kann man mit ihnen interagieren. Und Interaktion ermöglicht Phänomene, die man durch Eintippen von Befehlslisten niemals hätte erzielen können.

Programmiersprachen sind die Werkzeuge, die wir zum Codieren der Ideen einsetzen. Dank immer schnellerer Computer können wir Sprachen mit einem wesentlich höheren Abstraktionsgrad verwenden; dies war früher wegen der fehlenden Performance undenkbar. Somit lassen sich komplexere Welten mit immer weniger Aufwand kreieren. Unterschiedliche Sprachen setzen auf unterschiedliche Paradigmen und führen so zu unterschiedlichen Lösungsansätzen. Wer mit einer bestimmten Programmiersprache arbeitet, beginnt in dieser Sprache zu denken und sieht für Problemstellungen stets mögliche Lösungen in jener Sprache.

Das Selbst und die Gesellschaft als Fitness-Funktion

Die Schnelligkeit der Rechner und die Expressivität der Programmiersprachen erlauben es, die Sphären von möglichen Klängen, Klang- und Musikprozessen sowie kompositorischen Algorithmen in einer noch nie dagewesenen Tiefe und Breite auszuloten. Frühe Zufallsmusik von Cage und anderen baute auf einfachen Algorithmen auf, und viele dieser ersten Kompositionsalgorithmen benötigen in modernen Sprachen nur wenige Zeilen Code.

Sucht man mithilfe eines Computers eine Lösung für eine Aufgabe, so braucht man eine Funktion, um festzustellen, ob man den richtigen Weg eingeschlagen hat. Das ist die Grundlage für genetische Algorithmen oder den A-Suchalgorithmus. Man braucht aber zumindest eine Funktion, um festzustellen, ob die Suche Erfolg hatte. In der Kunst lässt sich keine derartige Funktion programmieren. Nicht einmal Menschen sind sich einig, ob ein Kunstwerk erfolgreich, interessant oder von einer gewissen Relevanz ist, weshalb jeder Einzelne und die Gesellschaft Fitness-Funktionen für Kunst einsetzen. Die Gesellschaft entscheidet über den Wert von Kunstwerken, der sich im Lauf der Zeit aufgrund von Modetrends oder der allgemeinen gesellschaftlichen Befindlichkeit ändern kann. Daher werden voll autonome Kompositionsprogramme so lange keinen Erfolg in der Gesellschaft haben, bis – falls überhaupt – sich Computer der menschlichen Beziehung zu Kunst und dem sozialen Kontext von Kunst bewusst werden.

Computermusik stellt das Publikum vor dasselbe Problem wie die moderne Kunst: Wie bewertet man ein Kunstwerk? Das Publikum kann oft gar nicht nachvollziehen, was in einem Computermusikstück gerade abläuft. Hat der Komponist alle Elemente selbst gewählt und verwendet er den Rechner nur zum Rendern? Oder ist ein Kompositionsalgorithmus mit im Spiel? Etwa ein interaktiver Algorithmus? Ein Zufallsalgorithmus? Ein deterministischer? Wie viele Entscheidungen hat das Programm getroffen und bei wie vielen hat der Komponist eingegriffen? Ohne Kommentare im Programm wird man vielleicht nie Antworten auf diese Fragen erhalten, da es möglicherweise keine Live-Prozesse gibt, die das Publikum sehen könnte. Selbst wenn Programmkommentare verfügbar sind, so ist der geniale Algorithmus des Komponisten vielleicht zu feinsinnig oder hinter oberflächlichen Details verborgen, als dass er wahrnehmbar wäre. Muss das Publikum die inneren Abläufe eines Kunstwerks kennen, um es wertschätzen zu können, oder reicht die sensorische Wahrnehmung des Endprodukts aus? Ein Komponist könnte seine Arbeit wegen der komplexen inneren Abläufe schätzen, doch beim Publikum findet es vielleicht wegen seines sensorischen Aspekts keine Zustimmung, da keine alternativen Verständnismöglichkeiten geboten werden.

Meta-Kompositionen

Jean Tinguelys *Méta-Matics* waren kinetische Skulpturen, die selbst Kunstwerke schufen. *AARON* von Harold Cohen oder *EMI* von David Cope sind von Künstlern geschriebene Programme, die Kunst produzieren. Wer Kompositionsalgorithmen in den Sprachen *MAX* oder *SuperCollider* schreibt, erzeugt Meta-Kunst. Der einzige Unterschied zwischen einer als Programm geschriebenen Komposition und einer aleatorischen besteht darin, dass wir anstelle eines Musikers einen Computer instruieren, welche Auswahlkriterien anzuwenden sind.

Ich habe *SuperCollider* entwickelt, weil ich an Musik interessiert bin, die bei jedem Abspielen anders wirkt. Ich wollte auch Kompositions-Klassen angeben und dann Beispiele dieser Klassen hören können. Computer zur Variantenerzeugung einzusetzen, ist eine Möglichkeit, die eigenen Werke nicht langweilig werden zu lassen. Dieses Verfahren bietet auch die emotionale Freiheit, nicht an jedem Entscheidungspunkt der Komposition sein Ego einbringen zu müssen, während man für die Regeln zur Entscheidungsfindung dennoch verantwortlich bleibt.

Das Erzielen schneller Ergebnisse

Wird ein neues Medium oder Werkzeug vorgestellt, müssen verschiedene Wege erkundet werden, wie man mit den gebotenen Möglichkeiten zu Rande kommt. Sehr oft wird dabei als erstes die Strategie des Erzielens schneller Ergebnisse verfolgt, d. h. man macht die einfachsten Dinge mit dem neuen Medium, sucht nach dem natürlichen Idiom des Mediums. Anfangs ist man sicher begeistert, doch dann werden diese Idiome zu Klischees. Diese Tendenz zeigt sich z. B. darin, dass in vielen Pop-Songs die neuesten Synthesizer immer nur mit den Werkseinstellungen verwendet werden. Oder wenn ich zu einem Konzert gehe oder mir jemand eine CD mit seinen Werken zuschickt, höre ich meine eigenen Demobeispiele. Oder ganze Stilrichtungen, die nur darauf aufbauen, dass ein Computer Loops aus Audio- oder MIDI-Daten bilden kann. „Wiederholung ist eine Art der Veränderung", wie die *Oblique Strategies*-Karte meint. Aber Veränderung ist oft die bessere Art der Veränderung, vor allem nach zwei Jahrzehnten extremer, repetitiver E-Musik. Auf einer Musikmesse pries jeder Hersteller vor einigen Jahren Software und Geräte für Loops an. Ich habe damals für mich entschieden, keine Loops mehr zu generieren. Ich kämpfe lieber mit der Veränderung.

Ausschöpfen der Grenzen

Einige Künstler versuchen die Grenzen digitaler Klangdarstellung auszuloten: Grenzen der Sample-Resolution, der Bandbreite, der Modelle oder der in Programmen enthaltenen Algorithmen zur Tonerzeugung oder -verarbeitung. Für einen Künstler mag es von Bedeutung sein, die Grenzen der für unsere Kultur so wichtigen digitalen Medien aufzuzeigen. Ich meine jedoch, dass die von den digitalen Medien gebotenen Möglichkeiten genauso bedeutend sind. Es ist oft einfacher, an die Grenzen zu gelangen, als die gebotenen Möglichkeiten zur Gänze auszuschöpfen.
Bedeutend interessanter ist es für mich, die Grenzen der menschlichen Wahrnehmung zu ergründen als die Einschränkungen der digitalen Medien. Wie kann man die Mehrdeutigkeit sensorischer Eindrücke nützen? Auf wie vielen Ebenen kann Information codiert und wahrgenommen werden? Komponisten nützen beim Schreiben eines Musikstücks ein intuitives Verständnis für den menschlichen Informationserwerb. Versuche, Informationstheorie Eins zu Eins in der Musik umzusetzen, resultieren in einem sehr dichten Musikstück, das nicht rezipiert werden kann. Die menschliche Wahrnehmung ist auf einer Ebene sehr rasch erschöpft, kann dafür jedoch auf mehreren Ebenen operieren. Fraktale stellen Informationen auf mehreren Ebenen dar; einfache Fraktalformeln bieten allerdings Informationen, die auf verschiedenen Ebenen zu ähnlich sind (entweder zu regelmäßig oder zu zufällig), so dass sie eher viele „Langeweile-Ebenen“ anstelle einer einzigen „Langeweile-Ebene“ ergeben.

Romantik des Naiven

Manchmal bin ich Zeuge, wenn ein Künstler sich brüstet, er verwende ein Tool in einer Weise, wie es nie vom Entwickler intendiert war. Ich halte das eher für Eigenlob als für einen rühmlichen Erfolg. Solche Menschen sehen sich als Künstler und den Entwickler als Techniker. Aber viele der Synthesizer- und Softwareentwickler sind auch Musiker, und hoch stehende Entwicklungen sind wie Kunst, weshalb dieses Konzept wohl kaum Gültigkeit hat. Sehr oft scheuen die Entwickler keine Mühen, um ein Tool so flexibel wie möglich zu gestalten, und solche User erkennen meist nicht einmal ansatzweise dieses Potenzial. Ja, vielleicht setzen sie das Tool auf eine Weise ein, für die es nicht konzipiert war. Aber ich bezweifle, dass der Entwickler davon beeindruckt wäre, kannte er doch die Möglichkeiten und Grenzen bereits vorher. Weiters bezweifle ich, dass dadurch etwas künstlerisch Großartiges geschaffen wurde, das der User nicht noch perfektionieren hätte können, hätte er das Tool besser beherrscht.

Terra Incognita

Mich interessiert vor allem, was es außer dem Erzielen immer schnellerer Ergebnisse, der Ausschöpfung aller Grenzen und der Romantisierung der Naivität noch geben könnte? Man könnte das als modernistische Haltung bezeichnen; die Haltung eines Menschen, der wie einst Schönberg noch immer an den unvermeidlichen Fortschritt in der Kunst glaubt. Dem stimme ich allerdings nicht zu. Das Resultat der modernen Kunstrevolution besteht darin, dass man jedes Mittel ohne jegliche Einschränkung zur Lösung eines künstlerischen Problems einsetzen kann (und das Publikum entscheidet über Ge- oder Missfallen). Es gibt jedoch noch unkartiertes Land. Neue Tools sind wie neue Vehikel, die uns ein Vordringen in dieses unerforschte Terrain ermöglichen. Und da ich gerne neue Klänge höre, möchte ich dieses Ziel erreichen.

Aus dem Amerikanischen von Michael Kaufmann

Design Noir
The Secret Life of Electronic Objects

Fiona Raby

Notopia

Beneath the glossy surface of official design lurks a dark and strange world driven by real human needs. A place where electronic objects co-star in a noir thriller, working with like-minded individuals to escape normalisation and ensure that even a totally manufactured environment has room for danger, adventure and transgression. We don't think that design can ever fully anticipate the richness of this unofficial world and neither should it. But it can draw inspiration from it and develop new design approaches and roles so that as our new environment evolves, there is still scope for rich and complex human pleasure.
Corporate futurologists force-feed us a "happy-ever-after" portrayal of life where technology is the solution to every problem. There is no room for doubt or complexity in their techno-utopian visions. Everyone is a stereotype, and social and cultural roles remain unchanged. Despite the fact that technology is evolving, the imagined products that feature in their fantasies reassure us that nothing essential will change, everything will stay the same. These future forecasters have a conservative role, predicting patterns of behaviour in relation to technological developments. They draw from what we already know about people, and weave new ideas into existing realities. The resulting scenarios extend pre-existent reality into the future and so reinforce the status quo rather than challenging it. Their slick surface distracts us from the dystopian vision of life they wish for. By designing the props for the videos produced to show us what the future could be like, design works to keep official values in place.
An occasional glance through almost any newspaper reveals a very different view of everyday life, where complex emotions, desires and needs are played out through the misuse and abuse of electronic products and systems. A mother shoots her son after an argument over which television channel to watch; a parent is outraged by a speaking doll made

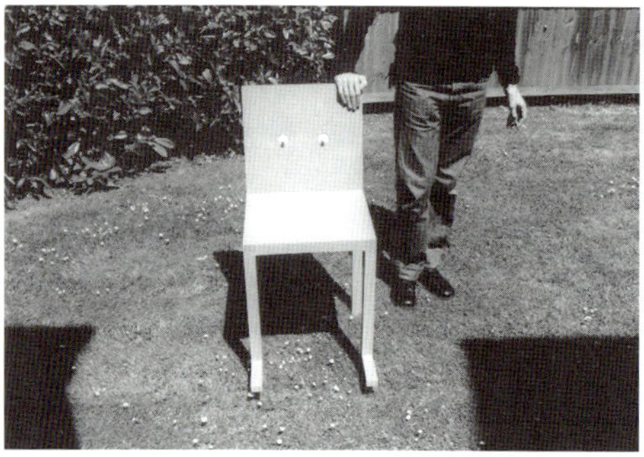

Nipple chair
Neil: When you come home at night, it speeds up and you think "Oh, it's pleased to see me." Poor deluded person that I am.

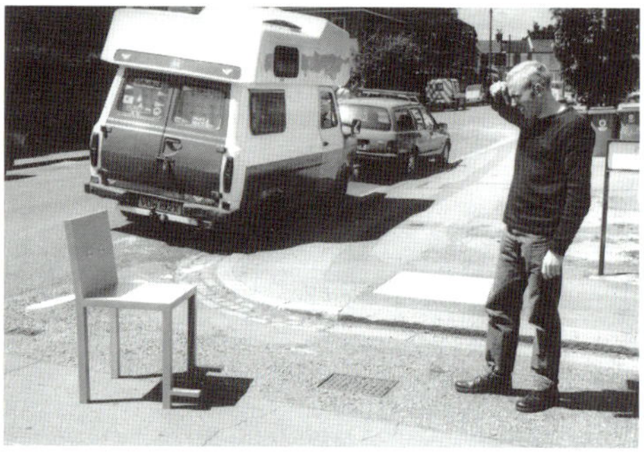

Nipple chair
Neil: When I'm not typing, I try and see if I can use my brain to change the rate it's vibrating at. Of course I can't, but I do try.

in China which sounds like it swears; the police set a trap for scanner snoopers—people who listen in to emergency radio frequencies illegally—by broadcasting a message that a UFO has landed in a local forest, within minutes several cars arrive and their scanners are confiscated. Many of these stories illustrate the narrative space entered by using and misusing a simple electronic product, how interaction with everyday electronic technologies can generate rich narratives that challenge the conformity of everyday life by short-circuiting our emotions and states of mind. They form part of a pathology of material culture that includes aberrations, transgressions and obsessions, the consequences of and motivations for the misuse of objects, and object malfunctions. They provide glimpses of another more complex reality hidden beneath the slick surface of electronic consumerism.

Amateur subversions and beta-testers

Some people already exploit the potentially subversive possibilities of this parallel world of illicit pleasures stolen from commodified experience. They seek out (ab)user-friendly products that lend themselves to imaginative possibilities for short-circuiting the combinatorial limits suggested by electronic products. This ranges from terrorists fashioning bombs and weapons out of mundane everyday objects, many of which are listed in the Anarchist Cookbook, to Otaku magazines showing Japanese gadget geeks how to modify standard electronic products to squeeze extra functionality out of them. There are no futurologists at work here. The main players in this world are beta-testers, tweaking and adjusting reality on a day-to-day basis. They are dissatisfied with the version of reality on offer, but rather than escaping or dropping out, they adjust it to suit themselves. They challenge the mechanisms that legitimise the conceptual models embodied in the design of the product or system and demonstrate behaviours towards technology that invite others to follow.

Beta-testers have learnt how to derive enjoyment from electronic materiality, from rejecting the material realities on offer and constructing their own. They display a level of pleasure in customisation currently limited to home DIY and custom car hobbyists. Many specialist magazines and books are already available that show readers how to modify or tweak everyday electronic products. An ever-growing number of home improvement magazines and TV programmes thrive on the pleasure people get from modifying their environments themselves—of customising reality.

Electronic product as neglected medium

The unique narrative potential of consumer electronic products has received surprisingly little attention from artists and designers. Even though industrial design plays a part in the design of extreme pain (e.g. weapons) and pleasure (e.g. sex aids), the range of emotions offered through most electronic products is pathetically narrow.

When the Sony Walkman was introduced in the early 1980s, it offered people a new kind of relationship to urban space. It allowed the wearers to create their own portable micro-environment, and it provided a soundtrack for travel through the city, encouraging different readings of familiar settings. It functioned as an urban interface. Nearly twenty years on, there are hundreds of variations on the original Walkman, but the relationship it created to the city remains the same. Product designers have accepted a role as a semiotician, a companion of packaging designers and marketeers, creating semiotic skins for incomprehensible technologies. The electronic product accordingly occupies a strange place in the world of material culture, closer to washing powder and cough mixture than furniture and architecture.

Product genres

This is just one approach to product design, one genre if you like, which offers a very limited experience. Like a Hollywood movie, the emphasis is on easy pleasure and conformist values. This genre reinforces the status quo rather than challenging it. We are surrounded by products that give us an illusion of choice and encourage passivity. But industrial design's position at the heart of consumer culture could be subverted for more socially beneficial ends by providing a unique aesthetic medium that engages the user's imagination in ways a film might, without being utopian or prescribing how things ought to be.

Electronic products and services could enrich and expand our experience of everyday life rather than closing it down; they could become a medium for experiencing complex aesthetic situations. To achieve this, designers would have to think about products and services very differently. There could be so many other genres of product beyond the bland Hollywood mainstream: arthouse, porn, romance, horror—noir, even—that exploit the unique and exciting functional and aesthetic potential of electronic technology. Although many products already fall into genres—Alessi products attempt design as comedy, designs for weapons and medical equipment can shock and horrify, sex-aids are obviously a form of design porn and white goods express a wholesome and romantic idea of settled domesticity—they do not aesthetically challenge or disturb.

Design Noir

If the current situation in product design is analogous to the Hollywood blockbuster, then an interesting place to explore in more detail might be its opposite: Design Noir. As a genre, it would focus on how the psychological dimensions of experiences offered through electronic products can be expanded. By referring to the world of product misuse and abuse, where desire overflows its material limits and subverts the function of everyday objects, this product genre would address the darker, conceptual models of need that are usually limited to cinema and literature.

Noir products would be conceptual products, a medium that fuses complex narratives with everyday life. This is very different from conceptual design, which uses design proposals as a medium for exploring what these products might be like. Conceptual design can exist comfortably in book or video form; it is about life, whereas conceptual products are part of life. With this form of design, the "product" would be a fusion of psychological and external "realities", the user would become a protagonist and co-producer of narrative experience rather than a passive consumer of a product's meaning. The mental interface between the individual and the product is where the "experience" lies. Electronic technology makes this meeting more fluid, more complex and more interesting.

Like in Film Noir, the emphasis would be on existentialism. Imagine objects that generate "existential moments"—a dilemma, for instance—which they would stage or dramatise. These objects would not help people to adapt to existing social, cultural and political values. Instead, the product would force a decision onto the user, revealing how limited choices are usually hard-wired into products for us. On another level, we could simply enjoy the wickedness of the values embedded in these products and services. Their very existence is enough to create pleasure.

The Truth Phone, a real product produced by the Counter Spy shop, is one example of how a Noir product might work. It combines a voice stress analyser with a telephone, and shows how electronic products have the potential to generate a chain of events which together form a story. If you consider products in this way, the focus of the design shifts from concerns of physical interaction (passive button pushing) to the potential psychological experiences inherent in the product. Imagine speaking to your mother or a lover while the Truth Phone suggests they are lying. The user becomes a protagonist and the designer becomes a co-author of the experience, the product creates dilemmas rather than resolving them. By using the phone, the owner explores boundaries between himself and the paranoid user suggested by the product, entering into a psychological adventure.

Design is ideological

Most designers, especially industrial designers, view design as somehow neutral, clean and pure. But all design is ideological, the design process is informed by values based on a specific world view, or way of seeing and understanding reality. Design can be described as falling into two very broad categories: affirmative design and critical design. The former reinforces how things are now, it conforms to cultural, social, technical and economic expectation. Most design falls into this category. The latter rejects how things are now as being the only possibility; it provides a critique of the prevailing situation through designs that embody alternative social, cultural, technical or economic values.

Critical design

Critical design, or design that asks carefully crafted questions and makes us think, is just as difficult and just as important as design that solves problems or finds answers. Being provocative and challenging might seem like an obvious role for art, but art is far too removed from the world of mass consumption and electronic consumer products to be effective in this context, even though it is of course part of consumerist culture. There is a place for a form of design that pushes the cultural and aesthetic potential and role of electronic products and services to its limits. Questions must be asked about what we actually need, about the way poetic moments can be intertwined with the everyday and not separated from it. At the moment, this type of design is neglected and regarded as secondary. Today, design's main purpose is still to provide new products—smaller, faster, different, better.

Critical design is related to haute couture, concept cars, design propaganda, and visions of the future, but its purpose is not to present the dreams of industry, attract new business, anticipate new trends or test the market. Its purpose is to stimulate discussion and debate amongst designers, industry and the public about the aesthetic quality of our electronically mediated existence. It differs too from experimental design, which seeks to extend the medium, extending it in the name of progress and aesthetic novelty. Critical design takes as its medium social, psychological, cultural, technical and economic values, in an effort to push the limits of lived experience, not the medium. This has always been the case in architecture, but design is struggling to reach this level of intellectual maturity.

(Un)Popular design

Developing a critical perspective in design is made difficult by the fact that the design profession, and product designers in particular, see the social value of their work as inextricably linked to the marketplace. Design outside this arena is viewed with suspicion as escapist or unreal. At the moment, the only alternatives to the Hollywood genre of corporate design are design consultancies promoting themselves to corporate clients with slick mocked-up products that are never intended to be developed any further. These objects are purely about PR, they are designed to sell the consultancy's potential for innovative and creative design thinking.

To be considered successful in the marketplace, design has to sell in large numbers, therefore it has to be popular. Critical design can never be truly popular, and that is its fundamental problem. Objects that are critical of industry's agenda are unlikely to be funded by industry. As a result, they will tend to remain one-offs. Maybe we need a new category to replace the avant-garde: (un)popular design.

Complicated pleasure

We believe that in order for conceptual design to be effective, it must provide pleasure, or more specifically, provide a type of experience that Martin Amis has called "complicated pleasure". One way this could happen in design is through the development of value fictions. If in science fiction, the technology is often futuristic while social values are conservative, the opposite is true in value fictions. In these scenarios, the technologies are realistic but the social and cultural values are often fictional, or at least highly ambiguous. The aim is to encourage the viewers to ask themselves why the values embodied in the proposal seem "fictional" or "unreal," and to question the social and cultural mechanisms that define what is real or fictional. The idea is not to be negative, but to stimulate discussion and debate amongst designers, industry and the public about electronic technology and everyday life. This is done by developing alternative and often gently provocative artefacts which set out to engage people through humour, insight, surprise and wonder.

The suspension of disbelief is crucial—if the artefacts are too strange they are dismissed, they have to be grounded in how people really do behave. The approach is based on viewing values as raw material and shaping them into objects. Materialising unusual values in products is one way that design can be a very powerful form of social critique. The design proposals portrayed in value fictions derive their interest from their potential functionality and use. One of the main challenges of using value fictions is how they are communicated: we need to see them in use, placed in everyday life, but in a way that leaves room for the viewer's imagination. We don't actually have to use the proposed products ourselves, it is by imagining them being used that they have an effect on us. Value fictions cannot be too clear or they blend into what we already know. A slight strangeness is the key—too weird and they are instantly dismissed, not strange enough and they're absorbed into everyday reality.

Is this a role for "academic" designers? Rather than writing papers and seeking conventional academic approval, they could exploit their privileged position to explore a subversive role for design as social critique. Free from commercial restrictions and based in an educational environment, they could develop provocative design proposals to challenge the simplistic Hollywood vision of the consumer electronics industry. Design proposals could be used as a medium to stimulate debate and discussion amongst the public, designers, and industry. The challenge is to blur the boundaries between the real and the fictional, so that the conceptual becomes more real and the real is seen as just one limited possibility among many.

From: Anthony Dunne and Fiona Raby
Design Noir. The Secret Life of Electronic Objects, Birkhäuser 2001

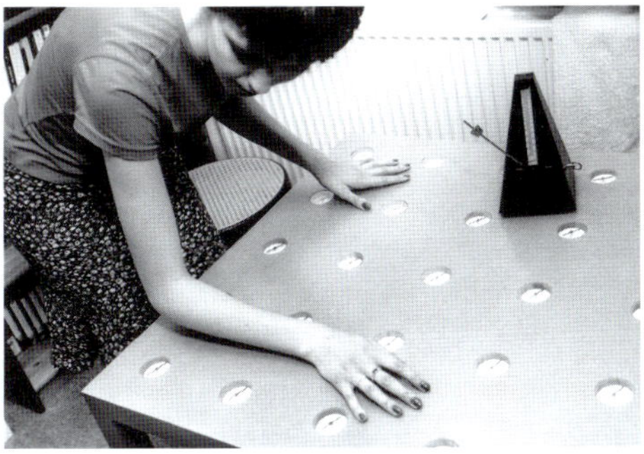

© Jason Evans

Compass table (Kompass-Tisch)
Arabella: „Ich glaube, es wäre ziemlich langweilig, wenn es nur rein funktionale Möbel gäbe."

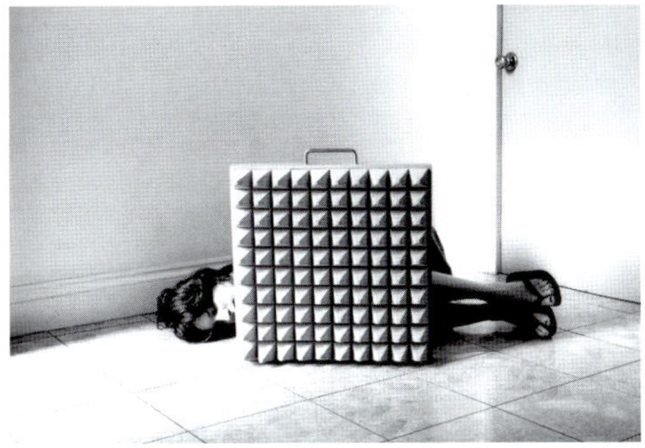

Electro-draught excluder (Strahlenwindabweiser)
Lauren: „Ich glaube, nach einer Weile hatte ich es satt, das Gerät zu verwenden."

Design Noir
Das geheime Leben elektronischer Objekte

Fiona Raby

Notopia

Unter der glänzenden Oberfläche des offiziellen Designs lauert eine dunkle und eigenartige Welt, die von wirklichen menschlichen Bedürfnissen gesteuert wird. Eine Welt, in der elektronische Objekte eine Hauptrolle in einem Film-Noir-Thriller spielen und von einer Gruppe Gleichgesinnter benützt werden, die der Normung entkommen und gewährleisten wollen, dass selbst eine durch und durch industrialisierte Umwelt Raum für Gefahr, Abenteuer und Überschreitung bietet. Wir glauben nicht, dass Design je die Vielfalt dieser inoffiziellen Welt vorwegnehmen kann oder sollte. Aber es kann sich davon inspirieren lassen und neue Ansätze und Rollen entwickeln, damit im Zuge der Erneuerung der Umwelt zugleich auch Raum für intensive und vielschichtige Freude geschaffen wird.
Der Berufsstand der Zukunftsforscher mästet uns permanent mit dem Bild eines „endlos glücklichen" Lebens, in dem die Technologie die Lösung jedes Problems darstellt. Ihre techno-utopischen Visionen lassen keinen Raum für Zweifel oder Komplexität. Jeder verhält sich stereotyp und die sozialen und kulturellen Rollen bleiben unverändert. Trotz der Tatsache, dass sich die Technologie entwickelt, wollen uns die imaginären Produkte ihrer Fantasie vorgaukeln, dass sich nichts Wesentliches ändern wird und alles beim Alten bleibt. Diese Zukunftsforscher haben eine konservative Funktion, sie prognostizieren Verhaltensmuster unter Bezugnahme auf technologische Entwicklungen. Sie berufen sich auf das, was wir bereits über Menschen wissen, und flechten neue Ideen in vorhandene Realitäten ein. Die Szenarien, die sich daraus ergeben, extrapolieren die vorgegebene Realität in die Zukunft und konsolidieren auf diese Weise den Status quo, anstatt ihn zu hinterfragen. Ihre glatte Oberfläche lenkt uns von der dystopischen Vision des Lebens ab, das sie sich erhoffen. Indem sie die Requisiten für die Videos entwerfen, die uns zeigen sollen, wie die Zukunft aussehen könnte, fungiert das Design als Bewahrer offizieller Werte.
Ein Blick in diverse Zeitungen zeigt sehr unterschiedliche Bilder des Alltags, in denen komplexe

Emotionen, Sehnsüchte und Bedürfnisse über den Missbrauch elektronischer Produkte und Systeme ausgetragen werden. Eine Mutter erschießt ihren Sohn nach einem Streit über die Wahl des Fernsehkanals; jemand empört sich über eine sprechende Puppe *made in China,* die so klingt, als ob sie fluchen würde; die Polizei stellt Menschen, die illegal Notruffrequenzen abhören, eine Falle, indem sie eine Meldung durchgibt, dass ein UFO in einem Wald gelandet ist. Innerhalb weniger Minuten treffen mehrere Autos an besagtem Ort ein, und ihre Scanner werden konfisziert. Viele dieser Geschichten illustrieren den narrativen Raum, der sich eröffnet, wenn man ein einfaches elektronisches Produkt ge- oder missbraucht, und zeigen, wie die Interaktion mit den elektronischen Alltagsgeräten dichte Erzählungen generieren kann, die die Konformität des Alltags hinterfragen, indem sie unsere Emotionen und unsere Geisteshaltung kurzschlussartig unterbrechen. Sie sind Teil einer Pathologie der Materialkultur, die Anomalien, Überschreitungen und Obsessionen impliziert, die Konsequenzen von und Motivationen für den Missbrauch von Gegenständen und ihren Fehlfunktionen. Sie geben Einblick in eine andere, komplexere Realität, die sich unter der glatten Oberfläche des Konsumverhaltens am elektronischen Markt verbirgt.

Amateurhafte Umstürze und Beta-Tester

Manche Menschen nutzen die potenziell subversiven Möglichkeiten dieser Parallelwelt verbotener Freuden, die sie der zur Ware gewordenen Erfahrung entreißen, bereits aus. Sie suchen nach missbraucher-/verbraucherfreundlichen Produkten, die sich dafür eignen, die kombinatorischen Grenzen, welche die elektronischen Produkte vorgeben, auf erfinderische Weise kurzzuschließen. Das Spektrum reicht von Terroristen, die Bomben und Waffen aus Alltagsobjekten basteln – viele davon sind im *Anarchistischen Kochbuch* aufgelistet –, bis hin zu Otaku-Magazinen, die japanischen Gadget-Freaks zeigen, wie elektronische Standardprodukte modifiziert werden können, um ihnen eine zusätzliche Funktion zu entlocken. Da sind keine Zukunftsforscher am Werk. Die Protagonisten in dieser Welt sind Beta-Tester, die die Realität justieren und an tägliche Bedürfnisse anpassen. Sie sind unzufrieden mit der ihnen gebotenen Version der Realität, doch anstatt ihr zu entfliehen oder auszusteigen, passen sie diese ihren Bedürfnisse an. Sie hinterfragen die Mechanismen, die die konzeptuellen Modelle legitimieren, welche im Produkt- oder Systemdesign verkörpert sind, und haben eine Einstellung zur Technologie, die zur Nachahmung einlädt.
Beta-Tester haben gelernt, wie der Elektronik Vergnügen abzugewinnen ist, indem sie die angebotenen materiellen Realitäten verwerfen und eigene konstruieren. Sie zeigen eine Freude an kundenspezifischer Anpassung, die derzeit auf Heimwerker und Autobastler beschränkt ist. Es gibt bereits zahlreiche Fachzeitschriften und Bücher, die den Lesern zeigen, wie elektronische Produkte des Alltags modifiziert oder justiert werden können. Eine wachsende Anzahl an Magazinen für ein schöneres Zuhause und TV-Programmen profitiert von der Freude, die Menschen daran haben, ihre Umgebung selbst zu gestalten – die Realität an ihre Bedürfnisse anzupassen.

Das elektronische Produkt als vernachlässigtes Medium

Dem einzigartigen narrativen Potenzial der elektronischen Konsumgüter wurde seitens der Künstler und Designer überraschend wenig Aufmerksamkeit zuteil. Obwohl das Industrial Design im Design von extremem Schmerz (z. B. Waffen) und extremer Freude (z. B. Sex-Spielzeug) eine nicht unwichtige Rolle spielt, ist das Spektrum der Emotionen, das durch die meisten elektronischen Produkte angeboten wird, erschütternd klein.
Als der Sony-Walkman Anfang der 80er Jahre auf den Markt kam, erschloss er den Menschen eine neue Beziehung zum urbanen Raum. Er ermöglichte dem Besitzer, sich eine eigene trag-

bare Mikro-Umgebung zu schaffen und lieferte den Soundtrack für die Reise durch die Stadt, wobei er zu unterschiedlichen Interpretationen vertrauter Umgebungen einlud. Er fungierte als urbanes Interface. Heute, fast zwanzig Jahre später, gibt es Hunderte von Variationen des ursprünglichen Walkman, aber die Beziehung, die er zur Stadt herstellt, bleibt dieselbe. Produktdesigner haben ihre Rolle als Semiotiker akzeptiert, als Kollegen der Designer und Händler, die eine semiotische Hülle für unverständliche Technologien kreieren. Das elektronische Produkt hat demzufolge eine seltsame Stellung in der Welt der materiellen Kultur, es ist eher mit Waschpulver und Hustensaft verwandt als mit Ausstattung oder Architektur.

Produktgenres

Dies ist nur eine Annäherung an das Produktdesign, ein Genre, wenn man so will, das eine sehr begrenzte Erfahrung bietet. Wie in einem Hollywood-Film liegt die Betonung auf schnellem Genuss und konformistischen Werten. Dieses Genre bekräftigt den Status quo, statt ihn zu hinterfragen. Wir sind von Produkten umgeben, die uns lediglich die Illusion einer Wahlmöglichkeit vermitteln, eigentlich aber die Passivität fördern. Doch die Stellung des Industrial Design im Zentrum der Konsumkultur könnte zum Wohle der Gesellschaft eingesetzt werden, da es ein einzigartiges ästhetisches Medium darstellt, das die Fantasie des Benutzers wie ein Film fesselt, ohne dabei utopisch zu sein oder vorzuschreiben, wie die Dinge sein sollten. Elektronische Produkte und Dienste könnten unsere Alltagserfahrung bereichern und erweitern, statt sie zu beschränken. Sie könnten ein Medium zur Erfahrung komplexer ästhetischer Situationen werden. Doch um dahin zu gelangen, müssten Designer über Produkte und Dienstleistungen ganz anders nachdenken. Es könnte neben dem verbindlichen Hollywood-Mainstream – Arthouse, Porno, Romantik, Horror, sogar Noir-Thriller, – so viele andere Produktgenres geben, die das einzigartige und aufregende funktionale und ästhetische Potenzial elektronischer Technologie nutzen. Wobei anzumerken ist, dass viele Produkte bereits in Genres eingeteilt werden: Alessi-Produkte inszenieren Design als Komödie, das Design für Waffen und medizinische Geräte kann schockieren und ängstigen, Sex-Spielzeug ist offenkundig eine Art Design-Porno, und Elektrohaushaltsgeräte vermitteln ein angenehmes und romantisches Konzept von situierter Häuslichkeit – sie sind keine ästhetische Herausforderung oder Störung.

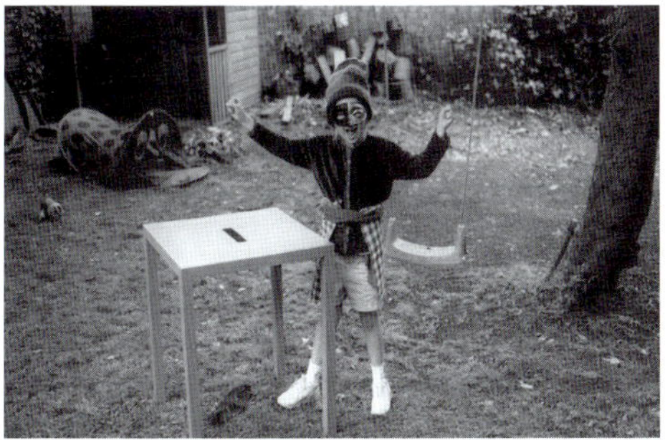

© Jason Evans

GPS table (GPS-Tisch)
Lorna: „Ist schon komisch, weil wir unseren Möbeln im Allgemeinen keine menschlichen Gefühle zusprechen."
Dick: „Als du gekommen bist und ihn installiert und angeschlossen hast, und er dann ‚verloren' meldete, war ich völlig schockiert.
Ich weiß nicht genau, warum ich schockiert war. Ich dachte mir: „Verdammt, das arme Ding ist verloren."

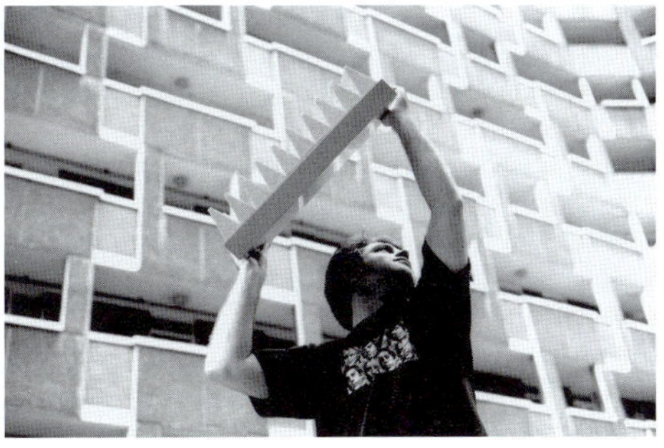

Electro-draught excluder (Strahlenwindabweiser)
Jan: „Alles was recht ist – jeder, der das Ding regelmäßig zu seinem Schutz benützt, entwickelt bedenkliche Gewohnheiten. Man kann nicht mit dem Schild herumspazieren, um sich vor Strahlung zu schützen. Was ist draußen auf der Straße, wo es Unmengen von Strahlung gibt? Gehst du durch die Straße und streckst es jeder Antenne oder was auch sonst immer entgegen, um dich zu schützen?"

Design Noir

Entspricht die gegenwärtige Situation im Produktdesign dem Hollywood-Blockbuster, dann bietet sich als Gegenmodell für eine detaillierte Untersuchung das Design Noir an. Im Zentrum dieses Genres stünde die Frage, wie die psychologischen Dimensionen von Erfahrungen, die durch elektronische Produkte geboten werden, erweitert werden könnten. Mit Bezugnahme auf die Welt des Produktmissbrauchs und der Zweckentfremdung, in der das Begehren sich über materielle Grenzen hinwegsetzt und die Funktion von Alltagsobjekten umkehrt, würde dieses Produktgenre die dunkleren konzeptuellen Modelle von Bedürfnissen ansprechen, die im Allgemeinen auf das Kino und die Literatur beschränkt sind.

Produkte des Design Noir wären konzeptuelle Produkte, ein Medium, das komplexe Erzählstränge mit dem Alltagsleben verknüpft. Darin unterscheidet es sich vom konzeptuellen Design, das Design-Vorschläge als Medium zur Erforschung des Inhalts dieser Produkte benutzt. Konzeptuelles Design kann bequem im Buch- oder Videoformat vertrieben werden, es handelt vom Leben, während konzeptuelle Produkte Teil des Lebens sind. Mit dieser Art von Design wäre das „Produkt“ eine Verschmelzung der psychologischen und äußerlichen „Realitäten“, der Benutzer würde zum Protagonisten und Co-Produzenten einer narrativen Erfahrung, anstatt passiver Konsument der Bedeutung eines Produkts. Das mentale Interface zwischen dem Individuum und dem Produkt ist dort, wo „Erfahrung“ stattfindet. Elektronische Technologie gestaltet diese Begegnung effizienter, komplexer und interessanter.

Wie im Film Noir würde der Existentialismus eine zentrale Rolle spielen. Man stelle sich Objekte vor, die „existenzielle Momente“ – etwa einen Konflikt – inszenieren oder dramatisieren. Diese Objekte würden den Menschen nicht helfen, sich an die herrschenden sozialen, kulturellen und politischen Werte anzupassen. Das Produkt würde dem Benutzer vielmehr eine Entscheidung abverlangen und aufdecken, wie begrenzte Möglichkeiten gewöhnlich in Produkte einprogrammiert sind. Auf einer anderen Ebene könnten wir schlicht und einfach die Boshaftigkeit der in diesen Produkten und Dienstleistungen integrierten Werte genießen. Ihre Existenz allein bereitet Freude.

Das Truth Phone, ein tatsächlich existierendes Produkt, das der Counter-Spy-Laden produzierte, ist ein Beispiel für die Funktionsweise eines Produit Noir. Es kombiniert einen Stimmenstressanalysator mit einem Telefon und zeigt, dass elektronische Produkte das Potenzial haben, eine Kette von Ereignissen auszulösen, die sich zu einer Geschichte verdichten. Bei einer solchen Produktauffassung verlagert sich der Schwerpunkt des Designs von den Interessen an physikalischer Interaktion (passivem Knopfdrücken) auf potenzielle psychologische Erfahrungen, die dem Produkt inhärent sind. Man stelle sich vor, mit der Mutter oder dem Geliebten zu sprechen, und das Truth Phone zeigt an, dass gelogen wird. Der Benutzer wird zum Protagonisten und der Designer zum Co-Autor der Erfahrung, das Produkt erzeugt Konflikte, statt sie zu lösen. Durch Verwendung des Telefons erforscht der Besitzer die Grenzen zwischen sich und dem paranoiden Benutzer, für den das Gerät gedacht ist, und er lässt sich auf ein psychologisches Abenteuer ein.

Design ist ideologisch

Für die meisten Designer, vor allem Industrial Designer, ist Design in gewisser Weise neutral, sauber und rein. Aber jedes Design ist ideologisch, der Designprozess wird von Werten getragen, die auf einer bestimmten Weltsicht, einem Verständnis von Realität basieren. Design lässt sich in zwei sehr breit gefasste Kategorien einteilen: affirmatives Design und kritisches Design. Ersteres konsolidiert den Ist-Zustand der Dinge, bestätigt kulturelle, soziale, technische und ökonomische Erwartungen. Der Großteil des Designs ist dieser Kategorie zuzurechen. Letztes lehnt den Ist-Zustand als einzige Möglichkeit ab, es bekundet Kritik an der vorherrschenden Situation durch ein Design, das alternative soziale, kulturelle, technische und ökonomische Werte verkörpert.

Kritisches Design

Kritisches Design oder Design, das sorgsam ausformulierte Fragen stellt und uns zum Denken anregt, ist ebenso schwierig und wichtig wie Design, das Probleme zu lösen oder Antworten zu finden vermag. Provokant zu sein und die Dinge zu hinterfragen, scheint eine prädestinierte Rolle für die Kunst, doch hat sich diese zu weit von der Welt des Massenkonsums und der elektronischen Konsumprodukte entfernt, als dass sie in diesem Kontext wirksam sein könnte, auch wenn sie natürlich Teil der Konsumkultur ist. Es gibt Raum für eine Form des Designs, die das kulturelle und ästhetische Potenzial und die Rolle elektronischer Produkte und Dienste an ihre Grenzen bringt. Wir müssen uns die Frage stellen, was wir wirklich brauchen, wie poetische Augenblicke nicht vom Alltag abgekoppelt, sondern in diesen integriert werden können. Derzeit wird diese Art von Design vernachlässigt und als zweitrangig betrachtet. Heute ist es der Hauptzweck von Design, neue Produkte zu liefern – kleiner, schneller, anders, besser lautet die Devise.
Kritisches Design wird mit Haute Couture, Konzeptautos, Design-Propaganda und Zukunftsvisionen in Beziehung gesetzt, sein Zweck besteht aber nicht darin, die Träume der Industrie zu zeigen, neue Geschäftsfelder zu erschließen, Trends vorwegzunehmen oder den Markt zu testen. Sein Ziel ist vielmehr, zu Diskussionen und Auseinandersetzungen zwischen Designern, Industrie und Öffentlichkeit über die ästhetische Qualität unserer elektronisch vermittelten Existenz anzuregen. Es unterscheidet sich auch von experimentellem Design, das eine Erweiterung des Mediums im Namen von Fortschritt und ästhetischer Neuheit sucht. Das Medium für kritisches Design sind soziale, psychologische, kulturelle, technische und ökonomische Werte; es versucht, die Grenzen gelebter Erfahrung, nicht jene des Mediums zu erweitern. Dies ist seit jeher eine Prämisse für die Architektur, während das Design noch um diese geistige Reife kämpft.

(Un)Populäres Design

Die Entwicklung einer kritischen Perspektive wird im Bereich des Designs durch die Tatsache erschwert, dass die Designer und insbesondere die Produktdesigner den sozialen Wert ihrer Arbeit als untrennbar mit dem Markt verbunden sehen. Design, das sich außerhalb dieser Arena bewegt, wird argwöhnisch als eskapistisch oder unrealistisch betrachtet. Derzeit sind die einzigen Alternativen zum Hollywood-Genre des Corporate Design eigene Design-Beratungsunternehmen, die sich den Kunden mit glatten Vorzeigeprodukten präsentieren, deren Weiterentwicklung nicht geplant ist. Diese Objekte werden nur von Public Relation bestimmt, sie werden entworfen, um das innovative und kreative Design-Potenzial des Beratungsunternehmens zu vermarkten. Um als erfolgreich am Markt zu gelten, muss Design sich in großer Stückzahl verkaufen, es muss populär sein. Kritisches Design kann nie wirklich populär sein, das ist sein fundamentales Problem. Gegenstände, die gegenüber der Agenda der Industrie eine kritische Haltung einnehmen, werden von dieser meist nicht finanziert. Die Folge ist, dass sie eine Einzelerscheinung bleiben. Vielleicht brauchen wir eine neue Kategorie, die die Avantgarde ersetzt: (un)populäres Design.

Komplizierte Freude

Wir glauben, dass effizientes konzeptuelles Design Freude bereiten oder, um genauer zu sein, eine Art der Erfahrung vermitteln muss, die Martin Amis „komplizierte Freude“ nannte. Dies könnte einerseits über die Entwicklung von Werte-Fiktionen geschehen. Während in der Science Fiction die Technologie oft futuristisch, soziale Werte hingegen konservativ dargestellt werden, gilt das Gegenteil für Werte-Fiktionen. In diesen Szenarien sind die Technologien realistisch, während die sozialen und kulturellen Werte oft fiktional oder zumindest höchst verschwommen sind. Das Ziel ist es, die Betrachter zu ermutigen, sich zu fragen, warum die in dem Vorschlag verkörperten Werte „fiktional" oder „irreal" erscheinen, und die sozialen und kulturellen Mechanismen zu hinterfragen, die definieren, was real oder fiktional ist. Es geht nicht um Negation, sondern darum, eine Diskussion und Auseinandersetzung unter Designern, Industrie und der Öffentlichkeit über elektronische Technologie und Alltagsleben anzuregen. Dies geschieht durch die Entwicklung alternativer und oft etwas provokanter Artefakte, die die Menschen durch Humor, Einsicht, Überraschungseffekte und Staunen für sich einnehmen. Die Ausschaltung der Unglaubwürdigkeit ist ein wesentlicher Moment – wenn Artefakte zu fremd sind, werden sie abgelehnt, sie müssen im tatsächlichen Verhalten der Menschen verankert sein. Diesem Ansatz zufolge sind Werte das Rohmaterial, das dann zu Gegenständen geformt wird. Die Materialisierung ungewöhnlicher Werte zu Produkten ist eine Möglichkeit, dass Design zu einer starken Form sozialer Kritik wird. Die Design-Vorschläge, die in Werte-Fiktionen porträtiert werden, sind durch ihre potenzielle Funktionalität und Verwendung interessant. Eine der größten Herausforderungen der Verwendung von Werte-Fiktionen ist die Art und Weise ihrer Kommunikation: Wir müssen sie in Verwendung sehen, im Alltagsleben, aber auf eine Weise, die der Fantasie des Betrachters Raum lässt. Wir müssen die vorgeschlagenen Produkte nicht wirklich selbst benützen, allein durch die Vorstellung, dass sie verwendet werden, wirken sie auf uns ein. Werte-Fiktionen dürfen nicht zu konkret sein, sonst vermischen sie sich mit bereits Bekanntem. Eine leichte Fremdheit ist der Schlüssel zum Erfolg – sind sie zu fremd, werden sie abgelehnt, sind sie nicht fremd genug, werden sie von der Realität des Alltags absorbiert. Wäre dies nicht eine Rolle für „akademische Designer"? Anstatt Artikel zu schreiben und konventionelle akademische Bestätigung zu suchen, könnten sie ihre privilegierte Position dazu nutzen, die subversive Rolle von Design als Sozialkritik zu erforschen. Frei von kommerziellen Beschränkungen und in einem Bildungsumfeld verankert, könnten sie provokante Designvorschläge entwickeln, um die vereinfachende Hollywood-Vision der Elektronikkonsumwelt in Frage zu stellen. Design-Vorschläge könnten als Medium verwendet werden, um die Diskussion zwischen der Öffentlichkeit, den Designern und der Industrie anzuregen. Die Herausforderung besteht darin, dass die Grenzen zwischen dem Realen und dem Fiktionalen verschwimmen, sodass das Konzeptuelle realer wird und das Reale nur als eine begrenzte Möglichkeit von vielen betrachtet wird.

Aus dem Englischen von Martina Bauer

Aus: Anthony Dunne and Fiona Raby:
Design Noir. The Secret Life of Electronic Objects, Birkhäuser 2001

Printing Out Buildings
Code—Printer—Buildings

Oliver Fritz

Since the beginning of the 20th century, architects have been experimenting with industrial methods of construction to build residential housing. Experimental projects like Gropius' Dessau-Törten as well as constructive experiments by Wachsmann and Prouvé provided the basic insights that led to prefabrication as practiced in the construction industry today. The various design and production methods that have resulted from this effort encompass a broad spectrum ranging from prefab homes—uniform and ready for occupancy—to highly developed modular construction systems, all the way to façade elements that are prefabricated in the workshop and installed in a large-scale application process on site. These systems assume fundamentally different forms but display a number of shared characteristics and objectives: shorter time spent on the building site, higher degree of precision, increased security, and reduced costs of planning and construction. Conventional prefabricated housing construction is extremely limited and practically no customizing by either the client or the architect is possible, while modular construction systems are distinguished by their regularities and uniform patterns. Building elements individually prefabricated in the workshop are generally not restricted to a predetermined form or mode of installation.

On the other hand, construction costs are usually proportional to the flexibility of the construction method. As a rule, traditional and less flexible planning and construction methods are more economical. A real challenge for the future of industrial construction is to enable builders to react to clients' individual wishes and needs. In the industry, there is an increasingly widespread orientation on individually customized mass-produced structures. In the past, this was practiced only in cases of cost-intensive products (like those of the auto industry) available with limited configuration options; now, there are firms that are customizing small, lower-priced products. This tendency is being made possible, above all, by new types of information technology, new forms of communication (like the Internet), as well as modern, individualized fabrication techniques.

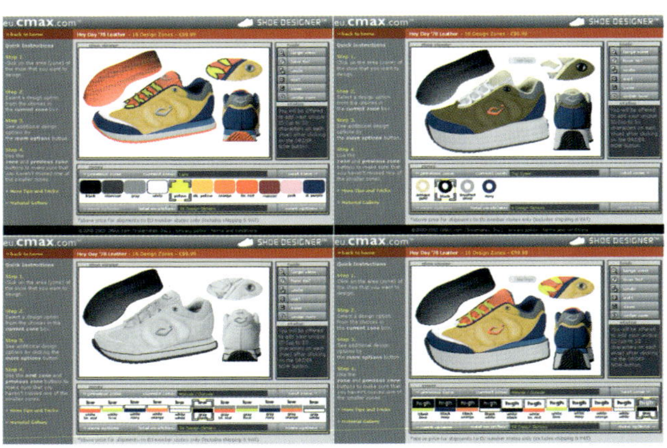

http://eu.cmax.com/
Customized Footwear

For the last two years or so, the Department of Computer Aided Architectural Design (CAAD) at the Swiss Federal Institute of Technology in Zurich (ETHZ) under the direction of Prof. Ludger Hovestadt has been conducting research on the integration of state-of-the-art information technologies into architectural production and design processes. The aim of this research is neither the formal development of a new type of architecture nor the definition of stylistic or formal characteristics; rather, the point here is the structural development of buildings in a way that proceeds from their essential "core" and the formulation of this process in a unified code that no longer provides an exact rendering describing a piece of architecture but rather fixes it as a program in a set of data—as what might be termed a "genetic code" that contains all relevant information about a building but no prescribed form of representation. This set of data can be configured, displayed or produced by any output device: in the Internet, via plotter, or directly as a structural component.

Programmed Architecture

Previous attempts to program software to generate architecture to some extent independently have run up against a very generalized problem in the field of architectural design: objectifiability. To what extent can the solutions generated in this way be objectively assessed? Issues of a functional nature—such as keeping distances that users have to walk within the building as short as possible—can indeed be analyzed adequately, but not the question of whether the windows on a particular façade ought to be rectangular or square. The problem that usually arises in evaluating architecture is that there frequently is no clearly "right" or "wrong" solution, but rather only one that someone likes or not. The assessment cannot always be supported with objective criteria; subjective taste is often the determining factor. Efforts to equip programs with learning algorithms—akin to genetic algorithms or neuronal networks—have not been an unqualified success thus far. Obviously, the interrelationships among aspects like physical setting, analysis, idea, style, space utilization program and choice of materials are too complicated to be succinctly summarized. And every designer has a different conception of the hierarchy and the importance of the individual aspects. Similar problems arise in the field of computer-generated music with the attempt to simulate classical composers, whereas new compositions not subject to these restrictions can be programmed very easily. Accordingly, there can be no generally applicable software or universal machine to design architecture.
How, then, could the computer—as a tool with great promise for the future, and beckoning areas of deployment that go beyond the electronic drawing machine, communications manager and archiving system—serve as a means to support the design process, and what consequences would such use have for architecture?
One of the first "programs to generate architecture" was described by Jean Nicholas Louis Durand in his 1819 book *Marche à suivre. Précis des Leçons d'Architecture données à l'Ecole Royale Polytechnique.* In it, Durand derived the construction of a detailed building from a few simple, multi-step rules. He formulated the axes of reflection and the minutest commonalities in his program and, in this way, unmistakably described the architecture. The result with which we are confronted is a plan in which, for one thing, elements are arranged in a way that is by no means haphazard and, for another, it is very easy to discover errors. This is not a program that generates architecture; rather, this is a case of programmed design—a description of a building that could not be more compact and one that avoids redundancies.
As far as the description of objects is concerned, modern object-oriented programming languages have a crucial advantage over Durand's linear (procedural) descriptions. With

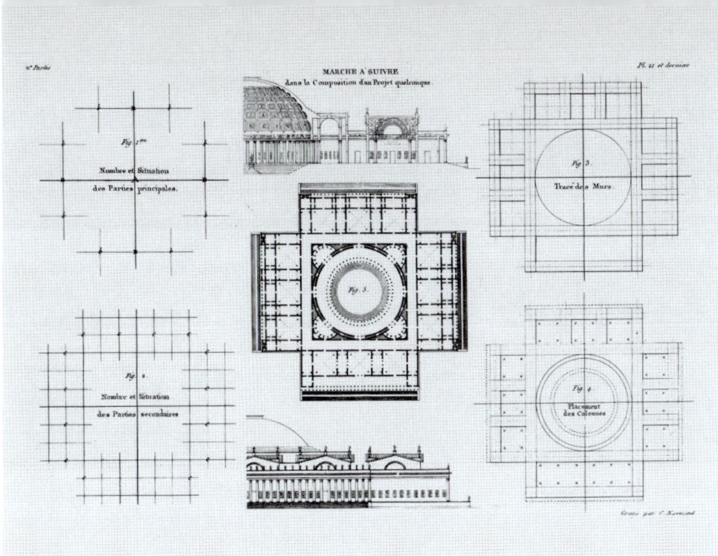

From: J. N. L. Durand, *Marche à suivre*

them, exceptions as well as rules are described in such a way that characteristics of a precursory object can be overwritten. In this way, it is relatively easy to build up very compact and yet highly adaptable structures that can be used both descriptively and operationally. This mode of programming is most convenient for the task of architectural design since structures can be described in detail without a definite solution to a superordinate problem having to be found.

Laser Printers and CNC Machines, Programmed Objects and Postprocessors

Only a few years ago, producing a single copy of a book, for instance, or a limited number of color postcards was a rather highly involved undertaking, since such jobs only made economic sense with print runs over 1,000 copies. Approximately 10 years ago, the first color laser and inkjet printers came onto the market. A laser printer was a considerable advance over its forerunners such as offset printing machinery. With this new technology, it makes no difference whether one prints out a single copy or multiple copies of a page. A new typeface or a completely different layout can be selected for every page. The laser printer is a flexible output device for any content whatsoever, whereas offset printing machinery is set up to turn out a single page at a time. These functions can also be usefully applied in architectural production processes, assuming compatibility between the descriptive format and the output device is achieved.
As previously mentioned, architecture can now also be designed as a program instead of, as is usually the case, as a blueprint. The essential innovation here as far as architecture is concerned is the ability to take the code that describes a building and, through the use of so-called postprocessors, to generate a variety of different forms of representation: a CAD rendering, a print file, a data sheet featuring a list of components, or an invitation for tender offers. In most cases, postprocessors are small translation programs that produce the necessary data from the code.
If the programmed architectural object offers a "print" option and if the program can execute it, a CAD rendering is generated from the code and sent to a laser printer. The printer, in turn, carries out this program in step-by-step fashion and produces a drawing of the programmed object on paper. In doing so, it makes no difference to the laser printer which printing instructions have been sent by which object, just as long as it is able to execute the program. Furthermore, the above-mentioned program can also feature a production

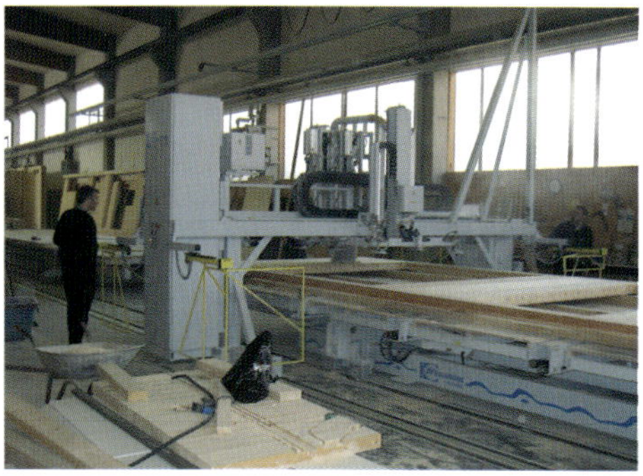

digitales bauen, Volkmar Hovestadt
The graphic shows a 30-meter-long machine for molding wood
CAAD.ETHZ.CH

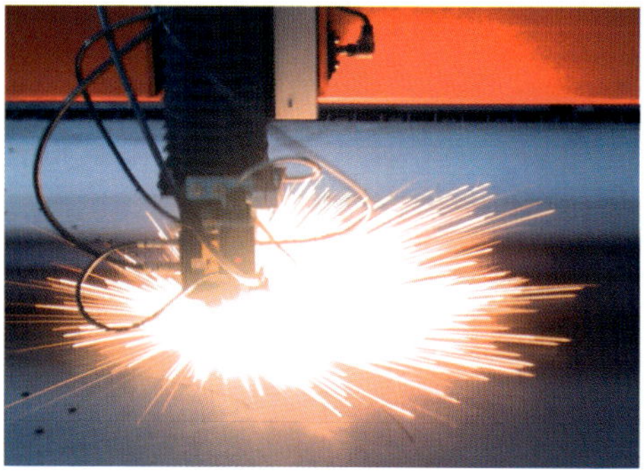

Cutting head of a laser cutting machine
plate size: 3 x 1.5 meters, plate thickness: up to 1 centimeter

option, whereby the necessary production data are calculated from the code and sent to the corresponding production machinery.

Thus, if the laser printer as a machine is capable of printing onto paper, it follows that there must also be computer-controlled machinery capable of directly "printing" a construction. With respect to technique and content, the problem of "printing out buildings" seems to have been solved. Just as a programmed object can be printed to paper with a laser printer, the same object can now be "printed out" in concrete with a concrete plotter. Metals and plastics can be cut with laser cutting machines; any imaginable form can be produced from glass or stone with water-jet cutting machines; plastics and wood can be worked with computerized numerical control (CNC) molding machines.

In accordance with this line of thinking, a current challenge for the field of architecture is to develop and implement structures that are compatible with these principles and can be produced on such machinery.

Here is brief but easily understood example meant to clarify the idea of a parametrized object and the series of steps involved in producing one. A rack for hanging up clothing is described in a program; entering the corresponding parameters—e.g. its length or the minimum distance between the individual notches that anchor the hooks of whatever sort of clothes hangers are used with it—makes it possible to generate a specific object that can be produced directly by means of a laser cutting device. Whether three of the same objects or three different ones are to be produced does not have a material effect upon their price: a rack costs about 100 Swiss Francs per linear meter. This is a programmed design from which, in a matter of seconds, an unlimited number of different objects can be produced.

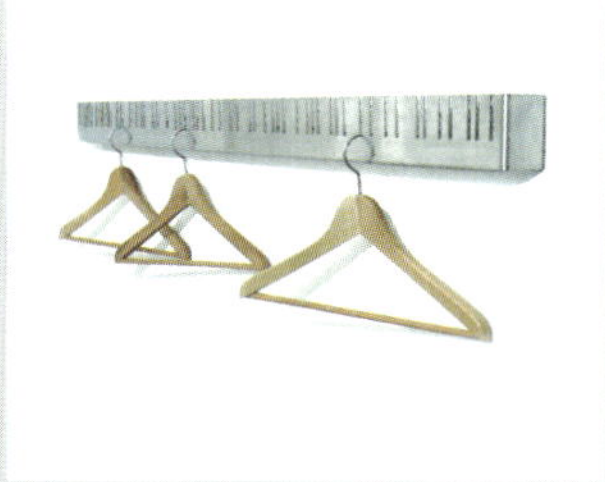

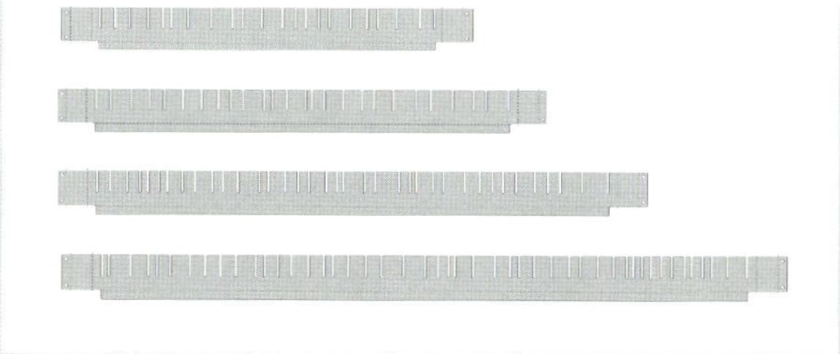

Parametrized Objects
Design: Christoph Schindler, CAAD ETHZ

From this, it follows that the economic viability of a piece of architecture is no longer proportional to its uniformity. If a design consists of many different objects of the same type and it can be described and designed in this way, then this has far-reaching consequences for the organization, construction and design of architecture.

Prototype = Series

When CNC machinery is used, the production costs of a prototype differ only slightly from the costs of producing a component in serial production (assuming that the concept of serial fabrication still even plays a role in this type of development and production process). With these design and production principles in force, very small production runs can be economically set up, produced and marketed with the use of very limited personnel resources. From the architect's point of view, the blending of a form of organization derived from the crafts and trades with industrial production methods could open up attractive new possibilities. After all, why shouldn't he go ahead and create a prototype of the façade component he developed himself, and, ultimately, produce it himself too?
According to the principles of conventional industrial construction, the development of a building component means a high initial investment which can only be amortized through big production runs, an elaborate marketing campaign and a large working group; here, however, it is conceivable to generate constructions and details that are highly individually adapted to a particular piece of architecture.

Summary / Work in Progress

Works of architecture can be programmed both generatively as well as descriptively and in a way that is economically viable. By way of illustration, I present several projects with which I have been associated—one involving the firm *digitales bauen* and the collaborative project entitled *"KaisersRot"* carried out by the ETHZ and the Dutch architectural firm KCAP Rotterdam.

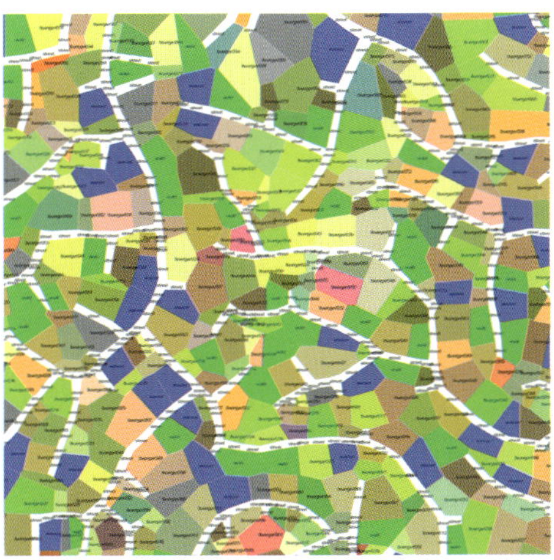

"KaisersRot." A collaborative project of KCAP Rotterdam and ETHZ. A computer-generated lot layout plan. Software: Markus Braach, ETHZ

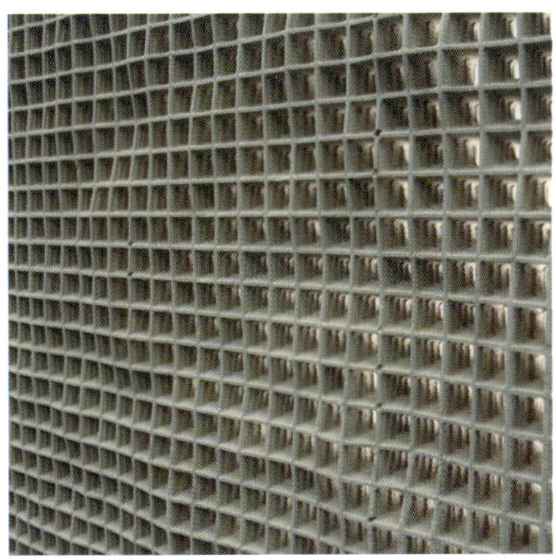

Façade element. Work by student Matthias Heberie in the course "Surface Light," Russell Loveridge, CAAD ETHZ. The image hidden within the structure becomes visible under different lighting conditions.

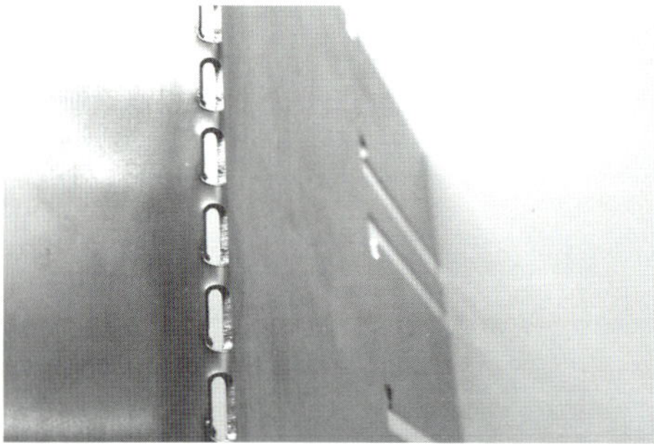

Milled Eternit plate
Christoph Schindler and Russell Loveridge, CAAD ETHZ.

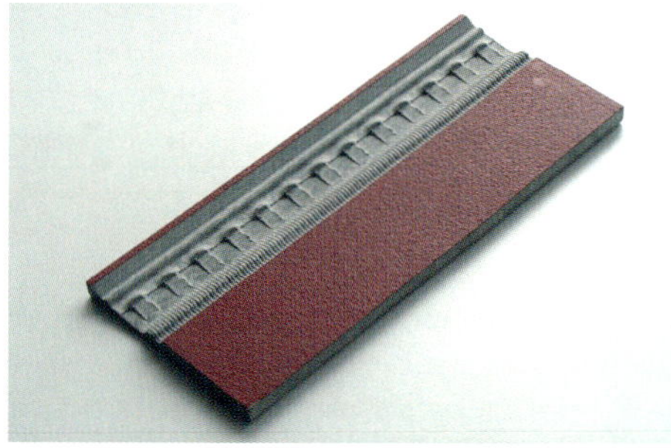

Perforated bend detail, CAAD booklet rack
Oliver Fritz, CAAD ETHZ

Structures are generated and described in both examples, and this is done more economically and more efficiently than with conventional methods. Projects like the clothes rack or the NDS Pavilion, in which the generated code—uniform for the design itself and the drawings of it—is also carried over into the CAM process, show how the future of an integrated design, description and production process for architecture might look.
Accomplishing this, however, will necessitate gaining additional experience with a wide range of "printing technologies." For example, a new printer driver for the concrete plotter will be written in the coming months, which will make it possible to produce walls directly from CAD programs or from the code.
Aside from the technical issues involved, these production processes also exert a not inconsiderable influence upon the design of architecture. For example, what might the details and exterior surfaces of computer-programmed and computer-produced architectural works look like? Could this possibly give rise to a new type of ornamentation?
The range of possibilities discussed above opens up a great deal of room for new experiments of a technical and formal nature. The decisive aspect of this effort will be to pragmatically pursue the objective of "printing out buildings" and its consequences for architecture in a manner that is free from ulterior motives of an esoteric nature.
After all, in the past, changes in construction technology usually manifested themselves very directly in the design of architecture.

Translated from the German by Mel Greenwald

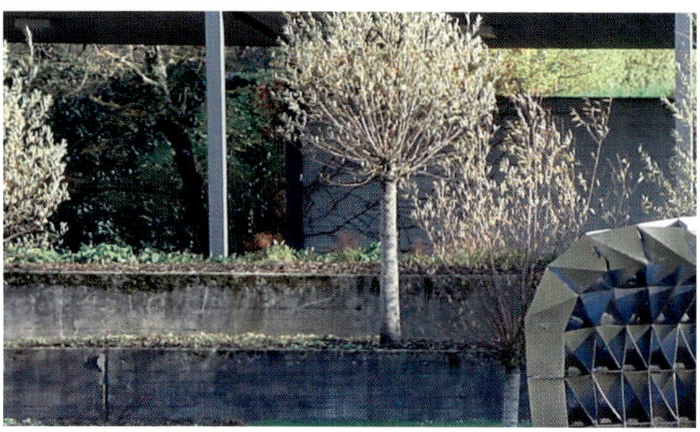

NDS Pavilion 2001 / 2002, CAAD ETHZ.
Seven postgraduate students are designing and building a structure consisting of 418 different parametrized and programmed components.

Häuser drucken
Code – Drucker – Häuser

Oliver Fritz

Seit Beginn des 20. Jahrhunderts experimentieren Architekten im Wohnungsbau mit industrieller Bauweise. Versuchssiedlungen wie Dessau-Törten von Gropius und Wachsmanns und Prouvés konstruktive Experimente lieferten die Grundlage zum heutigen Verständnis von Vorfertigung im Bauwesen. Die daraus resultierenden unterschiedlichen Entwurfs- und Produktionsmethoden umfassen ein weites Spektrum: Es reicht vom Fertighaus – uniform und von der Stange – über hoch entwickelte Baukastensysteme bis zu in der Werkstatt vorgefertigten Fassadenelementen, die großflächig auf der Baustelle montiert werden. Diese Systeme unterscheiden sich grundsätzlich in ihrer Ausprägung, zeichnen sich jedoch durch gemeinsame Eigenschaften und Ziele aus: kürzere Baustellenzeiten, höhere Präzision, größere Sicherheiten, geringere Planungs- und Fertigungskosten.
Während der klassische Fertighausbau sehr eingeschränkt ist und praktisch keine Anpassungen durch den Kunden oder den Architekten möglich sind, zeichnen sich Baukastensysteme durch Regelmäßigkeiten und Raster aus. Praktisch ungebunden an eine vorbestimmte Form und Konstruktion sind die in der Werkstatt individuellen vorgefertigten Bauelemente.
Umgekehrt proportional zur Flexibilität der Bauweise verhält es sich meist mit den Baukosten. Die traditionellen und weniger flexiblen Planungs- und Fertigungsmethoden sind in der Regel die günstigeren. Eine tatsächliche Herausforderung für die Zukunft des industriellen Bauens stellt die Reaktionsmöglichkeit auf die individuellen Wünsche und Bedürfnisse der Bauherren dar. In der Industrie findet eine Orientierung zu individuell angepassten Massengütern statt. Wurde das bisher nur bei kostenintensiven Produkten (z. B. in der Automobilindustrie) mit geringen Konfigurationsmöglichkeiten praktiziert, gibt es inzwischen auch Firmen, die kleine, preisgünstige Produkte an individuelle Bedürfnisse anpassen. Diese Tendenz wird vor allem auch durch neue Zweige der Informationstechnologien, neue Kommunikationsformen – wie das Internet –, aber auch durch die aktuellen individualisierten Fertigungstechniken ermöglicht.

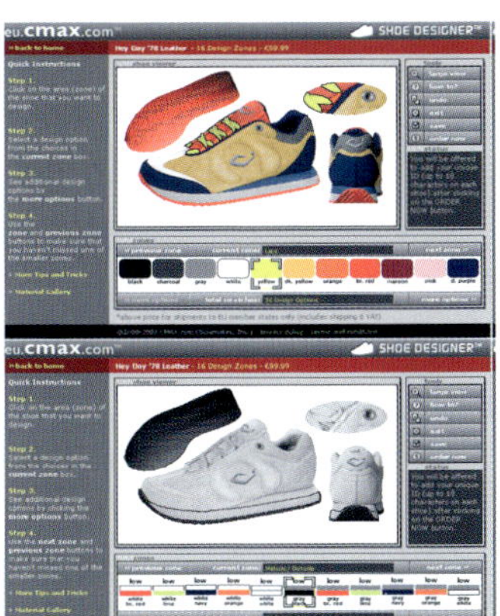

http://eu.cmax.com/
Customized Footwear

Seit ungefähr zwei Jahren forscht die Professur für CAAD unter der Leitung von Prof. Ludger Hovestadt an der ETH Zürich an der Integration aktueller Informationstechnologien in architektonische Entwurfs- und Produktionsvorgänge. Ziel dieser Forschung ist nicht die formale Entwicklung einer neuen Architektur oder die Definition von Stil- oder Formmerkmalen. Es geht vielmehr um die strukturelle Entwicklung von Gebäuden aus dem Kern heraus und um die Formulierung dieser in einem einheitlichen Code, der die Architektur nicht mehr zeichnerisch beschreibt, sondern programmiert in einem Datensatz fixiert – sozusagen als „Gencode" beinhaltet er alle relevanten Gebäudeinformationen, aber keine vorgegebene Repräsentationsform. Dieser Datensatz kann von beliebigen Ausgabegeräten konfiguriert, dargestellt oder produziert werden: im Internet, auf dem Plotter oder direkt als Bauteil.

Bei den bisherigen Versuchen, eine Software zu programmieren, die Architektur einigermaßen selbstständig generieren kann, stieß man auf ein sehr allgemeines Problem von Architekturentwürfen: die Objektivierbarkeit. Inwiefern können die generierten Lösungen objektiv beurteilt werden? Fragen funktionaler Natur, beispielsweise nach möglichst kurzen Wegen innerhalb eines Gebäudes, können zwar noch gut analysiert werden; nicht aber die Frage, ob die Fenster einer Fassade quadratisch oder rechteckig sein sollen. Das Problem, das sich üblicherweise beim Bewerten von Architektur ergibt, ist, dass es für Entscheidungen häufig kein eindeutiges „Richtig" oder „Falsch" gibt, sondern nur „gefällt" oder „gefällt nicht": Die Bewertung kann nicht immer auf objektive Kriterien gestützt werden, sie ist oft vom subjektiven Geschmack geleitet. Bemühungen, Programme mit Lernalgorithmen zu versehen – wie genetische Algorithmen oder neuronale Netze –, sind bisher noch nicht überzeugend gelungen. Offenbar sind die Zusammenhänge zwischen Aspekten wie Umfeld, Analyse, Idee, Stil, Raumprogramm und Materialwahl zu kompliziert, als dass sie sich zusammenfassen ließen. Und jeder Entwerfer beurteilt Hierarchie und Wichtigkeit der einzelnen Aspekte unterschiedlich. Ähnliche Probleme finden sich in der computergenerierten Musik beim Versuch, klassische Komponisten zu simulieren, während neue Kompositionen ohne diese Einschränkungen sehr einfach programmierbar sind. Folgerichtig kann es keine allgemeingültige Software oder universelle Maschine geben, die Architektur entwerfen kann.
Wie also könnte der Computer als ein weitergehendes Werkzeug – über die elektronische Zeichenmaschine, die Kommunikationszentrale und das Archivierungssystem hinweg – als Entwurfsunterstützung dienen und welche Auswirkungen hätte sein Einsatz auf die Architektur? Eines der ersten „Generierungsprogramme" für Architektur beschreibt Jean Nicholas Louis Durand in seinem 1819 erschienenen Buch *Marche à suivre. Précis des Leçons d'Architecture données à l'Ecole Royale Politechnique.*

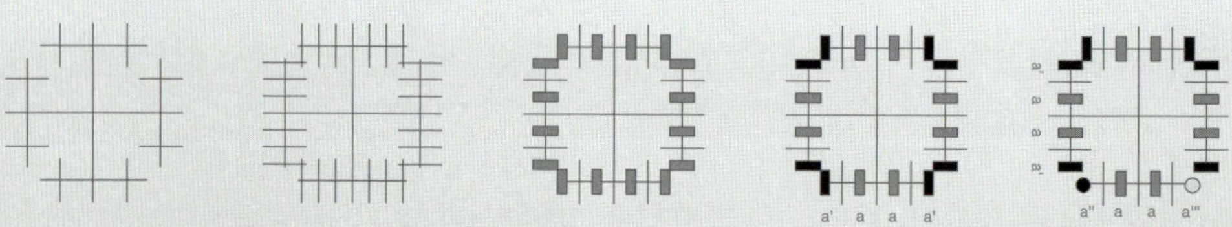

Aus: J. N. L. Durand: *Marche à suivre*

Durand leitet aus wenigen einfachen und mehrstufigen Regeln die Konstruktion eines detaillierten Gebäudes ab. Er formuliert die Spiegelachsen und kleinsten Gemeinsamkeiten in seinem Programm und beschreibt auf diese Weise unmissverständlich die Architektur. Als Ergebnis finden wir einen Plan, bei dem es zum einen nicht beliebig ist, wo welches Element angeordnet ist, und es zum anderen sehr leicht möglich ist, Fehler zu finden. Es handelt sich hier nicht um ein Programm, das Architektur generiert, sondern vielmehr um einen programmierten Entwurf – und um eine Beschreibung des Gebäudes, die kompakter nicht sein könnte und Redundanzen vermeidet.
Moderne objektorientierte Progammiersprachen haben, was die Beschreibung von Objekten betrifft, einen wesentlichen Vorteil gegenüber den linearen (prozeduralen) Beschreibungen Durands. Mit ihnen werden Ausnahmen wie Regeln beschrieben, indem Merkmale eines Vorgängerobjektes überschrieben werden können. Auf diese Art und Weise ist es relativ leicht, sehr kompakte und dennoch anpassungsfähige Strukturen aufzubauen, die sowohl beschreibend

als auch operational genutzt werden können. Diese Art des Programmierens kommt dem architektonischen Entwurf entgegen, da Strukturen im Detail beschrieben werden können, ohne dass ein übergeordnetes Problem bereits endgültig gelöst zu sein braucht.

Laserdrucker und CNC-Maschinen, programmierte Objekte und Postprozessoren

Vor wenigen Jahren war beispielsweise das Produzieren eines einzelnen Buches oder einer geringen Stückzahl farbiger Postkarten eine verhältnismäßig aufwändige Lösung, da sich eine Auflage erst ab einer Stückzahl von mehr als 1000 rentiert hat. Vor circa zehn Jahren kamen die ersten Farblaserdrucker und Tintenstrahldrucker auf den Markt. Ein Laserdrucker unterscheidet sich beträchtlich von seinen Vorgängern, z. B. den Offsetdruckmaschinen. Bei dieser Technik ist es nicht wesentlich, ob man eine oder mehrere gleiche Seiten druckt. Für jede neue Seite kann ein beliebiger Schrifttyp oder eine unterschiedliche Gestaltung gewählt werden. Der Laserdrucker ist ein flexibles Ausgabegerät für beliebige Inhalte, während eine Offsetdruckmaschine für jeweils nur einen Druckbogen gerüstet wird. Diese Funktionsweisen können auch für Produktionsabläufe in der Architektur nutzbar gemacht werden, wenn ein vergleichbares Verhältnis zwischen Beschreibungsformat und Ausgabegerät gefunden wird.
Es wurde bereits erwähnt, dass Architektur statt üblicherweise als Zeichnung nun auch als Programm entworfen werden kann. Das für die Architektur grundsätzlich Neue daran ist, dass aus dem Code, der ein Gebäude beschreibt, nun mit so genannten Postprozessoren verschiedene Repräsentationsformen generiert werden können: eine CAD-Zeichnung, eine Druckdatei, ein Datenblatt mit Stückteillisten oder eine Ausschreibung. In den meisten Fällen sind Postprozessoren kleine Übersetzungsprogramme, die aus dem Code die benötigten Daten erzeugen. Besitzt das programmierte Architekturobjekt die Methode „Drucken“ und wird diese vom Programm ausgelöst, so wird aus dem Code eine CAD-Darstellung zusammengestellt und an einen Laserdrucker gesendet. Der Drucker wiederum führt dieses Programm schrittweise aus und erstellt auf einem Papier die Zeichnung des Programmierobjektes. Dabei ist dem Laserdrucker egal, welches Objekt welche Druckanweisungen geschickt hat, solange das Programm für ihn ausführbar ist. Ebenso kann das erwähnte Programm jedoch als Eigenschaft die eigene Produktion haben. Die Methode „Produktion“ würde aus dem Code die notwendigen Produktionsdaten errechnen und an die entsprechende Produktionsmaschine gesendet werden.
Wenn also der Laserdrucker als Maschine in der Lage ist, auf Papier zu drucken, müsste es schlussfolgernd auch computergesteuerte Maschinen geben, die direkt eine Konstruktion „drucken“ können.

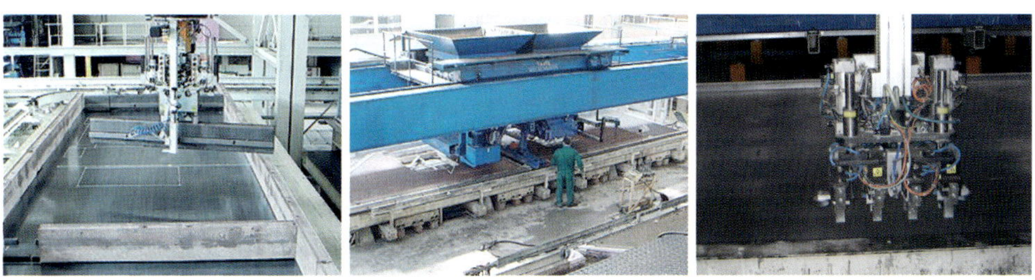

http://www.betonkemmler.de

digitales bauen: Das Bild zeigt z. B. ein „Druckwerk“ für jede Betonwand. Diese Maschine kostet zur Zeit zwischen 10 und 15 Mio. Euro, kann pro Jahr die Wände von 400 bis 500 individuellen Einfamilienhäusern (die z. B. von einem Architekten entworfen sind) ausdrucken und benötigt zur Bedienung vier Personen.

Technisch und inhaltlich ist das „Drucken von Häusern" scheinbar gelöst. So wie sich ein Programmierobjekt mit einem Laserdrucker auf Papier ausdrucken lässt, kann dasselbe Objekt nun mit dem Betondrucker in Beton ausgedruckt werden. Bleche und Kunststoffe lassen sich mit Laserschneidemaschinen schneiden, beliebige Formen aus Glas und Stein können mit Wasserstrahlschneidemaschinen produziert werden, Kunststoffe und Holz können mit CNC-Fräsen bearbeitet werden.
Diesem Gedankengang folgend ist es nun die Herausforderung für die Architektur, Konstruktionen zu entwickeln und einzusetzen, die sich mit diesen Prinzipien vereinbaren lassen und auf solchen Maschinen produziert werden können.

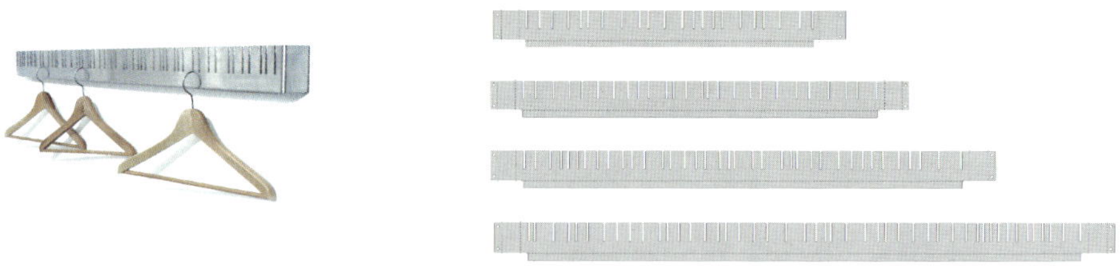

Parametrisierte Objekte
Entwurf: Christoph Schindler, CAAD ETH Zürich

Ein kleines, aber verständliches Beispiel soll Idee und Produktionskette eines parametrisierten Objektes verdeutlichen. Eine Kleiderleiste wurde in einem Programm beschrieben; durch Eingabe von entsprechenden Parametern wie beispielsweise Länge oder Mindestabstand der einzelnen zufällig erzeugten Einhänger wird eine Instanz – ein individuelles Objekt – erzeugt, das direkt mit einer Laserschneidemaschine produziert werden kann. Ob drei gleiche oder drei verschiedene Objekte hergestellt werden sollen, macht sich im Preis nur unwesentlich bemerkbar: Die Leiste kostet etwa 100.– CHF pro Laufmeter. Hier handelt es sich um einen programmierten Entwurf, von dem in Sekunden beliebig viele unterschiedliche Instanzen erzeugt werden können.
Daraus folgt, dass Wirtschaftlichkeit einer Architektur ist nicht mehr proportional zu ihrer Regelmäßigkeit ist. Wenn ein Entwurf aus vielen unterschiedlichen Objekten gleicher Art besteht und auf diese Art und Weise beschrieben und entworfen werden kann, hat das weit reichende Konsequenzen für die Organisation, den Bau und die Gestaltung von Architektur.

Prototyp = Serie

Die Herstellungskosten des Prototyps unterscheiden sich bei der Verwendung von CNC-Maschinen unwesentlich von den Kosten eines Serienteils (solange bei dieser Art des Entwicklungs- und Herstellungsprozesses überhaupt noch der Gedanke der Serienproduktion eine Rolle spielt). Mit diesen Entwurfs- und Produktionsprinzipien können kleine Stückzahlen mit geringem Personalaufwand wirtschaftlich konstruiert, produziert und verkauft werden. Aus der Sicht des Architekten könnte die Mischung von handwerklicher Organisationsform und industrieller Fertigung einen neuen reizvollen Aspekt liefern. Warum sollte er das selbst entwickelte Fassadenteil nicht gleich „prototypen" und letztendlich selbst produzieren?
Während die Entwicklungsprinzipien des klassischen Industriellen Bauens für ein Bauteil hohe Anfangsinvestitionen bedeuteten, die sich nur durch große Stückzahlen, einem aufwändigen Vertrieb und einer großen Arbeitsgruppe amortisierten, sind hier Konstruktionen und Details vorstellbar, die individuell und im hohen Maße an die Architektur angepasst sind.

Resümee / Work in Progress

Architekturen können – sowohl generativ als auch beschreibend – wirtschaftlich sinnvoll programmiert werden, wie einige Beispiele aus den eigenen Reihen – z. B. die der Firma digitales bauen – oder das Kooperationsprojekt „KaisersRot" zwischen der ETH Zürich und dem holländischem Architekturbüro KCAP Rotterdam zeigen.

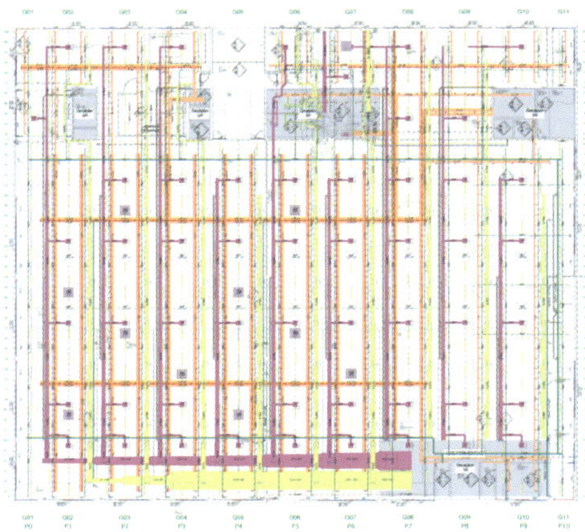

digitales bauen: Ein programmierter Grundriss,
Roche Diagnostics, Mannheim,
Architekten: Schmidt&Schmidt Architekten, Karlsruhe

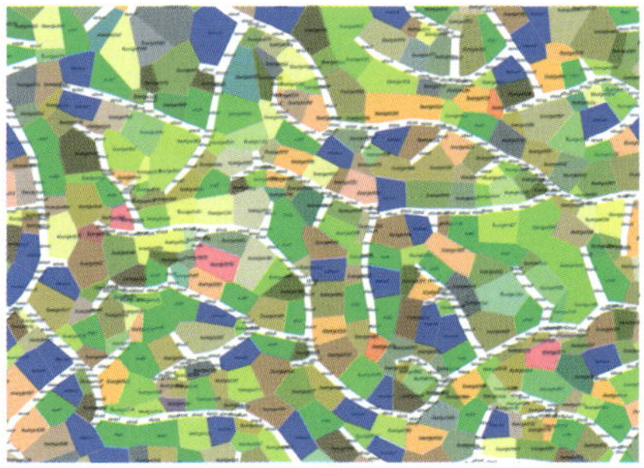

„KaisersRot". Kooperation KCAP Rotterdam NL und ETH Zürich.
Ein generierter Parzellierungsplan.
Software: Markus Braach, ETHZ

In beiden Beispielen werden Strukturen generiert und beschrieben, und zwar günstiger und leistungsfähiger als auf die herkömmliche Art und Weise. Anhand von Projekten wie der Kleiderleiste oder dem NDS-Pavillon, bei denen sich der generierte Code – einheitlich für Entwurf und dessen Zeichnung – auch in die computergestützte Produktion zieht, zeigt sich, wie die Zukunft eines integrierten Entwurfs-, Beschreibungs- und Produktionsprozesses für Architektur aussehen könnte.
Hierfür sind jedoch noch weitere Erfahrungen mit den unterschiedlichen „Drucktechniken" erforderlich. So soll z. B. in den kommenden Monaten ein Druckertreiber für den Betondrucker geschrieben werden, der es ermöglicht, direkt aus CAD-Programmen oder aus dem Code Wände zu produzieren.
Neben den technischen Fragestellungen haben diese Produktionsverfahren auch auf die Gestaltung von Architektur einen nicht unwesentlichen Einfluss: Wie könnten beispielsweise die Details und die Oberflächen programmierter und mit Computern produzierter Architekturen aussehen? Entsteht hier möglicherweise eine neue Art von Ornament?

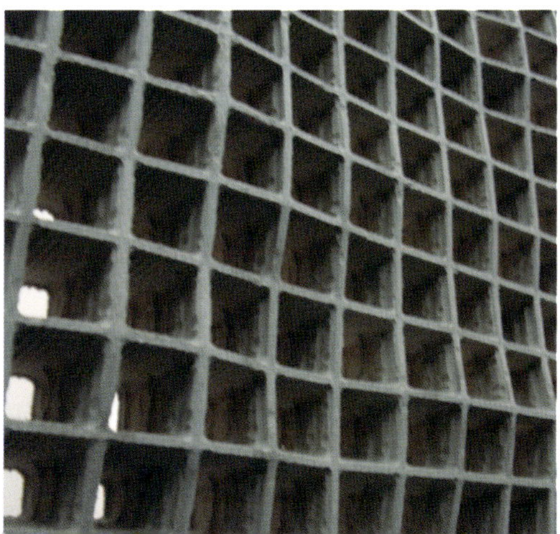

Fassadenelement. Studentenarbeit von Matthias Heberle, im Kurs „Surface Light", Russell Loveridge, CAAD ETH Zürich.
Unter verschiedenen Lichtbedingungen wird das in der Struktur verborgene Bild sichtbar.

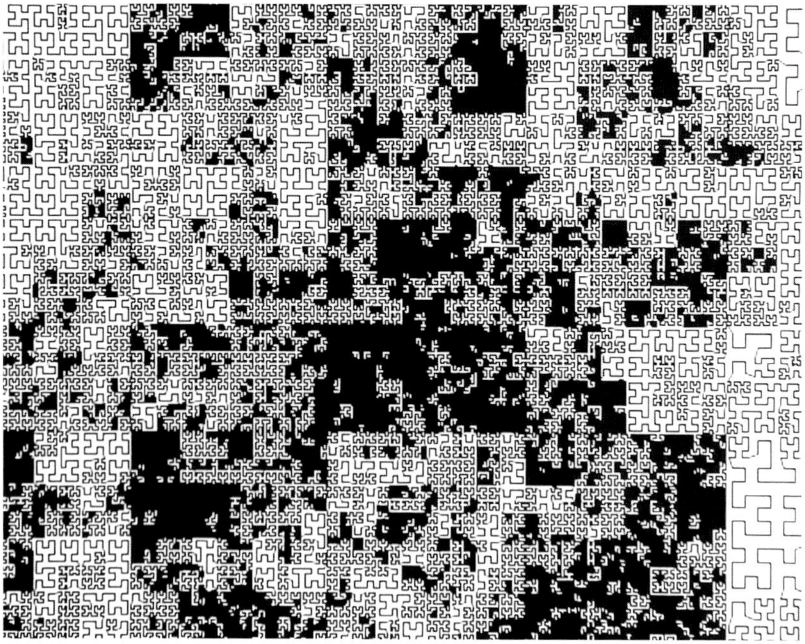

Programmiertes Ornament, Kai Strehlke, CAAD ETH Zürich

Innerhalb des angesprochenen Spannungsfeldes öffnet sich ein weiter Raum für neue Experimente technischer und formaler Natur. Dabei ist es entscheidend, pragmatisch das Ziel „Häuser auszudrucken"und dessen Auswirkungen auf die Architektur frei von esoterischen Hintergedanken zu verfolgen.
Üblicherweise haben sich ja Veränderungen in der Bautechnologie sehr unmittelbar in der Gestaltung von Architektur bemerkbar gemacht.

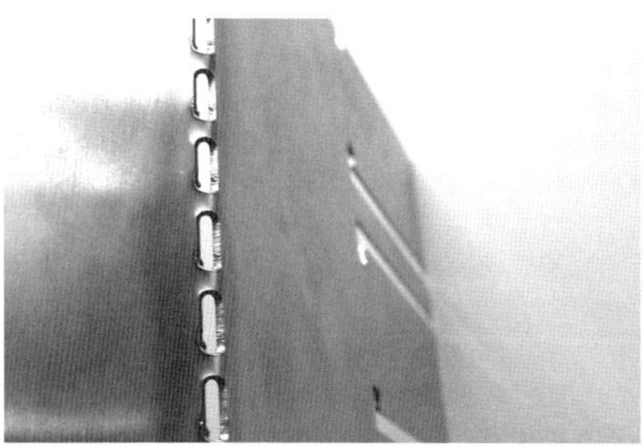

Perforiertes Biegedetail, CAAD-Bookletständer
Oliver Fritz, CAAD ETH Zürich

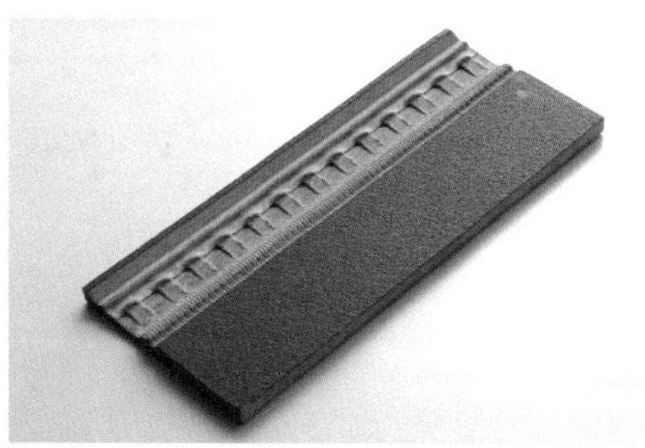

Gefräste Eternitplatte
Christoph Schindler und Russell Loveridge,
CAAD ETH Zürich.

Code and Music: Technology and Creativity in Composing

Jonathan Norton

Since the first singing of "Daisy" echoed through the halls of Bell Laboratories from their mainframe, computers and their software code have become an integral part of how music is created and, for better or worse, distributed. In today's world there is almost no area of music that has not been touched by technology. As Gerfried Stocker has observed, "Artistic expression no longer arises solely as the result of artists' talent and mastery of their craft, rather, program codes describe parameters and processes in accordance with dynamic visual, and sound environments are generated via computer ... serious and popular alike."

(Ars Electronica Festival, Press Release, Linz, March 25, 2003.)

The symposium has asked me to consider the role of code in music. Since this is a daunting task, I will examine briefly how code touches and even shapes certain aspects of music composition, and pose some questions for exploration. We cannot put the genie back into the bottle, nor do we wish to, but we should think about the way code has been fused into art and music to free our own creativity.

A specific question was posed recently in an Ars Electronica press release this Spring: "How do software and digital codes impact the essence and identity of media art as 'art created out of code', that is, as a generative and processual art form that has developed from and consists of algorithmic and computational processes?" This question is very much on target.

Some of the larger changes have occurred in algorithmic composition. Although lower level programming environments based on Lisp, C and C++ still exist and are still commonly used, such as Common Lisp Music (CLM), Csound, and the Synthesis ToolKit in C++ (STK), they are mainly the playground for academic institutions that cater to research and the further development of the genre. Only within the last several years has this begun to change. The computing power that was once only available to these institutions a mere ten years ago has dramatically changed. Today the typical home computer is powerful enough to run just about any programming environment with room to spare. This has unlocked a whole new market of potential users.

Along with less expensive and faster computers, the advent of higher level GUI programming environments such as PD and in particular MAX/MSP, have allowed more people access to computer music than ever before. Since it is no longer only the realm of academics, the mainstream now has a chance to enter the domain of computer music. Opening the doors to the more mainstream also yields the side benefit of innovations developing more quickly. Composers, academic and non-academic alike, who once hesitated to attempt to create computer music, due in part to lower level languages, are now able to let their imaginations soar in an entirely new area of music. This has profoundly changed the musical landscape.

For example, about nine or ten years ago when I wanted to write algorithmic composition I mainly used Rick Taube's Stella program which was based on Lisp. It was a powerful program tailor-made for this type of composition that was relatively easy to learn for anyone with knowledge of Lisp. MAX was available at that time, but its capabilities were limited as a more general programming environment. Both Stella and MAX, however, were limited because they could only use MIDI. When I wanted to write music that entailed computer generated and manipulated audio I would have to switch to a program such as CLM. Yet, Stella and CLM environments still required writing many lines of computer code that ran on the NeXT computer. Today, if I want to create this type of music, I normally use MAX/MSP, which now combines the qualities of algorithmic composition and audio together in one package, and it runs on my laptop.

With the help of faster computers and GUI programming environments, another area of rapid growth is in the field of musical controllers and interfaces. In fact, it has become so popular in the past few years that a new international conference has sprung up to address the topic—the New Interfaces for Musical Expression conference (NIME) held at McGill University in Montreal, Canada this year.

Many of these controllers are cross-pollinations from different fields that take objects from their normally intended environment and use them in a novel way. BioControl's BioMuse was one of the first systems to employ bioelectric transdermal electrodes—normally used for biofeedback and medical therapy—for musical applications. The system could measure electromyograms (muscle movement), electrooculograms (eye movement), electrocardiograms (heart), and electroencephalograms (brain waves) from eight different sensors at once. While this was great at the time, its application was pretty much limited to academic use and composition because of lack of knowledge among and, thus, access to those outside of academic and medical circles.

More recently, Infusion Systems' I-Cube and similar products have entered the scene. The I-Cube system does not work with bioelectric sensors like the BioMuse, but has a more flexible design that allows the use of up to 32 sensors at once. It also features a wider array of sensors that measure such parameters as bend, touch, light, tilt, magnetic field, orientation, temperature and pressure. An important advantage and time saver of these systems is that they automatically translate the raw sensor information into MIDI data. This in and of itself makes them much more user friendly. When combined with a GUI programming environment they lend themselves well to reaching a larger population due to this environment's accessibility and ease of use.

Not only do the controllers and software code allow for more organic and evolving sound, but they also allow for the sound to evolve in a real-time performance setting. This new possibility was not available in the past or at least not as easily accessible. Previously, in a live situation, sound had to be physically produced either by miking an instrument or played from tape before it could be altered through EQ, filters, tape manipulation, or the use of many outboard effect boxes. However, the sound source itself could not adapt. Currently, the sounds themselves can be completely adaptive and the parameters that affect them can be spontaneously produced on the command of the performer.

So, in the larger context of music with all of these advances in technology, how has the position of the artists changed by their use of software? For traditional composers it means that they no longer have to write music with pencil and paper only. While traditional pencil and paper are still used, software has allowed them to create, audition and generate music and musical scores faster, with more diversity, and in more directions than ever before. Sequencer programs make it easier to audition different textures and arrangements before committing oneself to them. Most of these programs also allow the integration of audio files into the sequences, which further enhances the composer's palette of possibilities as never before. Notation programs, once learned, are also invaluable time savers. Entire sections of music can be entered, altered, cut and pasted, transposed and checked for range, all with relative ease. Once completed, the individual parts can be extracted and printed automatically from the score. For orchestral scores and other large works, notation programs are worth their weight in gold.

For modern composers, the proliferation of software choices means that they have become part composer and part programmer. In addition to digital audio, sequencer programs can import a plethora of plug-ins for effects, sound manipulation, samplers and virtual instruments, just to name a few. For composers who are not satisfied with the limitations of existing programs and plug-ins, high and low level programming environments are the tools of choice. This is the realm of algorithmic composition, acoustic models, physical models, digital signal processing and unique controllers. Here, every parameter and nuance of sound can be dictated and tailor made for specific situations, sonorities and musical ideas. Of course this flexibility comes with a price. The more nuances composers want to control, the deeper their understanding must be in terms of synthesis techniques, acoustic modeling, digital signal processing, and how the parameters of each affect one another.

For artists in other disciplines, software has allowed them to become composers and vice versa. In the past, without software a person truly had to be a composer. In order to write music, pencil and paper were needed to create a score and then shown to a musician to be played. This required certain mastery at the very least of how to notate music as well as knowledge of the capabilities and limitations of the instruments for which the pieces were being written. Through the use of software, hardware and computer-generated or computer-controlled sounds this is no longer the case. Most art in one form or another can be translated into almost any other art form. An artist can take an image of his/her art, be it a photograph, a drawing, or a form of video and, through a scanner or video camera connected to translation software, map the pixel density or rate of movement into raw MIDI data. This data in turn could be sent to a synthesizer or any other sound source or programming environment to create sound. Another example would be a sculptor who uses light, heat, touch or bend sensors attached to his/her sculpture to generate raw MIDI data which is patched to a sound source. The possible combinations are endless.

Conversely, a composer could take an existing composition or a live performance and through the use of MIDI to video or audio to video converters create a graphic representation of his/her music in real-time based on some predetermined parameter mappings.

As I conclude, I come back to specific concerns with code and creativity. As stated above, most modern composers and especially computer music composers have become part composer and part programmer. Some people might say that such a composer's music is not musical, but most people will not argue about the music being a form of art. But what about the code used to produce the music? With an increased reliance on computers and software is it possible to say that the code itself has become an art form in its own right? If so, at what point does software stop being simply code and cross the line into art? Do these rules change for different creators or do they stay the same across the board? For example, if a computer programmer writes, say, an algorithm that generates music, is that program considered to be art? What if on the other hand a composer writes the exact same algorithm? Is the composer's program considered art and the computer programmer's program seen merely as code, as a means to the end product of music, or are they seen on equal footing? Is either one considered art? Is a program that has been labeled as art truly art or is it just merely because someone says, "This is art?" Are there any concrete criteria on which to base such a decision on or is it merely subjective? These are questions that move us toward the heart of the integration of technology and art.

Although I have only talked about code, technology and music composition, the concept of code and music has many levels that will probably affect us all in the future. As I mentioned in the beginning, computer technology and software have become an integral part not only of how music is created, but also how it is distributed. The current controversy about the distribution of music and file swapping through the Internet involves law, code and individual creation of art at an even broader level. Technology and code that broaden the art of individual creativity, as I have discussed, also threaten to change individuals' rights to their art.

Code und Musik
Technik und Kreativität beim Komponieren

Jonathan Norton

Seit erstmals „Daisy, Daisy" bei *Bell Laboratories* aus dem Großrechner ertönte, sind Computer und Softwarecode zu einem bedeutenden Einflussfaktor bei der Schaffung und Verbreitung von Musik geworden. Es gibt heute fast keinen Bereich der Musik, der nicht von Technik beeinflusst wäre. Wie Gerfried Stocker ausführt, „[entsteht] künstlerischer Ausdruck [...] nicht mehr ausschließlich durch Können und Handwerk des Künstlers, sondern über Programmcodes werden die Parameter und Prozesse beschrieben, entsprechend derer vom Computer dynamische Bild- und Klangwelten generiert werden – ... [in] Bereichen der U- [ebenso wie der] E-Musik."

(Ars Electronica, Presseaussendung, Linz, 25. März 2003)

Ich wurde gebeten, im Rahmen der Ars Electronica 2003 die Rolle von Code in der Musik zu untersuchen. Dies stellt eine reizvolle Herausforderung dar und erlaubt mir, kurz die Berührungspunkte und Zusammenhänge zwischen Code und Musik darzulegen und abschließend einige Fragen zu formulieren. Weder können noch wollen wir den Geist zurück in die Flasche verbannen; wir sollten jedoch überlegen, wie Code Eingang in die Kunst und Musik gefunden und unserer Kreativität neue Impulse verliehen hat.

In einer Presseaussendung der Ars Electronica vom Frühjahr 2003 wurde folgende Frage aufgeworfen: „Welche Rolle spielen Software und digitale Codes für das Wesen und die Identität von digitaler Medienkunst als einer ‚Kunst aus Code', also einer generativen, aus computativen Prozessen entwickelten und entstehenden Kunst?" Diese Frage berührt den Kern des Problems.

Einige der umfassendsten Innovationen zeigen sich im Bereich der algorithmischen Komposition. Obwohl auf Lisp, C und C++ basierende Low-Level-Programmierumgebungen wie z. B. Common Lisp Music (CLM), Csound und die Synthesis ToolKit-Funktion von C++ (STK) weiterhin häufig zum Einsatz kommen, werden sie hauptsächlich im akademischen Bereich für Forschungszwecke und zur Weiterentwicklung des Genres verwendet. Geändert hat sich dies erst in jüngster Zeit. Die Rechnerleistung hat sich dramatisch erhöht; während vor nur zehn Jahren fast ausschließlich die oben erwähnten Institutionen ausreichend leistungsstarke

Rechner besaßen, ist heute die Rechnerleistung von typischen Heimcomputern so hoch, dass jede Programmierumgebung genutzt werden kann und dennoch freie Kapazitäten zur Verfügung stehen. Dadurch konnte ein völlig neues Marktsegment von potenziellen Anwendern erschlossen werden.
Neben einem breit gefächerten Angebot an günstigeren und schnelleren Computern hat die Entwicklung von komplexeren GUI-Programmierumgebungen wie PD und besonders MAX/MSP dazu beigetragen, dass heute mehr Menschen als jemals zuvor Zugang zu Computermusik haben. Computermusik ist nicht länger eine Domäne von Akademikern, nun kann auch die breite Masse die Welt der Computermusik für sich erschließen. Ein positiver Effekt dieser Öffnung ist, dass Innovationen sich rascher durchsetzen. Komponisten, Akademiker und Nicht-Akademiker, die früher vor Computermusik zurückschreckten, weil u. a. die Programmiersprachen für ihre Zwecke nicht komplex genug waren, lassen nun ihrer Fantasie freien Lauf. Dies hat zu einer tief greifenden Veränderung der Musikszene geführt.
Wenn ich beispielsweise vor neun oder zehn Jahren eine algorithmische Komposition schreiben wollte, verwendete ich primär Rick Taubes auf Lisp basiertes Programm *Stella,* das maßgeschneidert für diese Art von Komposition war und mit Lisp-Grundkenntnissen relativ leicht erlernt werden konnte. MAX war zu jener Zeit ebenfalls bereits am Markt erhältlich, beschränkte sich jedoch eher auf eine allgemeine Programmierumgebung. Sowohl MAX als auch *Stella* waren nur eingeschränkt verwendbar, da sie ausschließlich MIDI verarbeiten konnten. Wollte ich Kompositionen schreiben, die computergenerierte und manipulierte Audiosequenzen enthielten, musste ich auf Programme wie CLM zurückgreifen. Sowohl *Stella* als auch CLM-Umgebungen erforderten viele Zeilen Computercode, die auf einem NeXT-Computer ausgeführt werden mussten. Möchte ich heute diese Art von Musik komponieren, verwende ich üblicherweise MAX/MSP; dieses Programm vereint bereits algorithmische Komposition und Audiokomposition und läuft auf meinem Laptop.
Durch den Einsatz von schnelleren Computern und GUI-Programmierumgebungen konnten auch im Bereich der Musik-Controller und Interfaces umfangreiche Neuerungen erzielt werden. Dieser Bereich zog in den letzten Jahren derart viel Aufmerksamkeit auf sich, dass eine internationale Konferenz zu diesem Thema initiiert wurde – die *New Interfaces for Musical Expression Conference* (NIME) wird heuer an der McGill University in Montréal, Kanada, stattfinden.
Viele Controller kombinieren Techniken aus verschiedenen anderen Bereichen; sie lösen Objekte aus ihrer natürlichen Umgebung heraus und nutzen sie auf neue Art. *BioMuse* von BioControl war eines der ersten Systeme, das bioelektrische, transdermale Elektroden, die normalerweise für Biofeedback und medizinische Therapien eingesetzt werden, für Musikapplikationen nutzte. Das System konnte über acht Sensoren gleichzeitig Elektromyogramme (Muskelbewegung), Elektrookulogramme (Augenbewegung), Elektrokardiogramme (Herz) und Elektroenzephalogramme (Hirnströme) aufzeichnen. Obwohl es einzigartig für seine Zeit war, blieb die Nutzung auf akademische Zwecke und Komposition beschränkt, da außerhalb des universitären und medizinischen Bereichs das Wissen über derartige Systeme fehlte und Interessierten daher der Zugang verwehrt blieb.
Seit einiger Zeit sind *I-Cube* von Infusion und ähnliche Produkte verfügbar. Das *I-Cube*-System verwendet keine bioelektrischen Sensoren wie *BioMuse,* sondern weist ein flexibleres Design auf, das die gleichzeitige Nutzung von 32 Sensoren ermöglicht. Das Programm verfügt auch über eine Vielzahl von Sensoren, die Parameter wie z. B. Biegung, Berührung, Lichteinfall, Neigung, magnetische Felder, Orientierungssinn, Temperatur und Druck messen. Ein bedeutender Vorteil dieser Systeme ist die automatische Umwandlung der Sensorrohdaten in MIDI-Daten, was eine Zeitersparnis bewirkt und die Programme wesentlich benutzerfreundlicher macht. In Kombination mit einer GUI-Programmierumgebung sind sie aufgrund ihrer leichten Zugänglichkeit und Benutzerfreundlichkeit auch für andere potenzielle Anwender interessant.

Controller und Softwarecode unterstützen nicht nur die Schaffung von organischeren und innovativeren Musikformen, sondern ermöglichen auch Klangentwicklung in einer Echtzeitumgebung. Dies war in der Vergangenheit nicht oder nur sehr schwer möglich. Früher mussten Töne in einer Live-Situation physisch erzeugt werden, indem Musik aufgenommen oder vom Band gespielt wurde, bevor die Musik durch EQ, Filter, Manipulationen von Aufnahmen oder Outboard-Effekte verändert wurde. Die Klangquelle selbst konnte allerdings nicht manipuliert werden. Heute können Töne selbst verändert werden, und die sie beeinflussenden Parameter können spontan auf Befehl des Künstlers erzeugt werden.
Wie hat sich also die Position des Künstlers in einem Musikumfeld, das von derart tief greifenden technischen Fortschritten geprägt ist, durch die Verwendung von Software verändert? Traditionelle Komponisten halten ihre Musik mittlerweile nicht länger ausschließlich auf Papier fest. Zwar werden Papier und Bleistift auch weiterhin verwendet, doch können sie ihre Musik und Partituren heute mittels spezifischer Software auf schnellere, komplexere und diversere Art gestalten, präsentieren und arrangieren. Sequencer-Programme ermöglichen das Abspielen verschiedener Sequenzen und Arrangements, bevor diese endgültig in der Partitur festgehalten werden. Viele dieser Programme erlauben auch die Einbindung von Audiodateien in einzelne Musiksequenzen, was die Palette an Ausdrucksmöglichkeiten, die dem Komponisten zur Verfügung stehen, stark erweitert. Vorausgesetzt man kann mit ihnen umgehen, bringen Notationsprogramme eine große Zeitersparnis. Ganze Sequenzen können relativ einfach eingegeben, verändert, ausgeschnitten, kopiert, transponiert und auf ihren Tonumfang hin überprüft werden. Nach Fertigstellung können einzelne Teile extrahiert und direkt über die am Bildschirm zu sehende Partitur ausgedruckt werden. Für Orchesterpartituren und andere große Werke sind Notationsprogramme unendlich wertvolle Hilfsmittel.
Für zeitgenössische Komponisten bedeutet das reichhaltige Softwareangebot, dass sie nicht nur Komponisten, sondern auch Programmierer sind. Neben digitalen Audiosequenzen können Sequencer-Programme eine Fülle von Plug-Ins importieren, um Effekte, Klangmanipulationen, Sampler und virtuelle Instrumente nutzen zu können. Für Komponisten, die mit den eingeschränkten Funktionen mancher Programme und Plug-Ins nicht zufrieden sind, sind High- und Low-Level-Programmierumgebungen die perfekte Wahl. Sie verschaffen ihnen Zutritt zum Reich der algorithmischen Komposition, der akustischen und physikalischen Modelle, der digitalen Signalverarbeitung und der einzigartigen Controller. Jeder Parameter und jede Klangnuance kann kontrolliert und exakt an spezifische Situationen, Klangfüllen und Musikideen angepasst werden. Allerdings hat diese Flexibilität ihren Preis. Je mehr Nuancen Komponisten über den Computer steuern wollen, desto größer muss ihr Wissen über Synthesetechniken, akustische Modellierung, digitale Signalverarbeitung und die Schnittstellen zwischen diesen einzelnen Parametern sein.
Künstler aus anderen Disziplinen macht die Software zu Komponisten. Als es noch keine entsprechende Software gab, mussten Komponisten „echte" Komponisten sein. Musikpartituren wurden händisch niedergeschrieben und dann von Musikern aufgeführt. Dies erforderte zumindest Wissen über die Notation von Musik und die Klangfülle bzw. den Tonumfang jener Instrumente, für die die Stücke geschrieben wurden. Mit der Verwendung von entsprechender Soft- bzw. Hardware und computergenerierten oder computergesteuerten Tönen ist dies nicht länger nötig. Die meisten Kunstformen können auf die eine oder andere Weise in alternative Kunstformen umgewandelt werden. Ein Künstler kann ein Abbild von seinem Kunstwerk machen, sei es ein Foto, eine Zeichnung oder eine Videoaufnahme, und mittels eines Scanners oder einer Videokamera, die an eine spezifische Bearbeitungssoftware angeschlossen sind, die Pixeldichte oder die Bewegungsdichte des Bildes auf MIDI-Rohdaten mappen. Diese Daten können zu einem Synthesizer oder einer anderen Klangquelle oder Programmierumgebung übertragen werden, die dann Musik generiert. Ein anderes Beispiel wären Bildhauer, die Licht-, Wärme-, Berührungs- oder Bewegungssensoren an ihrem Kunst-

werk anbringen, um MIDI-Rohdaten zu generieren, die dann an eine Klangquelle angeschlossen werden. Die Kombinationsmöglichkeiten sind schier unendlich.

Umgekehrt könnten Komponisten eine existierende Komposition oder Live-Performance verwenden, um durch MIDI/Video-Converter oder Audio/Video-Converter auf der Basis bestimmter vorprogrammierter Parameter-Mappings eine grafische Repräsentation ihrer Musik in Echtzeit zu schaffen.

Abschließend möchte ich nochmals auf spezifische Aspekte des Codes und der Kreativität zurückkommen. Wie bereits erwähnt, sind die meisten zeitgenössischen Komponisten – und besonders jene von Computermusik – Komponisten und Programmierer in Personalunion. Manche behaupten vielleicht, dass das Musikschaffen dieser Komponisten keine echte Musik sei, nur wenige werden allerdings bestreiten, dass Musik eine Kunstform ist. Was charakterisiert also den Code, der zur Schaffung von Musik verwendet wird? Darf behauptet werden, dass der Code aufgrund der zunehmenden Nutzung von Computern und Software zu einer eigenständigen Kunstform geworden ist? Ist dies der Fall, wann ist Software dann nicht einfach nur Code, sondern Kunst? Gelten diese Grundsätze für alle Kunstschaffenden oder gibt es Unterschiede? Programmiert z. B. ein Computerprogrammierer einen Algorithmus, der Musik erzeugt, sollte dieses Programm dann als Kunst betrachtet werden? Was, wenn etwa ein Komponist exakt den gleichen Algorithmus schreibt? Wird das Programm des Komponisten als Kunst, das Programm des Programmierers hingegen lediglich als Code zur Generierung von Musik betrachtet, oder sind die Programme gleichwertig? Wird vielleicht keines der Programme als Kunst akzeptiert? Ist ein Programm, das als Kunst bezeichnet wird, tatsächlich Kunst oder wird es nur als Kunst angesehen, weil jemand behauptet „Das ist Kunst"? Gibt es konkrete Kriterien, die einen derartigen Standpunkt rechtfertigen, oder handelt es sich um subjektive Werturteile? All diese Fragen berühren Kernpunkte der Fusion von Technik und Kunst.

Ich habe mich in diesem Kontext auf die Zusammenhänge zwischen Code, Technik und Komposition beschränkt, das Thema „Code und Musik" ist aber wesentlich vielschichtiger und wird uns in der Zukunft vermutlich alle in den verschiedensten Lebensbereichen berühren. Wie eingangs erwähnt, sind Computertechnik und Software zu einem integralen Bestandteil der Schaffung und Verbreitung von Musik geworden. Die anhaltende Kontroverse um die Verbreitung von Musik und das Kopieren von Dateien über das Internet greift Fragen des Rechts, des Codes und der individuellen künstlerischen Schöpfung aus einer weitaus vielschichtigeren Perspektive auf. Technik und Code fördern die individuelle Kreativität, wie ich aufzuzeigen versucht habe, drohen jedoch gleichzeitig das Recht des Individuums auf seine eigene Kunst einzuschränken.

Aus dem Amerikanischen von Sonja Pöllabauer

Pixelspaces 2003
Sensory Environments – Immaterial Interfaces

Heimo Ranzenbacher / Horst Hörtner

The Ars Electronica Futurelab's symposium entitled *Pixelspaces—Sensory Environments–Immaterial Interfaces* focuses on a field of concentration of the lab's current work and simultaneously on an area in which the classical performing arts have of late displayed certain tendencies bringing them in closer proximity to leading edge media art. On the basis of current projects and concepts that can be subsumed within the thematic range defined in the symposium's title—for example, Joachim Sauter's work on the opera *The Jew of Malta* (Opera Biennale Munich), Klaus Obermaier's *Dave* (Ars Electronica 2002) and installations like Justin Manor's *Key Grip—Pixelspaces 2003* will be scrutinizing artistic and technical production methods. In doing so, the symposium will also be looking into the question of the extent to which institutions in the traditional arts such as musical theater and dance are indicating their readiness to take into account the media-aesthetic implications of this development or are even capable of doing so.
Moreover, Klaus Obermaier's current project entitled "Dance and Media Performance Fusions" [DAMPF, see p. 301], an interdisciplinary project dealing with the (performance) stage as a sensory environment, makes available a forum in which theory formation and practical experimentation blend into real performances. *Pixelspaces 2003* will complement them by providing basic research in the sense of relevant experience in artistic and technical practice.
Parallel to demonstrations of interest on the part of the arts—represented first and foremost by dance companies and the theater (understood in the broadest sense)—it is technology itself that nurtures and supports this process of convergence through availability on one hand and through the accompanying feasibility (of the concepts) on the other. Nevertheless, for media art on the technological leading edge, the most important reason for the relevance of the traditional arts' increased interest in new systems that has accompanied this greater feasibility is that it signals the emergence and acknowledgement of a media-specific way of doing art. Speaking in favor of this view is not only the very fact of the use of these means but also that the means themselves determine the content which is being taken into account by their use. Thus, what is called for first of all is competence in media art, and this is simultaneously the source of the challenge and the problems.
Media-aesthetic competence has not remained without influence on the contents presented at classical venues. This is presumably so to an even greater extent than is the case with a conventional set designer, who implements his skills not only as a structural engineer, interior designer etc. following the instructions of the director but also in collaboration with him in the process of making an impact upon what transpires on stage and thus its aesthetic. This is inherent in the constitutive nature of media. For the fusion being addressed through DAMPF, the model of the traditional partnership between direction and set design will be the minimum precondition—with, in accordance with their nature, new consequences. Through projects like *Gulliver's Box* (Adrian Cheok, Hirokazu Kato, Ars Electronica Futurelab) [see p. 326], *Can you see me now?* (Blast Theory / Mix Media

Lab), *Key Grip* (Justin Manor) [see p. 330] and *co.in.cide* (Heimo Ranzenbacher, x-space & Ars Electronica FutureLab) [see p. 332], these consequences are gaining entry into the discourse of DAMPF.

For this reason, *Pixelspaces 2003* is also investigating the potential effects of an upload of physical programming environments on classical forms of representation and performance spaces, and is thus simultaneously attempting to formulate approaches to a theoretical figure (for instance, in the type of music as movement of sound in time) that are necessary as references for the aesthetic process of coming to terms with performance spaces that are new for both partners.

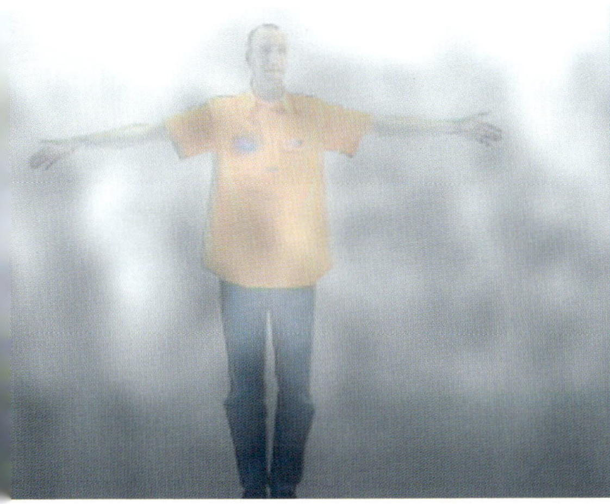

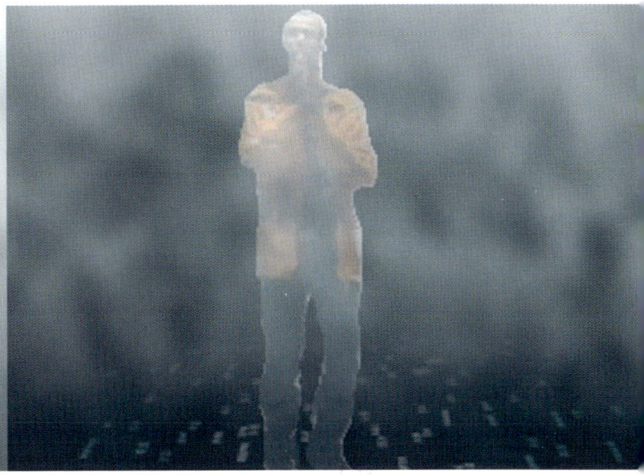

Pixelspaces_DAMPF

Pixelspaces 2003

Sensorische Umgebungen – immaterielle Interfaces

Heimo Ranzenbacher / Horst Hörtner

Das Symposion des Ars Electronica Futurelab, *Pixelspaces – Sensorische Umgebungen – immaterielle Interfaces,* nimmt mit einem Arbeitsschwerpunkt des Lab zugleich Bezug auf Tendenzen einer Annäherung der klassischen darstellenden Künste an die avancierte Medienkunst. Anhand aktueller Projekte und Konzepte, die sich in dieser thematischen Klammer des Titels zusammenfassen lassen – etwa Joachim Sauters Arbeit für die Oper *Der Jude von Malta* (Opernbiennale München), Klaus Obermaiers *Dave* (Ars Electronica 2002) oder installativer Projekte wie Justin Manors *Key Grip,* – untersucht Pixelspaces 2003 künstlerische und technische Methoden der Realisierung. Pixelspaces 2003 geht damit auch der Frage nach, wie weit Institutionen aus dem Bereich der traditionellen Künste – etwa Musik- und Tanztheater – Bereitschaft zeigen (können), den medienästhetischen Implikationen Rechnung zu tragen. Mit Klaus Obermaiers aktuellem interdisziplinären Projekt „Dance and Media Performance

Fusions“, kurz DAMPF [s. Seite 302], das sich mit der (Performance-)Bühne als sensorische Umgebung befasst, steht darüber hinaus ein Forum zur Verfügung, in dem Theoriebildung und praktische Erprobung in reale Aufführungen münden. *Pixelspaces 2003* liefert dazu im Sinne der Grundlagenforschung einschlägige Erfahrungswerte aus der künstlerischen und technischen Praxis.

Parallel zu Interessensbezeugungen seitens der vor allem durch Tanz und (im weitesten Sinn) Theater repräsentierten Künste, ist es die Technik selbst, die diese Annäherung einerseits durch Verfügbarkeit, andererseits durch die damit assoziierte Machbarkeit (der Konzepte) unterstützt.

Für die technisch avancierte Medienkunst ist das damit gewachsene Interesse der traditionellen Kunst an neuen Systemen vor allem aber deshalb relevant, weil es mittlerweile das Verständnis einer medienspezifischen *Machart* signalisiert. Sprich dafür, dass nicht nur der Einsatz der Mittel, sondern die Mittel selbst schon Inhalte determinieren, welchen der Einsatz Rechnung trägt. Gefragt ist also erstmals auch Medienkunst-Kompetenz. Darin liegen zugleich die Herausfordung und die Probleme.

Medienästhetische Kompetenz bleibt nicht ohne Einfluss auf die Inhalte der klassischen Spielräume. Sie wird vermutlich in einem noch höheren Maß als ein herkömmlicher Bühnenbildner, der seine Kompetenzen nicht nur als Statiker, Raumgestalter etc. im Auftrag, sondern in Verbindung mit der Regie umsetzt, das Bühnengeschehen und damit seine Ästhetik prägen. Das liegt in der konstitutiven Natur der Medien. Für die durch DAMPF angesprochene Fusion wird das Modell der traditionellen Partnerschaft zwischen Regie und Bühnenbild die Mindestvoraussetzung sein – mit, ihrer Natur nach, neuen Konsequenzen. Durch Projekte, wie *Gulliver's Box* (Adrian Cheok, Hirokazu Kato, Ars Electronica Futurelab) [s. Seite 328], *Can you see me now?* (Blast Theory / Mixed Media Lab), *Key Grip* (Justin Manor) [s. Seite 331] und *co.in.cide* (Heimo Ranzenbacher, x-space & Ars Electronica Futurelab) [s. Seite 334] finden diese Konsequenzen Eingang in den Diskurs von DAMPF.

Pixelspaces 2003 untersucht daher auch mögliche Auswirkungen eines Uploads physikalischer Programmierumgebungen auf klassische Darstellungsformen und Bühnenräume und versucht damit zugleich Ansätze einer theoretischen Figur (etwa in der Art von Musik als Bewegung von Klang in der Zeit) zu formulieren, die als Referenz für die ästhetische Bewältigung der für beide Partner neuen Spielräume nötig sind.

DAMPF Lab
Dance and Media Performance Fusions

Scott deLahunta

DAMPF Lab is an interdisciplinary collaborative project dedicated to fostering new and distinctive art works of high quality that integrate interactive computer technologies with performing arts practices. Critically rigorous and informed by a broad set of research perspectives, DAMPF Lab will investigate the relation between developing technologies and body-based performance, seeking new insight into e.g. the impact on creative processes and shifting relations between maker (author), performer and audience.
DAMPF Lab has been made possible by a grant from the European Union's Culture 2000 programme for annual projects in support of a partnership involving *tanz performance köln,* the *Ars Electronica Futurelab Linz, V2_Lab Rotterdam* and the *Animax Multimedia Theater Bonn.* This partnership will contribute experience, expertise and facilities to a series of ongoing events in 2003-2004 within the framework of two complementary strands: (1) research labs and (2) co-productions.
The co-productions are aimed at the nurturing and realisation of specific art works. There are two of these currently in development: one is led by composer/director and media artist Klaus Obermaier working in close collaboration with the *Ars Electronica Futurelab* to investigate the effective implementation of interactive technologies in the context of a new performance for the stage; the other is led by choreographer Angelika Oei collaborating with the *V2_Lab* on the creation of a series of prototypes heading towards the production of a large scale performance/interactive media installation work.
The main aim of the research labs is to generate a range of diverse and shareable outcomes to include: drawing questions from and in turn supporting the creative work of the co-productions; the stimulation of other new artistic work; the development of reusable technology solutions (found in extant or newly developed hardware and software); and the devising of unique dramaturgical and user testing approaches to the artistic process. In addition, the research labs aim to disseminate documentation and writings that will contribute to conceptual, theoretical and educational approaches to this area of work.
There are three research labs currently being planned to take place over the next several months, the first in the context of this year's Ars Electronica 2003. The second will take place at V2_Lab in Rotterdam and the third at the Animax Multimedia Theater in Bonn. In June/ July 2004, there will be a presentation of resulting artistic prototypes and previews in the context of the DAMPF Festival organised by *tanz performance köln.*

DAMPF Lab at Ars Electronica

The first DAMPF Research Lab will be organised in a close relation to the Ars Electronica *Pixelspaces* conference (8 and 9 September 2003). The theme of the *Pixelspaces* conference this year is the relation between the programmable (as different from the navigable) interface and an interactive physical environment. A number of DAMPF related research lines can be developed within this theme; e.g. connections between code and choreographic processes, complex perceptive/receptive modes, generative performing systems, etc. In order to further develop these lines and fine tune questions and responses in relation to them, the DAMPF Lab at Ars Electronica will participate in the conference and practical hands-on sessions as well as organise a series of smaller dialogues and discussions with invited guests selected in part from the larger Ars Electronica programme.

Further information can be accessed at this URL: *http://dampf.v2.nl*

Collaborating on DAMPF are: tanz performance köln, Animax Multimedia Theater Bonn, V2_Lab Rotterdam, Ars Electronica Center Linz.
With the support of the Culture 2000 programme of the European Union.

DAMPF Lab
Dance and Media Performance Fusions

Scott deLahunta

DAMPF Lab ist ein interdisziplinäres Gemeinschaftsprojekt zur Förderung innovativer und herausragender Kunstprojekte, die interaktive Computertechnologien mit darstellender Kunst verbinden. Mit kritischer Gründlichkeit untersucht DAMPF Lab verschiedene Perspektiven der Beziehung zwischen innovativen Technologien und körperorientierten Performances, um neue Erkenntnisse über bestimmte Phänomene, wie etwa die Auswirkungen kreativer Schaffensprozesse und das wechselnde Beziehungsgefüge zwischen Produzent (Autor), Darsteller und Publikum, zu erlangen.
DAMPF Lab wird über Mittel des EU-Programms „Kultur 2000“ finanziert, das die Zusammenarbeit zwischen Kulturschaffenden aus mehreren EU-Mitgliedstaaten fördert; die Partner von DAMPF Lab sind tanz performance köln, das Ars Electronica Futurelab Linz, das V2_Lab Rotterdam und das Animax Multimedia-Theater Bonn. Die Erfahrungen, das Know-how und die Ressourcen aller Partner fließen 2003 und 2004 in verschiedene Events zweier sich ergänzender Veranstaltungsreihen ein: (1) Research Labs und (2) Co-Productions.
In den Co-Productions werden spezifische Kunstprojekte geplant und umgesetzt. Zurzeit befinden sich zwei Projekte in der Entwicklungsphase: Eines wird vom Komponisten, Dirigenten und Medienkünstler Klaus Obermaier geleitet, der bei seinen Untersuchungen zur adäquaten Umsetzung von interaktiven Technologien im Kontext einer innovativen Bühneperformance eng mit dem Ars Electronica Futurelab zusammenarbeitet. Das zweite Projekt wird von der Choreografin Angelika Oei geleitet, die bei der Herstellung verschiedener Prototypen zur Gestaltung einer Mega-Performance bzw. interaktiven Medieninstallation mit dem V2_Lab zusammenarbeitet.
Das Hauptziel der Research Labs ist es, ein breites Spektrum an verschiedensten vielseitig nutzbaren Forschungsergebnissen zu gewinnen; aus den Co-Productions sollen neue Forschungsfragen abgeleitet werden, die umgekehrt dem Schöpfungsprozess in den Co-Pro-

ductions neue Impulse verleihen. Die Research Labs sollen Impulse für neue innovative Kunstprojekte setzen. Ein weiteres Ziel ist die Entwicklung von wiederverwertbaren Techniklösungen (anhand bestehender oder neu entwickelter Hard- und Software) und schließlich die Entwicklung von dramaturgischen Konzepten und Möglichkeiten zur Bewertung des künstlerischen Schaffensprozesses. Die Research Labs sind auch bestrebt, Dokumentationsmaterial und neue Literatur zum konzeptionellen, theoretischen und pädagogischen Hintergrund dieser Projekte zur Verfügung zu stellen.
In den nächsten Monaten sind drei Research Labs geplant: das erste im Rahmen der Ars Electronica 2003 stattfinden, das zweite beim *V2_Lab* in Rotterdam und das dritte im Animax Multimedia-Theater in Bonn. Im Juni / Juli 2004 werden die in den Research Labs entwickelten Prototypen und eine Vorschau auf weitere Neuentwicklungen beim von der *tanz performance köln* organisierten DAMPF-Festival präsentiert werden.

DAMPF Lab im Rahmen der Ars Electronica

Das erste DAMPF Research Lab findet in enger Zusammenarbeit mit der Ars-Electronica-Konferenz *Pixelspaces* (8. und 9. September 2003) statt. Übergeordnetes Thema der diesjährigen *Pixelspaces*-Konferenz ist die Beziehung zwischen programmierbaren (im Unterschied zu navigierbaren) Interfaces und einer interaktiven physischen Umgebung. Unter diesem Gesichtspunkt wurden verschiedene DAMPF-Forschungsfragen diskutiert, wie etwa die Verbindungen zwischen Code und choreografischen Prozessen, komplexen perzeptiven / rezeptiven Verfahren, generativen Performing Systems etc. Zur Weiterentwicklung und Feinabstimmung der Reaktionen auf diese Forschungsfragen wird *DAMPF Lab* an der Konferenz und einigen Übungsseminaren teilnehmen und Diskussionsrunden mit ausgewählten Gästen organisieren, die u. a. selbst an der Ars Electronica mitwirken.
Weitere Informationen finden sich unter folgender URL: *http://dampf.v2.nl*

Aus dem Englischen von Sonja Pöllabauer

An Dampf sind beteiligt: tanz performance Köln, Animax Multimedia Theater Bonn, V2_Lab Rotterdam, Ars Electronica Center Linz.
Mit Unterstützung des Culture 2000 Programm der Europäischen Union.

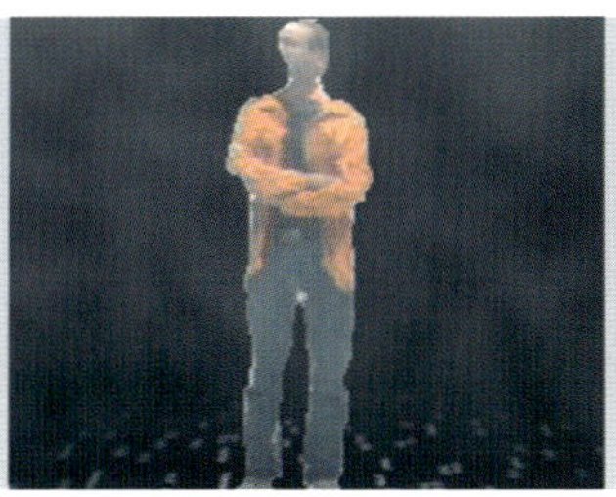
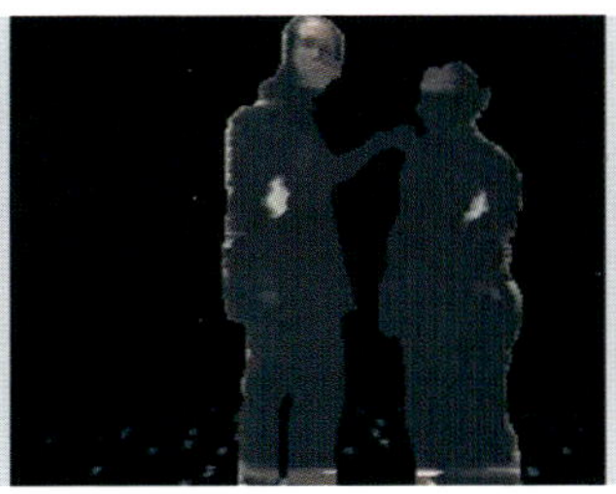
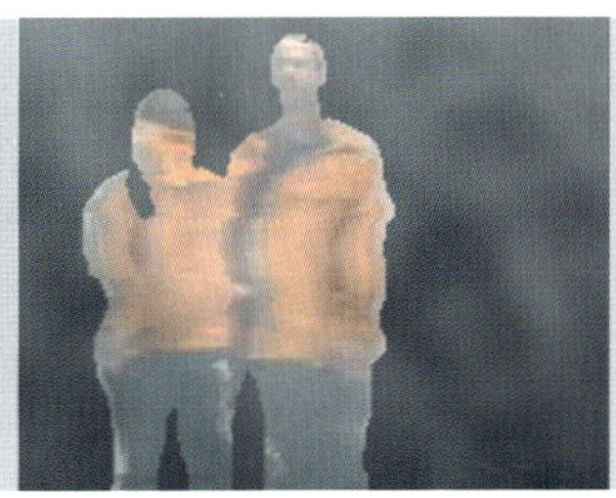

Open Source Choreography?

Scott deLahunta

This essay is an exercise in applying concepts derived from the Open Source software movement to the creative processes and products of contemporary choreography.[1] Across its three sections, comparison and contrast is used to open up and explore some questions related to issues of authorship and originality, whether or not choreographic methods are decoded through forms of discourse, and if the sharing of these methods could constitute a form of Open Source.

The Art of Making Dance

The history of contemporary, modern or "post modern" dance is usually written as a 20th century affair that originates in America and Western Europe and has a canonical sequence beginning at the turn of the century with Isadora Duncan. There is a tendency to organise this canon in two parts, early modern dance and post modern dance, along the lines of the general shift from modernism to postmodernism in the arts and architecture and on either side of a particularly iconoclastic rupture in the early 1960s known as the Judson Church movement that broadened tremendously the scope for choreographic methods.[2]
Prior to the 1960s, documentation of specific choreographic methods for contemporary dance is minimal. Just before her death in 1958, a member of the early canon of modern dance, choreographer and teacher Doris Humphrey, completed a small book entitled *The Art of Making Dances.* This book, published in 1959 and again in 1987, is widely perceived to be the "first" book to comprehensively present the art of choreography in a "how to manual" for dance making.[3] As such it is likely to be found in the bibliography of most dance composition courses in higher education in the United States, the United Kingdom and some dance programs in continental Europe.
In her introduction to the book, Humphrey contends that there were no theories of craftsmanship or form for dance making before the 1930s. Missing, she writes, was something equivalent to what music had "with its counterpoint and harmony, or painting with its laws of perspective and proportion". In *The Art of Making Dances,* Humphrey produces her theory on the "craft" of choreography organised around the concepts of ingredients and tools, design and dynamics, rhythm, motivation and gesture, words, music, sets and props and form.
As it is one of the original reference points for the discourse on how to make dances, the book marks the beginning of a period when the compositional techniques, strategies and methods of dance making begin to gather momentum. Interestingly, new books written by subsequent generations of choreographers do not follow. What does is that the discourse begins to evolve through the multiple accumulating acts of writing and publishing of a growing number of dance writers, critics and increasingly scholars. Sometimes the writings are explicitly "about" choreographic methods, such as Sally Banes on the "Choreographic Methods of the Judson Dance Theatre".[4] Insight into how a particular choreographer makes dances occasionally comes through in an interview with a writer; at other times a close description of the work carries methodological information.[5] It is

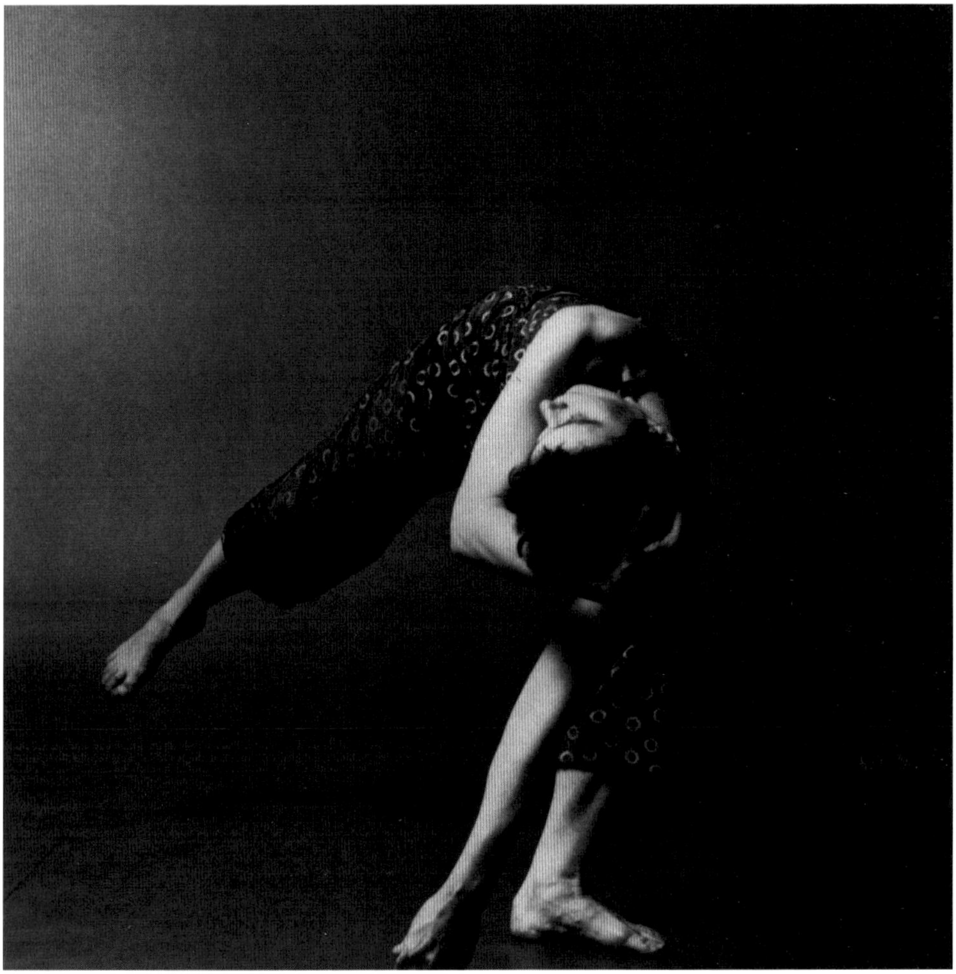

Photographer Lois Greenfield

important to note that plenty of choreographers were also involved in documenting their making processes, and some were producing sizeable publications either solely or in edited collections filled with scores, sketches, notes, etc. However, the point I wish to make is that this figure of the writer / interviewer, someone standing alongside and observing the actual practice, becomes instrumental in exposing and disseminating the methods of choreography without them our collective understanding of how to make dances would be significantly diminished.

To summarize briefly up to this point: Prior to the 1960s, lacking a discourse, information about how to make dances would have come from watching dances or taking workshops with the artist. Subsequent to the publication of *The Art of Making Dances* there begins a collective process of knowledge building about choreographic process through the growth of a variety of forms of discourse in the field of dance (in parallel with a growth in the practice of making dances and public interest in the art form). Some choreographers contribute documentation, notes and some larger works to this discourse, but much of its production enters the domain of the writer / interviewer.

Collective Creativity

Open Source Software is software that is freely available not only as its executable binary code, but also as its source code. This way the software can be modified and used for other programs by anyone. Within the concept of Open Source resides the notion that some form of collective creativity produces and maintains the software product. This product is owned by everyone and no one—as intellectual property this software can be protected by various licensing agreements that preserve this freedom of ownership and the rights of the user to adapt the software to his or her needs. It would be difficult to apply this concept of collective creativity as it might relate to choreography. I have suggested that choreographers and writers / interviewers work together collectively to provide open access through discourse to explanations and explications of choreographic method (a type of intellectual property), but I would not refer to this as a form of collective creativity as the dances that are made are almost always reconfigured as objects of individual choreographic authorship. As such, in fact, copyright law in many countries protects these dances, a topic I will address below.

Neither could one say that "open access" to discourses about dance making is anything like open access to software code despite some correspondence between choreographic methods and code that can be teased out by looking at the work of choreographers who have at some point in their career made dances based almost entirely on a set of rules or instructions or an "algorithm" and as such their "source code" is freely available. In the 1970s, New York choreographer Trisha Brown and member of the Judson Church group did two performances in particular which were based on instructions. These were *Accumulation* and *Locus* (and their various manifestations). The instructions for these dances are published in several books, and nothing prevents me from placing the algorithm for *Accumulation* here in this text with the appropriate citation:

> The accumulation is an additive procedure where movement 1 is presented; start over. Movement 1; 2 is added and start over. 1,2; 3 is added and start over, etc., until the dance ends. Primary Accumulation accumulates thirty movements in eighteen minutes. The 29th and 30th movements each cause the figure to revolve 45 degrees, making a 90-degree turn with each completion of the sequence. Therefore, a 360-degree revolution occurs in the last two minutes of the dance, giving the audience three alternate views of the dance before finally stopping.[6]

Despite the fact that with this algorithm, the "source code" so to speak, one could recreate a dance that was performed in 1975, only Trisha Brown is entitled to compile and perform it as *Accumulation,* due to the extending of American copyright law to protect abstract choreography in 1976. Prior to 1976, copyright protection could be extended to dance works if they could be classified as "dramatic or dramatico-musical compositions".[7] However, the copyright in either case has only applied to the finished work, not to its underlying rules.[8] This further interrupts any direct correspondence between software source code that can be protected by law and choreographic methods that would not be considered intellectual property at the point prior to the finished performance. On the other hand, the "algorithm" for *Accumulation* can be pulled from the field of discourse around making dances (just as I have done here in this essay) and used to generate movement material that is going to be transformed in subsequent stages of the making process into something unique to another choreographer. Seen in this light, it is possible to suggest that there is some aspect of Open Source software in operation in the practice of sharing choreographic methods. I will return to this notion at the end of the essay.

In order to identify a dance so as to defend a copyright, there must be some objective method of fixing the choreography in a stable form as evidence. The Copyright Office in Washington D.C. distributes the following guidelines: "for choreography, the work may be embodied in a film or video recording or be precisely described on any phonorecord or in written text or any dance notation system such as Labanotation, Sutton Movement Shorthand or Benesh Notation." The notation systems listed here come closest to the concept of software in terms of intellectual property. Unlike the audio video recording devices, dance notation systems are made up of a flexible classification of discrete symbols that can be recombined to form increasingly larger units of information relating to particular movements over time. The simplest unit of information in Labanotation for example is referred to as the "staff" (as in music) and within this staff one can combine the symbols necessary to indicate the direction, part of body, level and length of time. Out of the syntactical combinatorial strength of this fairly simple symbol language, complex information about movement can be represented.

This description of how dance notation works bears similarities to how software code functions. However, what distinguishes the dance notation system from software code is that in the practice of making dances, dance notation is not used as a generative device while software code is by its nature inherently generative; it produces the effect. Notation systems were created with the intention of preserving and restaging choreographies, not generating them. Choreographers would not devise a dance by writing it out in dance notation symbols first. However, in intellectual property terms notation functions as part of the system of owning choreographies; and this is similar to software code.

To review briefly from the last summary: The way that information about making dances is collectively aggregated from a variety of individual sources is not the same as the collective creativity practiced in the creation of Open Source software. Dances ultimately tend to resolve into objects of individual authorship and can be protected as such by recent copyright adaptations. While some choreographers may work with rule based systems for making dances, these algorithms themselves are not likely to be considered as intellectual property. In order for the copyright act to be used to protect a finished dance, the choreography of that dance must be fixed in the form of an audio and / or video recording or some form of written dance notation. Dance notation systems by their nature perhaps bear a closer resemblance to software than other features of dance—but they are used primarily to record choreographies, not to generate them.

Choreography and Open Source

Just as particular choreographers have worked with rule based systems in their dance making, something approximating a "copy" of a dance may be used by some choreographers to explore the philosophical implications of intellectual property laws applied to dance. Well known now in Europe for creating provocative conceptual dance works, French choreographer Jérôme Bel intended his 1998 piece *The Last Performance* to be made up of short sections or "quotes" from dances by other choreographers that have influenced him in some way.[9] He obtained permission to use some of this material, but also some rejection letters citing copyright laws. These were read aloud at the first performances of *The Last Performance.*

One of the choreographers who provided permission for Bel to use her material was German choreographer Susanne Linke, and one of the dancers in *The Last Performance* wears a white dress and states, "I am Susanne Linke." In this context, the significance of the "copy" is the set of references it holds for the viewers at the moment of its representation in the performance. No longer bound by the logical structures of language or the code of software or law, this "copy" begins to play on the blurry edge of mimesis—to claim to be the original performer is to perhaps step into the role as an actor or as an imitator. Dancing bodies are extremely complex in informational terms and will resist reified readings. *The Last Performance* illustrates the point at which the relationship between contemporary choreography and Open Source diverges and a comparison becomes too inconsistent to be worthwhile. To bring this essay to a close, just as the example of *The Last Performance* can be used to illustrate a situation in which comparisons between choreography and Open Source can unravel, another choreographer can provide a clear case for carrying through with the exercise. I wish to return to the suggestion that some aspect of Open Source software is in operation in the practice of sharing choreographic ideas of which the following is an example.

William Forsythe, the artistic director and primary choreographer of the Frankfurt Ballet since 1984, has made elements of his choreographic process available through the distribution of an interactive multimedia CD-ROM entitled *Improvisation Technologies: A Tool for the Analytical Dance Eye.*[10] His motivation for starting the CD-ROM project was to provide new dancers to the company with a way of studying the basics of his innovative improvisation techniques. Unlike Doris Humphrey's *The Art of Making Dances,* Forsythe had no intention of producing a publication that would address all aspects of dance making, but to provide information about what he refers to as "building blocks" for developing a way of analysing motion while moving improvisationally. In Forsythe's view, these building blocks represent concepts or ideas more than techniques or strategies. From this perspective, choreographic methods resolve into choreographic thinking.

The CD-ROM presents four categories of information: lines, additions, reorganising and writing. Within each category there are up to five subcategories (e.g. point point line, rotating inscription, isometries, etc.) and within these several more. This hierarchical organisation of the information allows the reader / user to proceed easily along a learning trajectory that goes from simple to more complex principles. The reader / user also has the option of entering the information through watching these building blocks or ideas danced by members of the company. There are a total of sixty-three separate building blocks represented on the CD-ROM and many of these contain other building blocks within them. They represent a small but important portion of William Forsythe's choreographic thinking. Because they are disseminated and made accessible through this electronic document, they are in the public domain as a form of Open Source code not only providing insight for those who wish to understand more about the process of making dances in general, but making the building blocks themselves available for anyone else to use.

When asked if he felt he is giving something away by publishing this information in the form of the CD-ROM, Forsythe has responded:

> Well, the CD-ROM doesn't tell you how I choreograph, it doesn't teach you anything other than how to observe motion. (...) It shows just some of the ways of thinking about analyzing motion. I think there is a whole new attitude towards work. Put it this way: work is not some sort of secret. It's rather superstitious to think one has to keep one's method secret. (...) At the end of the 20th century, work doesn't need to be kept secret. It won't disappear just because we communicate. We might be apprehended, so to speak, and that could force us to abandon our own methods, which is not such a bad thing either. (...) I would hope that the users would actually discover their own dancing en route to understanding ours.[11]

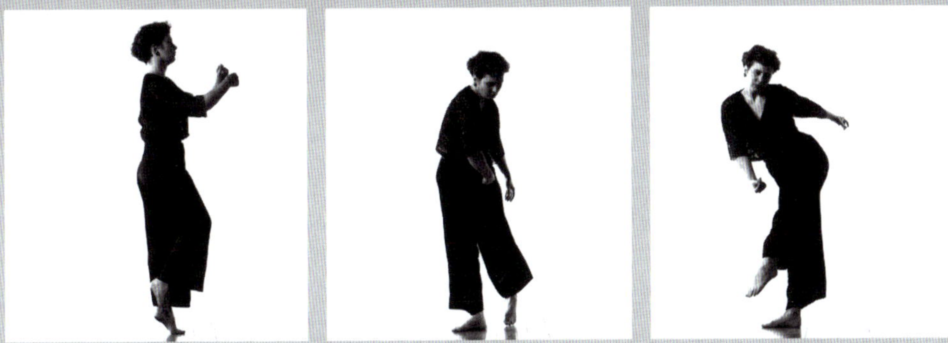

Dance critic Jennifer Dunning describing a choreography by Susan Rethorst in the *New York Times*, 21 September 1995: "The dance is packed with exquisite movement phrases and striking small gestures, fleeting though they may be."

To review briefly from the last summary: when finally produced as a performance, a dance can be registered for copyright, and it is possible for the choreographer to refuse to allow other choreographers to reproduce any section of that dance as happened with *The Last Performance* by Jérôme Bel. However, when on stage the dancing body does not easily conform to the neat fixed entity that the institution of copyright might prefer. The dancing body on stage also resists being compared to the dynamics of Open Source. Connections between choreography and Open Source as a particular set of concepts and practices are more likely to be found in the conditions of openness as manifest in the *Improvisation Technologies* CD-ROM of William Forsythe.

Conclusion

The creative processes and products of contemporary choreography practice can only be inconsistently aligned with those of the Open Source software movement. Forsythe suggests that the days of keeping one's methods secret are disappearing, but I am not sure to what degree this is contingent upon or simply coincident with the Open Source movement (both are in the same historical time frame). Different types of questions emerge: do the software licenses that preserve free access to source code suggest any adaptations to the choreography copyright law? In seeking to answer this question, we would find our comparison rapidly breaking down as it has occasionally in this essay. Another type of question: wouldn't one need to know how to choreograph or be a choreographer to make use of the source code of a particular dance? This asks us to consider the possibilities of knowledge as something other than property. Perhaps understanding how a dance is made, having access to its "source code", could help us deepen our grasp of creative processes in general. A dance performance then might begin to be widely perceived as inseparable from the process—an executable of choreographic thinking. Perhaps if choreographic processes are better understood, they could be used to produce things other than performances. If comparing the world of choreography to the world of Open Source software inspires this shift, then it's an exercise well worth doing.

1 This essay was originally written for an MIT Press book (as yet unpublished) inspired by the CODE conference organised in April 2001 *(http://www.cl.cam.ac.uk/CODE/)*. I have chosen Open Source rather than Free Software as my term of reference for the concept of software that is freely available not only as its executable binary code, but also as its source code. However, it's important to note that while both may fit this same technical description, Open Source and Free Software have divergent histories and in some contexts are ideologically opposed. Both have their own websites, and for additional clarifying reading I suggest some of Florian Cramer's essays: *Free Software (http://www.fsf.org);* Open Source *(http://www.opensource.org/);* Florian Cramer *(http://userpage.fu-berlin.de/~cantsin/).*

2 The Judson Church movement refers to a series of dance composition classes and performances in New York City that took place in the 1960s. At the start of the decade at the suggestion of John Cage, the composer Robert Dunn conducted a small number of influential composition classes in New York City out of which some of the best-known and most innovative contemporary choreographers of the second half of the 20th century emerged. The classes created the conditions for moving away from the choreographic formulas that had been developed by early 20th century theorists like Doris Humphrey. Names of dance artists who participated in the classes include Trisha Brown, Lucinda Childs, David Gordon, Douglas Dunn, Kenneth King, Yvonne Ranier, Steve Paxton, Simone Forti and Deborah Hay. A selection of this group gave their first in a famous series of performances that would last four years on 6 July 1962 at the Judson Memorial Church in Lower Manhattan, thus earning them the title of the Judson Dance Theater group.

3 Doris Humphrey. *The Art of Making Dances.* Edited by Barbara Pollack. Princeton Book Company, Hightstown, NJ, 1959 / 1987.

4 Sally Banes. "Choreographic Methods of the Judson Dance Theater". in *Writing Dancing in the Age of Postmodernism.* pp. 211-226. Wesleyan University Press, February 1994.

5 For example see: 1) this edited book of interviews with choreographers: Jo Butterworth and Gill Clarke, eds. *Dance Makers Portfolio: conversations with choreographers.* Bretton Hall, Wakefield, UK: Centre for Dance and Theatre Studies, 1998.; and 2) any issue of a dance journal that often includes feature articles on particular choreographers such as *Ballet International / Tanz Aktuell (http://www.ballet-tanz.de/)* or *Dance Theatre Journal (http://www.laban.org/dance_theatre_journal.phtml).*

6 One source for this dance "algorithm" can be found in an interview with Trisha Brown in *The Drama Review, Post-modern Dance Issue.* T-65, March 1975.

7 Julie Van Camp. "Copyright of Choreographic Works." *1994 – 95 Entertainment, Publishing and the Arts Handbook.* edited by Stephen F. Breimer, Robert Thorne, and John David Viera. pp. 59 – 92. Clark, Boardman and Callaghan, New York,1994. This article can be found on line at *http://www.csulb.edu/~jvancamp/copyrigh.html.*

8 Actual litigation involving dance and copyright law has only occurred occasionally. One example is a written court case over the use of the name of iconic modern dance figure Martha Graham. David Finkle. "The Future of Dance's Past: Graham Center Wins a Round in Court and Wakes Up Choreographers". *The Village Voice.* Week of August 15-21, 2001. This can be found on line by searching on David Finkle at *http://www.villagevoice.com/.*

9 Gerald Siegmund. "The Endgame of Dance: 'The Last Performance' by Jérôme Bel in Nuremberg." *Ballett International Tanz Aktuell.* January 1999.

10 William Forsythe. *Improvisation Technologies: A Tool for the Analytical Dance Eye* (CD-ROM). Hatje Cantz Verlag (ISBN: 3775708502), Ostfildern, June 2000.

11 These quotations are extracted from an interview with William Forsythe conducted by Nik Haffner on 22 April 1999 that is published in the booklet that accompanies the *Improvisation Technologies* CD-ROM. Nik Haffner, Volker Kuchelmeiser and Christian Ziegler made major contributions to the conceptual and technical aspects of the CD-ROM.

Open-Source-Choreografie?

Scott deLahunta

Dieser Text ist ein Versuch, Konzepte aus der Bewegung der Open-Source-Software auf kreative Prozesse und Produkte zeitgenössischer Choreografie zu übertragen.[1] In drei Abschnitten werden mittels Vergleich und Gegenüberstellung Fragen zu Autorschaft und Originalität angeschnitten und Untersuchungen angestellt, ob choreografische Methoden durch Diskursformen dekodiert werden und der freie Zugang zu diesen Methoden eine Art „Open Source" darstellt.

Die Kunst, Tänze zu machen

Die Geschichte des Contemporary Dance, des Modern oder „Postmodern" Dance wird meist als ein Phänomen des 20. Jahrhunderts beschrieben, das in Amerika und Westeuropa entstand und einen Kanon ausgebildet hat, der um die Jahrhundertwende mit Isadora Duncan begann. Es besteht die Tendenz, diesen Kanon in zwei Abschnitte zu gliedern – den frühen Modern Dance und den Postmodern Dance –, die dem allgemeinen Übergang von der Moderne zur Postmoderne in den Künsten und der Architektur entsprechen und vor und nach jenem ikonoklastischen Bruch in den frühen 1960er Jahren anzusiedeln sind. Diesen Bruch markiert die Judson-Church-Bewegung, die das Spektrum choreografischer Methoden enorm erweiterte.[2] Vor 1960 wurden spezielle choreografische Methoden für den Contemporary Dance kaum dokumentiert. Kurz vor ihrem Tod im Jahr 1958 vollendete die Choreografin und Lehrerin Doris Humphrey, eine Vertreterin des frühen Kanons des Modernen Tanzes, ein kleines Buch mit dem Titel *Die Kunst, Tänze zu machen: Zur Choreographie des Modernen Tanzes.* Dieses 1959 erschienene und 1987 neu aufgelegte Werk gilt weithin als das erste Buch, das die Kunst der Choreografie umfassend in Form eines „praktischen Handbuchs" des Tanzes präsentiert.[3] Als solches ist es ein fixer Bestandteil der Tanzausbildung in den Vereinigten Staaten, Großbritannien und auch in Kontinentaleuropa.

Humphrey behauptet in der Einleitung ihres Buchs, dass vor den 1930er Jahren keine handwerklichen oder formalen Theorien für den Tanz existierten. Es fehlte, wie sie schreibt, ein Bezugsrahmen wie es für die Musik „Kontrapunkt und Harmonie oder für die Malerei die Gesetze der Perspektive und Proportion sind". In *Die Kunst, Tänze zu machen* entwickelt Humphrey ihre Theorie zum „Handwerk" der Choreografie anhand von Komponenten und Instrumenten wie Design und Dynamik, Rhythmus, Motivation und Gestik, Worte, Musik, Bühnenbild sowie Requisiten und Form.

Das Buch kennzeichnet als einer der ersten Bezugspunkte für den Diskurs über den Entstehungsprozess von Tänzen den Beginn einer Periode, in der Kompositionstechniken, Strategien und Methoden der Tanzproduktion eine Eigendynamik zu entwickeln beginnen. Interessanterweise folgten keine neuen Bücher von den nachfolgenden Choreografengenerationen. Doch begann sich durch die zahlreichen Schriften und Publikationen einer wachsenden Anzahl von Autoren, Kritikern und zunehmend auch Wissenschaftlern ein Diskurs zu entfalten. Einige dieser Texte behandeln explizit choreografische Methoden, wie etwa Sally Banes in den „Choreografic Methods of the Judson Dance Theatre".[4] Einblicke, wie gewisse Choreografen Tänze gestalteten, bekam man hin und wieder durch Interviews; methodologische Informationen wurden mitunter durch genaue Beschreibungen des Arbeitsprozesses vermittelt.[5]

Festzuhalten ist, dass viele Choreografen an der Dokumentation ihrer kreativen Prozesse Anteil hatten – manche brachten als Einzelautoren oder in Zusammenarbeit mit anderen umfangreiche Publikationen heraus, die Partituren, Skizzen, Anmerkungen etc. enthielten. Worauf ich aber hinaus will ist, dass diese Figur des Autors/Interviewers, eines Außenstehenden, der die Praxis beobachtet, an der Darstellung und Verbreitung der choreografischen Methoden zunehmend mitwirkte. Ohne sie wäre unser Wissen über den Entstehungsprozess von Tänzen deutlich geringer.
Das bisher Gesagte kurz zusammengefasst: In Ermangelung eines Diskurses informierte man sich vor 1960 über die Entstehung von Tänzen, indem man sich diese ansah oder an Workshops mit dem Künstler teilnahm. Nach der Veröffentlichung des Buchs *Die Kunst, Tänze zu machen* begann durch die Entwicklung einer Vielfalt von Diskursen über das Tanzen (parallel zum Anwachsen der diversen Tanzformen und des öffentlichen Interesses an dieser Kunstform) ein kollektiver Prozess der Wissensbildung über den choreografischen Prozess. Manche Choreografen beteiligten sich an diesem Diskurs durch Dokumentationen, Anmerkungen und einige größere Arbeiten, der Großteil dieser Produktion fällt jedoch in den Bereich des Autors/Interviewers.

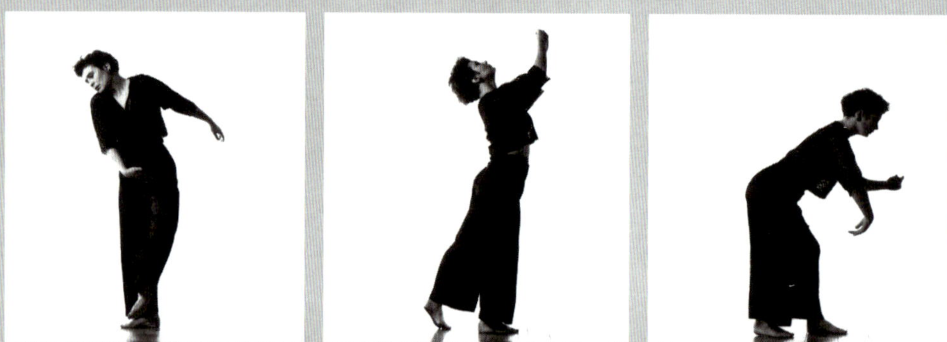

Fotos: Lois Greenfield

Die Tanzkritikerin Jennifer Dunning beschreibt eine Choreografie von Susan Rethors in der New York Times vom 21. September 1995 wie folgt: „Der Tanz ist voller exquisiter Bewegungsphrasen und kleiner Gesten, die trotz ihrer Flüchtigkeit überaus faszinierend sind."

Kollektive Kreativität

Open-Source-Software ist eine Software, von der nicht nur der ausführbare Binärcode, sondern auch der Quellcode frei verfügbar ist. Die Software kann daher modifiziert und von jedem für andere Programme verwendet werden. Das Open-Source-Konzept beruht darauf, dass das Softwareprodukt von einer Art kollektiver Kreativität produziert und weiterentwickelt wird. Dieses Produkt gehört jedem und niemandem – als geistiges Eigentum kann die Software durch diverse Lizenzvereinbarungen geschützt werden, die diese „Eigentumsfreiheit" und die Rechte des Users, die Software an seine bzw. ihre Bedürfnisse anzupassen, gewährleisten. Dieses Konzept kollektiver Kreativität lässt sich nur schwer auf die Choreografie übertragen. Ich habe vorgeschlagen, dass Choreografen und Autoren/Interviewer als Kollektiv zusammenarbeiten, um mittels eines Diskurses freien Zugang zu Erläuterungen und Erklärungen choreografischer Methoden (einer Form geistigen Eigentums) zu gewähren. Ich würde dies nicht als eine Form kollektiver Kreativität bezeichnen, da die Tänze, die geschaffen werden, fast immer Produkte einer individuellen choreografischen Autorschaft und Neugestaltung sind. Als solche werden diese Tänze in vielen Ländern durch das Urheberrechtsgesetz geschützt, mit dem ich mich in der Folge beschäftigen werde.

Man kann auch nicht sagen, dass der „freie Zugang" zu den Diskursen über den Entstehungsprozess von Tänzen mit dem freien Zugriff auf einen Softwarecode vergleichbar ist – obwohl man einige Übereinstimmungen zwischen choreografischen Methoden und einem Code finden könnte, wenn man die Arbeit an Choreografien beobachtet, die fast zur Gänze auf einem Regelwerk, auf Instruktionen oder einem „Algorithmus" basieren, deren „Quellcode" frei verfügbar ist. In den 1970er Jahren hat die New Yorker Choreografin und Mitglied des Judson Church-Kollektivs Trisha Brown zwei Performances gestaltet, die auf Instruktionen basierten: *Accumulation* und *Locus* (und deren diverse Erscheinungsformen). Die Instruktionen für diese Tänze wurden in mehreren Büchern publiziert – und nichts hindert mich daran, den Algorithmus für *Accumulation* in diesem Text mit dem entsprechenden Quellennachweis zu zitieren.

> Die Akkumulation ist ein additives Verfahren. Bewegung 1 wird präsentiert – und wiederholt. Bewegung 1; 2 wird hinzugefügt, das Ganze wird wiederholt. 1, 2; Bewegung 3 wird hinzugefügt und das Ganze wiederholt etc., bis der Tanz beendet ist. Die ursprüngliche Akkumulation umfasst dreißig Bewegungen in achtzehn Minuten. Die 29. und 30. Bewegung ziehen eine 45-Grad-Drehung nach sich, was bei jeder Vollendung der Sequenz eine 90-Grad-Drehung ergibt. Daher kommt es in den letzten zwei Minuten des Tanzes zu einer 360-Grad-Drehung, die dem Publikum drei unterschiedliche Ansichten des Tanzes gewährt, bevor er schließlich endet.[6]

Obwohl man mit diesem Algorithmus, dem „Quellcode" sozusagen, einen Tanz aus dem Jahr 1975 nachgestalten könnte, ist der Erweiterung des amerikanischen Urhebergesetzes auf den Schutz abstrakter Choreografie aus dem Jahr 1976 zufolge nur Trisha Brown berechtigt, dieses Stück unter dem Titel *Accumulation* zu inszenieren und zur Aufführung zu bringen. Vor 1976 konnte der Urheberrechtsschutz nur auf Tanzproduktionen angewendet werden, die als „dramaturgische oder dramaturgisch-musikalische Kompositionen" einzuordnen waren.[7] In beiden Fällen galt das Copyright nur für das Endprodukt, nicht für die ihm zugrunde liegenden Regeln.[8] Dies widerspricht ebenfalls einer direkten Übereinstimmung zwischen dem Quellcode einer Software, der gesetzlich geschützt werden kann, und choreografischen Methoden, die vor Vollendung der Performance nicht als geistiges Eigentum gelten. Andererseits kann der „Algorithmus" für *Accumulation* dem Diskurs um die Tanzproduktion entnommen und verwendet werden (wie ich es in diesem Text getan habe), um Bewegungsmaterial zu generieren, das von einem anderen Choreografen in etwas Neues verwandelt werden kann. So gesehen ist der Hinweis legitim, dass der eine oder andere Aspekt der Open-Source-Software im offenen Zugang zu choreografische Methoden Anwendung findet. Ich werde darauf gegen Ende dieses Essays zurückkommen.

Um einen Tanz so zu definieren, dass er dem Urheberschutz unterliegt, ist eine objektive Methode erforderlich, um eine Choreografie so zu fixieren, dass sie identifizierbar ist. Die Richtlinien des Urheberrechtssamts in Washington D.C. lauten wie folgt: „Für die Choreografie kann das Werk in einem Film oder einem Video, mit einem Recorder aufgezeichnet oder in einem Text oder Tanznotationssystem wie etwa Labanotation, Sutton Movement Shorthand oder Benesh-Notation präzise beschrieben sein". Die hier aufgelisteten Notationssysteme kommen dem Begriff von Software als geistigem Eigentum sehr nahe. Im Unterschied zu Audio-Video-Aufnahmegeräten bestehen Tanznotationssysteme aus einem flexiblen Register mit einzelnen Symbolen, die zu immer größeren Informationseinheiten neu kombiniert werden können, die sich auf bestimmte Bewegungen im Zeitablauf beziehen. Die einfachste

Informationseinheit der Labanotation ist (wie in der Musik) ein Liniensystem. Auf diesen Linien kann man die Symbole kombinieren, die benötigt werden, um die Richtung, den Körperteil, die Position und den Zeitraum anzuzeigen. Mit der syntaktischen kombinatorischen Intelligenz dieser relativ einfachen Symbolsprache können komplexe Bewegungsinformationen dargestellt werden.

Diese Funktionsbeschreibung der Tanznotation weist Ähnlichkeit mit jener des Softwarecodes auf. Das Tanznotationssystem unterscheidet sich jedoch insofern vom Programmcode, als die Tanznotation bei der Produktion von Tänzen nicht als ein generatives Instrument verwendet wird, während der Softwarecode seinem Wesen nach inhärent generativ ist; er produziert Wirkung. Notationssysteme wurden mit der Absicht geschaffen, Choreografien zu bewahren und wieder zur Aufführung bringen zu können, nicht sie zu erzeugen. Choreografen erfinden einen Tanz nicht, indem sie diesen vorab in den Symbolen der Tanznotation niederschreiben. Doch in den Begriffen des geistigen Eigentums ist die Notation Teil des Systems, das den Besitz von Choreografien definiert; und darin ist sie dem Softwarecode wiederum ähnlich.

Eine kurze Zusammenfassung des Kapitels: Die Art und Weise, wie Informationen über die Produktion von Tänzen aus einer Vielzahl individueller Quellen kollektiv gesammelt werden, ist nicht zu vergleichen mit der kollektiven Kreativität, die bei der Erzeugung von Open-Source-Software praktiziert wird. Tänze werden letztlich zu Produkten individueller Autorschaft und können als solche durch neuere Copyright-Adaptationen geschützt werden. Obwohl einige Choreografen in ihren Tanzproduktionen mit auf Regeln basierenden Systemen arbeiten, können diese Algorithmen kaum als geistiges Eigentum betrachtet werden. Damit ein Copyright zum Schutz eines Tanzes zur Anwendung kommen kann, muss die Choreografie dieses Tanzes in Form einer Audio- und/oder Videoaufnahme oder in irgendeiner Form von schriftlicher Tanznotation festgehalten werden. Tanznotationssysteme haben ihrem Wesen nach eine größere Ähnlichkeit mit Software als andere Charakteristika des Tanzes – sie werden aber in erster Linie verwendet, um Choreografien aufzuzeichnen, nicht um sie zu schaffen.

Choreografie und Open Source

Während gewisse Choreografen bei ihren Tanzproduktionen mit Systemen gearbeitet haben, die auf einem Regelwerk basierten, verwenden andere gleichsam „Kopien" eines Tanzes, um die philosophischen Implikationen geistigen Eigentums in Bezug auf den Tanz zu erforschen. Das Stück *The Last Performance* aus dem Jahr 1998 des in Europa für seine provokanten konzeptuellen Tanzproduktionen bekannten französischen Choreografen Jérôme Bel besteht aus kurzen Sequenzen oder „Zitaten" von Tänzen anderer Choreografen, die ihn auf die eine oder andere Weise beeinflusst hatten.[9] Er erhielt die Genehmigung, Teile dieses Materials zu verwenden, bekam aber auch Ablehnungsbriefe, die Zitate des Urheberrechtsgesetzes enthielten. Diese wurden bei den ersten Aufführungen des Stücks „The Last Performance" laut vorgelesen.

Unter den Choreografen, die Bel gestatteten, ihr Material zu verwenden, war auch die Deutsche Susanne Linke. Eine in einem weißen Kleid auftretende Tänzerin aus *The Last Performance* sagt den Satz: „Ich bin Susanne Linke." In diesem Kontext ist die Bedeutung der „Kopie" für den Betrachter der Performance das Bezugssystem. Nicht länger an die logischen Strukturen von Sprache oder Code, von Software oder Gesetz gebunden, beginnt diese „Kopie" an den verschwimmenden Rändern der Mimesis zu spielen – wobei die Behauptung, die Urheberin der Performance zu sein, hier vielleicht bedeutet, in die Rolle eines Schauspielers oder Imitators zu schlüpfen. Tanzende Körper sind in informationellen Begriffen äußerst komplex und sperren sich gegen eine konkrete Auslegung. *The Last Performance* illustriert den Punkt, an dem die Beziehung zwischen zeitgenössischer Choreografie und Open Source auseinanderstrebt und zu inkonsistent wird, als dass sich ein Vergleich noch lohnen würde. Während *The Last Performance* eine Situation illustriert, in der Vergleiche zwischen Choreografie und Open Source klarer werden, eignet sich das Beispiel eines weiteren Choreografen für eine Fortsetzung dieses Gedankenspiels. Ich möchte auf die Vermutung zurückkommen, dass einige Aspekte der Open-Source-Software im Austausch choreografischer Ideen gegeben sind, wofür das Folgende ein Beispiel ist.

William Forsythe, künstlerischer Leiter und seit 1984 erster Choreograf des Frankfurter Balletts, stellte Komponenten seiner choreografischen Arbeit durch die Verbreitung einer interaktiven Multimedia-CD-ROM mit dem Titel *Improvisation Technologies: A Tool for the Analytical Dance Eye zur Verfügung.*[10] Er wollte mit seinem CD-ROM-Projekt neuen Tänzern der Kompanie ein Trainingsinstrument zur Verfügung stellen, das es gestattete, die grundlegenden Aspekte seiner innovativen Improvisationstechniken zu studieren. Im Unterschied zu Doris Humphreys *Die Kunst, Tänze zu machen* wollte Forsythe mit seiner Publikation nicht alle Aspekte der Tanzproduktion berühren, sondern lediglich über die so genannten Bausteine informieren, die zur Entwicklung einer Analysemethode der Improvisation geeignet sind. Forsythe zufolge sind diese Bausteine eher als Konzepte oder Ideen denn Techniken oder Strategien zu verstehen. Aus dieser Perspektive betrachtet gehen choreografische Methoden in choreografisches Denken über.

Die CD-ROM präsentiert vier Informationskategorien: Linien, Additionen, Reorganisation und Text. Innerhalb jeder Kategorie gibt es bis zu fünf Subkategorien (z. B. Punkt-Punkt-Linie, grafische Animationen, Isometrien etc.), die sich weiter unterteilen. Dieser hierarchische Informationsaufbau ermöglicht es dem Leser / User, bequem einem roten Faden von Bewegungen zu folgen, der von einfachen zu komplexeren Prinzipien führt. Der Leser / User hat auch die Möglichkeit, die Informationen aufzunehmen, indem er sich ansieht, wie diese Bausteine oder Ideen von Mitgliedern der Kompanie getanzt werden. Es gibt insgesamt 63 verschiedene Bausteine auf der CD-ROM, wobei viele davon weitere enthalten. Sie repräsentieren einen kleinen, aber bedeutenden Ausschnitt von William Forsythes choreografischem Denken. Da sie durch dieses elektronische Medium verbreitet und zugänglich gemacht werden, sind sie eine Art Open-Source-Code in öffentlichem Besitz, der nicht nur allen an der Entstehung von Tänzen Interessierten entsprechende Einblicke gewährt, sondern die Bausteine auch jedem zur eigenen Verwendung zur Verfügung stellt.

Als Forsythe gefragt wurde, ob er das Gefühl hätte, durch die Publikation dieser Informationen in Form der CD-ROM etwas zu verschenken, antwortete er:

> Nun, durch die CD-ROM erfährt man nicht, wie ich choreografiere, sie zeigt lediglich, wie Bewegung zu beobachten ist. (...) Sie zeigt nur einige Denkansätze zur Analyse von Bewegung. Ich glaube, es gibt eine ganz neue Einstellung zur Arbeit: Lassen Sie es mich so ausdrücken: Arbeit ist kein Geheimnis. Es ist irgendwie abergläubisch zu denken, dass man seine Methode geheim halten müsste. (...) Gegen Ende des 20. Jahrhunderts sollte Arbeit nicht geheim gehalten werden. Sie verschwindet nicht, nur weil wir kommunizieren. Wir könnten sozusagen verstanden und dadurch gezwungen werden, unsere eigenen Methoden aufzugeben, was auch nicht das Schlechteste wäre (...) Ich hoffe, dass die User ihren eigenen Tanz entdecken, indem sie unseren verstehen.[11]

Eine kurze Zusammenfassung des Kapitels: Wenn ein Tanz schließlich zur Aufführung kommt, kann er urheberrechtlich geschützt werden, und die Choreografen können Kollegen die Genehmigung verweigern, einen Ausschnitt dieses Tanzes zu reproduzieren, wie es bei *The Last Performance* von Jérôme Bel geschah. Doch lässt sich der tanzende Körper auf der Bühne nicht so leicht in das starre Korsett pressen, das die Einrichtung des Copyrights gerne hätte.

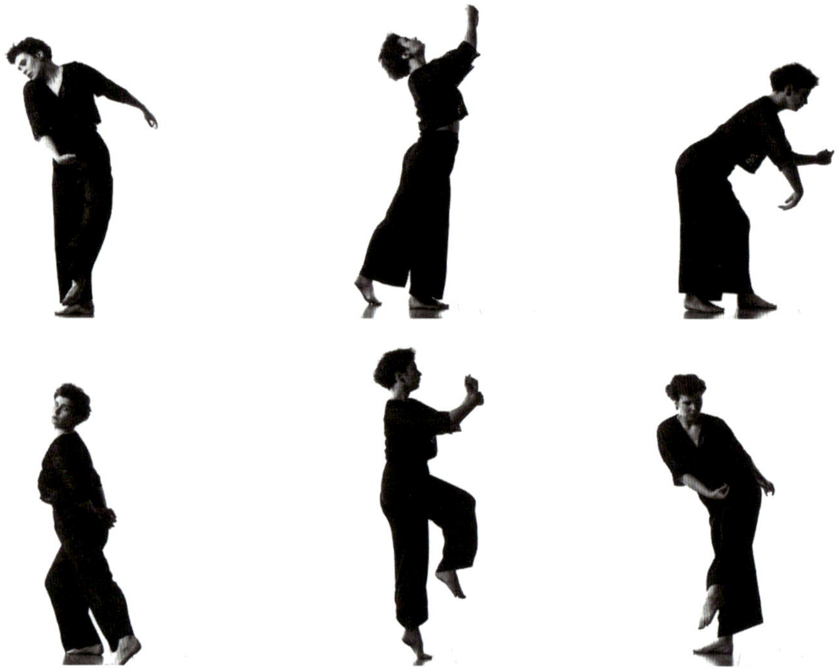

Fotos: Lois Greenfield

Der tanzende Körper auf der Bühne lässt sich auch nicht mit der Dynamik von Open Source vergleichen. Zusammenhänge zwischen Choreografie und Open Source als eine bestimmte Sammlung von Konzepten und Praktiken finden sich eher in der manifesthaften Offenheit der CD-ROM *Improvisation Technologies* von William Forsythe.

Schluss

Die kreativen Prozesse und Produkte der zeitgenössischen Choreografiepraxis decken sich nur teilweise mit jenen der Bewegung der Open-Source-Software. Forsythe zufolge ist die Zeit, in der man aus seinen Methoden ein Geheimnis machte, vorbei, doch bin ich mir nicht sicher, in welchem Ausmaß dies von der Open-Source-Bewegung herrührt oder einfach nur ein zufälliges Zusammentreffen ist (bedingt durch denselben historischen Zeitrahmen). Verschiedene Fragen stellen sich: Geben die Software-Lizenzen, die freien Zugang zum Quellcode gewährleisten, einen Anstoß zur Adaptation der Urheberrechtsgesetze für Choreografie? Auf der Suche nach einer Antwort zeigt sich alsbald, dass eine derartige Verknüpfung nicht möglich ist, wie sich auch an mancher Stelle in diesem Essay gezeigt hat. Eine andere Frage: Müsste man nicht wissen, wie eine Choreografie gemacht wird oder selbst Choreograf sein, um den Quellcode eines bestimmten Tanzes verwenden zu können? Dies wäre eine Aufforderung an uns, die Möglichkeiten des Wissens als etwas anderes als Eigentum zu betrachten. Vielleicht könnte das Verständnis, wie ein Tanz gemacht wird, der Zugang zu seinem Quellcode, dazu führen, dass wir generell ein größeres Verständnis für kreative Prozesse entwickeln. Man würde beginnen, eine Tanzperformance als untrennbar von ihrem Entstehungsprozess zu sehen – als eine Anwendung choreografischen Denkens. Ein größeres Verständnis choreografischer Prozesse könnte vielleicht dazu führen, auch anderes als Performances zu schaffen. Wenn ein Vergleich der Welt der Choreografie mit jener der Open-Source-Software zu einer solchen Verlagerung inspiriert, sind die Überlegungen der Mühe wert.

Aus dem Englischen von Martina Bauer

1 Dieser Essay wurde ursprünglich für ein (noch nicht veröffentlichtes) Buch der MIT Press geschrieben, das von der CODE-Konferenz, die im April 2001 stattfand, angeregt wurde *(http://www.cl.cam.ac.uk/CODE/.* Ich habe mich für den Begriff „Open Source" statt „Freier Software" entschieden, um das Konzept einer Software mit freiem Zugang nicht nur zum ausführbaren Binärcode, sondern auch zum Quellcode zu beschreiben. Ich möchte darauf hinweisen, dass diese technische Beschreibung zwar für beide Konzepte zutrifft, Open Source und Freie Software jedoch eine unterschiedliche Geschichte haben und in mancher Hinsicht auch ideologische Unterschiede aufweisen. Beide haben eigene Websites, als weiterführende Lektüre empfehle ich einige Texte von Florian Cramer: „Freie Software" *(http://www.fsf.org),* Open Source *(http://www.opensource.org/);* Florian Cramer: *http://userpage.fu-berlin.de/~cantsin/.*

2 Die Judson-Church-Bewegung bezeichnet eine Reihe von Tanzprojekten und Performances in New York, die in den 1960er Jahren stattfanden. Anfang des Jahrzehnts leitete der Komponist Robert Dunn auf Anregung von John Cage einflussreiche Choreografieklassen in New York, aus denen einige der bekanntesten und innovativsten Choreografen der zweiten Hälfte des 20. Jahrhunderts hervorgingen. Die Klassen schufen die Voraussetzungen, um sich von dem choreografischen Standardrepertoire wegzubewegen, das von den Theoretikern des frühen 20. Jahrhunderts wie Doris Humphrey entwickelt worden war. Unter den Tanzkünstlern, die an diesen Klassen teilnahmen, finden sich berühmte Namen wie: Trisha Brown, Lucinda Childs, David Gordon, Douglas Dunn, Kenneth King, Yvonne Ranier, Steve Paxton, Simone Forti und Deborah Hay. Einige Mitglieder dieser Gruppe traten ab dem 6. Juli 1962 mit einer Reihe von Performances in der Judson Memorial Church in Lower Manhattan auf. Die Auftritte erstreckten sich über vier Jahre, weshalb die Gruppe als „Judson Dance Theater" bezeichnet wurde.

3 Humphrey, Doris: *Die Kunst Tänze zu machen: Zur Choreographie des modernen Tanzes.* Aus dem Amerikanischen übersetzt und herausgegeben von Karin Vial, Verlag der Heinrichshofen-Bücher, Wilhelmshaven 1998, S. 16.

4 Banes, Sally: „Choreografic Methods of the Judson Dance Theater" in *Writing Dancing in the Age of Postmodernism,* S. 211 – 226, Wesleyan University Press, Februar 1994.

5 Siehe beispielsweise 1) folgendes Buch, das Interviews mit Choreografen bringt:
Butterworth, Jo und Clarke, Gill, Hrsg., *Dance Makers Portfolio: conversations with Choreografers,* Bretton Hall, Wakefield, GB: Centre for Dance and Theatre Studies, 1998
sowie 2) diverse Ausgaben von Tanzjournalen, in denen häufig Artikel über bestimmte Choreografen erscheinen, etwa *Ballet International/Tanz Aktuell (http://www.ballet-tanz.de/)* oder *Dance Theatre Journal (http://www.laban.org/dance_theatre_journal.phtml)*

6 Mehr über diesen Tanz-Algorithmus ist in einem Interview mit Trisha Brown in *The Drama Reviews, Post-modern Dance issue* nachzulesen. T-65, März 1975.

7 Van Camp, Julie: „Copyright of Choreografic Works", in *1994–95 Entertainment, Publishing and the Arts Handbook,* S. 59 – 92, Hrsg.: Stephen F. Breimer, Robert Thorne und John David Viera; Clark, Boardman und Callaghan, New York 1994. Dieser Artikel ist online abrufbar unter: *http://www.csulb.edu/~jvancampcopyrigh.html.*

8 Prozesse im Zusammenhang mit Tanz und Urheberrechtsgesetz gab es nur gelegentlich. Ein Beispiel dafür ist die schriftliche Aufzeichnung eines Gerichtsfalls über die Verwendung des Namens von Martha Graham, der Ikone des modernen Tanzes. Finkle, David: „The Future of Dance's Past, Graham Center Wins a Round in Court and Wakes up Choreografers", in *The Village Voice,* August, Woche 15 – 21. 2001. Der Text ist auf *http://www.villagevoice.com online* abrufbar, wenn man in das Suchfeld „David Finkle" eingibt.

9 Siegmund, Gerald: „The Endgame of Dance: ‚The Last Performance' von Jérôme Bel in Nürnberg" in *Ballett International/Tanz Aktuell,* Januar 1999.

10 Forsythe, William: *Improvisation Technologies: A Tool for the Analytical Dance Eye* (CD-ROM), Hatje Cantz Verlag (ISBN: 3775708502), Ostfildern Juni 2000.

11 Diese Zitate sind einem Interview mit William Forsythe entnommen, das Nik Haffner am 22. April 1999 führte und in dem Booklet der CD-ROM *Improvisation Technologies* veröffentlicht ist. Nik Haffner, Volker Kuchelmeiser und Christian Ziegler leisteten in konzeptueller und technischer Hinsicht wesentliche Beiträge zu der CD-ROM.

(sämtliche URLs datieren vom 14. Mai 2003)

Messa di Voce
A Performance of Visualized Speech and Song

Tmema / Jaap Blonk / Joan La Barbara

Messa di Voce is a new concert performance in which the speech, shouts, barks and songs produced by a duet of experimental vocalists are augmented in realtime by custom interactive visualization software. The forty-minute performance touches on themes of abstract communication, synaesthetic relationships, cartoon language and writing and scoring systems, within the context of a sophisticated, playful and virtuosic audiovisual narrative.

Messa di Voce lies at an intersection of human and technological performance extremes, melding the unpredictable spontaneity and extended vocal techniques of two masterful composers/improvisers with the latest in computer vision and speech recognition technologies. Utterly wordless, yet profoundly verbal, *Messa di Voce* is designed to provoke questions about the meaning and effects of speech sounds, speech acts and the immersive environment of our language.

The core technologies which scaffold the performance are computer vision and speech recognition. A computer incorporates a video camera in order to locate and track the positions of the vocalists; it also analyses the speech and song coming from their wireless microphones. In response, the computer projects various kinds of visualizations on a projection screen behind the performers. These visualizations are synthesized in direct response to the sounds spoken and sung by the performers. With the help of the computer-vision tracking system, these visualizations are projected in such a way that they appear to emerge directly from the performers' heads or mouths. Where and when circumstances permit, stereographic projections are used to enhance the illusion that the vocal figurations are hovering in the same space as the performers. The end result presents the fiction that speech can be truly visible.

LETTERS: The singer speaks short phonemes. The computer recognizes these phonemes and places large letters in the screen. The letters crowd around the singer, but never touch him.

Messa di Voce emerges from a pair of commissions created by Golan Levin and Zachary Lieberman as Artists-in-Residence at the Ars Electronica Futurelab. During July and August 2002, we produced two new installations for the Ars Electronica Museum, called *Re:mark* and *The Hidden Worlds of Noise and Voice.* These artworks combined state-of-the-art speech analysis technologies (such as vocal stress estimation, pitch tracking, and realtime phoneme recognition) with camera-based motion tracking, augmented reality displays, and other sensing techniques, in order to allow museum-goers to engage vocally and viscerally with different sorts of highly reactive speech visualizations. Participants in the Hidden Worlds exhibit, for example, are able

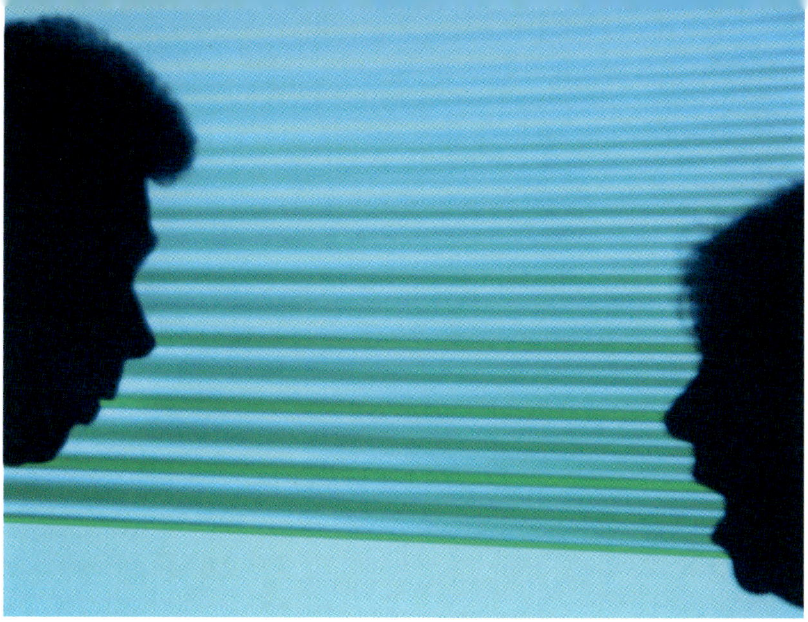

to "see" each others' voices, made visible (through stereographic VR glasses) in the form of animated graphic figurations that appear to emerge from the participants' mouths. For the *Messa di Voce* performance, we have developed these core technologies into a "professional" version, customised for a duet of vocalists well known for their experimental repertoires and extended vocal techniques: Joan La Barbara (USA) and Jaap Blonk (Holland). In *Messa di Voce,* Joan and Jaap engage in abstract dialogues with themselves and each other. Visual representations of their speech and song are computed in real-time, appropriately positioned around their heads and bodies by a computer-vision algorithm, and projected onto a series of spatially contiguous video screens.
The visual representations are "aware" of the locations of the performers, and also aware of the other visual representations. In this way, it is possible for the performers/interactants to conduct a "game" with their speech-gestures. Over the course of the performance, increasingly sophisticated forms of speech recognition are employed, and used to develop an overall narrative from purely formal abstraction to symbolic representations and transcriptions.

Tmema is: Golan Levin and Zachary Lieberman.
Commissioned by Ars Electronica with the support of SAP, la Fondation Daniel Langlois pour l'art, la science et la technologie, Eyebeam Atelier, The Rockefeller MAP Fund, and the Arts Council England.

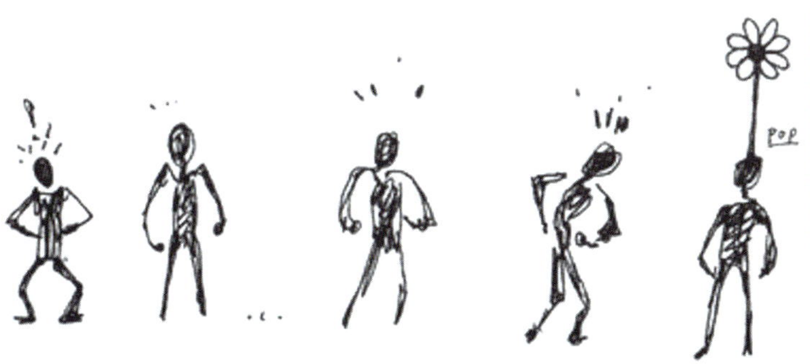

FLOWER: This idea is a really silly one-liner. After struggling and groaning and grunting for a while, a flower is abruptly released from the singer's head when he creates a loud "POP" sound.

Messa di Voce

Visualisierte Sprache und Gesang – eine Performance

Tmema / Jaap Blonk / Joan La Barbara

Messa di Voce ist eine neue Konzertform, bei der zwei Experimentalvokalisten sprechen, schreien, bellen und singen und diese Laute in Echtzeit per interaktiver Visualisierungssoftware augmentiert werden. Eingebettet in eine elaborierte, verspielt virtuose audiovisuelle Erzählung, behandelt die 40-minütige Performance Themen wie abstrakte Kommunikation, synästhetische Beziehungen, Comic-Sprache sowie Zeichen- und Notationssysteme. Bei *Messa di Voce* verschwimmen die Grenzen zwischen menschlicher und technischer Leistungsfähigkeit. Hier verschmelzen die unvorhersehbare Spontaneität und die bravouröse Stimmtechnik zweier Meisterkomponisten/-improvisatoren mit den allerneuesten Computertechnologien im Bereich der Bild- und Spracherkennung. Völlig wortlos und doch zutiefst verbal, soll *Messa di Voce* zum Nachdenken über Sinn und Wirkung von Sprachklängen bzw. Sprechakten und die immersive Atmosphäre unserer Sprache anregen.
Bild- und Spracherkennung sind die Kerntechniken, die die Performance tragen. Ein mit einer Kamera ausgestatteter Computer verfolgt die Bewegungen der Vokalisten und analysiert gleichzeitig die per Funkmikrofon übertragenen Sprachlaute und Gesänge. Als Reaktion projiziert der Computer unterschiedlichste Bildkompositionen auf eine Leinwand hinter den Sängern. Diese Bilder werden als direkter Response auf die gesprochenen und gesungenen Klänge synthetisiert. Dank eines ausgefeilten Trackingsystems scheinen der Kopf oder Mund der

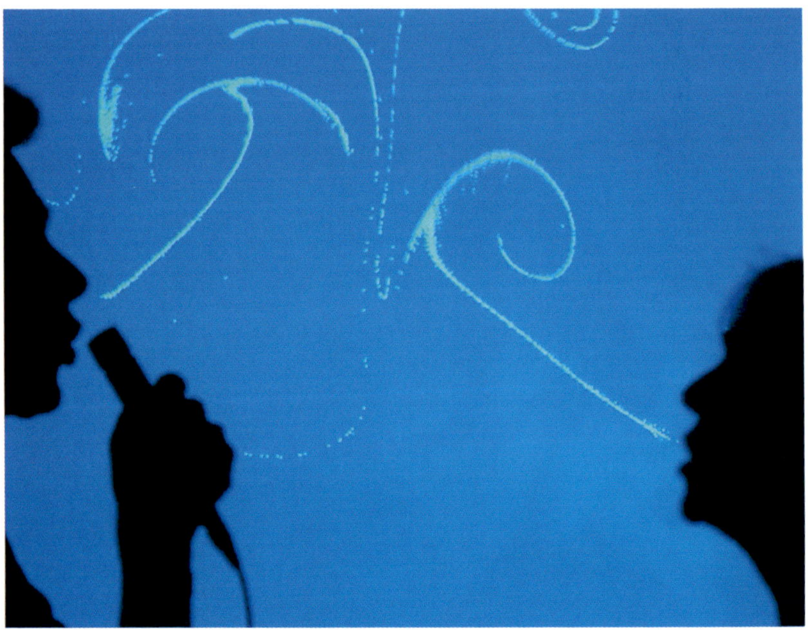

Sänger diese Bilder selbst zu projizieren. Sofern möglich, werden stereografische Projektionen eingesetzt, um die Illusion zu verstärken, dass diese Vokaldarstellungen im selben Raum wie die Sänger schweben. Das Ergebnis ist die Fiktion einer in der Tat sichtbaren Sprache. *Messa di Voce* ist eine Weiterentwicklung zweier Auftragsarbeiten, die Golan Levin und Zachary Lieberman als Artists-in-Residence für das Ars Electronica Futurelab entwickelt haben. In den Monaten Juli und August 2002 haben wir für das Ars Electronica Center die Installationen *RE:MARK* und *The Hidden Worlds of Noise and Voice* geschaffen. Diese Arbeiten vereinten hochmoderne Spracherkennung (u. a. Stimmstressanalyse, Tonhöhen- und Echtzeit-Phonemerkennung) mit optischem Motion-Tracking, Augmented-Reality-Displays und anderen sensorischen Technologien. Damit ist der Museumsbesucher in der Lage, sich vokal und emotional mit verschiedensten sensibel reagierenden Sprachvisualisierungen auseinanderzusetzen. So können z. B. die Protagonisten in den *Hidden Worlds* die Stimmen der anderen, die mittels Stereo-VR-Brillen sichtbar gemacht werden, als animierte grafische Darstellungen aus dem Mund des jeweiligen Sprechers strömen „sehen".
Für *Messa di Voce* haben wir aus diesen Kerntechnologien eine „Professional"-Version entwickelt und auf das Gesangsduo Joan La Barbara (USA) und Jaap Blonk (Holland) zugeschnitten. Beide sind für ihr experimentelles Repertoire und ihre exzellente Stimmtechnik bekannt. In *Messa di Voce* führen Joan und Jaap abstrakte Dialoge mit sich selbst und miteinander. Die visuelle Darstellung ihrer Sprache und ihres Gesangs wird in Echtzeit errechnet, mittels Computeralgorithmus passend um ihre Köpfe und Körper positioniert und auf eine Reihe von nebeneinander angeordneten Leinwänden projiziert.
Die Projektionen „erkennen" sowohl die Position der Sänger als auch die Form der übrigen visuellen Darstellungen. Somit können die Protagonisten / Interagierenden mit ihren Sprach-Gebärden „spielen". Im Verlauf der Performance werden immer bessere Spracherkennungsmethoden eingesetzt, wodurch sich die Erzählung von rein formaler Abstraktion hin zu symbolischer Darstellung und Transkription entwickelt.

Aus dem Amerikanischen von Michael Kaufmann

Tmema sind Golan Levin und Zachary Lieberman.
Commissioned by Ars Electronica with the support of SAP, la Fondation Daniel Langlois pour l'art, la science et la technologie, Eyebeam Atelier, The Rockefeller MAP Fund, and the Arts Council England.

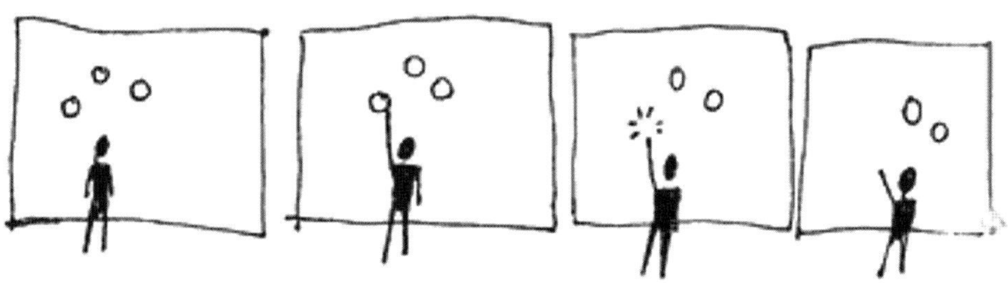

BUBBLES (Seifenblasen): Hier kann der Vokalist seine Lautäußerungen erneut abspielen.
Jede kurze Vokalisierung wird als Seifenblase oder in ähnlicher Form dargestellt. Langt der Sänger mit dem Schatten seiner Hand nach oben, so „zerplatzt" die jeweilige Seifenblase und man hört (zum zweiten Mal) den Laut, der die Seifenblase ursprünglich erzeugt hat..

POL. A Mechatronic Show

Marcel·lí Antúnez Roca

POL is a tale told in the form of a mecatronic show: an ironic and poetic fable for all audiences. An interactive story, a product of the dialogue between machines and performers. A new form of technology, a mutation of stage production.

Although inspired in the genre, *POL* isn't a reworking of any particular popular tale. The story of *POL* traces the perilous journey of a rabbit in search of love. The loss of his teeth, a biological accident of his infancy and physiological change akin to that which the body undergoes in other stages of life, emerges as one of the leitmotifs of the odyssey. His quest for love is another. *POL* is staged in a rectangular space bounded by three vertical screens at the back and the computer system on the sides at the front. Four robots and two *dresskeletitzed* performers provide the action on stage.

The kinetic backdrop is made up of three vertical backprojections, creating a wide-screen image. The visual universe is made up of two- and three-dimensional interactive images. The robotic automatons are made of animal skins, plastic and metal. With the exception of Cervosatán, who moves autonomously, they are fed through cables connected to the computer system. The robots are included in the fable's cast of characters.

The *dresskeletons* translate the movements executed by the performers and send them via radio modem to the computers, which in turn control the image, sound and robots. A development of the prototype used in *Afasia* from 1998, the *dresskeleton* is the system's chief interface. It is equipped with on/off switches, mercury switches (signalling position), a selecting switch, level potentiometers and a microphone.

In some scenes the performers' voices are used as level sensors, the volume generating or deforming certain images.

The interactive and interdisciplinary grammar of *POL* is made possible by our own software written specifically for the show. The program allows the sensors to be linked to the variables of image, sound and robots. Through this program, a sort of editor, the more than seventy sensors on the *dresskeletons* and totems are linked up with commercial programs and MIDI protocols.

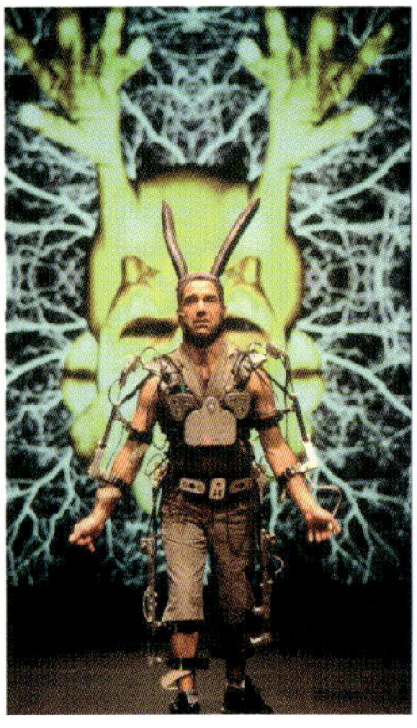

POL examines the specific arguments that technology brings to artistic discourse and its means of representation. The use of such concepts as juxtaposition, synchrony and interaction permits a new form of narration. As in *Afasia,* the interaction in *POL* is at the service of the story. Other interactive forms pursue different objectives—in videogames, for example, where interactivity provides the means to overcome obstacles, or on the Internet, where interaction is the engine for information exchange. None of this happens in this performance.

The interactive narration in *POL* occurs on a broad and specific platform. The interface prototypes—*dresskeleton*—tend to generate a specific body action, quite different from the other interactions—mice, keyboards. The body expands in a cause/non-effect relation towards such new means as robots or inter-

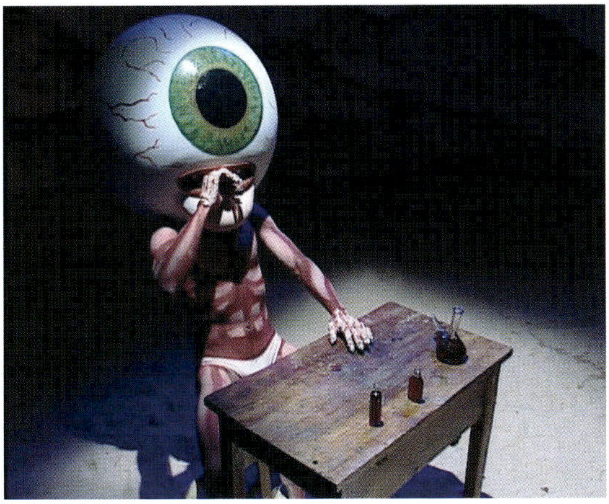

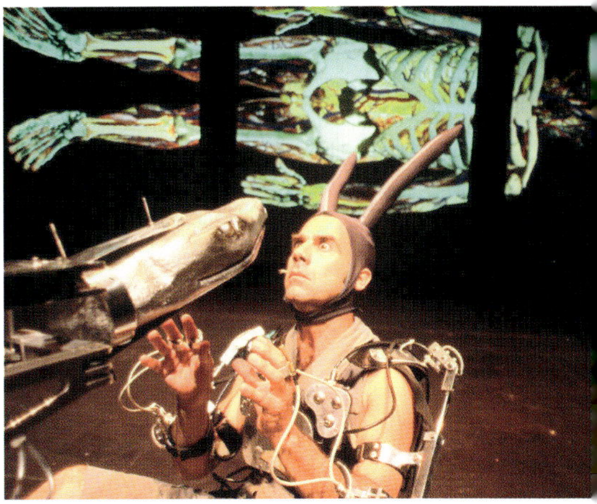

active image and sound. An arm movement can determine things as arbitrary as the modulated frequency of a sound, the horizontal direction of a virtual landscape or the speed with which a robot moves.

This mechatronic event is the foundation of the interactive drama. The spoken dialogue underpinning traditional drama is either relegated to a secondary plane or disappears. The drama is a chain reaction that links body, interface, computer and setting in interactive dialogue. And this discourse juxtaposes gesture, apparatus, noise and icon, engendering a new form without known standards and offering vast potentials. The story emerges from the means that the executor anticipates from his interface, administering a torrential flow of information. And thus flows the fable. The interaction in *POL* doesn't produce random events, but rather a malleable, entertaining and flexible narrative line. And, hopefully, a cathartic rite.

POL has been awarded a Honorary Mention at Prix Ars Electronica in the category "Interactive Art".

POL
Direction & Conception: Marcel·lí Antúnez Roca / Performers: Piero Steiner & Marcel·lí Antúnez / Virtual performer: Silvia García / Music: Alain Wergifosse / Robots: Roland Olbeter / Computer Graphics Head: Alvaro Uña / Software Head: Jesus de la Calle / Photo: Darius Koehli / Costumes: Josep Abril / Lighting: Ramón Rey / Dresskeletons: EBA-studio (Christian Konn, Carlos Jovellar, Dani) / 3D Studio: SU-Studio (Marko Brajovic, Richard Porcher, Stefanie Alice Vandendriessche & Luka Brajovic) / Technical Head: Paco Beltran / Scene assistant: Joan Baixas / Management: Marta Oliveres—*MOM* / Production Head: Dietrich Grosse—*MONDIGROMAX* / Computer graphics: David Aja, Marcel·lí Antúnez / Flash animation: Nacho Vilaro, Eva Vázquez / Flash Editing: Angelika Orf, Gaetano Mangano / Video & 3D graphics: Nicolás García Graphics assistants: Marcelo Dematei, Gerard Bosch, Silvia Adell, Lluís Alba y Cristina Torron / MIDI software: Eugenio Tisselli / Flash sound: Mitos Colom / Story: Marcel·lí Antúnez Roca, Luís Miguel Rubio Software assistant: Joan Coll / Hard comunications: Jordi Montoya & Esteva Amo / Midi file robots: Sebastian Harms / Sculpture animals: Esterina Zarrillo / Atrezzo, poupet: Nico Nubiola / Administration:Toñi Santos

Image Bank
Make up: Gema Planchadell & Samanta Crescente. Light Technician: Ramón Rey & Carlos Lucena. Operator: Antoni Anglada, Camera Laura, Sigon Atrezzo, Nicolas Nubiola, Assistant Nicolas, García Fernández. Sound Technician: José Ignacio Ortuzar. Direction assistant: Maria Torrent.
Thanks to: Begoña Egurbide, Adelaida Antunez, Alvar Antunez, Gori Casas.

POL produced by *PANSPERMIA S.L.* coproducers: *Festival d'Estiu de Barcelona Grec 2002, Mercat de les Flors, MEDIA-EUROPA, Fira de Teatre de Tàrrega.* Supported: *Institut Català de les Indústries Culturals–ICIC de la Generalitat de Catalunya i SGAE* Sponsors: *FESTO, Josep Abril, Sanyo, Native Instruments, Vegap, New Balance, Fundición Ubach, Mecanitzats EBLAN.*

PANSPERMIA SL Supported by *INAEM-Ministerio de Educación, Deporte y Cultura, ICUB-Ajuntament de Barcelona, Departament de Cultura-Generalitat de Catalunya.*

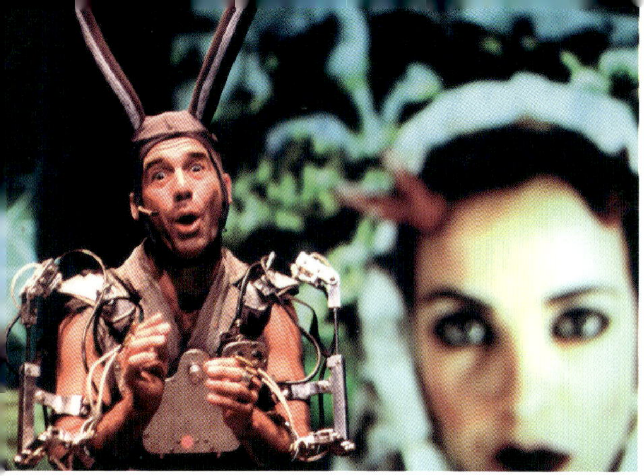

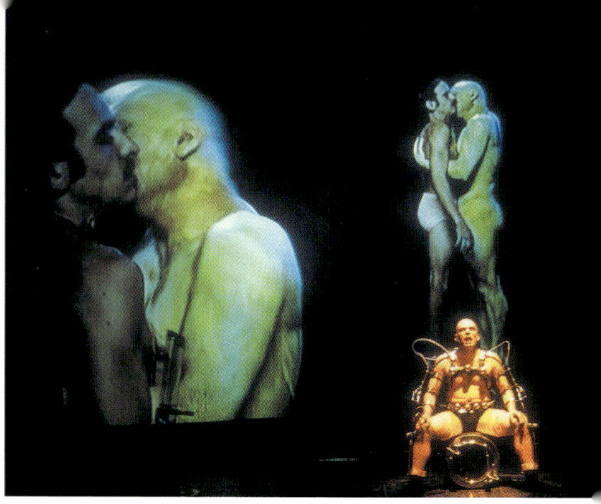

POL. Eine mechatronische Show

Marcel·lí Antúnez Roca

POL erzählt eine Geschichte in Form einer mechatronischen Show: ein ironisches und poetisches Märchen für ein breites Publikum. Eine interaktive Fabel, Produkt eines Dialogs zwischen Maschinen und Performance-Künstlern. Eine neue Technologie, Mutation eines Bühnenstücks.

Seine Wurzeln hat *POL* in der europäischen Fabel. Wir haben uns nicht wegen einer nostalgischen Sehnsucht nach Kindergeschichten oder dem Wunsch nach Aufrechterhaltung einer volkstümlichen Tradition, sondern wegen seiner narrativen Gestaltung für dieses Genre entschieden. Fabeln haben eine einfache Struktur, mit einer klar geordneten und temporeichen Abfolge von – magischen, unerwarteten, aufwühlenden – Geschehnissen, die sie für die Konstruktion eines bestimmten real anmutenden Universums und die prägnante interaktive Darstellung von Schlüsselmomenten sehr geeignet erscheinen lassen.

POL wird auf einer rechteckigen Bühnen aufgeführt, die von drei vertikalen Leinwänden an der Rückseite und einem Computersystem vorne an den Seiten begrenzt wird. Vier Roboter und zwei Darsteller, die mit einem Exoskelett – einer Synthese aus Skelett und orthopädischem Stützkorsett, die außen am Körper getragen wird – bekleidet sind, vollziehen die Handlung auf der Bühne. Die kinetische Kulisse besteht aus drei vertikalen Projektionen an der Rückwand der Bühne, die zu einer Breitbildprojektion verschwimmen. Das visuelle Universum besteht aus zwei- und dreidimensionalen interaktiven Bildern. Die Roboter sind aus Tierhäuten, Kunststoff und Metall zusammengesetzt. Mit Ausnahme von Cervosatán, der sich autonom bewegt, sind sie über Kabel an das Computersystem angeschlossen. Die Roboter sind wie die Darsteller Teil der Bühnenbesetzung.

Die Exoskelette übertragen die Bewegungen der Künstler und übermitteln sie via Funkmodem an die Computer, die Ton, Bild und Roboter steuern. Sie sind das Hauptinterface des Systems und eine Weiterentwicklung des Exoskelett-Prototypen, der bereits 1998 für die Show *Afasia* verwendet wurde. Sie sind mit Ein-/Aus-Schaltern, Quecksilberschaltern (zur Positionsbestimmung), Wahlschaltern, Level-Potentiometern und je einem Mikrofon ausgestattet. In einigen Szenen dienen die Stimmen der Darsteller als Pegelsensoren, indem die Lautstärke bestimmte Bilder erzeugt oder deformiert.

Die interaktive und interdisziplinäre Grammatik von *POL* wird durch eine eigens für die Show entwickelte Software ermöglicht. Das Programm ermöglicht eine Verknüpfung der Sensoren mit den Variablen Bild, Klang und Roboter. Dieses Programm, einer Art von Editor, verbindet die mehr als siebzig Sensoren der Exoskelette und Totems mit kommerziellen Programmen und MIDI-Protokollen.
POL untersucht jene spezifischen Aspekte, die dem künstlerischen Diskurs und dessen Ausdrucksmöglichkeiten durch die Technik eröffnet werden. Die Verwendung von Gestaltungsformen wie Juxtaposition, Synchronie und Interaktion ermöglicht eine neue Erzählform. Wie in *Afasia* ist auch in *POL* die Interaktion der eigentlichen Handlung untergeordnet. Andere interaktive Formen verfolgen unterschiedliche Ziele: In Videospielen bedeutet Interaktivität etwa eine Möglichkeit zur Überwindung von Hürden, im Internet ist Interaktion der Motor des Informationsaustauschs. Nichts davon ereignet sich in dieser Performance.
Die interaktive Erzählung in *POL* nutzt eine breite und spezifische Plattform. Die Interface-Prototypen – die Exoskelette – generieren ein spezifisches körperbasiertes Handlungsgefüge, das sich von den anderen Interaktionsmöglichkeiten – Maus, Tastatur –deutlich unterscheidet. Der Körper öffnet sich in einer Ursache-/Nichtwirkung-Beziehung gegenüber neuen Medien wie Robotern oder interaktiven Bildern und Klängen. Eine Bewegung des Arms kann so arbiträre Phänomene wie die modulierte Frequenz eines Tons, die horizontale Ausdehnung einer virtuellen Landschaft oder die Bewegungsgeschwindigkeit eines Roboters beeinflussen. Diese mechatronische Installation ist das Fundament des dargestellten interaktiven Dramas. Der gesprochene Dialog, der Grundlage des traditionellen Dramas ist, wird auf eine untergeordnete Ebene verbannt oder verschwindet zur Gänze. Das in dieser Performance aufgeführte Drama besteht aus einer Kettenreaktion, in der Körper, Interface, Computer und Setting miteinander in einen interaktiven Dialog treten. Dieser Diskurs lässt Gestik, Maschinerie, Geräusche und Bilder nebeneinander bestehen und verkörpert eine neue Erzählweise, die vertraute Richtwerte aufgibt und schier unermessliches Potenzial in sich birgt.
Der Handlungsstrang entspinnt sich über die vielfältigen Ausdrucksmöglichkeiten, die der ausführende Darsteller über sein Interface antizipiert, indem er eine wahre Flut von Informationen verwaltet. Auf diese Weise wird die Rahmenhandlung der Fabel konstruiert. Die Interaktion in *POL* erzeugt keine Zufallsereignisse, sondern einen beliebig formbaren, unterhaltsamen und flexiblen Erzählstrang – und resultiert hoffentlich in einer Kartharsis.

Aus dem Englischen von Sonja Pöllabauer

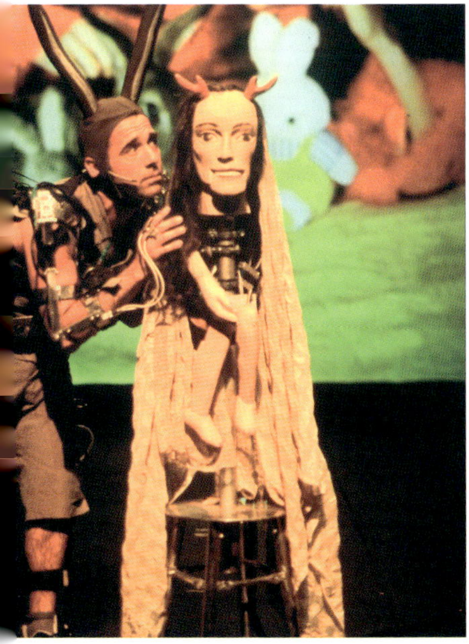

Gulliver's Box

Adrian David Cheok, Hirokazu Kato and Ars Electronica Futurelab

Gulliver's Box is a result of the Ars Electronica Futurelab's collaboration with Prof. Adrian Cheok (National University of Singapore) and Prof. Hirokazu Kato (Osaka University). With the Futurelab focusing increased attention over the last two years on Mixed Reality applications—including the technology to run them and their potential areas of utilization in artistic and scientific fields—an initial meeting with Cheok and Kato was held in conjunction with *Pixelspaces 2002,* where they presented their work at a symposium. Then as well, they offered visitors to the OpenLab Exhibition the opportunity to try out Mixed Reality applications they had developed. Visitors' positive experiences and reactions and the discussions triggered by their presentation ultimately gave rise to the idea of a joint project.

The developments that have been brought together in this installation represent the effort to pursue new approaches to dealing with Mixed Reality content. The challenge at the core of this project was to position an innovative medium somewhere between theater, film and installation. The result is an infrastructure that offers artists new opportunities to convey audiovisual information, and one that ought to encourage creatives in every discipline to work with these new approaches. Seen from this perspective, the platform that has been created in this way generates an experimental laboratory situation for a broad spectrum of forms of artistic expression. With it, performances by dancers, singers or actors can be recorded, transferred to avatars, and enhanced with any kind of computer animation. The application on display in the Ars Electronica Center also provides visitors with the opportunity to customize recordings of their own actions and subsequently to undertake a very special process of self-reflection. This unique aspect arises from the perspective of the viewer—just like in the world of huge Brobdignagians and tiny Lilliputians in *Gulliver's Travels,* quantum dimensional leaps and the play of scale and relation are what shatter accustomed modes of seeing. Ultimately, the various approaches that go into *Gulliver's Box* seem just as fantastic and horizon-expanding as the visions in Jonathan Swift's novel. The performances rendered by this medium and the recordings of the visitors themselves are an inviting chance for viewers to fundamentally change their points of view or to reconsider them for once. The possibility of observing and manipulating the mise-en-scène from any desired position external to the action goes beyond the God-mode of computer games and seems to be unique in a media context. Interaction with characters—either those captured live or animated ones—used to be necessarily bound to monitors or projection screens, but Mixed Reality technology now gives rise to forms of artistic expression and reception in an intimate—albeit likewise projected—situation involving protagonists and viewers. In *Gulliver's Box,* the processes of creative design, display and perception are brought together in a single environment.

Portions of the installation are, in turn, reminiscent of elements of the theater. These include a stage with a set, actors and a framework plot. The scene consists of animated characters, pre-produced footage and shots of the visitors that appear by means of head mounted displays on the stage—in this case, a table. The shots are made possible by the "3DLive" system[1] developed by Cheok that computer-generates a 3-D sequence out

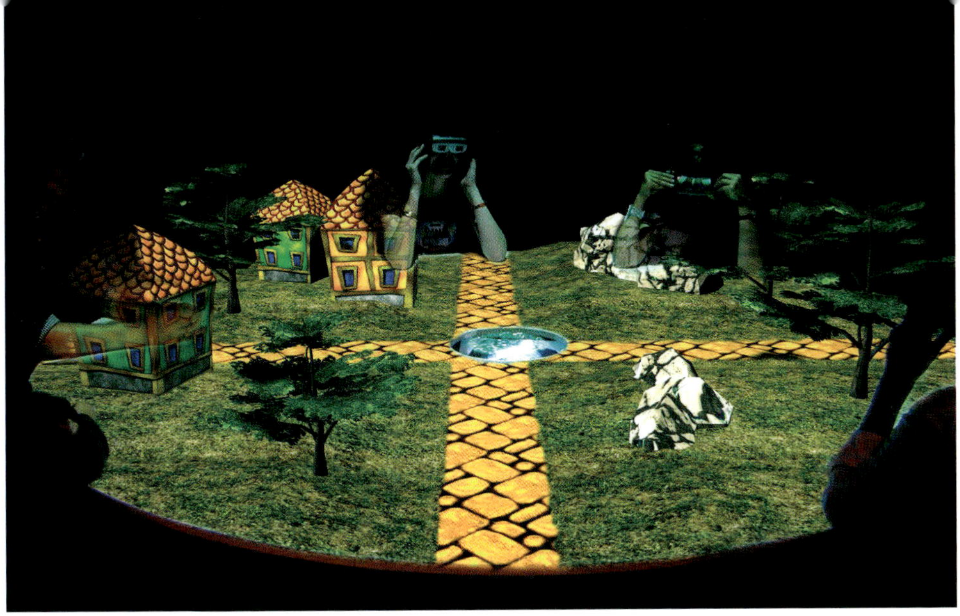

of numerous video images. The recording process is an integral part of the installation, and, in the Recording Area, visitors are given an introduction to this extremely promising form of data preservation. Then, with the help of optical markers, the video and audio information recorded in this way can be positioned on the play level however the user desires and played back.

The modular mode of scene construction allows the observer to intervene in the situation, modify it and determine the playback sequence. The tool to perform these manipulations is "MagicCup",[2] a tangible interface that combines a number of features. The interface consists of a simple transparent cube whose position and movements are recognized and interpreted by an optical system. The user grasps the cube and places it on top of a virtual object being displayed in order to reposition it, move it to the foreground or background, copy it or delete it. Switching among the individual functional features is done by simply shaking the cube.

This ongoing project is testing a wide variety of procedures and seeking to identify the system's full capabilities. But it will only be the process of gaining experience with the interplay of spontaneous, live 3-D recordings, artistic performances and animated characters and the public's dealings in actual practice with the system's technical tools for manipulation and interaction that will deliver a clearer picture of the implications of this Mixed Reality approach for future applications.

Translated from the German by Mel Greenwald
Text by Pascal Maresch / Christopher Lindinger

1 S.J.D. Prince, A.D. Cheok, F. Farbiz, T. Williamson, N. Johnson, M. Billinghurst and H. Kato. "3D Live: Real time captured content for mixed reality," International Symposium on Mixed and Augmented Reality, 2002.

2 H.Kato, M.Billinghurst, I.Poupyrev, K.Imamoto, K.Tachibana, "Virtual Object Manipulation on a Table-Top AR Environment," Proc. of IEEE and ACM International Symposium on Augmented Reality 2000, pp.111–119 (2000).

Conception: Adrian David Cheok, Hirokazu Kato, Christopher Lindinger, Horst Hörtner, Nina Wenhart, Gerfried Stocker / Content: Li Yu, Pascal Maresch, Andreas Jalsovec, Christine Pilsl / Softwaredevelopment: Dan Borthwick, Simon Prince, Adrian David Cheok, Hirokazu Kato, Gernot Ziegler, Roland Haring, Wolfgang Ziegler, Stefan Feldler / Production: Rudolf Hanl, Martin Honzik, Gerold Hofstadler, Stefan Mittelböck-Jungwirth
Exhibition Design: Scott Ritter

Supported by the funding of DSTA Singapore and the National Arts Council Singapore

Gulliver's Box

Adrian David Cheok, Hirokazu Kato und Ars Electronica Futurelab

Gulliver's Box ist eine Kooperationsarbeit des Ars Electronica Futurelab mit Prof. Adrian Cheok (National University of Singapore) und Prof. Hirokazu Kato (Osaka University). Nachdem das Futurelab in den letzten zwei Jahren sein Forschungsinteresse verstärkt auf Technologien und Einsatzmöglichkeiten von Mixed-Reality-Anwendungen im künstlerischen und wissenschaftlichen Bereich gerichtet hatte, kam es im Rahmen von *Pixelspaces 2002* zu einem ersten Treffen der Kooperationspartner. Cheok und Kato präsentierten ihre Arbeit im Symposium und gaben auch damals schon den Besuchern der OpenLab-Ausstellung die Gelegenheit, ihre Mixed-Reality-Applikationen auszuprobieren. Die positiven Erfahrungen mit den Besuchern und die durch die Präsentation ausgelösten Diskussionen führten schließlich zu der Idee eines gemeinsamen Projekts.
Mit den in der Installation kombinierten Entwicklungen werden neue Ansätze verfolgt, mit Mixed-Reality-Inhalten umzugehen. Die zentrale Herausforderung des Projekts bestand in der Positionierung eines neuartigen Mediums irgendwo zwischen Theater, Film und Installation. Das Ergebnis ist eine Infrastruktur, die Künstlern neue Möglichkeiten bietet, audiovisuelle Infor-

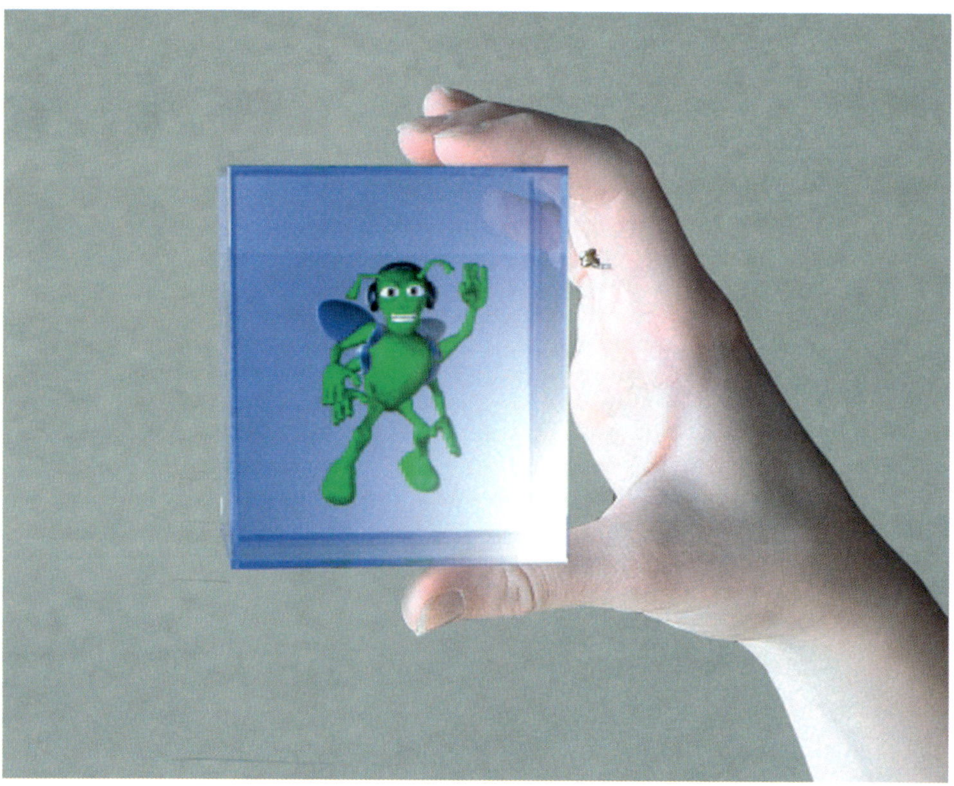

mation zu transportieren, und Kreative jeder Disziplin ermutigen soll, mit diesen neuen Ansätzen zu Arbeiten. So gesehen, generiert die geschaffene Plattform eine experimentelle Laborsituation für eine große Bandbreite künstlerischer Ausdrucksformen. Die Perfomances von Tänzern, Sängern oder Schauspielern können aufgenommen und, auf Avatare übertragen, mit beliebigen Computeranimationen konfrontiert werden. Der Zugang im Ars Electronica Center bietet darüber hinaus auch jedem Besucher die Möglichkeit, Aufnahmen von eigenen Aktionen zu gestalten und in der Folge eine spezielle Art der Selbstreflexion. Dieser besondere Aspekt ergibt sich aus dem Blickwinkel des Betrachters. Wie in der Welt der Riesen und Zwerge in *Gullivers Reisen,* sind es die Dimensionssprünge, das Spiel mit Maßstäben und Relationen, die gewohnte Seeweisen aufbrechen. Letztendlich erscheinen die verschiedenen Ansätze in *Gulliver's Box* genauso phantastisch und horizonterweiternd wie die Visionen im Roman von Jonathan Swift. Die über das Medium wiedergegebenen Performances und die Aufzeichnungen der Besucher selbst laden ein dazu, die Perspektive einmal grundlegend zu wechseln bzw. zu überdenken. Die Möglichkeit der Beobachtung und Manipulation der Szene, von einer erhöhten und frei wählbaren Position heraus, übertrifft den God-Mode von Computerspielen und scheint im Medienkontext einzigartig. Interaktion mit „live captured" oder animierten Charakteren war im Regelfall an Bildschirme oder Projektionswände gebunden. Mit der Mixed-Reality-Technologie ergeben sich nun Formen des künstlerischen Ausdrucks und der Rezeption in einer intimen, wenn auch projizierten, Situation zwischen Akteur und Betrachter. In *Gulliver's Box* werden die Prozesse des Gestaltens, der Darbietung und der Wahrnehmung in einem Environment vereint.
Teile der Installation erinnern wiederum an Elemente des Theaters. Es gibt eine Bühne mit Bühnenbild, Akteure und eine Rahmenhandlung. Die Szene besteht aus animierten Charakteren, vorproduzierten Aufnahmen und Aufnahmen der Besucher, die mittels Head Mounted Displays auf der Bühne, in diesem Fall einem Tisch, erscheinen. Die Aufnahmen werden ermöglicht durch das von Cheok entwickelte 3DLive-System,[1] das aus mehreren Videobildern eine dreidimensionale Sequenz errechnet. Der Aufnahmeprozess ist ein integrierter Bestanteil der Installation; in der Recording Area wir der Besucher an diese zukunftsträchtige Form der Konservierung herangeführt. Die so aufgezeichneten Bild- und Toninformationen können anschließend mit Hilfe von optischen Markern beliebig auf der Spielebene platziert und abgespielt werden. Der modulare Aufbau der Szene erlaubt es dem Beobachter in die Situation verändernd einzugreifen und den Ablauf zu bestimmen. Ein Werkzeug für diese Manipulationen ist das Tangible Interface „MagicCup",[2] das eine Reihe von Optionen in sich vereint. Das Interface besteht aus einem schlichten transparenten Würfel, dessen Position und Bewegungen von einem optischen System erkannt und interpretiert werden. Der Benutzer nimmt den Würfel, setzt ihn über ein eingeblendetes virtuelles Objekt und kann es so aufheben, bewegen und absetzen, kopieren oder löschen. Der Wechsel zwischen den einzelnen Funktionalitäten erfolgt durch einfaches Schütteln des Würfels.
Im Rahmen des fortlaufenden Projekts werden unterschiedlichste Verfahren erprobt und die Grenzen des Systems ausgelotet. Erst die Erfahrungen, die im Zusammenspiel von spontanen 3D-Live-Aufnahmen, künstlerischen Performances und animierten Charakteren gemacht werden können, und der praktische Umgang mit den technischen Manipulations- und Interaktionswerkzeugen im Publikumsverkehr werden zeigen, was dieser Mixed-Reality-Ansatz für zukünftige Anwendungen bedeutet, kann.

Text von Pascal Maresch / Christopher Lindinger

1 S.J.D. Prince, A.D. Cheok, F. Farbiz, T. Williamson, N. Johnson, M. Billinghurst und H. Kato. „3D Live: Real time captured content for mixed reality," International Symposium on Mixed and Augmented Reality, 2002.
2 H.Kato, M.Billinghurst, I.Poupyrev, K.Imamoto, K.Tachibana, „Virtual Object Manipulation on a Table-Top AR Environment," Proc. of IEEE and ACM International Symposium on Augmented Reality 2000, pp.111–119 (2000).

Key Grip

Justin Manor

The Key Grip project is an attempt to combine the entertainment and expressive possibilities of television, video gaming, and audiovisual performance into a single platform. The user can manipulate live and recorded media streams in a fully three dimensional environment via an arcade gamepad. Video and audio can be scratched, looped, and extruded into an expansive virtual space with the gamepad controls.
As the nature of visuals created for live performances becomes more complex and three dimensional, the use of a videogame input device becomes very natural and useful. PC and console games now take place in accuratere constructions of real cities, richly decorated landscapes, and across whole galaxies. And with this explosion of scale and realism, the ability of users to fluidly navigate and view their surroundings has blossomed with the advent of creative control metaphors and high-bandwidth input devices.
The player ceases to register individual button presses and joystick twiddles; they simply "become" the character in the game and proceed to jump, dodge, and shoot their way towards victory. This control transparency coupled with the ease of three dimensional navigation made the gamepad a natural choice for realtime audiovideo manipulation, or VJing.
By programming command over spatial and temporal presentation of live video into the Key Grip system, the control convenience of computer modelling software was combined with the expressive possibilities of direct scene manipulations. Key Grip users can loop interesting footage or zoom into a tiny portion of a scene from any angle or velocity.
With the ability to introduce time changes and three dimensional distortions to live video subtly or abruptly, viewers can be drawn into a world that is simultaneously real and unreal. The shared surroundings of performer and audience are easily reinterpreted at will to exaggerate prominent features or introduce new meaning.

Realized with support of the Siemens Artist in Residence Project at Ars Electronica.

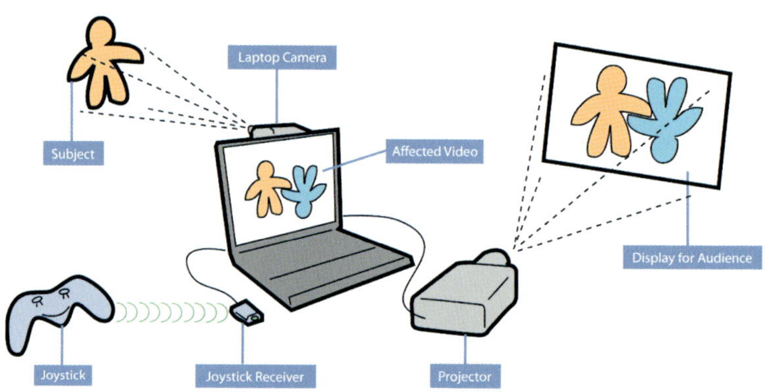

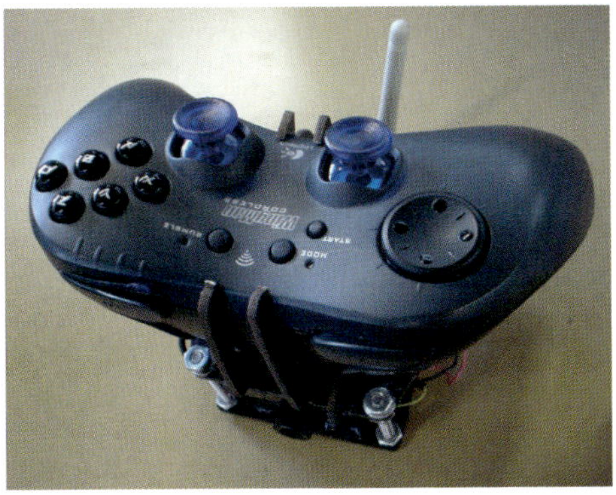

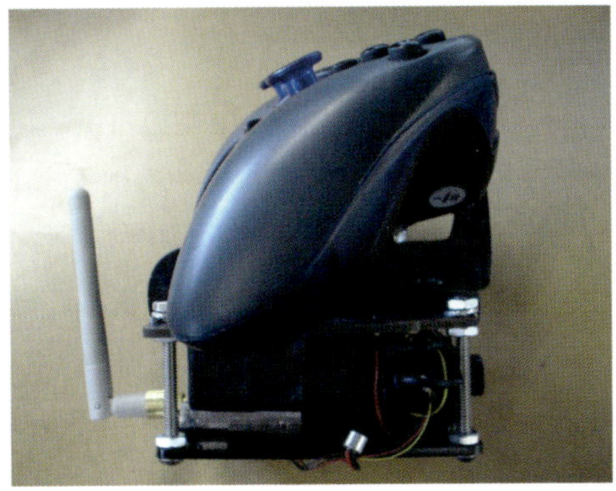

Key Grip

Justin Manor

Das Projekt *Key Grip* will die unterhaltenden und expressiven Elemente von Fernsehen, Videospielen und audiovisuellen Performances in einer Plattform vereinen. Per Arcade-Gamepad kann der User aufgezeichnete und Live-Streams in einer dreidimensionalen Umgebung manipulieren. Mithilfe der Gamepad-Tasten kann er die Video- und Audiosequenzen scratchen, loopen und in einen expansiven virtuellen Raum überführen.

Da für Live-Performances kreierte Visuals immer öfter dreidimensional sind und ständig komplexer werden, eignen sich die Input-Elemente von Videospielen bestens für diese Art der Manipulation. Die PC- und Konsolen-Games der jüngsten Generation spielen in naturgetreuen Nachbildungen von Städten und Landschaften oder in den Weiten ferner Galaxien. Dank maßstabgetreuerer und realistischerer Darstellungen und kreativer Steuerungsmetaphern und Breitband-Eingabegeräten kann der User nun wesentlich flüssiger durch das Envirnoment navigieren und die Umgebung besser betrachten.

Der Spieler nimmt das Drücken der Knöpfe und die Bewegungen des Joysticks gar nicht mehr wahr: Er „wird" die Figur im Spiel, die springt, geschickt ausweicht und sich den Weg zum Sieg freischießt. Mit seiner transparenten Steuerung und der einfachen dreidimensionalen Navigation ist das Gamepad das ideale Input-Device für die Audio-Video-Manipulation in Echtzeit oder für VJ-ing.

Indem wir die Steuerung der räumlichen und zeitlichen Darstellung von Live-Videosequenzen direkt ins *Key Grip*-System einprogrammierten, konnten wir die Bedienungsfreundlichkeit einer Modelling-Software mit den gestalterischen Möglichkeiten direkter Szenenmanipulation kombinieren. User von *Key Grip* können interessante Filmausschnitte loopen oder aus einem beliebigen Winkel mit beliebiger Geschwindigkeit in einen winzigen Ausschnitt einer Szene zoomen. Dadurch, dass zeitliche Änderungen und dreidimensionale Verzerrungen der Live-Videosequenzen fein dosiert oder abrupt vorgenommen werden können, taucht der Zuseher in eine Welt ein, die zugleich real und irreal ist. Und da sich Performer und Publikum in ein und derselben Umgebung befinden, kann diese beliebig neu interpretiert werden, um hervorstechende Merkmale zu überzeichnen oder ihnen eine neue Bedeutung zu verleihen.

Aus dem Amerikanischen von Michael Kaufmann

Realisiert im Rahmen des Siemens Artist in Residence Project at Ars Electronica.

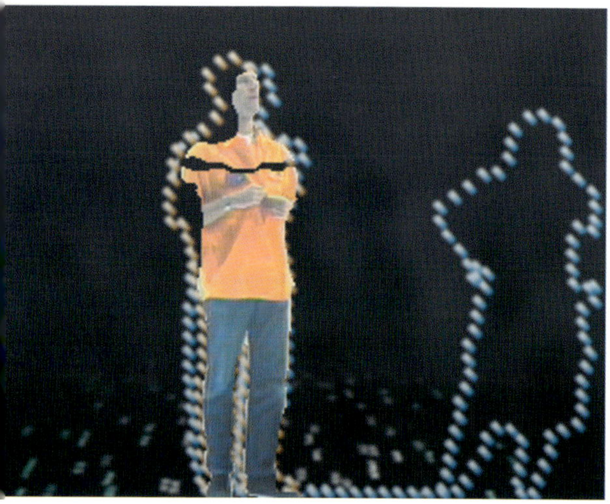

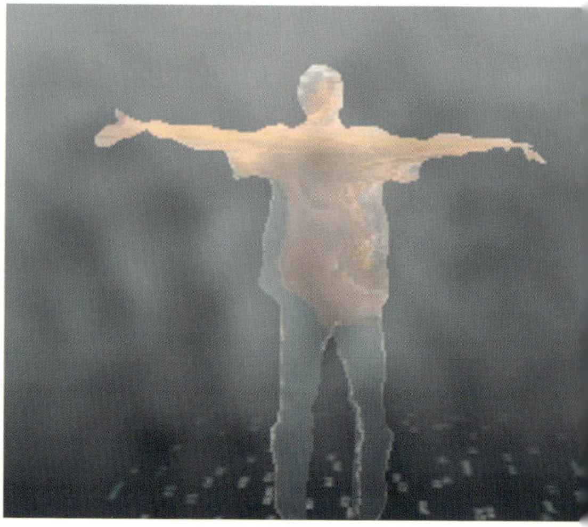

co.in.cide—The Third Place

x-space | Heimo Ranzenbacher

co.in.cide formalizes the interrelationship of two "places" by means of a system of interaction that mediates between them—the "third place." Whenever the visualizations of visitors' bodies/movements coincide with those of their telematic counterparts, they can open up a channel of verbal communication and establish eye contact. Only those who behave according to the conditions of the "third place" can reach that goal. When congruity is attained, the full image of the particular user's counterpart appears and replaces (assumes the place of) that user's own reflection. Saving and storing the images of the protagonists along with their voices concludes the process. The automatic upload of the file sets up an additional "place" in the Internet *(http://residence.aec.at/coincide)* made up of visual and acoustic evidence (tracks + traces) of the interaction.
The idea of the third place—the concept of decisive importance for *co.in.cide*—posits that the relationship that two places establish between themselves (or in which they are placed) creates for these places, even independently of the actual reference, binding conditions for the respective actions and activities carried out "on site."
Despite the effects of globalization teaching us something that is quite the contrary nearly every day, there are still many who cling to the habit of, for example, regarding one's place of residence as the center*point* of one's life. In doing so, we are presumably being taken in by the illusion of a close-up image, by the proximity of mere topography (topographical illusions). From this intimate relationship, (politically formative) on-site actions and activities are derived. (The greater the supposed sovereignty of a place, the more pronounced its tendency to derive from this illusion of concreteness the mandate and the modes of treating that place.)
Nevertheless, places tend to behave in a way that is contrary to the traditional demands placed on them. Commuters, for example, are only a consequence of this tendency. If

one takes three steps back and imagines the routes of commuters as a form that shapes the *image* of a cityscape, the way one imagines the center*point* of one's life also changes. Aspects that had previously been left out of consideration emerge: relationships, relations to other *points*. The image of the place "radiates" forth ...

If a place establishes a relationship to another place via commuters, then this circumstance produces, among other effects—for example, due to municipal expenses and revenues, increased traffic flows, etc.—the "third" place in relation to these two places. It emerges "on site" as a result of certain types of actions or activities having to do with anything from political policymaking to topography. (If, for example, the problem of increasing traffic is solved with a traffic circle or an express bypass, then this can, in turn, have an impact on businesses that are dependent upon high traffic on the old street, etc.) With respect to the cityscape, for example, if the actions or activities were oriented on a particular place's striking cityscape, then this would only be based on appearances. A place is always theory as well—something the faculty of sight might be blind to.

The third place is, to a certain extent, the power at work behind its concrete manifestations, a virtuality that is fed by reality/realities and that, in turn, feeds back on reality to realize itself. The place turns out to be a theoretical (topological) object. Art traditionally operates as it were from the state into which the theorization of things successively leads. The way in which images that make a strong impression on our conceptions of things come about says, as a rule, much more about their content than the pictures themselves. Art is directly addressed here: not as the producer of images (which it basically never was) but rather in its traditional role of focusing attention upon the non-visible aspects of what it shows, and from which what is visible draws its meaning. And this is the reason why the so often evoked school of seeing in art is also a school of political action. Not seeing what is visible but rather recognizing the forces that become visible is the basis of its aesthetic.

Places are communities, people, ideas, projects ...

Translated from the German by Mel Greenwald

The programmatic context of *co.in.cide* is *Liquid Music (http://www.liquid-music.org),* a project that has been manifesting itself since 1998 primarily in the form of a small annual festival in the City of Judenburg (in the Austrian Province of Styria, *http://www.judenburg.at).* Just as the city is an integral part of *Liquid Music,* artistic contributions are integral parts of the project. In response to an invitation from Graz 2003 – Cultural Capital of Europe, *co.in.cide* was developed further as Judenburg's contribution to the STADT_LAND_KUNST (City_Province_Art) program being presented as part of the Graz 2003 festivities. The considerations with respect to the significance of Graz as European cultural capital and Judenburg, which has established an artistic relationship with Graz, have gone into the formulation of "The Third Place" as the theme of *Liquid Music 2003.*

A *Liquid Music* project for Graz 2003—Cultural Capital of Europe in conjunction with STADT_LAND_KUNST.
Realized at the Ars Electronica Futurelab, Linz.
Software: Robert Praxmarer, Stage: Stefan Mittlböck-Jungwirth, Martin Honzik, Christoph Scholz.
Web/3D-Client: Helmut Höllerl, Florian Landerl

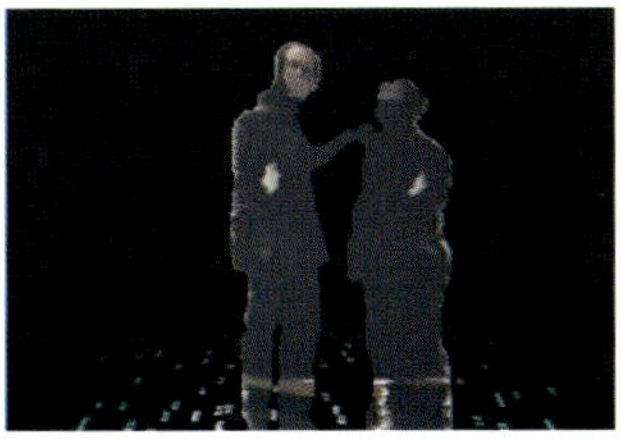

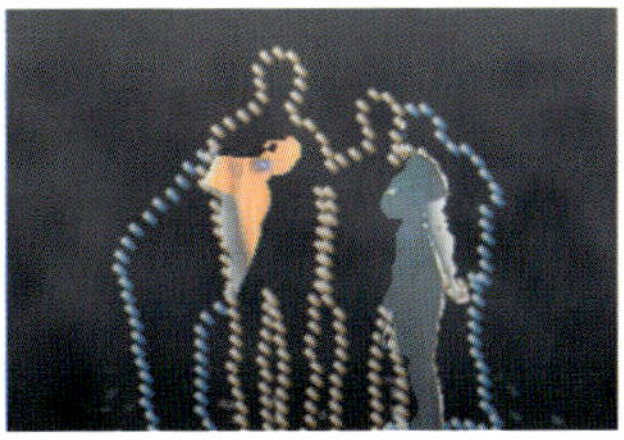

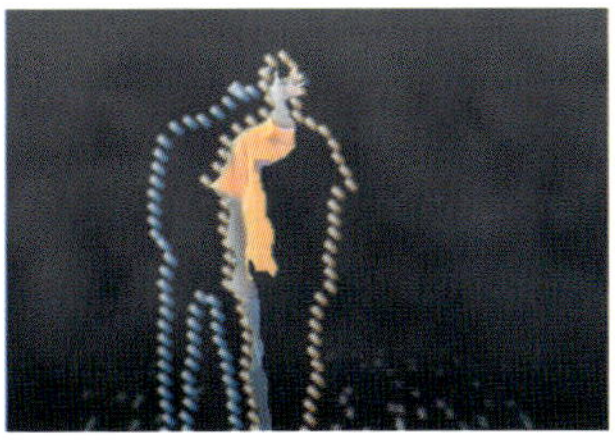

co.in.cide – der dritte Ort

x-space | Heimo Ranzenbacher

co.in.cide formalisiert die Beziehung zweier „Orte" durch ein zwischen beiden vermittelndes Interaktionssystem, den „dritten Ort". Indem die BesucherInnen die Visualisierungen ihrer Körper / Bewegungen mit ihrem telematischen Gegenüber zur Deckung bringen, können sie einen Sprachkommunikationskanal öffnen und Blickkontakt herstellen. Das Ziel kann nur erreichen, wer sich nach den Bedingungen des „dritten Ortes" verhält. Bei Deckungsgleiche erscheint das Vollbild der jeweiligen Gegenseite und ersetzt das eigene Spiegelbild, es nimmt dessen Platz ein. Die Speicherung des Bildes der Akteure mit deren Stimmen beendet den Prozess. Der automatische Upload des Files etabliert im Web einen weiteren „Ort" *(http://residence.aec.at/coincide)* aus visuellen und akustischen Spuren („Tracks + Traces") der Interaktion.
Die Idee des dritten Ortes, wie sie für *co.in.cide* maßgeblich war, besagt, dass die Beziehung, in die sich Orte zueinander setzen (bzw. in die sie gesetzt werden), für diese Orte auch unabhängig von den eigentlichen Bezugnahmen verbindliche Bedingungen für die jeweiligen Handlungen „vor Ort" erzeugt.
Obwohl von Globalisierungseffekten nahezu täglich eines Besseren belehrt, wird (z. B.) gemeinhin an der Gewohnheit festgehalten, Wohnorte als Lebensmittel*punkt* zu begreifen. Dabei sitzen wir vermutlich der Illusion eines Nahbildes auf, der Nähe zur bloßen Topografie (topografische Illusionen). Aus diesem Naheverhältnis werden „vor Ort" – politisch-gestaltende – Handlungen abgeleitet. (Je höher die vermeintliche Souveränität eines Ortes, desto ausgeprägter die Neigung, aus der Illusion des Konkreten das Mandat und die Modi der Behandlung des Ortes abzuleiten.)

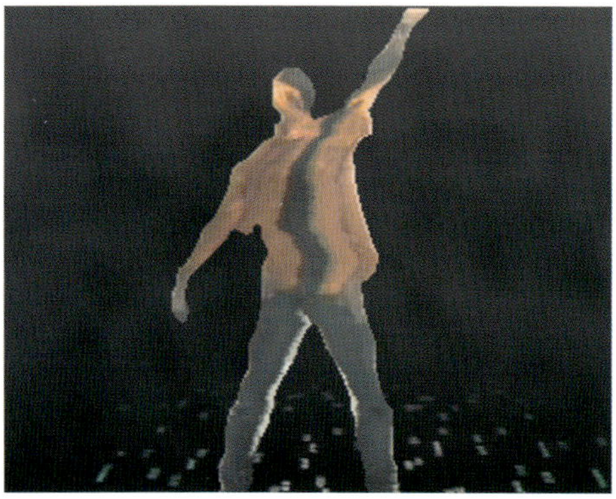

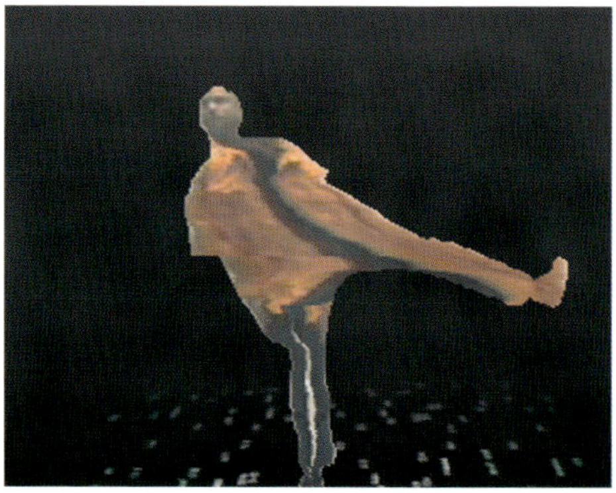

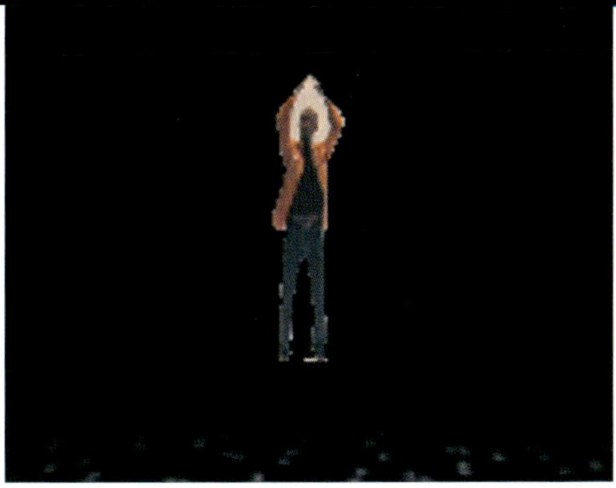

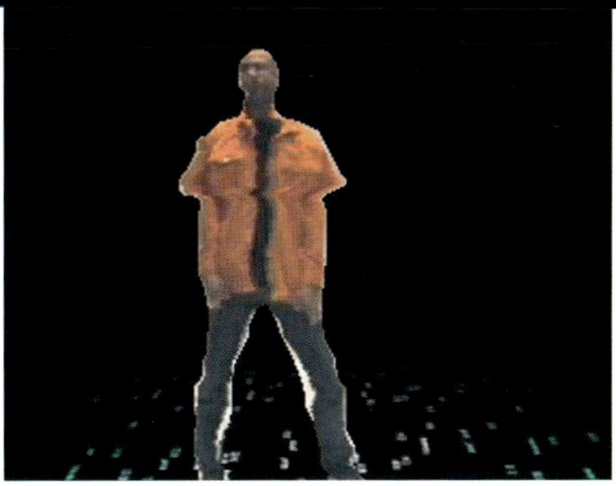

Orte neigen jedoch dazu, sich gegen den traditionellen Anspruch an sie zu verhalten. Pendler sind z. B. nur eine Folge dieser Tendenz. Tritt man drei Schritte zurück und stellt man sich die Wege der Pendler als Ausformung eines Orts*bildes* vor, ändert sich auch die Vorstellung von einem Lebensmittel*punkt*. Es tauchen zuvor unbeachtete Aspekte auf, Verhältnisse, Beziehungen zu anderen *Punkten.* Das Bild des Ortes „strahlt" aus ...
Wenn sich ein Ort durch Pendler zu einem anderen Ort in Beziehung setzt, dann erzeugt dieser Umstand u. a. durch Kommunalabgaben bzw. -einnahmen, durch Verkehrsaufkommen etc. den diesbezüglich „dritten" Ort dieser beiden Orte. Er tritt „vor Ort" durch bestimmte, von der Tagespolitik bis in die Topografie hinein wirkende Handlungsmodalitäten zu Tage. (Wenn z. B. das Problem zunehmenden Verkehrs durch einen Kreisverkehr oder eine Umfahrung gelöst wird – was wiederum Auswirkungen auf Wirtschaftsbetriebe haben kann, die von der Frequenz der alten Straße abhängig ist – etc. etc.) Würde sich z. B. in Sachen Ortsbild das Handeln für einen Ort an seinem Bild orientieren, das sich augenfällig erschließt, hätte es nur das Scheinbare zur Grundlage. Ein Ort ist immer auch, was sich dem Blick verschließt – Theorie.
Der dritte Ort ist gewissermaßen die hinter seinen konkreten Manifestationen wirkende Kraft, eine aus Realität(en) gespeiste Virtualität, die auf die Realität zurück wirkt, sich realisiert ...
Der Ort entpuppt sich als theoretisches (topologisches) Objekt. Die Kunst operiert gewissermaßen traditionell aus dem Zustand heraus, in den die Theoretisierung der Dinge sukzessive führt.
Der Modus, wie die Bilder, die unsere Vorstellungen von den Dingen prägen, zustande kommen, sagt in der Regel weit mehr über deren Inhalte aus als die Bilder selbst. Die Kunst ist da direkt angesprochen: nicht als Bild-Produzentin, die sie im Grunde nie war, sondern in ihrer Tradition, die Aufmerksamkeit durch das, was sie zeigt, auf das Nicht-Sichtbare zu lenken, aus dem das Sichtbare dann seinen Sinn bezieht. Deshalb ist die viel beschworene Schule des Sehens der Kunst auch eine Schule des politischen Handelns. Nicht im Sichtbaren, sondern im Erkennen der Kräfte, die sichtbar werden, begründet sich ihre Ästhetik.
Orte sind Kommunen, Menschen, Ideen, Projekte ...

co.in.cide steht im programmatischen Kontext von *Liquid Music (http://www.liquid-music.org),* einem Projekt, das sich seit 1998 primär in Form eines jährlichen kleinen Festivals in der Stadt Judenburg (Steiermark / A, *http://www.judenburg.at)* manifestiert. Ebenso wie die Stadt integrierender Teil von *Liquid Music* ist, sind die künstlerischen Beiträge integrierende Teile des Projektes. *co.in.cide* wurde auf Einladung von Graz 2003 – Kulturhauptstadt Europas, Judenburg durch *Liquid Music* am Programm STADT_LAND_KUNST von Graz 2003 zu beteiligen, konzipiert. Die Überlegungen im Hinblick auf die Bedeutung von Graz als europäische Kulturhauptstadt und Judenburg, das sich künstlerisch in Beziehung zu Graz setzt, haben das Thema von *Liquid Music 2003,* den dritten Ort, bestimmt.

Ein *Liquid-Music*-Projekt für Graz 2003 – Kulturhauptstadt Europas im Rahmen von STADT_LAND_KUNST.
Realisiert im Ars Electronica Futurelab, Linz.
Software: Robert Praxmarer, Stage: Stefan Mittlböck-Jungwirth, Martin Honzik, Christoph Scholz.
Web/3D-Client: Helmut Höllerl, Florian Landerl

Colophony Circuit

Electric Indigo / Mia Zabelka

Mia Zabelka and Electric Indigo met up in April 2002 and began a "co-opération électrique": via interfaces that assume a whole range of different forms, they create acoustic continua in space evoked by the famously anarchic behavior of Mia Zabelka, who, with lusty aggressiveness and point-blank physical immediacy, produces complex, multi-layered musical images on the electronic violin that blend with the syncopated rhythms and bass-heavy grooves of Electric Indigo. The duo jams like human rhythm machines that form melodies and turn sounds into music. Their interplay, their compelling stage presence and the musical results of their collaboration engender a level of intensity that the audience feels like a high-voltage charge. Her performance will be enhanced with visuals by the video artist Glam Fatal.

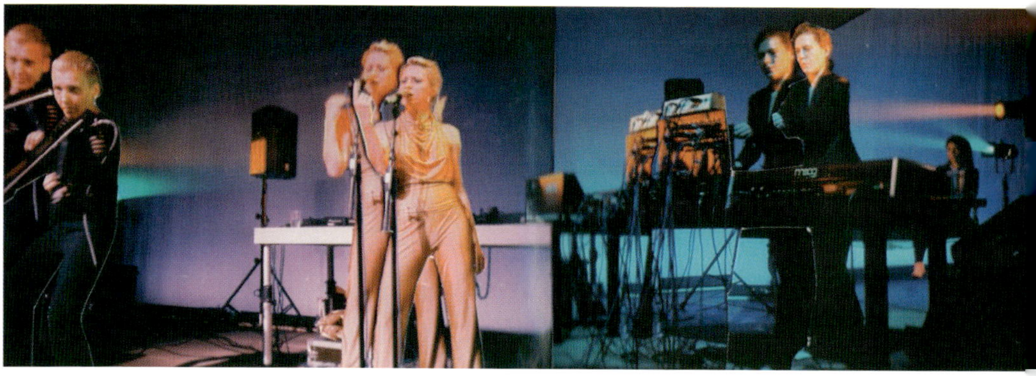

Mia Zabelka und Electric Indigo begegneten sich im April 2002 und starteten eine „coopération électrique": Über vielgestaltige Schnittstellen schaffen sie akustische Verläufe im Raum, evoziert durch die bekannt anarchische Verhaltensweise der Mia Zabelka, die auf ihrer Electronic Violin auf angriffslustige Weise mit körperlicher Unmittelbarkeit vielschichtige musikalische Bilder erzeugt, gepaart mit den synkopisierten Rhythmen und basslastigen Grooves von Electric Indigo. Sie agieren wie menschliche Rhythmusmaschinen, die Melodien bilden und Geräusche zu Musik werden lassen. Das Zusammenspiel der beiden, ihre unmittelbar wirksame Bühnenpräsenz und das musikalische Ergebnis dieser Kooperation erzeugen eine Intensität, die das Publikum gleichsam unter Strom setzt. Ihr Auftritt wird durch Visuals der Videokünstlerinnen Glam Fatal ergänzt.

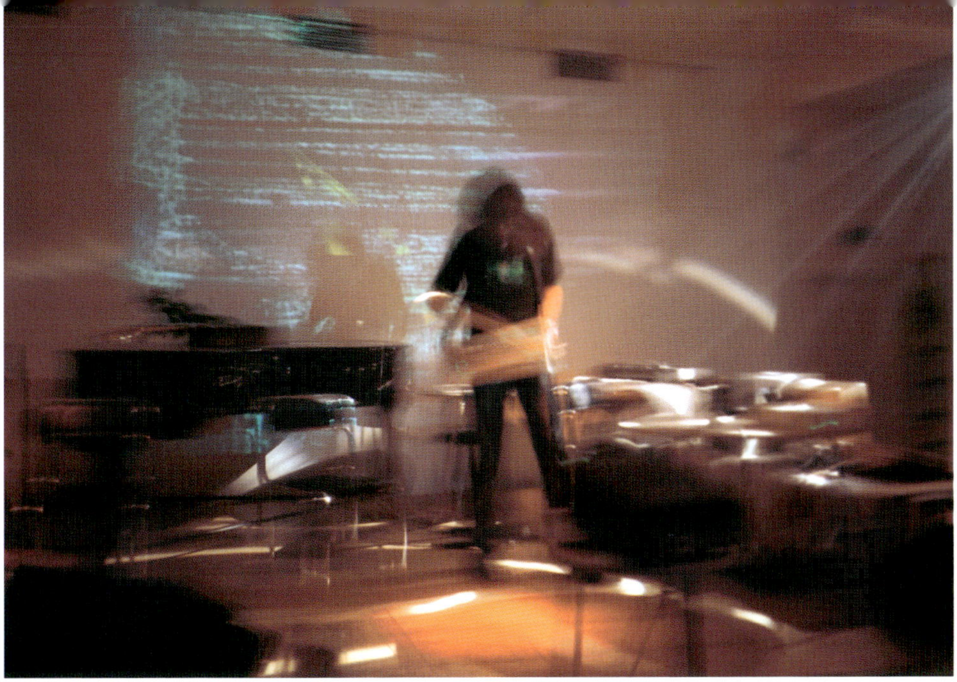

Pixelspaces_DAMPF

386 dx

Alexei Shulgin

386 dx is undeniably humorous
386 dx is the world's first cyberpunk rock band
386 dx is a computer
386 dx is available via staalplaat records at
386 dx is based on an archaic computer
386 dx is a rock band that consists of the only obsolete computer which sings and plays guitars and drums
386 dx is the name of the old pc that is used in this work
386 dx is not yet settled
386 dx is the world's first cyberpunk rock band
386 dx is a 32 bit machine
386 dx is the world's first cyberpunk electrorockband
386 dx is a 132 pin pga
386 dx is the true 32
386 dx is not a very

From: *http://www.googlism.com/who_is/3/386_dx/*

Principles of Indeterminism

Heimo Ranzenbacher

Code–Notation

With software, graphic artists have at their disposal for the first time a tool comparable to musicians' systems of notation, a tool that not only is able to bring production and performance into congruence but also one that intensifies the process of bringing the two disciplines methodologically into line with one another and thereby formalizes interdisciplinarity beyond the interaction of diverse interests through a grammar shared by their various languages. Thus far, the clearest manifestation of this phenomenon has emerged within the framework of the open source movement with the development—motivated (in no small measure) over the course of art projects—of separate programming languages that, as publicly available reference sources, have become the basis—the source code—of other individual applications. However, an additional consequence of codes binding among disciplines is the dynamization of the systems involved, and this is precisely the constitutive core of the concepts and undertakings subsumed under the heading media art.
Ars Electronica is staging *Principles of Indeterminism* as an evening spent concentrating on the theme of this year's festival, "Code—The Language of Our Time." With its primary focus on music, the program will attempt to take a historical approach to identifying principles of media art in paradigmatic works of modern classicism and to establish their affinity to current strategies of real-time processing in the graph arts. The leitmotif here is the principle of transformation and metamorphosis alluded to in the title, which, as the artistic credo of composer, tonal experimenter and architect Iannis Xenakis, also applies to the concept underlying art forms characterized by interdisciplinarity, synesthesia and technique (or interactivity, generativity and multimediality). The evening's program will range from analog to electronic to digital music, from composed to programmed music, from orchestral and instrumental ensemble playing to live electronics and digital sound synthesis, as well as from sound to image. Xenakis' ideas are both the crux and the point of departure of these concert and performance events.

Parametrization

Iannis Xenakis (1922–2001) is considered a creative pioneer and is much admired by many contemporary digital musicians for his inimitable electronic worlds of sound that reflect his radical understanding of music as an algorithmically based, open process. But even beyond the approach of this conceptualization whereby music is to be understood as a sort of software, not the least of the reasons why Xenakis' oeuvre continues to fascinate is the psycho-acoustic, spatially formative dimension of much of his music. Xenakis, in his work as a composer, utilized his competence as an architect to create, as it were, acoustic metaphors for conceptions of space that have been thematicized and formalized in the media arts repeatedly since their inception.
The search for a leading light from the century just past was substantially motivated by

the festival's intention to document the fact that the process of opening up the uncharted territory of digital code did not in fact represent the invention of a whole new world. Rather, the concepts that constitute what is tantamount to a leitmotif running through the works of the current generation of digital artists most certainly do have a past history, and, in point of fact, many of the concepts dating back to the '50s and '60s were not able to be implemented in suitable fashion until the advent of the instruments and tools of information technology and the development of the computer as a freely programmable device. Thus, with its focus on the role of software in art, the didactic arc of the program lined up for presentation in conjunction with *Principles of Indeterminism* begins with the parametrization and production of sound, and ranges over developments in the thematic context of the parametrization of interpretation including its ultimate phase in which performance too mutates into a real-time process. It proceeds from the instrument to electronics to the laptop; from the composer who works "offline" with notation systems recorded on paper, to the composer who indeed does work with the computer but does so offline, and all the way to current tendencies—represented by programs like Supercollider and various configurations of MAX—that set up a sort of real-time developmental environment in which the composer's work in writing software and performing music are blended together into a single process and distinctions between the disciplines of music and media art start to become obsolete.

Principles of Indeterminism takes a number of different approaches to spanning this arc with illustrative pieces by Edgar Varése, Morton Subotnick and Iannis Xenakis, Steve Reich—in light of his iconic role for minimal music, which can be interpreted as a forerunner of generative music—and Marco Stroppa. These are pieces that, analogously to the paradigmatic strategies of composition, have, on one hand, been remixed by representatives of the digital music generation, and, on the other hand—as illustrated by the work of Bill Viola, Sue Constabile, Lia, Martin Wattenberg, Marius Watz, Justin Manor, Gerda Palmetshofer and Stefan Mittlböck—are accompanied by visualizations that exemplify, as it were, the affinity of the strategies. For the lineup of digital musicians, Rupert Huber / Tosca, Ryoji Ikeda, Otomo Yoshihide and Naut Human have been engaged. Their advancing, enhancing remixing of these remixes is, in theoretically consistent fashion, just as much a part of their work as the performance of their own pieces, which draw their principle conception of self from precisely this sort of metamorphosis.

Didactic intentions are likewise behind the shifting of performance venues—from the Main Hall of the Brucknerhaus to its Middle Hall, on to the Klangpark and back again—that go along with these changing strategies.

Visualization

Synaesthesia is one of the leitmotifs of media art and probably the quality in which the fundamental principles that differentiate it from the traditional arts stand out most strongly. So then, if ones goal is to design an evening's program featuring statements that deal with the essence of the current state of media art, then synaesthetic qualities are by definition among ones central intentions, and these are manifested in *Principles of Indeterminism* in the form of perceptual and strategic linkage of sound and image.

The second matter of concern has to do with a question that has been addressed over and over again in the context of the discussion of the role of software in art—whether software is merely another system of notation, and, if it is, then at what point does it become an artistic work in its own right? In principle, notation functions only when there is general agreement about it or—with respect to new systems—when it is so meaningfully expressive that it produces general agreement.

In this connection as well, the history of music delivers analogies based on the development of new systems of notation. These were born of the necessity to come up with a corresponding set of characters to record in writing its newly discovered tonal worlds and to provide for a suitable expansion of interpretational latitude. Prominent examples are to be found in the work of Iannis Xenakis and Varése as well as that of Ligeti, for instance, and, more recently, Logothetis, who took notation far beyond its conventional function of an exact or even merely associative set of instructions to become a largely autonomous graphic vocabulary.
Nowadays, the question of notation systems is simultaneously a question of visualization, or rather one of the power of expression of visual or—in the realm of software—text-based systems for the resulting sensorially determined processes. To what extent is the graphic quality of a score in a position to no longer be just an explanatory adjunct to the music but rather to expand or possibly even to replace it? Thus, artists who work with (real-time) software—that is, those who program their graphics and how they behave—have also been invited to visualize pieces of music. An additional precondition for this engagement was to showcase their work live on stage as an integral part of the musical performance.

Principles of Indeterminism

Heimo Ranzenbacher

Code – Notation

Mit Software haben bildende KünstlerInnen erstmals ein den Notationssystemen der Musiker vergleichbares Werkzeug, das nicht nur Produktion und Performance zur Deckungsgleiche zu bringen vermag, sondern auch die methodische Angleichung der Sparten forciert und damit Interdisziplinarität über das Maß des Zusammenwirkens verteilter Interessen hinaus – durch eine ihren Sprachen gemeinsame Grammatik – formalisiert. (Seine bislang deutlichste Ausprägung erfährt dieser Umstand etwa im Rahmen der Open-Source-Bewegung durch die – auch – in Kunstprojekten motivierte Entwicklung eigener Programmiersprachen, die als öffentlich verfügbare Bezugsquelle zur Grundlage, zum „Quellcode", für weitere individuelle Anwendungen werden.) Interdisziplinär verbindliche Codes haben jedoch auch die Dynamisierung der beteiligten Systeme zur Folge, und gerade darin haben unter Medienkunst subsumierte Konzepte und Unternehmen ihren konstitutiven Kern.
Mit *Principles of Indeterminism* gestaltet Ars Electronica einen Themenabend zum diesjährigen Festivalschwerpunkt „Code – The Language of Our Time". Angesiedelt im Bereich der Musik, versucht das Programm Prinzipien der Medienkunst in paradigmatischen Werken der modernen Klassik historisch zu verorten und deren Verwandtschaft mit aktuellen Strategien des Realtime-Processing in der bildenden Kunst zu verknüpfen. Leitthema ist das mit dem Titel angesprochene Prinzip der Transformation und Metamorphose, das als das künstlerische Credo

des Komponisten, Klangforschers und Architekten Iannis Xenakis auch den Begriff von Interdisziplinarität, Synästhesie und Technik beziehungsweise Interaktivität, Generativität und Multimedialität geprägter Künste betrifft. Das Programm führt von analoger über elektronische zu digitaler Musik, von komponierter zu programmierter Musik, vom Orchester und Instrumentalensemble über Live Electronics zur digitalen Klangsynthese, von Klang zu Bild. Xenakis' Ideen sind sowohl Angel- als auch Ausgangspunkt dieser Konzert- und Performance-Events.

Parametrisierung

Iannis Xenakis (1922 – 2001) gilt wegen seiner unverwechselbaren elektronischen Klangwelten, die sein radikales Verständnis von Musik als algorithmisch basierter, offener Prozess dokumentieren, als Leitfigur vieler zeitgenössischer Digital-Musiker. Über den Ansatz der Idee, Musik als eine Art Software zu verstehen, hinaus fasziniert Xenakis' Oeuvre nicht zuletzt auch durch den Aspekt der psychoakustisch räumlich gestaltenden Dimension vieler seiner Werke. Der Komponist Xenakis hat gleichsam mit der Kompetenz des Architekten Klangmetaphern für Raumvorstellungen geschaffen, wie sie seither immer wieder in den Medienkünsten thematisiert und formalisiert werden.

Die Suche nach einer Leitfigur aus dem vergangenen Jahrhundert war nicht zuletzt von der Absicht des Festivals motiviert, zu dokumentieren, dass mit dem Neuland des digitalen Codes nicht die ganze Welt neu erfunden wurde, sondern dass Konzepte, die nahezu leitmotivisch die digitale Kunst der aktuellen Generation durchziehen, ihre Vergangenheit haben; dass jedoch viele aus den 50er und 60er Jahren datierende Ideen erst mit den Instrumenten und Werkzeugen der Informationstechnologie, dem Computer als frei programmierbarem Gerät, adäquat realisierbar wurden.

Mit seinem Fokus auf die Rolle von Software in der Kunst setzt daher der didaktische Bogen des Programms *Principles of Indeterminism* bei der Parametrisierung des Klanges und der Erzeugung des Klanges an und spannt sich über Entwicklungen im thematischen Kontext der Parametrisierung der Interpretation bis hin zur letzten Phase, in der auch die Performance zu einem Echtzeit-Prozess mutiert; vom Instrument über die Elektronik zum Laptop; vom Komponisten, der „offline“ auf Papier mit Notationssystemen arbeitet, zum Komponisten, der schon am Computer, aber offline arbeitet, hin zu den aktuellen, durch Programme wie Supercollider oder verschiedene Konfigurationen von MAX repräsentierten Tendenzen, die eine Art Realtime-Entwicklungsumgebung etablieren, in der für Komponisten das Schreiben von Software und die Aufführung von Musik zu einem Prozess verschmelzen und disziplinäre Unterscheidungen zwischen Musik und Medienkunst obsolet zu werden beginnen.

Diesen Bogen spannt *Principles of Indeterminism* in verschiedener Hinsicht mit exemplarischen Stücken von Edgar Varèse, Morton Subotnick und Iannis Xenakis, Steve Reich – im Hinblick auf seine ikonischen Rolle für die Minimal Music, die als ein Vorläufer für die generative Musik interpretiert werden kann – und Marco Stroppa – Stücken, die in Analogie zu den paradigmatischen Strategien des Komponierens einerseits Remixes durch Vertreter der Generation der Digital Music unterzogen, andererseits – durch Beiträge von Bill Viola, Sue Constabile, Lia, Martin Wattenberg, Marius Watz, Justin Manor, Gerda Palmetshofer und Stefan Mittlböck – von Visualisierungen begleitet werden, an denen die Verwandtschaft der Strategien gleichsam exemplifiziert wird. Als Digital Musicians wurden Rupert Huber / Tosca, Ryoji Ikeda, Otomo Yoshihide und Naut Humon engagiert. Ihr weiter führender Remix dieser Remixes ist konsequenterweise ebenso Teil ihrer Arbeit wie die Aufführung eigener Stücke, die ihr prinzipielles Selbstverständnis aus solchen Metamorphosen beziehen. Didaktische Absichten liegen auch den mit wechselnden Strategien wechselnden Schauplätzen – vom Großen Saal des Brucknerhauses, in den Mittleren Saal, den Klangpark und zurück – zu Grunde.

Visualisierung

Synästhesie ist eines der Leitmotive der Medienkunst und wahrscheinlich die Eigenschaft, in der ihre grundlegenden Prinzipien den Unterschied zu den traditionellen Künsten am besten charakterisieren. Will man einen Abend zu Kernaussagen über den Status quo der Medienkunst programmieren, dann sind synästhetische Eigenschaften per definitionem eine seiner zentralen Intentionen, die in *Principles of Indeterminism* in Form der perzeptiven und strategischen Verknüpfung von Klang und Bild verfolgt werden.
Das zweite Anliegen betrifft die im Kontext der Diskussion um die Rolle von Software in der Kunst immer wieder erörterte Frage, ob Software lediglich ein anderes Notationssystem sei oder, und wenn ja, ab welchem Moment sie zu einem eigenständigen künstlerischen Werk werde.
Notation funktioniert im Prinzip nur, wenn es eine Übereinkunft über sie gibt oder sie – im Hinblick auf neue Systeme – so aussagekräftig ist, dass sie eine Übereinkunft erzeugt.
Die Musikgeschichte liefert auch in diesem Zusammenhang Analogien durch die Entwicklung neuer Notationssysteme. Aus der Notwendigkeit heraus entstanden, die neuen Klangwelten, die man entdeckt hat, entsprechend niederzuschreiben und für eine adäquate Erweiterung des interpretatorischen Spielraums zu sorgen, finden sich prominente Beispiele bei Iannis Xenakis und Varèse ebenso wie etwa bei Ligeti oder, in jüngerer Zeit, Logothetis, der die Notation weit abseits ihrer herkömmlichen Funktion einer exakten oder auch nur mehr assoziativen Handlungsanweisung, zu einem weitgehend autonomen Grafik getrieben hat.
Die Frage nach den Notationssystemen ist heute zugleich eine Frage der Visualisierung beziehungsweise eine Frage nach der Aussagekraft von visuellen oder – im Bereich Software – von textbasierten Systemen für die daraus folgenden sinnlich bestimmten Prozesse: Inwieweit ist die bildhafte Qualität einer Partitur imstande, nicht mehr nur Erklärung zur Musik zu sein, sondern sie zu erweitern oder eventuell sogar abzulösen?
Für den Part der Visualisierung der Musikstücke wurden daher auch KünstlerInnen eingeladen, die mit (Realtime-)Software arbeiten, also ihre Grafiken und deren Verhalten programmieren. Eine weitere Bedingung für das Engagement war, als integrierender Teil der musikalischen Performance live auf der Bühne zu agieren.

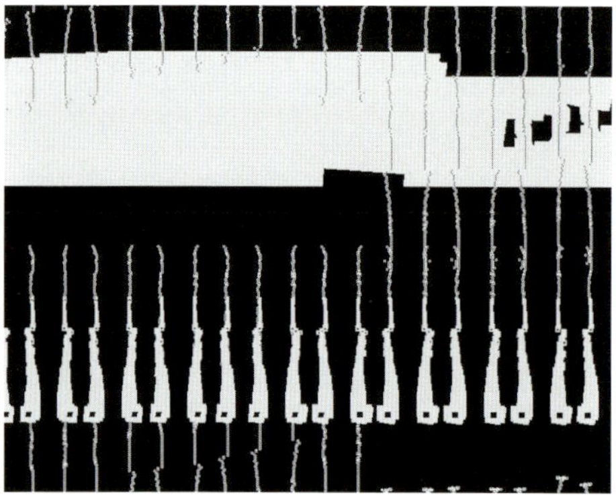

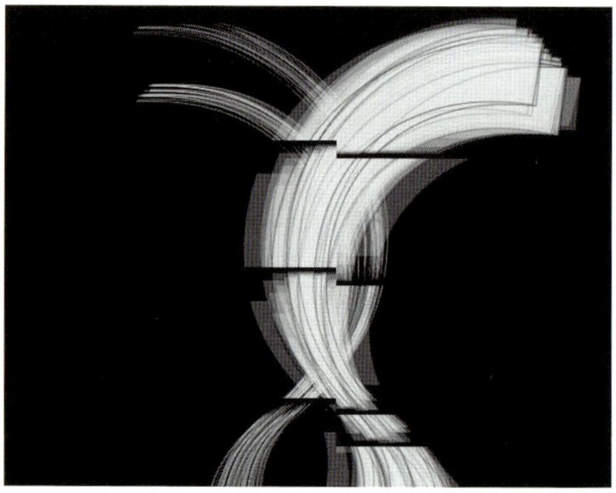

© by Lia

Geste Electronique

Gerda Palmetshofer

Analogique A (1958), a composition for nine string instruments, is dedicated to Fred Goldbeck. It is an abstract structure based on probability computation. Eight different tonal states are interlinked using the methods of Markov.
Analogique B (1959), dedicated to Oliver Messian, is electronic music on a magnetic tape that has been cut up into hundreds of tiny pieces and then reassembled in a new sequence—one of the first musical compositions to use the method of granulation.
The concept calls for performing *A* and *B* together—originally directly, in a situation of "call response"; here through the playback of the piece heard previously. Thus, it is one of the few works (aside from *Kraanerg)* that places two media which Xenakis normally preferred to use separately—electronic music and the orchestra—in a situation of juxtaposition and confrontation. The string instruments are set off by sinusoidal tones.

Persepolis and *Mycenae Alpha* are both pieces for "polytopes," those audiovisual mise-en-scènes in which numerous spatial configurations consisting of sound, light and architecture overlay one another at a single physical location. The various dimensions of the space are not synchronous but rather independent of one another. According to Xenakis' view, tonal masses and masses of visual elements are equivalent with respect to their structure and can therefore be treated with the same principles, the implementation of which is referred to as a "geste electronique."
"Graphic densities"—that is, sketches of a graphic nature (with reference to his work as an architect)—preceded the process of writing down the score. They varied in form and gestalt; the most outstanding of them were renderings in tree-like form, the so-called "arboresences" that were brachiated curves drawn on graph paper as the written manifestations of mathematical formulas and matrices. Mathematical theories were drawn upon for the purpose of mastering clouds (or Milky Ways) of sound. What Xenakis himself termed "stochastic music" had recourse to the theory of probability; game theory engendered "strategic music"; set theory led to "symbolic music."
In 1979, Xenakis produced the first example of a UPIC (Unité Polygogique Informatique de CEMAMu), a "composing machine" that turned the curves drawn on a light shade into sounds in real time. Interesting sounds are generated by dense notations and curves assuming complex shapes. Well-known processes including granular synthesis and frequency modulation synthesis were utilized.
Mycenae Alpha (1978) was the first work entirely composed with the UPIC system. *Gendy* ("general dynamic stochastic synthesis") is the next step, in that composition was done with the help of software. Here, though, there was no longer a need for a graphic interface; rather, the work is hard coded.

Geste Electronique

Gerda Palmetshofer

Analogique A (1958). Diese Komposition für neun Streichinstrumente ist Fred Goldbeck gewidmet. Es ist eine abstrakte Struktur auf Basis der Wahrscheinlichkeitsrechnung. Acht verschiedene Klangzustände werden durch die Methode von Markov miteinander verkettet.
Analogique B (1959), Oliver Messian gewidmet, ist elektronische Musik auf einem Magnetband, welches in Hunderte von kleinen Stückten zerschnitten wurde, um dann in einer neuen Ordnung wieder zusammengesetzt zu werden – eine der ersten musikalischen Kompositonen, welche die Methode der Granulation benutzte.
Gedacht ist, *A* und *B* gemeinsam aufzuführen – ursprünglich direkt, in einer Situation des „Call Response" – hier durch die Wiedergabe des zuvor gehörten Stückes. Es ist somit eines der wenigen Werke (neben *Kraanerg),* das zwei Medien, die Xenakis normalerweise lieber getrennt verwendet – elektronische Musik und Orchester – in eine Situation des Nebeneinander und der Konfrontation versetzt. Die Steichinstrumente werden sinusoidalen Klängen gegeneinander gestellt.

Persepolis und *Mycenae Alpha* sind beides Stücke für Polytope – jene audiovisuellen Rauminszenierungen, bei denen sich an einem Ort zahlreiche Räume aus Klang, Licht und Architektur überlagern. Die verschiedenen Dimensionen des Raumes sind nicht synchron, sondern voneinander unabhängig. Xenakis' Ansicht nach sind Klangmassen und Massen visueller Elemente hinsichtlicher ihrer Struktur gleich und können daher mit den gleichen Prinzipien behandelt werden – bei einer Umsetzung dessen spricht dabei von einer „Geste Electronique".
„Graphic densities" – also Skizzen grafischer Art (mit Bezug auf seine Arbeit als Architekt) sind der Partiturniederschrift vorausgegangen. Verschieden in ihrer Form und Gestalt, kann man vor allem die Skizzen in Gestalt baumartiger Formen, so genannte „Arboresences", hervorheben: verästelte Kurven auf Milimeterpapier, die Niederschrift von mathematischen Formeln und Matrizen. Mathematische Theorien wurden zur Beherrschung von Klangwolken oder –milchstraßen herangezogen. Die von Xenakis selbst benannte „stochastische Musik" griff auf die Theorie der Wahrscheinlichkeiten zurück, Spieletheorie ergab die „strategische Musik", während die Gruppentheorie zur „symbolischen Musik" führte.
1979 entstand das erste Exemplar von UPIC (Unité Polygogique Informatique de CEMAMu), eine „Komponiermmaschine", durch welche die auf einem Lichtschirm aufgezeichneten Kurven in Realzeit zu Klang werden. Interessante Klänge werden durch eine dichte Notationen und komplexe Kurvenverläufe erhalten. Es werden bekannte Prozesse u. a. wie Granulare Synthese und Frequenzmodulationssynthese benutzt.
Mycenae Alpha (1978) ist das erste Werk, welches vollständig mit dem UPIC-System komponiert wurde. *Gendy (General Dynamic Stochastic Synthesis)* ist der nächste Schritt, bei welchem mit Hilfe von Software komponiert wird. Hier allerdings bedarf es nicht mehr eines grafischen Interface, sondern es wird hardgecoded.

Fluid Neon Bright Shadows: The Music of Iannis Xenakis

Paul D. Miller

"I originated in 1954 a music constructed from the principle of indeterminism; two years later I named it 'Stochastic music.' The laws of the calculus of probabilities entered the composition through musical necessity ... But other paths also led to the same stochastic cross-roads—first of all, natural events such as the collision of hail or rain with hard surfaces, or the song of cicadas in a summer field. These sonic events are made out of thousands of isolated sounds; this multitude of sounds, seen as a totality, is a new sonic event. This mass event is articulated and forms a plastic mold of time, which itself follows aleatory and stochastic laws. If one then wishes to form a large mass of point-notes, such as string pizzicati, one must know these mathematical laws, which, in any case, are no more than a tight and concise expression of a chain of logical reasoning. Everyone has observed the sonic phenomena of a political crowd of dozens or hundreds of thousands of people. The human river shouts a slogan in a uniform rhythm. Then another slogan springs from the head of the demonstration; it spreads towards the tail replacing the first. A wave of transition thus passes from the head to the tail. The clamor fills the city, and the inhibiting force of voice and rhythm reaches a climax. It is an event of great power and beauty in its ferocity. Then the impact between the demonstrators and the enemy occurs. The perfect rhythm of the last slogan breaks up in a huge cluster of chaotic shouts, which also spreads to the tail.
Imagine, in addition, the reports of dozens of machine guns and the whistle of bullets adding their punctuations to this total disorder. The crowd is then rapidly dispersed, and after sonic and visual hell follows a detonating calm, full of despair, dust and death. The statistical laws of these events, separated from their political or moral context, are the same as those of the cicadas or the rain. They are the laws of the passage from complete order to total disorder in a continuous or explosive manner. They are stochastic laws. Here we touch on one of the great problems that have haunted human intelligence since antiquity: continuous or discontinuous transformation ... Transformation."

(Iannis Xenakis, "Formalized Music" 1955)

Amongst his many other achievements, Iannis Xenakis was one of the first composers to truly engage the notion of being a polymath, of allowing a cross-fruition of different metiers to fully fertilize expression. To understand the music of Iannis Xenakis, you have to understand this. All else is an elaboration of this step towards a translatability between codes, of carrying the structures of thought through different media. Xenakis, along with physicist Herman Helmholtz, Erik Satie (with his *musique d''ameublement)* and Edgar Varese, significantly focused on the similarity between physicality and metaphor, organized sound verging on noise and its translation into signal. His presentation of "Metastasis" in 1954 was the first instance of achieving the effect of mass through the use of organized glissandi, and from that point on, he pursued his interests in sound media in a number of different ways: orchestral, electro-acoustic (electronic and concrete), and numerical (from computers and digital to analog converters). He likes to describe his music as being based on what he called a "principle of indeterminism." In his work one finds the turbulent aftereffects of an encounter with something that seems to be a new art form, yet, conversely, one also is confronted with the echoes of ancient value systems as core elements of his compositional techniques: signal into music, music into concrete form, concrete form into transcendent engagement with the cosmos. In his Thesis defense, Xenakis was asked by the renowned philosopher of science, Michel Serres, "Why is a fugue an automaton?" and his reply speaks volumes about the cybernetic implications this style of creating music has on human consciousness. The conversation, in its own way, sums up his continual dialog with the notion that music and science go in cycles—for Xenakis, music is usually the forerunner of other conceptual developments that occur in society. Their conversation was as follows:

Michel Serres: Once again, musical thinking is in the forefront. What do you mean when you say that the fugue is an automaton, that "the fugue is an abstract automaton conceived two centuries before automated science?" I don't believe this is true. I think they coincided, if science didn't appear first.

Iannis Xenakis: Oh no, not automated science. Automated science was born in the 20th century.

Michel Serres: Not automated, but the construction of automatons.

Iannis Xenakis: That makes a difference, because the use of automatons dates from Alexandrian times.

Michel Serres: In *A Thousand and One Nights,* for example, there are automatic fountains, water machines.

Iannis Xenakis: Yes, but *A Thousand and One Nights* dates from the 12th century, the use of automatons occurs much earlier than that. The Alexandrian period already knew Heron and the first steam engine.

Michel Serres: Yes, even Archytus's Dove.

Iannis Xenakis: All of these are concrete inventions. It was music, however, which introduced its abstraction.

Michel Serres: So then, why is a fugue an automaton?

Iannis Xenakis: I think that it corresponds more or less to the definition of a scientific automaton which came about in the twenties, thanks to Weiner and cybernetics. It can be summarized in the following manner: An automaton is a network of causes and effects, meaning a temporal chain of events, eventually coupled or multicoupled with certain liberties. An automaton can be closed. It suffices to plug in energy and it works cyclically. It can be relatively open, complete with data entries and external actions, thanks to the help of buttons, for example. Every time new data entries are given, an automaton can produce different results, despite the internal rigor which defines it.

Michel Serres: Its syntaxes are repetitive but not its performances.

Iannis Xenakis: Yes, its syntaxes are repetitive. Why? Because there is an internal structural rigor.

Michel Serres: Is the fugue's syntax always stable?

Iannis Xenakis: The fugue does not constitute such an absolute automaton; it is a relative automaton, especially when compared to the automatons studied by science, which are relatively rigorous in relation to musical ones. When I say musical automaton, I consider that a minuet is also an automaton. The value specific to musical invention is that it was the first to give, to create an abstract automaton, meaning that it produced nothing except music ...

(From *Arts/Sciences: Alloys, The Thesis Defense of Iannis Xenakis, 1976)*

Open yourself to the sounds of total war: not war as a physical embodiment of the political differences between obsolete nation-states, but war as an engagement with technological acceleration. War as a questioning of the human condition. War as the sounds of primal fear stitched across the empty spaces of the mind. (It has been said that Xenakis' music could only have been composed by someone whose flesh had been traumatized by steel, pierced by the stupidity of any one group of humans that try to impose their will on another.) War as the numbers at the core of human expression, a binary dissonance between presence and absence, an expression of a metalanguage we all know, but very few of us can pronounce.

In the multiplicity of sound, everything is disentangled, nothing is deciphered, "run" through (like thread in a stocking, or the glissandi of Xenakis's stochastic structures) at every point and every level, but there is nothing beneath; the space of music is to be ranged over, not violently pierced, music ceaselessly posits meaning to ceaselessly evaporate it, carrying out a systematic exemption. Letting the numbers at the core of consciousness shine through, a perpetual play and instability occurs in the unending drift across the transverse. Sound and signification? Sound and its deployment in space? This flickering of the signifier, fissuring and retarding any signified ... Xenakis's gleaming mathematical constructs, his ruptured and fractured sounds: thought dissolves in the reverie, emotion unfolds in the glitter of the algorithms he uses to produce his music ... This vertiginous music lies beyond conventional narrative.

Xenakis often writes about his experiences during World War II—the great social upheaval that brought us computers and refined nuclear physics, and that exposed the world to some of the greatest carnage in human history—as a kind of abstract crucible, a place that forged his fascination with turbulence. But the "stochastic method" Xenakis employs (stochastic here refers to the notion of change as a series of contingencies), has deeper roots in his own continuous engagement with extreme change.

"In my music," he wrote many years ago, "there is all the anguish of my youth, of the resistance (the Greek anti-Fascist movement) and the aesthetic problems they posed, together with the gigantic street demonstrations or the rarified mysterious noises, the mortal noises of the cold nights of December 1944, in Athens. Out of this was born my mass conception, and in turn, stochastic music." Later, he cited Harry Neville as saying, "The explanation of the world and consequently of the sound phenomenon that surrounds us, or that may be created, required an enlargement of the causal principle, the basis of which is formed by the law of the great numbers." Stochastic (derived from the Greek "stochos"—"to aim") music for him was a path away from the deterministic realm of "neo-serialism" that was so prevalent in the works of composers of that time. What he would eventually describe in a 1955 article entitled "The Crisis of Serial Music", was what he felt was an ossification in the Western classical world that he saw himself as having to break out of.

As Maurice Fleuret wrote in the liner notes of a release of *The Polytope of Montreal:* "Other times, other customs: to the young, who question formerly sacred values and revolt against the confines of society, this music expresses the rage to live and think. Better still: by fusing art and science, for the service of mankind, it symbolizes the new conscience of our times."

But to stick with Xenakis's own words [...], here is his account of a future defined and circumscribed by extreme flux, an epoch on the edge of continuous cultural upheaval:

"In barely three generations, the population of the globe will have passed 24 thousand million. 80 per cent will be aged under 25. The result will be fantastic transformations in every domain. A biological struggle between generations unfurling all over the planet, destroying existing political, social, urban, scientific, artistic and ideological frameworks

on a scale never before attempted by humanity, and unforeseeable. This extraordinary multiplication of conflict is prefigured by the current youth movements throughout the world. These movements are actually the beginnings of this biological turmoil which awaits us, irrespective of the ideological contents of these movements. [...]"
The mechanical implementation of sequential and non-sequential forms of text, music as a reference to other zones of human expression, an engagement with culture as a collective archive, asymmetries in sound as it translates into cultural signifiers, aural metonymy, electronic means of composing and deploying sound, and a host of other characteristics link the experimental compositional structures of 20th century avant garde classical music to the art form of DJ'ing. Indeed, when seen in this light, the vernacular of DJ culture has absorbed almost all of the previous art movements of the 20th century.
Excerpt from the liner notes of *Kraneerg,* Asphodel

Principles of Indeterminism

Fließende neon-grelle Schatten: Die Musik von Iannis Xenakis

Paul D. Miller

„1954 begründete ich eine Musikrichtung, die auf den Prinzipien der Unbestimmtheit aufbaut. Zwei Jahre später nannte ich sie ‚Stochastische Musik'. Die Gesetze der Wahrscheinlichkeitsrechnung fanden aufgrund musikalischer Notwendigkeit Einzug in die Komposition ... Doch auch andere Wege führten zur selben stochastischen Kreuzung – allen voran Naturereignisse wie der Aufprall von Hagel oder Regen auf einer harten Oberfläche oder das Zirpen der Zikaden in einer Sommerwiese. Diese Klangereignisse bestehen aus tausenden Einzelklängen und bilden in ihrer Gesamtheit ein neues Klangereignis. Diese Klangmasse wird artikuliert und schafft eine plastische Form der Zeit, die aleatorischen und stochastischen Gesetzen folgt. Will man eine große Masse von Einzelnoten z. B. für ein Streicher-Pizzicato formen, muss man diese mathematischen Gesetze beherrschen, die jedoch immer nur ein exakter Ausdruck einer logischen Folgerungskette sind."
Jeder hat wohl schon die Klangphänomene gehört, die Dutzende, Hunderte oder Tausende Demonstranten verursachen können. Ein Menschenstrom skandiert im einförmigen Rhythmus eine Parole. Dann kommt am Beginn des Demonstrationszugs ein neuer Slogan auf, pflanzt sich bis zum Ende fort und ersetzt den ersten. Eine Welle erfasst die Menschenmenge und wogt von vorne nach hinten. Die Protestrufe hallen durch die Stadt und die alles unterdrückende Intensität der rhythmischen Stimmen erreicht ihren Höhepunkt – ein in seiner Wildheit beeindruckend machtvolles und schönes Schauspiel. Dann kommt es zum Zusammenstoß zwischen den Demonstranten und dem Feind. Der perfekte Rhythmus der letzten Parole zerbirst in chaotische Rufe, die sich ebenfalls bis zum Ende hin fortpflanzen.
Man stelle sich dazu noch Salven von Dutzenden Maschinenpistolen und das Pfeifen der Kugeln vor, die diese totale Unordnung kontrapunktieren. Die Menge ist schnell auseinander gesprengt und nach der klanglichen und visuellen Hölle folgt eine sich explosionsartig ausbreitende Stille voll Verzweiflung, Staub und Tod. Losgelöst von ihrem politischen oder moralischen Kontext

folgen solche Ereignisse den selben statistischen Gesetzen wie die Zikaden oder der Regen. Es sind die Gesetze des stetigen oder abrupten Wechsels von völliger Ordnung zu totaler Unordnung. Es sind die Gesetze der Stochastik. Und damit stoßen wir auf eines der großen Probleme, die die menschliche Intelligenz seit der Antike verfolgt: kontinuierliche oder diskontinuierliche Transformation ...Transformation."

Iannis Xenakis, *Formalized Music,* 1955

Neben all seinen anderen Verdiensten war Iannis Xenakis einer der ersten Komponisten, der wirklich interdisziplinär arbeitete, indem er Querverbindungen der verschiedenen Fächer zuließ und damit seine Ausdruckskraft befruchtete. Für ein Verständnis von Iannis Xenakis' Musik ist dies unerlässlich. Alles weitere sind Details auf seinem Weg zur Übersetzbarkeit verschiedener Codes und zum Beibehalten der gedanklichen Struktur in verschiedenen Medien. Gemeinsam mit dem Physiker Hermann Helmholtz, Erik Satie (und dessen *„Musique d'ameublement")* und Edgar Varese konzentrierte sich Xenakis vor allem auf die Ähnlichkeit zwischen dem Dinglichen und der Metapher, auf organisierte Klänge nahe am Lärm und deren Umsetzung in ein Signal. Bei der Aufführung von *Metastaseis* 1954 setzte er zum ersten Mal Klangmassen ein, die er durch organisierte Glissandi erzielte. Von da an verfolgte er seine Interessen an Klangmedien auf verschiedenste Weise: orchestral, elektro-akustisch (elektronische und traditionelle Instrumente) und rechnerisch (mit Computern und Digital-Analogwandlern). Er beschrieb seine Musik gerne als auf dem „Prinzip der Indeterminiertheit" fußend, wie er es nannte.
In seinem Werk finden sich turbulente Nachwirkungen eines Zusammentreffens mit einer offensichtlich neuen Kunstform, man sieht sich aber auch mit Nachklängen alter Wertesysteme konfrontiert, die Kernelemente seiner Kompositionstechnik darstellen: Signal zu Musik, Musik zu konkreter Form, konkrete Form zur transzendenten Auseinandersetzung mit dem Kosmos. Im Rahmen der Verteidigung seiner Doktorarbeit fragte der bekannte Wissenschaftsphilosoph Michel Serres Xenakis: „Warum ist eine Fuge ein Automat?" Seine Antwort spricht Bände über die kybernetischen Implikationen, die diese Musikform auf das menschliche Bewusstsein hat. Diese Unterhaltung fasst auf ihre Art Xenakis immerwährenden Dialog zusammen, dass Musik und Wissenschaft zyklisch seien. Er sieht in der Musik für gewöhnlich den Vorboten für weitere konzeptuelle gesellschaftliche Entwicklungen. Ihre Unterhaltung verlief folgendermaßen:

Michel Serres: Noch einmal, musikalische Gedanken stehen im Vordergrund. Was meinen Sie damit, dass die Fuge ein Automat sei, dass „eine Fuge ein abstrakter Automat ist, der bereits zwei Jahrhunderte vor der Atuomatisierungswissenschaft erfunden wurde?" Ich glaube das nicht. Ich denke, dass dies zufällig zugleich geschah, wenn nicht sogar die Wissenschaft zuerst da war.

Iannis Xenakis: Oh nein, nicht die Automatisierungswissenschaft. Die wurde erst im 20. Jahrhundert geboren.

Michel Serres: Nicht die Wissenschaft, aber die Konstruktion von Automaten.

Iannis Xenakis: Das macht einen Unterschied, denn der Einsatz von Automaten datiert aus der Alexandrinischen Zeit.

Michel Serres: In *Tausend und einer Nacht* gibt es beispielsweise automatische Brunnen und Wassermaschinen.

Iannis Xenakis: Ja, aber *Tausend und eine Nacht* stammt aus dem 12. Jahrhundert, während Automaten bereits viel früher verwendet wurden. Bereits die Zeit Alexanders kannte Heron und die erste Dampfmaschine.

Michel Serres: Ja, und sogar die Taube des Archytas.

Iannis Xenakis: Das waren alles konkrete Erfindungen, aber erst die Musik brachte die Abstraktion.

Michel Serres: Warum ist dann eine Fuge ein Automat?

Iannis Xenakis: Ich meine, sie entspricht im Großen und Ganzen der Definition eines wissenschaftlichen Automaten, die in den Zwanzigern dank Weiner und der Kybernetik aufgekommen ist. Zusammenfassend kann man sagen: Ein Automat ist ein Netzwerk von Ursachen und Wirkungen, die eine temporale Verkettung von Ereignissen bedeuten, die mit bestimmten Freiheiten gekoppelt oder sogar mehrfach gekoppelt sind. Ein Automat kann abgeschlossen sein. Es genügt, Energie zuzuführen, und er arbeitet zyklisch. Er kann aber auch vergleichsweise offen sein, über Möglichkeiten der Dateneingabe und externe Ausgaben, etwa durch Schaltknöpfe, verfügen. Bei jeder neuen Dateneingabe kann ein Automat, trotz seiner inhärenten Starrheit, unterschiedliche Ergebnisse erzielen.

Michel Serres: Die Syntax wiederholt sich, nicht aber die Ausführungen.

Iannis Xenakis: Genau, die Syntax wiederholt sich. Warum? Wegen der inhärenten strukturellen Starrheit.

Michel Serres: Ist die Syntax einer Fuge immer dieselbe?

Iannis Xenakis: Die Fuge stellt keinen absoluten Automaten dar. Sie ist ein relativer Automat, besonders im Vergleich mit den wissenschaftlich untersuchten, die im Verhältnis zu musikalischen ziemlich starr sind. Wenn ich musikalischer Automat sage, so meine ich, dass ein Menuett auch ein Automat ist. Der besondere Wert musikalischer Erfindungen besteht im erstmaligen Geschenk, der Kreation eines abstrakten Automaten, der nichts als Musik erzeugte ...

Aus *Arts/Sciences: Alloys, The Thesis Defense of Iannis Xenakis,* 1976

Öffnen Sie sich den Klängen des totalen Kriegs: Nicht Krieg als physische Verkörperung politischer Differenzen zwischen obsoleten Nationalstaaten, sondern Krieg als Auseinandersetzung mit technologischer Beschleunigung. Krieg als In-Frage-Stellens der Conditio humana. Krieg als der Klang einer Urangst, die in allen Winkeln des menschlichen Verstands steckt. (Man sagt, Xenakis' Musik konnte nur von jemandem komponiert werden, dessen Fleisch traumatisiert war, durchbohrt von der Dummheit von Menschen, die anderen ihren Willen aufzwingen wollen.) Krieg als Synonym für die Zahlen im Zentrum menschlichen Ausdrucks, eine binäre Dissonanz zwischen Präsenz und Absenz, ein Ausdruck einer uns allen bekannten Metasprache, die jedoch nur wenige beherrschen.
In der Vielfalt des Klangs wird alles befreit, dabei aber nichts entziffert, es „läuft" (wie ein Faden in einer Socke oder die Glissandi von Xenakis' stochastischen Strukturen) an jedem Punkt und in jeder Ebene, aber es liegt nichts dahinter. Der musikalische Raum ist zu durchwandern, nicht gewalttätig zu durchbohren; Musik postuliert unaufhörlich Bedeutung, um sie unaufhörlich wieder in Nichts aufzulösen, indem sie eine systematische Befreiung vornimmt. Während die Zahlen im Kern des Bewusstseins durchschimmern, ist die unendliche Drift über die Transversale von ewigem Spiel und ewiger Instabilität gekennzeichnet. Klang und Bedeutung? Klang und sein Einsatz im Raum? Das Aufflackern des Signifikanten, der alle Signifikate spaltet und verzögert ... Xenakis' schimmernde mathematische Konstrukte, seine geplatzten und gebrochenen Klänge. Ein Gedanke löst sich in Visionen auf, Emotionen entfalten sich im Glitzerschein der Algorithmen, aus denen er Musik generiert ... Diese schwindelerregende Musik geht über jede konventionelle Narration hinaus.

Oft beschreibt Xenakis seine Erfahrungen während des Zweiten Weltkriegs – jene enorme soziale Umwälzung, die uns Computer bescherte, die Atomphysik revolutionierte und die Welt mit einigen der größten Massaker in der menschlichen Geschichte konfrontierte – oft als eine Art abstrakten Schmelztiegel, in dem seine Faszination für das Aufgewühlte geschmiedet wurde. Aber die von Xenakis verwendeten „stochastischen Methoden" („stochastisch" bezieht sich hier auf die Bedeutung von Änderung als eine Abfolge von Eventualitäten), wurzeln wohl tiefer in seiner beständigen Auseinandersetzung mit extremen Veränderungen.
„In meiner Musik", schrieb er vor vielen Jahren, „liegt der ganze Schmerz meiner Jugend und des Widerstands (der griechischen Antifaschisten) sowie die damit aufgeworfenen ästhetischen Fragen, zusammen mit den gewaltigen Straßendemonstrationen oder jenen mysteriösen Geräuschen – den Geräuschen des Todes in den kalten Nächten Athens im Dezember 1944. Daraus hat sich mein Verständnis von Massen und letztlich die stochastische Musik entwickelt." Später zitiert er Harry Neville, indem er sagt: „Die Erklärung der Welt und in Folge auch des Klangphänomens, das uns umgibt bzw. das kreiert werden kann, bedurfte einer Expansion des Kausalprinzips, dessen Grundlage auf den Gesetzen der Zahlen basiert." Stochastische (abgeleitet vom griechischen *stochos* – „zielen") Musik bedeutete für ihn die Abwendung von der deterministischen „neo-seriellen Musik", die in den Werken der damaligen Komponisten vorherrschend war. In dem 1955 veröffentlichten Aufsatz „Die Krise der seriellen Musik" beschrieb er sein Gefühl von der Verknöcherung der westlichen klassischen Welt, aus der er ausbrechen musste.
Wie Maurice Fleuret im Begleittext zu einer Ausgabe von „Le Polytope de Montreal" schrieb: „Andere Zeiten, andere Sitten: Für die Jugend, die ehemals heilige Werte in Frage stellt und gegen die Enge der Gesellschaft revoltiert, drückt diese Musik ein unbändiges Verlangen nach Leben und eigenem Denken aus. Noch besser: Indem sie Kunst und Wissenschaft im Dienst der Menschheit miteinander verschmilzt, symbolisiert sie das neue Gewissen unserer Zeit." Aber um bei Xenakis' eigenen Worten zu bleiben [...], folgt seine Beschreibung einer Zukunft, die durch extreme Veränderungen definiert und umschrieben wird, eine Epoche am Rand permanenten kulturellen Aufruhrs:
„Nach kaum drei Generationen wird die Erdbevölkerung mehr als 24.000 Millionen Menschen betragen. 80 Prozent werden unter 25 Jahren alt sein. Daraus werden fantastische Veränderungen in allen Bereichen resultieren. Ein unvorhersehbarer biologischer Kampf wird zwischen den Generationen entbrennen, der sich über den gesamten Planeten ausbreiten und die bestehenden politischen, sozialen, urbanen, wissenschaftlichen, künstlerischen und ideologischen Rahmenbedingungen in einem noch nie von der Menschheit versuchten Umfang sprengen wird. Diese außergewöhnliche Konfliktvermehrung kündigt sich bereits durch die weltweiten Jugendbewegungen an. Diese Bewegungen sind der Anfang jenes biologischen Umsturzes, der uns ungeachtet des ideologischen Inhalts dieser Bewegungen bevorsteht. [...]"
Die mechanische Implementierung sequenzieller und nicht-sequenzieller Textformen, Musik als Referenz für andere menschliche Ausdrucksformen, eine Auseinandersetzung mit Kultur als kollektivem Archiv, Asymmetrien von Klang bei dessen Umsetzung in kulturelle Signifikanten, akustische Metonymien, elektronische Werkzeuge zum Komponieren und Erzeugen von Klängen sowie eine Reihe weiterer Merkmale verbinden die experimentellen kompositorischen Strukturen der Klassik-Avantgarde des 20. Jahrhunderts mit der Kunstform des DJ-ing. Unter diesem Aspekt betrachtet, hat sich das Vokabular der DJ-Kultur beinahe alle künstlerischen Strömungen des 20. Jahrhunderts bereits einverleibt.

Aus dem Amerikanischen von Michael Kaufmann

Aus dem Booklet zur CD *Kraneerg* von Iannis Xenakis, veröffentlicht auf Asphodel.

Schedule

metamorph #1
Brucknerhaus / Großer Saal
Bruckner Orchester Linz, Conductor: Dennis Russell Davies
Music : Edgar Varèse, *Déserts*—Video: Bill Viola
Music: Morton Subotnick, *Before the Butterfly*—Visuals: Sue Costabile
Maki Namekawa (piano and computer)
Music: Marco Stroppa, *Traiettoria ... deviata*—Visuals: Marius Watz
Bruckner Orchester Linz, Conductor: Dennis Russell Davies
Music: Iannis Xenakis, *Analogique A*—Visuals: Lia

metamorph #2
Brucknerhaus / Mittlerer Saal
Dennis Russell Davies (piano), Maki Namekawa (piano)
Music: Steve Reich, *Piano Phase*—Visuals: Martin Wattenberg
Studio Percussion Graz
Music: Steve Reich, Drumming—Visuals: Justin Manor
Rupert Huber / Tosca, *I Could Be You*–Visuals: Justin Manor

metamorph #3
in Klangpark
Music: Iannis Xenakis, *Analogique B*–2 Channel Tape
Music: Iannis Xenakis, *Persepolis*–4 Channel Tape
Visuals: Gerda Palmetshofer, Stefan Mittlböck

metamorph #4
Brucknerhaus / Großer Saal
Persépolis
Remix by Otomo Yoshihide—Visuals by Lia
Remix by Ryoji Ikeda–Visuals by Ryoji Ikeda
Remix of the Remixers by Naut Humon—Visuals: Sue Costabile

metamorph #5
Brucknerhaus / Großer Saal
Data Spectra—Music and Visuals by Ryoji Ikeda
Multiple Otomo—Music and Visuals by Otomo Yoshihide
 # dominant, Music by Rupert Huber—Visuals by Marius Watz

The idea leading to this project resulted from many conversations involving Dennis Russell Davies, Gerfried Stocker, Naut Humon and Rupert Huber. First and foremost, we wish to thank all participating artists who, without exception, committed spontaneously to making this extraordinary evening possible. For the extensive support they provided, we wish to thank the Bruckner Orchestra Linz, Dennis Russell Davies, Dr. Heribert Schröder, ORF Upper Austria, Österreich 1, Claude Mussou / INA (Groupe de Recherches Musicales), Steven Joyce / Boosey & Hawkes, Andreas P. Leitner / Universal Edition AG, Rudolf Andrich / Sacem, Madame Françoise Xenakis, Dianna Santillano / Bill Viola Office / Arcotel Nike.
Supported by PANI Projection & Lighting
Audio/technical concept: Naut Humon and Hubert Havel
Project/technical director: Magnus Hofmüller
Production director: Manu Pfaffenberger
This concert is a cooperative production of the Ars Electronica Festival and the Brucknerhaus Linz.

REMIX OF THE REMIXES

Naut Humon

One of Iannis Xenakis's first "polytope" multimedia pieces *Persepolis* was chosen for re-interpretation with customized live remixes by Ryoji Ikeda, Otomo Yoshihide, and Naut Humon. In Naut Humon's segment there are added remix representations from Zbigniew Karkowski, Rechenzentrum, Merzbow, Ulf Langheinrich, antimatter, Laminar, Richard Devine, Paul Dolden, Francisco Lopez , Construction Kit and others in which he blends these sources that consider the spirit and influence of Xenakis' more massive electro-acoustic excursions. Many of these re-workings are actual excerpts from the recently released *Persepolis* CD on Asphodel which contains the original INA-GRM mix engineered by Daniel Teruggi and consultation from Xenakis himself in Paris over a decade ago.

This overall reconfiguration of the remixed remixes and added outside materials was realized at the Recombinant Media Labs compound in San Francisco on a portion of the Surround Traffic Control AV system. The photographic imagery that accompanies the music comes from the actual documentation of the live evening event at the Persepolis ruins in the southern Iran desert during 1971. From the central position of the site, where 59 loudspeakers projected the eight channels of sound throughout the audience area, the spotlights and lasers swept upward and out creating luminous patterns on the ancient hillside tombs of Darius and Artaxerxes. There, in the distance, bonfires were burning and parades of children carrying lighted torches wended their way around the surrounding heights displaying an ever-changing, linear tableau.

The interlacing of the remix "modules" draws largely from the original 56-minute work, emphasizing its noisy sonorities and overlapping waves of intensity. As the aged nature of the master recordings from that era can occasionally reveal their brittle fidelity, the remixers move in to creatively compound the initial fracture. While sustained string, woodwind and percussive source entities stochastically collide with clashing metallic material, the sonic incision often seems overly dense or overwhelming. Add to that the transformative process of today's digital signal processing to take this ancient audio and turn it into pure frequencies or rhythmic pulse waves (plus many of the remixer's own personalized audentities) and what we're left with are intricate, glacier-like soundscapes of fluid proportions.

The compositions here aren't merely depicting a "Then versus Now" dynamic, which has been incongruently ascribed to numerous remix and tribute models over the years. Rather, the interpretations are reflective of certain sound-worlds that the Xenakis example continues to inspire and foster offspring from which bear witness to alternative aesthetics and deeper microsonic explorations.

Thus these realizations are dedicated to the future memory of Iannis Xenakis.

Thanks to Peter Segerstrom (STC engineer) and Sue Costabile (visual program interface).

Otomo Yoshihide, Naut Humon und Ryoji Ikeda wählten *Persepolis,* das erste Multimedia-Werk aus Iannis Xenakis' *Polytope*-Zyklus, um es mit eigenen Live-Remixes neu zu interpretieren. Naut Humon verwendet dabei Remix-Zitate von Zbigniew Kakowski, Rechenzentrum, Merzbow, Ulf Langheinrich, Antimatter, Laminar, Richard Devine, Paul Dolden, Francisco Lopez, Construction Kit und anderen, die er mit jenen Passagen mischt, die dem Geist und Einfluss von Xenakis' massiveren elektro-akustischen Ausflügen Tribut zollen. Viele dieser Bearbeitungen verwenden Ausschnitte des Original-Mix der kürzlich bei Asphodel erschienenen CD *Persepolis,* die unter der Aufnahmeleitung von Daniel Teruggi und Xenakis eigenen Anweisungen vor mehr als einem Jahrzehnt am INA-GRM in Paris entstand.

Die gesamte Bearbeitung der neu gemischten Remixes und der ergänzenden Aufnahmen erfolgte auf dem *Surround Traffic Control*-AV-System in den *Recombinant Media Labs* in San Francisco. Die Bilder zur Musik entstammen der Dokumentation zur Live-Aufführung, die 1971 in den Ruinen von Persepolis in der südpersischen Wüste stattfand. Vom Zentrum des Aufführungsorts, wo 59 Lautsprecher das Publikum mit acht Klangkanälen beschallten, malten die Scheinwerfer und Laserkanonen leuchtende Muster auf die am Berghang gelegenen Grabstätten von Darius und Artaxerxes. In einiger Entfernung brannten mehrere Feuer, und Abordnungen von Kindern wandelten mit brennenden Fackeln den nahen Höhenzug entlang, einem sich ständig ändernden, linearen Tableau gleich.

Die Remix-„Module" sind in erster Linie durch das 56-minütige Originalwerk untereinander verwoben, indem sie dessen geräuschvolle Sonorität und sich überlappende Intensitätswellen betonen. Klingen die mittlerweile in die Jahre gekommenen Masterbänder an manchen Stellen spröde, kitten die Remixer die ursprüngliche Fraktur kreativ. Während anhaltende Klangentitäten von Streichern, Holzbläsern und Perkussion stochastisch mit dröhnenden Schwermetall-Elementen kollidieren, erscheinen diese Klangeinschnitte oft zu dicht und überwältigend. Führt man diese Transformation noch fort, indem man diese alte Aufnahme mittels digitaler Signalbearbeitung in reine Frequenzen oder rhythmisch gepulste Waves (oder eine der vielen persönlich gestalteten „Audio-Entitäten" der Remixer) verwandelt, so erhält man komplexe, gletscherähnliche „Klangschaften" mit fließenden Proportionen.

Diese Kompositionen beschreiben nicht nur eine Dynamik des „Damals versus Jetzt", was im Lauf der Jahre verschiedenen Remix- und Tribute-Modellen nicht immer gleichermaßen nachgesagt wurde. Vielmehr sind diese Interpretationen Reflexionen bestimmter Klang-Welten, deren Abkömmlinge, von Xenakis' Beispiel inspiriert, Zeugnis von alternativer Ästhetik und weitreichenden mikroklanglichen Entdeckungsreisen ablegen.

Somit sind diese Werke dem zukünftigen Gedenken an Iannis Xenakis gewidmet.

Aus dem Amerikanischen von Michael Kaufmann

Thanks to Peter Segerstrom (STC engineer) and Sue Costabile (visual program interface).

Marius Watz

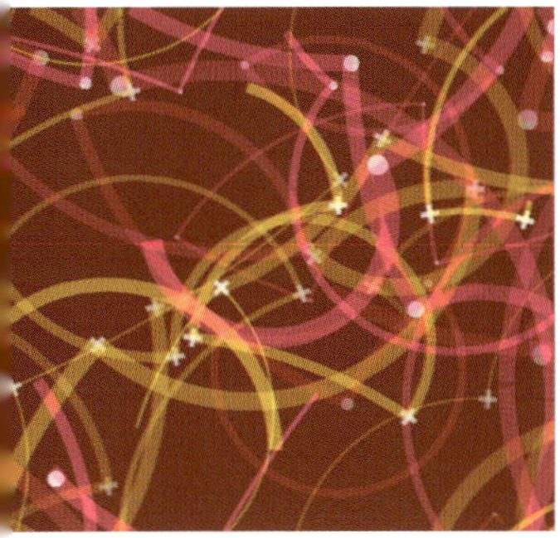

"When creating visuals for live music (or VJ'ing), my approach is to synthesize rather than to sample found or prerendered video. I create a visualisation tool in the form of a piece of software, specifically adapted to the music at hand, as opposed to being a generic VJ tool. Simple sound analysis is used to map from aural parameters, such as spectral characteristics, beats etc., to algorithmically generated visual shapes.
The issue of improvisation is important. Parameters of the software can be adjusted interactively to account for changes in tempo or mood. In some cases it is even possible to program live. This makes it possible to play the visualisation tool like an instrument—a synthesizer of shapes rather than of sounds."

Martin Wattenberg

My piece is a visual meditation on the transition between being in and out of phase. Drawing on inspirations ranging from traditional quilting patterns to acoustical waveforms, I have coded an algorithmic narrative, meant to complement Steve Reich’s music, based on the idea of changing phase. Reich’s music is elegantly mathematical, which makes it a natural fit for software art; yet at the same time there is a subtle challenge: how also to convey its beautiful non-mathematical rhythms. In all my work I invite the viewer to see the invisible. Viewers of this piece will see a journey from symmetry to complexity and back again.

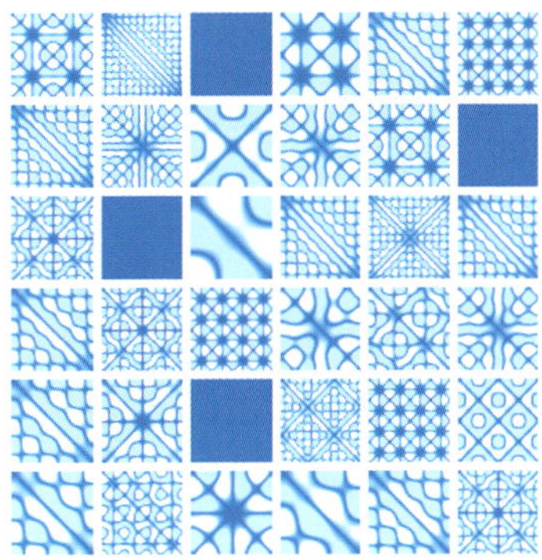

Gerda Palmetshofer

This segment could also be entitled "The Architecture of Music, The Music of Architecture." Midway through the evening, in an allusion to the spectacle in Persepolis and the work of the same name, the audience will be asked to make its way outside to the park along the banks of the Danube, where they will experience recorded versions of *Analogique A+B, Persepolis"* and *Mycenae Alpha* accompanied by large-format projections. Linear elements emerge; visual similarities between the images evoked by the compositions and architectural design plans manifest themselves. Ultimately, they bring to light structural reciprocities between music and architecture, and illustrate Xenakis' contributions to the transformation of precisely this interrelationship. Simultaneously displaying visual and acoustic elements is by no means an effort to achieve a synesthetic effect; instead, the tension between the two is meant to remain intact. What is being sought after and represented here is not the connection that binds them but rather the one that goes beyond them or that is hidden in their shadows.

Morton Subotnick

Before the Butterfly was completed and premiered in 1976. With it, I created the first of a series of works based on the notion that, since a major limiting factor to the orchestral sound is balance between quiet and loud instruments, the orchestral palette of the future could be transformed by a live partnering of the recording studio, the electronic music studio and the symphony orchestra. In order to avoid the mechanical limitations of studio machines, I created a living mixer by using the amplitude envelope of "control" violins to amplify, modify and pan a group of solo instruments. Thus, the quietist sound, even a breath, can become equal to the entire orchestra. Since the control instruments are often playing independently of the solo instruments, unexpected moments of amplification and sound transformation occur in each performance. It is as if the normal studio machines have become living and responsive partners to the orchestral performers.

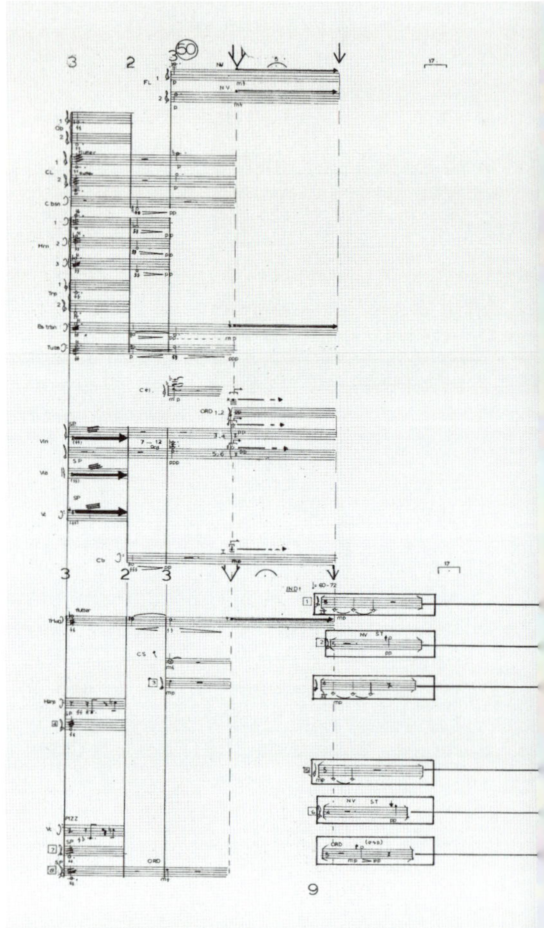

© Copyright 1976 by Morton Subotnick/excerpt of the score of "Before the Butterfly"

Justin Manor

During the original and remix versions of Steve Reich's Drumming piece Justin Manor will be performing visuals on the four screens in the Middle Hall of the Brucknerhaus. Several cameras will be placed around the percussionists and the Hall itself. The video shown on the projection screens will be controlled by a custom built drum set built and performed by Justin. He will affect what the audience sees on the displays by playing the drums himself and feeding the audio into a computer system running audiovisual software written for the show.

The visuals will accentuate the rhythmatic and cyclic nature of the score by displaying the relative phases of the performers in combination with reinterpreted live feeds of their actions. During the presentation of Reich's original piece the visuals will be in an analog style and as Rupert Huber begins his electronic remixing, the displays will take on a more digital look introducing exotic temporal and spatial effects.

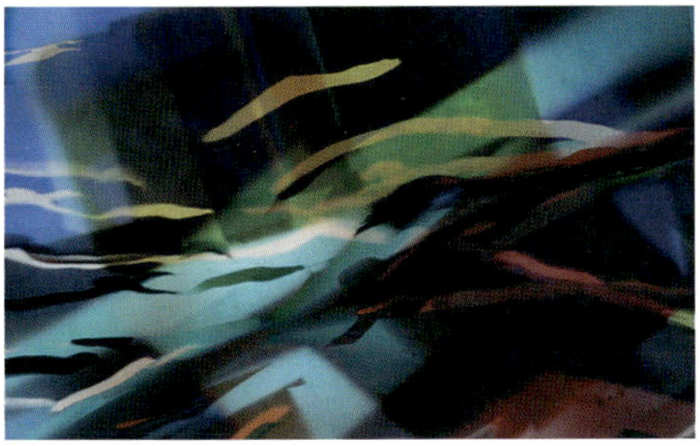

Sue Costabile

Humans process visual information in individual contexts. Abstract imagery stimulates personal experience, memory recall, associations and connections unique to each living system. In cooperation with music, the visual experience can become more suggestive and associative; sound and picture communicating through artistic and personal interpretation. As a visual artist working in the live-improv setting I build associations between sound and image that develop into a language of sorts. This language grows out of physical objects, illuminated and animated in real-time, playing the role of score and instrumentation. Tonight this language will emerge from Morton Subotnick's score for "Before the Butterfly", a musical code transformed into a visual one.

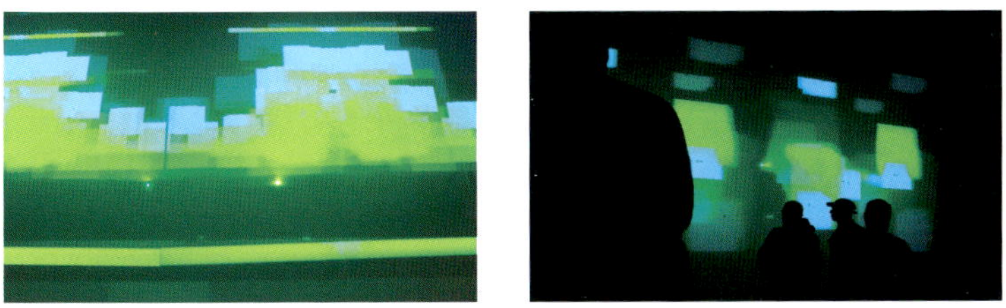

photos by Jan-Peter van der Wenden, taken at Scnic Light 2003, amsterdam

Lia

In Lia's online pieces interaction takes place mainly on the visual level, while the soundtrack is in most cases present as an overall support element to the image(s) created, and not as plastic as the images themselves.
This led Lia to work to more complex musical elements, both in linear videos or on live presentations. In these, music is fed into the system, playing a much greater role in the outcome, since during the performance, Lia interacts with them at the same level as through the music the musicians make. In this way, and with sound being allowed to enter the system, both the music performed and the images projected merge into a complete audio-visual performance. Ultimately "live visuals" are not much more than Lia's interactive pieces manipulated by their author, and this adds another layer of meaning to something that otherwise is already complete. After creation, the author manipulates and re-interprets the tool which then perhaps loses its completeness and is left unfinished, until the moment the performance ends.

miguel carvalhais, 07/2003

Rupert Huber

WRITTEN MUSIC II

1 the beauty of a wild flower,
notwithstanding its intelligence

2 instructions for controlled sound propagation

3 consistency as gauge for the recognition of an essence

4 can our perception come to terms with leaps, leaps into
linear thinking, linguistic leaps,
shifts of meaning?

5 in piano phase the people run away from each other and catch
up to one another again.

6 new music like dance choreography—we've practiced long and hard,
now we can run away from each other perfectly—

7 a variation a dedication a tribute a rearrangement
a variant a paraphrase a persiflage a remix
a caricature a reference a borrowing
an answer an inspiration
a composition a piece
a work
a tool

8 a question a sensation a brief feeling of happiness

9 a seedling box made of words

10 words describe, but ought not to have been meant
by our thinking

11 intention process result lost in words

the pauses between the riffs:
1-2--3-4---5-6-7--8--9---10---11

pauses: - one beat
-- two beats
--- three beats

one beat = 60 bpm
at a steady rhythm—all syllables of the same length and equally loud—the following tones of a temperate mood can be allocated to the riffs:
1 - c
2 - c#
3 - d
4 - d#
5 - e
6 - f
7 - f#
8 - g
9 - g#
10 - a
11 - a#
(the octave register may be chosen freely as long as all riffs are in one octave)

The riffs can be said/sung in any desired sequence and number,
together or sequentially

the fundamental stipulation is:
one riff, labeled by a number in the text, is the smallest unit and cannot be subdivided.

Floating Points in the OMV Klangpark

In a programmatic allusion to the intentions of Linz's famed Klangwolke, the Ars Electronica Festival initiated the *OMV Klangpark* four years ago as the launch of an ongoing series of annual events.

Based on the idea of underscoring the connection between the stylistically formative processes and concepts of leading edge Digital Music and established, artistically "serious" music by showcasing the work of one of the "masterminds" and leading creative protagonists of advanced Sound Art, the Klangpark's annual setting since its inception has been the space between the Brucknerhaus and the riverbank. This "stage"—a 160,000-Watt tonal space—is marked off by four loudspeaker towers that fill the Danube Park with sound throughout the Festival.

Michael Nyman was the "mastermind" of the first *OMV Klangpark* in 1999. This year, it's KOAN music software: in a cooperative effort curated by Tim Didymus,13 "KOAN composers" have collaborated on the development of a *Dark Symphony* under Didymus' direction.

At the 2003 *OMV Klangpark*, the methods of music generation and composition—as they are transported and extrapolated with historic ambitions by the *Principles of Indeterminism* project (see p. 338)—are distilled down to the point of code itself as it were in the form of four 12-hour real-time soundtracks.

Unter Bezugnahme auf die Intentionen der Klangwolke rief das Festival Ars Electronica vor vier Jahren das als Reihe angelegte Projekt *OMV Klangpark* ins Leben.

Basierend auf der Idee, die Verbindung von stilprägenden Verfahren und Konzepten der avancierten Digital Music und der etablierten E-Musik durch einen ihrer „Masterminds" und Vertreter der avancierten Sound Art herauszustreichen, hat der Klangpark seither jährlich zwischen Brucknerhaus und der Donau seine Bühne. Diese „Bühne" – einen 160.000-Watt-Klangraum – markieren vier Lautsprechertürme, die während des Festivals den Donaupark beschallen.

1999 war Michael Nyman „Mastermind" des *OMV Klangpark,* heuer ist es die Musiksoftware KOAN. 13 „KOAN-Komponisten", kuratiert von Tim Didymus, sind unter der Regie von Didymus an der Entwicklung einer *Dark Symphony* engagiert.

Methoden der Musikgenerierung und Komposition, wie sie das Projekt *Principles of Indeterminism* (siehe S. 340) mit einem historischen Ehrgeiz transportiert und extrapoliert, werden im *OMV Klangpark* 2003 in Form von vier 12-stündigen Realtime-Soundtracks gleichsam auf den Punkt des Codes selbst gebracht.

Koan
Early History

Tim Cole

In 1986 Tim Cole had the idea for what would become Koan. It was a handheld device that would generate subtle and continuous, ever-changing "context sensitive" music, either under the direct control of an artist and/or responding to environmental inputs.

In 1990 Tim, joined by Jon Pettigrew, founded SSEYO. Peter Cole, the Koan Music Engine architect, joined the company as Technical Director during its first year. The crucial component turned out to be the real-time "content engine" that would need to collate the inputs and create an integrated and coherent output. Hence arose the Koan Music Engine (an "integrator"), which, from sets of rules and parameters, created continuously generated music (generative music). As Koan was a real-time music engine that could additionally be externally directed, it was also capable of generating music that was continually morphing from one space / shape to the next, an extra behaviour which SSEYO termed "intermorphic".

By 1994 SSEYO had started trading with the release of the Koan music player "Koan Plus", soon followed by the first version of Koan Pro in 1995. By 1996 Koan had become the first European-developed plugin for Netscape and SSEYO had published Brian Eno's seminal *Generative Music 1,* and Tim Didymus' *Float.*

From 1996-2000, SSEYO was heavily influenced by developments in the Internet and browsers. SSEYO's goal was to open up access to the Koan system so that webpage designers and developers could create their own tools and applications. Through the auspices of the (even today) free Koan Plugin and a comprehensive JavaScript API, it became a highly programmable music engine that could be used in webpages, could drive animations and even be controlled by Flash. Over this period SSEYO also attempted to move away from the limitations of MIDI sound palettes on computer soundcards, so it developed its own integrated modular software synthesiser and a text-based parameter format called "Vector Audio."

From 2000 to 2002, SSEYO's primary focus was in developing audio frameworks for mobile devices, to provide the necessary foundation for an open environment for music engines and sound generators.

Following a successful merger with Tao Group in 2002, and the integration of its audio technologies and frameworks into the intent Sound System (announced July 2003), the original dream is close to fruition!

Many artists today are developing their own music systems and software, a challenging task indeed. From the first release of Koan Pro in 1995, it has always been SSEYO's goal to create platforms, tools and players that could be used and enjoyed by the public, musicians and music software developers. Ultimately, to do this properly, it realised it had to create an open platform which others could extend, and this meant getting into an Operating System. The new intent Sound System (iSS) is now the culmination of many years of work to this end. It is an open, cross-language, cross-platform high performance audio framework for mobile devices to desktops. The comprehensive iSS is easily extendable, allowing music software developers to add their own audio components, FX, modular synthesisers and music engines (written in C, C++, Java or Virtual Processor). The full power of the iSS can be accessed through the intent browser Qi, so it is easy to build tool front ends with DHTML, HTML, XML and JavaScript. And, just for completeness, Koan now runs on intent, too!

Tao Group: *http://www.tao-group.com*
SSEYO: *http://www.sseyo.com*

intent Sound System (iSS):
http://withintent.biz/index2.php?Cat=4&AntX=67
iSS Technical documentation:
http://www.sseyo.com/tao_group/ave/iss/api.html
Koan Generative Music Engine:
http://www.sseyo.com/koan/koanVectorAudio_GenerativeMusic.html

Principles of Indeterminism–OMV Klangpark

Koan
Die Entstehung

Tim Cole

1986 hatte Tim Cole jene Idee, aus der sich später *Koan* entwickeln sollte. Es handelte sich dabei um ein Handheld-Gerät, das fortwährend sanfte, sich ständig verändernde "kontextsensitive" Musik erzeugt, wobei es entweder von einem Künstler gesteuert wird und/oder auf Umgebungseinflüsse reagiert.

1990 gründete Tim gemeinsam mit Jon Pettigrew SSEYO. Peter Cole, der Architekt der *Koan Music Engine,* trat noch im ersten Jahr als technischer Direktor dem Unternehmen bei. Als wichtigster Bestandteil erwies sich die in Echtzeit laufende „Content Engine“, deren Aufgabe es war, die verschiedenen Inputs zusammenzustellen und zu vergleichen und einen einheitlichen und kohärenten Output zu erzeugen. Daraus entstand die *Koan Music Engine* (ein "Integrator"), der auf der Basis von bestimmten Regeln und Parametern ständig fortlaufende Musik erzeugte (generative Musik). Da es sich bei *Koan* um eine Echtzeit-Engine handelte, die auch von außen zu steuern war, konnte damit auch Musik generiert werden, die ständig von einem Raum/einer Form zur nächsten morphte. Dieses zusätzliche Feature bezeichnete man bei SSEYO als "intermorphisch".

Bereits 1994 brachte SSEYO den Koan Music-Player *Koan Plus* auf den Markt, und kurz darauf folge die erste Version von *Koan Pro* (1995). 1996 war Koan das erste in Europa entwickelte Netscape-Plugin, und SSEYO hatte Brian Enos bahnbrechende Arbeit *Generative Music 1* und *Float* von Tim Didymus herausgebracht.

In den Jahren von 1996 bis 2000 wurde SSEYO stark von Entwicklungen im Internet- und Browser-Bereich beeinflusst. SSEYO wollte das Koan-System allgemein zugänglich machen und so Webdesignern und Entwicklern ermöglichen, ihre eigenen Tools und Applikationen zu entwickeln. Dank des (noch heute) kostenlosen Koan-Plugins und eines umfassenden JavaScript-APIs entstand so eine einfach zu programmierende Engine, die auf Webseiten eingesetzt werden, Animationen unterstützen und sogar über Flash gesteuert werden konnte. Gleichzeitig versuchte SSEYO, die beschränkten Möglichkeiten von MIDI-Soundpaletten hinter sich zu lassen, und entwickelte einen eigenen integrativen Softwaresynthesizer und das textbasierte Parameterformat *Vector Audio.*

Zwischen 2000 und 2002 konzentrierte sich SSEYO hauptsächlich auf die Entwicklung von Audio-Frameworks für Mobilgeräte, um eine offene Umgebung für Engines und Soundgeneratoren zu schaffen.

Nach dem erfolgreichen Zusammenschluss mit der *Tao Group* im Jahr 2002 und der Integration der Audiotechnologien und -Frameworks des Unternehmens in das *intent Sound System* (angekündigt für Juli 2003) steht der ursprüngliche Traum knapp vor der Vollendung!

Heute entwickeln viele Künstler ihre eigenen Musiksysteme und die dazugehörige Software, was eine große Herausforderung darstellt. Seit dem Erscheinen von Koan Pro 1995 hat SSEYO es sich zum Ziel gesetzt, Plattformen, Tools und Player zu entwickeln, die von der breiten Öffentlichkeit, von Musikern und Musiksoftwareentwicklern eingesetzt werden können. Um diesem Vorhaben jedoch den nötigen Rahmen zu geben, musste eine offene Plattform geschaffen werden, die von anderen Benutzern erweitert werden konnte. Das war nur über ein Betriebssystem möglich. Das neue *intent Sound System* (iSS) ist das Ergebnis langjähriger harter Arbeit. Es handelt sich dabei um ein offenes, sprach- und plattformübergreifendes leistungsfähiges Audioframework für Mobilgeräte bis hin zu PCs. Das iSS-Gesamtsystem ist einfach auszubauen und erlaubt Musiksoftwareentwicklern, ihre eigenen Audiokomponenten, FX, Modularsynthesizer und Engines (geschrieben in C, C++, Java oder Virtual Processor) zu integrieren. Das gesamte Spektrum des iSS ist über den intent-Browser Qi zugänglich, Tool-Frontends lassen sich mit DHTML, HTML, XML und JavaScript einfach schreiben. Der Vollständigkeit halber sei noch erwähnt, dass Koan jetzt auch auf intent läuft!

Aus dem Amerikanischen von Elisabeth Wiellander

Floating Points—Dark Symphony

Tim Didymus

A rare and unique opportunity to hear four Koan music engines in "the ecstasy of communication." (Jean Baudrillard)

Music engine 1 representing *Noise*
Music engine 2 representing *Voice*
Music engine 3 representing *Rhythm*
Music engine 4 representing *Tonality*

4x12 hour performances
Transmitted via 4 towers at the "Klangpark", an open-air acoustic projection space in Linz.

Each tower will be assigned a simultaneous signal.
The distance between the towers:
2 towers near the Brucknerhaus: 60 meters
2 towers near the River Danube: 80 meters
Distance between the Brucknerhaus and the river: 120 meters

DARK SYMPHONY—if you want to see, first you must hear.
"Music is in advance, because music reaches the limits of any given code before the rest of society does.
You can create different possible musics within a given code much more rapidly than you can explore the possible ways of organising realities. Matter is more difficult to transform." (Jacques Attali)

Why has the music engine appeared at this point in history?
Has it found any value yet, as a mass cultural identity?

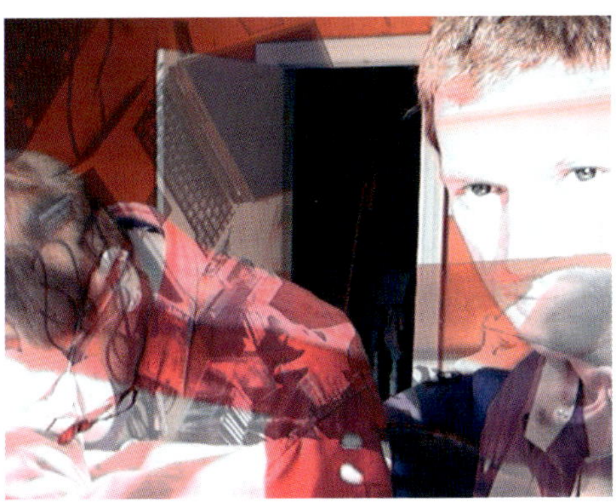

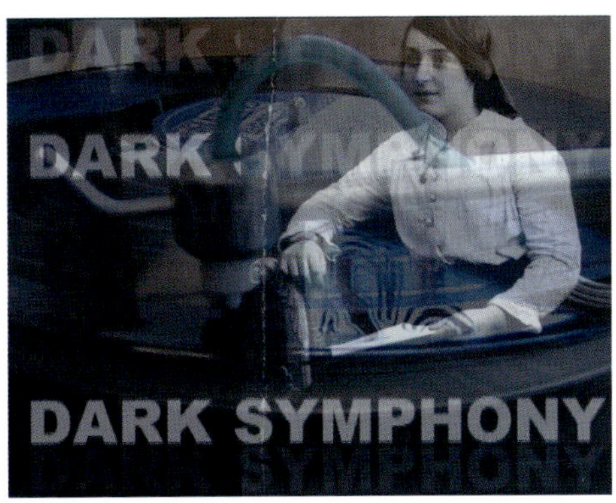

DARK SYMPHONY—Image=signifier
The music engine is a composing/erasing image.
"When it's new there's less instruction, it's not that there's less law, it's just not written down yet. When it's new, you have to find new rules in yourself, when to work, when to love more." (Jean-Luc Godard)

My concern here is what images can in and of themselves best communicate the phenomenon of the music engine.
And can this phenomenon stand out alone, as truly as say, the cinema does from painting?

DARK SYMPHONY—in a state of disappearing
The music engine, like the search engine, is a device for the selection and erasure of memory.
For each image it presents, we should also consider that far more potential information is being forgotten,
the music engine is not merely affirming existence, but also erasing it.

DARK SYMPHONY—the image is always after the fact.
In the moment of singularity, in that frame, we name "the present."
Where the gaze rests, the music engine has made its choice, and all further potential is erased.

The music engine cannot stop projecting images until you turn it off.
The output has many varying risks.

When we listen to it, what will it say?

Eine seltene und einzigartige Gelegenheit, vier Koan-Music-Engines in „der Ekstase der Kommunikation" zu hören. (Jean Baudrillard)

Music-Engine 1 steht für *Geräusch*
Music-Engine 2 steht für *Stimme*
Music-Engine 3 steht für *Rhythmus*
Music-Engine 4 steht für *Tonalität*

4 x 12-stündige Performances
Wird von vier Türmen im Linzer „Klangpark", einem akustischen Open-Air-Projektionsraum, übertragen.

Jedem Turm wird ein simultanes Signal zugewiesen.
Entfernung zwischen den Türmen:
Zwei Türme in der Nähe des Brucknerhauses: 60 Meter
Zwei Türme in der Nähe der Donau: 80 Meter
Entfernung zwischen Brucknerhaus und Fluss: 120 Meter

DARK SYMPHONY – Will man sehen, muss man zuerst hören.
„Die Musik hat immer einen Vorsprung, denn sie stößt an die Grenzen eines jeden Codes, bevor der Rest der Gesellschaft diese erreicht.
Man kann innerhalb eines jeden Codes verschiedene Arten von Musik schaffen, und zwar viel schneller, als man alle möglichen Organisationsformen von Wirklichkeiten erforschen kann, da Materie um vieles schwieriger umzuformen ist."
(Jacques Attali)

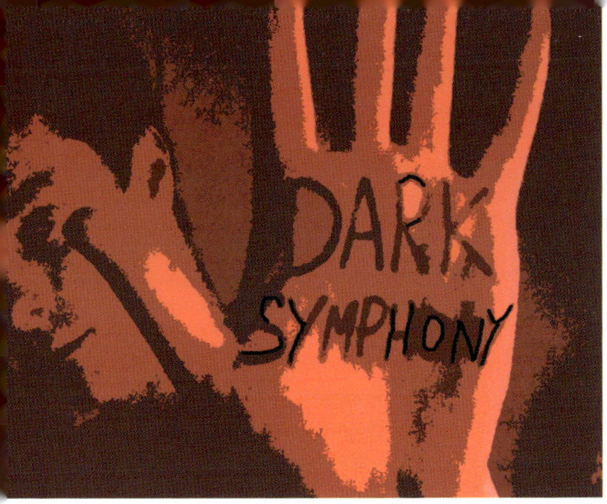

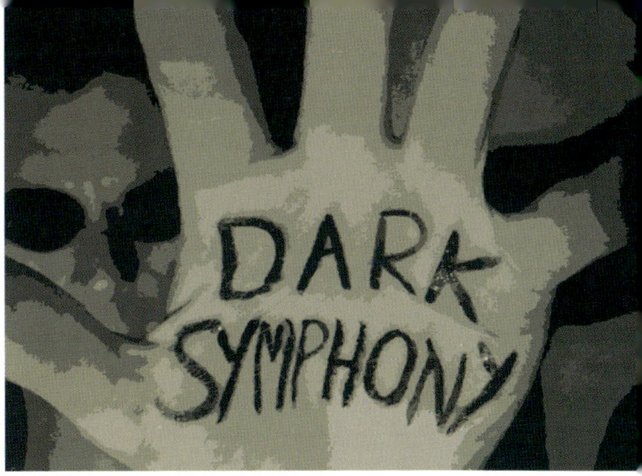

Warum ist die Engine gerade an diesem Punkt in der Geschichte entstanden?
Hat sie als breite kulturelle Identität überhaupt schon Gewicht erlangt?

DARK SYMPHONY – Bild = Signifikant
Die Engine als komponierendes / löschendes Bild.
„Wenn etwas neu ist, dann gibt es weniger Vorschriften; das heißt nicht, dass es keine Gesetze gibt, sie sind nur noch nicht niedergeschrieben worden; ist etwas neu, muss jeder seine eigenen Regeln festlegen, wann wird gearbeitet, wann wird eher geliebt."
(Jean-Luc Godard)

Mich interessiert, welche Bilder können das Erlebnis Music-Engine an und für sich am besten transportieren?
Ich frage mich, ob die Engine-Erfahrung für sich selbst stehen kann, so wie sich z. B. das Kino neben der Malerei behauptet?

DARK SYMPHONY – in einem Zustand des Verschwindens
Wie die Suchmaschine ist auch die Music-Engine ein Werkzeug zum Auswählen und Löschen von gespeicherten Informationen.
Bei jedem Bild, das sie präsentiert, darf man nicht vergessen, dass weit mehr potenzielle Information vergessen wird; die Engine bestätigt nicht nur die Wirklichkeit, sondern löscht sie auch aus.

DARK SYMPHONY – Das Bild folgt immer dem Fakt.
Im Moment der Singularität, in diesem Frame, geben wir „der Gegenwart" einen Namen. Wohin der Blick auch gefallen ist, in diesem Moment hat die Engine ihre Wahl schon getroffen und alle weiteren Möglichkeiten sind ausgelöscht.

Die Engine hört erst dann auf, Bilder zu projizieren, wenn sie abgeschalten wird.
Der Output birgt verschiedene Risiken.
Was wird er sagen, wenn wir ihm zuhören?

Aus dem Amerikanischen von Elisabeth Wiellander

Contributors:
Paul Cohen, Tim Cole, Tim Didymus, Brian Eno, Andrew Garton, Richard Garrett, Michael Hagleitner, Mark Harrop, Al Jolley, Yoshio Machida, Kelvin L. Smith, Emilia Telese, Mashashi Genzan Yano
Editing: Al Jolley / Tim Didymus
Curated by Tim Didymus

How Code Made its Way into My Music

AGF ::: Antye Greie

As a singer and producer, I rely primarily on content, and that can get to be a real encumbrance. After many years of creating music, I feel that I'm being confronted over and over again with the fact that listeners—and especially when it comes to Germans dealing with the German language—have problems getting to the music. Content always comes first—the message, the brain. In cutting the tracks for my album *head slash bauch,* I wanted to use my voice more like an instrument. I wanted to free myself from this coercive pressure to have to say something understandable and emotional. On my way to becoming an independent producer, I geeked my way through the process of self-education in matters of hardware, software, user's manuals and all the other stuff that goes with it. And that's how the computer/laptop came to exert an extremely positive—except for the chronic back pain—influence on my working and lifestyle options, my communication and production possibilities, and makes possible more and more flexibility, speed and personal control. More and more mixtures of "think in code" lead to phenomena like "when I go to bed, I'm shifting into sleep mode, etc." and user's manuals suddenly become good friends *(joke).*
So, that's how I discovered the poetry and beauty of this technically practical programming language. Since then, I've been experimenting with this tension between technical coolness and rhythm and melody in connection with reality/feeling/vision.
For the opening of the Klangpark at Ars Electronica 2003, I'll present a 30-minute live performance featuring some of this work and integrate into it a composition especially for the festival based on the dictionary entry for "CODE."

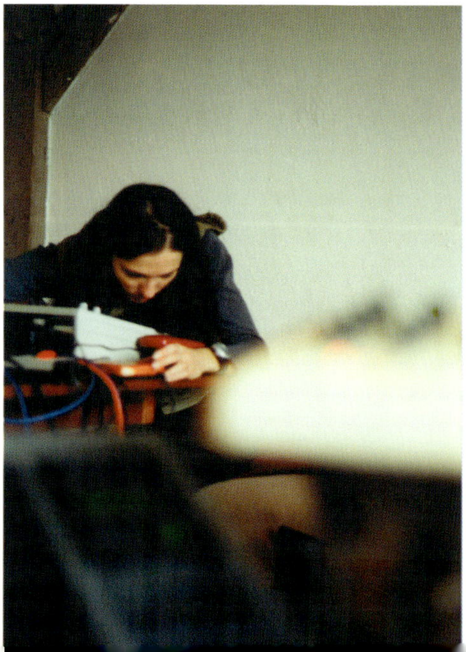

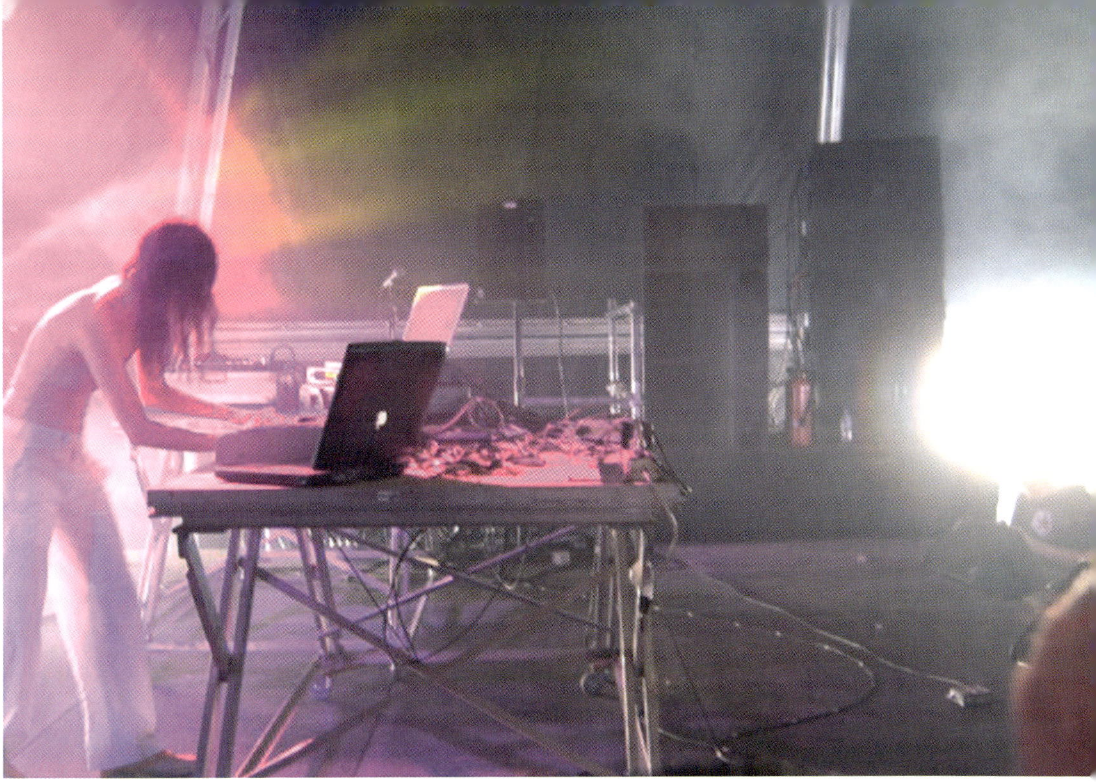

als sängerin und produzentin ist man überwiegend auf inhalte angewiesen, und das kann eine ganz schön bürde sein. nach vielen jahren musikschaffen fühle ich mich immer wieder damit konfrontiert, dass vor allem im deutschen umgang mit deutscher sprache die zuhörer probleme haben, die musik zu erreichen. zuerst kommt immer der inhalt. die aussage. das gehirn. bei den aufnahmen zu meinem album *head slash bauch* wollte ich meine stimme eher wie ein instrument einsetzen. ich wollte mich befreien von diesem zwang, verständliches und emotionales sagen zu müssen. auf dem weg, ein „independent producer" zu werden, „geekte" ich mich durch den prozess der selbstausbildung in hardware. softwares. bedienungsanleitungen und allem, was man so braucht. und so hat der computer/laptop meine arbeits- und lebens-/kommunikation und produktionsmöglichkeiten extrem und bis auf chronische rückenschmerzen positiv beeinflusst und ermöglicht immer mehr flexibilität. schnelligkeit und selbstbeherrschung. mehr und mehr vermischungen von „denke in code" führen zu phänomenen wie „wenn ich schlafen gehe, geh ich über in den sleep mode. usw." und plötzlich werden bedienungsanleitungen zu guten freunden *(joke).*
so entdeckte ich die poesie und schönheit dieser technischen praktischen programmiersprache. seitdem experimentiere ich mit dieser spannung zwischen technischer kühle und rhythmus und melodie im zusammenhang mit realität / gefühl / vision.
zur eröffnung des klangparks der ars electronica 2003 stelle ich in einer 30-minütigen live-performance teile dieser arbeit vor und binde auch eine komposition für das festival basierend auf dem lexikontext zu „CODE" ein.

Media | Art | Education
Working on and with *Eigensinn*

Giaco Schiesser

The Department <Media & Art> at the University of Art and Design Zurich

In 2002, as part of the restructuring of the University of Art and Design Zurich *(Hochschule für Gestaltung und Kunst Zürich,* HGKZ) that had been underway since 1997, the Departments of Film/Video, Photography, and New Media as well as the Fine Arts program were merged together into the Department of Media & Art, in which approximately 300 full-time students are currently enrolled. Since early 2002, the department has been going about opening up the previously quite self-contained curricula of the individual programs and working out an educational concept that maintains the quality of the training provided heretofore—for example, the Departments of Film and Photography here in Zurich are the only ones of their kind in Switzerland and the Department of New Media's focus is unique in Europe—and that, at the same time, takes into account changed circumstances with respect to the role of information, networks and knowledge in modern society. The aim has been to offer students an attractive, highly self-determined course of study that can be pursued either vertically within one of the majors or laterally in interdisciplinary fashion.

Guiding Precepts or *On Eigensinn* as Artistic Productive Force

Three fundamental precepts—unique in Europe, it may well be said—guide the work on this concept, a process that will be completed in early 2004:[1]

1. Training in individual and collective *media authorship*
2. Working on and with the *Eigensinn* (approx.: willful obstinacy) of film, photography, computers / networks and the fine arts as media
3. *Art as process, art as method*

"Training in individual and collective media authorship" means that students ought to develop and pursue their own themes, interests and issues, which they are then to execute in a way that is appropriate to the medium in which they are working. An advantage of the concept of media authorship is that it avoids establishing a fruitless distinction between artistic and applied works. Whether students go on to careers as artists or in private enterprise—either as employees or entrepreneurs—is their decision. The key factor here is that students do not assume the role of an operator who executes prescribed assignments; rather, they act as producers who, with independence and media competence, process content and realize it as a finished project or product. Furthermore, it is highly desirable for all of us to get, besides art, for example, other photographs custom-tailored to the potential of their media in magazines and advertisements, other films on TV, or other computer games that go against the grain and get away from conventional uses of media.

"Working on and with the *Eigensinn* (willful obstinacy) of computers and networks as media" proceeds under the assumption that computers and networks have their own individually specific potentials, structures and limitations. You are all familiar with works of literature, the fine arts, photography, music, film and video. From your everyday experience—whether as specialists or laymen—you are aware that each one of these media has something about it that is essentially its own. What can be written in literature is something different than what can be shown on film. What a photograph captures differs from what a piece of music expresses. All these media possess different possibilities and limitations that make them unique and inimitable by any other. With the term *Eigensinn* of a medium," I attempt to capture this complex differentiation. And for each of these media, there is a series of specific aesthetics that have emerged over the course of centuries in some cases, over several decades in others. In the cinema, for instance, from the silent film aesthetic of artists like George Méliès to the first French avant-garde works to contemporary splatter movies; in literature, from the Entwicklungsroman to Dadaism and the automatic style of writing of the surrealists all the way to current, collectively authored Internet literature; and in music, from Italian opera to twelve-tone music and Jazz to Hip-Hop and ambient, to cite just a few examples.
Without working on and with this *Eigensinn,* it is impossible to attain media authorship that exhibits originality, radicality and promise.
"Art as process, art as method," a concept that can be traced back to Russian formalist Viktor Slovski, refers to the fact that it is only by means of project-oriented education and ongoing, astute and media-customized artistic experimentation—the process of incessantly going deeper into a subject, of going against the grain and of subverting commonplace uses of media—that new and innovative artistic and design projects, and thus new possibilities of perception and insight, can be conceived, executed and experienced.

A Media and Art Education in Keeping with the Times

Willful obstinacy (Eigensinnigkeit) and artistic acumen (Scharfsinnigkeit) in both individual and collective media authorship / appropriate use of media / art as a process—I consider these the strategic elements in a model of a media and art education that is in keeping with the times.
In addition, an education that is conceived in terms of the future but one that also includes, takes seriously and works through experience with tradition will provide students with latitude for experimentation in which, curiously, radically and uncompromisingly, the individual and collective work of creative media authorship done by students on interests, content and topics of their own choosing or on assigned projects as well as their work on and with *Eigensinn* with a whole spectrum of individual and hybrid media is demanded and encouraged.
Moreover, a media education today must at the same time be transmedial, meaning that students are put in a position to be able to work both in and with a particular medium as well as to learn to think in terms of and work at its interface with other media. Authorship in a media- and technology-based age—precisely what our post-industrial epoch constitutes—means not only individual or collective authorship in which everyone brings his/her own specific areas of competence to bear but also collaborative authorship in which everyone is capable of setting up their own linkages between their specific fields of competence and those of others and, in doing so, repeatedly emerge as having been themselves thoroughly transformed by this process. Besides the development of social, communicative and, to an increasing extent, analytical skills, however, this also presupposes profound

insights into ones own medium as well as the media of others. The meaning of an education that includes both in-depth work in one medium and transdisciplinary work in others—and one that must necessarily go beyond that which is offered by a university of media and art—is, in my opinion, enabling art students to find a way that is in keeping with the times, or, as is increasingly called for in this Information Society, to become flexible and multi-dimensional media authors who, as individuals and as team members, are capable of assuming responsibility for content, conception, realization, the production process and budgeting in confident, masterly fashion.

If it is true that any new medium has a double impact on old media, in that it forces them into a new conception of their possibilities under new circumstances and, at the same time, transforms them as well, then one of the essential challenges to and opportunities of a media and art education at art universities is also—and perhaps even essentially—to enable and encourage hybrid or cross-over works of art such as interactive audio installations, video essays, media architecture, transmedial interfaces, interfaces in urban spaces, DJ events, digital poetry, new aesthetics of the performative, SMS visuals for clubs, parties, intercity streams from DJ events, Internet TV, cultural software, radio concerts for cell phones or many, many other possibilities. Transmedial or hybrid art demands—and over the intermediate term, this is the central challenge for art education—that we work in, impart and utilize a whole series of complex specialized fields like neurophysiology, cognitive sciences, architecture, nanotechnology, theories of informatics, aesthetics, cognition and perception, as well as the life sciences that are not taught at a single university but rather at a number of different institutions. A key reason for this is the fact that, whereas the technology-based nature of the media has indeed been constantly increasing since the invention of photography, this process has taken a quantum leap as a result of digitization. Thus, the dispositive has also changed fundamentally and dramatically for the arts as well. In a detailed and comprehensive work published a number of years ago, Hans-Peter Schwarz traced the eventful history of the various arts and technology since the 18th century and established the indisputable significance of technology for media art now and in the future. The linkage of art, technology and science—which, in the Renaissance, became a matter taken completely for granted during a short historical epoch—will, without a doubt, be a precondition for art and media work in the future and thus for an adequate education.

---

1 Due to space constraints, my remarks here can only briefly touch on the social framework conditions, content, objectives and guiding principles of the education that the Department of Media and Art will provide in the future. For a more detailed and comprehensive elaboration, see: Giaco Schiesser: Medien | Kunst | Ausbildung. Über den *Eigensinn* als künstlerische Produktivkraft. (Media | Art | Education. On Eigensinn as a Force in Artistic Production.) In: *Schnittstellen.* Edited by Sigrid Schade, Thomas Sieber, and Georg Christoph Tholen. (Basler Beiträge zur Medienwissenschaft. Vol. 1). Basel: Schwabe 2004.

Media | Art | Education
Arbeit am und mit dem Eigensinn

Giaco Schiesser

Das Departement Medien & Kunst der Hochschule für Gestaltung und Kunst Zürich

Im Rahmen der seit 1997 laufenden Restrukturierung der Hochschule für Gestaltung und Kunst Zürich wurden 2002 die Studienbereiche Film / Video, Fotografie, Neue Medien und der Studiengang Bildende Kunst zum Departement <Medien & Kunst> zusammengefasst, an dem zur Zeit rund 300 Vollzeitstudierende studieren. Seit anfang 2002 ist das Department dabei, die bis anhin stark autark angelegten Curricula der einzelnen Studienbereiche zu öffnen und ein Ausbildungskonzept zu erarbeiten, das die Qualitäten der bisherigen Ausbildung – so existieren etwa die Studienbereiche Film und Fotografie schweizweit nur in Zürich und der Studienbereich Neue Medien hat einen europaweit einmaligen Fokus – erhalten bleiben und zugleich den veränderten Bedingungen der Informations-, Netzwerk- oder Wissensgesellschaft Rechung getragen wird. Für die Studierenden soll ein attraktives, stark selbst bestimmtes Studium angeboten werden, das entweder stärker vertikal in einem der Bereiche oder mehr transversal quer zu den Bereichen gemacht werden kann.

Leitideen oder *Vom Eigensinn* als Produktivkraft

Leitend für das bis Anfang 2004 erarbeitete Konzept sind dabei, europaweit wohl einmalig, drei Leitideen:[1]

1. Ausbildung zur individuellen und / oder kollektiven *MedienautorIn*
2. Arbeit am und mit dem *Eigensinn der Medien* Film, Fotografie, Computer / Netzwerke und der bildenden Künste
3. *Kunst als Verfahren,* Kunst als Methode

„Ausbildung zur eigensinnigen, individuellen oder kollektiven Medienautorschaft“ bedeutet, dass die StudentInnen ihre eigenen Themen, Interessen, Fragestellungen erarbeiten und verfolgen sollen, die sie medienadäquat realisieren. Ein Vorteil des Begriffs der Medienautorschaft ist, dass er die unselige Trennung zwischen künstlerischen und angewandten Arbeiten unterläuft. Ob die Studierenden später als KünstlerInnen tätig sind oder in Unternehmen arbeiten bzw. solche gründen, ist ihre Entscheidung. Beide, und das ist zentral, verhalten sich aber nicht als Anwender (Operators), die gestellte Aufgaben ausführen, sondern sind als ProduzentInnen tätig, die eigenständig und medienkompetent Inhalte erarbeiten und umsetzen. Zudem wäre es wünschbar und dringlich, neben der Kunst andere, eigensinnige Fotografien in Zeitschriften und in der Werbung, andere Filme im Fernsehen oder andere, gegen den Strich-gebürstete Computergames zu sehen und zu hören zu bekommen.
„Arbeit am und mit dem Eigensinn des Mediums“ geht davon aus, dass Computer und Netzwerke je spezifische, eigene Potenziale, Strukturen und Beschränkungen eignen.
Sie alle kennen Werke der Literatur, der bildenden Kunst, der Fotografie, der Musik, des Films, Videos. Ob als Spezialistin oder ob als Laie: Aus Ihrer Alltagserfahrung wissen Sie,

dass alle diese Medien etwas je Eigenes haben. Was in Literatur geschrieben werden kann, ist etwas anderes, als im Film gezeigt wird. Was die Fotografie erfasst, unterscheidet sich von dem, was ein Musikstück ausdrückt.
Alle diese Medien besitzen unterschiedliche Möglichkeiten und Grenzen, die sie einmalig und wechselseitig unersetzbar machen. Mit dem Begriff „Eigensinn eines Mediums" versuche ich dieses komplexe Unterschiedliche zu fassen. Für alle diese Medien gibt es ein Reihe je spezifischer, zum Teil über Jahrhunderte, zum Teil über einige Jahrzehnte gewachsene Ästhetiken. Im Film etwa von der Stummfilmästhetik eines George Méliès über die erste französische Avantgarde bis zum zeitgenössischen Splatter-Movie, in der Literatur vom Entwicklungsroman über den Dadaismus und die automatischen Schreibweise der Surrealisten hin zur aktuellen, kollektiv verfassten Netzliteratur, in der Musik von der italienischen Oper über Zwölftonmusik und Jazz bis hin zu Hip-Hop und Ambient, um nur einige wenige Beispiele zu nennen.
Ohne Arbeit am und mit diesem Eigensinn ist originelle, radikale und weiterführende Medienautorschaft nicht zu haben.
„Kunst als Verfahren bzw. Kunst als Methode", ein Konzept, das auf den russischen Formalisten Viktor Slovskji zückgeht, verweist darauf, dass nur über den Projektunterricht und das permanente – eigensinnige und scharfsinnige – künstlerische Experimentieren – das unablässige Sichvertiefen-in, das Gegen-den-Strich-Bürsten, das Unterlaufen gang-und-gäber Mediennutzung - neue und neuartige künstlerische und gestalterische Erfahrungen, Projekte und damit neue Wahrnehmungs- und Erkenntnismöglichkeiten denk-, mach- und erlebbar werden.

Eine Medien- und Kunstausbildung auf der Höhe ihrer Zeit

Eigensinnigkeit und die Scharfsinnigkeit künstlerischer – individueller und kollektiver - Autorschaft / Eigensinn der Medien / Kunst als Verfahren halte ich für die strategischen Momente in einem Modell einer Medien- und Kunstausbildung, die sich auf der Höhe ihrer Zeit bewegt. Eine Medien- und Kunstausbildung auf Augenhöhe mit ihrer Zeit, eine Ausbildung, die von der Zukunft her gedacht wird und zugleich die Erfahrungen der Tradition ernst nimmt und durcharbeitet, wird den Studierenden Experimentierräume zur Verfügung stellen. Experimentierräume, in denen neugierig, radikal und kompromisslos die individuelle und kollektive, eigensinnige Arbeit der StudentInnen an selbst gewählten oder auferlegten, Interessen / Inhalten / Themen und ihre Arbeit am und mit dem Eigensinn unterschiedlicher Einzel- und Hybrid-Medien gefordert und gefördert wird.
Zu einer medialen gehört heute zugleich auch eine transmediale Ausbildung. Transmediale Ausbildung heißt, dass die Studierenden in die Lage versetzt werden, gleichzeitig in und mit einem Medium arbeiten zu können und die Schnittstelle zu anderen Medien denken und künstlerisch bespielen zu lernen. Autorschaft in einem medien- und technologiebasierten Zeitalter, wie es die postindustrielle Epoche darstellt, bedeutet nicht nur individuelle oder kollektive Autorschaft, in der jeder seine spezifische Kompetenzen einbringt, sondern kollaborative Autorschaft, in der jeder und jede seine spezifischen Kompetenzen mit den Kompetenzen anderer selbst zu vernetzen imstande ist und dadurch selbst immer wieder gründlich transformiert aus diesem Prozess hervorgeht. Dies setzt aber neben der Entwicklung sozialer, kommunikativer und zunehmend auch analytischer Kompetenzen vertiefte Kenntnisse des eigenen und Kenntnisse der anderen Medien voraus. Die Bedeutung einer zugleich medial vertiefendenden und transmedial vernetzenden Ausbildung – die bald auch über das Angebot der einer Medien- und Kunsthochschule hinausgreifen muss – sehe ich darin, dass sie den Studierenden ermöglicht, einen Weg als KünstlerInnen auf der Höhe ihrer Zeit oder als in der „Informationsgesellschaft" zunehmend und dringlich gebrauchte, flexible und vielseitig anschlussfähige MedienautorInnen zu

gehen, die als Einzelne und im Team in der Lage sind, Verantwortlichkeit über Inhalt, Konzeption, Realisation, Produktionsablauf und Budgetierung souverän wahrzunehmen.
Wenn es richtig ist, dass ein jeweils neues Medium in doppelter Weise Auswirkung auf alte Medien hat, indem es diese zu einem neuen Verständnis ihrer Möglichkeiten unter neuen Bedingungen zwingt und sie zugleich auch transformiert, dann liegt eine wesentliche Herausforderung und Chance der Medien- und Kunstausbildung an Kunsthochschulen auch und gerade in der Ermöglichung und Förderung hybrider oder Cross-over-Kunstwerke, handle es sich dabei um interaktive Audioinstallationen, Videoessays, Medienarchitektur, transmediale Schnittstellen in urbanen Räume, DJ-Events, digitale Dichtung, neue Ästhetiken des Performativen, um SMS-Visuals für Clubs, Parties, Intercity-Streams von DJ-Events, Netz-TV, kulturelle Software, Radiokonzerte für Handys oder, oder, oder. Eine transmediale oder hybride Kunst erfordert – und das ist für eine Kunstausbildung mittelfristig die zentrale Herausforderung – die Erarbeitung, Vermittlung und die Nutzung einer Reihe von komplexen Fachgebieten wie Neurophysiologie, Kognitionswissenschaften, Architektur, Nanotechnologie, Informatik-, Ästhetik-, Erkenntnis- und Wahrnehmungstheorien, Life Sciences, die nicht an einer, sondern verstreut an unterschiedlichen Hochschulen gelehrt werden. Ein wesentlicher Grund dafür ist, dass die Technologiebasiertheit der Medien seit der Erfindung der Fotografie zwar stetig zugenommen, durch die Digitalisierung aber einen eigentlichen Sprung erfahren hat. Das Dispositiv hat sich damit auch für die Künste grundlegend und dramatisch verändert. In einem materialreichen Beitrag hat Hans-Peter Schwarz vor einigen Jahren die wechselvolle Geschichte der unterschiedlichen Künste und der Technologie seit dem 18. Jahrhundert nachgezeichnet und die unhintergehbare Bedeutung der Technologie für eine aktuelle und zukünftige Medienkunst festgehalten. Die Verknüpfung von Kunst, Technologie und Wissenschaft – die in der Renaissance für eine kurze historische Epoche zu einer Selbstverständlichkeit wurde - wird, das ist heute unabweisbar, zu einer Voraussetzung zukünftiger Kunst- und Medienarbeit und damit auch einer adäquaten Ausbildung.

1 Aus Platzgründen kann ich im Folgenden nur in der gebotenen Verkürzung auf die gesellschaftlichen Rahmenbedingungen, auf die Inhalte, Ziele und Leitideen der zukünftigen Ausbildung im Departement <Medien & Kunst> eingehen. Ausführlich habe ich sie dargelegt in: Giaco Schiesser: „Medien | Kunst | Ausbildung. Über den *Eigensinn* als künstlerische Produktivkraft". In: *Schnittstellen,* hrsg. von Sigrid Schade, Thomas Sieber, Georg Christoph Tholen. (= Basler Beiträge zur Medienwissenschaft. Bd. 1). Basel: Schwabe 2004.

Media | Art | Education

Cecilia Hausheer

The *Media | Art | Education* exhibition deals with digitization's impact on the arts and the future consequences of this phenomenon. It features the latest trends to emerge from the experimental laboratories of the Department of Media and Art at the School of Art and Design Zurich.
The exhibition's organizers have intentionally avoided producing a "Zurich's Greatest Hits"—type showcase. Instead, this compilation gives viewers in Linz a look at degree projects by the Class of 2003, recently completed undergrad classwork, as well as current works-in-progress from different fields of instruction and experimentation—in concrete terms, Internet-based works, interactive installations (including audio, multimedia and cross-media applications), computer animation, films, video documentaries and performance works. Topics/themes include constructions of meaning, perception of shifting sounds/spaces/contexts, power/control, high/low tech, hybrid, recycling/recombinant, open source, and media-historical memory.
The Department of Media and Art's collaborating partner is Linz's University of Art, which has made space available for the exhibition on three floors of its premises.
During the festival, the University of Art's façade will become a public interface. This interface—the *Teleklettergarten* portal project—emerged as the winner of a competition held by the Zurich school for the design of the façade in accordance with CODE, the festival theme. Finally, in Kino Moviemento, the School of Art and Design presents a program on the manifold effects that digitization has been having on film (see page 391).

Die Ausstellung *Medien | Kunst | Ausbildung* beschäftigt sich mit dem Einfluss und den Auswirkungen der Digitalisierung auf die Künste. Sie stellt aktuelle und jüngste Tendenzen aus den experimentellen Labors des Departements Medien & Kunst DMK der Hochschule für Gestaltung und Kunst Zürich vor.
Die Ausstellung will bewusst keine Leistungsschau à la Best-of sein. Sie präsentiert aktuelle Diplomarbeiten des Jahres 2003, abgeschlossene Semesterprojekte sowie verschiedene Work-in-Progress aus Lehre und Forschung vor Ort in Linz. Konkret zu sehen sind Netzwerk-basierte Arbeiten, interaktive Installationen (von Klang über Multi- bis Cross-Media), Computeranimationen, Filme, Videodokumente und Aktionen. Themenfelder der Ausstellung sind Sinn-Konstruktionen, Wahrnehmung zwischen Tönen / Räumen / Kontexten, Macht / Kontrolle, High / Low Tech, Hybrid, Recycling / Recombinant, Open Source, medienhistorisches Gedächtnis.
Kooperationspartner des Departements Medien & Kunst ist die Kunstuniversität Linz, in deren Gebäude die Ausstellung auf drei Stockwerken gezeigt wird.
Während des Festivals wird die Fassade der Kunstuniversität zum öffentlichen Interface. Dieses Interface – das Portalprojekt *Teleklettergarten* – ging als Gewinner eines an der Hochschule für Gestaltung und Kunst ausgeschriebenen Wettbewerbs für die Gestaltung der Fassade zum Festivalthema CODE hervor.
Im Kino Moviemento schließlich präsentieren wir ein Programm zu den unterschiedlichen Auswirkungen, die die Digitalisierung auf den Film hat (siehe Seite 391).

BEATWEEN–Impulse in the Pulse
Interactive Sound Installation, 2003 / SNM

Michael Hampel

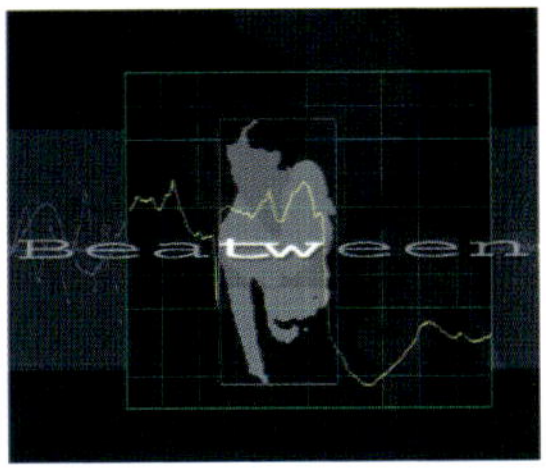

In a darkened room, video cameras shooting simultaneously from different angles capture the impulses triggered by the movements of visitors. Out of granulated, quantized samples, they form polymorphous, fluid constructions between rhythm and sound. The indistinct, grinding contours in between (interpolation, morphing) are like wind-born sand that gets in ones eyes and sensitizes one to the interaction and reciprocal effects of different porous levels of time that are inseparably bound to movement and space. Beatween: being the impulse in the pulse.

FAX.BOOT.FORCE: Become an Engine of One
Interactive Installation, 2003 / SNM

Felix Eggmann/Max Rheiner

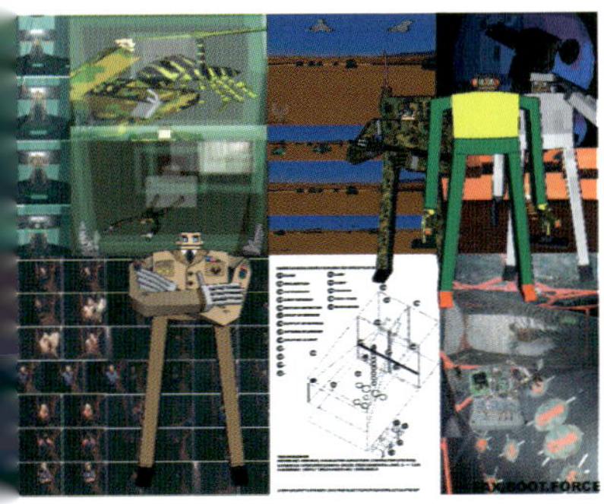

The Pentagon paid $7 million to develop "America's Army: Operations," an online video game designed to train young Americans and to give them a realistic view of a modern army.
FAX.BOOT.FORCE deals with interfaces at the nexus of society, army and the entertainment industry. In a playful installation, visitors to the exhibit are recruited as FAX ARMY SOLDIERS and assigned to a unit of the virtual army. Recruits' behavior during the enlistment process influences their army career ...

Heimatwerk
Action September 2003 / SNM

Gregor Huber/Ivan Sterzinger

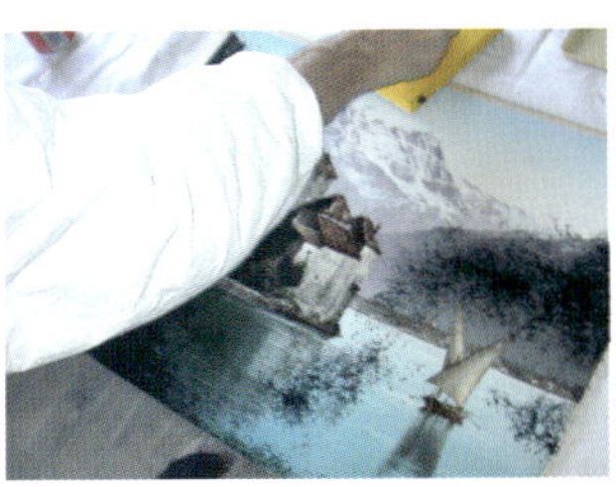

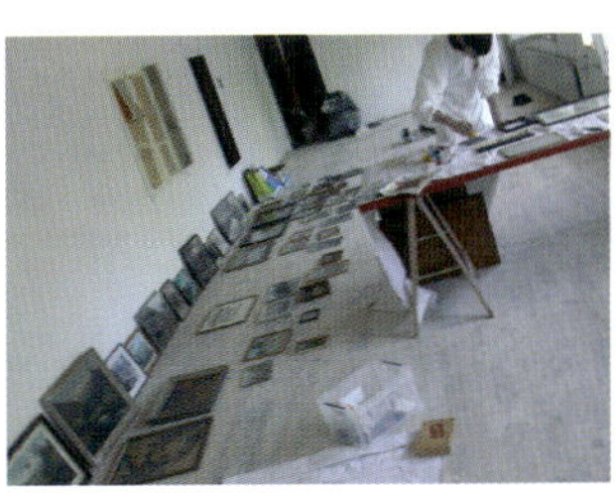

Homeland as canned goods put up in times of the mental defense of the country. Today, their best-before dates long since expired, they sit in storage at the nation's dealers in second-hand wares. *Heimatwerk* (in German-speaking Europe, a quasi-official purveyor of native folkloric costumes and handicrafts) promotes a discourse about the changing image of homeland by using a process of re-adaptation and a public mise-en-scène to recontextualize homeland-related subjects that used to have a powerfully identity-endowing effect. The material for the graphics was acquired at local second-hand dealers and reads like a historical film script of a previously institutionally subsidized staging of Switzerland in a pictorial language.

loogie.net tv

Internet application for television, 2003 / SNM

Marc Lee

loogie.net tv displays current TV news reportage on user-selected subjects at the press of a button. By entering a keyword by means of a special remote control device, the user can determine the topic of the material appearing on TV and thus view a custom-tailored news program. In a second step, the program currently appearing can also be thematically focused in accordance with the user's own interests. *loogie.net tv* takes advantage of the abundant resources of the Internet to satisfy TV viewers' needs more optimally than ever.

ImageWriter

Interactive Installation, 2002 / SNM

Silvan Leuthold

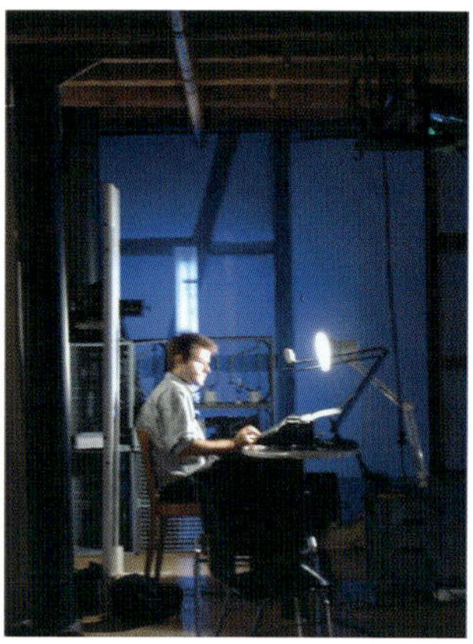

The typewriter as a familiar medium for writing text is combined with a computer to become an input/output interface that dictates to the user his/her own portrait as an ASCII image. *ImageWriter* is characterized by the confrontation of the typewriter with the computer and by the encounter of low-tech and high-tech. It illustrates the shortcomings as well as the charm of the predecessor of the modern-day keyboard as an input interface—the battle of the generations, retro-cult and ASCII-art. The end product, entered on the typewriter by the sweat of the typist's brow, is hardly conceivable independent of the controlling computer; nevertheless, the print-out made by a typewriter differs significantly from a computer print-out.

Jusqu'ici tout va bien

Installation, 2003 / SNM

Anne-Lea Werlen / Carmen Weisskopf

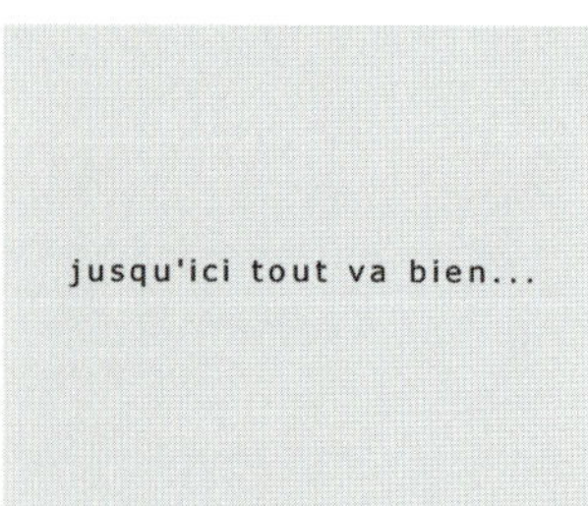

"We want neither to punish the machine for its inability to win a beauty pageant nor to punish the human being for losing a race with an airplane." (Alan Turing)

When a human being and a machine stand face to face in an elevator, will they see eye to eye? *Jusqu'ici tout va bien* ("so far, so good") sheds light on how understanding functions and meaning emerges in the interplay of man and machine. What is the meaning of the human need by all means to endow with meaning our dealings with machines? This installation takes a measure of that sphere between sense-endowing interpretation and the crash beyond the pale of understanding and access.

Luxus4all – open office

Internet Installation, 2003 / SNM

Mario Purkathofer / Doma Smoljo

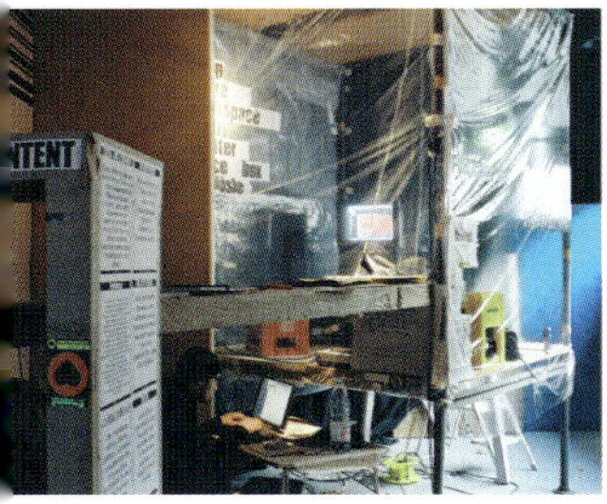

Luxus4all.org is a Web interface offering open access to free informational products. Luxury for all—a free market for information, concepts and their users. Producers of information, ideas and creative theories are invited to make their unfinished works available under an open license. In the open office, this information can be obtained as open products. Anyone who acquires such a product does not obtain ownership of a piece of merchandise but rather assumes shared responsibility for its publication, distribution, exploitation or cooperation.

Mommy, I want superalgorithms too...!

Interactive Installation, 2003 / SNM

Niki Schawalder

A super-switchbox provides—in a most charming way—access to the interior of a digital system and insight into how software thinks. In contrast to common, everyday access via mouse and keyboard, a lamp-switch interface gives non-programmers an opportunity to get a close-up look at the inner workings of a digital system and to write a piece of super-software themselves. Through five windows, the box provides a glimpse into its program-specific logic. Some curious souls might start getting bright ideas.

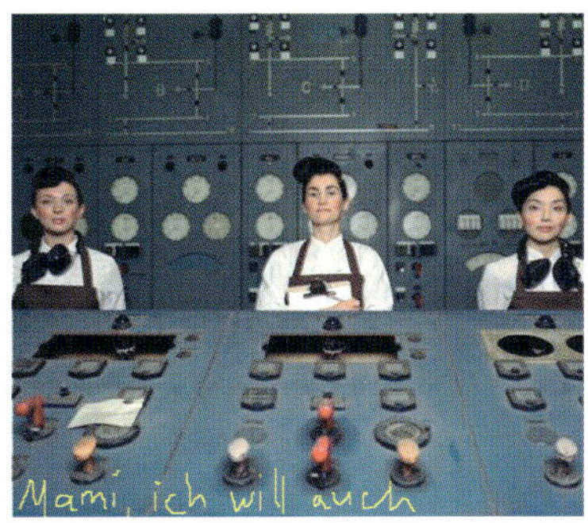

Desktop Hardware Orchestra

Interactive Sound Installation, 2003 / SNM

Roger Wigger/Mascha Leummens

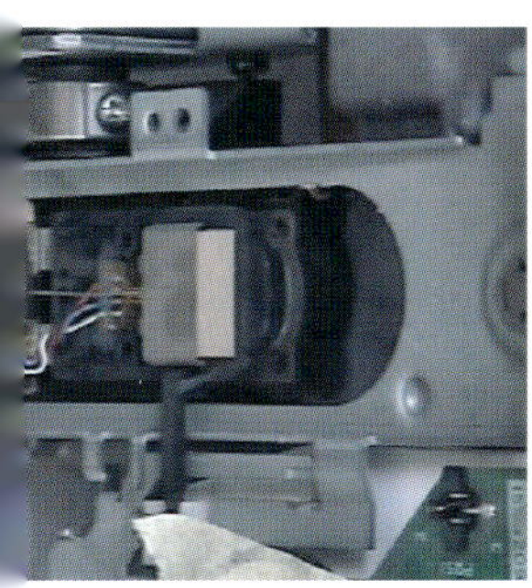

The distinctive sounds made by the hardware components of a conventional desktop computer (hard disk drive, floppy disk drive, CPU, fan, etc.) comprise the acoustic instrument with which visitors can create their own compositions or listen to those composed by others. The software does not emulate "hardware" (for instance, a guitar); instead, it only regulates the sounds made by the components themselves. The results are musical structures played on devices that were not built for this purpose.

Recombinant_Hardware Hacker Project

Action Video, 2002 / SNM

Students who collaborated on this project in their major field of study: Anne-Lea Werlen, Carmen Weisskopf, Christoph Burgdorfer, Cindy Aebischer, Marco Klingmann, Mascha Leummens, Roger Wigger, Thomas Comiotto, Nico Dreher, Andrea del Carmen Cruz Gonzales
Project Directors: Prof. Margarete Jahrmann; Prof. Giaco Schiesser

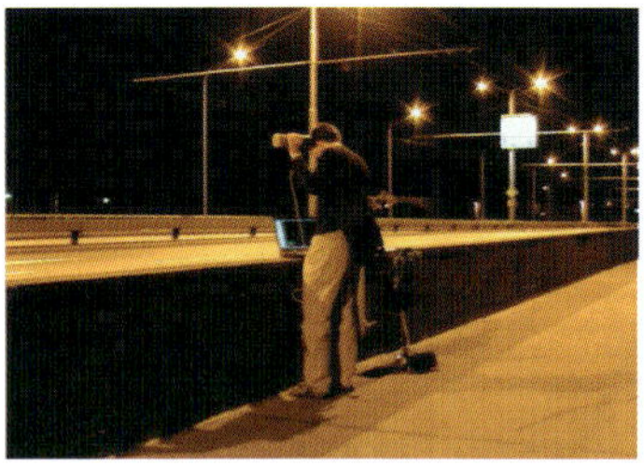

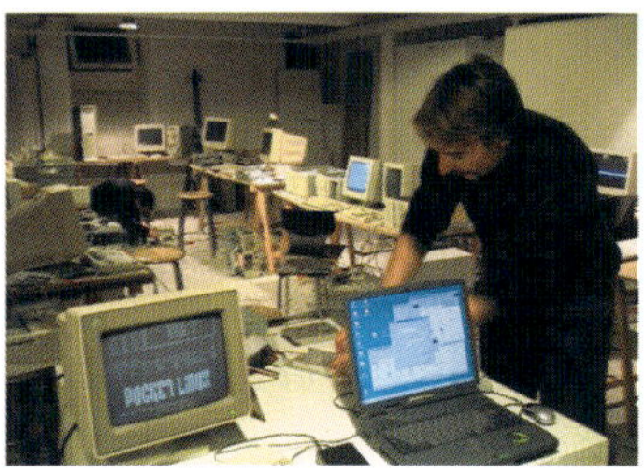

Recombinant is a live video recording of an action in an urban setting that was conducted as the conclusion of a study project by students majoring in New Media. The idea behind the project was to collect and readapt old, obsolete hardware. What in another context is considered techno-junk was collected and reprocessed into individual hardware modules. The first step was to check out the various individual projects to determine—in a reinterpretation of the "hardware handshake"—if they could be compatibly hooked up with each other, and then they were analyzed with the aim of establishing what can be generated with the material itself without any further input. The spectrum ranges from sound that can be extracted directly via microphone from various different hardware components (Desktop Hardware Orchestra) to homemade wave LAN antenna modules, and all the way to a compacted computer that can be exhibited in the context of a work of art and thereby newly encoded.

SuPerVillainizer–Conspiracy Client

Website, 2002 / SNM

LAN / Annina Rüst

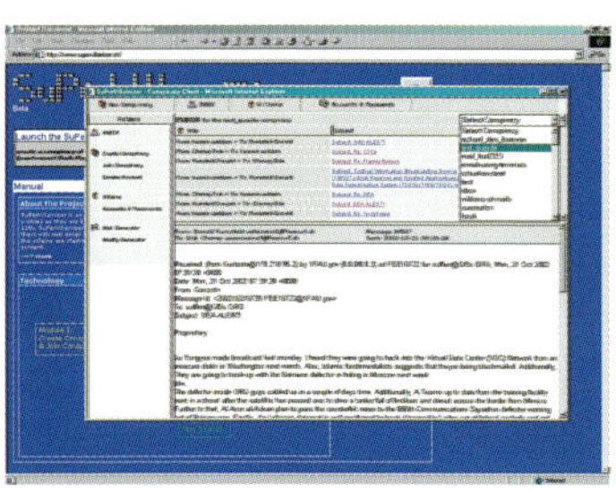

SuPerVillainizer is an interactive Web project that takes a stand against thinking in terms of the cliché-ridden images of the bad guys that are the basis of new surveillance scenarios. By generating artificial villains, *SuPerVillainizer* calls conventional concepts of friend and foe into question. The way it does this is by designing profiles of desperados, rogues and scapegoats, setting them up with real e-mail accounts at Swiss providers, getting them hooked up in conspiracies and then watching how the rogues start passing conspiracy content generated by *SuPerVillainizer* back and forth to each other. Users can have input into the conspiratorial e-mails and choose the language of the conspiracy. In this way, the carefully planned surveillance databanks get infiltrated, bewildered and filled up with conspiratorial connections.

Swiss Dotcoms in Retrospect

Video, 2003 / SNM

Thomas Comiotto/Niki Schawalder

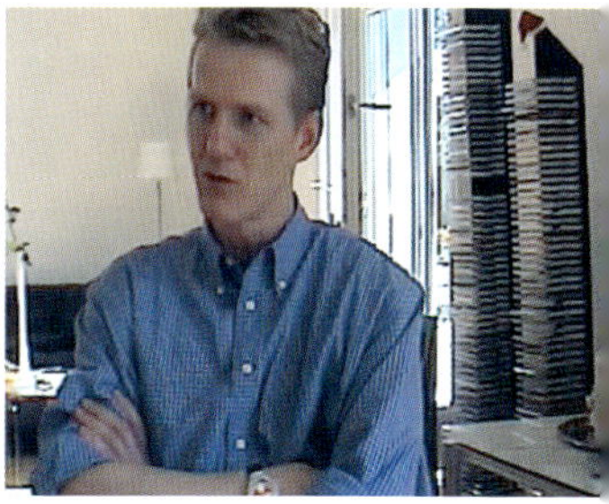

Interviews focusing on the Internet boom in Switzerland, with those actually involved in a variety of different positions giving accounts of their experiences. Of principle interest here is not so much the fates of the various firms as individual ideas, motives and visions, and the participants' career paths. Where did these people come from? What were their reasons for joining Internet start-ups? What conceptions did they have of the work, the sector, the market and their own chances of success? What are these people doing today?

track-the-trackers---

Installation with Mobile Components, 2003 / SNM

Annina Rüst

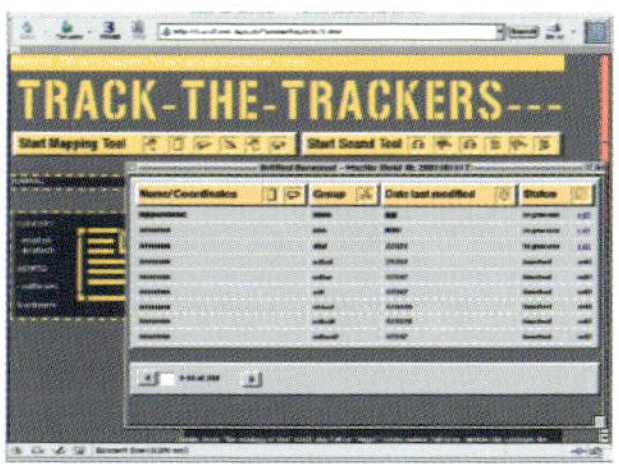

track-the-trackers--- offers an expanded experience of the proliferation of video surveillance in the urban public sphere on an auditory basis. At the same time, it is a less-than-pragmatic cartographic device for producing individual and collective cartographic works, which in turn are fed back into the system. *track-the-trackers---* is an installation with mobile components: the mobile unit, the *track-the-trackers---bag,* is borrowed and taken along on a journey through the urban space. The data gathered in this way are sent to the *track-the-trackers---station* and made available to the other participants via Internet platform. The installation prompts participants to think beyond the protection of their own private sphere and to invest in the public sphere.

16elemente

Interactive "Audio Play" Installation 2003 / SNM

Christine Szabo / Valentina Vuksic

The installation is a cylindrical space outfitted with a computer screen whose user interface can be navigated by means of a joystick. *16elemente* stages various elements of science fiction, belles-lettres and computer games on four different levels. The centerpiece of the work consists of fragments of four novels that have been orchestrated into an audio play. The various fields on the computer screen record the stories' main themes and make available quotations and sound material on an interactive basis. Users can also select from among lighting and texture options to customize the atmosphere.

Compiler: Magazine for Contemporary Art
DVD, 2003 / SBK

Research Director: Susann Wintsch; Concept: Milica Tomic, Susann Wintsch; Project Director: Hildegard Spielhofer; Private Sector Associates: Tweaklab AG, Basel, Hanspeter Giuliani; Graphics/Screen Design: Thomas Bircher; Programmer: Hannes Rüttimann

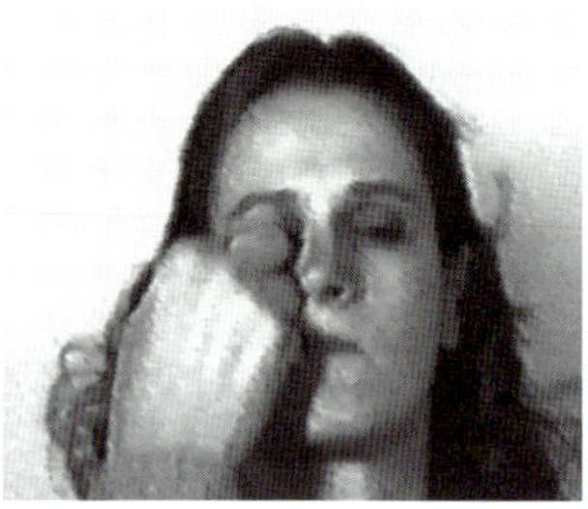

This DVD magazine is a new platform showcasing contemporary art and especially video and audio works, short films, performances, actions and processes. *Compiler* defines itself as a collection of data compiled to investigate key issues in international contemporary art. Each issue focuses on a selected region, whereby the featured works of art and statements contributed by cultural producers implicitly or explicitly reflect aspects of their particular society and thus call attention to distinctive features or differences within the globalized system.

Forum
DVD, 2000 / SBK

Gabriela Gerber/Lukas Bardill

"There are wonderful opportunities to do business in Singapore."—"Yes, and Hong Kong is even better."—"… but you're forgetting something—Beijing is the emerging city." (quoted by C. Seibt)
Gerber / Bardill gathered the material for *Forum* at the 2000 World Economic Forum in Davos. The on-screen sequences are superimposed upon one another on multiple video tracks. They create a turbulent flow of events featuring animalized helicopters. Large and small, near and far—like swarming insects, the helicopters float through the air, jabbing at or reconciling with one another. More and more of them, louder and louder—as their numbers increase, the rhythm accelerates. Wild rotor blades flap around like wings in a playful battle.

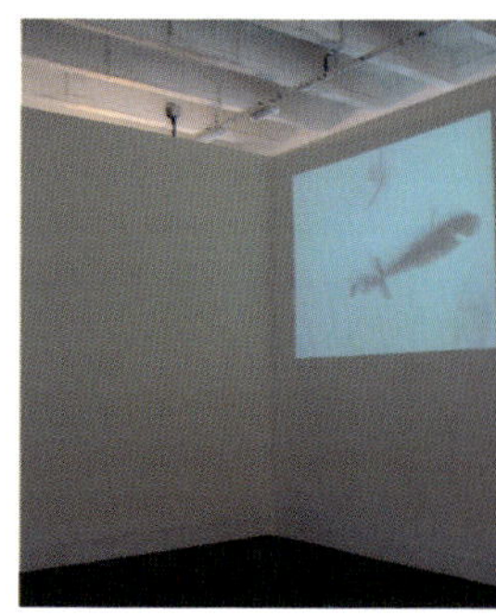

Schatten-tv (Shadow TV)
Media Event, 2003 / SBK

Jörg Köppl

The soundtrack of a selected TV channel gets processed, taken out of its original context, enhanced and broadcast on the radio. Listeners at home can enjoy a work of media art by turning on the TV, shutting off the sound, and tuning it the radio instead. The processing of the soundtrack is done with a computer program and by vocalists representing a number of different genres who improvise in the radio studio to the television images.

Schatten-tv is produced in cooperation with Radio FRO, Free Radio Upper Austria.
Concept: Jörg Köppl / Musical director: Philipp Schaufelberger

public plaiv

Contemporary Art in the La Plaiv Region of Oberengadin, Switzerland, 2003 / SBK

An interdisciplinary research project by the Department of Fine Arts of the School of Art and Design Zurich in cooperation with the Chair in Modern and Contemporary Art of the University of Zurich.Project Director: Christoph Schenker; Project Staff: Lilian Pfaff, Susann Wintsch, Tim Zulauf

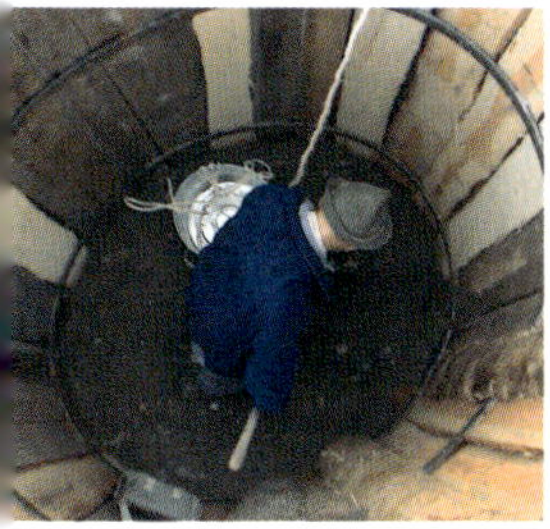

During the installation work

public plaiv investigates the culture and the economy of La Plaiv, an alpine region of Oberengadin in which tourism plays an important role. There, the competition to attract new businesses and the marketing/sell-out of local resources and traditions threaten to increasingly polarize the locals' image of themselves and how outsiders perceive them, and to drive a wedge between natives, tourists and guest workers. Invited artists conceptualize artworks that open up fields of new social functions. The first series of works premiered in July 2003.
http://www.publicplaiv.ch

Edit:MountainView

Competition entry for public plaiv / SBK

Felix S. Huber /Florian Wüst, in collaboration with Daniel Burckhardt

Edit:MountainView is the design of a constantly changing collage of images and texts that can be viewed both as a real on-site installation and live in the Internet. The broadcast of a video stream from a plaza below the village of S-chanf is the point of departure. This 24/7 real-time document is constantly being interrupted, enhanced, commented upon and contrasted by the playback of video sequences and the interaction possibilities of the Internet. *Edit:MountainView* is based on the concept of the re:site project realized in 2002 by kunstprojekte_riem, Munich.
http://www.resiteprojects.de

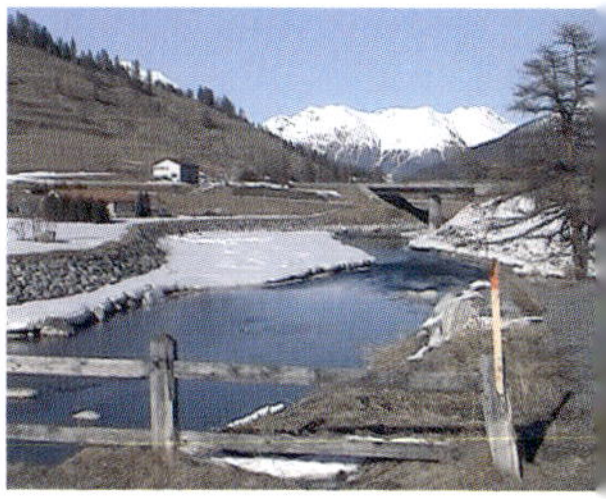

Sitzungszimmer (Conference Room)

Computer animation, 2001 / SBK

Cornelia Heusser

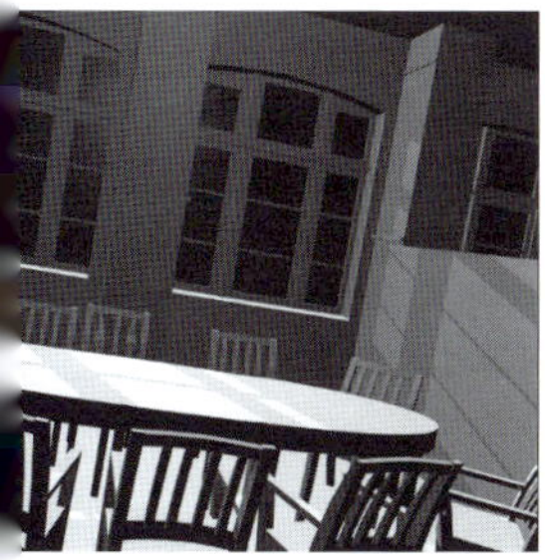

A real historical space, the former chambers of a justice of the peace, has been computer-modeled and placed in a new spatial context. The room is empty except for a long table with a couple of chairs. Even though there are no historical figures to be seen, the room nevertheless seems to have been brought to life by its long history. This impression of liveliness is realized graphically in the realm of virtuality—the room begins to rock and pitch like a galley ship; the chairs follow the movements, sliding slowly back and forth.
The digital space and the real one jointly determine the observer's perception. The boundaries between virtuality and reality get a bit shaky as well. The point is for the observer to have to discover his own balance between the two worlds.

VonZeit zuZeit (FromTime toTime)

Video Installation, 2002 / SBK

Tom Karrer

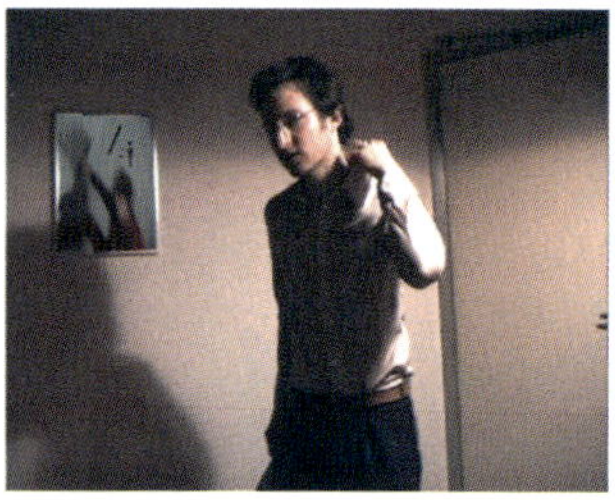

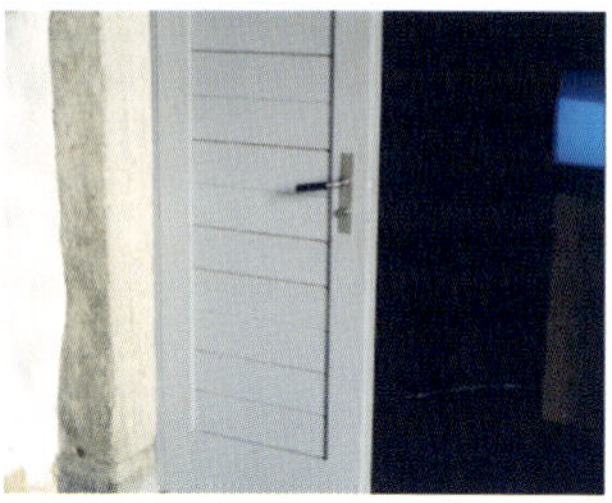

A TV sits in a room; a light switch is located next to it. There is no picture to be seen on the set and no sound to be heard. When someone presses the button, a picture can be seen and a text heard as long as the button remains depressed.

The person on the TV screen recites an endless text; as soon as it ends, it immediately starts from the beginning again. Each sentence of the text segues immediately into the next one without a transitional pause in between; the next sentence seizes upon the previous one and, in this way, modifies its meaning. With each word he speaks, the person is standing at another spot within the room. In the background, a picture is visible in which a person is collapsing in slow motion.

Jubilee. Zehn Jahre Studienbereich Film / Video

(10th Anniversary of the Film / Video Department)
DVD, 2002 / SFV

Concept and Realization: Flavia Caviezel, Bernhard Lehner, Thomas Schärer, Ronnie Wahli, Barbara Weber

Since this department was first established in 1992, more than 60 students have completed this four-year (up to 2002: five-year) program. The course of study trains generalists who do not approach film from the perspective of a specialized sub-discipline but rather as a cultural phenomenon whose sub-disciplines achieve consummation only in collaboration. Since 1992, over 400 films have been made as undergraduate assignments or as master's thesis projects. The 10th Anniversary DVD brings together a selection of these dramatic films, documentaries, works of experimental cinema and animated shorts, complemented by added features such as the TV project *Literaturquiz* and alumni interviews.

forschungsgruppe_f
Open Situation Room

Action Research, September 6-11, 2003 / SFO

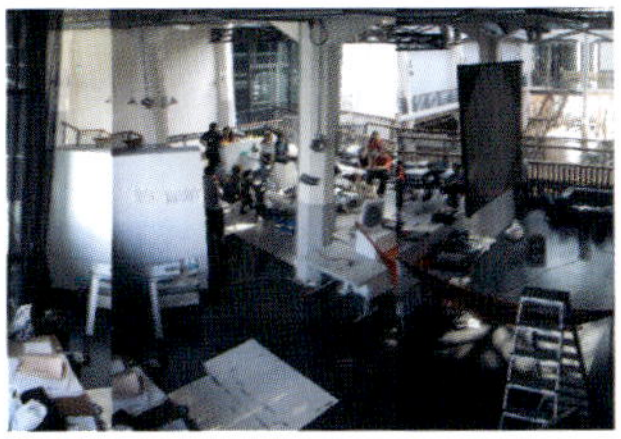

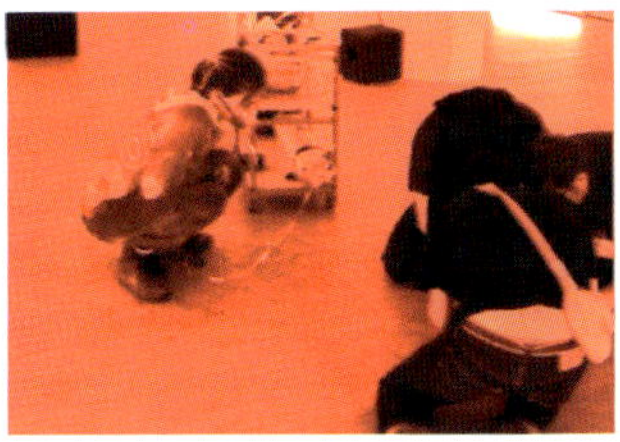

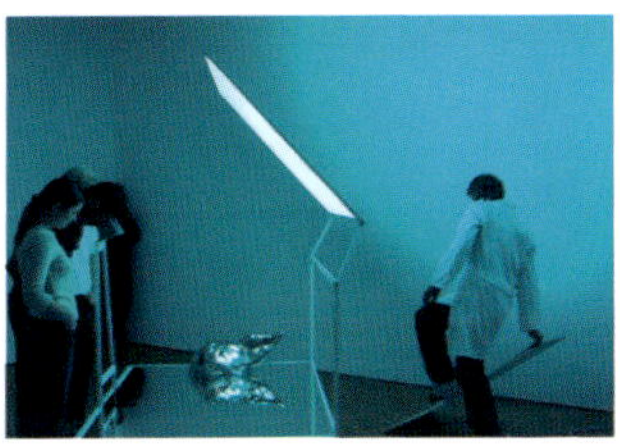

Students taking an experimental lab at the School of Art and Design Zurich's Department of Photography set up this research group in 2000. An expanded investigation of the circumstances in which images are organized and displayed, and how they are received by those viewing them made in necessary to question prevailing conditions and to process the results of this inquiry in the sense of performing action research. This open working group is made up of students at various institutions of higher education; it works in project-oriented fashion with a variety of different media.

For the exhibition *Iconoclash – Beyond the War of Images in Science, Religion and Art* presented in 2002 at the Center for Art and Media Technology (ZKM) in Karlsruhe, Germany, forschungsgruppe_f developed a contribution in the form of a temporary lab and office from which situational interventions into the exhibition were undertaken. The rituals and codes of displaying and viewing works as well as the consensuses and conflicts of opinion resulting from these activities were investigated and questioned with active involvement by visitors to the exhibition.

For Ars Electronica 2003 in Linz, forschungsgruppe_f is planning an open research station that takes the festival theme "Code—The Language of Our Time" into account with the focus on human factors in processes of designation. With performative means and corresponding personnel, a "tool" will be fashioned in collaboration with the audience on site and situationally utilized. Current issues like "friendly fire" will be part of the mix.

Project Management: Cecilia Hausheer
Curator: Cecilia Hausheer
Selection / Coordination of the Departments:
Fine Arts: Nadia Gisler, Felix S. Huber, Prof. Christoph Schenker
Film / Video: Prof. Marille Hahn
New Media: Prof. Christian Hübler, Alexander Tuchacek
Photography: Georg Winter, Prof. Ulrich Görlich
Best Boy: Prof. Giaco Schiesser
Film Programm for the Moviemento Cinema: Prof. Marille Hahne, Barbara Weber

HGKZ ...seit 125 jahren
HOCHSCHULE FÜR GESTALTUNG UND KUNST ZÜRICH
>>DEPARTEMENT MEDIEN & KUNST

MEDIA | ART | EDUCATION is supported by Pro Helvetia and the Embassy of Switzerland, Vienna
MEDIEN | KUNST | AUSBILDUNG wird unterstützt von Pro Helvetia und der Schweizer Botschaft, Wien

Teleklettergarten

Gruppe F.O.K.

The room between the characters of our character input machines is too small. There's hardly any space for bodies. With the world's largest keyboard, we're making room. The world's largest keyboard is a public interface that provides free access to a processor and the Internet. Teleklettergarten's input device is a Kletterwand (an indoor climbing wall like the ones used by Alpinists to train for a vertical ascent) connected to a monitor.
Visitors go through a trainee program to learn software development skills. Programmers and climbers work collaboratively in an oversized programming environment.
We program codes, scripts and tools, and demonstrate functions. In times of software patenting, digital rights management and access controls, one is no longer guaranteed to be able to write and run a function without running the risk of committing illegal acts thereby.

Der Abstand zwischen den Zeichen unserer Zeichenmaschinen ist zu klein. Es bleibt kein Raum für die Körper. Mit der größten Tastatur der Welt schaffen wir diesen Raum. Die größte Tastatur der Welt ist ein öffentliches Interface, das freien Zugang zu einem Rechner und ins Netz bietet. Als Eingabegerät des *Teleklettergartens* dient eine Kletterwand, die mit einem Monitor verbunden ist.
Die Besucherinnen durchlaufen ein Trainee-Programm und werden zu Software-Entwicklern ausgebildet. Programmierer und Kletterer agieren kollaborativ in einer überdimensionierten Programmierumgebung.
Wir programmieren Codes, Scripts und Tools, demonstrieren Funktionen. In Zeiten von Softwarepatentierung, Digital Rights Management und Zugangskontrollen ist es nicht länger gewährleistet, dass man eine Funktion schreiben und ausführen kann ohne Gefahr zu laufen, illegale Handlungen zu begehen.

Gruppe F.O.K, Kunstverein Freunde der Informatikerinnen, luxus4all.org, bitnik.org. Mit Doma Smoljo, Silvan Leuthold, kiilo, Mario Purkathofer, Phillip Oettli, Carmen Weisskopf, Valentina Vuksic, Marc Widmer, Florian Merkur, Margit Greinöcker, Aron, u. v. a. In Kooperation mit Mammut, Naturfreunde Oberösterreich, Kunstuni Linz u. a.

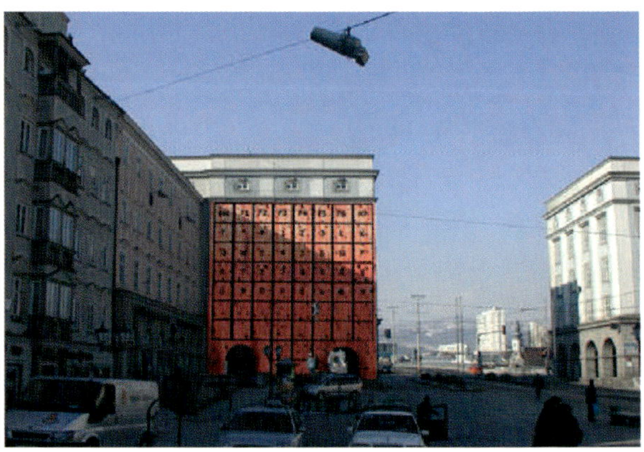

»digital sparks«—Crowning Outstanding Student Media Projects

MARS–Exploratory Media Lab of the Fraunhofer-Institute for Media Communication

»digital sparks« is a competition among undergraduates and recent grads majoring in media art, media design, media informatics and media communication at German-language academies and universities. Works that display an innovative approach to dealing with digital cultural technologies are singled out for recognition in this competition. Each year, 421 prizes designed to foster talented individuals in the plastic arts are awarded in Germany; however, only 20 of them go to recipients in media art fields and, of these, fewer than a half dozen are expressly meant for young artists. Therefore, the mission of »digital sparks« is to further the careers of gifted students in the media arts and, at the same time, to showcase outstanding work being done at teaching and research facilities in the German-speaking regions of Europe.
The entire competition—from submission to assessment and judging by experts and all the way to archiving the works—is conducted online. The competition is also distinguished by its high level of transparency in that all submitted works are presented online and the experts' commentary is likewise available for all to see.
»digital sparks« is one of the active modules of the *netzspannung.org* Internet platform, the objective of which is to spotlight developments in digital cultures and to compile an up-to-date, network-linked information pool dealing with media art, science and technology. More than 150 institutions of higher education in Germany, Austria and Switzerland were invited to participate in 2003. Prerequisites for a student submission are an accompanying commentary by the professor who acted as project advisor as well as that professor's elaborations on the teaching context in which the project was done. This results in not only a collection of especially interesting projects but also an overview of current curriculum content. A cartographic depiction of all submissions is available at *netzspannung.org.* This interactive map that has been growing year by year provides a picture of innovative places for teaching, research and production in German-speaking Europe, and thus offers users access to information about educational opportunities *(http://netzspannung.org/digital-sparks/flashmap/).* The three best works each receive a prize of 2,500 Euros. This year, the students have the opportunity to publicly present their works in conjunction with the awards ceremony at Ars Electronica Festival 2003.
Production prizes that are also awarded in special cases enable prizewinners to rework their projects or to develop them further. Thus, »digital sparks« is more than just a competition—it is also a media strategy to nurture and support leading-edge media culture *http://netzspannung.org/digital-sparks/*

»digital sparks« is conducted by the MARS‹Exploratory Media Lab of the Fraunhofer Institute for Media Communication under the direction of Monika Fleischmann and Wolfgang Strauss, and is produced by Diane Müller (project coordinator) and the staff of netzspannung.org: Gabriele Blome, Katja Heckes, Kai-Uwe Kunze, Daniel Pfuhl, Felix Schmitz-Justen; »digital sparks« is made possible by a grant from Germany's Federal Ministry of Education and Research. *http://www.imk.fraunhofer.de/mars; http://www.bmbf.de/*
The Info-Jukebox was produced by: Monika Fleischmann, Wolfgang Strauss, Yinlin Li, Christoph Grönegress, Jochen Denzinger, Ansgar Himmel,Lina Lubig, Gabriele Blome. *http://www.imk.fraunhofer.de/de/jukebox/*

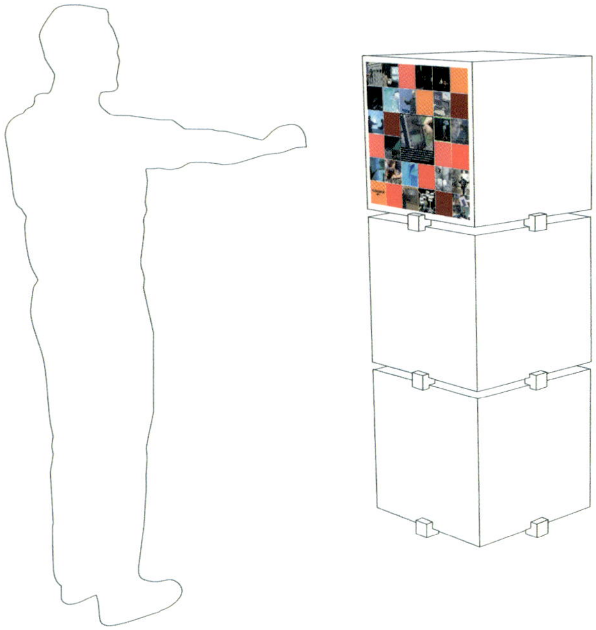

The Mars- Exploratory Media Lab presents all projects on the Info-Jukebox which received the >digital sparks< award in 2001–2003. The Info Jukebox is a digital enquiry kiosk system which allows an intuitive and playful access to multimedia contents. The installation is operated by a touchless pointscreen interface, which allows the user to control the screens with simple hand gestures. The Info-Jukebox will be on display during the festival on the ground floor of the Ars Electronica Center.
http://www.imk.fraunhofer.de/de/jukebox/

»digital sparks« – Wettbewerb studentischer Medienprojekte

MARS–Exploratory Media Lab des Fraunhofer-Instituts für Medienkommunikation

»digital sparks« ist ein Wettbewerb für Studierende und Absolventen in den Bereichen Medienkunst, Mediengestaltung, Medieninformatik sowie mediale Inszenierung und Vermitllung an deutschsprachigen Hochschulen. Arbeiten, die einen innovativen Umgang mit digitalen Kulturtechniken zeigen, werden mit diesem Hochschulwettbewerb ausgezeichnet. In Deutschland werden jährlich 421 Förderpreise für Bildende Kunst vergeben. Davon entfallen jedoch nur 20 auf den Medienkunstbereich, und von diesen sind weniger als ein halbes Dutzend Nachwuchsförderpreise. »digital sparks« möchte daher insbesondere Studierende der Medienbereiche fördern und zugleich einen Einblick in Forschung und Lehre an Hochschulen im deutschsprachigen Raum geben.

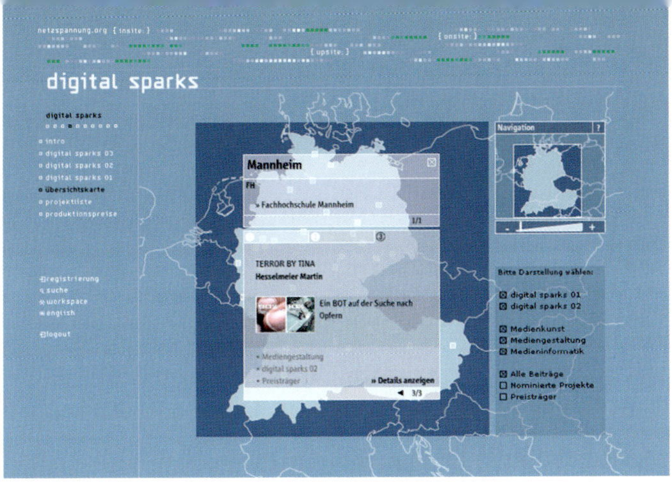

Der gesamte Wettbewerb, von der Einreichung der Projekte bis zur Begutachtung und ihrer Archivierung, wird online durchgeführt. Der Wettbewerb zeichnet sich zudem durch besondere Transparenz aus: Alle eingereichten Arbeiten werden online präsentiert und die Gutachterkommentare sind einsehbar.
»digital sparks« ist eines der aktiven Module der Internetplattform *netzspannung.org,* die zum Ziel hat, die Entwicklungen digitaler Kulturen darzustellen und einen aktuellen und vernetzten Informationspool der Medienkunst, Wissenschaft und Technologie aufzubauen. Mehr als 150 Hochschulen in Deutschland, Österreich und der Schweiz wurden 2003 aufgerufen, sich zu beteiligen. Voraussetzung für die Einreichung eines studentischen Beitrags war der Kommentar des betreuenden Professors sowie dessen Erläuterungen zum Kontext der Lehre. Dadurch entsteht nicht nur eine Sammlung besonders interessanter Projekte, sondern auch eine Übersicht aktueller Lehrinhalte.
Alle Beiträge sind auf *netzspannung.org* in einer kartografischen Darstellung publiziert. Diese jährlich wachsende interaktive Karte macht innovative Lehr-, Lern- und Produktionsorte im deutschsprachigen Raum sichtbar und bietet somit Zugang zu Informationen über Ausbildungsmöglichkeiten *(http://netzspannung.org/digital-sparks/flashmap/).*
Die drei besten Arbeiten werden mit Preisen von je 2.500 Euro ausgezeichnet. Die Studenten haben in diesem Jahr die Gelegenheit, ihre Projekte im Rahmen der Preisverleihung auf der „Ars Electronica“ zu präsentieren.
Die in besonderen Fällen vergebenen Produktionspreise ermöglichen den Preisträgern die Weiter- oder Neuentwicklung ihrer Projekte. »digital sparks« ist daher mehr als nur ein Wettbewerb: Es ist eine mediale Strategie, um die aktuelle junge Medienkultur zu unterstützen.

Alle in den Jahren 2001 bis 2003 ausgezeichneten Arbeiten werden während des gesamten Festivals auf der *Info-Jukebox* im Erdgeschoss des Ars Electronica Centers gezeigt. Die *Info-Jukebox* ist ein digitales Kiosk-System, das einen intuitiven und spielerischen Zugang zu multimedialen Inhalten erlaubt. Die Benutzer interagieren mittels Gesten durch bloßes Zeigen auf digitale Artefakte – völlig ohne Berührung.
http://netzspannung.org/digital-sparks/
http://www.imk.fraunhofer.de/de/jukebox/

»digital sparks« wird vom MARS – Exploratory Media Lab des Fraunhofer-Instituts für Medienkommunikation unter der Leitung von Monika Fleischmann und Wolfgang Strauss veranstaltet und von Diane Müller (Projektkoordination) und dem netzspannung.org–Team durchgeführt: Gabriele Blome, Katja Heckes, Kai-Uwe Kunze, Daniel Pfuhl, Felix Schmitz-Justen. »digital sparks« wird vom deutschen Bundesministerium für Bildung und Forschung gefördert. *http://www.imk.fraunhofer.de/mars/; http://www.bmbf.de/*
Die Info-Jukebox wurde produziert von: Monika Fleischmann, Wolfgang Strauss, Yinlin Li, Christoph Grönegress, Jochen Denzinger, Ansgar Himmel, Lina Lubig, Gabriele Blome. *http://www.imk.fraunhofer.de/de/jukebox/*

Codes did not come into existence with the advent of programmable machines; long before this, the cinema itself, as a still largely non-digital medium, had developed codes, which we now regard as something to be taken completely for granted and which are therefore difficult to reflect upon.
But the history of film is, among other things, always a history of the depiction of codes—of communication that accompanies the language, that gets around it and transcends it. This series of films attempts to open up a realm in which code is defined and interpreted in highly diversified fashion, and where it can become apparent that every code bears complex possibilities as well as secrets for its users.

Codes gibt es nicht erst, seit es programmierbare Maschinen gibt. Das Kino selbst, als größtenteils immer noch nicht-digitales Medium, hat längst Codes entwickelt, die wir für selbstverständlich nehmen und die deshalb schwer zu reflektieren sind. Die Geschichte des Films ist aber immer auch eine Geschichte der Abbildung von Codes: von Kommunikation, die die Sprache begleitet, sie unterläuft und sie transzendiert. Die Filmreihe versucht einen Raum zu öffnen, in dem „Code" vielfältig verortet wird und wo sichtbar werden kann, dass jeder Code für seine BenutzerInnen komplexe Möglichkeiten aber auch Geheimnisse birgt.

Program

Jenseits der Stille

D 1996. 100 min. Director: Caroline Link.

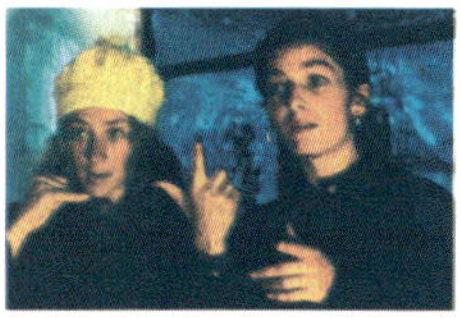

Laura grows up as a non-hearing-impaired daughter of deaf parents. In this melodrama, she moves back and forth between a speaking world and a silent one, and must ultimately defend her love for playing the clarinet against her father's lack of understanding.

Kira (Dogma #21)

DK 2001. 94 min. Director: Ole Christian Madsen.

The Austrian premiere of a drama shot according to the rules of Dogma 95. Following her stay in a psychiatric facility, Kira's behavior calls into question bourgeois conceptions of marriage, motherhood and the representation of social status.

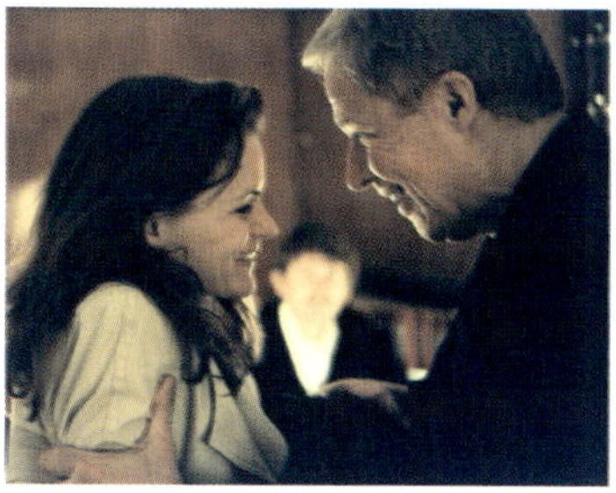

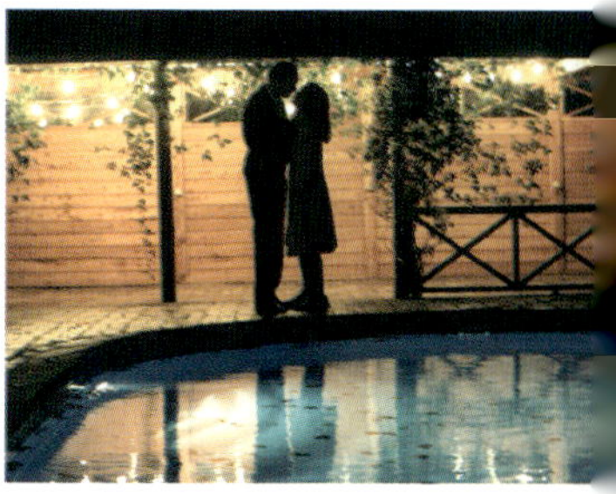

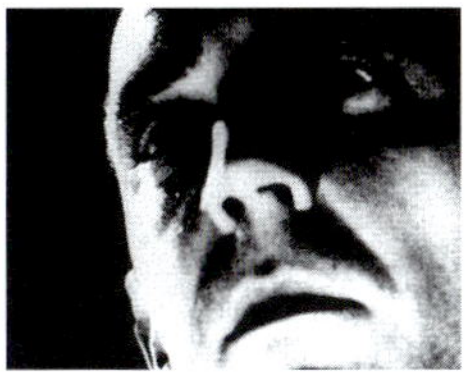
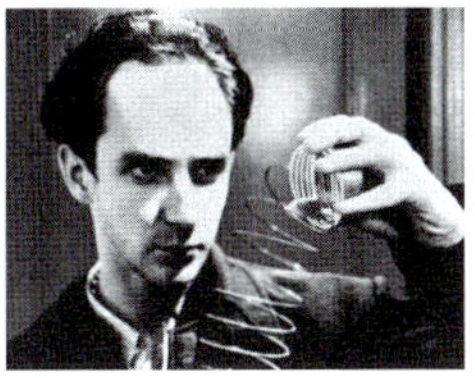

Pi
USA 1997. 85 min. Director: Darren Aronofsky.

With the help of Cabala and the Pi constant, Max Cohen is attempting to discover a mathematical code that explains the world. Meanwhile, he's being pursued by an unscrupulous Wall Street firm and a Jewish sect. When he finally succeeds in breaking the code, Max makes a discovery for which all are ready to kill him.

The Pillow Book
GB/NL/F 1996. 123 min. Director: Peter Greenaway.

Greenaway's visually opulent and expressive tribute to the art of calligraphy. A young Japanese woman whose father paints her body with pictograms every year on her birthday until she becomes an adult flees from an arranged marriage. Then she finds a man whose own body awakes in her the desire to begin writing herself.

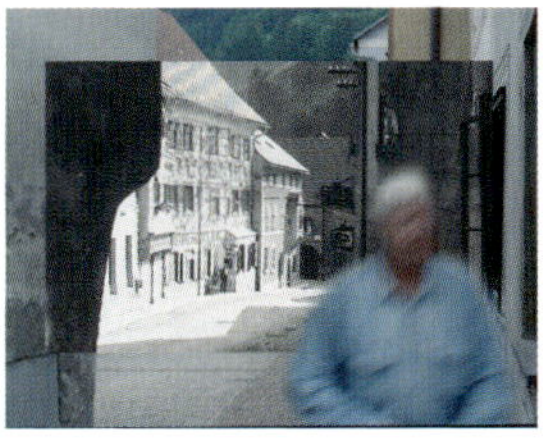
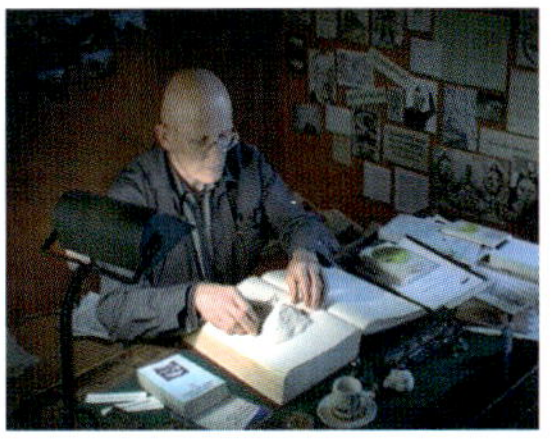

Im Anfang war der Blick
A/LUX 2002. 45 min. Director: Bady Minck.

The avant-garde filmmaker has assembled thousands of postcards into a critical reconquest of idyllic Biedermeier landscapes. In breathtaking montages, she penetrates the sultry colorfulness of the postcards without ever succumbing to their campy charms.

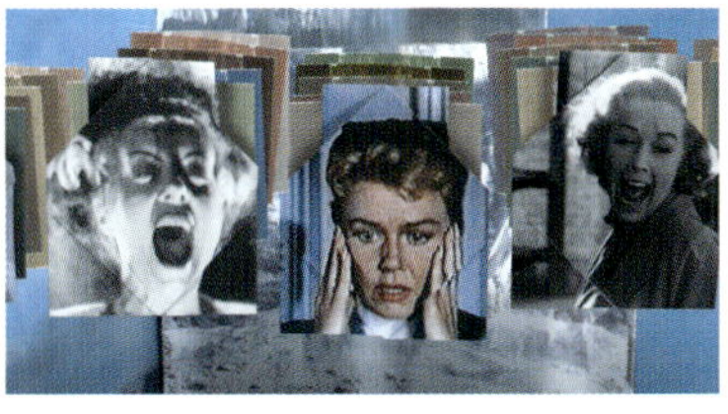
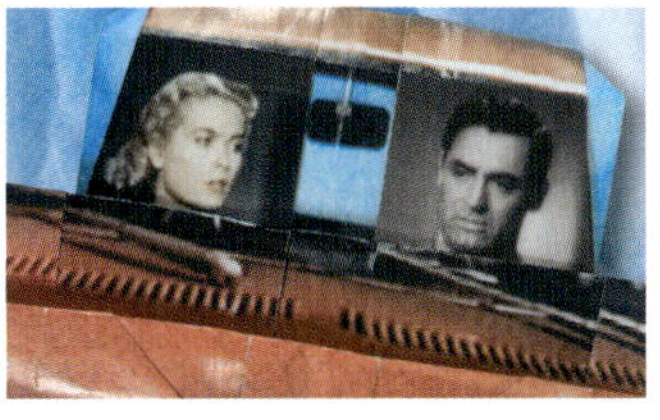

Preliminary Short: Fast Film.
A/Lux 2003. 14 min. Director: Virgil Widrich.

A chase scene through film chase scenes, staged with found footage consisting of individual images of chase scenes that have been printed out and animated on paper.

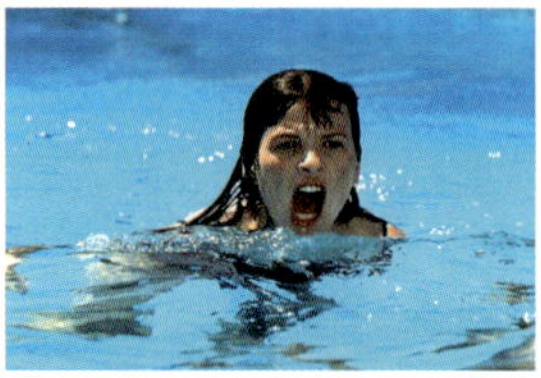

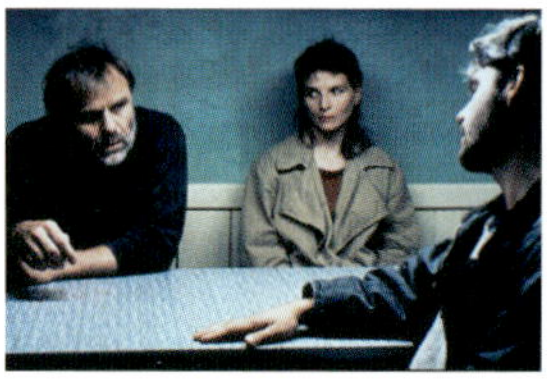

Code inconnu
F/D 2000. 116 min. Director: Michael Haneke

Michael Haneke's theme is communication and how it doesn't come about (any more), or does so only through acts of violence. In fragmentary, brilliantly narrated episodes, he plumbs the depths of various codes in this puzzling game in search of their relevance to the present.

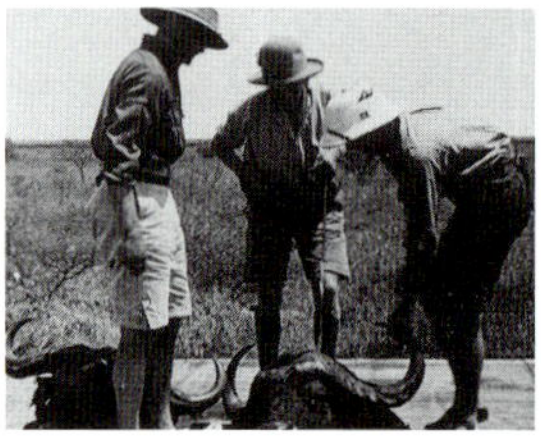

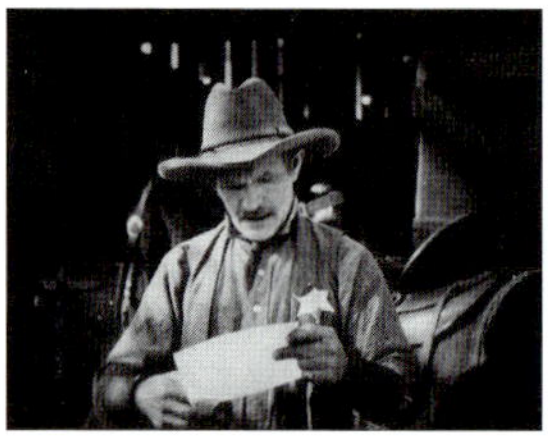

Film ist. 1- 6 / 7 – 12
A 1998 / 2002. 60 min / 93 min. Director: Gustav Deutsch.

This gigantic tableau film presented as a work in progress focuses on a number of different aspects of film and its history—for example, movement and time, light and darkness, a mirror, magic, conquest, feeling and passion.

Die Schönste
East Germany 1957. 86 min / 58 min. Director: Ernesto Remani.

The loss of a valuable necklace transforms a spoiled West Berlin socialite; she then vows to give up the wasteful lifestyle she's been leading and to place kindness and goodness above wealth and possessions.
On hand are the 1957 original version (86 min.) that was not approved by the Communist Party's Central Committee, as well as the abridged version (58 min) that also includes an additional subplot featuring actor Manfred Krug but otherwise has been radically cut. The comparison of the two is a fascinating exercise that enables viewers to take a retrospective look at the big picture of cultural policymaking in East Germany.

Line-up of Films from the Film/Video Program at the School of Art and Design Zurich

This line-up of films was put together especially for presentation at Ars Electronica by the staff of the Film/Video Program in the Department of Media and Art at the School of Art and Design Zurich. It features a representative sample of student films ranging from early undergraduate exercises to degree projects produced at the conclusion of a four-year course of study.

Enhanced digital tools certainly have had an impact on the latest work being done by Swiss student filmmakers; nevertheless, most of the productions by film students in Zurich—dramatic features as well as documentary filmmaking—display a rather stronger interest in narrative plot structures. Many convey the filmmaker's pursuit of his/her own personal form of aesthetic expression.

Thus, the undergrad exercise *wald.exe* is a response to new compositing possibilities using simple digital means. *Faster Movie Kill Kill Kill,* on the other hand, represents an oppositional attitude towards digital techniques, and this work intentionally thematicizes filmmaking on celluloid. *Amnesie* attempts to use an idiosyncratic video aesthetic to enable its audience to cinematically experience the state of unconsciousness of the film's female protagonist. The trio of degree projects on the program displays the broad spectrum of approaches possible in such films. *Timing* is a work in the sci-fi genre dealing with the manipulation of time (including "film-time"). *Der Komplex* is a documentary film in the form of a collage expressing the simultaneity of the real situation of many residents of a high-rise housing project. Finally, *Wunderland* is a cinematic essay created with minimal production resources; unencumbered by laborious shooting techniques, the filmmaker has created—in the form of a cinematic postcard—a poetic documentation of his personal father-son relationships.

Das Filmprogramm wurde speziell für die Präsentation an der Ars Electronica vom Studienbereich Film / Video im Departement Medien und Kunst an der Hochschule für Gestaltung und Kunst in Zürich zusammengestellt. Es präsentiert einen kleinen Querschnitt durch studentische Filmproduktionen mit Übungen aus den unteren Semestern wie auch Diplomfilmen am Ende der vierjährigen Ausbildung.

Erweiterte digitale Tools beeinflussen auch das Filmschaffen der jungen Schweizer FilmstudentInnen. Die meisten studentischen Produktionen an der Züricher Filmausbildung deuten jedoch mehr noch auf ein vorrangiges Interesse an narrativen Erzählstrukturen im fiktionalen wie auch dokumentarischen Bereich hin. Viele Filme drücken die Suche nach einem eigenen ästhetischen Ausdruck aus. Dabei reagiert die Fingerübung *wald.exe* auf die neuen Möglichkeiten des Compositing mit einfachen digitalen Mitteln. *Faster Movie Kill Kill Kill* steht dagegen für eine Antihaltung zum Digitalen, der Film thematisiert bewusst das Filmemachen auf Zelluloid. „Amnesie" versucht mit einer eigenwilligen Videoästhetik, den Zustand der Bewusstlosigkeit der Protagonistin filmisch nachzuempfinden.

Die drei Diplomfilme im Programm zeigen die Bandbreite möglicher Diplomfilmproduktionen. Während *Timing* 1999 sich im Science-Fictiongenre mit der Manipulation von Zeit (auch der Filmzeit) beschäftigt, widmet sich der Dokumentarfilm *Der Komplex* collagenartig der Gleichzeitigkeit realer Situation vieler Hausbewohner einer Hochbausiedlung. *Wunderland* schließlich ist ein essayistischer Film, hergestellt mit minimalen Produktionsmitteln. Befreit von beschwerlicher Aufnahmetechnik entstand in Form einer filmischen Postkarte ein poetisches Dokument über die persönlichen Vater-Sohn-Beziehungen des Filmemachers.

(Prof. Marille Hahne)

Wald.exe

Thomas Gerber, 2002, Beta SP, color, 1:40 min.

By a pond on a sunny morning in May, a frog becomes a witness to how flora and fauna are slowly turning topsy-turvy.

Faster Movie, Kill Kill Kill

Thomas Isler, 1995, 16mm, b/w, 3:20 min.

A celebration in five acts of speed, aggression, intoxication and joy—an experimental attempt to reach the filmmaker's physical and mental limits.

Der Komplex

Fabienne Boesch, degree project 2002, 35mm (Faz), color & b/w, 30 min.

Approximately 800 people representing different ethnic groups and social classes live in Zurich's Lochergut high-rise housing project. A declaration of love of cultural exchange, neighborly tolerance and charming eccentricity.

Timing

Chris Niemeyer, degree project 1999, 35mm (Faz), b/w, 15 min.

A sci-fi thriller in which time has become merely a question of drugs. In CIP, a privately managed prison, Dr. Block manipulates an inmate's perception of time. When Claire Lobos, the facility's psychologist, finds out about it, she has to use Dr. Block's drugs to rescue the prisoner and herself.

Amnesie

Anne-Catherine Kunz, 1999, Beta SP, color, 7 min.

"My mother says I'm just like my grandmother—she simply went to sleep and didn't want to get up anymore."—Thoughts of a daughter in a hospital at 9:59 on a Sunday morning.

Wunderland

Michael Hertig, degree project 2000, 35mm (Faz), color, 11:20 min.

A postcard. A short story about a vacation in a land without borders. Images. A journey. Nothing is fixed, all is in motion. The only constant is that everything is undergoing change and doing so unremittingly. The wonderland is exploding.

Supplementary Notes:

The Film/Video Program has been offered for 11 years in Zurich. With 50 students, it provides the most comprehensive training in filmmaking available in Switzerland. The faculty members are Prof. Lucie Bader, Prof. Margit Eschenbach, Prof. Marille Hahne, Prof. Bernhard Lehner. The course of instruction also features numerous series of specialized seminars conducted by Swiss independent filmmakers. The "Jubiläum-Jubilee" DVD in the exhibition of works from the Department of Media and Art includes 17 additional student productions along with detailed and comprehensive supplementary material.

In cooperation with Moviemento, Linz.

Japanese Animation ACA Media Arts Festival

The ACA Media Arts Festival is an international festival to honor creative works that have developed new expression techniques for Web sites, games, CG, installations, animation, and manga and to introduce the latest media arts to the public and the world.

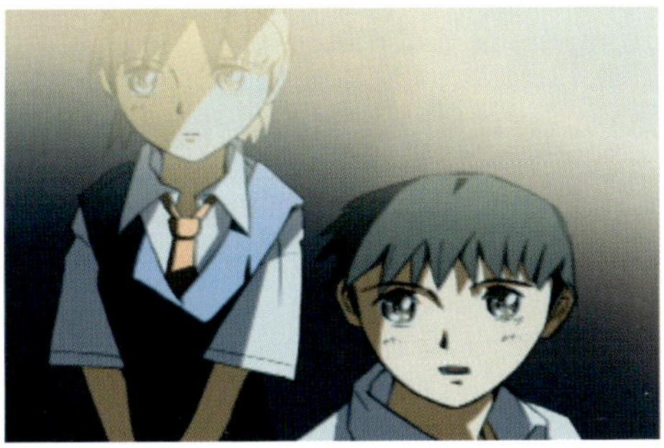

The voices of a distant star

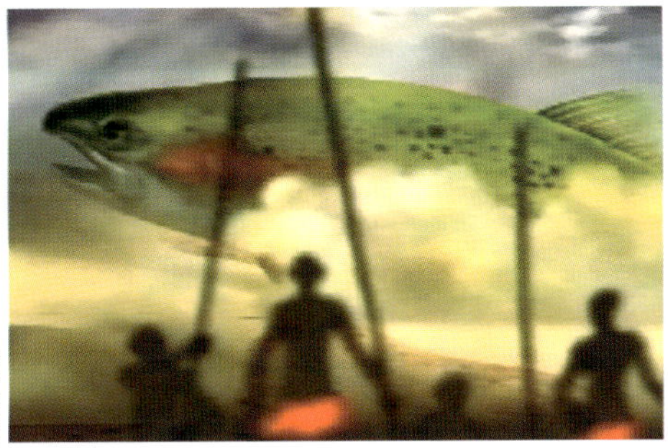

Fisher Man

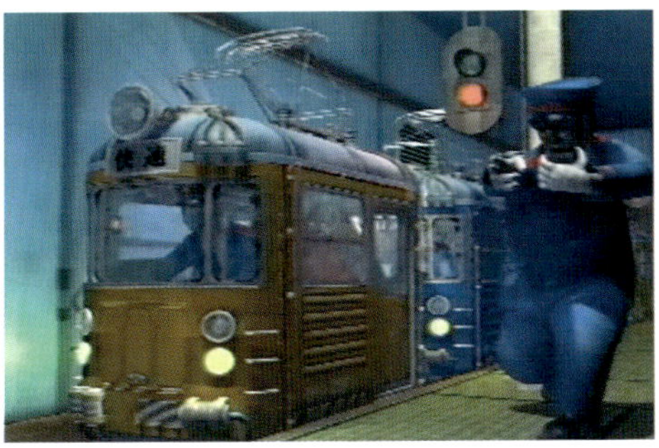

Justice Runners

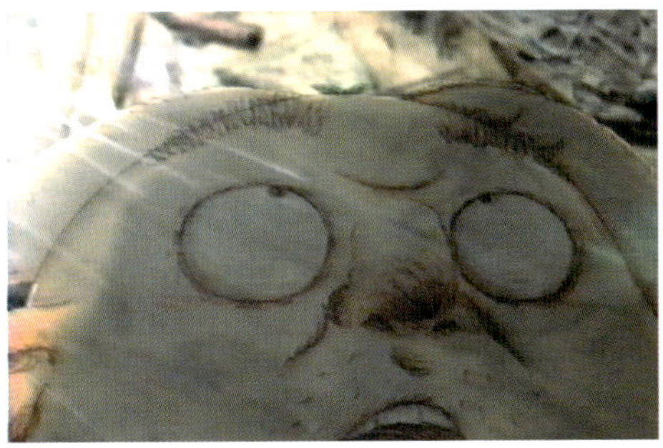

Mt. Head

Winning Works Animation Division 2003

Excellence Award

Justice Runners
Satoshi Tomioka / D's

Mt. Head
Koji Yamamura / Yamamura Animation

Mustafrog and Ninja Bunny
SCORT / Usagi Tanaka, Sayako Hirata

Encouragement Prize

Fisher Man
Saku Sakamoto

The Evening Traveling
Akino Kondoh

Special Prize

The voices of a distant star
Makoto Shinka / CoMix WAve

NOT TO SCALE

Isabelle Cornaro, Heman Chong, Daniel Kluge
Kunst Raum Goethestraße, Linz/Austria

NOT TO SCALE is a space in Ars Electronica 2003 where the word "code" is taken for granted and the terms "life, art and law" are translated into different sets of meanings. Developed by Isabelle Cornaro, Heman Chong and Daniel Kluge, *NOT TO SCALE* sets itself up to interpret the festival's theme in an alternative fashion, locating the works both inside and outside of the conventions of technology and art by way of metaphorical and poetic workings.

Isabelle Cornaro will be presenting a Quest for Reality, where reality occurs through abstract codes and laws. Lawyers, members of the armed forces, policemen, politicians or businessmen are the representatives of a social order which are defined by abstract laws. Often, they might even be the ones who define these laws, inventing them or imposing them. At the same time, they are submitted to external codes. By inserting real people belonging to these social categories and interviewing them in the public space of the KunstRaum, Cornaro seeks to create an enquiry into real characters, evolving in a real space. They will be asked about their social status, as representatives of powerful institutions, which subtly affects the image they have of themselves and also about the notions of authority and charisma that goes with their social function, and its external representation through a coded dressing.

In Heman Chong and Daniel Kluge's Adventure Code: The ACI/SCI worlds of Sierra On-Line, the 2 artists have chosen to explore a fraction of code in time, specifically from 1980 to1999. Through the games produced by Oakhurst based game company Sierra On-Line as a basis for thought on consumerism, miniature worlds and nostalgia, the work can be seen both as research on commercial coding and the world of adventure gaming. Between the imagined realities of King's Quest, Police Quest, Space Quest, Quest for Glory and Leisure Suit Larry, what occurs is a marketplace—communities consuming and developing ancient code. Is code a cultural commodity, similar to collectables like books or stamps or art? What equips code with this status? How is this sheltered from the conditions of acceleration and progress, the core idea behind technology?

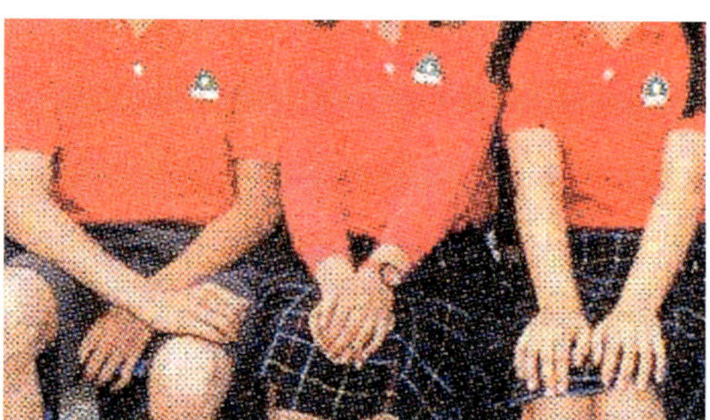

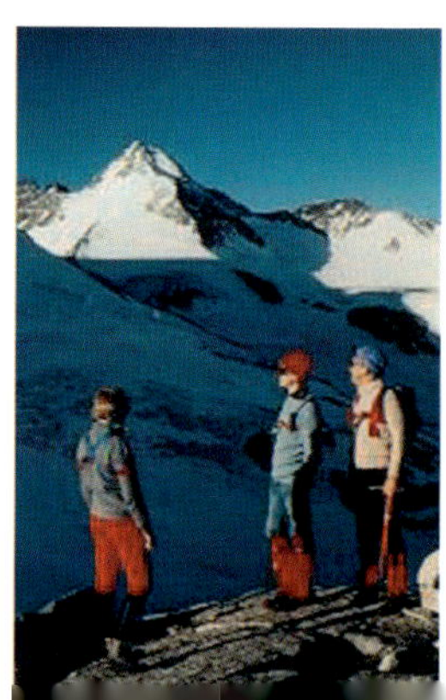

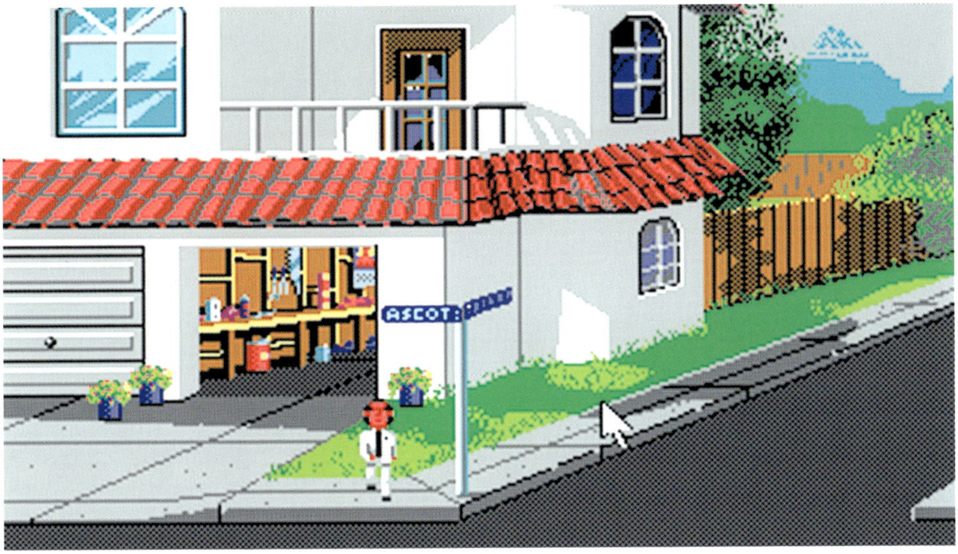

NOT TO SCALE ist ein Raum, indem das Wort „Code" als selbstverständlich betrachtet wird und die Begriffe „Leben, Kunst und Gesetz" auf verschiedene Bedeutungsebenen übertragen werden. *NOT TO SCALE* von Isabelle Cornaro, Heman Chong und Daniel Kluge entwickelt, interpretiert das Thema des Festivals Ars Electronica 2003 auf eine alternative Weise: Künstlerische Arbeiten werden in metaphorischer oder poetischer Form sowohl innerhalb als auch außerhalb der Konventionen von Technologie und Kunst positioniert.
Isabelle Cornaro stellt die „Suche nach der Wirklichkeit" an Orten, wo die Realität durch abstrakte Codes und Gesetze auftritt, vor. JuristInnen, Militärbedienstete, PolizistInnen, PolitikerInnen oder UnternehmerInnen sind VertreterInnen einer gesellschaftlichen Ordnung, die durch abstrakte Gesetze definiert ist. Oft sind diese VertreterInnen auch diejenigen, die diese Gesetze definieren, indem sie diese erfinden oder verhängen. Gleichzeitig sind diese RepräsentantInnen auch äußeren Codes unterworfen. Cornaro führt eine Untersuchung über Charaktere, die sich in einem realen Umfeld herausbilden, indem sie Menschen, die diesen gesellschaftlichen Kategorien angehören, in einen öffentlichen Raum, den „Kunst Raum", bringt und dort interviewt. Die Befragung zielt ab auf ihre gesellschaftliche Stellung als RepräsentantInnen von mächtigen Institutionen, dem Image, das sie von sich selbst haben, ihre Meinung zu Authorität und Charisma, das eine derartige gesellschaftliche Funktion mit sich bringt und auch über ihre Repräsentation nach außen durch eine kodierte Kleidung.
In Heman Chongs und Daniel Kluges Abenteuer *Code – Die ACI/SCI worlds of Sierra On-Line,* haben sich die beiden Künstler zum Ziel gesetzt, einen Bruchteil von einem Code eines Zeitabschnittes, speziell den zwischen 1980 und 1999, zu erforschen.Durch die Spiele, die von der in Oakhurst angesiedelten Game-Company produziert werden, postiert sich *Sierra On-Line* als Basis für Überlegungen zu Konsumverhalten, Miniaturwelten und Nostalgie durch die Untersuchung von Werbecodes einerseits und der Welt des „Spiels mit dem Abenteuer" andererseits. Zwischen den imaginären Welten von King's Quest, Police Quest, Space Quest, Quest for Glory und Leisure Suit Larry kommt ein Marktplatz vor, wo Bevölkerungsgruppen einen alten Code (aus der Antike) für sich in Anspruch nehmen und entwickeln.
Ist Code eine kulturelle Ware, ähnlich Sammelgegenständen wie Bücher, Briefmarken oder Kunstwerke? Was gibt Code diesen Status? Wie wird das vor Beschleunigung und Fortschritt, den Kernideen der Technologie, geschützt?

24!

Michael Aschauer / Norbert Pfaffenbichler / Lotte Schreiber

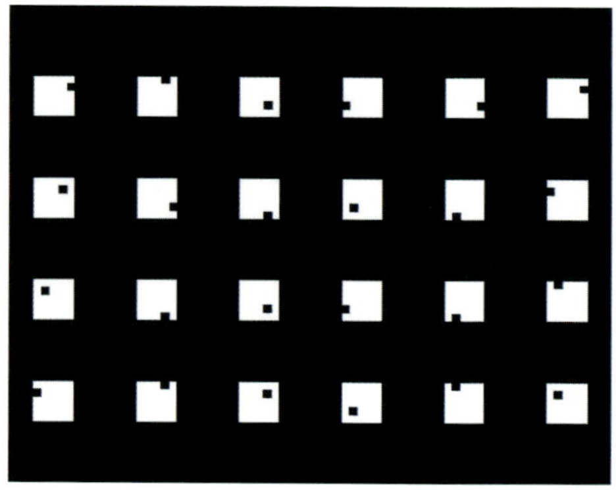

Fundamental Considerations

Binary code is the basis of every digital computer system. Data in and of themselves are neutral; it is only the process of updating them that calls for interpretation by programs—i.e. the stored information must be translated into an event that human beings can perceive. Thus, for example, both optical and acoustic results can be generated from one and the same batch of data. The installation on display here is a systematic and categorical treatment of this phenomenon—that is to say, a simple binary code is translated into spatial, acoustic and optical reference systems. In going about this, we have sought common denominators and dispensed with decorative elements so that the fundamental structure is identical with the final work. The installation presents itself in the form of its own skeleton. Music is by definition the deliberate organization of sound in time (and in space), just as a (motion) picture is the organization of forms on a physical surface (in time) and architecture is the plastic organization of space. A principle that could not conceivably be any simpler is invoked as the basis for a composition and applied in these three disciplines.

The System

This work is based on the bit system, and translates the four possible states that two bits can represent (00, 01, 10, 11) into the Cartesian system of coordinates. The result is the definition of four distinct points whose positions with respect to one another describe the form of a rectangle (which, in turn, corresponds to the shape of a pixel, the smallest visual entity of the computer system).

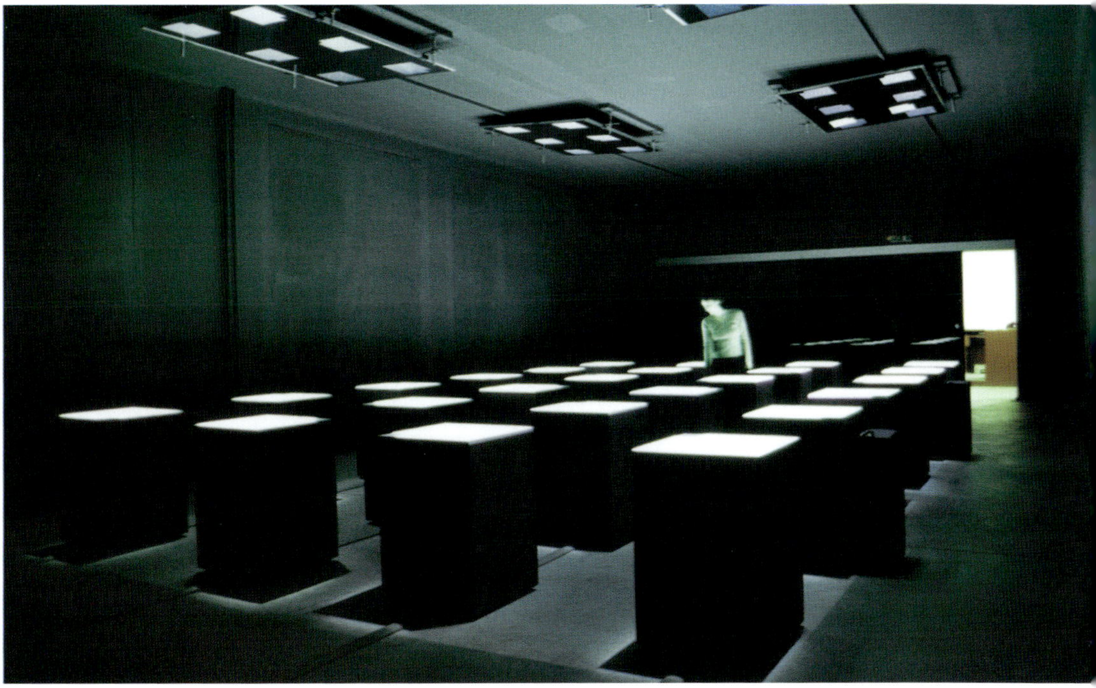

The establishment of six axes of movement lays down a finite number of possible position changes of the four defining points and thus yields 24 different sequences of movements within the specified geometric system (see the diagram). Every possible pattern of movement is combined with all others and played out in all variations with respect to one another, which yields a finite number of 24! (twenty-four factorial) different permutations.
Once a bloc of 24 permutations has been played out, the layout of the pixels is rearranged. Just as in a song's refrain, all visible pixels move in unison in order to then once again regroup and to begin with the next set of variations. The animation is played out alternately at six different speeds corresponding to the number of vectors.

The **installation** consists of 24 pedestals featuring a rectangular base measuring 50 x 50 x 75 cm, which are set up in a uniform matrix within the exhibition space. The top surface of each of these pedestals displays a single animated pixel that horizontally, vertically and diagonally scans the axes of the pedestal's rectangular upper surface. Visitors to the installation can move about freely among these pedestals.

The **audio composition** is based on the same system as the animation. Here, 24 loudspeakers playing a finite number of non-repeating combinations are mounted in the 24 pedestals. Serving as acoustic raw material are digitally generated wave forms—sine, sawtooth, noise—and a direct interpretation of the image movements into sound movements on the smallest digital-acoustic entity of a sample value.

It would take approximately 19,674,289,755,600,000 years to play out all possible combinations of this finite spatial/audio/visual composition.

24!

Michael Aschauer / Norbert Pfaffenbichler / Lotte Schreiber

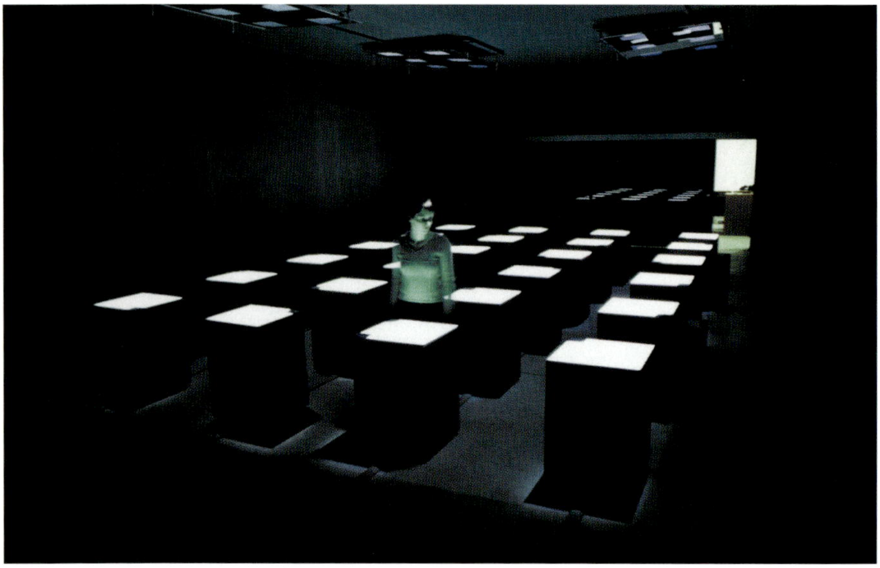

Der Ausgangspunkt

Der binäre Code liegt jedem digitalem Computersystem zugrunde. Daten an sich sind neutral, erst ihre Aktualisierung erfordert die Interpretation durch Programme; d. h. die gespeicherte Information muss in ein für den Menschen wahrnehmbares Ereignis übersetzt werden. So lassen sich z. B. aus ein und derselben Datenmenge sowohl optische als auch akustische Ergebnisse generieren. In der gezeigten Installation wird dieses Phänomen systematisch und kategorisch bearbeitet, d. h. ein simpler binärer Code wird in räumliche, akustische und optische Referenzsysteme übersetzt. Dabei wurde der kleinste gemeinsame Nenner gesucht und auf dekorative Elemente verzichtet, sodass die zugrundeliegende Struktur ident ist mit dem endgültigen Werk. Die Installation präsentiert sich in Form des eigenen Skeletts.
Musik ist per Definition die willentliche Organisation von Klang in der Zeit (und im Raum), so wie ein (Bewegungs-)Bild die Organisation von Formen auf einer Fläche (in der Zeit) ist und Architektur die plastische Organisation von Raum ist. Es wird ein denkbar einfaches Prinzip als Kompositionsgrundlage herangezogen und in diesen drei Disziplinen angewandt.

Das System

Die Arbeit basiert auf dem Bit-System und überträgt die vier möglichen Zustände, die 2 Bit beinhalten (00, 01, 10, 11) auf das kartesianische Koordinatensystem. So werden vier eindeutige Punkte definiert, deren Lage zueinander die Form eines Quadrats beschreibt (was

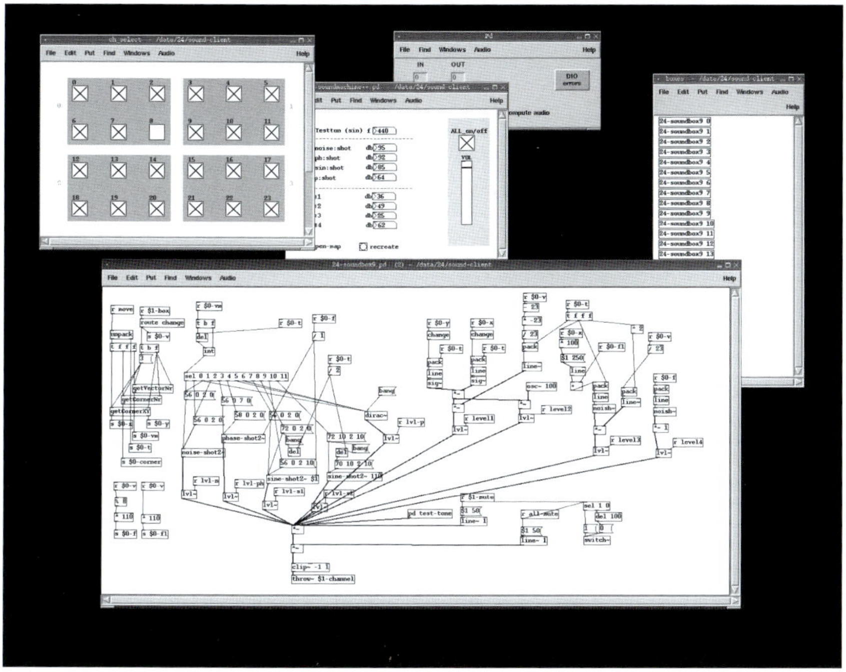

wiederum der Form des Pixels, der kleinsten visuellen Einheit des Computersystems, entspricht).

Die Festlegung von sechs Bewegungsachsen setzt eine endliche Anzahl von möglichen Positionsänderungen der vier Eckpunkte fest. Somit ergeben sich 24 unterschiedliche Bewegungsfolgen innerhalb des vorgegebenen geometrischen Systems. Jedes mögliche Bewegungsmuster wird mit jedem weiteren kombiniert und in allen Variationen zueinander abgespielt, was eine endliche Anzahl von 24! (vierundzwanzig Fakultät) sich nicht wiederholender Durchläufe ergibt.

Nach jeweils 24 abgespielten Permutationen werden die Pixel neu angeordnet. Vergleichbar einem Refrain bei einem Lied, bewegen sich alle sichtbaren Pixel unisono, um sich anschließend wieder neu zu gruppieren und mit dem nächsten Variationssatz zu beginnen. Entsprechend der Anzahl der Vektoren läuft die Animation alternierend in sechs unterschiedlichen Geschwindigkeiten ab.

Die **Installation** besteht aus 24 Podesten mit quadratischer Basis (50 x 50 x 75 cm), die in einem regelmäßigen Raster im Raum aufgestellt sind. Auf der Oberseite jedes dieser Sockeln ist jeweils ein animierter Pixel zu sehen, der die Achsen der quadratischen Sockeloberfläche horizontal, vertikal und diagonal abscannt. Der Besucher kann sich frei zwischen diesen Sockeln bewegen.

Der **Audiokomposition** liegt dasselbe System zugrunde wie der Animation. 24 Lautsprecher – die eine endliche Anzahl sich nicht wiederholender Kombinationen abspielen – sind in den 24 Sockeln angebracht. Als akustisches Rohmaterial dienen digital generierte Wellenformen – Sinus, Sägezahn, Noise – und eine direkte Interpretation der Bildbewegungen in Klangbewegungen auf der kleinsten digital-akustische Einheit eines Samplewertes.

Es würde rund 19.674.289.755.600.000 Jahre dauern um sämtliche möglichen Kombinationen dieser endlichen räumlich/audio/visuellen Gesamtkomposition abzuspielen.

Music Creatures

Marc Downie

This interactive installation consists of a colony of musical creatures that live within the sonic environment of the gallery. These autonomous, virtually embodied creatures have the ability to perceive, act and survive in musical worlds. They possess abstract, simple bodies, the control of which they learn, and the movement of which creates sound. Played out in a spatial representation, fragments of sound heard by the creatures are exchanged and distorted; retrograde variations and repeated sub-segments are swapped back and forth in an accidental, recombinant evolution; sounds from the environment are drawn into the knowledge that the creatures come to possess about their world and their bodies.
In this respect this audio-visual work does not present a *mapping* between sound and image, but rather draws parallels between human-musical problems and the problems of motor control and learning in animals, playing with the very physicality of the sound creation process. A dynamic, spatial arrangement of sonic elements allows us to recapture and recast many musical transformations—passages can be inverted, fused, or temporally manipulated. By transferring musical passages into space, musical problems are transformed into problems for these synthetic bodies. For these artificial intelligences do not dance *reactively,* but move because they are capable of predicting, and to some extent understanding, sound/body contingencies constructed from their own experience. Ultimately these creatures, who in their colony interact with each other, interact with us: we can use musical instruments to directly inject musical material into the colony or let the creatures work with the ambient sound in the gallery space. The adaptation and learning present in these creatures ensure that the colony maintains a position on an edge of musical complexity.

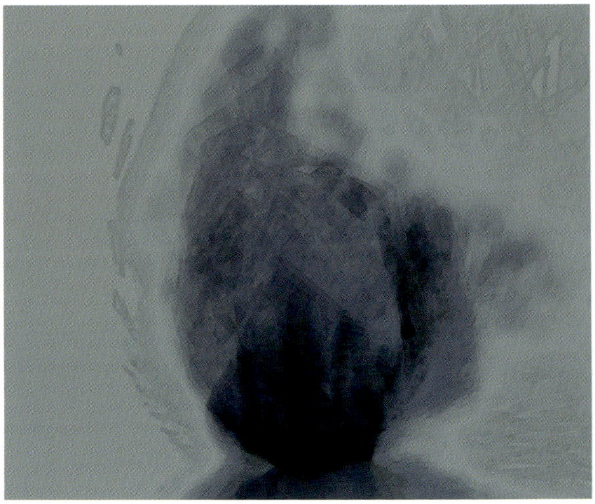

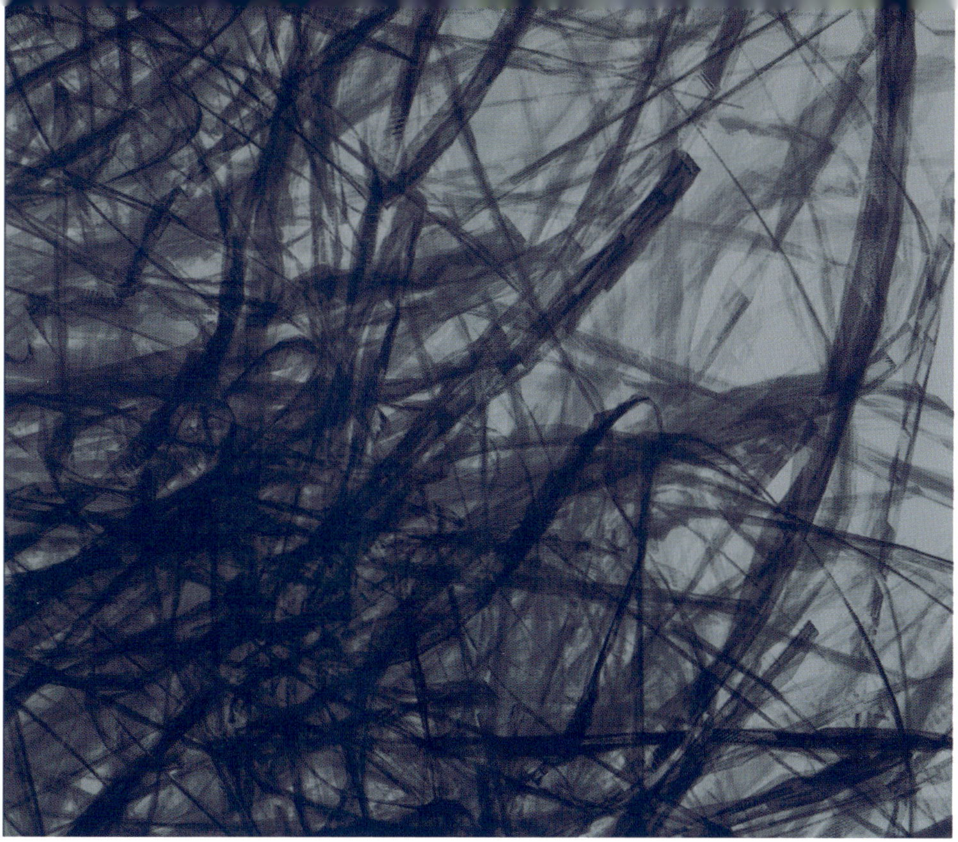

The work of the Synthetic Characters Group at the MIT Media Lab focuses on the creation of expressive, autonomous creatures in interactive installations. These creatures' personalities and interactions are authored in high level terms: drives and motivations, goals and expectations. Our research is grounded on a number of years of work on the design of such systems, and inspired by the study of real animals. In this work we are driven by the desire to investigate not only the relationship between musical problems and motor problems but to engage the (necessarily) biological roots of human music and press the field of artificial intelligence into the service of interactive music and digital animation. In this wider context, we have a bold hypothesis: only by beginning with a study of the animal roots of musical behavior—roots which may include the organization of both sound and gesture in time—can we begin to create systems with which we can interact musically. We further hypothesize that a study of *proto*-musical capabilities and the commonalities of animals may ultimately prove more useful for the creation of new interactive music and in the construction of primitive, artificial, interactive musical agency than any conventional music theory. Therefore, we make perceptive learning and motor representations of these music creatures biologically plausible, in the hope that they will be useful for artistic ends.

Despite a recent resurgence of interest in such *biomusicology,* science cannot yet provide a computationally constructive or artistically useful theory of musical production, consumption or collaboration. And it is unlikely that purely biological approaches will bear fruit without complementary constructive artistic experimentation. These musical creatures are early moves towards these goals.

Marc Downie with the Synthetic Characters Group at the MIT Media Lab.

Music Creatures

Marc Downie

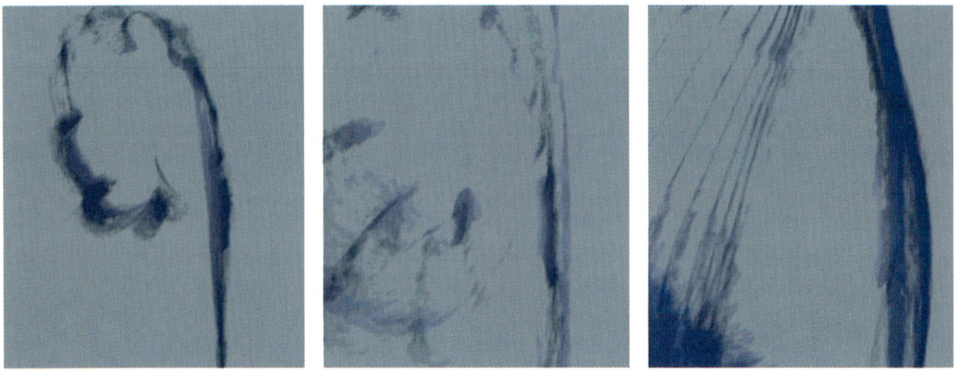

Die interaktive Installation *Music Creatures* präsentiert eine Kolonie von musikalischen Wesen, deren Lebenswelt die Klangatmosphäre des Ausstellungsraums ist. Diese autonomen, virtuellen Wesen können in Musikwelten Klänge wahrnehmen, interagieren und überleben. Sie verfügen über abstrakte, einfache Körper, die sie zu kontrollieren lernen und deren Bewegungen Klänge erzeugen. Räumlich wiedergegebene Klangfragmente werden vertauscht und verzerrt; retrograde Variationen und Wiederholungen von Teilsegmenten werden in einer arbiträren, rekombinanten Evolutionswelle durchmischt; aus der Umgebung gefilterte Töne verschmelzen mit dem Wissen, das diese Wesen über ihre Welt und ihren Körper erwerben. Diese audiovisuelle Installation zeigt keine Fusion von Klang und Bild, sondern zieht Parallelen zwischen menschlich-musikalischen Problemen und jenen der motorischen Kontrolle und des Lernvermögens von Tieren und spielt dabei mit der Körperlichkeit des Klangentstehungsprozesses selbst. Eine dynamische, räumliche Anordnung von Klangelementen erlaubt es, eine Vielzahl musikalischer Transformationen ins Gedächtnis zu rufen und umzuformen – Sequenzen werden invertiert, verschmolzen oder vorübergehend manipuliert. Durch die Beschallung des Raums mit Musikpassagen werden musikalische Probleme zu Problemen dieser synthetisch erzeugten Körper. Denn diese Künstliche Intelligenz tanzt nicht *reaktiv,* sondern die Wesen bewegen sich aufgrund ihrer Fähigkeit, aus ihrer subjektiven Erfahrung generierte klangliche / körperliche Kontingenzen vorherzusagen und bis zu einem gewissen Grad zu verstehen. Und schließlich kommunizieren diese Kreaturen, die in ihrer Kolonie miteinander interagieren, auch mit uns Menschen: Mit Instrumenten kann man Musikmaterial in die Kolonie einbringen oder die Wesen mit den Umgebungsgeräuschen der Galerie „füttern“. Dank ihres Anpassungs- und Lernvermögens nehmen die virtuellen Lebewesen einen Sonderplatz im Grenzbereich musikalischer Komplexität ein.

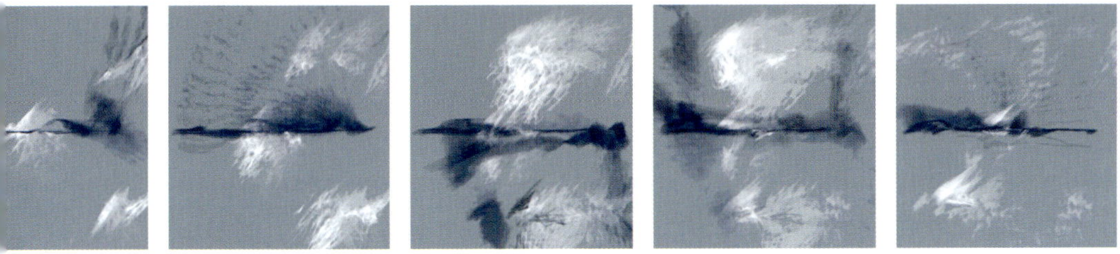

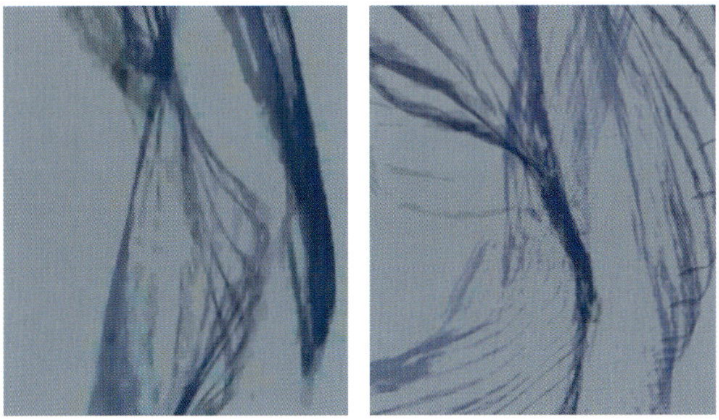

Die *Synthetic Characters Group* des MIT Media Lab beschäftigt sich mit der Schaffung von ausdrucksfähigen, autonomen Wesen in interaktiven Installationen. Die Persönlichkeit und Interaktionen dieser Wesen sind sehr komplex: Sie werden von Trieben und Motiven, Zielen und Erwartungen geleitet. Unsere Forschungsarbeit basiert auf unserer mehrjährigen Erfahrung in der Entwicklung solcher Systeme; Inspiration finden wir durch das Studium echter Lebewesen. Wir möchten nicht nur die Beziehung zwischen musikalischen und motorischen Problemen untersuchen, sondern die (notwendigerweise) biologischen Wurzeln der menschlichen Musik aufdecken und künstliche Intelligenz in den Dienst der interaktiven Musik und digitalen Animation stellen. Vor diesem Hintergrund formulieren wir eine kühne Hypothese: Nur durch die Erforschung der Wurzeln des Musikverhaltens von Lebewesen – Wurzeln, die vielleicht auch die Anordnung von Klängen und Bewegungen im Taktgefüge umfassen – können wir Systeme schaffen, mit denen wir musikalisch interagieren können. Wir nehmen weiter an, dass das Studium der *proto*-musikalischen Fähigkeiten und Ähnlichkeiten von realen Lebewesen letztlich zu wertvolleren Erkenntnissen hinsichtlich der Schaffung neuer interaktiver Musikformen führen wird und sich für die Konstruktion von primitiven, künstlichen, interaktiven musikalischen Welten brauchbarer als jede andere konventionelle Musiktheorie erweisen wird. In der Hoffnung, diese letztlich für künstlerische Zwecke nützen zu können, bemühen wir uns um eine biologisch glaubwürdige Gestaltung der rezipierenden Lernfähigkeit und der motorischen Repräsentationen der *Music Creatures.*

Trotz des neu erwachten Interesses an einer derartigen Bio-Musiklehre verfügt die Wissenschaft noch über keine rechnerisch nachvollziehbare oder künstlerisch sinnvolle Theorie zu Produktion, Konsumation und Kooperation im Bereich der Musik. Es ist auch unwahrscheinlich, dass ein rein biologischer Ansatz ohne ergänzende künstlerische Experimente Früchte tragen wird. Unsere *Music Creatures* sind ein erster Schritt in diese Richtung.

Projekt von Marc Downie und der Synthetic Character Group am MIT Media Lab.

Elevated Space

Thomas Lorenz

Elevated Space consists of films designed to be shown in the Ars Electronica Center's elevator. They were the subject of two classes in the CasinoIT / DV workshop at the University of Stuttgart's Department of Urban Planning and Architecture as well as of the Visual Culture module at the Technical University of Vienna's Department of Architecture and Spatial Planning. These films were made in cooperation with the Ars Electronica Futurelab in Linz and especially with Christopher Lindinger and Dietmar Offenhuber, who not only helped to resolve questions having to do with the equipment's technical specifications and made themselves available for the final installation but also provided valuable input in conjunction with the classroom instruction.

Elevated Space is a project that conforms to and also expands the pre-existing structure of the Ars Electronica Center's elevator. The floor of the elevator car is a plate of glass that serves as the projection surface for a film whose running speed is synchronized with that of the elevator. The film that is shown during a ride from the lowest underground level to the top floor is also interrupted by a brief intermediate sequence whenever the elevator makes a stop at one of the floors in between. This is why passengers do not always get to watch the whole film—all 30 seconds of it, which is not very much to begin with—but rather in many cases see only fragments of the work depending on where they get on and off. In addition to what is by nature an unusual perspective, the fact that viewers are standing upon the projection surface triggers, on one hand, the feeling of being "right in the middle of the action"; on the other hand, one's view is highly dependent upon how many other passengers happen to be riding in the elevator car at that moment.

This setup, in which the projection surface is not limited to a certain form but rather, due to its particular parameters, creates a unique setting that opens up possibilities as well as establishing limitations, emerges as a space in which literally everything can be seen and, at the same time, only certain things can work. Thus, there are actually several spaces superimposed upon each other at this site: the confined space of the elevator car, the space of the elevator shaft that is, in a certain sense virtual since although we know it exists, we never see it, and the graphic space, which can be identical with or totally different from the real space. And finally, there's the "space" that influences us through the fact that one of its facets is variable and can function as a limitation, as a means of making visible, or as an expansion. Moreover—and this seems to be an essential characteristic of this place—the elevator has an added significance: what takes place within it is, as a rule, "consumed" within a matter of only a few seconds. And even though one gets closer to the screen than is usually the case, there is no time to get involved in details. Therefore, producers of films for this installation must decide whether they want to reach their potential viewers as quickly as possible or if they want to take a chance that audience members will eventually figure out what they are being shown after several viewings.

In light of this limited number of possibilities, students at the University of Stuttgart and the Technical University of Vienna have created films that deal with these aspects. In doing so, they have come up with projects that are interrelated in many different ways and that indicate how many forms of images and spaces there can be.

Elevated Space

Thomas Lorenz

Elevated Space sind Filme für den Lift des Ars Electronica Center, die Thema zweier Lehrveranstaltungen am CasinoIT / DV-Werkstatt der Fakultät für Stadtplanung und Architektur der Universität Stuttgart sowie des Moduls Visuelle Kultur an der Fakultät für Architektur und Raumplanung an der Technischen Universität Wien waren. Diese Filme entstanden in Kooperation mit dem Ars Electronica Futurelab in Linz – insbesondere mit Christopher Lindinger und Dietmar Offenhuber, die nicht nur die technischen Randbedingungen zu klären halfen und für die letztendliche Implementierung zur Verfügung standen, sondern auch im Rahmen der Lehrveranstaltungen wertvollen Input lieferten.

Elevated Space ist ein Projekt, das sich in die bereits bestehende Struktur des Lifts des Ars Electronica Center einfügt und sie erweitert. Der Boden des Lifts besteht aus einer Glasplatte, auf die ein Film projiziert wird, dessen Abspielgeschwindigkeit mit der des Liftes synchron ist. Die Filme, die bei einer Fahrt vom untersten Geschoß bis ganz nach oben durchlaufen, werden zusätzlich immer dann unterbrochen und durch eine kurze Zwischensequenz ersetzt, wenn der Lift in einem Geschoß hält. Daher bekommt man nicht immer den gesamten Film, der mit 30 Sekunden Länge an sich schon eher kurz ist, zu sehen, sondern je nachdem, wo man ein- oder aussteigt, oft nur Fragmente der Arbeiten. Neben der an sich unüblichen Perspektive löst der Umstand, dass man auf der Projektionsfläche steht, einerseits das Gefühl aus, „mitten im Film" zu sein, andererseits hängt die Sicht sehr stark davon ab, wie viele Personen sich gerade in der Kabine befinden.

Dieses Setup, in dem die Projektionsfläche nicht auf eine bestimmte Erscheinungsform beschränkt ist, sondern durch ihre besonderen Parameter eine Umgebung schafft, die sowohl Möglichkeiten eröffnet als auch Grenzen setzt, erscheint als Raum, in dem buchstäblich alles zu sehen sein kann und gleichzeitig nur bestimmte Dinge funktionieren können.

So überlagern sich gleich mehrere Räume an diesem Ort: der enge Raum der Liftkabine, der Raum des Liftschachtes, der – in gewissem Sinne – virtuell ist, weil wir zwar wissen, dass er vorhanden ist, ihn aber nie sehen, und der Bildraum, der mit dem realen Raum ident oder von ihm vollkommen verschieden sein kann. Und schließlich der „Raum", der uns dadurch beeinflusst, dass eben eine seiner Seiten veränderlich ist und als Begrenzung, als Sichtbarmachung oder als Erweiterung fungieren kann.

Darüber hinaus – und das scheint ein wesentliches Charakteristikum dieses Ortes zu sein – verfügt der Lift über eine weitere Bedeutung: Was in ihm stattfindet, wird in der Regel in nur wenigen Sekunden „konsumiert". Und obwohl man der Bildfläche näher kommt als sonst üblich, bleibt keine Zeit, um sich auf Details einzulassen. Der Produzent eines Films für diese Installation muss also entscheiden, ob er seinen potenziellen Betrachter so schnell wie möglich erreichen will oder ob er damit spekulieren will, dass dieser das Gezeigte in mehreren Wiederholungen entschlüsseln wird.

Angesichts dieser eingeschränkten Vielzahl an Möglichkeiten haben StudentInnen der Universität Stuttgart und der TU Wien Filme erstellt, die sich mit diesen Aspekten auseinandersetzen, und dabei Projekte geschaffen, die zueinander in vielfältiger Beziehung stehen und andeuten, wie viele Formen von Bildern und Räumen es geben kann.

The Moon and the Soup
Karin Reisinger

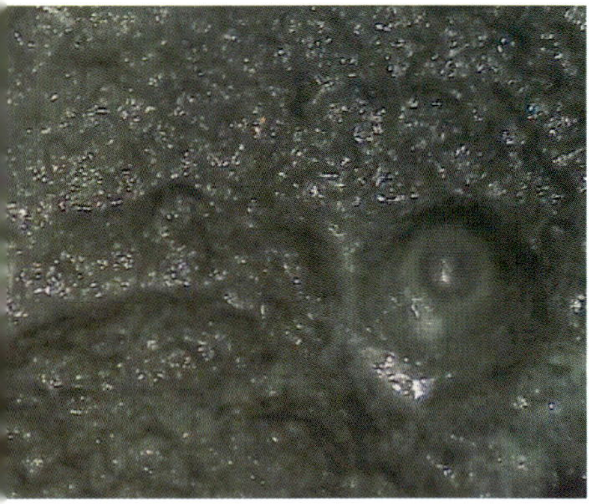

Just like moon formations, there are also soup formations, though they have been the focus of much less research than those of the moon in spite of the fact that, as objects of research, they are located much closer and can be reproduced at will. Thus, the (pseudo)-science of soup formations is also a story about tradition, the private sphere and everyday life, since the true soup movement—in contrast to the public projection space, the elevator—usually takes place at home. Research into soup formations can thus be conducted by anyone; trying out on ones own body the mass-in-motion with its private context can be done only in the elevator in which the film is being shown—and indeed, virtually, as a possibility.

EXIT
Margit Thieme

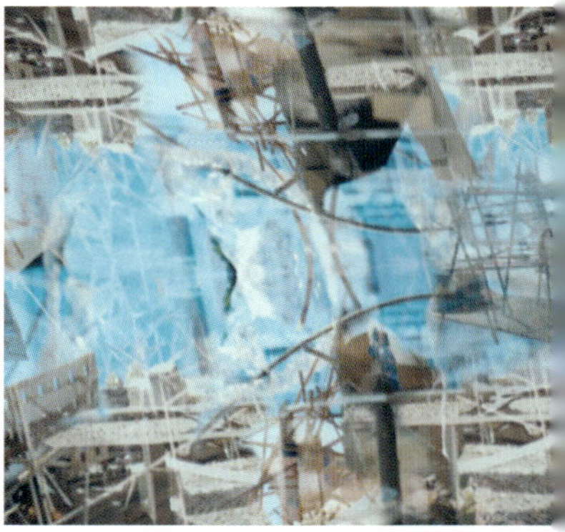

Horizon Line ... This still-widely-unnoticed artistic invention to differentiate every "form" and every "background" ... from one another ... as a result of which we so often lose sight of the zenithal perspective ... a battle waged by relentlessly stubborn surveyors ... for forgetting the differentiation between "above" and "below." All that is meant to remain is the differentiation between "near" and "far," the vanishing point.

Vanishing point ... the vanishing lines that run together at the horizon are not ... the first orientation point of our view, ... but rather the light pressure of a universal attraction that imposes upon us its orientation on the center of the earth and the danger of downfall .... the vanishing point of Quattrocento will now be complemented by the vanishing point of Novecento: Today there is an exit on top ...

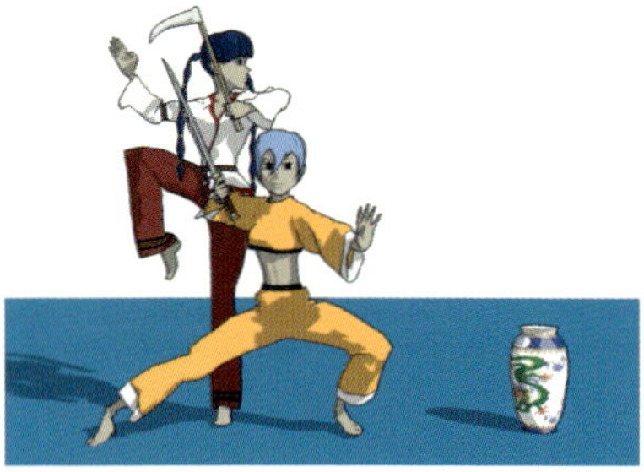

Um-Chi-Im e Je-Sul – The Art of Movement
Andreas Mäule

Due to human anatomy, traveling vertically through space forces man to make use of technical and architectural aids. The space generated by this vertical motion makes other forms of movement possible.

UZUMAKI – The Spiral
Volker Gebhard

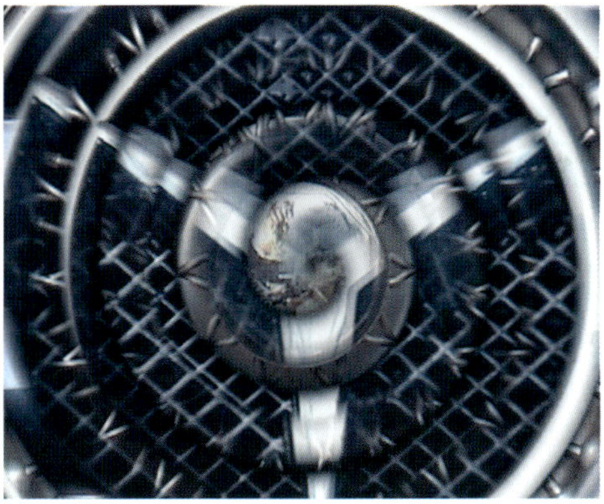

To escape the dogma of the horizontal, man invented the elevator. But this mode of transportation is also the most unnatural one for us. In order to break the vertical axis, it has to be overlaid with a second, undirected movement so that there is no longer a forward and backward, nor any more up and down ...

Pedestrian
Emilie Hagen & Minka Ludwig

Are you totally fit, or do you always feel a little bit lazy whenever you take the lift? Here, you can see in detail what you've been missing in the elevator. How indefatigably industrious people live.

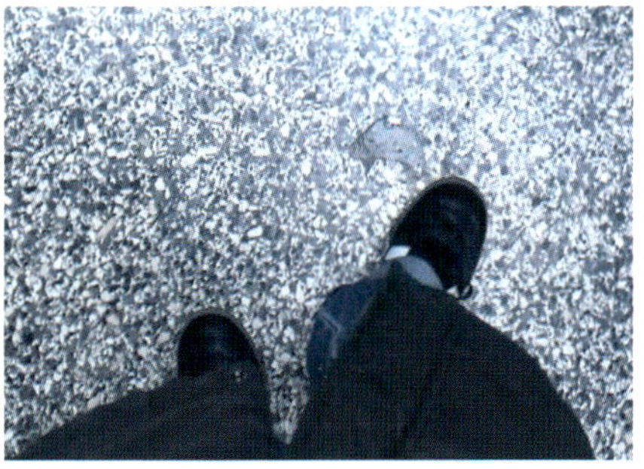

Video ohne Schildkröte (World without Tortoise), Agnes Liebsch & Judith Leitner; Konsumwelt (World of Consumption), Peter Swatschina; non stop, Marco Tschöp; XXX, Alexander Laber; BLACK HOLE / SHOP TILL YOU DROP, Emilie Hagen & Minka Ludwig
All projects at: *http://double-happiness.co.uk/lspace*

Translated from the German by Mel Greenwald

We wish to thank Gerfried Stocker from the Ars Electronica Center for his interest in and openness to the project concept, as well as Petra Gemeinböck, Ingrid Manka, Sven Pfeiffer and Peter Mörtenböck for their substantive suggestions and critique of the work.

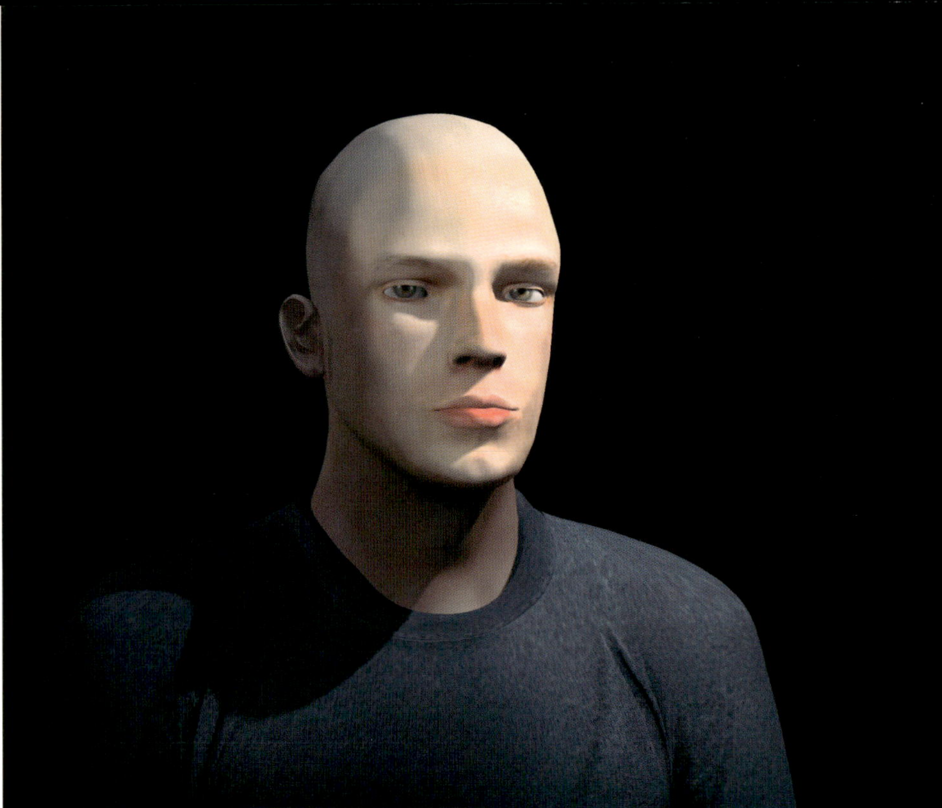

Florian (3D portrait)
Medium : 3D portrait derived from photographic source.
Date : 2003 (work in progress) © John Gerrard

Networked Portrait

John Gerrard

Networked Portrait presents a contemporary portrait diptych composed of two 3D models. The portraits appearance and orientation can be changed by the user in real-time. This is achieved by physically manipulating the surface of the portrait mesh through a touch screen interface.

The screens are hinged and can be turned toward one another, with a corresponding change in the position of the portraits. During this movement the models attention switches from looking at the viewer to looking at the companion portrait. From this point of "eye contact" over real space a series of reactions occur depending on the sort of expressions previously created. Using Ekman's Facial Action Coding System[1] as a source, the strength and nature of the new expressions are judged and a sliding scale of responses ensues, over which the user has no control beyond reframing.

The motivations behind the work were developed along several conceptual lines. One impetus was to reassess the notion of portraiture as static form, and to reconfigure the genre as one that is fundamentally changeable or adaptable. This can develop to include a wider range of stimuli, such as temperature, proximity or temporal aspects, in tandem with manual interventions, as showcased here. In the case of portraits that respond to time passing by incrementally changing, the ideal installation site for these works is the domestic space. This provides the opportunity for relationships to be developed with artworks that change slowly over decades.

A focus of the *Networked Portrait* project is the creation of highly charged, evocative portraits in 3D, from photographic sources, (but not per se photo-realistic).[2] These models were built from the ground up using a multiple of photographic references, rigged for the required animation and polygon honed for optimum performance. Photographic-type portraits existing in three dimensions such as these and in particular photographic 3D laser scans create a break in the history of photography, in which the single photographic moment, long since detached by computer technology from ideas of truthful representation, becomes an object. Sculpture and photography begin to merge and the opportunity to evolve from the collage basis of much work in new media becomes possible. In tandem with the development of appropriate and affordable display devices this trajectory away from frame based representations and the inclusion of real-time control of position and framing using gaming engines gives the contemporary artist the possibility to create what really are "moving pictures" in every sense.

1 Ekman, P. + Friesen, W. *The Facial Action Coding System.* Network Information Research Corporation
2 *Networked Portrait* showcases real people, with the names of the sitters to appear in brackets following the title. The images displayed here are work in progress concept renders, utilising photographic portraits.

Concept and 3D portraits: John Gerrard; Interaction design: Erwin Reitboeck; 3D development: Martin Bruner, Aga Jalsovec; Electronics: Christoph Scholtz; Project management: Christopher Lindinger, Pascal Maresch.

Realised within the Ars Electronica Futurelab artist in residence programme, made possible by Pépinières européennes pour jeunes artistes 2003.

Networked Portrait präsentiert ein Portrait-Diptychon aus zwei 3D-Modellen. Die Erscheinung und Orientierung der Portraits kann vom User in Echtzeit verändert werden. Dies geschieht durch physische Manipulation der Oberfläche des Portraitrasters mittels eines Touch-Screens.

Die Screens sind an Scharnieren befestigt und können zueinander gedreht werden, wobei sich auch die Position der Portraits entsprechend verändert. Bei dieser Bewegung verlagert sich die Aufmerksamkeit der Modelle: Sie schauen nicht länger den Betrachter an, sondern ihr Gegenüber. Von diesem (ersten) Kontakt im realen Raum wird eine Reihe von Reaktionen ausgelöst, die von dem vorher erzeugten Ausdruck abhängen. Anhand von Ekmans *Facial Action Coding System*[1] werden Fülle und Form der neuen Gesichtsausdrücke bewertet. Daraus resultiert eine Gleitskala mit Reaktionen, auf die der User, abgesehen von der Möglichkeit des Reframing, keine Kontrolle hat.

Mehrere konzeptuelle Fäden motivierten diese Arbeit. Einer davon ist eine Neubewertung des Begriffs der Portraitfotografie als einer statischen Form und ihre Neukonfiguration zu einem Genre, das potenziell veränderbar und wandlungsfähig ist. Eine solche Entwicklung könnte neben der hier gezeigten manuellen Intervention ein breiteres Spektrum von Stimuli umfassen wie etwa Temperatur, Nähe, Erregungsgrad etc. Im Falle der Portraits, die auf das Vergehen der Zeit durch wachsende Veränderung reagieren, wäre der ideale Ausstellungsort der individuelle Wohnbereich, denn so könnte sich eine Beziehung zu künstlerischen Arbeiten, die sich über die Jahre hinweg veränderen, aufbauen.

Ein Schwerpunkt von *Networked Portrait* ist die Schaffung von bedeutungsgeladenen, suggestiven 3D-Porträts auf der Basis von Fotografien (die aber nicht per se fotorealistisch sind).[2] Diese Modelle wurden ursprünglich anhand fotografischer 3D-Laserscans entwickelt, die sich

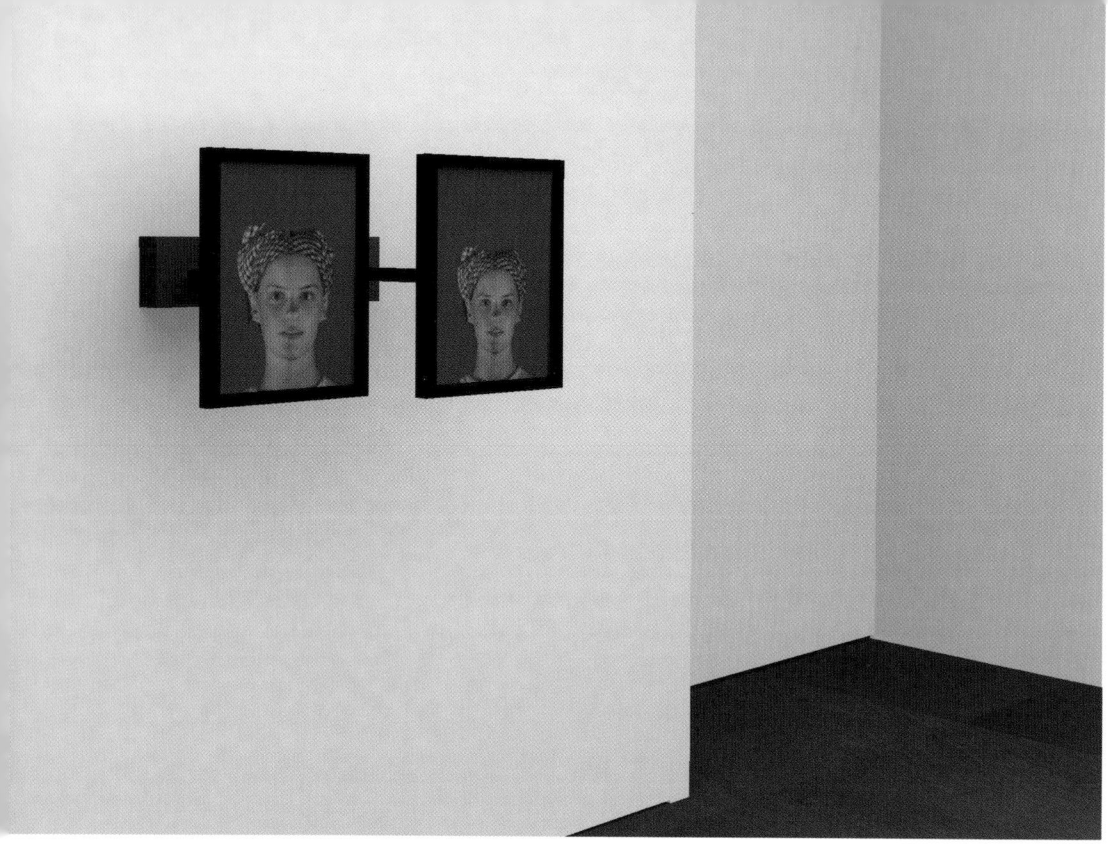

Networked Portrait (3D visualization)
Touch screens, support arm, 3D portraits, sensors, custom software 2003 (work in progress) © John Gerrard

aber rasch als schwerfällig und uninteressant erwiesen. Sie wurden nun durch Modelle ersetzt, die auf einer Vielzahl fotografischer Referenzen aufbauen und die für die erwünschte Animation manipuliert und durch Anpassung der Polygone auf bestmögliche Performance hin optimiert sind.

Derartige fotografische Porträts, die in drei Dimensionen existieren, und vor allem fotografische 3D-Laserscans bilden eine Zäsur in der Geschichte der Fotografie, weil der einzelne fotografische Moment, der seit langem durch die Computertechnologie von der Vorstellung einer wahrheitsgetreuen Abbildung losgelöst ist, zum Objekt wird. Skulptur und Fotografie beginnen zu verschmelzen, und für Arbeiten im Bereich der Neuen Medien, die oft eine Collage als Ausgangspunkt haben, tun sich neue Möglichkeiten auf.

Diese Entwicklung weg von rahmenbasierten Darstellungen und die Einbeziehung von Positions-kontrolle in Echtzeit mittels Game-Engines sowie die Entwicklung geeigneter und leistbarer Displays geben dem Künstler die Möglichkeit, in jeder Hinsicht „bewegte" Bilder zu schaffen.

Aus dem Englischen von Martina Bauer

1 Ekman, P. und Friesen, W.: *The Facial Action Coding System,* Herausgeber: Network Information Research Corporation
2 *Networked Portrait* zeigt wirkliche Menschen, die Namen der Sitzenden erscheinen in Klammer nach dem Titel.

Die hier gezeigten Bilder sind Konzeptentwürfe dieses Work-in-Progress, die mit fotografischen Portraits arbeiten.
Realisiert im Rahmen des Ars Electronica Futurelab Artist-in-Residence-Programms.
Ermöglicht durch Pépinières européennes pour jeunes artistes 2003

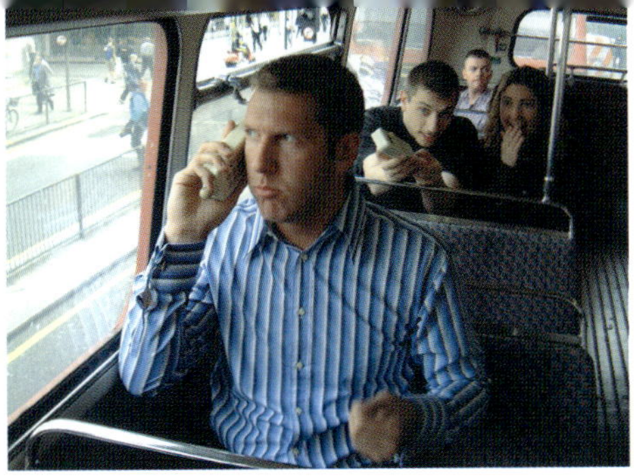

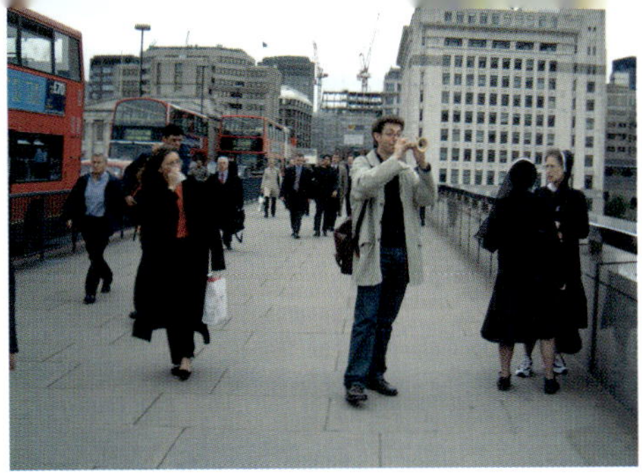

Social Mobiles

Crispin Jones with IDEO

We are interested in the frustration and anger caused by other people's mobile phones. *Social Mobiles* consists of five phones that, in different ways, modify their user's behaviour to make it less disruptive. All the *Social Mobiles* have been produced as working phones.

The mobile phone industry seems to us to be neglecting the problems that mobile phones have brought with them and we chose to focus on the irritation and social disruption that they manifest. Mobile phones were recently voted the third most hated invention of the past 100 years in a poll of Radio 4 listeners in the UK (interestingly the conventional telephone was in the top ten of most loved inventions in the same period). We felt that it would be interesting to design some phones specifically to address this social aspect of the technology, as a counterpoint to the industry's focus on providing new features as a way of enhancing their products.

We felt that the mobile phones had never undergone a period of radical diversion and exploration. This is different from, for example, the car industry, which enjoyed a sustained period of invention and supported plural approaches to the car—mechanism, engine style, carriage form etc. The period of divergence in the car industry gradually converged on an homogeneous approach (use of steering wheel; standardised pedal layout etc) which all manufacturers largely adhere to today. Mobile phones in contrast appear to have remained largely unchanged in form and interaction since the very earliest models. We felt that this resistance to exploration was limiting the possibilities for the interactive experience of the mobile phone. *Social Mobiles* is an attempt to redress this by introducing some radical new ideas to the interaction and function of the mobile phone.

Social Mobiles was undertaken in collaboration with international design consultancy IDEO. The project was realised with the collaboration of designers from a broad range of disciplines. Having this participation allowed us to produce some extremely sophisticated prototypes both in terms of their form and their function. The form of the phone was carefully considered so that it has a neutrality. We wanted it to be clear that these handsets are not presenting themselves as the "next" mobile phone. The handsets are designed to appear quite difficult to place in terms of when they were made—they look simultaneously old- fashioned and contemporary and utilise non-standard mobile phone materials: for example wood. We hoped that the neutrality of the handsets would make it clear to viewers that the focus was the interaction of the handset, rather than simply its form.

Core team: Crispin Jones, Graham Pullin, Mat Hunter, Anton Schubert

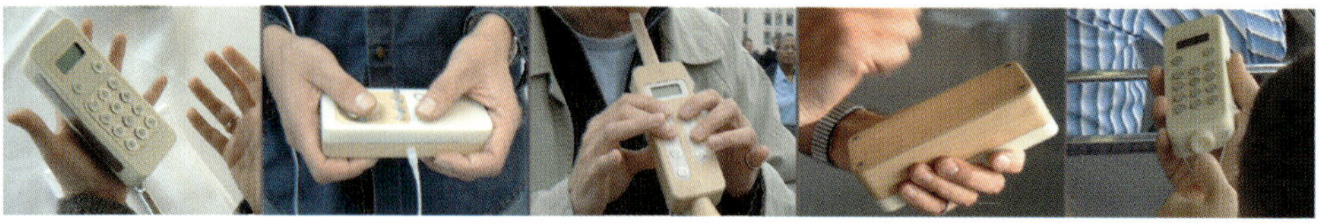

Social Mobiles

Crispin Jones / IDEO

Wir untersuchen die Frustration und Wut, die Mobiltelefone anderer Leute hervorrufen. *Social Mobiles* besteht aus fünf Mobiltelefonen, die mit unterschiedlichsten Methoden das Verhalten ihrer Benutzer so verändern, dass es weniger störend wirkt. Sämtliche *Social Mobiles* sind voll funktionsfähige Geräte.

Offensichtlich ignoriert die Handyindustrie die durch Mobiltelefone entstandenen Probleme, weshalb wir uns auf diese Irritationen und gesellschaftlichen Störmomente konzentrieren. In einer erst kürzlich im Vereinigten Königreich von *Radio 4* durchgeführten Umfrage belegten Mobiltelefone den dritten Platz unter den meistgehassten Erfindungen der letzten hundert Jahre (während das herkömmliche Telefon zu den zehn beliebtesten Erfindungen im selben Zeitraum gehörte). Daher wollten wir Telefone konstruieren, die genau diesen sozialen Aspekt der Technik ansprechen – als Gegenpol zum ständigen Bestreben der Industrie, ihre Produkte durch immer neue technische Spielereien aufzuwerten.

Mobiltelefone waren nie eine Spielwiese für äußerliche Innovationen. Darin unterscheiden sie sich z. B. von der Kfz-Industrie, die eine ausgedehnte Entwicklungsphase mitgemacht hat – mit unterschiedlichsten Ansätzen zu Mechanik, Motorkonzepten und Karosserieformen. Die Phase der Divergenz in der Autoindustrie wich allmählich einem homogenen Ansatz (Verwendung des Lenkrads, standardisierte Anordnung der Pedale usw.), dem heute sämtliche Hersteller im Großen und Ganzen folgen. Mobiltelefone blieben hingegen in Bezug auf Form und Bedienung seit den frühesten Modellen beinahe unverändert. Dieses entwicklerische Desinteresse führt zu einer Einschränkung der interaktiven Erfahrungen mit Mobiltelefonen. *Social Mobiles* will diesem Umstand durch die Einführung einiger radikaler neuer Ideen zur Interaktion und Funktion des Mobiltelefons begegnen.

Social Mobiles entstand in Zusammenarbeit mit der internationalen Design-Beraterfirma IDEO. Das Projekt wurde gemeinsam mit zahlreichen Designern aus den unterschiedlichsten Bereichen erarbeitet. Dadurch konnten wir einige in Form und Funktion ausgesprochen raffinierte Prototypen herstellen. Jedes Telefon wurde mit größter Sorgfalt neutral designt. Diese Geräte sollten nicht als die „nächste Generation" von Mobiltelefonen verstanden werden. Ihre Gestaltung sollte das Datum ihrer Herstellung möglichst gut verschleiern – sie sehen zugleich altmodisch und modern aus und es kommen ungewöhnliche Materialien wie etwa Holz zur Verwendung. Das neutrale Design der Geräte sollte den Betrachtern vor Augen führen, dass es hier hauptsächlich um Interaktion und nicht einfach um Form geht.

Das Team: Crispin Jones, Graham Pullin, Mat Hunter, Anton Schubert

Aus dem Amerikanischen von Susanne Steinacher

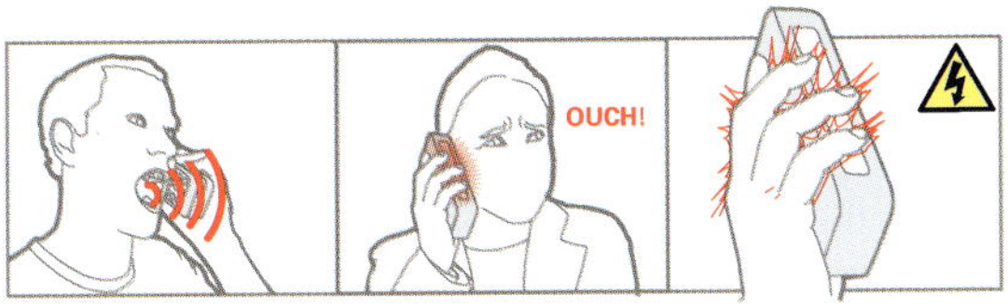

SoMo1
the electric shock mobile

This phone delivers a variable level of electric shock depending on how loudly the person on the other end is speaking. As a result the two parties are induced to speak more quietly. SoMo1 phones would be given to repeat offenders who persistently disturb others with their intrusive conversations.

SoMo2
the speaking mobile

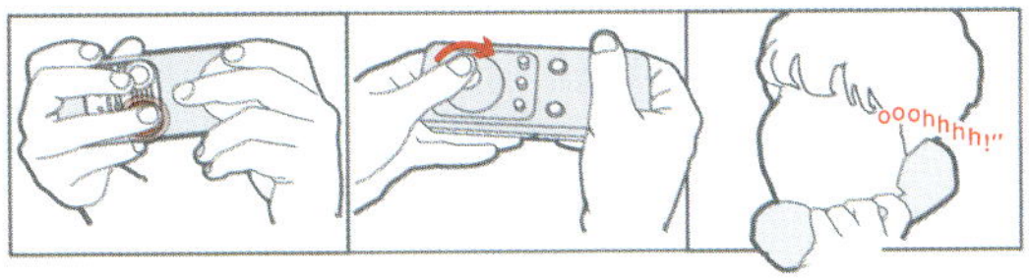

This phone allows a user to converse silently: a person receiving a call in a quiet space can respond with simple but expressive vowel sounds which they produce and subtly intone manually. SoMo2 is the antithesis of text messaging in that it conveys rich emotional nuance at the expense of textual information.

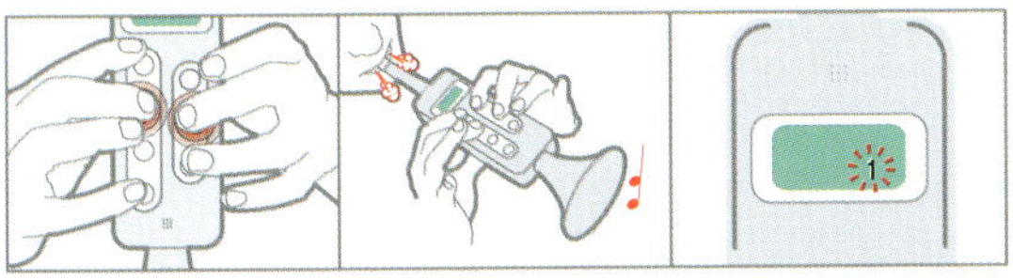

SoMo3
the musical mobile

This phone requires the user to play the tune of the phone number they wish to call. The public performance that dialling demands acts as a litmus test of when it is appropriate to make a call. Children would take phone lessons in order to learn to play their phone.

SoMo4
the knocking mobile

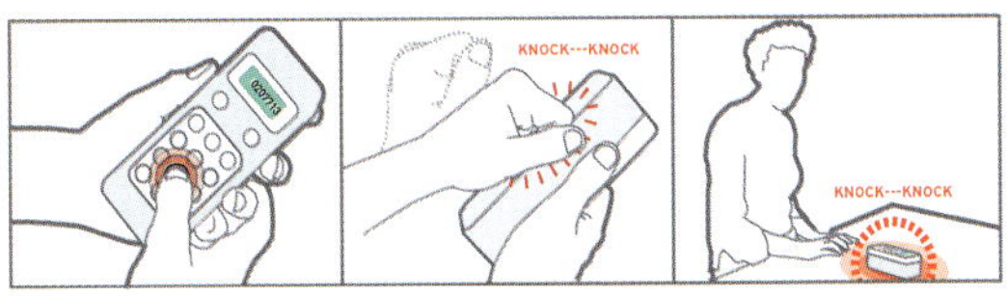

The user knocks on this phone to communicate the urgency of their call. The recipient hears this knock through their phone and can be discerning about which calls to answer. Given time people would learn to recognise each others' knocking mannerisms.

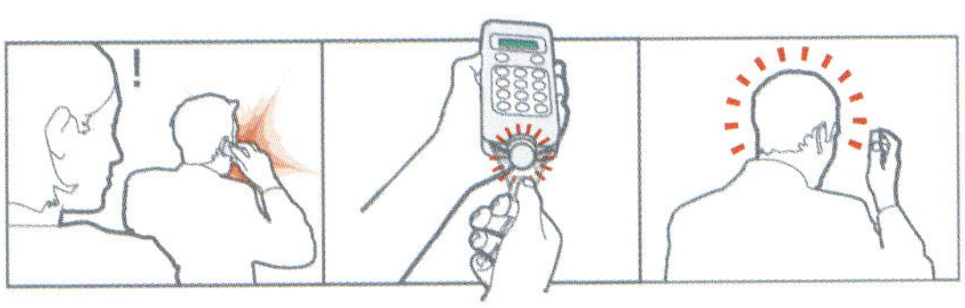

SoMo5
the catapult mobile

This phone can be used to launch sounds into other people's phone conversations. Firing the catapult transmits a sound into the offender's phone. This provides a direct yet discreet way of invading their space. Businesses supply users with a choice of interrupts to launch from their phones.

Audiopad

James Patten/Ben Recht

Audiopad is a composition and performance instrument for electronic music that tracks the positions of objects on a tabletop surface and converts their motion into music. One can pull sounds from a giant set of samples, juxtapose archived recordings against warm synthetic melodies, cut between drum loops to create new beats, and apply digital processing all at the same time on the same table. *Audiopad* not only allows for spontaneous reinterpretation of musical compositions, but also creates a visual and tactile dialogue between itself, the performer, and the audience.

The performer uses three types of objects to make sound on the *Audiopad* table. The "tracks" represent different pieces of the musical composition, for example melody and percussion. Each of these has a set of associated musical samples. The "microphone" controls the volume of each track: tracks that are closer to the microphone are louder than those that are far away. This spatial mixing metaphor lets the performer control the volume of many different tracks at the same time in a way that is difficult with a bank of knobs or sliders, and impossible with a computer keyboard and mouse. The performer uses the third type of object, the "modifier," to change how each of the tracks sounds. The modifier can control digital effects and select new samples for each track.

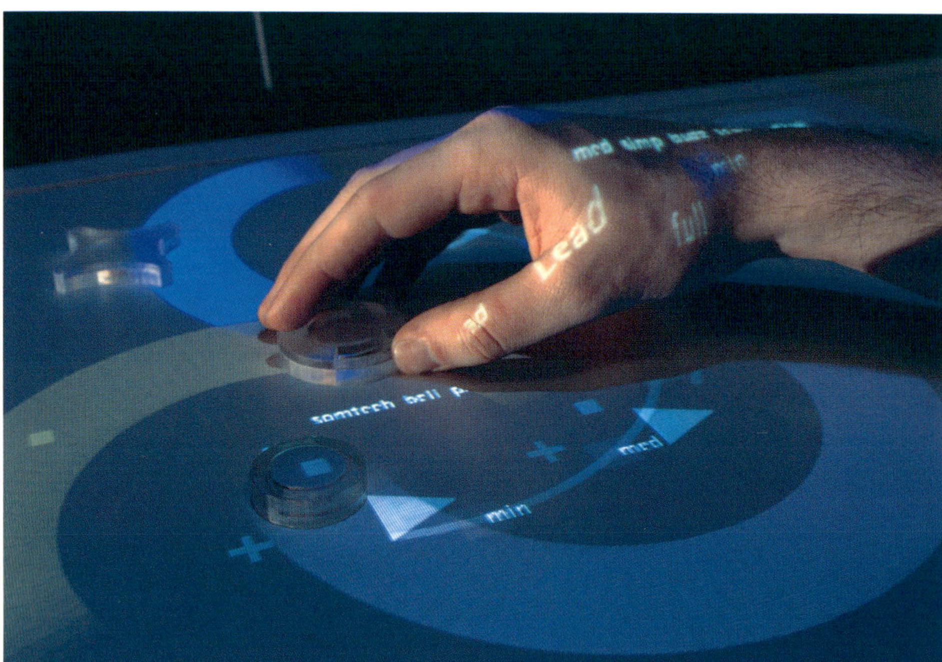

As one moves these objects, graphics on the table reflect what the performer is doing. For example, each track is surrounded by a spinning colored arc which changes to reflect the volume and tempo of the track. Samples related to the current sample (as determined by the composer) are displayed on an arc near the track. The performer can quickly switch between these related samples by moving the track between them. In this sense, *Audiopad* starts to become an embodiment of the composition being performed, rather than just an instrument with which to perform. The interaction between the graphics, the objects on the table and the performer give the audience a view into how the performance is realized.
Audiopad uses a matrix of specially shaped antenna elements built into a horizontal sensing surface that is built into a table. The resonance of these antenna elements can determine the position of a group of LC tags. Each LC tag is a small coil of wire attached to a capacitor that resonates at a specific RF frequency. Software running on a PC translates the position information from the antenna elements into graphics on the tabletop, and MIDI commands for various pieces of synthesizer software. The graphics are displayed using a video projector pointed down at the surface of the *Audiopad* table. The software that tracks the positions of the LC tags is written in C and C++. The remainder of the software is written in Python, and uses OpenGL for graphics.
In creating *Audiopad,* our aim was to combine the modularity of computer-based synthesis with some of the expressive power of traditional musical instruments. In addition, we wanted to create something through which audiences could begin to understand a process through which electronic music can be performed. Finally, we aimed to make *Audiopad* reconfigurable. To prepare for each performance, we rewrite portions of the *Audiopad* software to experiment with new performance techniques and tailor the software for the composition to be performed. In the context of the *Audiopad* installation at Ars Electronica, some of these interactions are not immediately apparent to one viewing the piece. Rather they reveal themselves gradually as one interacts with *Audiopad*.
Audiopad has been developed at the MIT Media Lab

Audiopad ist ein Kompositions- und Performance-Instrument für elektronische Musik, das die Position von Objekten auf einer Tischoberfläche verfolgt und deren Bewegungen als Musik wiedergibt. Man kann aus einer Vielzahl von Klangsamples wählen, gespeicherte Aufnahmen warmen synthetischen Melodien gegenüberstellen, Drum-Loops zu neuen Beats mischen und gleichzeitig auf dem selben Tisch Digitaleffekte einsetzen. *Audiopad* erlaubt nicht nur die spontane Neuinterpretation musikalischer Kompositionen, sondern ermöglicht außerdem den visuellen und taktilen Dialog zwischen Instrument, Künstler und Publikum.
Der Künstler kann drei verschiedene Objekte zur Klangerzeugung auf dem *Audiopad*-Tisch einsetzen. Ein „Track" steht für einen Teil der Komposition, wie z. B. Melodie oder Percussion, wobei jeder mehrere Klangsamples enthält. Das „Mikrofon" regelt die Lautstärke jedes Tracks: Liegt er näher am Mikrofon, so ist er lauter als jene, die weiter entfernt sind. Diese räumliche Mischtechnik erlaubt es dem Künstler, den Pegel vieler verschiedener Tracks gleichzeitig zu regulieren, was mit Dreh- oder Schiebereglern schwierig und mit Computertastatur und Maus unmöglich zu erreichen ist. Mit Hilfe des dritten Objekttyps, des „Modifikators", kann der Künstler den Klang jedes einzelnen Tracks verändern. Er kann damit digitale Effekte steuern und für jeden Track neue Samples wählen.
Jede Bewegung der Objekte wird auf dem Tisch grafisch dargestellt. So ist etwa jeder Track von einem rotierenden Farbbogen umgeben, der Änderungen in Lautstärke und Tempo des

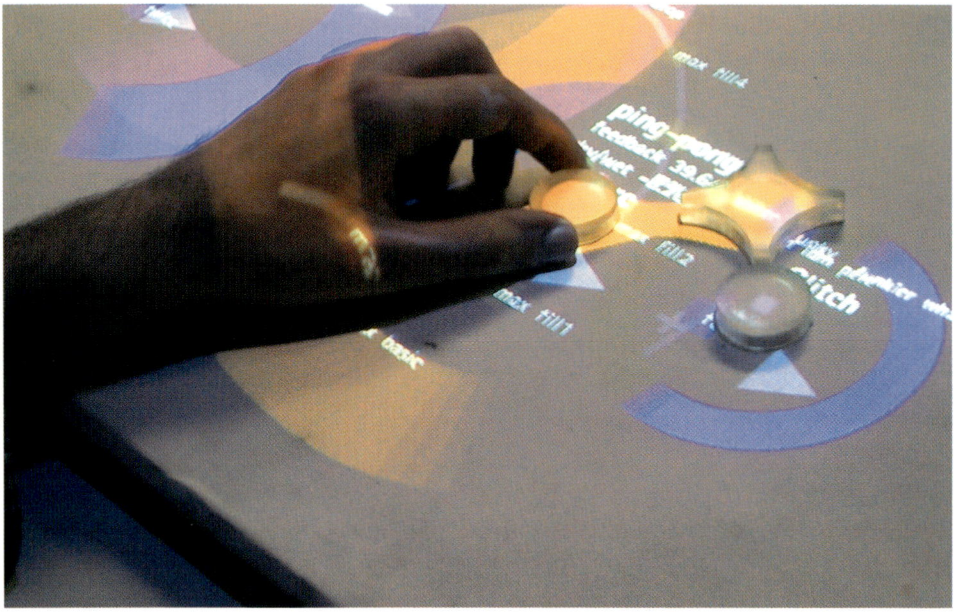

Tracks widerspiegelt. Samples, die mit dem jeweils laufenden verwandt sind (vom Künstler festgelegt), werden durch einen Bogen neben dem Track gekennzeichnet. Der Künstler kann schnell von einem verwandten Sample zum nächsten springen, indem er den Track zwischen ihnen verschiebt. *Audiopad* ist somit nicht nur das Instrument zur Wiedergabe der Komposition, sondern auch ihre Verkörperung. Die Interaktion zwischen der grafischen Darstellung, den Objekten auf dem Tisch und dem Künstler gewährt dem Publikum Einblick in die Realisierung des Musikstücks.

Audiopad nutzt eine Matrix speziell geformter Antennenelementen, die Teil einer in den Tisch integrierten horizontalen Sensoroberfläche sind. Die Resonanz dieser Antennenelemente kann die Position einer Gruppe von LC-Tags ermitteln. Jedes LC-Tag besteht aus einer kleinen, an einem Kondensator angebrachten Drahtspule, die bei einer bestimmten RF-Frequenz zu schwingen beginnt. Eine PC-Software stellt die über die Antennenelemente gesammelte Information auf der Tischoberfläche grafisch dar und wandelt sie in MIDI-Befehle für verschiedenste Synthesizer-Software um. Ein Videobeam projiziert die grafische Darstellung auf die Oberfläche des *Audiopad*-Tischs. Die Software zur Standortbestimmung der LC-Tags ist in C und C++ geschrieben, die übrige Software in Python und die Grafiken werden mittels OpenGL generiert.

Unsere Zielsetzung für *Audiopad* war die Modularität computerbasierter Synthese mit der Ausdruckskraft traditioneller Musikinstrumente zu kombinieren. Außerdem wollten wir dem Publikum einen kleinen Einblick gewähren, wie elektronische Musik wiedergegeben werden kann. Und *Audiopad* sollte rekonfigurierbar sein. Im Vorfeld jeder Performance werden Teile der *Audiopad*-Software umgeschrieben, wodurch wir mit neuen Performance-Techniken experimentieren und die Software an die zu präsentierende Komposition anpassen. Im Rahmen der *Audiopad*-Installation auf der Ars Electronica stechen einige dieser Interaktionen dem Besucher nicht unmittelbar ins Auge, sondern zeigen sich erst nach und nach in der persönlichen Auseinandersetzung mit *Audiopad*.

Aus dem Amerikanischen von Elisabeth Wiellander

Audiopad wurde am MIT Media Lab MIT Media Lab entwickelt.

Ars Electronica Center Exhibition

Han Hoogerbrugge / Wiggle: Flow in a Lift

Flow in a Lift is the porting of Hoogerbrugge and Wiggle's first interactive music video, "FLOW." Its visuals and musical phrases change to the users' actions—the music clip conforms to each and every user.
The Net based version *Flow* has been awarded a Honorary Mention in the category Net Vision / Net Excellence of Prix Ars Electronica 2003 (you find a detailed description of the project in the *Prix Ars Electronica Compendium CyberArts 2003,* pp 64).

LeCielEstBleu: Puppettool

PuppetTool is an experimental animation tool that allows users to generate highly expressive movements unhindered by limits of gravity or elasticity.
Puppettool has been awarded a Honorary Mention in the category Net Vision / Net Excellence of Prix Ars Electronica 2003 (you find a detailed description of the project in the *Prix Ars Electronica Compendium CyberArts 2003,* pp 72).

Henry Newton-Dunn / Hiroaki Nakano / James Gibson / Ryota Kuwakubo: Block Jam

Block Jam is a tangible interface consisting of block like objects used to interact with music. Each block represents a sound, so by simply arranging the blocks users can describe meaningful musical phrases and structures.
Block Jam has been awarded a Honorary Mention in the category Interactive Art of Prix Ars Electronica 2003 (you find a detailed description of the project in the *Prix Ars Electronica Compendium CyberArts 2003,* pp 116).

Iori Nakai: Streetscape

Streetscape is an installation that extracts the city in the form of sound and maps, immersing you in everyday scenes. When you trace the white map with a pen, you can hear the real sounds of a city.
Streetscape has been awarded a Honorary Mention in the category Interactive Art of Prix Ars Electronica 2003 (you find a detailed description of the project in the *Prix Ars Electronica Compendium CyberArts 2003,* pp 114).

Little Red MR

Kenji Iguchi (Needle) / Tomoki Saso

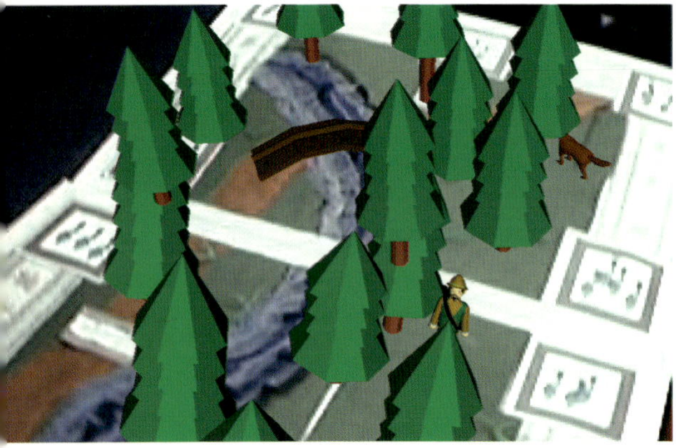

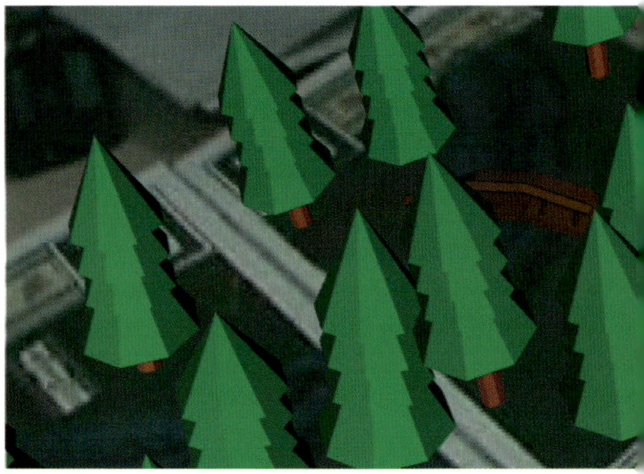

Little Red MR is an exploration in new methods of storytelling. It is a children's pop-up book that implements techniques of re-creating literary work in 3D using Mixed Reality, or MR technology. The user can read the book wearing a head-mounted display (HMD), and enjoy the story being told through a three-dimensional field.
The set-up of *Little Red MR* looks like a picture book, except with only the scene terrain depicted on the pages. The story begins when the user puts on the head-mounted display and opens the book. With an HMD on, animated 3D images of Little Red Riding Hood and her surroundings pop up on top of the book, telling her story. Each page contains a scene in Little Red Riding Hood's journey from the starting point, her house, to the destination, her grandmother's house. Dialogue and narratives are delivered aurally.
Since both the book (in real space) and the computer-generated graphics (in virtual space) hold three-dimensional information, the user can freely rotate or take a closer look at the book, and his / her field of view reacts accordingly. The terrain is made with materials such as felt and Japanese paper, giving the user a tangible feel of the 3D world. The 2D terrain features work in conjunction with the superimposed 3D animation to present the story to the user in one coherent whole.
Progression of the story in conventional books consists of turning the page, but this is not the case with *Little Red MR*. The story instead develops along with time, similarly to movies. In *Little Red MR,* turning the page amounts to the act of switching the in-storyworld location currently being viewed. For instance, if the user flipped to the page next to the page where Little Red Riding Hood currently is, he or she would actually be able to see the wolf running to get ahead of her. Events can be happening at multiple locations simultaneously, and the user can quickly flip back and forth through pages to experience more of the story than was previously possible with conventional books.
The storyline basically adheres to the original text of the Little Red Riding Hood story, but depending on the user's interaction, it can fork at certain points. For example, if the

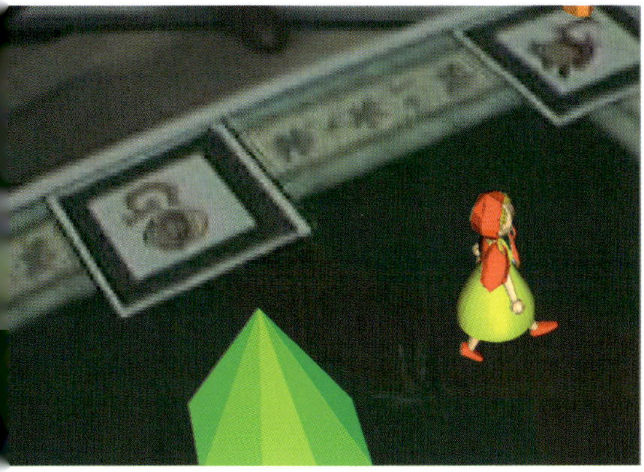

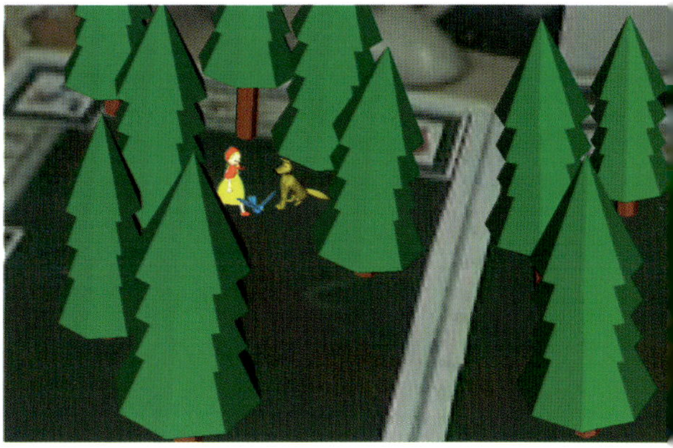

user takes the right actions, Little Red Riding Hood may be able to walk across a tree that has fallen over the river, instead of needing to take a detour around it. The story and ending can change depending on the actions the user may take.

In order to explore new possibilities of storytelling beyond what can be done with conventional books, *Little Red MR* interprets the physical form of the book itself as the interface. Therefore, actions such as closing the book, turning the page, and touching the page can be used as metaphoric ways to interact with the story. Also, presenting the story to the user by simultaneously utilizing both rendered 3D graphics and printed illustrations enable forms of expression that would otherwise have been impossible.

Augmented and Mixed Reality is entering the practical stage. Vision based Augmented Reality, which uses markers placed in real space to synchronize the coordinate axis between real space and virtual space, can be expected to be applied to the publishing field, as devices and markers for implementation can be obtained inexpensively. We decided that a book-reading style was suited for Mixed Reality storytelling, since the book, as an object, affords to the user many familiar actions (such as turning and page flipping) that can be used as devices for interaction with the MR scene.

We believe that establishing a new means of storytelling, one where the user views a 3D scene emerging amidst real space, and intervenes in the story using their own hands, will expand the realms of storytelling. *Little Red MR* can be represented as a publication of the next generation, and at the same time, an intuitive and tangible interface for enjoying interactive movies.

Tomoki Saso: Leader & Software Development, Kenji Iguchi: User Interface Design, Aska Morinobu: Software Development, Mizuho Hanazawa: 2D Artwork, Ayako Takagi: 2D & 3D Artwork, Satoshi Umase: 3D Artwork, Tomohiro Nishita: Sound Design, Eriko Matsumoto: Story & 2D Artwork, Mana Son: 3D Artwork, Yasuko Saito: Software Development, Kasumi Shigiyama: 2D Artwork, Yoko Muta: 2D Artwork, Mariko Takeuchi: 3D Artwork

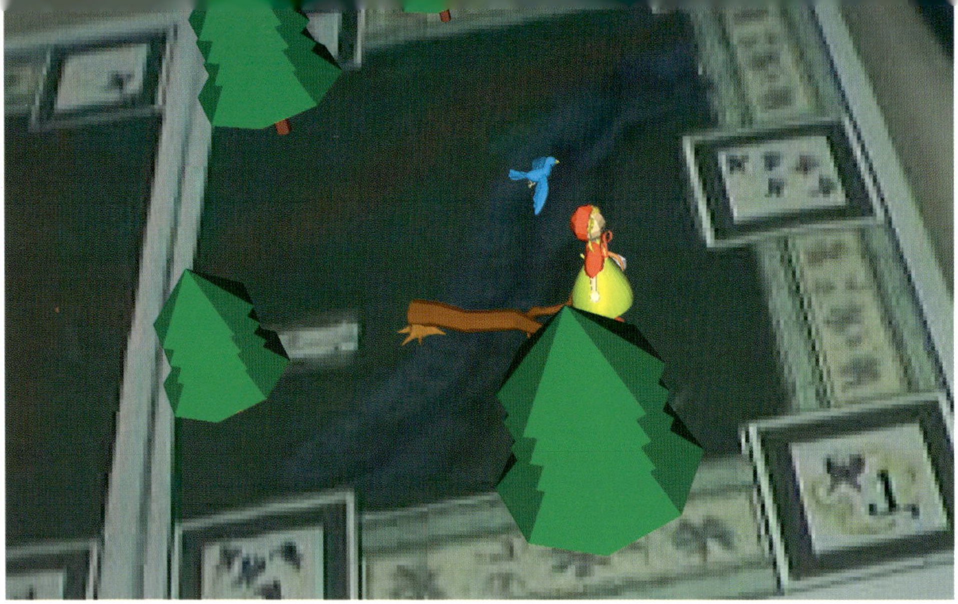

Little Red MR

Kenji Iguchi (Needle) / Tomoki Saso

Little Red MR erforscht neue Methoden des Märchenerzählens. Es ist ein Pop-up-Buch für Kinder, das mittels Mixed-Reality-Technologie (MR) die 3D-Nachbildung literarischer Werke ermöglicht. Der User setzt zum Lesen einen Datenhelm *(head-mounted display* – HMD) auf und kann so die Handlung in einem dreidimensionalen Raum ablaufen sehen.
Little Red MR sieht aus wie ein Bilderbuch – mit dem Unterschied, dass auf jeder Seite nur der Hintergrund zur jeweiligen Szene abgebildet ist. Die Geschichte beginnt erst, wenn der User das HMD aufsetzt und das Buch aufblättert. Animierte 3D-Bilder erzählen nun die Geschichte von Rotkäppchen. Jede Seite zeigt eine Szene, die Rotkäppchen auf dem Weg von zuhause (Ausgangspunkt) zum Haus der Großmutter (Ziel) erlebt. Dialoge und Erzähltext werden vorgelesen.
Da sowohl das Buch (im realen Raum) und die computergenerierten Grafiken (im virtuellen Raum) dreidimensionale Informationen enthalten, kann sich der User frei bewegen bzw. sich das Buch genauer ansehen, während sich sein Gesichtsfeld entsprechend mitbewegt. Der Hintergrund besteht aus Materialien wie Filz und Japanpapier und vermittelt so einen fühlbaren Eindruck von der 3D-Welt. Die Eigenschaften des 2D-Hintergrunds werden von der 3D-Animation überlagert; basierend auf dem Zusammenspiel der beiden Dimensionen wird dem User die Geschichte in einem kohärenten Ganzen präsentiert.
Bei herkömmlichen Büchern nimmt die Handlung durch das Umblättern der Seiten ihren Lauf, doch auf *Little Red MR* trifft dies nicht zu. Die Geschichte entwickelt sich vielmehr entlang einer Zeitachse, wie in einem Kinofilm. Bei *Little Red MR* entspricht das „Umblättern" einem Ortswechsel in der momentan dargestellten Erzählwelt. Wenn der User von der Seite, auf der sich Rotkäppchen gerade befindet, auf die nächste Seite blättert, so könnte er tatsächlich beobachten, wie der Wolf dorthin läuft, um noch vor Rotkäppchen anzukommen. Die Handlung kann sich an vielen Orten gleichzeitig abspielen, und der User kann durch rasches Vor- und Zurückblättern mehr aus der Erzählung herausholen als bei einem herkömmlichen Buch.

Die Handlung hält sich im Wesentlichen an den Originaltext von *Rotkäppchen,* doch können sich – in Abhängigkeit von der Interaktion des Lesers – an gewissen Punkten parallele Handlungsstränge entwickeln. Wenn ein User die entsprechenden Handlungen setzt, kann Rotkäppchen etwa auf einem Baumstamm über den Fluss balancieren, während in anderen Fällen ein Umweg notwendig ist. Der User kann durch sein Verhalten sowohl die Geschichte als auch ihr Ende verändern.

Mit dem Ziel, neue Möglichkeiten des Märchenerzählens zu erforschen, die über die Grenzen herkömmlicher Bücher hinausgehen, interpretiert *Little Red MR* die physische Form des Buchs selbst als Schnittstelle. Somit werden Akte wie das Schließen des Buchs, das Umblättern oder das Berühren der Seiten zu metaphorischen Möglichkeiten für die Interaktion mit dem Handlungsablauf. Außerdem werden durch die kombinierte Darstellung der Handlung mittels 3D-Grafiken und gedruckter Illustrationen Ausdrucksformen möglich, die sonst nicht realisierbar gewesen wären. Augmented Reality und Mixed Reality werden nun praktisch anwendbar. Man kann davon ausgehen, dass die auf visuelle Wahrnehmung gestützte Augmented Reality, bei der Markierungen im realen Raum dazu dienen, die Koordinatenachse zwischen realem und virtuellem Raum zu synchronisieren, im Verlagswesen Anwendung finden wird, da die erforderlichen Geräte und Markierungen zur Implementierung dieser Technik relativ kostengünstig sind. Für unsere Mixed-Reality-Anwendung erschien uns ein am Lesevorgang angelehnter Stil geeignet, da das Buch als Objekt dem User zahlreiche vertraute Handlungen erlaubt (wie Umblättern oder rasches Vor- und Zurückblättern), die auch zur Interaktion mit der MR-Szene genutzt werden können.

Wir sind überzeugt, dass die Einführung einer neuen Erzählform, bei der der User eine 3D-Szene sieht, die inmitten eines realen Raums entsteht, und zugleich im wahrsten Sinn des Worts in den Handlungsablauf ein*greifen* kann, den Handlungsspielraum des Märchenerzählens erweitert. *Little Red MR* kann als Publikation der nächsten Generation gelten und zugleich als intuitive und taktile Schnittstelle zum Betrachten interaktiver Filme.

Aus dem Englischen von Susanne Steinacher

Tomoki Saso: Leader & Software Development, Kenji Iguchi: User Interface Design, Aska Morinobu: Software Development, Mizuho Hanazawa: 2D Artwork, Ayako Takagi: 2D & 3D Artwork, Satoshi Umase: 3D Artwork, Tomohiro Nishita: Sound Design, Eriko Matsumoto: Story & 2D Artwork, Mana Son: 3D Artwork, Yasuko Saito: Software Development, Kasumi Shigiyama: 2D Artwork, Yoko Muta: 2D Artwork, Mariko Takeuchi: 3D Artwork

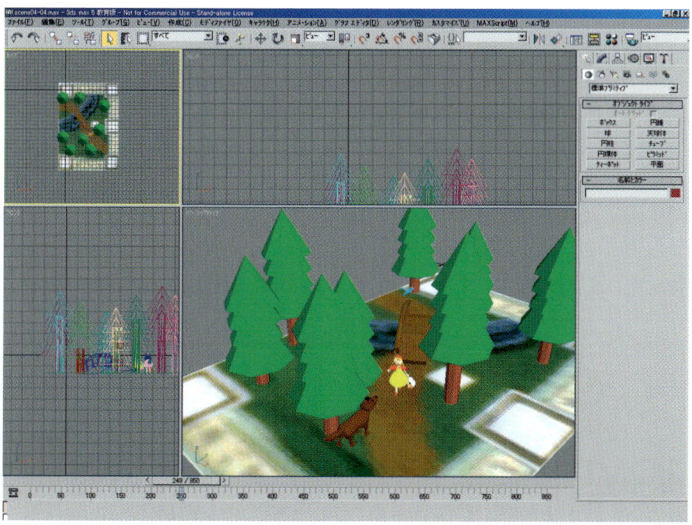

Protrude, Flow

Sachiko Kodama / Minako Takeno

We are attempting to create interactive installations to express our primitive feelings. The dynamic, organic shape and movement of the black lustrous fluid (magnetic fluid) is placed in some parts of the installation to express desire (passion) for life. The phenomenon of fluid rising against gravity reminds us of something living. Fluid moves according to the synchronous sound. These installations are not like machines, they remind us of the energy of pulsating fluid in the body of life.

Protrude, Flow

Modeling physical material more freely and making it move more flexibly is a dream long sought after by human beings, and many artists have created surreal illusions in pictures or moving images. But those were imaginary. Can we obtain a real object that transforms as we designed it? *Protrude, flow* is an interactive installation which expresses the dynamics of fluid motion of physical material, the dynamics of organic, wild shapes and movements of liquid by means of digital computer control.
Protrude, flow uses magnetic fluid, sound, and moving images. Affected by the sounds and spectators' voices where the exhibition is held, the three-dimensional patterns of magnetic fluid transform in various ways, and simultaneously its flowing movement and dynamic transformations are projected on the wide screen.

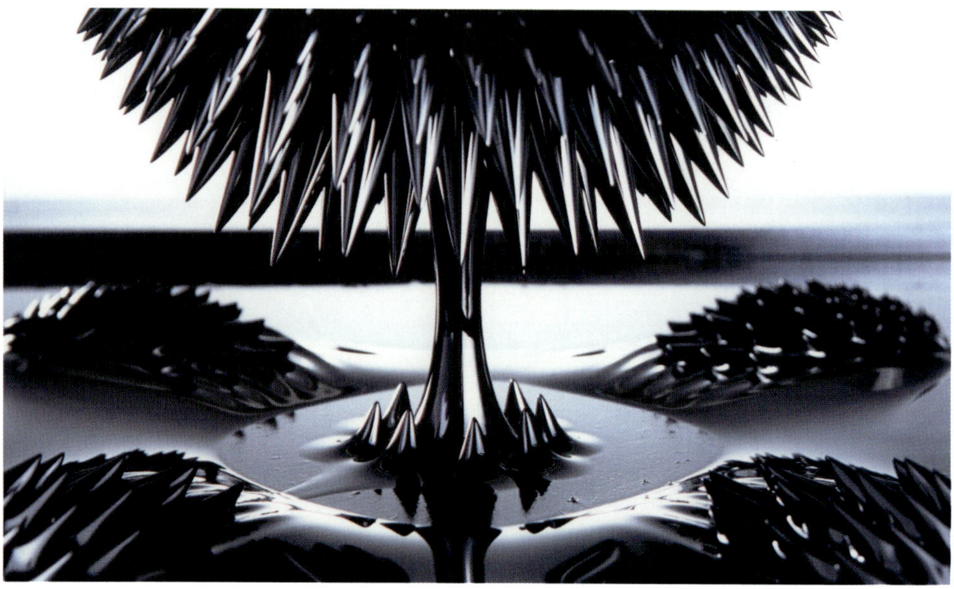

"Protrude, Flow" 2001 Photo: Yozo Takada

The magnetic fluid appears black. It is made by dissolving ferro-magnetic micro-powder in a solvent such as water or oil, and it remains strongly magnetic even in the fluid condition. Therefore it is more flexibly transformable than iron sand and so it is possible to create more complicated three-dimensional organic patterns. These appear occasionally as pointed mountains or pliable organic shapes, sometimes as flowing particle streams. The transformation of magnetic fluid is caused by the interaction with environmental sound. The sounds of the exhibition (sounds created by artists, and the voices of spectators) are caught by a microphone hanging from the ceiling, and then a computer converts the sound volume to electromagnetic voltage which determines the strength of the magnetic field. At the same time, the magnetic fluid changes its three-dimensional patterns sequentially. Each pattern appears synchronized to the environmental sound and the points of the shapes move correspondingly. As a result, magnetic fluid pulsates according to the sound. A digital video camera captures images of the moving magnetic fluid, and projects them onto the screen.

Pulsate 2002

In *Protrude, flow,* we attempted to present the dynamic movement and shape of magnetic fluid. The art formed organic abstract shapes that move smoothly.
In *Pulsate,* we put fluid in a familiar place where you can find things that have ordinary meanings. Here, fluid will become a place where peoples' thoughts mingle together.
The stage of *Pulsate* is a table. Eating is the most essential activity for human beings. Black fluid in a white dish develops waves on its surface when conversation between people around a table starts, and its movement stimulates their communication. The floor is covered with white sand. Fluorescent lamps are hung from the ceiling, and then the exhibition room is filled with white light. You can see a white table and several white chairs around it. At the center of the table, there is a large white dish holding black fluid. When people gather, the fluid pulsates calmly in sync with the sounds round about (spectators' voices, the sound of footsteps etc.). The louder the sound becomes, the more violently the waves pulsate, until at last they splash in the air.
Pulsate is an interactive installation that reflects, in the movement of fluid in a dish, our desire to communicate with other people.

Software: Shotaro Yamada, Photography: Yozo Takada, Sound: Ippei Oguta
This work was supported by Denshijiki Industry Co., Ltd.

"Pulsate" in *Zone Exhibit* (Tokyo) Photo: Yozo Takada

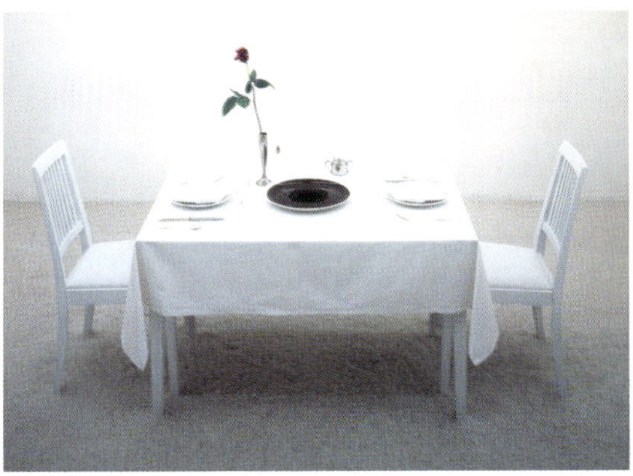

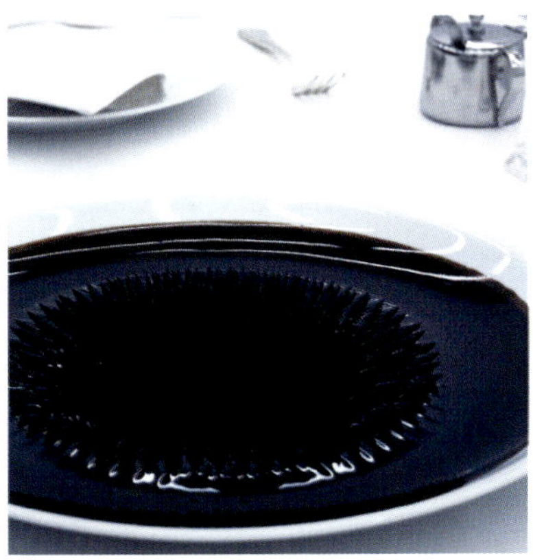

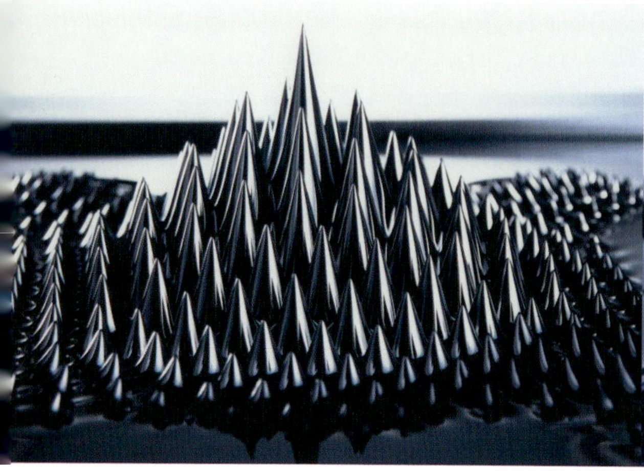

„Protrude, Flow“, 2001, Foto: Yozo Takada

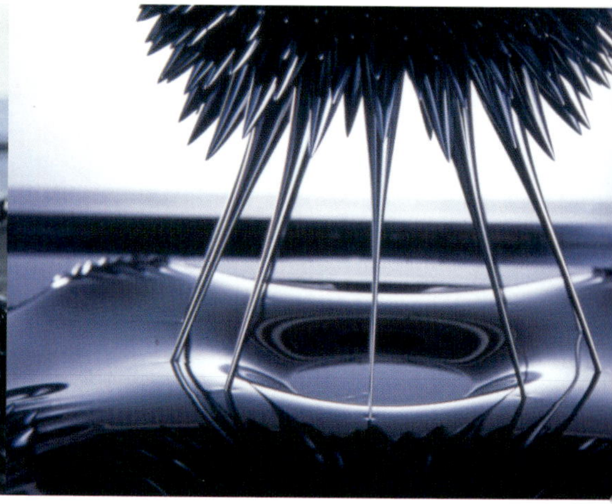

Protrude, Flow

Sachiko Kodama / Minako Takeno

Wir möchten mit unseren interaktiven Installationen unseren elementaren Gefühlen Ausdruck verleihen. Die dynamischen, organischen Formen und Bewegungen der schwarz schimmernden Flüssigkeit (Magnetofluid) werden in der Installation gezielt eingesetzt, um die Sehnsucht (das leidenschaftliche Verlangen) nach Leben auszudrücken. Die Eigenschaft der Flüssigkeit, entgegen dem Gesetz der Schwerkraft aufzusteigen, erinnert an etwas Lebendiges. Sie bewegt sich dabei synchron zu den Umweltgeräuschen. Diese Installationen haben nichts Maschinenähnliches, sondern erinnern an die Energie der pulsierenden Säfte im Körper des Lebens.

Protrude, Flow

Physikalische Materie freier formen und flexibler bewegen zu können ist schon seit langem ein Traum der Menschheit, und viele Künstler haben bereits ihre surrealen Fantasien in Bildern oder Bildsequenzen verwirklicht. Lässt sich ein reales Objekt erzeugen, das sich unseren Vorstellungen entsprechend verformt? *Protrude, Flow* ist eine interaktive Installation, die die Fließdynamiken physikalischer Materie, die per Computer gesteuerten Dynamiken organischer, urwüchsiger Formen und Bewegungen einer Flüssigkeit zum Ausdruck bringt.
Protrude, Flow verwendet Magnetofluide, Sound und Bildsequenzen. Unter Einwirkung von Klängen und Stimmen der Betrachter am Ausstellungsort verwandeln sich die dreidimensionalen Muster des Magnetofluids auf unterschiedliche Weise, während die fließende Bewegung und die dynamischen Transformationen gleichzeitig auf eine breite Leinwand projiziert werden. Das schwarz wirkende Magnetofluid besteht aus einer Suspension von fein verteilten ferromagnetischen Teilchen in einer Flüssigkeit wie Wasser oder Öl und behält sogar in flüssigem Zustand seine starke magnetische Wirkung. Es reagiert daher weniger träge als Eisensand, weshalb auch dreidimensionale organische Muster von größerer Komplexität erzeugt werden können. Diese können als spitz zulaufende Berge oder bizarre organische Formen, manchmal auch als fließende Partikelströme in Erscheinung treten.

Die Transformation des Magnetofluids wird durch die Interaktion mit Umweltgeräuschen bewirkt. Der Sound der Ausstellung (von Künstlern erzeugte Sounds und die Stimmen der Besucher) wird von einem von der Decke hängenden Mikrofon aufgenommen und von einem Computer in elektromagnetische Spannung verwandelt, die die Stärke des Magnetfelds reguliert. Gleichzeitig verändert das Magnetofluid fortlaufend seine dreidimensionalen Muster. Jedes Muster tritt synchron zu den Umgebungsgeräuschen in Erscheinung und auch die Spitzen der Formen bewegen sich entsprechend. In der Folge vibriert das Magnetofluid im Einklang mit dem Sound. Eine digitale Videokamera nimmt Bilder des sich bewegenden Magnetofluids auf und projiziert sie auf eine Leinwand.

Pulsate

In *Protrude, Flow* haben wir versucht, die dynamische Bewegung und Form des Magnetofluids zu zeigen – abstrakte Formen, die sich geschmeidig bewegen.
In *Pulsate* wird eine Flüssigkeit an einem vertrauten Ort präsentiert, an dem alltägliche Dinge zu finden sind. Die Flüssigkeit wird zu einem Medium, in dem die Gedanken der Menschen gleichsam ineinander fließen. Die Bühne von *Pulsate* ist ein Tisch. Die Nahrungsaufnahme ist die wichtigste Tätigkeit der Menschen. Sobald die Konversation zwischen den um den Tisch versammelten Personen beginnt, entwickelt die schwarze Flüssigkeit in der weißen Schüssel Oberflächenwellen, eine Bewegung, die wiederum die Kommunikation stimuliert. Der Boden ist mit weißem Sand bedeckt. Fluoreszierende Lampen hängen von der Decke, der Ausstellungsraum ist in weißes Licht getaucht. Ein weißer Tisch und mehrere weiße Stühle sind zu sehen. In der Mitte des Tisches steht eine große, weiße Schüssel, die eine schwarze Flüssigkeit enthält. Sobald sich einige Personen einfinden, beginnt die Flüssigkeit synchron zu den Umgebungsgeräuschen (Stimmen der Zuseher, Schritte etc.) leicht zu vibrieren. Je lauter es wird, desto heftiger vibrieren die Wellen, bis sie schließlich über den Rand klatschen. Die interaktive Installation *Pulsate* spiegelt unseren Wunsch, mit anderen zu kommunizieren, in der Bewegung von Flüssigkeit in einer Schüssel wider.

Aus dem Englischen von Martina Bauer

Software: Shotaro Yamada, Photography: Yozo Takada, Sound: Ippei Oguta
Dieses Projekt wurde von Denshijiki Industry Co., Ltd. unterstützt.

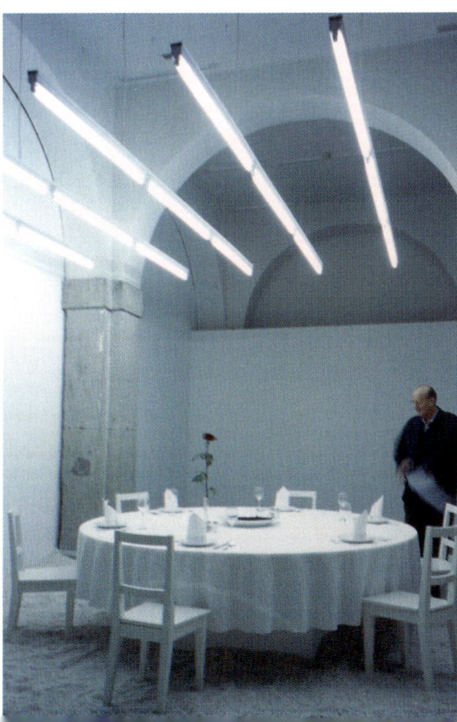

„Pulsate“ 2002 im Rahmen von *Cibervision*

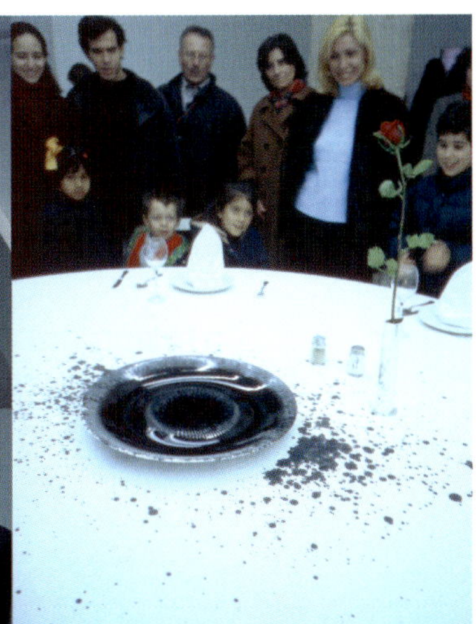

„Pulsate“ 2002 im Rahmen von *Cibervision*
(Centro Cultural Conde Duque, Madrid)

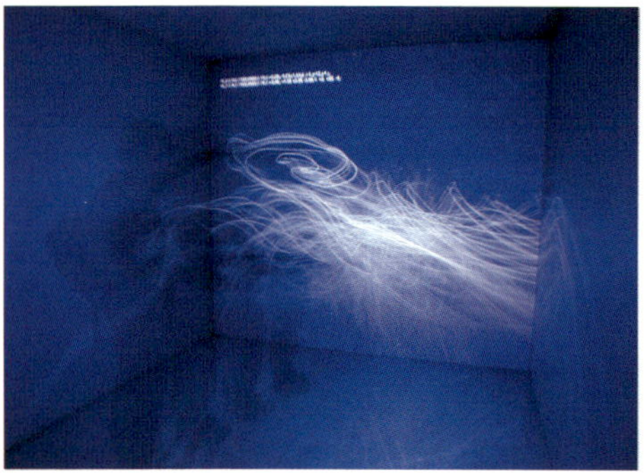

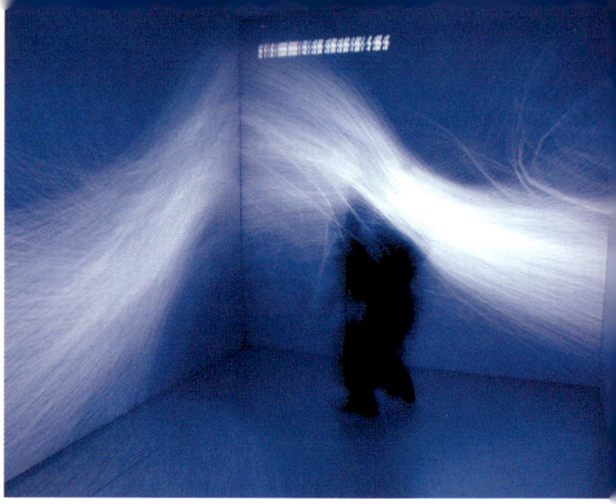

Foto: Victor S. Brigola

Ars Electronica Center Exhibition

Uzume

Petra Gemeinböck / Roland Blach / Nicolaj Kirisits

Uzume is named after a Japanese Shinto goddess and means "whirling." The story of Uzume tells of her strange dance that lured the sun goddess Amaterasu out of the cave where she had hidden herself.

Immersed in *Uzume,* a sensitively responsive, dynamic environment surrounds the visitor, unfolding the communicative nature of a strange, virtual entity. To communicate with *Uzume* is similar to pursuing a dialogue without knowing the language of the other. Although the environment responds subtly to every movement of the participant, it evolves to some extent self-independently and challenges the user to explore its strange language code. Input and response become thus a dynamic interplay, creating a transformative mirror, in which users are able to discover their own selves, as well as the others'.

Uzume's world is bound to the physical projection space of the CAVE. Its appearance is based on spatial representations of the temporal behavior of nonlinear chaotic systems, so called 'Strange Attractors'. By physically moving around inside the projection space, participants affect the current state of their surrounding, traversing the attractors' parametric fields. At the same time their presence subtly transforms *Uzume's* medium, a viscous fluid-like force field, in which both the visitors and the whirling structures are embedded.

The virtual environment involves the aspects of presence, reflectivity, and otherness as they evolve in immersive, interactive environments. Its responsive—yet unpredictable—behavior unveils the ambiguous nature of computer controlled systems, in particular the illusion of control. *Uzume* unfolds its meaning in the performative element of the evolving dialogue between the temporary inhabitant and the virtual opposite.

Uzume was implemented at the CC Virtual Environments, IAO Fraunhofer Stuttgart, Germany.

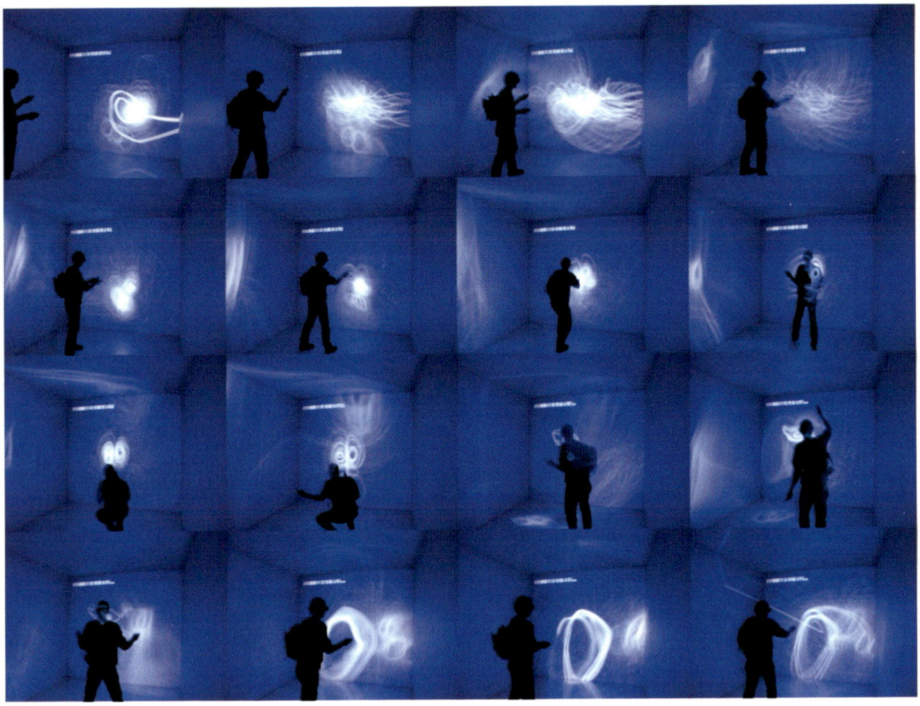
Foto: Victor S. Brigola

Uzume ist nach einer japanischen Shinto-Göttin benannt und bedeutet „wirbelig“. Die Geschichte erzählt von Uzumes eigenwilligem Tanz, der die Sonnengöttin Amaterasu aus der Höhle lockte, in der sie sich versteckt hatte.

Der Besucher taucht in *Uzume* in eine sehr empfindlich reagierende, dynamische Umgebung ein und erlebt dabei die kommunikative Ader einer seltsamen, virtuellen Entität. Diese Kommunikation ähnelt dem Versuch, ein Gespräch zu führen, ohne die Sprache des Gegenübers zu kennen. Obwohl die Umgebung auf jede kleinste Bewegung des Benutzers reagiert, entwickelt sie sich doch bis zu einem gewissen Grad eigenständig und fordert den Besucher heraus, ihren eigentümlichen Sprachcode zu erforschen. Input und Reaktion werden so zu einem dynamischen Wechselspiel und schaffen einen transformativen Spiegel, in dem die Benutzer sich selbst und das Gegenüber erkennen können.

Uzumes Welt ist an den physischen Projektionsraum des CAVE gebunden und basiert auf der räumlichen Darstellung des zeitlichen Verhaltens nichtlinearer chaotischer Systeme, sogenannter „seltsamer Attraktoren“. Wenn sich die Besucher innerhalb des Projektionsraums bewegen, durchqueren sie die Parameterfelder der Attraktoren und verändern dadurch den jeweiligen Zustand ihrer Umgebung. Zugleich löst ihre Anwesenheit kleinste Veränderungen in *Uzumes* Medium aus, einem zähflüssig wirkenden Kraftfeld, in das sowohl die Besucher als auch die wirbelnden Strukturen eingebettet sind.

Die virtuelle Umgebung wird zum Schauplatz für Präsenz, Reflektivität und Andersheit, die sich in immersiven, interaktiven Umgebungen entwickeln. Ihr reaktives – aber unvorhersehbares – Verhalten entlarvt die Ambivalenz computergesteuerter Systeme, und insbesonders die Illusion von Kontrolle. *Uzumes* tiefere Bedeutung entfaltet sich mit der Darbietung des sich zwischen dem Kurzzeitbesucher und seinem virtuellen Gegenüber entwickelnden Dialogs.

Uzume wurde am CC Virtual Environments des Fraunhofer IAO Stuttgart entwickelt.

CITYCLUSTER
From the Renaissance to the Gigabits Networking Age

Franz Fischnaller

CityCluster is a virtual networking matrix, a creative high-tech container with original technological features such as navigation, interactivity and its own graphic and style. Within this container, multiple environments, ambiences or cities both real and imagined, can be hosted, coexist and relate to one another through a common, virtual territory, interconnected by high-speed network, enabling remote participants to interact and collaborate in a single shared environment. This framework may be expanded, modified, enriched, developed, and produced ad hoc in accordance with the nature and typology of the environment to be incorporated. Visitors, with their own creativity and communicative skills, can become protagonist and/or free citizen: navigate, interact, intervene, exchange structures, objects and ideas and or create their own ideal environment. A virtual-reality networking interface display, a VR-pathfinder called Meta-Net-Page was designed and implemented ad hoc for *CityCluster* as the main interactivity tool for the user.
"From the Renaissance to the Megabyte Networking Age" is the first *CityCluster* virtual-reality networked application. The virtual application offers its visitors a thrilling interactive journey departing from the Renaissance and continuing to the super wideband networking of the Electronic Age, breaking the barriers of time and space in real time. Florence metaphorically represents the "Renaissance Age," Chicago the "Gigabits Networking Age." Each virtual city is inhabited by a group of avatars: David, Venus and Machiavelli in Florence and Mega, Giga and Picasso in Chicago.
The system has been designed to produce an integrated computing facility and to implement a high speed digital container in which multiple environments may coexist and be interconnected within a common, virtual territory. *CityCluster* can be adapted to a number of diverse cities or virtual environments. Local and non-local interactive visitors can experience a shared environment in local and in remote locations through high speed networking.

Lead technical advisor: Alex Hill, EVL, University of Illinois at Chicago, USA.
Producer and Project coordinator: F.A.B.R.I.CATORS, Milan, Italy
Partner: Electronic Visualization Lab (EVL), University of Illinois at Chicago, USA

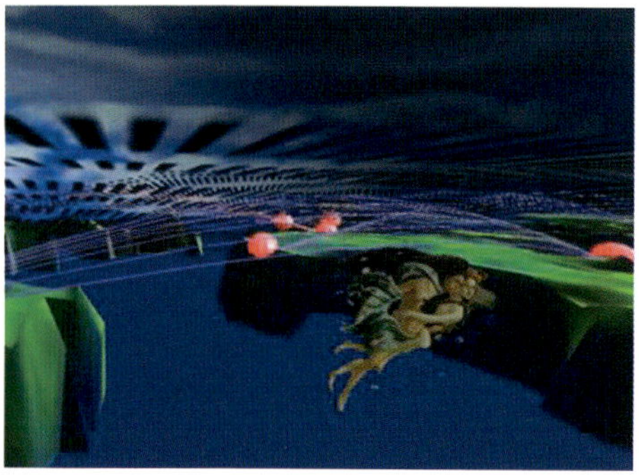

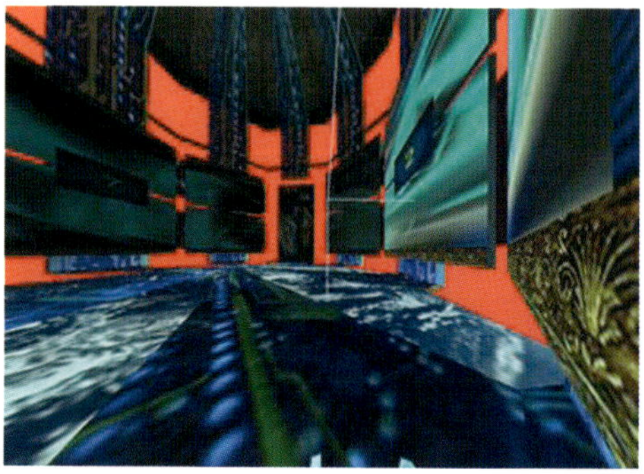

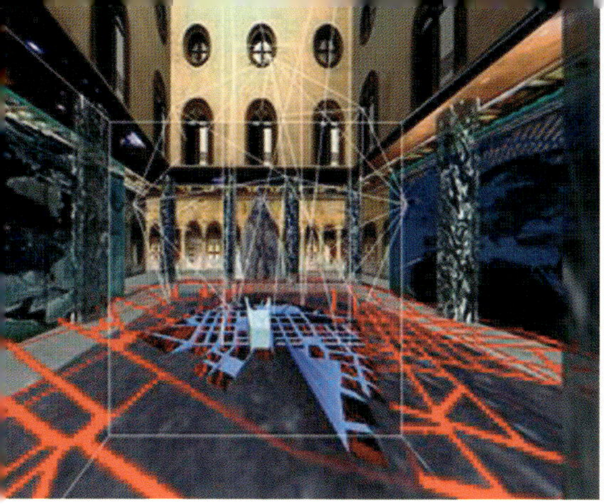

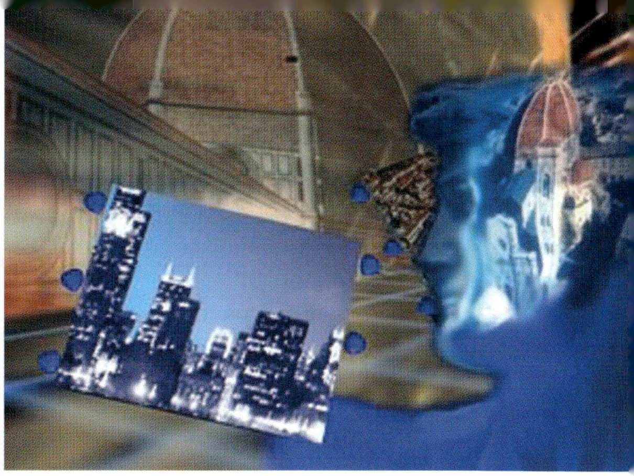

CITYCLUSTER Von der Renaissance bis ins Zeitalter des Gigabit-Networkings

Franz Fischnaller

CityCluster ist eine virtuelle Netzwerkmatrix, ein kreativer Hi-Tech-Container mit originellen technischen Eigenschaften wie Navigation, Interaktion und eigenem grafischem sowie inhaltlichem Stil. Darin können multiple Umgebungen oder Cities – reale wie imaginäre – aufgenommen werden, nebeneinander bestehen und in Beziehung zueinander treten über ein gemeinsames virtuelles Terrain, welches durch ein Hochgeschwindigkeitsnetz verbunden ist und es den Usern an den remoten Orten ermöglicht, zu interagieren, zusammenzuarbeiten und ein und dasselbe Environment zu teilen. Dieser Rahmen kann erweitert, geändert, bereichert, entwickelt und ad hoc hergestellt werden – je nach Natur und Typologie der einzubindenden Umgebung. Kreative Besucher mit guten kommunikativen Fähigkeiten können Protagonist und / oder freie Bürger werden, d. h. navigieren, interagieren, intervenieren, Bauformen, Objekte und Ideen austauschen und ihre eigene ideale Umgebung schaffen.

Ein VR-Networking-Interface, ein VR-Pfad-Finder namens Meta-Net-Page, wurde ad hoc für *CityCluster* konzipiert und implementiert und dient als wichtiges Interaktionstool für den User. „Von der Renaissance bis zum Zeitalter des Megabyte-Networkings“ ist die erste VR-Networking-Applikation von *CityCluster.* Die virtuelle Anwendung bietet den Besuchern eine spannende interaktive Reise, die in der Renaissance anfängt und bis zum Superbreitband-Networking des elektronischen Zeitalters geht und die Grenzen zwischen Zeit und Raum in Realzeit durchbricht. Florenz repräsentiert metaphorisch das Zeitalter der Renaissance, Chicago das „Gigabit-Networking-Zeitalter“. In jeder virtuellen Stadt wohnt eine Gruppe von Avataren: David, Venus und Machiavelli in Florenz und Mega, Giga und Picasso in Chicago.

Mit dem System-Design wurde es möglich, ein integriertes Computing-Werkzeug zu erstellen und einen digitalen Hochgeschwindigkeits-Container zu implementieren, in dem multiple Umgebungen koexistieren und auf einem gemeinsamen virtuellen Territorium miteinander in Verbindung treten. *CityCluster* kann an eine große Zahl unterschiedlicher Städte oder virtueller Umgebungen angepasst werden. Lokale und auch andere Besucher können lokal oder remote über das Hochgeschwindigkeits-Networking in einer gemeinsamen Umgebung arbeiten.

Aus dem Englischen von Sigrid Dohmen Piola

raum.art
An Electronic Museum
Virtual Interactive 3-D CAVE Installation

A. Benjamin Spaeth

raum.art is an interactive virtual environment developed at the University of Stuttgart's High Performance Computing Center in cooperation with Erwin Herzberger and Uwe Wössner. The work makes a statement about the relationship of architecture, art and virtual space.

Virtual space with its electronic texts, sounds and images is a real part of our reality. The shifting of the realm of human activity into the digital domain is being prefigured by the world of art. This museum as a forum of art carries out this shift in an appropriate way. The consequences of this phenomenon are manifestly, palpably evident in the museum both conceptually and as an architectural presence. This raises the question of a museum that dispenses with the physical existence of both works on display in a museum context and visitors coming to view them.

To compensate for the absence of a *genius loci* in virtual space, there is the ephemeral presence of real places. The concrete architectural form takes shape by means of the network linkage of real locations and the inscription of significant processes and qualities of these locations upon the electronic presence. The absence of external parameters like gravity, rain and wind makes it possible to reduce the architecture to its pure content. This state of "being space" offers the opportunity to place the objects in relation to each other, to establish an order among them, and to allow them to enter one's faculties of perception. In its mode of manifestation, architecture in the electronic sphere reifies the specific characteristics of virtuality.

Idea, concept, programming: A. Benjamin Spaeth
Concept: Erwin Herzberger
Programming: Uwe Wössner

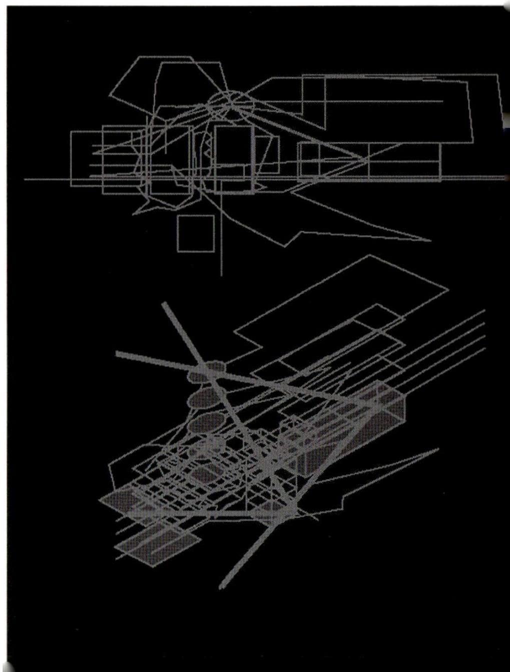

Inscription and manipulation of significant processes into the architectural form

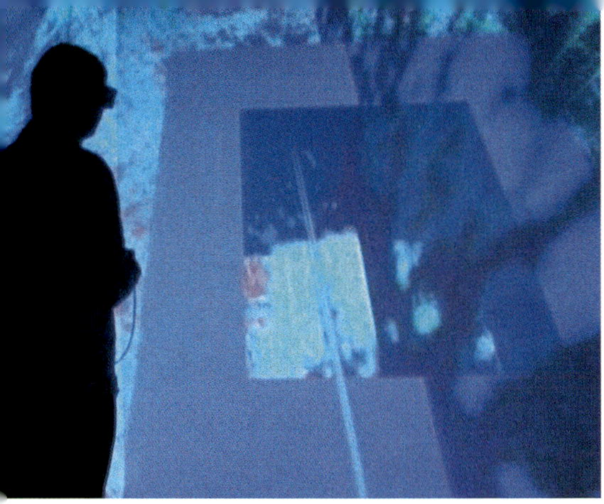
bildraum Objekt

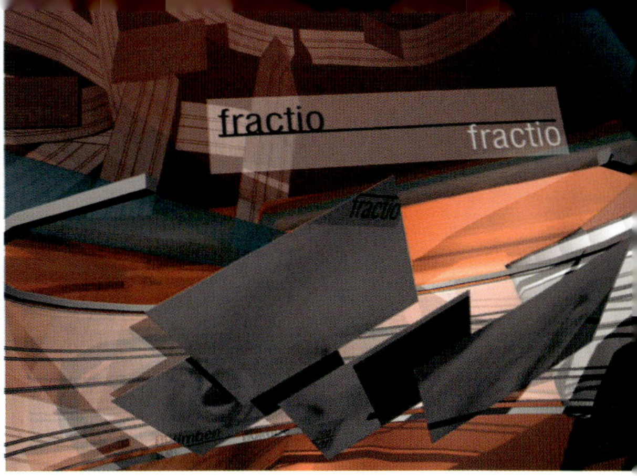

Zugang zum Objekt fractio

raum.art
ein elektronisches Museum
virtuelle interaktive 3D-CAVE-Installation

A. Benjamin Spaeth

raum.art ist eine interaktive virtuelle Umgebung, die am Höchstleistungsrechenzentrum der Universität Stuttgart (hlrs) in Zusammenarbeit mit Erwin Herzberger und Uwe Wössner entwickelt wurde. Die Arbeit nimmt Stellung zum Verhältnis von Architektur Kunst und virtuellem Raum.
Der virtuelle Raum ist mit seinen elektronischen Texten, Tönen und Bilder realer Bestandteil unserer Wirklichkeit. Die Verschiebung des Handlungsbereichs des Menschen ins Digitale wird von der Kunst vorgezeichnet. Das Museum – Forum der Kunst – vollzieht diese Verschiebung entsprechend. Die Auswirkung ist im Museum als Idee, aber auch in seiner architektonischen Präsenz spürbar und ablesbar. Es stellt sich die Frage nach einem Museum, welches der körperlichen Existenz seiner musealen Werke und seiner Besucher entbehrt.
Der Mangel des Genius loci im virtuellen Raum wird durch die ephemere Präsenz realer Orte ausgeglichen. Die konkrete architektonische Form entsteht durch die Vernetzung realer Orte und die Einschreibung signifikanter Prozesse und Eigenschaften dieser Orte in die elektronische Präsenz. Die fehlenden äußeren Parameter wie Gravitation, Regen oder Windkraft ermöglichten es der Architektur sich auf ihren reinen Inhalt zu reduzieren. Das Raum-Sein bietet die Möglichkeit die Objekte zueinander in Beziehung zu setzten, zu ordnen und zur Wahrnehmung zu bringen. Die Architektur im elektronischen Raum setzt die spezifischen Eigenschaften der Virtualität in ihrer Erscheinung um.

Idee, Konzept, Programmierung: A. Benjamin Spaeth
Konzept: Erwin Herzberger
Programmierung: Uwe Wössner

Humphrey

Heimo Ranzenbacher

In the beginning, there was Humphrey—a mechatronic device that worked in conjunction with a pair of data glasses to simulate flight in a 3-D environment.
This installation in the Ars Electronica Center has been a smash hit with visitors ever since the opening of the museum, which has replaced almost all of the "exhibits" on display there at least once over the past eight years. And, indeed, Humphrey will remain aloft in Ars Electronica's airspace, but his new design will greatly enhance and intensify the experience of flight. Continual improvements in processing capabilities make it possible to generate simulations that get closer and closer to perfection. Virtual reality systems use stereoscopic imagery to produce the illusion of a real, three-dimensional environment. By means of force feedback devices, even physical forces can be mechanically simulated in these virtual worlds.
As the outcome of R&D work in which Ars Electronica Futurelab engineers utilized an empirical design process, *Humphrey* has mutated into the prototype of an apparatus that uses a combination of virtual reality and force feedback technologies to impart a feeling of weightlessness that is as realistic as possible and of the centrifugal force generated by flying. An aspect that makes a key contribution to this is the innovative mode of navigation, which enables the user to steer through an artificial environment by means of intuitive arm movements.
The essential elements are a data helmet, specially reinforced overalls resembling a pilot's jumpsuit, and the equipment responsible for producing the force simulation. In designing the pneumatic components, engineers also took the factor of visual impact into consideration since one of their prime objectives was to enable users and observers alike to understand how the apparatus functions. The contracting muscles that produce flight also give viewers a direct impression of the forces at work upon the user.
For the process of immersion—that is, for the user to completely get into a virtual world—the most important component is the data helmet that stereographically visualizes an environment consisting of computer-generated data. In keeping with the state of the art, the helmet was designed to be as light as possible and reduced to its functional elements. Leading edge technology also went into the force-feedback-generated "physics" at work in these immersive worlds, as well as the new 3-D environments that will premier at the opening of the 2003 Ars Electronica Festival.

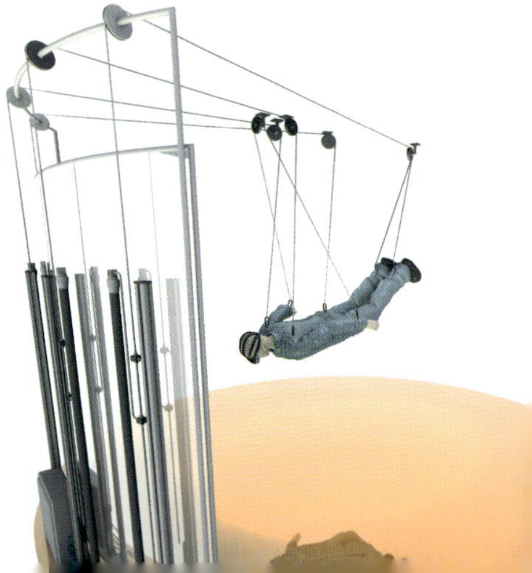

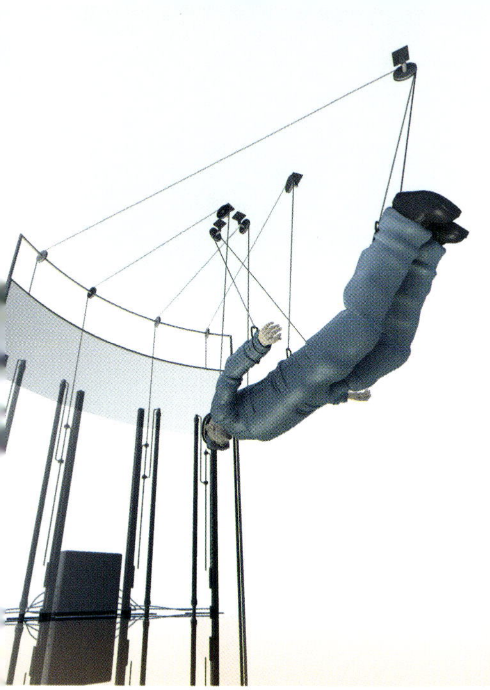

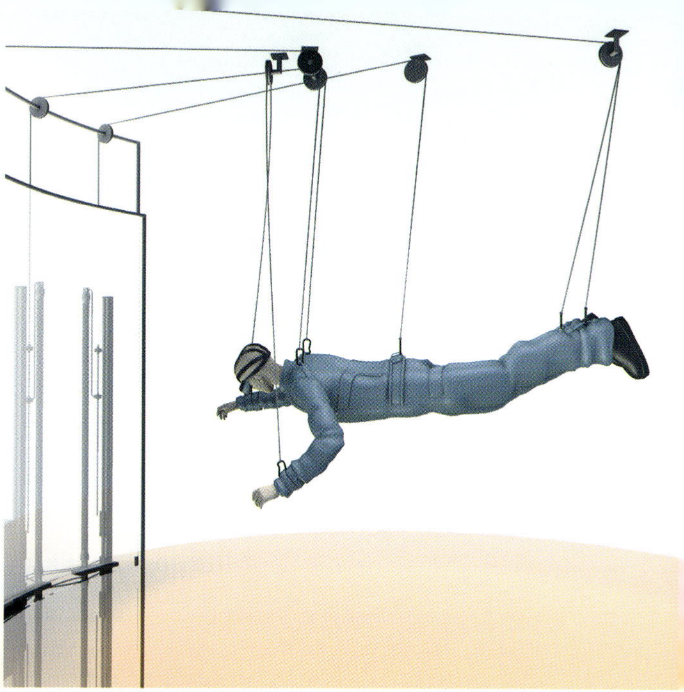

Am Anfang war *Humphrey* – eine mechatronische Vorrichtung, durch die in Verbindung mit einer Datenbrille das Fliegen in 3D-Umgebungen simuliert wurde.
Die Installation im Ars Electronica Center ist seit der Eröffnung ein Publikumsmagnet des Museums, das in den vergangenen acht Jahren nahezu sein gesamtes Inventar nicht nur einmal durch neue „Exponate" ersetzt hat. *Humphrey* bleibt den BesucherInnen auch weiter erhalten; sein aktuelles Design intensiviert jedoch die Erfahrung des Fliegens um ein Vielfaches.
Die stetig wachsenden Rechenleistungen ermöglichen immer perfektere Simulationen. Virtual-Reality-Systeme erzeugen durch stereoskopische Bilder die Illusion einer realen dreidimensionalen Umwelt. Mittels Force-Feedback-Apparaturen können auch physikalische Kräfte der virtuellen Welten mechanisch simuliert werden.
In Anwendung einer in einem empirischen Designprozess entwickelten Studie des Ars Electronica Futurelab mutiert *Humphrey* zum Prototyp einer Apparatur, die durch Kombination von Virtual-Reality- und Force-Feedback-Technologien ein möglichst realistisches Gefühl von Schwerelosigkeit und der durch Flugbewegungen aufkommenden Fliehkräfte vermittelt. Ein dafür wichtiger Aspekt ist die neuartige Steuerung, die es ermöglicht, mittels intuitiver Bewegungen der Arme durch das künstliche Environment zu navigieren.
Der Datenhelm, ein speziell verstärkter, an einen Pilotenoverall angelehnter Anzug und die für die Kräftesimulation verantwortlichen Antriebe sind die maßgeblichen Elemente. Bei den pneumatischen Bauteilen spielte deren optische Wirkung durchaus eine Rolle, da die Funktion der Apparatur für den Benutzer und Betrachter gleichermaßen begreiflich gemacht werden sollte. Die kontrahierenden Luftmuskeln geben auch dem Betrachter einen unmittelbaren Eindruck von den auf den Benutzer wirkenden Kräften.
Die für die Immersion, d. h. für das vollständige Eintauchen des Benutzers in die virtuelle Welt, wichtigste Komponente ist der Datenhelm, der die vom Computer berechnete Umgebung stereografisch visualisiert. Dem Stand der Technik entsprechend wurde der Helm möglichst leicht und auf seine funktionellen Teile reduziert gestaltet.
Dem Stand der Technik, einschließlich der durch Force-Feedback manifesten „Physik" der immersiven Welten, entsprechen auch neue 3D-Umgebungen, die zur Eröffnung des Festivals Ars Electronica 2003 erstmals zu erleben sind.

Interfacelifting

Heimo Ranzenbacher

Considering the infrastructure it houses, the Ars Electronica Center—Museum of the Future is actually a machine, one that is programmable and dynamic, a freely configurable "hall of mirrors" in the sense that the technological creativity of the present reflects the future. That is this facility's essential metaphor, imagery that corresponds to its programmatically derived inner workings. What is being programmed is neither the art nor the future but rather the reflection, and this is the basis of the facility's inherent creativity—technological creativity as the interface between today and tomorrow. "Face the future!"

When, however, media—via art—definitively evoke a facility, then *pro domo* to the extent that they produce its manifestation and function as a derivative of its organizing principles. The facility's exterior shell—beyond architectural-poetic practice whereby windows have already been designated as elements of transparency between interior and exterior domains—actually would assume the function of an interface. Dynamism, its most fundamental characteristic, represents what has been, in the case of the Ars Electronica Center, merely the entree.

After all, externally, the edifice—as the result of a process of rethinking/redefinition during the course of its construction—was just a building, which is to say a structure without correspondence to the facility's technical, aesthetic and educational—in short: dynamic—organization. The Center has signaled its singular status within the cityscape of Linz above all with the large-format graphics—embodying the slogan "Face the Future," changing each year with the respective Festival theme—that have adorned the building's façade overlooking the city's Main Square and most important bridge. The external shell, on the other hand, remained static, and would have continued to do so—theoretically—even if the graphics had changed more frequently, and even if the speed of the succession of images had increased to that of an animated film.

Thus, a sort of interfacelifting was undertaken with the installation of the media façade. The media façade is a projection screen encompassing three of the building's exterior walls. In line with its function as an interface, it is a freely programmable surface with the capability of visualizing "transparency between interior and exterior domains"—which it to say manipulation in a way that depends on content.

The images are to be projected during the evening hours until midnight by three synchronized projectors positioned on the east, south and west sides of the building. The columns and projector housings were designed by Scott Ritter.

The media façade will kick off by presenting a variation on Golan Levin and Zachary Lieberman's installation entitled *Hidden Worlds of Noise and Voice.* Indoors, it generates graphic objects out of voices; outdoors, the immediate surroundings of the Museum have been miked to pick up the *Noise and Voice* emanating from passers-by and the urban soundscape. Also linked sensorially to the environment in which it is set, this installation is not an application in the sense of a secondary accessory but rather an essential enhancement. With it, the Ars Electronica Center, as an architectural component of an urban public space and as part of its institutional mission, publicizes the "space" in which its relation to the city is played out.

Interfacelifting

Heimo Ranzenbacher

Das Ars Electronica Center – Museum der Zukunft ist seiner Anlage nach eine Maschine, programmierbar und dynamisch. Ein frei konfigurierbares „Spiegelkabinett" in dem Sinne, dass die technologische Kreativität der Gegenwart die Zukunft widerspiegelt. Das ist die Metaphorik des Hauses, der sein programmatisches Innenleben entspricht. Programmiert wird nicht die Kunst, auch nicht die Zukunft, sondern die Spiegelung; darin begründet sich die Kreativität des Hauses. Technologische Kreativität als das Interface zwischen Heute und Morgen. „Face the future!"

Wenn aber Medien – vermittels Kunst – von einem Haus sprechen, dann insofern *pro domo,* als sie dessen Erscheinung und Funktion aus ihren Organisationsprinzipien heraus erzeugen. Seine Hülle hätte abseits der architekturpoetischen Praxis, wonach Fenster schon einmal als Elemente der Transparenz zwischen Innen und Außen bezeichnet werden, wohl tatsächlich die Funktion eines Interface. Dessen grundlegende Eigenschaft, die Dynamik, repräsentierte im Falle des Ars Electronica Center bislang bloß der Eingang.

Denn außen war das Haus – Folge einer Umwidmung des Bauwerkes während seiner Errichtung – schlicht ein Gebäude, das heißt ohne Entsprechung seiner technischen, ästhetischen, edukativen – kurz: dynamischen – Organisation. Seinen besonderen Status im Stadtbild signalisierte es vor allem durch die den Slogan „Face the Future" veranschaulichenden und mit den Themen der Festivals wechselnden, großformatigen Bildmotive an der Stirnseite. Die Hülle war hingegen statisch, und wäre es – theoretisch – auch bei einem rascheren Wechsel der Motive geblieben; selbst dann, wenn sich die Geschwindigkeit des Wechsels bis zu einer Animation gesteigert hätte. Mit der Installierung der Medienfassade wurde demnach eine Art Interfacelifting vorgenommen.

Die Medienfassade ist eine Projektionsfläche, welche drei Seiten des Hauses umfasst. Ihre Interface-Funktion erfüllt sie als eine frei programmierbare Oberfläche, mit der Möglichkeit, „Transparenz zwischen Innen und Außen" zu visualisieren, das heißt auch Content-abhängig zu manipulieren.

Projiziert wird in den Abendstunden, bis 24 Uhr, von drei miteinander synchronisierten Projektoren aus auf die Ost-, Süd- und Westseite des Gebäudes; die Stelen und Projektoren-Gehäuse wurden von Scott Ritter gestaltet.

In Betrieb genommen wird die Medienfassade mit einer Variation über Golan Levins und Zachary Liebermans Installation *Hidden Worlds of Noise and Voice,* die – indoor – aus Stimmen grafische Objekte generiert. Outdoor werden für *Noise and Voice* durch die Mikrofonierung des näheren Umkreises des Museums Passanten ebenso wie das urbane Betriebsgeräusch engagiert.

Sensorisch auch an das Umfeld gekoppelt, ist die Installation nicht Applikation im Sinne eines Beiwerkes, sondern der Erweiterung: Damit betreibt das Ars Electronica Center als Objekt im öffentlichen Raum der Stadt in Anwendung seiner Programmatik die Veröffentlichung des „Raumes" seiner Beziehung zur Stadt.

Biographies

agf aka antye greie (D) is musician. producer. vocalist. author. artist and currently living in berlin. agf got internationally know by recording herself reading lines of code and then deconstructing them into sluice of broken syllables and bursts of breath. AGF takes what has been done before with DSP laptop electronics and turns it on its head electronic roar. subsonic beats. vocal processing. lyric sampling. multilingual.

Amy Alexander (USA) has worked in film, video, music, computer animation and new media. She holds a BA in Communications and Film from Rowan University and an MFA in Film and Video from the California Institute of the Arts. She is currently an Assistant Professor of Visual Arts at the University of California, San Diego. Since 1996, she has been working primarily in net art and software art, exploring dynamic processes, temporal structures, net politics and net culture. Much of her recent work has been in live Internet performance and software art, playing with the relationships between new media and early abstract animated filmmaking, as well as the juxtaposition of geek culture and pop culture.

Marcel.lí Antúnez Roca (E), born 1959, is well-known in the international art scene for his mechanotronic performances and robotic installations. A founding member of La Fura dels Baus, he worked in this company as art co-ordinator, musician and performer from 1979 to 1989, and presented the group's macro-performances *ACCIONS* (1984), *SUZ/O/SUZ* (1985) and *TIER MON* (1988). In the nineties his avantgarde mechatronic performances combined such elements as *Bodybots* (body-controlled robots), *Systematugy* (interactive narration with computers) and *dresskeleton* (the exoskeleton interfacing with the body). He is currently working on the spatial artwork *DEDALUS.*

Michael Aschauer (A), born in 1977; since 1999, master class in visual media design at the University of Applied Art; lives in Vienna where he works as an artist primarily with code in the Internet, image and sound; nominated for the 2003 International Media Art Prize of the ZKM, Karlsruhe, Germany. *http://m.ash.to, http://www.logicaland.net*

Peter J. Bentley (GB) is an Honorary Research Fellow at the Department of Computer Science, University College London (UCL), known for his prolific research covering all aspects of Evolutionary Computation and Digital Biology. His research investigates evolutionary algorithms, ecological modelling, artificial immune systems, computational embryology and swarming systems, applied to diverse applications including design, control, fraud detection, security, and music composition. He is editor of the books *Evolutionary Design by Computers* and *Creative Evolutionary Systems,* and author of the popular science book *Digital Biology.*

Roland Blach (D) has completed his studies of Control Engineering in Stuttgart in 1992 and since then works at the Virtual Environments Lab at the Fraunhofer IAO, Stuttgart (D). His work focuses on the development of the virtual reality core system software Lightning / Personal Immersion. For the last two years Roland worked on the government funded research project INVITE with the subject of "Interaction with information structures in immersive environments".

Jaap Blonk (NL), born 1953, is a composer, voice performer and sound poet. In reciting poetry, especially the works of Antonin Artaud and Kurt Schwitters, he discovered the directness and flexibility of vocal utterance, whether using meaningful words or not. At present, he has developed into a prolific writer/composer and a specialist in the performance of sound poetry, supported by a powerful stage presence and an almost childlike freedom in improvisation.

Marc Canter (USA). Founder of MacroMind, the company that went on to become Macromedia. As such, he was involved in the invention of Director, the world's first multimedia authoring tool. After leaving Macromedia, Marc started Canter Technology in 1992, which focused on developing interactive, scalable and networked multimedia products. Under Marc's leadership, Canter Technology created MediaBand, the world's first interactive music video (1992-1994), the Marc Canter Show, a scalable talk show delivered over the Internet (1995-1996) and the MediaBar, a cyber restaurant and club that explored the potential of location-based entertainment as a stepping stone to interactive TV (1996–1997). In 1998, Marc helped develop and deploy the ChoiceSeat system for Super Bowl XXXII and was instrumental in building a prototype of a digital city for Trieste, Italy. He has worked extensively Digiscents, the current leader in computer-controlled smell emission, on their early demonstrations. He continues to be an innovator and leader in the field of multimedia technologies.

Adrian David Cheok (SGP) has worked in real-time systems, soft computing, and embedded computing in both Mitsubishi Electric Research Labs (Osaka, Japan) and at the Depertment of Electrical and Computer Engineering, National University of Singapore (NUS) where he heads the Mixed Reality Lab. In NUS he has been working on research covering mixed reality, human-computer interaction, wearable computers and smart spaces, fuzzy systems, embedded systems, power electronics, and multi-modal recognition. The research output has included numerous high quality academic journal papers, research prototype deliverables, numerous exhibitions, keynote speeches, and international television worldwide broadcasts (including CNN/CNBC). He is currently Chairman of the IEEE Singapore Section, and President of ACM SIGCHI Singapore Chapter.

Heman Chong (SGP/D) is currently an Artist-in-Residence at the Künstlerhaus Bethanien (2003) in Berlin. His trans-disciplinary practice involves the use of graphics, photography, text, video in the exploration of mobility/nomadism, cinema/off-screen spaces, urbanity and, increasingly, socio-political issues concerning the production of contemporary visual art in Asia. He has exhibited in many countries including Belgium, Denmark, France, Japan, India, Spain, Singapore and the United Kingdom. He holds an MA in Communication Art and Design from the Royal College of Art, London.

Cindy Cohn (USA) is the Legal Director for the Electronic Frontier Foundation. She is responsible for overseeing the EFF's overall legal strategy. EFF has been actively involved in nearly all areas where civil liberties are impacted online. EFF has focused in the past few years on the challenge to the constitutional rights presented by recent changes and broad application of intellectual property laws. Key cases handled by the EFF in this area are Felten v. RIAA, focusing on the danger to scientific freedom posed by the anti-circumvention provisions of the DMCA, and Universal v. Reimerdes (2600) focusing on the danger to news reporting posed by the same laws. The EFF has also advised the criminal defense attorneys in U.S. v. Sklyarov, focusing on the criminal application of those same provisions to creators of format conversion software. The EFF has also worked to preserve the right to anonymous speech online, including bringing In Re 2TheMart.com, which established core legal standards for protecting the identity of online speakers sought by civil subpena. In addition, the EFF continues to defend those accused of various offenses based upon their protected speech activities. In the aftermath of the attacks of September 11, 2001, EFF has returned to its roots, focusing on the issues of government surveillance and other traditional civil liberties online.

Isabelle Cornaro (F) works primarily with drawings, text and video that are presented within a framework where one medium interacts with another. Her work deals with the concept of authority implied and imposed by constructed spaces (modern architecture, French gardens, etc) and is influenced by the work of science-fiction writers. She has exhibited in Belgium, Denmark, France, Germany, Singapore and the United Kingdom. Cornaro studied at École Nationale Supérieure des Beaux-Arts, Paris and École du Louvre (History of Art), Paris.

Florian Cramer (D), born 1969, lecturer in Comparative Literature at Freie Universität Berlin, writer on literature and computing, Free Software, code poetry and software art, administrator (with Tilman Baumgärtel) of the mailing list *rohrpost,* editor (with Alan Sondheim) of the „unstable digest" on the mailing list *Nettime,* member of the transmediale.01 software art jury and the *read_me/runme.org* expert group.
http://userpage.fu-berlin.de/~cantsin/homepage/
http://www.complit.fu-berlin.de/institut/lehrpersonal/cramer.html

Scott deLahunta (NL/UK) is a writer and researcher (with Writing Research Associates and Dartington College of Arts) in the field of overlap between the practices associated with live performance and emerging technologies.

Tim Mark Didymus (UK) has been realising generative audio works since 1993 releasing his first album "Float" in 1996. He is Principal Musician for Sseyo, Bafta award winning multimedia / software technologists.

Marc Downie (UK) is an artist and artificial intelligence researcher who lives and works in Massachusetts, USA. Educated at the University of Cambridge, he is currently a doctoral candidate and a member of the Synthetic Characters Group at The Media Lab, MIT. Marc has collaborated with a number of artists and scientists, creating both installations and digital projections with Merce Cunningham, Paul Kaiser and Shelley Eshkar and is currently constructing new works for dance theater with choreographers Bill T. Jones, Trisha Brown and Bebe Miller. His work has been shown internationally at venues including Ars Electronica, SIGGRAPH, ICA London and the Barbican Centre.

Kenji Iguchi (Needle) (J). First used a computer back in 91, and has been using one ever since. For someone tinkering with a computer so long, has pretty low programming skills and doesn't know C. Right now is rather interested in graphic design using Photoshop and other tools.

Electric Indigo (A), DJ and musician, has rocked clubs, raves, and festivals in more than 31 countries. Her name stands for an intelligent interpretation of the terms „techno" and „party". She started her DJ-career in 1989 in Vienna, Austria, lived in Berlin, Germany, from 1993 to 1996 and has been based in Vienna since. In recent years she has extended her activities to several media fields like television, radio and internet. In 1998 she started *female:pressure,* an internet-database for female DJs, producers, and visual artists in the electronic music scene.

Leo Findeisen (A), Academic Teacher, Writer, Musician, Networker. Studied a.o. old languages, composition and philosophy in Germany, Israel and Austria. Has been teaching since 1996 at the Chair for Cultural Philosophy and Media Theory at the Academy of Fine Arts Vienna; Assistent to german philosopher and writer Peter Sloterdijk at the same instiute. Engaged in cross-border networking in the fields of art, architecture, media and science for Western and Eastern Europe. Texts in several international publications.

Franz Fischnaller (I) is the art-director and project-coordinator of F.A.B.R.I.CATORS, an interdiciplinary group concerned with the integration of technology + communication + art + design. The group carries out research activities in the artistic and technological fields. Fischnaller + F.A.B.R.I.CATORS have produced installations in collaboration with various institutions,including EVL (Electronic Visualisation Lab) Illinois University at Chicago, USA; Centro Enrico Piaggio, University of Pisa (Italy); Laboratoy Eidomatica-University of Milan.

Oliver Fritz (D), born 1967. Studies of architecture (1990 – 1997) at the university of kaiserslautern. Since 2000 assistant at the chair of CAAD at ETH Zürich.

Benjamin Fry (USA) is a doctoral candidate at the M IT Media Laboratory. His research focuses on methods of visualizing large amounts of data from dynamic information sources. At MIT, he is a member of the Aesthetics and Computation Group, led by John Maeda. Ben received an undergraduate degree from the School of Design at Carnegie Mellon University, with a major in Graphic Design and a minor in Computer Science.

Alexander R. Galloway (USA) is an artist and computer programmer. He lectures frequently on issues of electronic art ans technological culture. Alex's first book, *PROTOCOL, or, How Control Exists After Decentralization,* will be published in 2003 by The MIT Press.

John Gerrard (IRL), born in 1974, is an artist and technologist working in video, interactive video, responsive 3D and photography, with a significant emphasis on portraiture. In 2003 Gerrard was the Pepineres artist in residence to the AEC Futurelab. Gerrard has received a BFA from the Ruskin School of Oxford University, UK, an MFA from the Art Institute of Chicago, and an MSc from Trinity College, Dublin, Ireland. See www.johngerrard.net

Olga Goriunova (RU) is a media researcher, organizer, writer, teacher of the new media history and theory. Born in 1977 in Ulan-Ude, USSR. Lives and works in Moscow and Helsinki. Olga co-organizes the international artistic software festival *read_me.*

Cecilia Hausheer (CH), born in 1958; film scholar, exhibition designer/producer and university lecturer; 1995-2002: curator for media at Zurich's Museum of Design, responsible for such exhibitions as "Ich & Du. Kommunikation und Neue Medien" (1996), "GAME_OVER. Version 1.0," *www.gameover.org* (1999) and "Bollywood" (2002); 1996-7: member of "Information Society Switzerland," a blue-ribbon panel commissioned by the Swiss Bundesrat (federal council).

Horst Hörtner (A) studied telematics at the Technical University of Graz and worked as a freelance developer of realtime control systems as well as for art projects. Co-founder of the group "x-space". He has worked for EXPO Sevilla, documenta IX, austromir, etc. Since 1995, he is technical director of the Ars Electronica Center in Linz and director of the Ars Electronica Futurelab.

Erkki Huhtamo (SF), Associate Professor, UCLA. Researcher, Writer & Curator. Specialities include media archaeology and the history of media art. Writings translated in 11 languages. Books (in Finnish) include „The Archaeology of Virtuality“ (1995), „The Archaeology of the Moving Image“ (1996) and „Phantasmagoria“ (2000). Curator of many exhibitions, including Digital Mediations (Art Center, Pasadena 1995), Unexpected Obstacles—Perry Hoberman (ZKM Karlsruhe, 1998) and Alien Intelligence (KIASMA Museum of Contemporary Art, Helsinki 2000). Creator of the installation „Ride of Your Life“ (SurroGate2, ZKM, Karlsruhe, 1998). Director and script writer of TV series for YLE (The Finnish TV). Member of media festival organizing committees and juries, including Interactive Media Festival (L.A., 1995) and Portraits in Cyberspace (MIT Media Lab, 1996).

Naut Humon (USA) is the director of operations for the Recombinant Media Labs in San Francisco. This network of A/V based actions houses the Surround Traffic Control cinesonic system for performance exhibitions and international residencies. He is also the producer and curator for the Asphodel label along with his own projects for speaker-screen installations.

Crispin Jones (UK) is an artist and designer based in London. He graduated from Kingston University with a degree in Fine Art in 1996 and subsequently gained an MA in Computer Related-Design from the Royal College of Art in 2000. Since then he has been dividing his time between working as an interaction designer for Philips and Ideo and furthering his own artistic practice.

Hirokazu Kato (J) is an associate professor in Osaka University. He has been studying image processing, computer vision and human computer interaction. He developed a software library called ARToolKit which is useful for development of Augmented Reality applications. It is used by many researchers, artists and designers in the world.

Friedrich Kittler (D), Ph.D. studied German language and literature, Romance languages and literature, and philosophy at the University of Freiburg/Breisgau; since 1993, occupant of the Chair in Aesthetics and the History of Media in the aesthetics program at Humboldt University, Berlin; staff member of the Hermann von Helmholtz Zentrum für Kulturtechnik and the research group "Bild Schrift Zahl" (DFG).

Daniel Kluge (D) is a visual artist based in Munich, where he develops video performances and interactive sound installations. He has worked closely with the ZKM in developing graphic design materials, as well as on several live video performances. The notion of fractured narratives and loop aesthetics form the core of his artistic investigations. Recent directions include the use of programming in the control of spatial triggers in creating sonic environments.

Sachiko Kodama (J), 1993 B.A., Hokkaido University (Division of Physics). 2000 Completed Doctoral Program in Art and Design, University of Tsukuba.

Richard Kriesche (A), born 1940, worked as professor already in the 60s within the area of audiovisual media. In 1969 he founded the art society "pool" and four years later the media gallery "poolerie" for photography, film and video. In the following years he was involved in the formation of several art labs and artists' syndicates. Since the end of the 80s Richard Kriesche held several teaching posts, among others for the Technical University Vienna and the École supérieure des beaux arts in Paris. Kriesche serves an an expert in several European commissions. Beside international exhibitions he already took part in Ars Electronica in 1989 and 1994.

Joan La Barbara (USA), born 1947, has been called one of the great vocal virtuosas of our time. A pioneer in the field of contemporary and sound art, she has developed a unique vocabulary of experimental and extended vocal techniques, including multiphonics, circular singing, ululation and glottal clicks. In addition to her own compositions, she has premiered landmark compositions written for her by noted American composers, including Robert Ashley, John Cage, Rhys Chatham, Charles Dodge, Morton Feldman, Philip Glass, Steve Reich, Morton Subotnick and James Tenney.

Golan Levin (USA) is an artist, composer and designer interested in developing artifacts and experiences which explore supple new modes of computational expression. His work has focused on the design of systems for the creation, manipulation and performance of simultaneous image and sound, as part of a more general examination of communications protocols for individual engagement and non-verbal dialogue. Levin's work spans a variety of online, installation and performance media, and includes such pieces as the *Dialtones Telesymphony* (2001), a concert the sounds of which are wholly performed through the carefully-choreographed ringing of the audience's own mobile phones. Levin was granted an Award of Distinction in the Prix Ars Electronica for his *Audiovisual Environment Suite* interactive software (2000) and its accompanying audiovisual performance, *Scribble* (2000). Most recently, Levin and collaborator Zach Lieberman developed *RE:MARK* and *Hidden Worlds* (2002), a pair of permanent installations commissioned by the Ars Electronica Center in Linz.

Pierre Lévy (F/CDN) is considered one of the most influential theoreticians of cyberculture. The Tunesian-born philosopher is currently working at the Université du Québec in Canada. One of his best known books is *Collective Intelligence: Mankind's Emerging World in Cyberspace.* He trained as a researcher with Michel Serres and Cornelius Castoriadis, and continued in Montreal, specialising in hypertextual approaches. With Michel Authier, he developed a network concept known as „Arbres de connaissances" (Trees of Knowledge.) Lévy is also interested in collective intelligence studied in an anthropological context and is one of today's leading media philosophers.

Zachary Lieberman (USA). Artist-engineer. Concerned with themes of kinetic and gestural performance, interactive imaging and sound synthesis. Graduated with a BA in Printmaking from Hunter College, New York in 2000; received an MFA degree in Design and Technology at Parsons School Of Design, NY in 2002. Since 2001, adjunct faculty in the Design and Technology department at Parsons. In 2002, Siemens Artist-in-Residence at the Ars Electronica Futurelab, Linz, Austria; in 2003, Artist-in-Residence at the Summer Workshop In Performance Telematics (SWIPT-2), Arizona State University. Upcoming commissions include Issue 12 of the Remedi project, and the 2002/Doublecell volume of Singlecell.org. Other projects include contributions to Mark Napier's *net.flag,* commissioned by the Guggenheim Museum, and *My News/Your News,* a reactive sculpture developed with Romy Achituv for the Gwangju Biennial, Korea.
http://www.thesystemis.com/

John Maeda (USA) is Muriel Cooper Professor of Media Arts and Sciences at the MIT Media Laboratory in Cambridge, Massachusetts. Maeda's early work redefined the use of electronic media as a core material for expression by combining skilled computer programming with sensitivity to traditional artistic concerns. He is the 2001 recipient of the nation's highest career honor in design—the National Design Award—and Japan's highest honor—the 2001 Mainichi Design Prize. Maeda is author of two books: *MIT Press,* and the 480-page retrospective *Rizzoli/Thames & Hudson. Listed by* as one of the "21 Most Important People of the 21st Century," in 2001 Maeda was honored with the world's largest solo digital media exhibition, "Beyond Post Digital," at the NTT InterCommunication Center in Tokyo, Japan. Maeda's work has been exhibited at the Museum of Modern Art, New York and the San Francisco Museum of Modern Art, and was the subject of two simultaneous one-man shows at the California College of Arts and Crafts Logan Galleries in 2000. Maeda is currently scheduled for a retrospective at the Institute of Contemporary Art, London, England in the summer of 2003, and an exhibition at the Fondation Cartier pour l'Art Contemporain, Paris, France in 2005.

Justin Manor (USA) has recently completed his studies under John Maeda in the Aesthetics and Computation Group at the MIT Media Lab. His work there focused on the realtime manipulation of video and audio, and the use of the body as a controller of media events. He also received a Bachelor's Degree in Astrophysics from MIT, and modelled the collisions of neutron stars and black holes. Between his stints at MIT he worked under designer David Small building museum installations and physical information browsers. Justin's work has been shown in the London ICA, the Chicago Museum of Science and Industry, the Asia Society Museum, and the Museum of Sex in New York.

Jonathan Norton (USA), born 1966. He is currently studying at the Center for Computer Research in Music and Acoustics (CCRMA) at Stanford University working towards a Ph.D. in computer-based music theory. During his time at Stanford he studied with John Chowning, Julius Smith, Max Mathews, Chris Chafe, and Jonathan Harvey. Before CCRMA, he received his masters in music composition at Northwestern University. His works for dance, acoustic instruments, tape, and soundtracks have been performed and heard extensively. His most recent soundtrack for „Dreams of a City: Creating East Palo Alto“ has been shown on PBS and recently entered into several film festivals. His soundtrack for „ENDGAME“ had its world premiere at Siggraph '94 in Orlando, Florida and has since been in festivals and on television in the USA, Russia, Spain, Japan, Monaco, Italy, France, and Switzerland.

James McCartney (USA), composer and author of the object oriented synthesis language *SuperCollider.*

Pascal Maresch (A) studied journalism, communications and art history at the Paris-Lodron University of Salzburg; his master's thesis was entitled "Virtual Reality–The Artificial Paradise?" He has worked in advertising and on photo-documentation assignments in connection with the fashion industry, concerts and events. Since 1998, he has been a staff member of the Ars Electronica Futurelab; since 2001, as content manager. In this function, he works on the conceptualization and design of project content, and is also in charge of public and press relations.

James Patten (USA) is PhD candidates at the MIT Media Laboratory. He designs new ways for people to interact with computers using physical objects, for tasks such as electronic music and interactive simulations. Together with Ben Recht, he has performed with the *Audiopad* throughout the Boston area, and their installation work has been exhibited at the Museu d'Art Contemporani de Barcelona as part of the Sonar Festival of Advanced Music and Multimedia Art, the NTT Inter-Communication Center in Tokyo, Japan, and the Cyberarts Festival in Boston, USA.

Christiane Paul (USA) is the Adjunct Curator of New Media Arts at the Whitney Museum of American Art and the director of Intelligent Agent, a service organization and information resource dedicated to digital art. She has written extensively on new media arts and her book „Digital Art“ (part of the World of Art Series by Thames & Hudson, UK) was published in May 2003. She has also been working with Victoria Vesna and Margot Lovejoy on an essay collection focusing on context and meaning in digital art. She teaches in the MFA computer arts department at the School of Visual Arts in New York and has lectured internationally on art and technology. Her first show at the Whitney, „Data Dynamics“ (March–June, 2001), dealt with the mapping of data and information flow on the Internet and in the museum space. She was one of the co-curators of the New York Digital Salon's 10th anniversary exhibition (April, 2003) and also curated the net art selections for the 2002 Whitney Biennial (March, 2002); for Fotofest (Houston, Texas, March, 2002); and the exhibition „Evo1“ (Gallery L, Moscow, October 2001); as well as the online exhibitions „CODeDOC“ (Whitney Artport, September 2002) and „Mapping Transitions“ at the University of Boulder, Colorado (September 2002). She is responsible for Artport, the Whitney's online portal to Internet art.

Norbert Pfaffenbichler (A), born 1967, lives and works as an artist and curator in Vienna; founding member of vidok and lanolin; member of Sixpackfilm; master class in visual media design at the University of Applied Art; numerous exhibitions and works on display at festivals in Linz, Graz, Geneva, New York, Tokyo, Berlin, Venice, Osnabrück, Paris, Nyon, Basel, Barcelona, et al.

Fiona Raby (UK) is a senior research fellow and founding member of the Research Studio. She has worked in a cross-disciplinary architectural practice in Tokyo, and has taught in the both the Architecture and Interaction Design departments at the RCA. She headed the FLIRT project at the RCA, and has also collaborated with Anthony Dunne in research into the cultural role of electronic products and systems, resulting in international exhibitions and, most recently, the book Design Noir: The Secret Life of Electronic Objects (August/Birkhäuser, 2001).

Casey Reas is an associate professor at the newly established Interaction Design Institute Ivrea in northern Italy. With Ben Fry of the MIT Media Lab, he is currently developing Processing, a platform for learning fundamentals of computer programming within the context of the media arts. Reas' work explores kinetic systems through diverse digital media including software art, prints, animation, installations, and responsive sculpture. In 2001, Casey received his M.S. degree in Media Arts and Sciences from the MIT Media Laboratory, where he was a member of the Aesthetics and Computation Group (ACG). Casey has lectured and exhibited in Europe, Asia, and the United States. His work has recently been shown at the American Museum of the Moving Image, Ars Electronica, New York Digital Salon, Museum of Modern Art, P.S.1, and Siggraph. *http://www.groupc.net, http://www.proce55ing.net, http://www.interaction-ivrea.it, http://acg.media.mit.edu*

Ben Recht (USA) is a PhD candidates at the MIT Media Laboratory. He spends his days constructing circuits and deconstructing sounds, and has released recordings on the American imprint Adhesive under the moniker localfields. Together with James Patten, he has performed with the *Audiopad* throughout the Boston area, and their installation work has been exhibited at the Museu d'Art Contemporani de Barcelona as part of the Sonar Festival of Advanced Music and Multimedia Art, the NTT InterCommunication Center in Tokyo, Japan, and the Cyberarts Festival in Boston, USA.

Heimo Ranzenbacher (A), born 1958, journalist, art critic, theorist and artist. Various publications in catalogues and specialized journals; diverse addresses at symposia. In 1993, he founded TXTD.sign, a studio for aesthetic services. Diverse art projects *(Klang Figur,* 1991; *Lichtzeichen,* 1994; *Sonderartikel,* 1995; *Ipzentrum,* 1997; *Liquid Space,* 1999; *Wet_Ware,* 2000; *Klimakonverter,* 2002; *R.E.M., 2002).*

Howard Rheingold (USA) is one of the world's foremost authorities on the social implications of technology. Over the past twenty years he has traveled around the world, observing and writing about emerging trends in computing, communications, and culture. One of the creators and former founding executive editor of HotWired, he has served as editor of *The Whole Earth Review,* editor-in-chief of *The Millennium Whole Earth Catalog,* and on-line host for *The Well.* The author of several books, including *The Virtual Community, Virtual Reality,* and *Tools for Thought.*

Daniel Rozin (USA), born 1961, is an artist, educator and developer, working in the area of interactive digital art. As an interactive artist Rozin creates installations and sculptures that change and respond to the presence and point of view of the viewer. As an educator, Rozin is the Director of Research and Adjunct Professor at Interactive Telecommunications Program, Tisch School Of The Arts, New York University where he teaches such classes as Interaction Design and Expressing with Technology. As developer, Rozin owns Smoothware Design, a software company that creates tools for the interactive art and multimedia authoring community. His work has been exhibited widely and featured in publications such as *The New York Times, Wired, ID, Spectrum* and *USA Today.* His work has earned him numerous awards including Prix Ars Electronica, ID Design Review and the Chrysler Design Award.

Steve Sacks (USA), Web developer, founder and director of Bitforms Gallery, New York, devoted to digital and digitally influenced art. The space is designed by the New York architecture firm Archi-Tectonics, and includes an Interactive Digital Catalogue touch screen archive of the artists' works.

Giaco Schiesser (CH) is professor for the theory and history of the media as well as head of the department „New Media“ at the „University of Art and Design Zurich“ (Hochschule für Gestaltung und Kunst Zürich, HGKZ). He studied philosophy and German studies at the Freie Universität (FU) in Berlin. From 1984 to 1987, he was a junior lecturer for New German Literature in the German Seminar at the University of Basel. From1983 to1993, he was co-editor of the magazine "Widerspruch" (Zurich) and between 1989 and 1994 he was scientific editor of the "WochenZeitung". From 1991 to 1996, he was a member of the Institute for Migration and Racism Research in Hamburg. Since 1994, he has been a senior lecturer in the history and theory of visual communication at the "School of Design Zurich" (SfGZ). From 1996 to 1997, he assisted assisted in establishing the university department "New Media" at the "University of Art and Design Zurich" (HGKZ) as head of the university department, and in autumn 1998, he was also appointed professor of this department. His work focuses on the culture of media, ideology, democracy, subject theory and everyday life.

Lotte Schreiber (A), born 1971, lives and works as an artist in Vienna; studied architecture at the Technical University in Graz and the Universities of Edinburgh and Naples; since March 2001, assistant professor in the Department of Architecture at the University of Art in Linz; numerous exhibitions and works on display at festivals in Linz, Graz, Geneva, New York, Tokyo, Berlin, Osnabrück, Paris, Nyon, Basel, Barcelona, et al.; award for Best Experimental Film at the 2003 New York Underground Film Festival; nominated for the 2003 International Media Art Prize of the ZKM, Karlsruhe, Germany.

Alexei Shulgin (RUS) is a Moscow based artist, musician, curator, activist and professor. In his work he explores the boundaries between art, culture and technology in their relation to "real life" effects and vice versa. His favorite methods are mixing contexts and questioning the existing states of things. Shulgin has participated in numerous exhibitions and symposiums on photography, contemporary art and new media.

Christa Sommerer (A) and Laurent Mignonneau (F) are internationally renowned media artists working in the field of interactive computer installation. They currently work as researchers and artistic directors at the ATR Media Integration and Communications Research Lab in Kyoto, Japan and as Associate Professors at the IAMAS International Academy of Media Arts and Sciences in Gifu, Japan. They also hold a position of Visiting Research Fellows at MIT Center for Advanced Visual Studies in Boston USA. Mignonneau and Sommerer have collaborated since 1992, and their interactive artworks have been called "epoch making" (Toshiharu Itoh, NTT-ICC museum) for pioneering the use of natural interfaces to create a new language of interactivity based on artificial life and evolutionary image processes. Their collaboration has been influenced by the combination of their different fields of interest, including art, biology, modern installation, performance, music, computer graphics and communication.

A. Benjamin Spaeth (D) was born in 1973; after vocational training in carpentry, he studied architecture and urban planning at the University of Stuttgart and the École d'architecture in Paris; lectureship at the Institute for Representation and Design; in 2002, he founded *gedanken_gebaeude,* a source of virtual environments, architectural concepts and multimedia architectural representations.

Minako Takeno (J), born 1969 in Tokyo, graduated from Tama Art University. 1995 M.A., University of Tsukuba (Master's Program in Art and Design).

Eugene Thacker (USA) is a cultural theorist and net.artist currently teaching at Rutgers University. He is director of [techne] New Media + Digital Arts and his work has been featured on Alt-X, Ars Electronica 99, Ctheory, Body & Society, Leonardo Electronic Almanac, mute, Semiotext(e)'s "Flesh Eating Technologies" issue, and Theory & Event. He is a contributing editor to The Thing and a collaborator with Fakeshop.

Otto Leopold Tremetzberger (A), born in 1974; studied cultural and media management, theater and philosophy; cultural and media projects with an emphasis on regional development, marketing and organizational development; journalistic activities, literary publications and prizes; mediator and chief executive of Radio FRO 105.0 MHz in Linz.

Roman Verostko (USA), artist, historian, and MCAD Professor Emeritus, was born in 1929 in the coal fields of Western Pennsylvania (USA). As a child he made his first paintings using a mail-order paint set. In the early 1980's, following 30 years of painting, he began executing algorithmic drawings with a pen plotter. Today his studio includes a network of computers coupled to pen plotters driven with his own original software. By 1987 he had created the world's first software driven "brushed" paintings with oriental brushes mounted on his pen plotter. His studio integrates coded digital procedure with fine arts traditions.

Fred von Lohmann (USA) is a senior staff attorney with the Electronic Frontier Foundation, specializing in intellectual property issues. In that role, he has represented programmers, technology innovators, and individuals in litigation against every major record label, movie studio, and television network (as well as several cable TV networks and music publishers) in the United States. In additon to litigation, he is involved in EFF's efforts to educate policy-makers regarding the proper balance between intellectual property protection and the public interest in fair use, free expression, and innovation.

Otomo Yoshihide (J) has always been very active in playing free improvisation—using oscillators, tapes, radios, etc. during his early years in Japan. Until his own signature band, Ground Zero, disbanded in March 1998, the group was always at the core of his musical creativity. Otomo has created and organized various groups and projects in addition to Ground Zero, among others the Double Unit Orchestra and Celluloid Machine Gun. Another of Otomo's major projects at that time was the *Sampling Virus Project* ('92 to '98), in which sampling processes were applied to musical works which were "passed around" among musicians. Otomo has demonstrated an exceptional talent as a composer of movie /TV/ video sound tracks. He has in particular enjoyed an excellent relationship with creators in the Chinese and Hong Kong film worlds. He also served as music director of the theater group Rinkogun from '92 to '95, creating the music for such works as Bird Man, Inu no Seikatsu, Hamlet Symbol, and Picnic Conductor.

Mia Zabelka (A), electric violinist, multimedia artist and curator, studied music, the violin, composition, electro-acoustic music and journalism in Vienna, Cologne, Berlin and New York. Numerous concerts and intermedial performances in Austria and abroad, in addition to CD, video, radio and TV productions.